The Complete Book of Maps & Geography

Table of Contents

Section 1:

Introduction to Maps and Map Skills

Floor Plans 4-13
Map Keys 14-24
Map Routes 25-36
Compasses 37-61
City/State/National Maps 62-74
Map Scales 75-86
Population Maps 87-88

Section 2:

United States Geography

Introduction to the U.S. and States 91-112
Boundaries and Rivers 113-121
Kinds of Maps 122
Political Maps 123-127
Physical Maps 128-137
Product Maps 138-147
Climate Maps 148-150

Section 3:

United States Regions

Pacific States 152-159
Mountain States 160-170
North Central States 171-180
South Central States 181-186
Midwest States 187-193
Northeastern States 194-206
Southeastern States 207-220

Section 4:

North and South America

Introduction to North and South America 222-225
Canada 226-230
Mexico 231-233
Central America 234-237
South America 238-240

Section 5:

Grid Maps 242-250

Section 6:

Global Geography

The Globe 252-255
Continents and Oceans 256-267
Hemispheres 268-275
Meridians of Longitude 277-285
Lines of Latitude 286-293
Latitude and Longitude 294-310
Time Zones 311-316

Map and Geography Review Sheets 317-322

Section 1

Introduction to Maps & Map Skills

Name____

The Mole Family

A floor plan shows where things are placed in a room. The Mole Family has just had all of their new living room furniture delivered. Now they have to arrange it. Help them decide where to put each piece of furniture. Color and cut out the pictures of the furniture. Glue the pictures on the drawing of the Mole Family's living room to make a floor plan.

Mole Family's Floor Plan

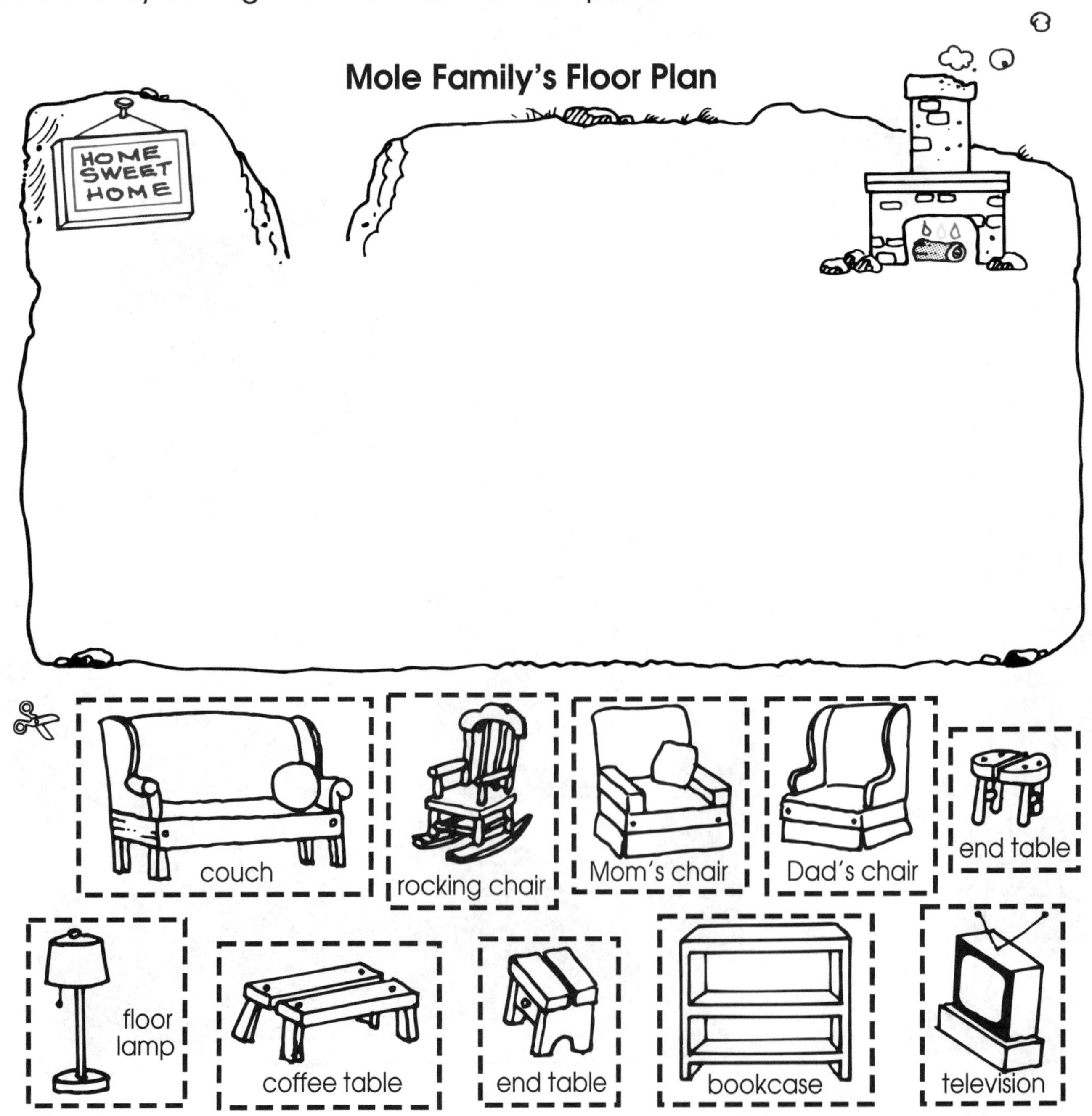

Name ________________________________

A Picture From Above

A floor plan looks like a picture someone drew looking down from the sky. It shows you where things are.

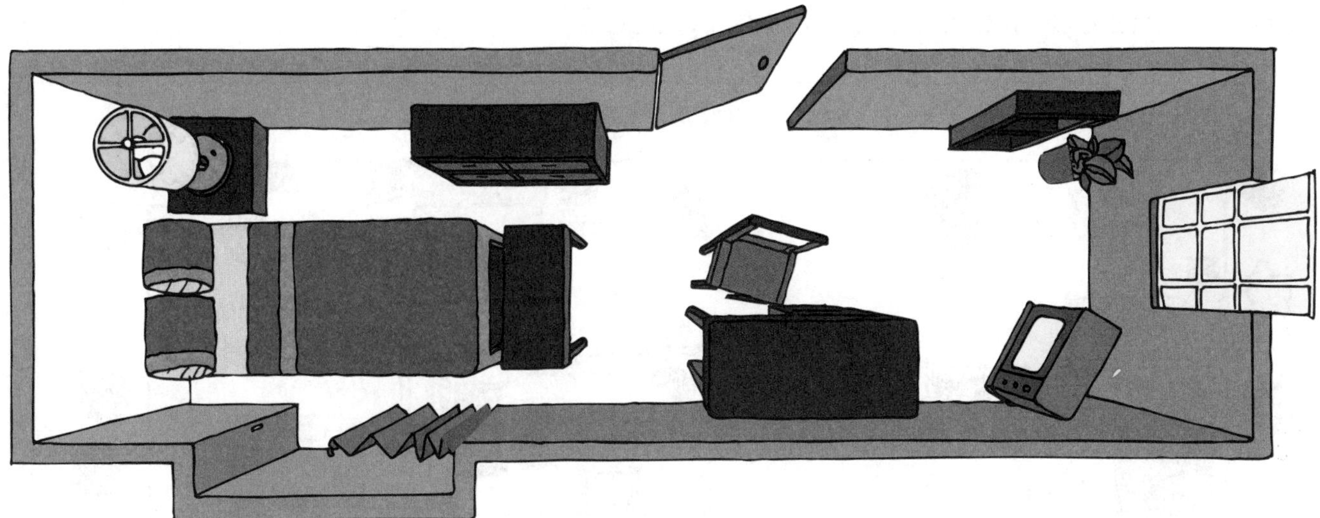

Circle the word which correctly completes each statement.

	a.	b.	c.
1. The TV is near the...	a. door	b. window	c. bed
2. The dresser is near the...	a. window	b. door	c. TV
3. Next to the bed is a...	a. TV	b. window	c. table
4. The bench is at the end of the...	a. bed	b. bookshelf	c. closet
5. The plant is by the...	a. dresser	b. bed	c. bookshelf
6. The bookshelf is next to the...	a. bed	b. closet	c. door
7. The lamp is on the...	a. table	b. TV	c. dresser

Follow these directions.

1. Draw a red circle around the TV.
2. Draw a black **X** on the desk.
3. Draw an oval rug in front of the bench using a color of your choice.
4. Draw a stuffed animal in the center of the bed.

Fill in these blanks with the correct word.

1. Between the closet and the TV is a ________________.
2. The window is between the ________________ and the TV.
3. When you walk in the door, the ________________ is to your right.
4. There is/are ______________________ lamp(s) in the room.

Name____

Hannah's New House

Hannah's family just moved into a new house. It is very different from their other house. Hannah drew a floor plan of her new house. Use the floor plan to answer the questions here and on page 7.

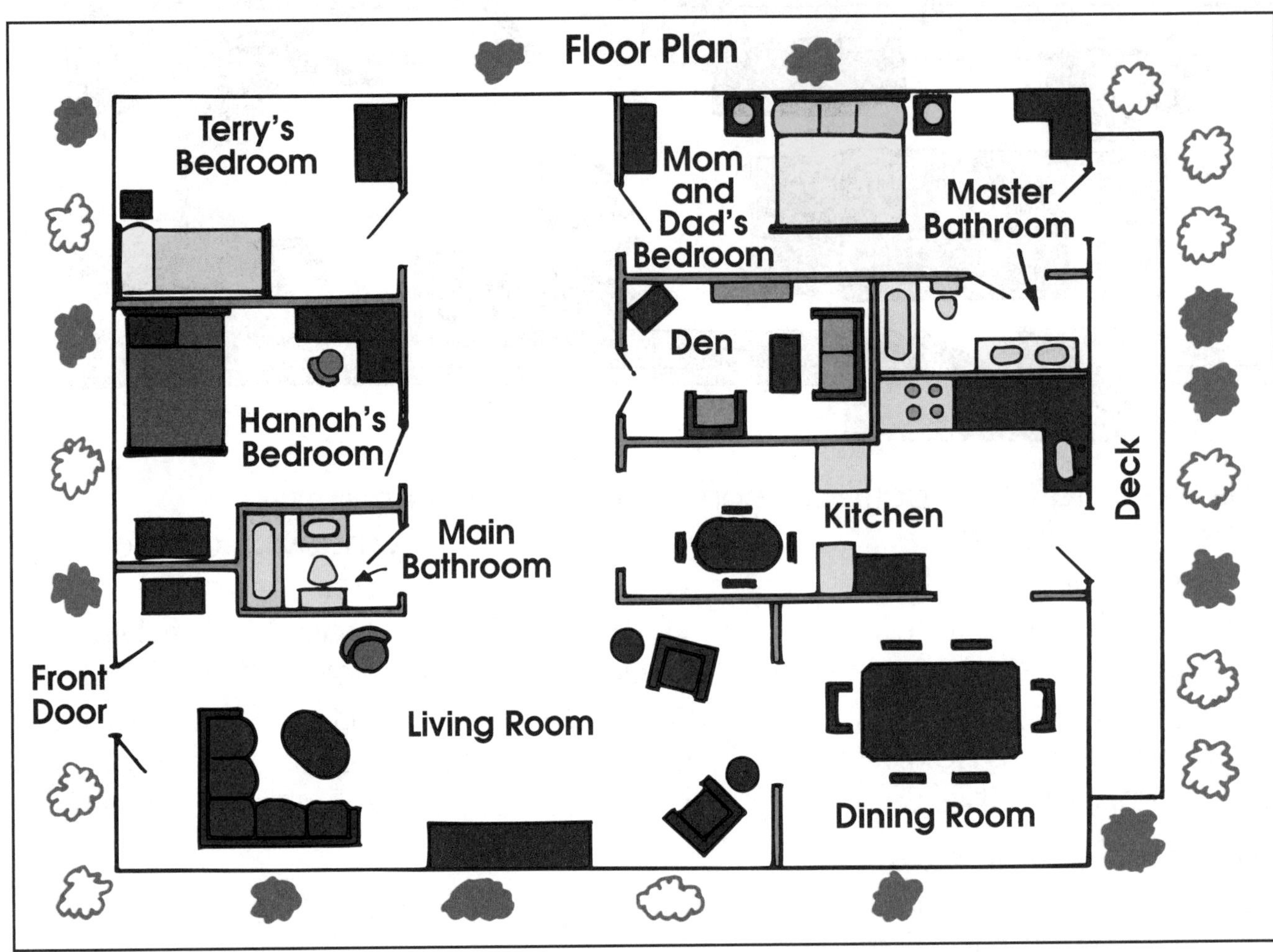

1. How many rooms does the house have? ____________________________

2. Which room is the smallest? ____________________________

3. Which room is the largest? ____________________________

Name ______________________

Hannah's New House

4. Who has a room across from Mom and Dad's bedroom?

____

5. Which rooms does Hannah walk past to go from the living room to her own bedroom?

____

6. How many bedrooms are there? ______________________

7. Which rooms have a door leading onto the deck?

____

8. The front door opens into what room?

____

9. On the floor plan on page 6, use a red crayon to draw the routes Hannah could take from her room to a door leading outside in case of an emergency.

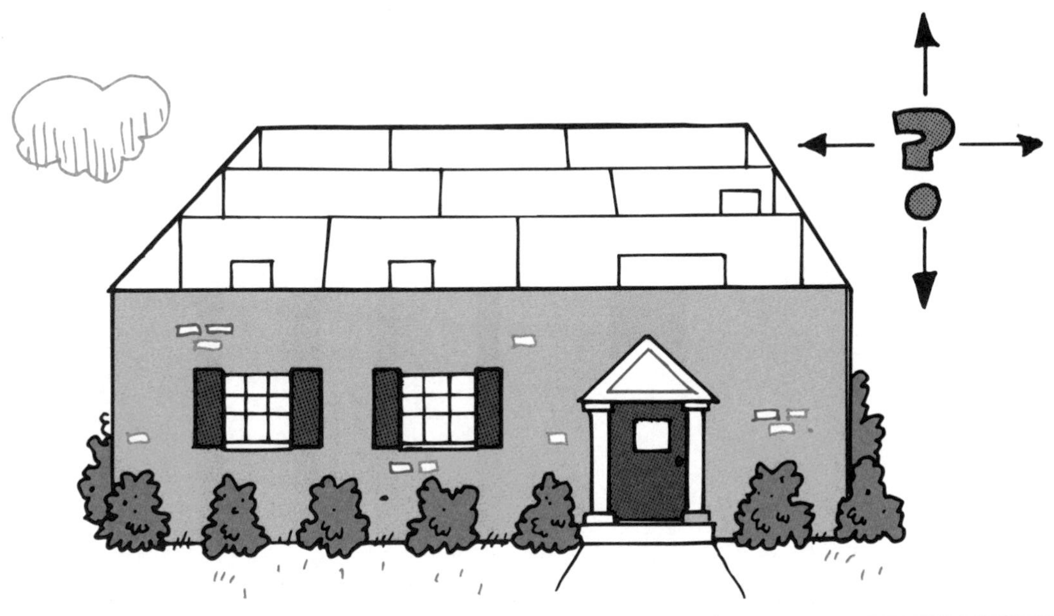

This page has been intentionally left blank.

Name ____________________

Fantastic Seats!

A floor plan can help you find your seat at a sports arena, concert hall or any place where you may go to see a special event.

Read each ticket. Find the seat on the floor plan. Color the seat on the floor plan the correct color.

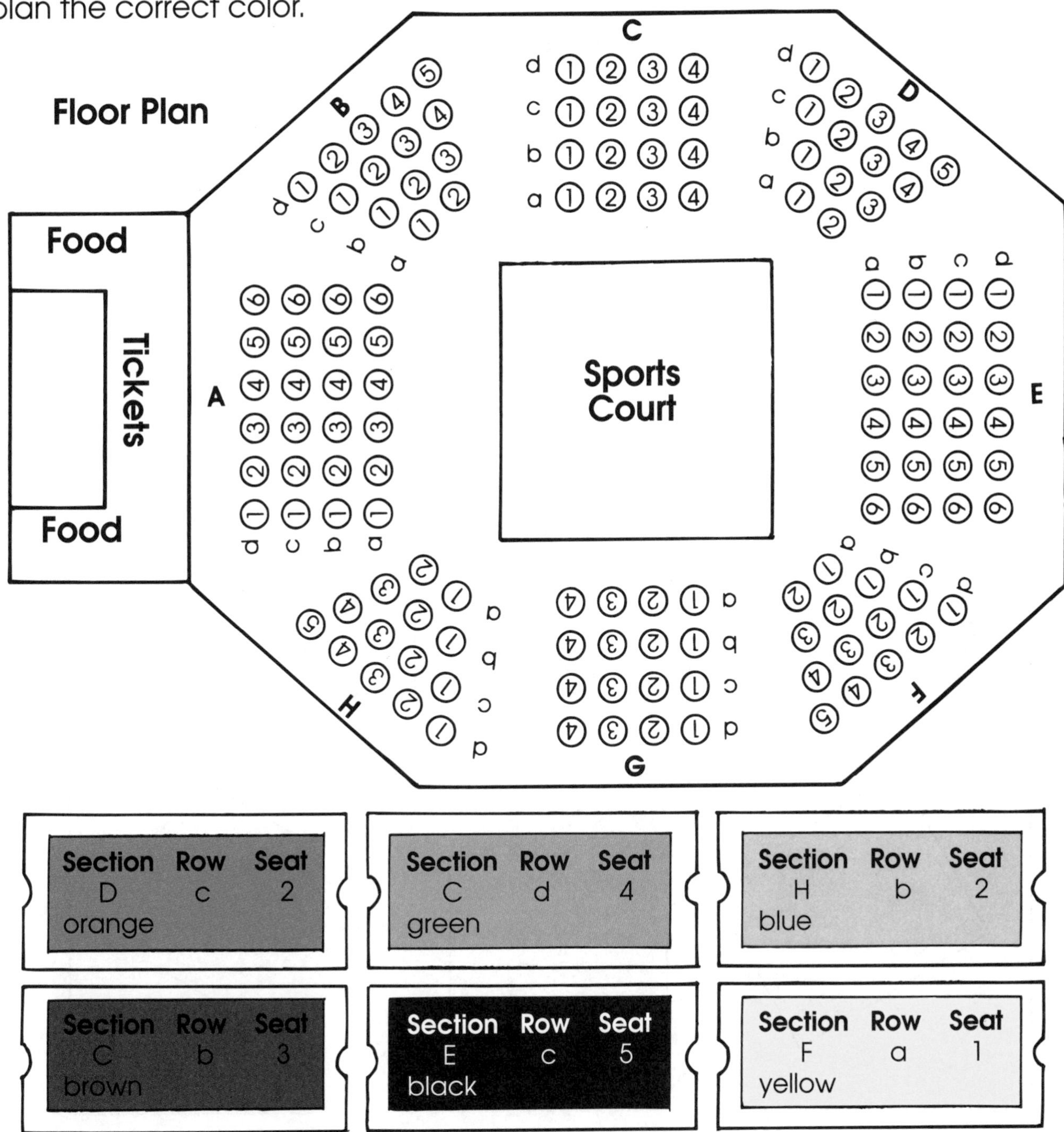

Section	Row	Seat	Color
D	c	2	orange
C	d	4	green
H	b	2	blue
C	b	3	brown
E	c	5	black
F	a	1	yellow

Name________________________________

Prepare for the Show

It's the big event of the year! Old cars from all over the United States are being put on display. The boxes on the floor plan show the spaces where cars will be placed. Follow the directions on page 11 to complete the floor plan.

Car Display Floor Plan

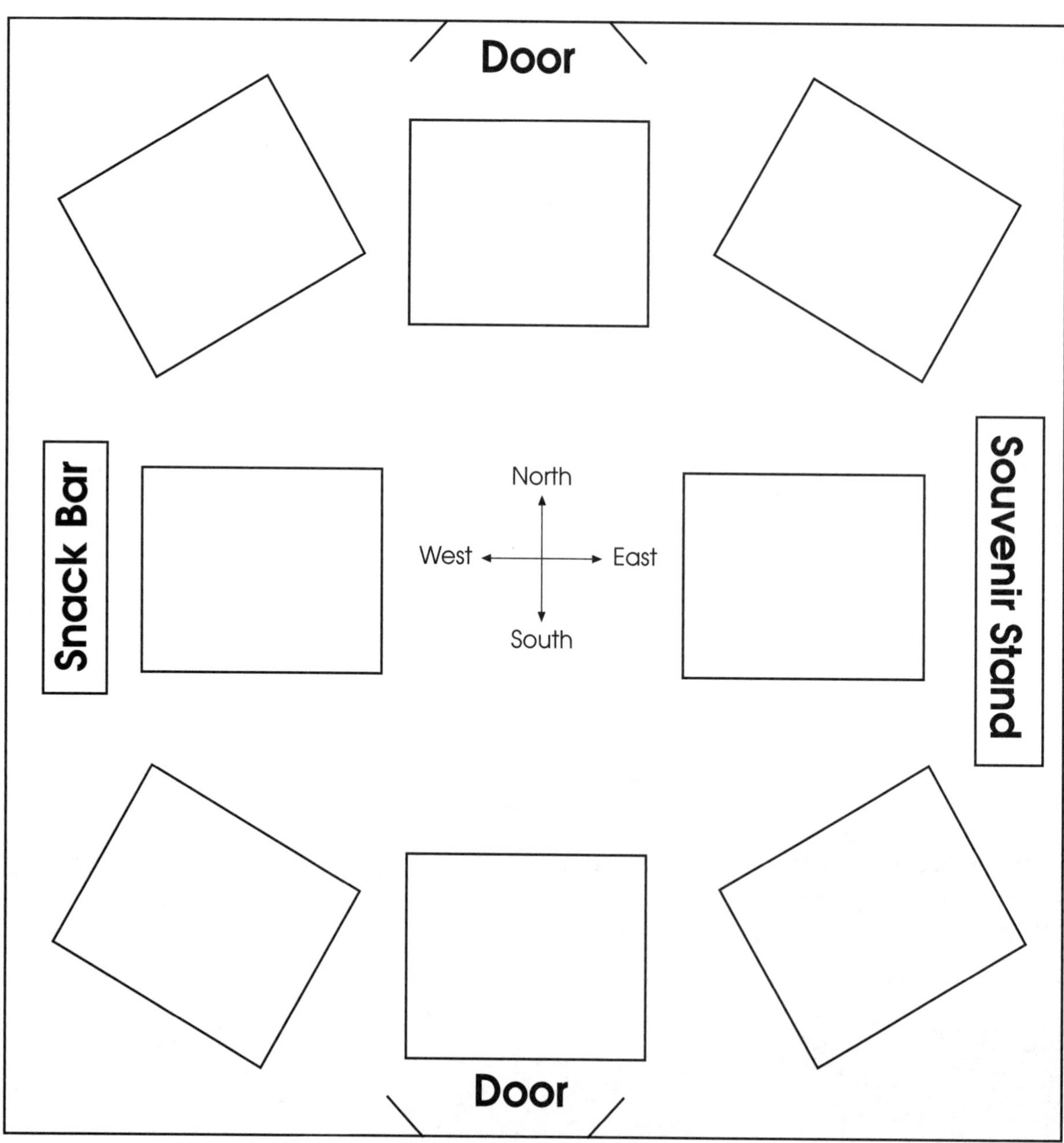

Name________________________________

Prepare for the Show

Color and cut out the pictures of the cars at the bottom of the page. Read the directions below to glue the pictures where they belong on page 10.

Directions:

1. The station wagon is in the space near the north door.
2. The roadster is in the space near the south door.
3. The van is in the space east of the station wagon.
4. The pickup is in the space west of the roadster.
5. The coupe is in the space west of the station wagon.
6. The carriage is in the space east of the roadster and south of the Souvenir Stand.
7. The Model A is east of the Snack Bar.
8. The Model T is east of the Model A.

Page is blank for cutting
exercise on previous page.

Name______________________________

Creating a Floor Plan

Pretend you are looking at your classroom or a room in your home from high atop the lighting fixtures. Draw how the room looks.

Name____

Picture This

This is a photograph that shows part of what is left of the town of Bodie, California. It was a mining town long ago. The photo shows a house, a barn and an old wagon. It also shows where a fence once was.

This is a map, or drawing, of the photo. It shows where the things in the photo can be found.

Bodie Map

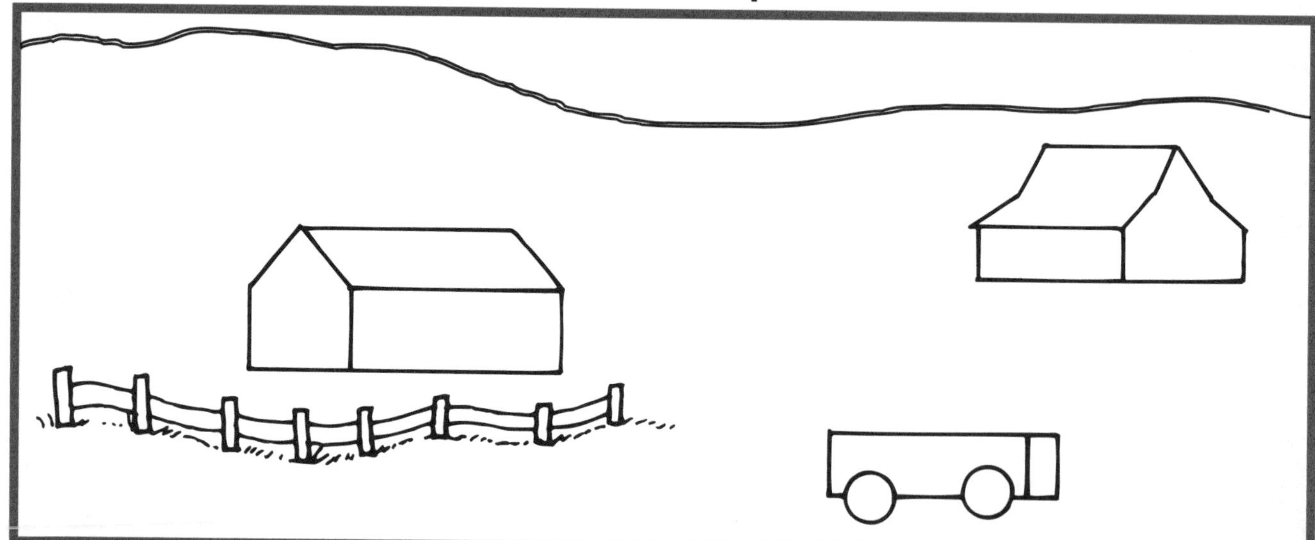

Directions:

1. Color the wagon red.
2. Color the fence brown.
3. Color the house yellow.
4. Color the barn blue.

Name ______________________________

Make a Map

Look closely at this photograph of an old pioneer schoolhouse and playground.

Directions:

In the box, draw a map to show what is in the photograph. Use the shapes to help you draw the pictures on your map that stand for things in the photo.

Pioneer Map

Name________________________________

Symbols on Maps

A symbol is a picture that stands for something that is shown on a map. Symbols used in a map are shown in the Map Key. Look at the symbols. Draw a line from each symbol to what it stands for in the drawing below.

Name________________________________

Symbols Replace Words

Symbols on a map show you where things are located.

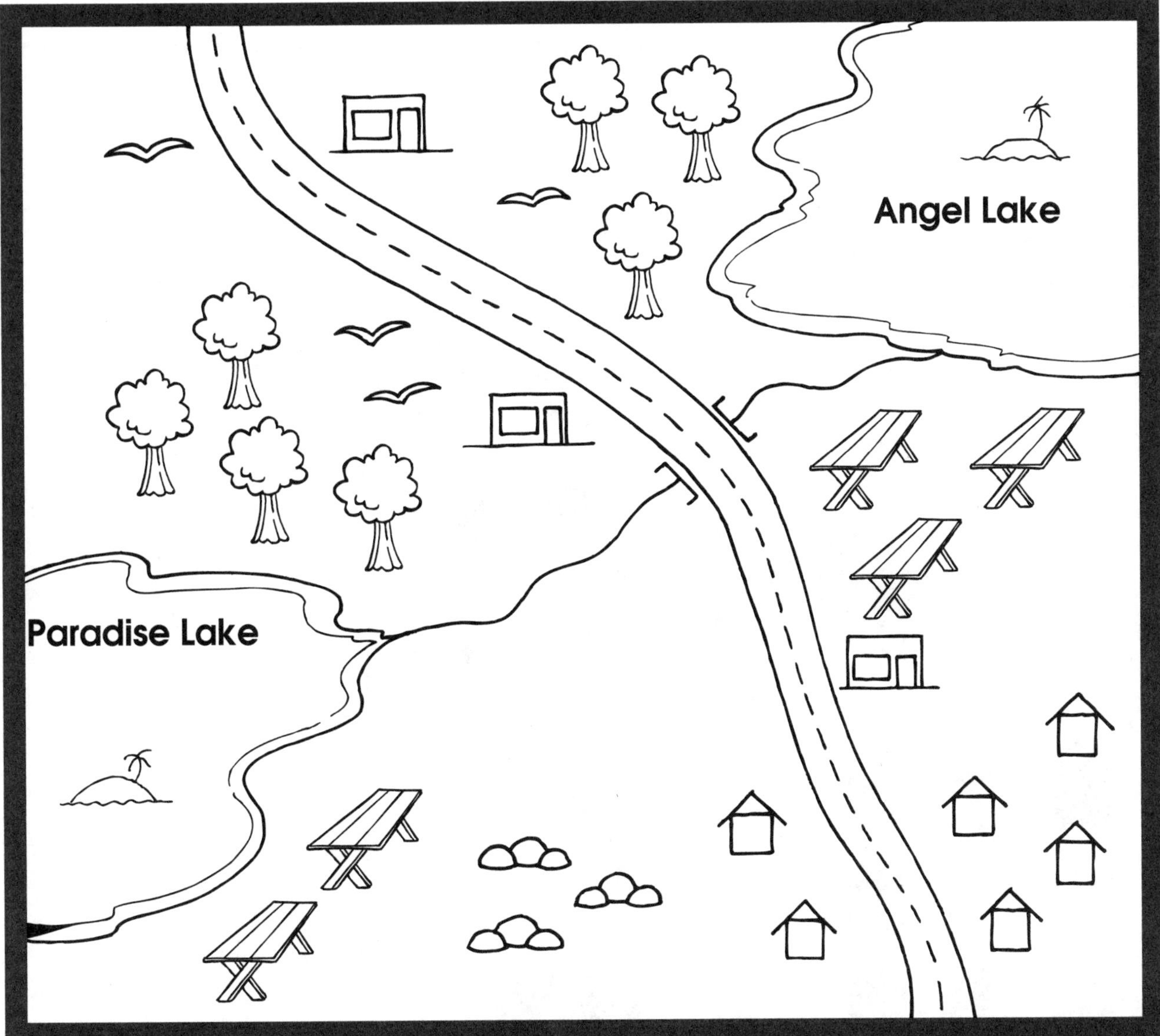

Directions: Use crayons or markers to complete the map.

1. Color the islands brown.
2. Color the trees green.
3. Color the rocks black.
4. Color the houses blue.
5. Color the stores orange.
6. Color the birds purple.
7. Color the picnic tables red.
8. Color the road yellow.

Name________________________________

The Wild Geese

Twice a day the wild geese fly from the river to a farm. Use this map with page 19.

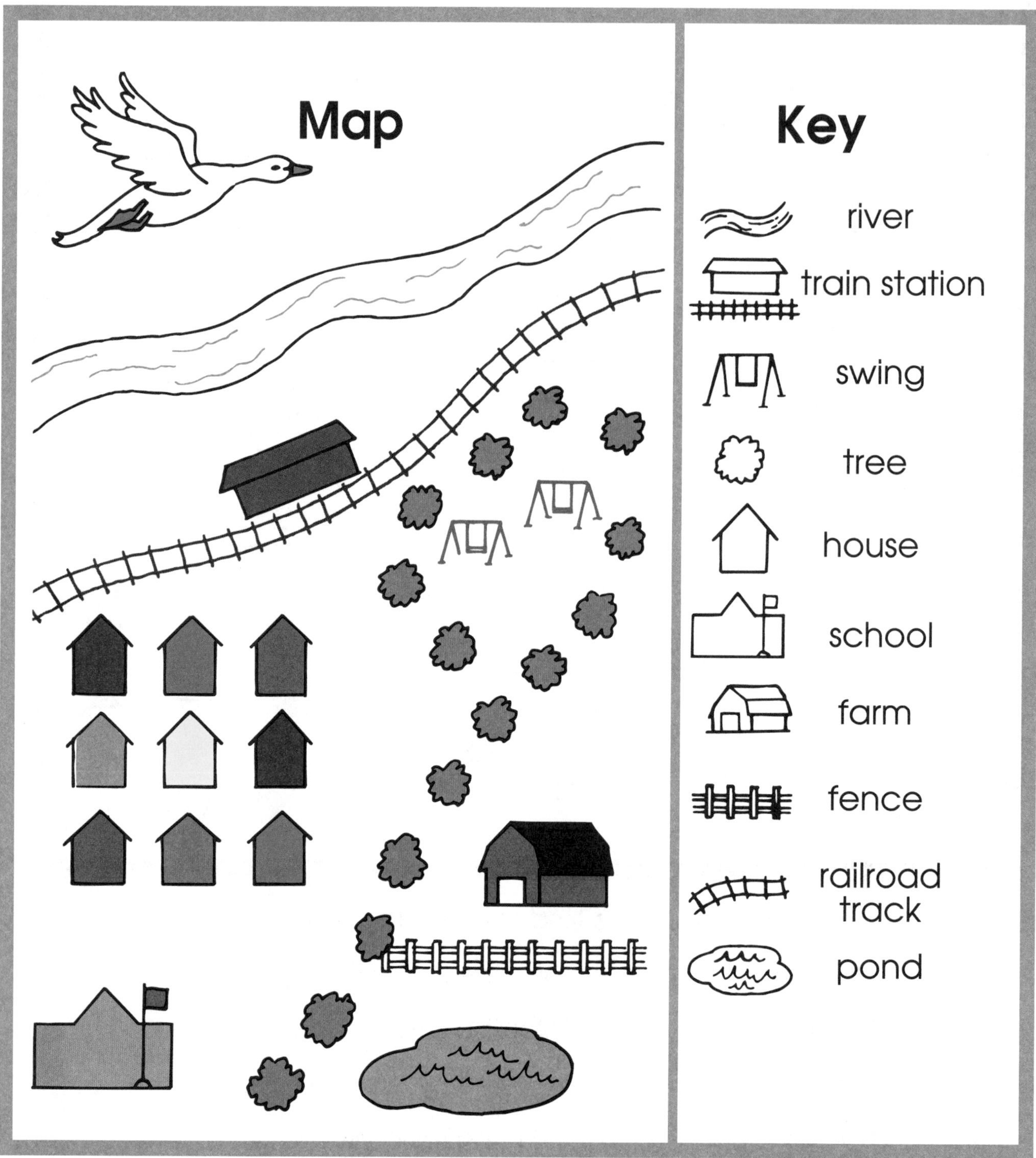

Name____________________________________

The Wild Geese

Directions: Write the word on the lines that tells what each symbol from the map key stands for.

1. ___ ___ ___ ___ ___
   1

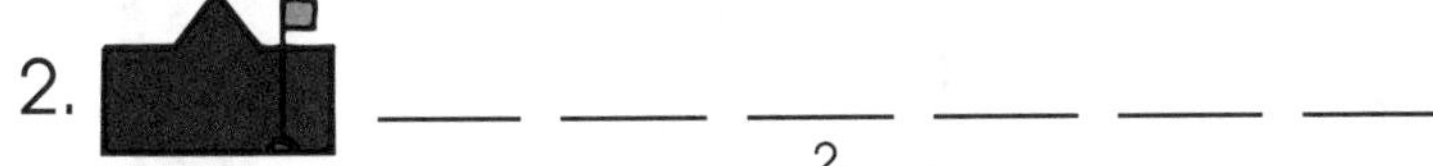

2. ___ ___ ___ ___ ___ ___
   2

3. ___ ___ ___ ___
   3 4

4. ___ ___ ___ ___ ___
   5

5. ___ ___ ___ ___
   6

6. ___ ___ ___ ___
   7

7. ___ ___ ___ ___ ___
   8

8. ___ ___ ___ ___ ___ ___ ___ ___ ___ ___ ___ ___
   9 10

9. ___ ___ ___ ___ ___
   11 12

10. ___ ___ ___ ___ ___ ___ ___ ___
    13 14
    ___ ___ ___ ___ ___
    15

Use the numbered letters to solve the puzzling question. Why do the geese fly this path twice a day?

___ ___ ___ ___ ___ ___ ___
10 3 13 9 4 12 14

___ ___ ___ ___ ___ ___ ___ ___ ___.
11 5 6 7 8 15 2 1 4

Name________________________________

Kool Kids Mall

Mall Map

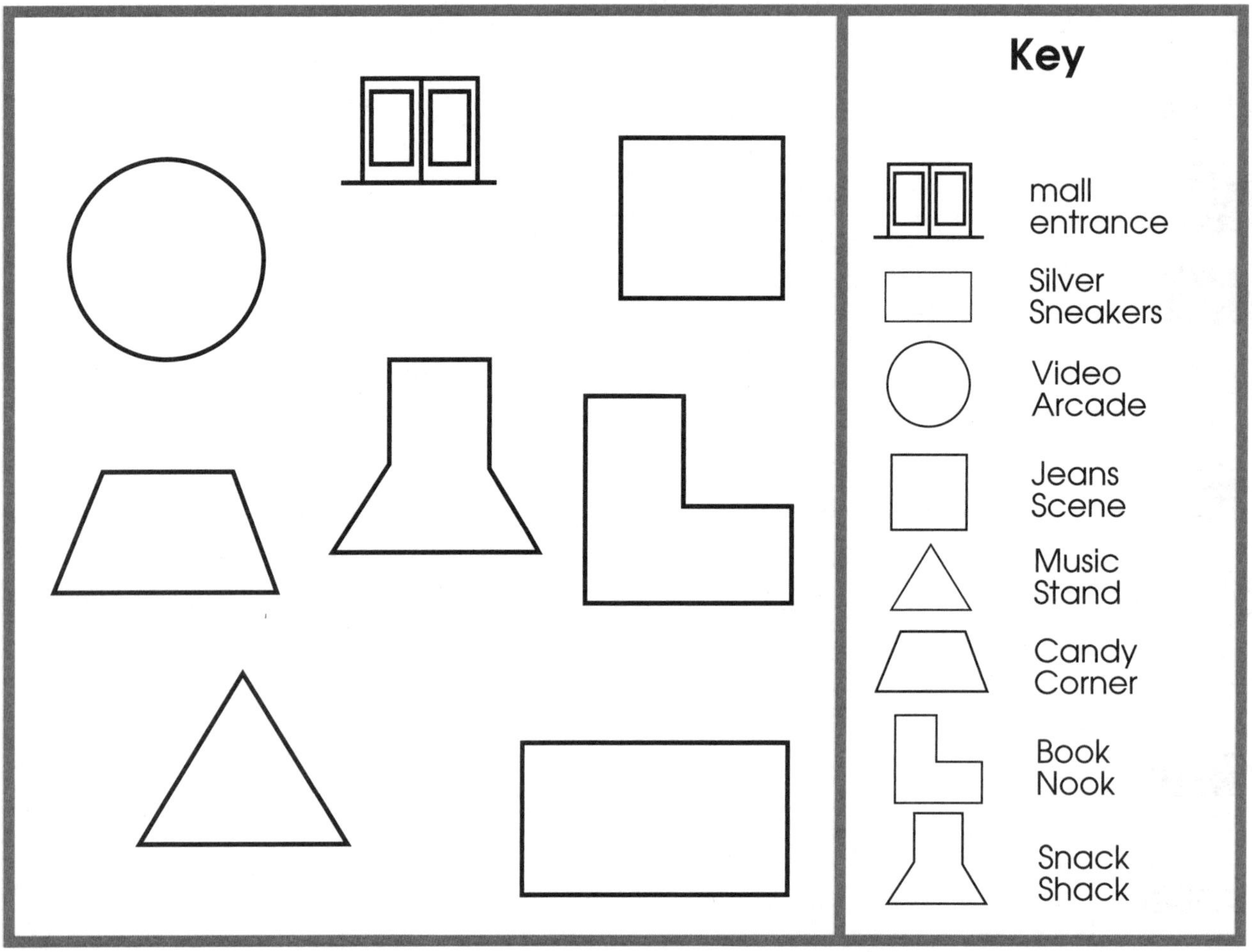

Key

- mall entrance
- Silver Sneakers
- Video Arcade
- Jeans Scene
- Music Stand
- Candy Corner
- Book Nook
- Snack Shack

Directions: Use the key to locate the stores. Draw the following:

1. a red and blue sneaker in Silver Sneakers
2. a black musical note in the Music Stand
3. a pair of blue jeans in the Jeans Scene
4. a green tree on each side of the mall entrance
5. a red piece of pizza in the Snack Shack
6. a pair of eyes in the Video Arcade
7. a yellow book and a blue book in the Book Nook
8. an orange lollipop in the Candy Corner

Name________________________________

Science Sense

This is a floor plan of the Science Sense Museum. Use the floor plan and key to complete this page.

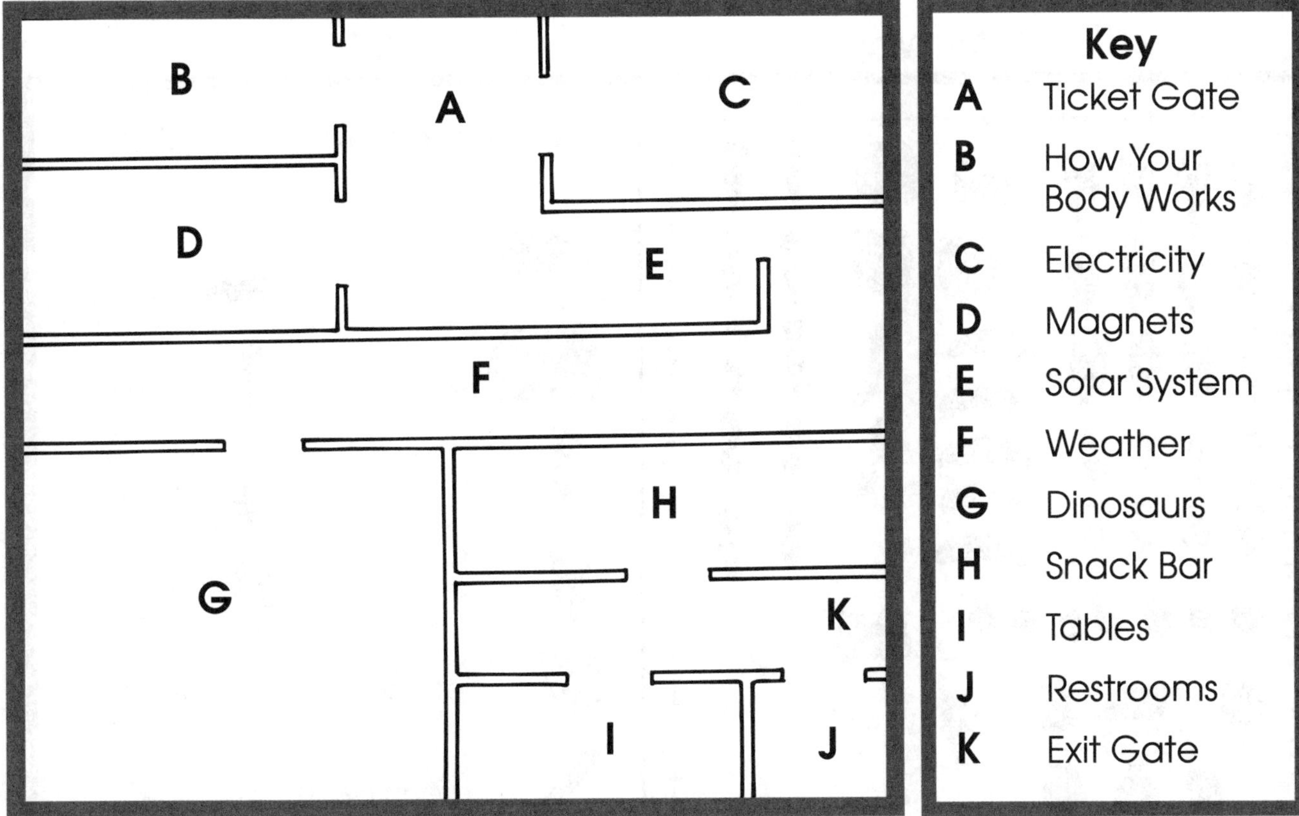

Key

A	Ticket Gate
B	How Your Body Works
C	Electricity
D	Magnets
E	Solar System
F	Weather
G	Dinosaurs
H	Snack Bar
I	Tables
J	Restrooms
K	Exit Gate

1. In which room would you go to see dinosaurs? ____________________
   Color the room brown.
2. In which room would you go to try using magnets? ________________
   Color the room blue.
3. Draw a hot dog in the snack bar.
4. Draw a table in the area in which tables are located.
5. Draw an **X** where you would buy a ticket to the museum.
6. If you go to room E, what will you learn about? ____________________

Name___________________________________

Farmer Fritz

Map symbols can tell us how many of something there are. Each symbol can stand for 1 or any number of that item. This map shows Farmer Fritz's crops. Each vegetable or fruit stands for 1 plant. Use the map and key to answer the questions.

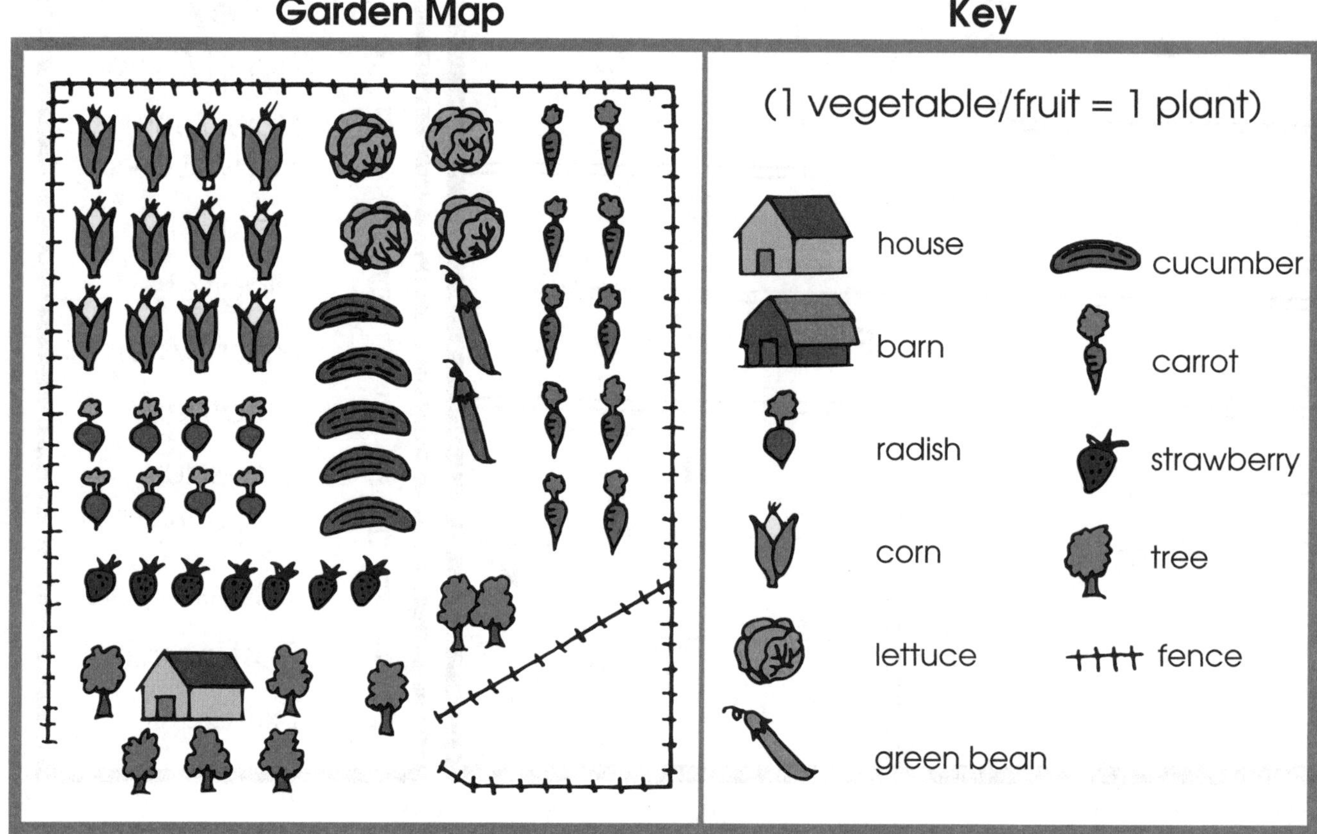

1. How many plants of each vegetable does Farmer Fritz have?

   radish ________ cucumber ________ corn ________

   carrot ________ green bean________ lettuce________

2. What fruit did Farmer Fritz plant? ______________________

   How many of these plants did he have? ______________________

3. Farmer Fritz planted the most of which vegetable? ______________

Name ___________________________

Carmella's Candy

Carmella made a map of her candy store so that her customers could easily find their favorite candy. Use the map and key to answer the questions.

Candy Store Map

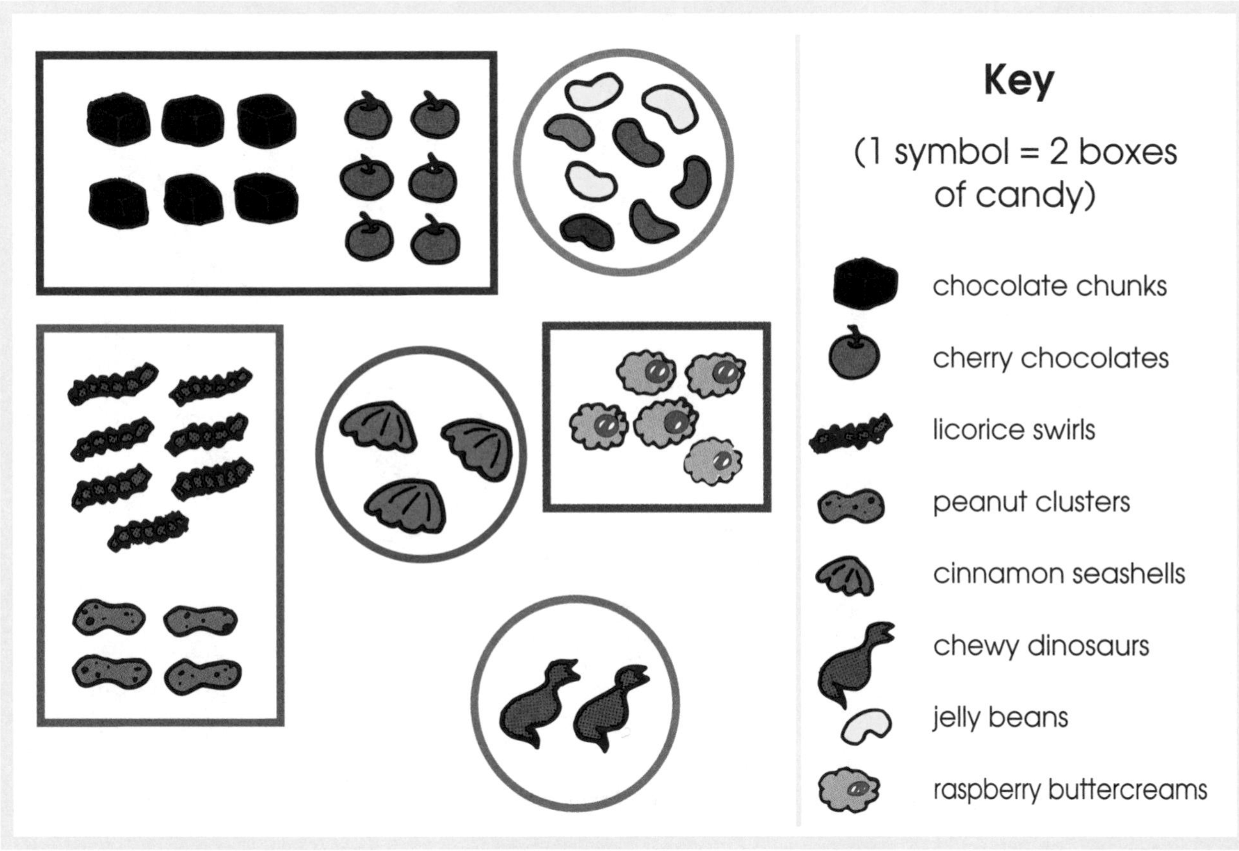

1. Each symbol equals how many boxes of candy? ________________

2. How many boxes of each kind of candy are there?

jelly beans	______	licorice swirls	______
chocolate chunks	______	cherry chocolates	______
peanut clusters	______	chewy dinosaurs	______
raspberry buttercreams	______	cinnamon seashells	______

3. Carmella has the greatest number of boxes of which candy?

____

Name____

Map Keys

Mixed-Up Map Maker

Mattie Map Maker goofed when creating a map of the state of Oopsylvania. Circle her mistakes and put a number by each one. Then, describe each error on the line with the matching number. (Hint: The key shows the correct map symbols.)

Oopsylvania Map

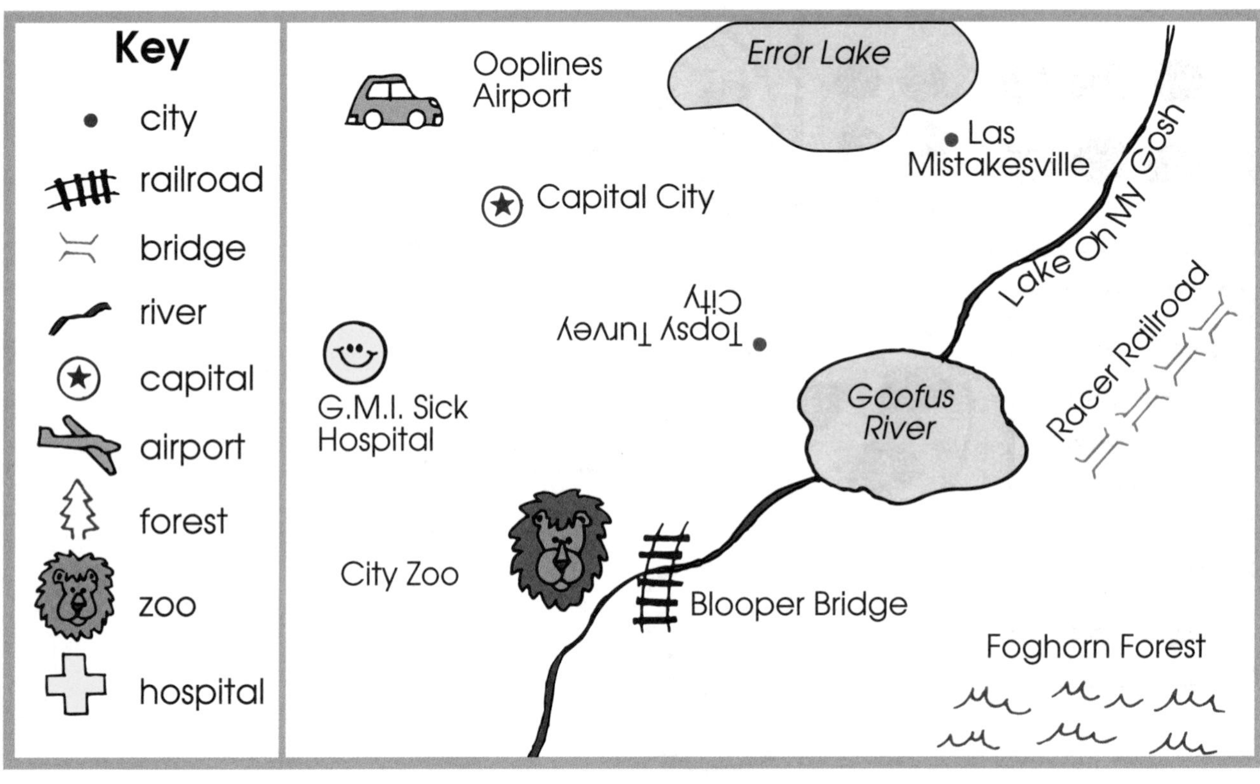

1. ____

2. ____

3. ____

4. ____

5. ____

6. ____

7. ____

8. ____

Name ____________________

Time to Go Home

This map shows routes the dinosaur can take to get to its cave. Use the key to find each symbol on the map. Then, follow the directions.

Dinosaur Cave Map

Directions:

1. Write the word **H O M E** on the dinosaur cave.
2. Color the volcano red.
3. Color the trees green.
4. Draw a blue line to show a route the dinosaur can take home that goes past the volcano.
5. Draw a yellow line to show a route the dinosaur can take home. Make the route go past the rocks.

Name_______________________________________

Seeing the Wildlife

Martin and Norma are excited about visiting the Wildlife Safari. It is different from a zoo. Here they drive slowly along a road to see the animals run freely in large fenced areas. They stop at the gate to buy tickets and to get a map. They will use the map so that they will be sure to see all the animals.

Safari Map

Directions: Follow Martin and Norma's route. Write the names of the animals in the order they will see them.

1.____________________ 4.____________________

2.____________________ 5.____________________

3.____________________ 6.____________________

Name ______________________________

Take a Hike

This is a map showing three hiking trails.

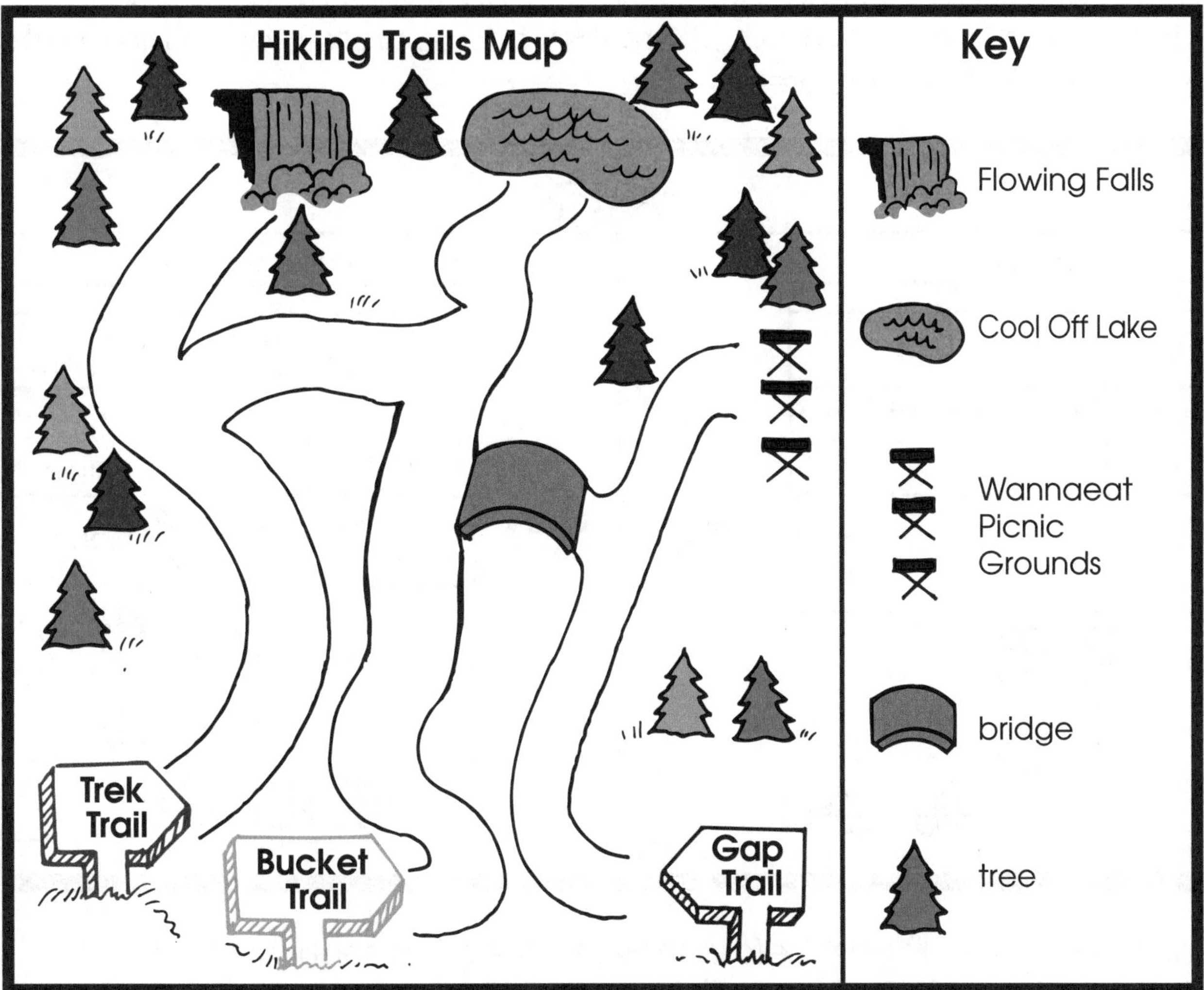

Directions:

1. Draw a red line along the trail that leads to the Wannaeat Picnic Grounds.
2. Draw a yellow line along the trail that leads to Flowing Falls.
3. Draw a green line along the trail that leads to Cool Off Lake.
4. Draw a blue line to show how you can go from Trek Trail to Cool Off Lake.
5. Draw an orange line to show how you can go from Bucket Trail to the Wannaeat Picnic Grounds.

Name ______________________________

Waiting at the Airport

Jenny and Carl went to the airport to pick up their grandparents. Dad let Mom and the kids out in front of the airport doors while he went to park the van. The dotted line (- - -) shows where they had to walk to go to the correct gate to meet their grandparents.

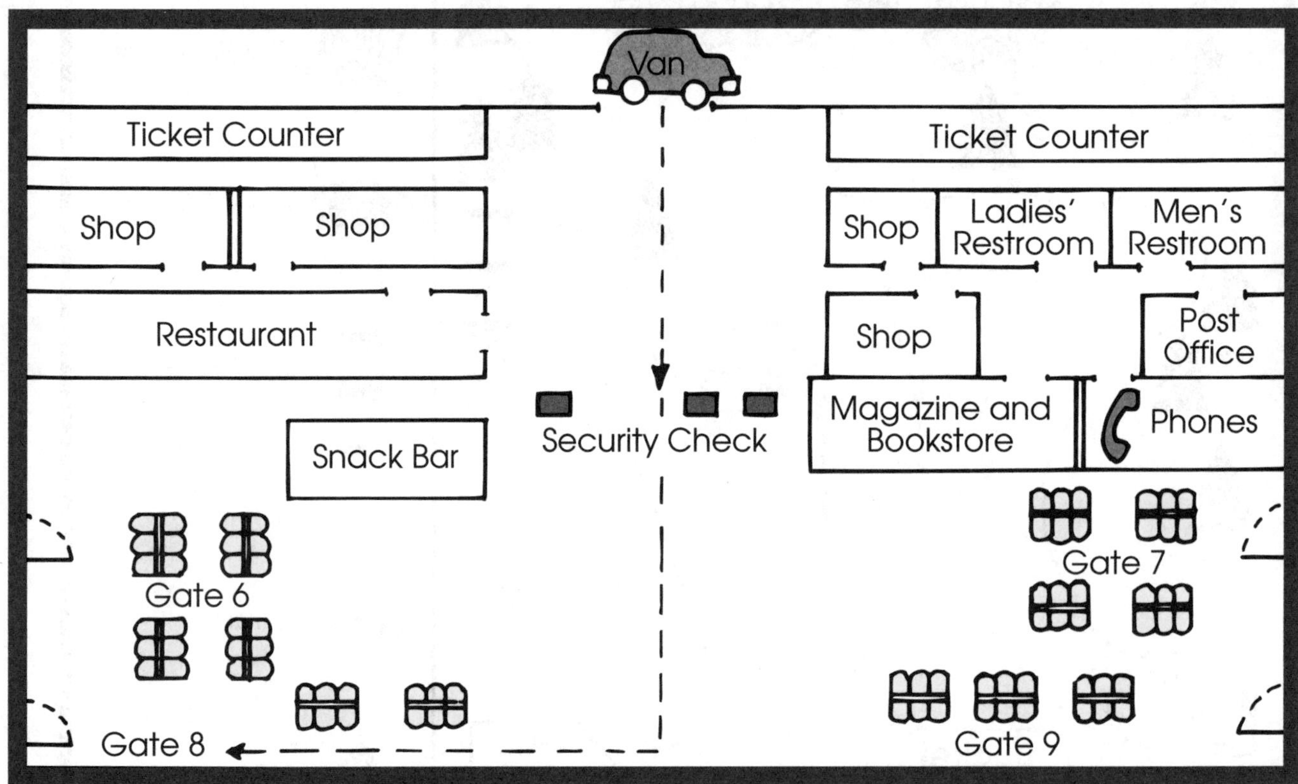

1. What did they walk past before they reached the security check?

____

____

2. Soon Dad joined them at the gate. Mom remembered she had to make a telephone call. Use an orange crayon to show the route she took to go from the gate to the telephones.

3. At what gate number will Jenny and Carl's grandparents arrive? _______

Name________________________________

A Real "Moose-tery"

Horrible Harvey Hunter has disappeared somewhere in the Mysterious Moosehead Mansion. Detective Dimwitt is trying to find him. Use the key to identify rooms in the mansion. Then, use a pencil to trace the route Detective Dimwitt took to locate the hapless Harvey.

Moosehead Mansion Map

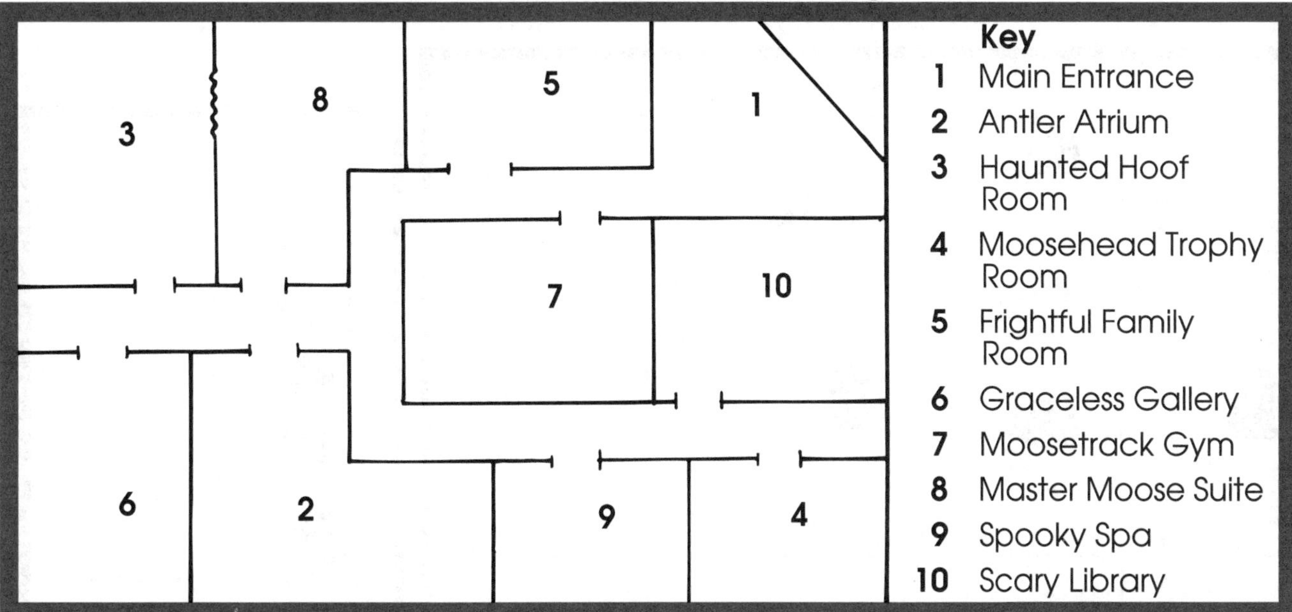

Detective Dimwitt's Route:

1. He enters the mansion at the Main Entrance.
2. Next, he checks out the Moosetrack Gym.
3. Then, he sneaks down the hall to the Antler Atrium.
4. From there he checks the Spooky Spa.
5. No luck, so on to the Scary Library he goes.
6. Next, the detective scans the Moosehead Trophy Room.
7. Then, he walks along the hall to look in the Frightful Family Room.
8. No Harvey there, so he moves on to the Graceless Gallery.
9. Could he be in the Master Moose Suite? He checks there.
10. Then, he looks in the Haunted Hoof Room.
11. There he discovers a secret room. Inside he finds Harvey reading a hunting magazine. The search is over!

Name________________________________

Find It There

To find your way around a town or city you can use a street map.

Find the bookstore on the key. Now, find it on the map. Look at the name of the street that goes past the bookstore. If you want to go to the bookstore, you will have to go to Smelt Street.

Street Map

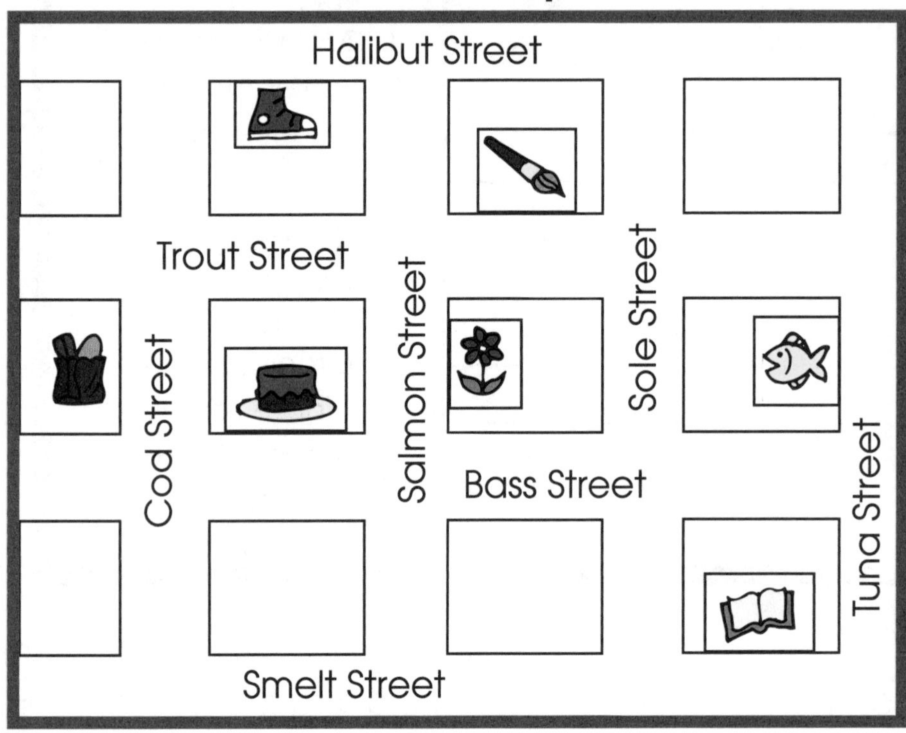

Directions:

Use the street map and map key. Fill in the blanks.

1. You can buy a cake on ____________________ Street.
2. You can buy new shoes on ____________________ Street.
3. You can buy a new fish tank on ____________________ Street.
4. What store is on Salmon Street? ____________________

Name ____________________

Going from Place to Place

Some maps show you where places are located in a town.

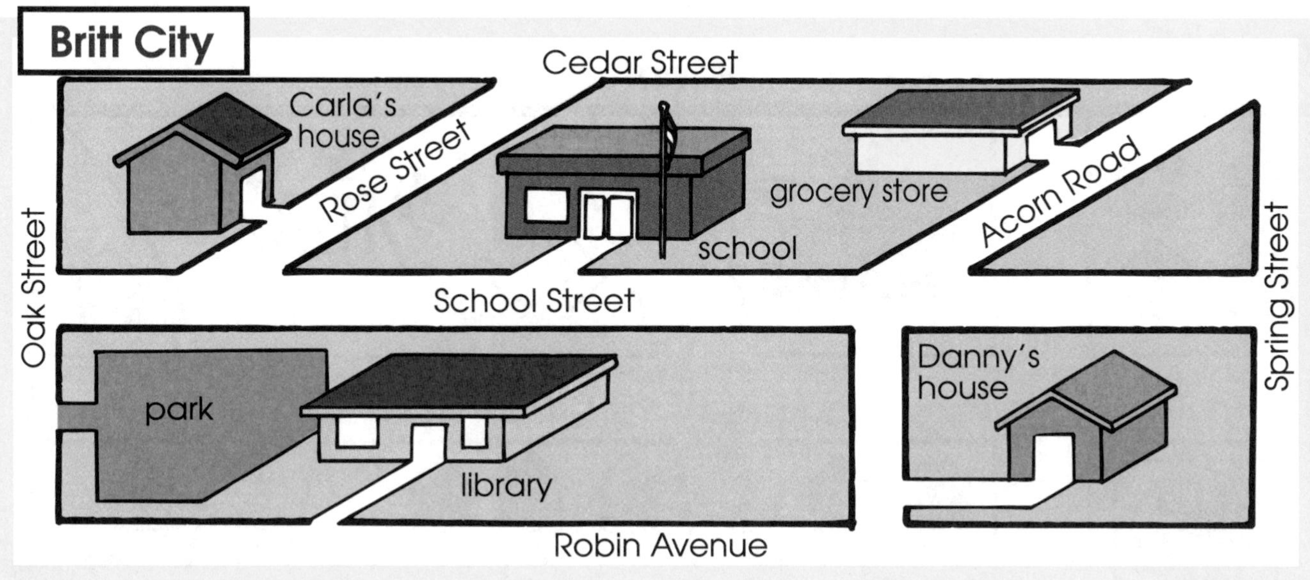

Circle the word that tells which is **closest** to Danny's house.

1. Carla's house	OR	the library
2. Robin Avenue	OR	Oak Street
3. the park	OR	the grocery store
4. Spring Street	OR	Cedar Street

Circle the word that tells which is **farthest** from Carla's house.

1. Spring Street	OR	Rose Street
2. the park	OR	Danny's house
3. the school	OR	the library
4. Oak Street	OR	Acorn Road

Add the following items to the map of Britt City.

1. Draw a flower garden on the corner of Spring Street and Robin Avenue.
2. Draw a swimming pool behind Carla's house.
3. Draw a baseball or football field behind the school.
4. Draw a car in front of Carla's house.
5. Draw a school bus on School Street.
6. Use a red crayon to draw the shortest path from Carla's house to Danny's.

Name________________________________

Map Routes

Victory Celebration

Betsy, Rachel and Pat were so happy! They won their first baseball game. To celebrate, they wanted to have pizza and ice cream. Use this map and key to complete page 33.

Map

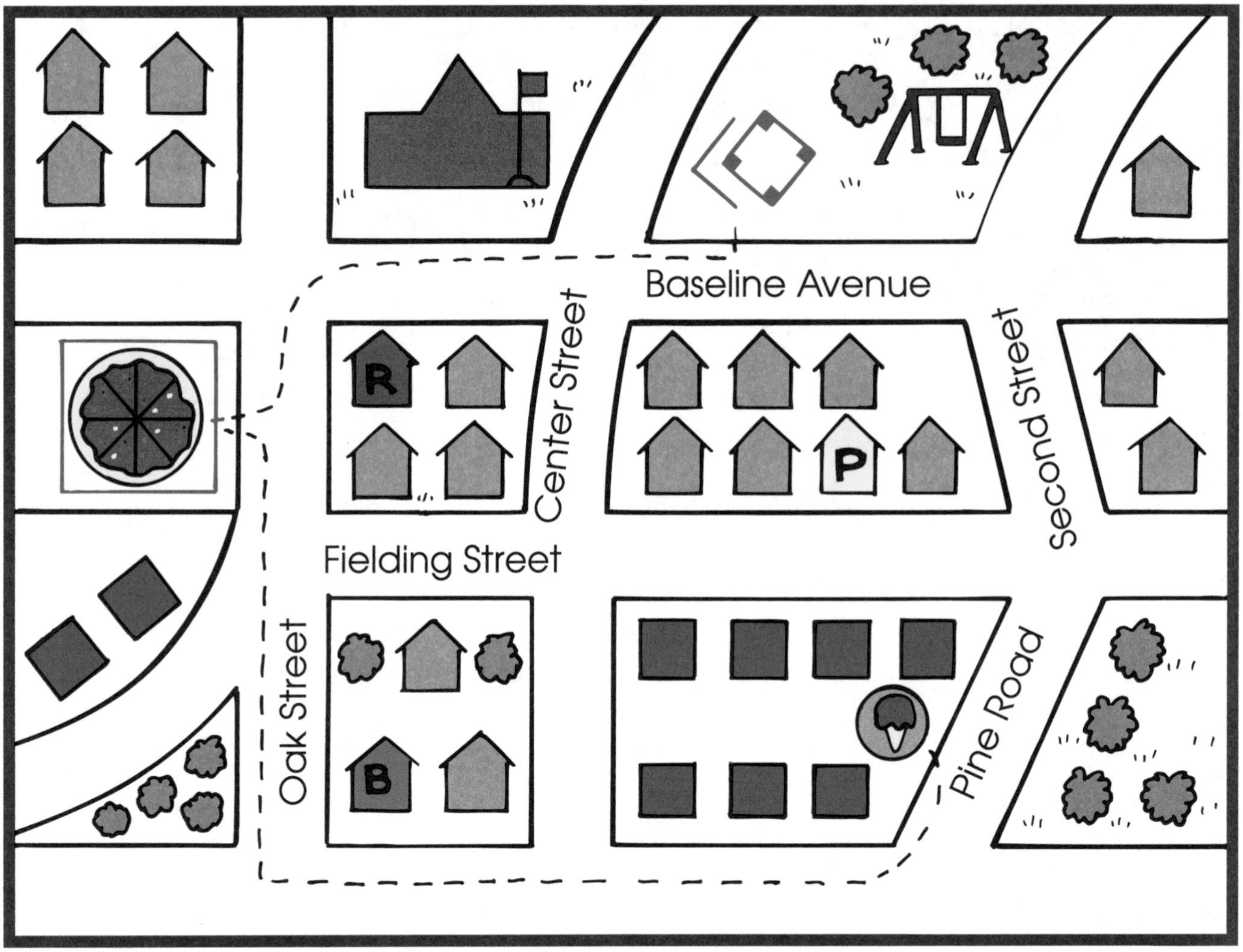

Baseline Avenue

Center Street

Second Street

Fielding Street

Oak Street

Pine Road

Key

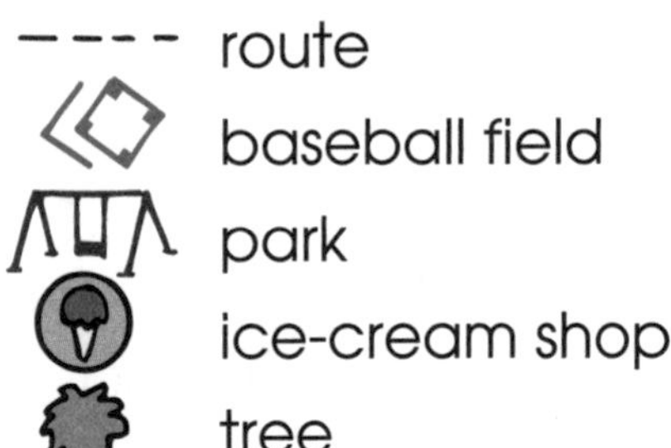

route

baseball field

park

ice-cream shop

tree

school

store

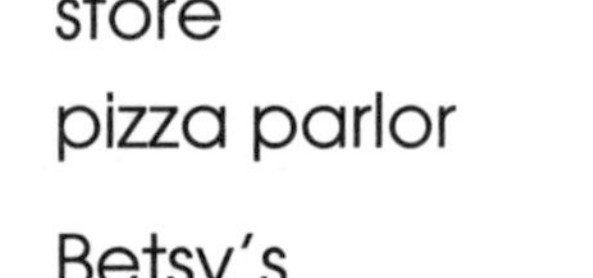

pizza parlor

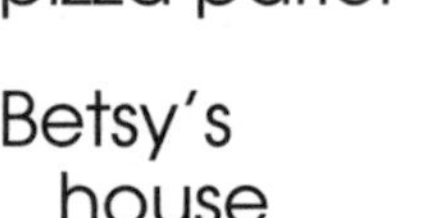

Betsy's house

house

Rachel's house

Pat's house

Name________________________________

Victory Celebration

1. Use your finger to follow the route the girls took from the baseball field to the pizza parlor. On what street did they walk when they first left the baseball field?

____

2. Did they walk past the school?________________________________

3. Did they walk past a park? ________________________________

4. On what street is the pizza parlor?________________________________

5. Use your finger to trace their route to the ice-cream shop. On what street is the ice-cream shop?

____

6. Then, it was time to go home. Use a blue crayon to mark a route Betsy might have taken home.

7. Use a red crayon to mark a route Rachel might have taken home.

8. Use a purple crayon to mark a route Pat might have taken home.

Name ________________________________

Map Routes

A New Puppy

Mike's dog had puppies. Jason and his parents are going to Mike's house to get one of the puppies. Use the street map and key to help you answer the questions.

Map

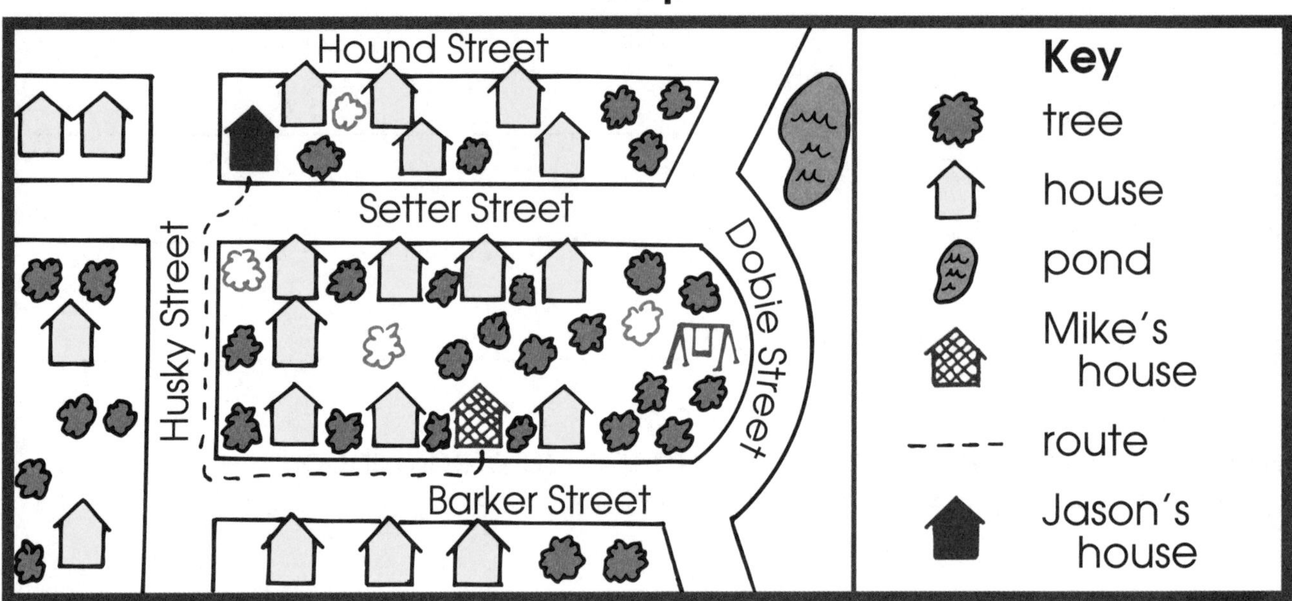

1. Find Jason's house. On what street does he live?

   ____

2. Find Mike's house. On what street does he live?

   ____

3. Use a red crayon to trace the route Mike drew for Jason to follow.

4. Which streets will Jason use to get to Mike's house?

   ____

5. Use a blue crayon to draw a different route Jason could use to get to Mike's house.

Name________________________________

Places to Go

Mrs. Nelson needs to do many errands this afternoon. She only has a short time in which to do everything. Read Mrs. Nelson's list of things to do. Use the street map and key to answer the questions.

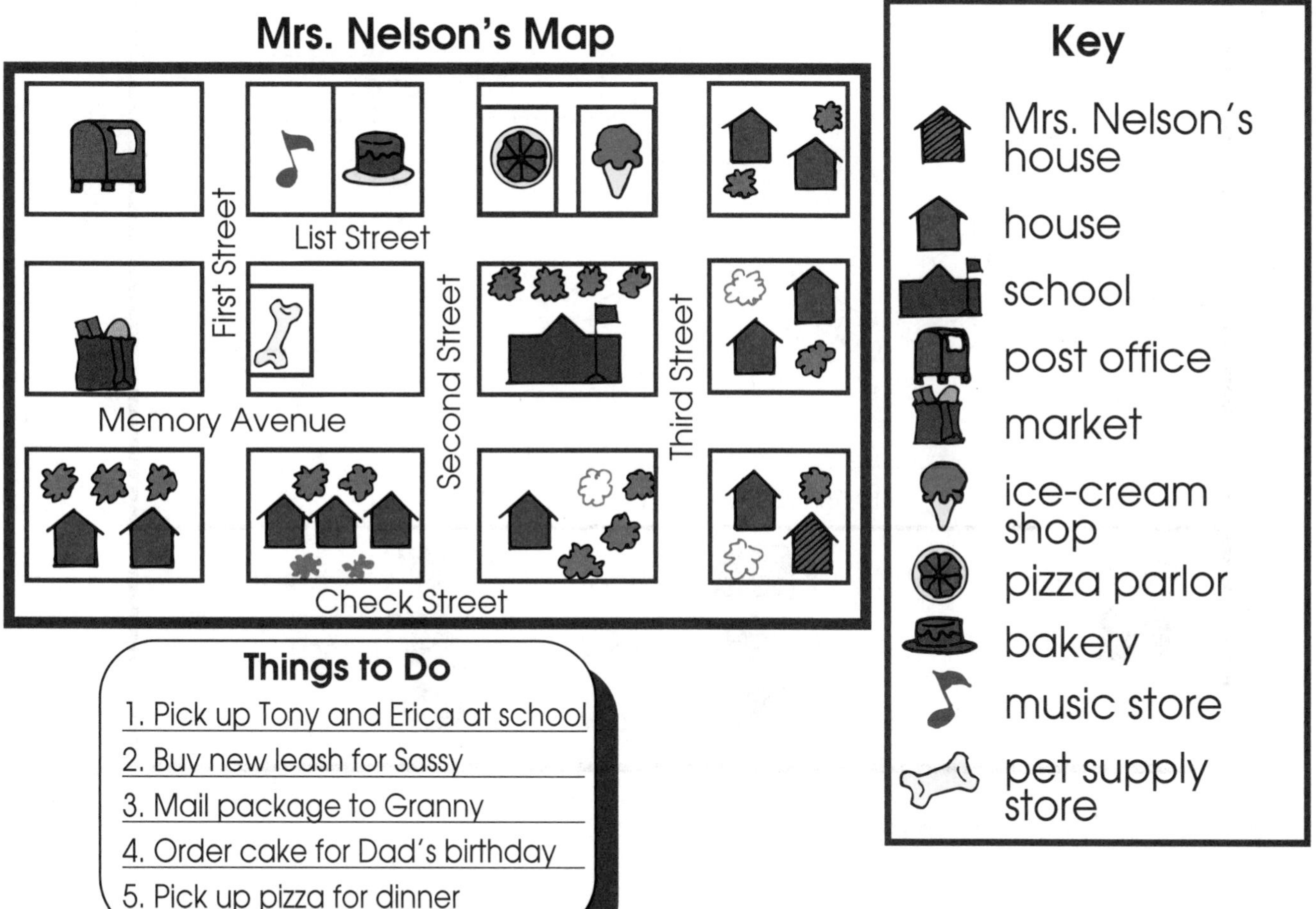

1. On the map, find the places Mrs. Nelson needs to go.
2. Mrs. Nelson will go to these places in the same order as her list of things to do. Write the number on each place on the map to show the order in which she will go to these places.
3. Start at Mrs. Nelson's house. Use a red crayon to draw the route Mrs. Nelson will take to do all of her errands.

Name________________________________

My Home Town

Complete the map by drawing the symbols from the key by each matching number on the map.

Map

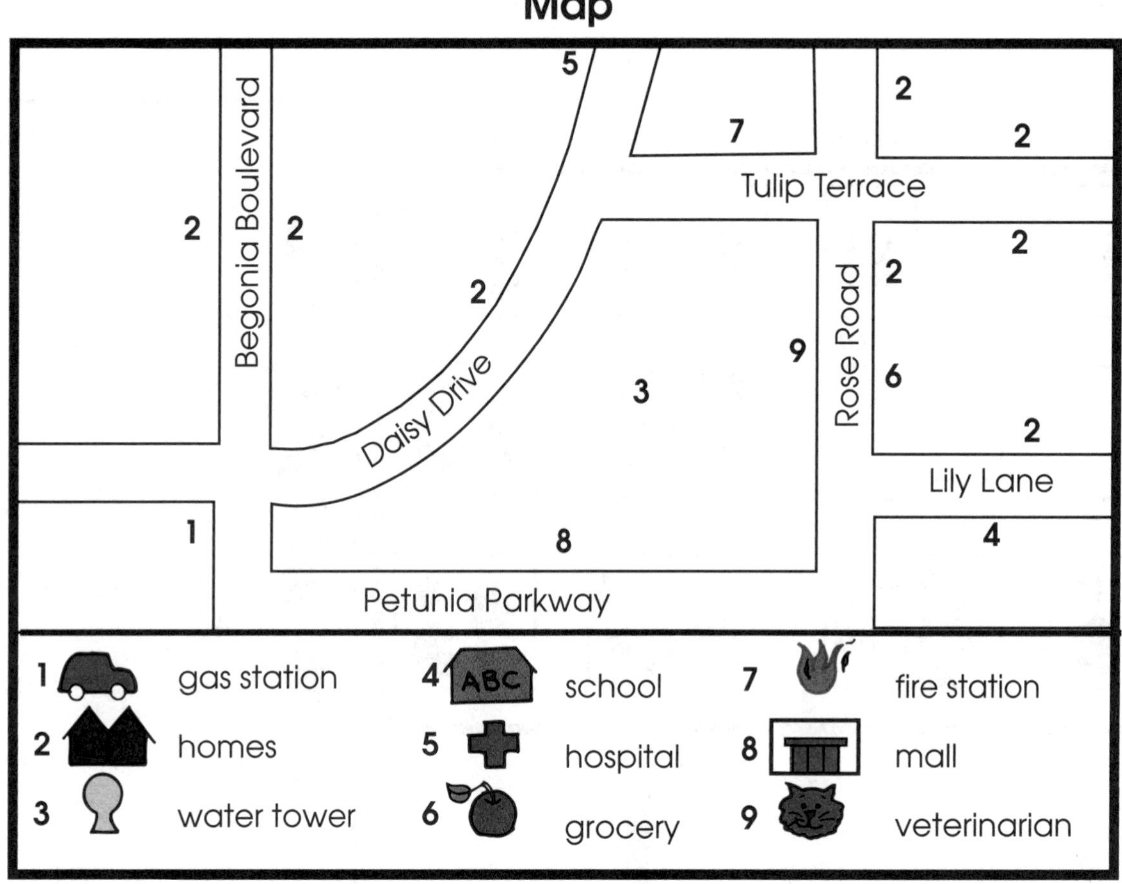

Directions: Write the name of the streets.

1. The gas station is on the corner of ______________________________

   and ______________________________.

2. The vet is on ______________________________.

3. The fire station is on ______________________________.

4. There are no homes on ______________________________.

5. The school is on ______________________________.

6. The grocery store is on______________________________.

Name_______________________________________

The Compass Rose

This is a compass rose. It tells the directions on a map. There are four arrows. Each arrow points in a different direction. These are called **cardinal** directions.

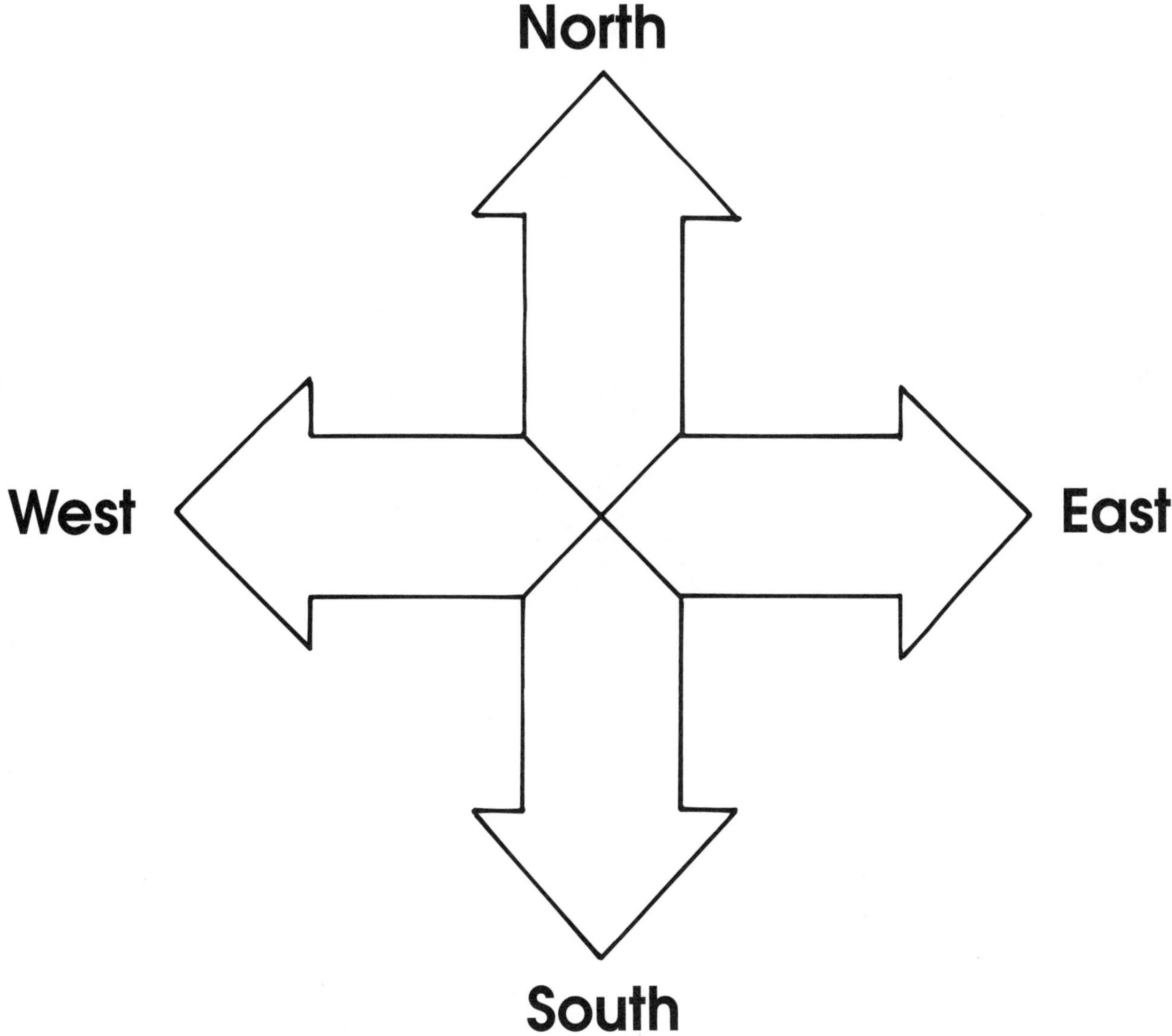

1. The arrow that points up is **north**. Color it blue.
2. The arrow that points down is **south**. Color it red.
3. The arrow that points to the right is **east**. Color it green.
4. The arrow that points to the left is **west**. Color it brown.

Name____

Compasses

Finding a Snack

The little bear cub is hungry for a snack. Read the clues. In each bear paw print, draw a picture of the snack he will find if he goes in that direction. Use the compass rose to help you.

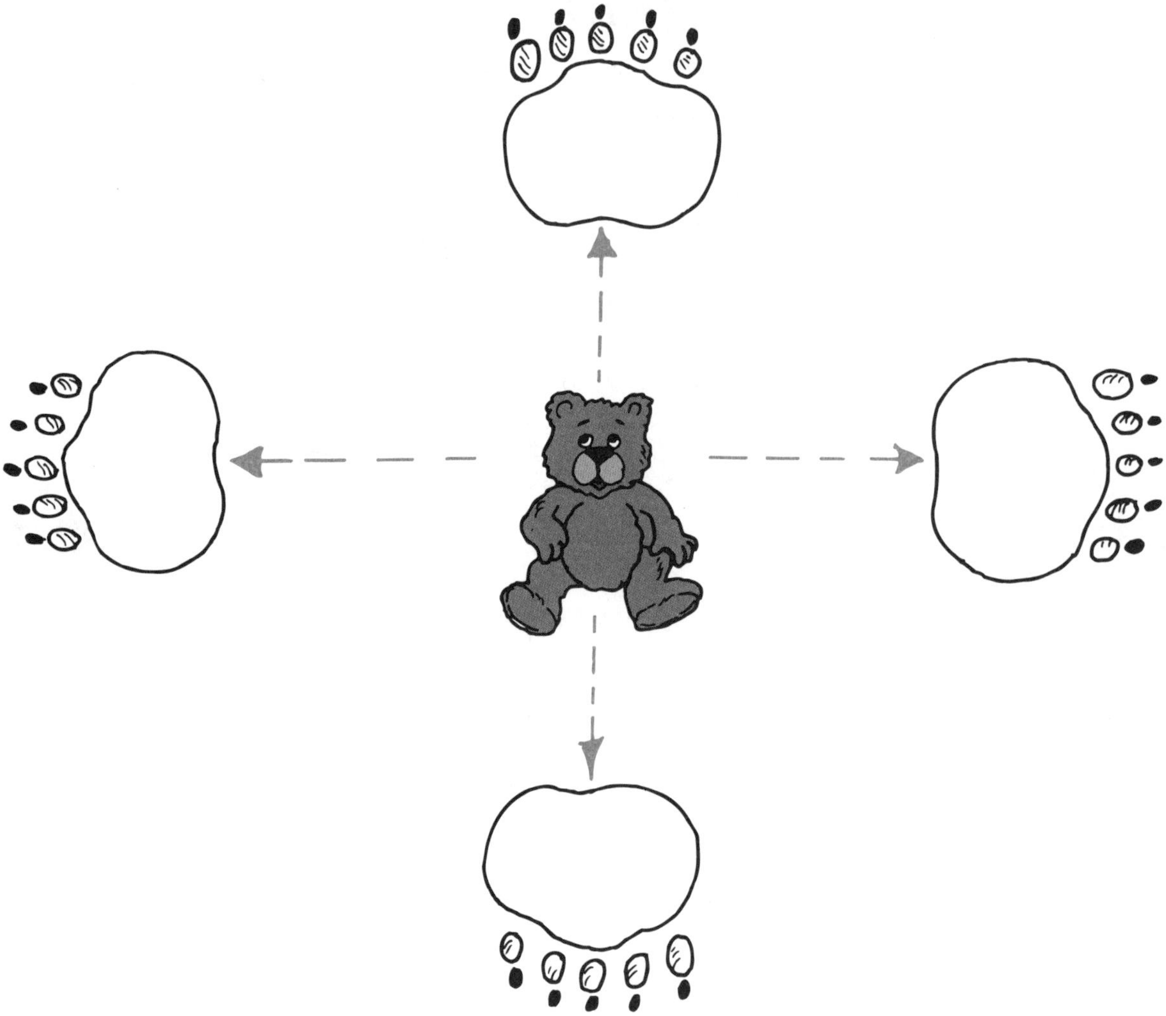

1. He will find [grapes] to the **west**.
2. He will find [cookie] to the **south**.
3. He will find [fish] to the **north**.
4. He will find [honey jar] to the **east**.

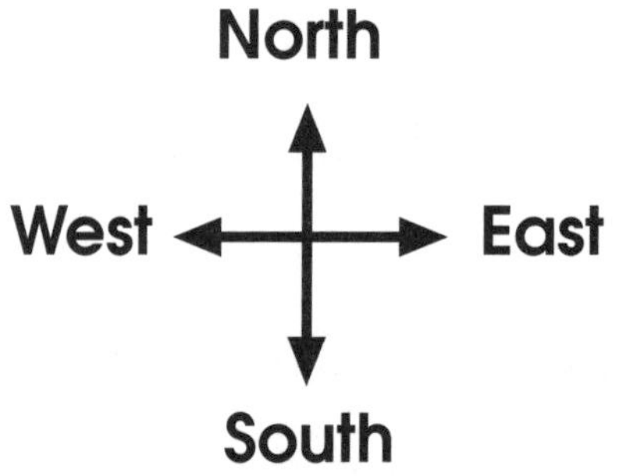

Name________________________________

Pirate's Booty

Sedgewick the Pirate must be able to find his buried treasure when he returns to the island. Read the sentences. Write the words **north**, **south**, **east** and **west** in the blanks to help Sedgewick locate his treasure. Use the compass rose to help you.

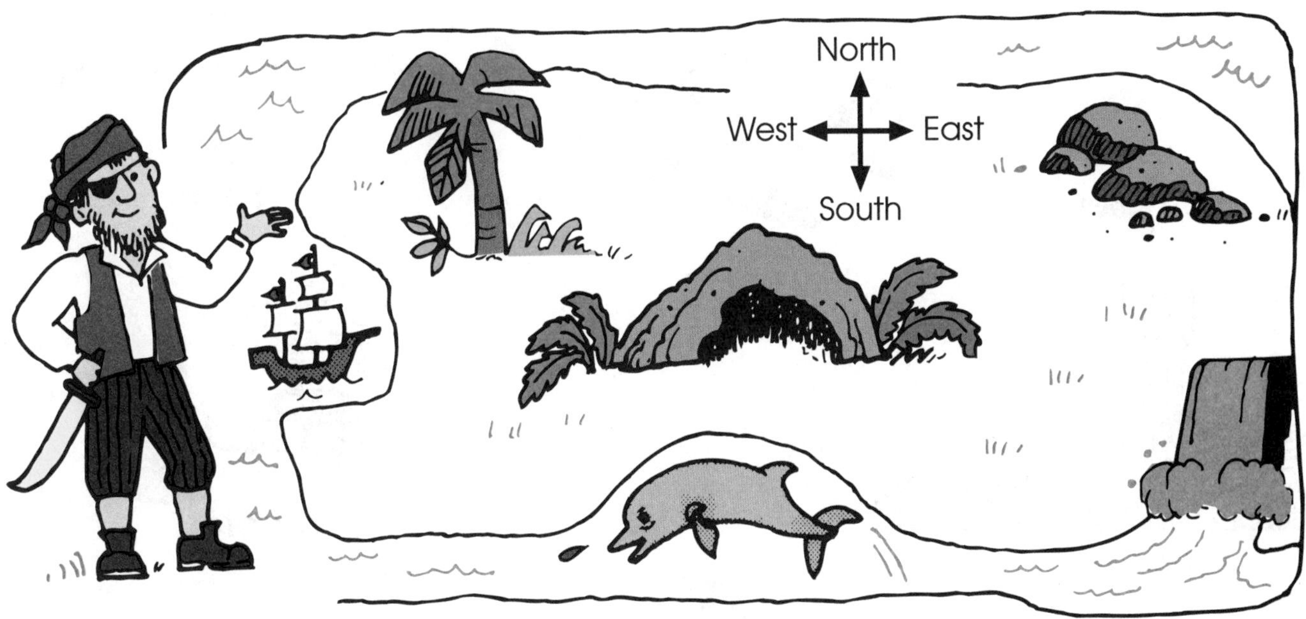

1. Dock the ship on the____________________ side of the island.

2. Walk____________________ to the cave.

3. Then, walk____________________ to Dolphin Cove.

4. Go ____________________ to the waterfall.

5. Go____________________ to the rocks.

6. Then, go____________________ to the palm tree.

7. Draw an **X** below the palm tree to show where the treasure is buried.

Name ______________________________

Look to the Sky

Mr. McGill took his students on a field trip to the airport. A boy in his class drew this map of things they saw.

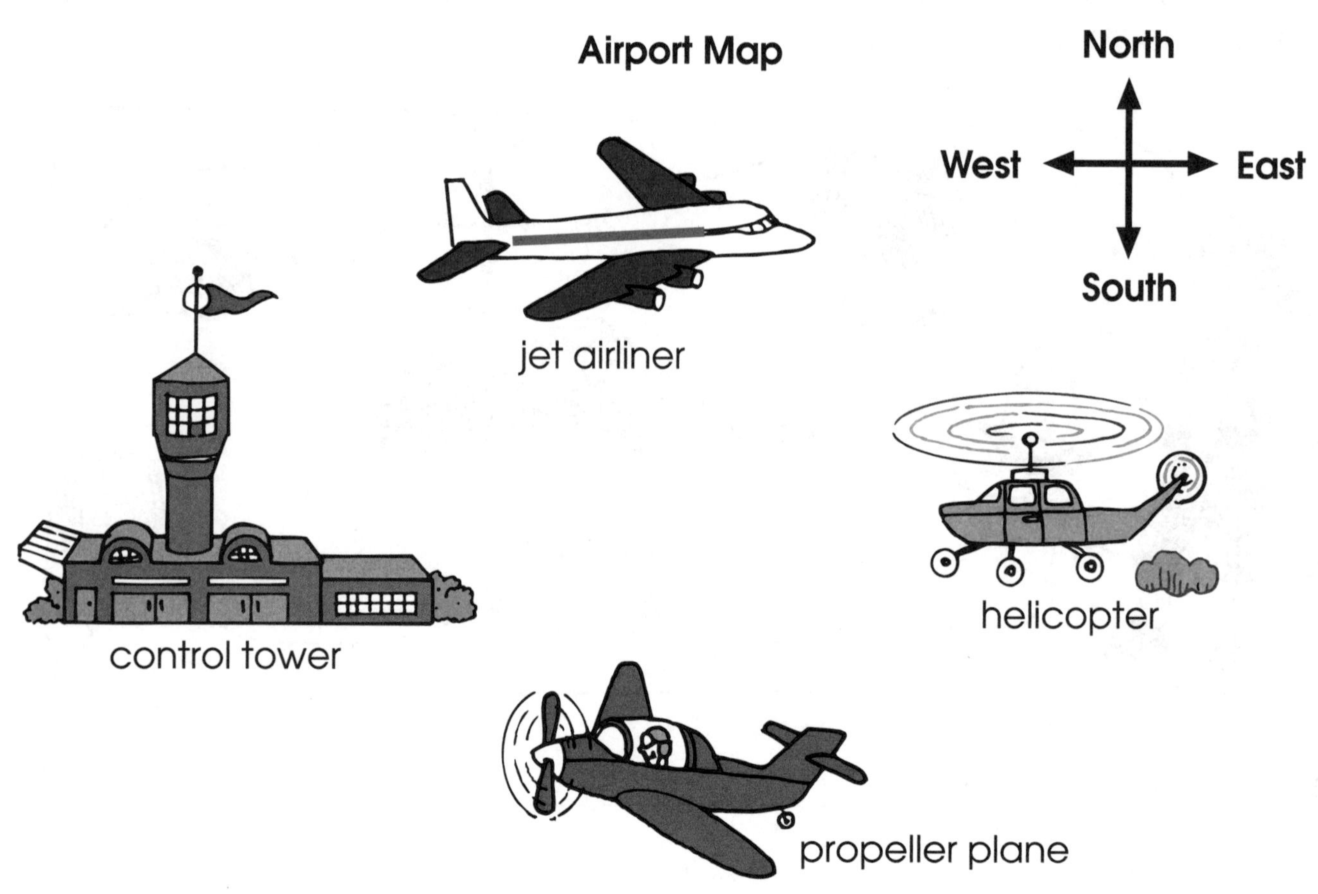

Directions: Write **north, south, west** or **east** to complete each sentence.

1. Look ______________________ to see the jet airliner.
2. Look ______________________ to see the control tower.
3. Look ______________________ to see the propeller plane.
4. Look ______________________ to see the helicopter.

Name______________________________________

Sign Search

Gina went for a hike. She found a piece of paper. There were strange directions written on it. Then, she looked around and saw pictures drawn on the rocks in the area. Aha! The paper she had found was a route to follow. Read the directions and draw the route on the map.

Map

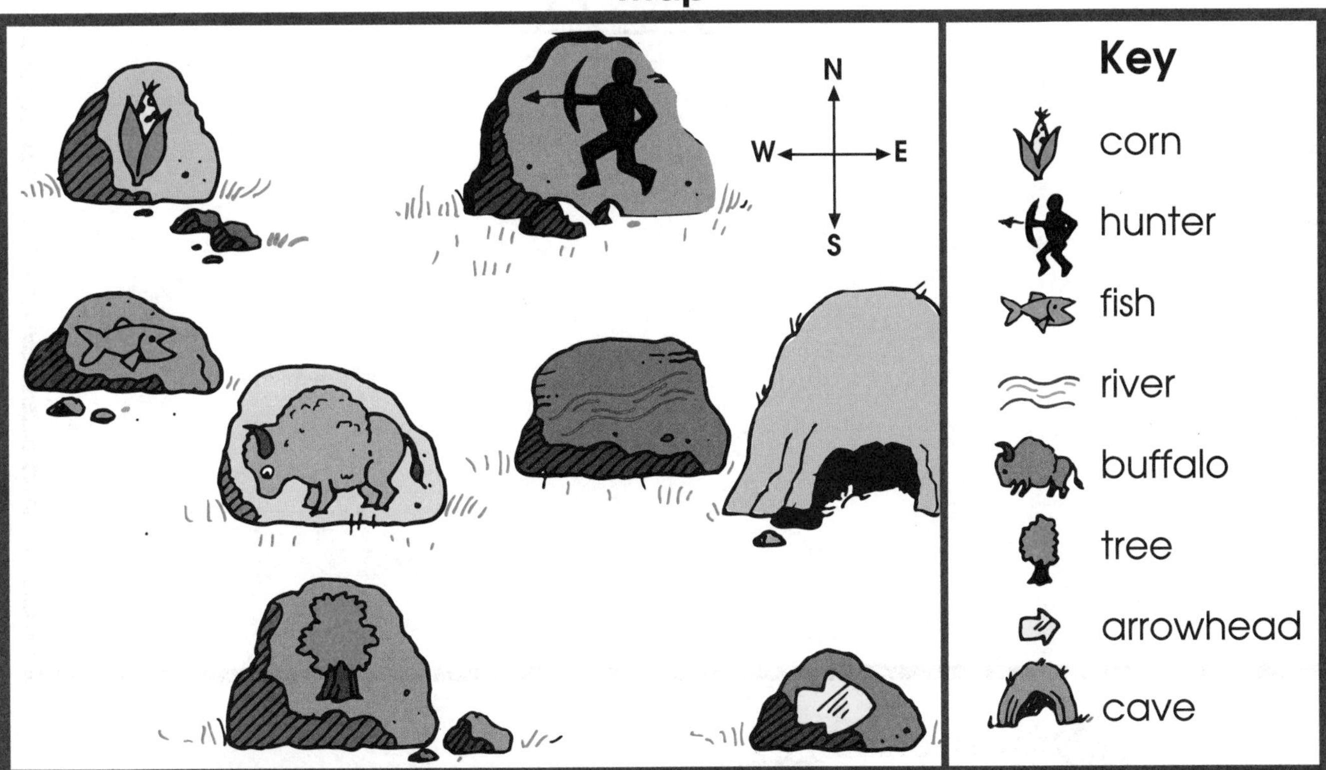

1. Start at the fish.
2. Go north to the corn.
3. Then go east to the hunter.
4. Go south to the river.
5. Go west to the buffalo.
6. Go south to the tree.
7. Go east to the arrowhead.
8. Go north to the cave. Draw a picture on the cave to show the treasure chest Gina finds there.

Name____

What Do Hikers See?

Follow the directions to complete this area map.

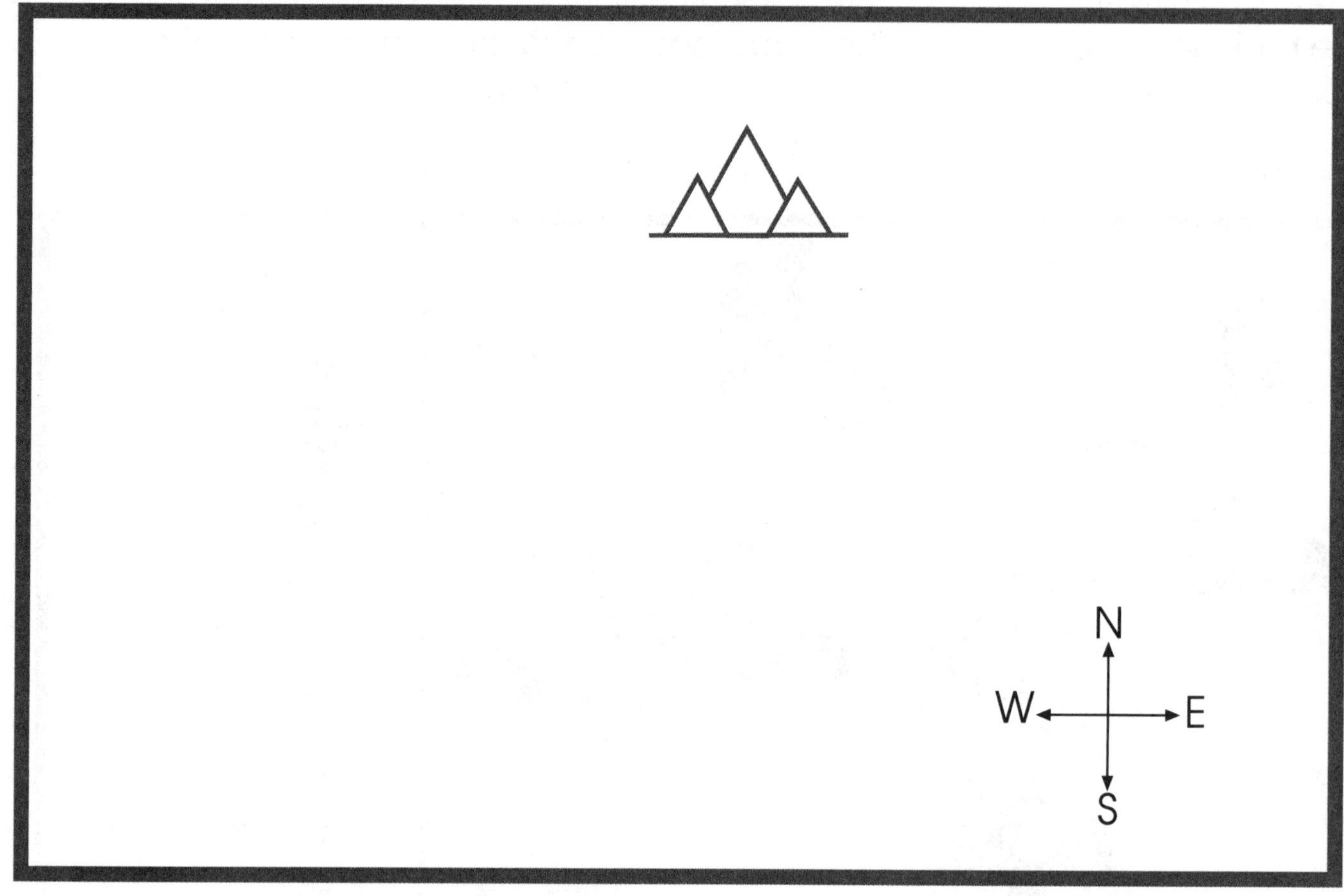

1. Draw a west of the .
2. Draw 6 south of the .
3. Draw an in the middle of the .
4. Draw 10 south of the .
5. Draw a between the and the .
6. Draw 2 on the east side of the .
7. Draw 2 south of the 6 .
8. Draw 3 south of the .

Name ____________________

You're Invited

Liz sent out invitations to her birthday party. She drew a map to show how to go from school to her house.

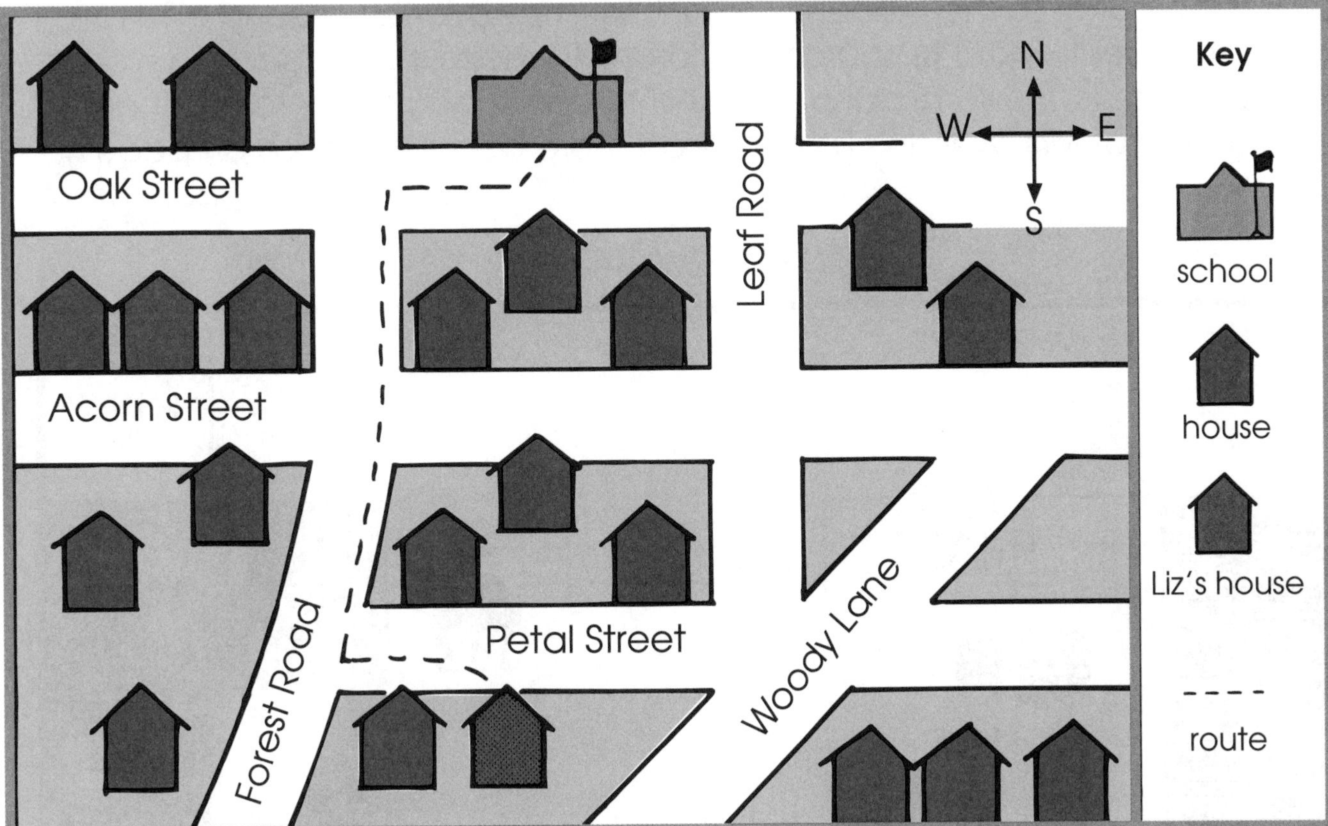

Directions:

Write **north**, **south**, **east** or **west** and the street name to complete the sentences.

1. Leave the school and go____________ along ____________________.

2. Turn________________ onto ______________________________.

3. Then, turn _______________ onto ____________________________.

Name____

Missing Diamonds

Mrs. Wently's diamonds are missing. Seth Sleuth has been hired to find them. He listens to Mrs. Wently's story. She had seen the robber run through the library and out onto the balcony. Then, he jumped to the ground and ran away. Seth Sleuth went to search the library. Perhaps the robber had hidden the diamonds in the library and planned to come back later to get them. This is a map of Mrs. Wently's library. Read more about the case on page 45.

Library Map

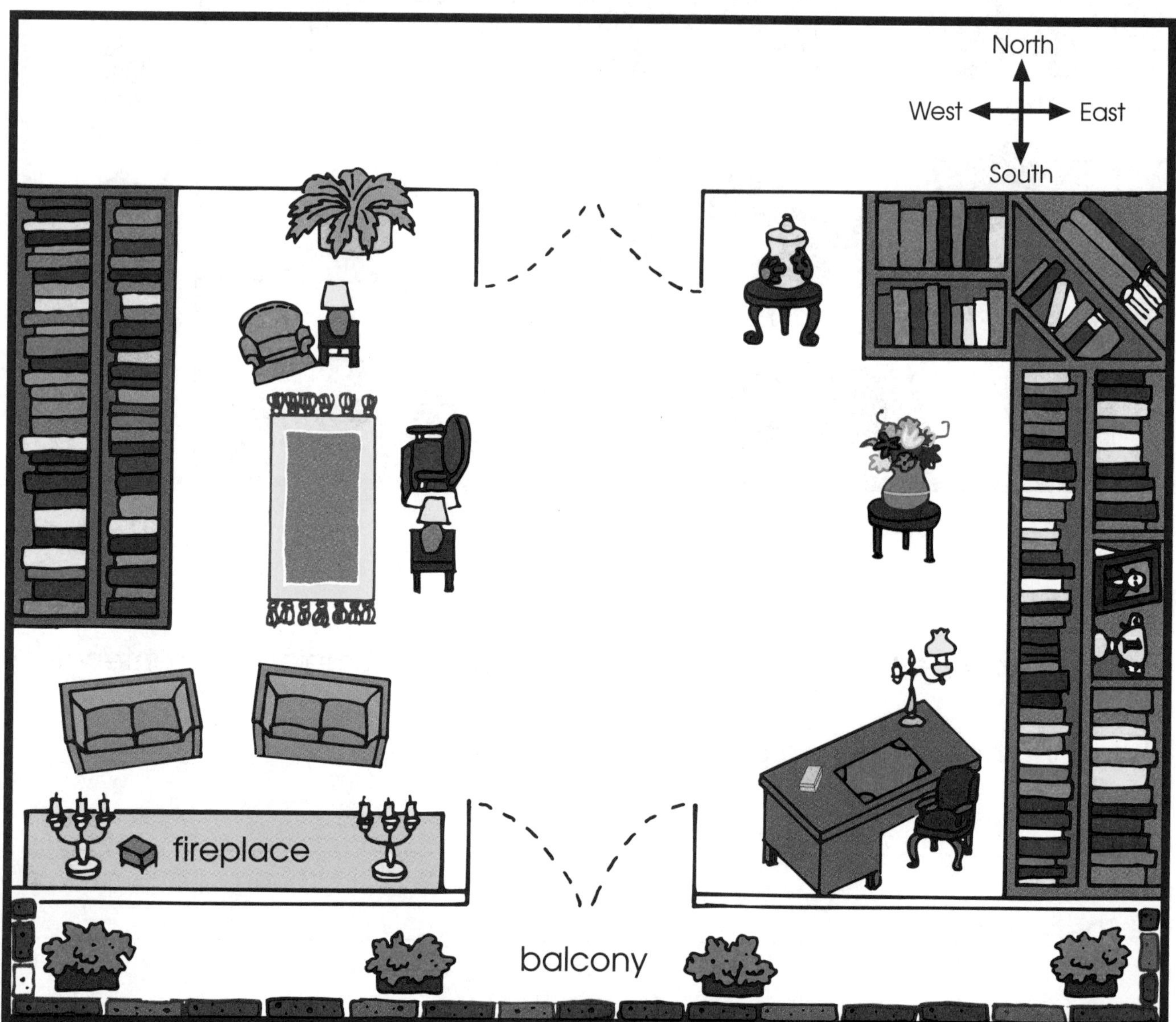

Name ___________________________

Missing Diamonds

Can you find the missing diamonds? Help Seth Sleuth search the library. Read the directions. Use the compass rose to help you. Use a red crayon to draw the route on the library map to show where you search.

1. You walk through the doors at the north end of the library.
2. Walk west to the bookcase and look behind every book.
3. Now, walk south to the fireplace. Look around the things on the mantel.
4. Walk north to the rug. There's a lump! Lift the rug. It is only the cat's toy mouse.
5. Walk east and then south to the balcony doors. Maybe the robber hid the diamonds outside. Look out on the balcony. No diamonds there.
6. Hmmmm. The diamonds must be in the library. Go back inside the balcony doors. Walk east to the desk. No diamonds in sight.
7. Walk north and look behind every book. Look inside the vase on the small table. Nothing there.
8. Head west and then north to look at the beautiful jar. Lift the lid. Inside are the sparkling diamonds. Draw a ◊ where you found the missing diamonds. Congratulations! You solved the case.

Name________________________________

Ice Cream!

Ding. Ding. Ding-a-ling! Here comes the ice-cream truck. On hot summer days, Stan drives his ice-cream truck around the neighborhood. He takes the same route every day. This map shows the neighborhood where Stan drives. Follow the directions on page 47.

Ice-Cream Truck Route Map

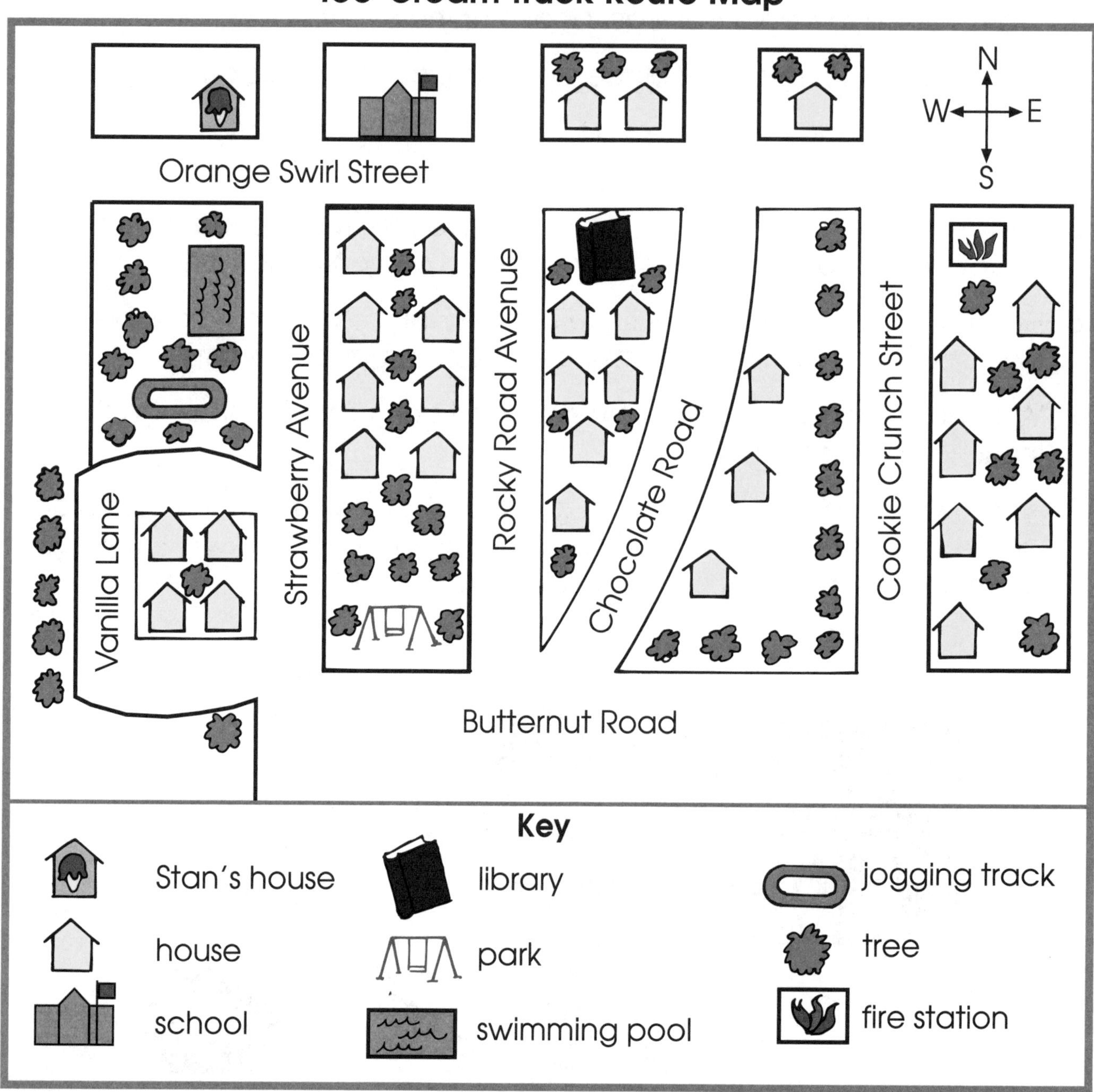

Name________________________________

Ice Cream!

Draw Stan's route on the map on page 46. To do this, read the information below. Use the map key and compass rose to help you.

1. Stan backs out of his driveway onto Orange Swirl Street.
2. He goes east.
3. Then, he turns south onto Strawberry Avenue.
4. He drives past the swimming pool. After he passes the jogging track, he turns west onto Vanilla Lane.
5. He drives around Vanilla Lane. Then, he drives east on Butternut Road past the park.
6. He turns and drives north along Rocky Road Avenue.
7. At the corner he turns and drives east along Orange Swirl Street.
8. He passes the library and drives south along Chocolate Road.
9. He turns east onto Butternut Road and drives past the row of trees.
10. Then, he turns north and drives along Cookie Crunch Street.
11. He passes the fire station and turns west and drives along Orange Swirl Street until he reaches his home.

Name____

Secret Mission

Sam Super Spy is on a mission. He must get the secret papers and deliver them to his boss as soon as possible. This is a map of where the mission is to take place. Follow the directions on page 49 to help Sam.

Name____

Secret Mission

Directions: Use a red crayon to mark the route Sam will take.

1. Enter the park through the entrance at the north end of the park.
2. Turn and walk east and then south past the swings and jungle gym.
3. Turn and go west to the fountain.
4. Walk to the south side of the fountain.
5. Walk to the bench south of the fountain.
6. You will find the papers you want under the wastebasket to the west of the bench. Draw a red **X** on where Sam finds the secret papers.

Now, Sam must deliver the secret papers to his boss. Use a blue crayon to mark the route Sam will take. Start at the red **X** you drew.

1. Walk south to the path.
2. Turn and walk east along the path to the wastebasket.
3. Turn and walk south near the duck pond.
4. Walk south to the path.
5. Turn and walk west toward the bridge.
6. There is a man standing under the tree north of the bridge. Sam hands the secret papers to him. Mission completed! Draw a blue **X** to show where Sam delivered the secret papers.

Name____

Connect - A - Dot

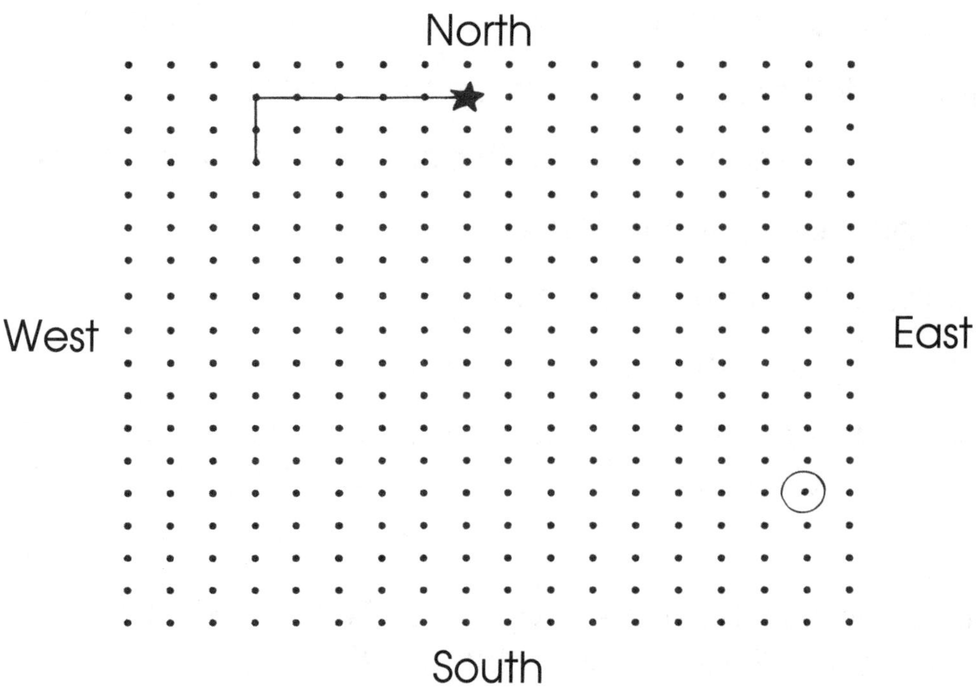

Directions: Follow the instructions below to complete a drawing. Begin at the star. The first two steps are done for you.

Draw a straight line . . .

1. Five spaces west.
2. Two spaces south.
3. Four spaces east.
4. Nine spaces south.
5. Two spaces east.
6. Nine spaces north.
7. Four spaces east.
8. Two spaces north.
9. Five spaces west.

What letter did you draw? ____________

Begin at the circle to complete another drawing.

Draw a straight line . . .

1. Four spaces south.
2. One space west.
3. Three spaces north.
4. One space west.
5. One space north.
6. Two spaces east.

What number did you draw? __________

Name ____________________

Finding Your Way Around Town

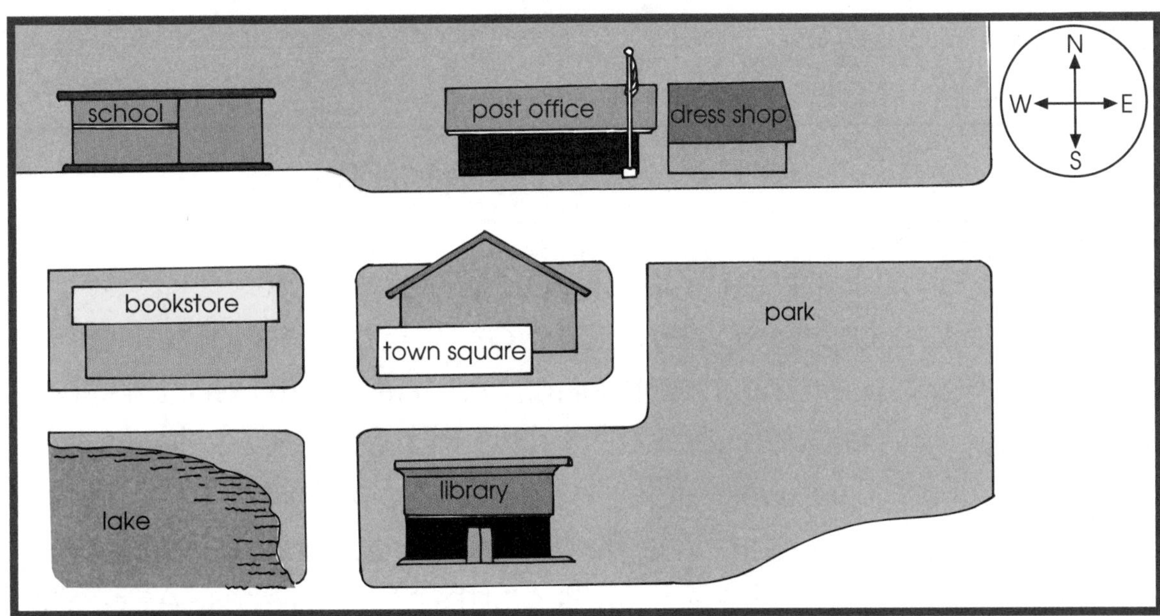

Directions: You are in the middle of the town square. Circle the correct answer to each question.

1. What direction is the library from you?	north	west	south
2. What direction is the bookstore from you?	west	east	south
3. What direction must you go to reach the post office?	east	north	west
4. Which direction must you go to get to the park?	north	west	east

Use crayons or markers to complete the map.

1. Place a red **X** on the first place north of the library.
2. Place a black **X** on the place east of the post office.
3. Draw a red circle on the place west of the dress shop.
4. Draw a blue fish on the place south of the bookstore.
5. Draw three trees east of the library.
6. Draw a movie theater east of the dress shop.
7. Draw a car south of the dress shop.
8. Draw a slide east of the school and west of the post office.
9. Draw doors and windows on the first building north of the lake.
10. Draw a yellow bus south of the place which is west of the post office.

Name________________________________

A Great Camp!

Read the letter. Then, draw a map to show what the camp looks like. Make a key for the map.

June 20, 2009

Dear Elizabeth,

This camp is great! I'll tell you what is here.

There is a big wooden gate as you come into the campground at the north end. At the south end there is a lake where we swim and ride in boats. We sleep in five tents on the west side. A big log cabin on the east side is where we eat. We make necklaces and other things under a big tree that is north of the tents. At night we sing songs and tell stories around a campfire south of the log cabin.

Hope you are having fun at home. See you soon.

Your friend,

Sandy

Camp Map

N

W E

S

Key

Name ______________________________

Making a Compass

A compass is a magnet that can identify geographic direction. It is very easy and a lot of fun to make your own compass!

You will need:
magnet
steel sewing needle
piece of thin plastic foam
(from fast-food packaging)
shallow glass or plastic bowl
masking tape
water

Directions:

1. Pull the sewing needle toward you across the magnet. Repeat this 20 times. Be sure to always pull in the same direction.

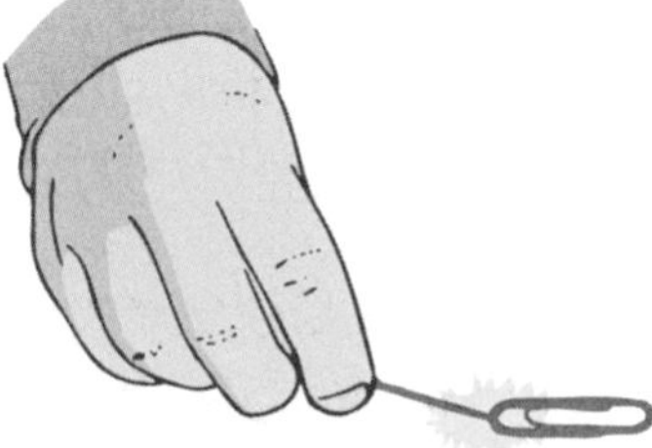

2. Test your needle on a steel object. If it is not yet magnetized, repeat step #1.

3. Tape the needle to a small piece of plastic foam.

4. Float your magnet in a dish of water.

What happened?

Wait for your floating needle to stop spinning. In what direction is it pointing?

____

Try giving the floating needle a little spin. Wait for it to stop spinning.

Now what direction is it pointing? ______________________

Name____

Drawing a Compass Rose

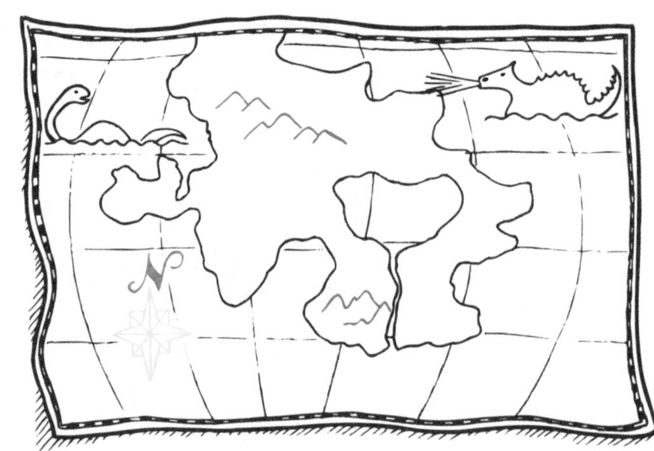

The maps of the early explorers were beautiful pieces of art. Their maps would often have pictures of fire-breathing dragons and sea monsters warning of dangers where they were traveling.

In a corner of their map would be a beautiful compass rose. The compass rose indicated the four cardinal directions—north, south, east and west. The compass rose also indicated four intermediate directions which are halfway between the four cardinal directions. They are northwest (NW), northeast (NE), southwest (SW) and southeast (SE).

Follow the steps below to draw a **compass rose** in the upper right-hand corner of the map. Indicate the cardinal **directions** on your rose. Then, draw a map of your own make-believe land.

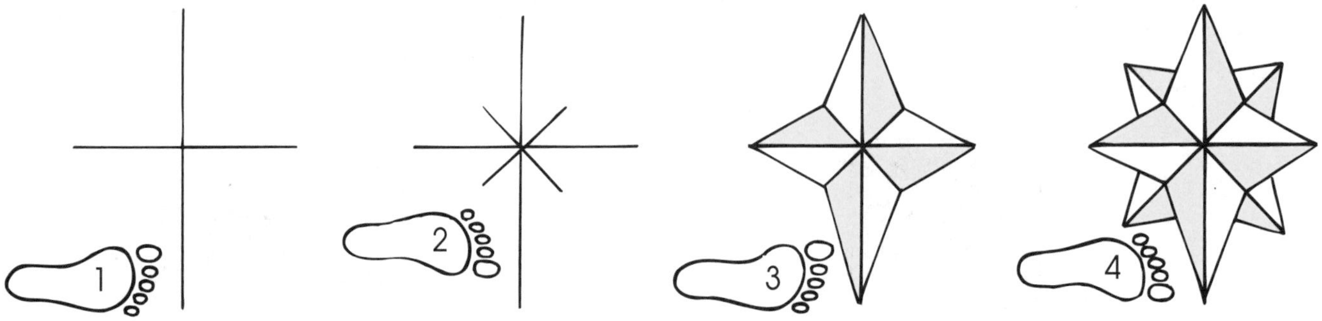

1 2 3 4

Name______________________________

Dizzy Designers

Decorate the compass rose boxes by following the directions below.

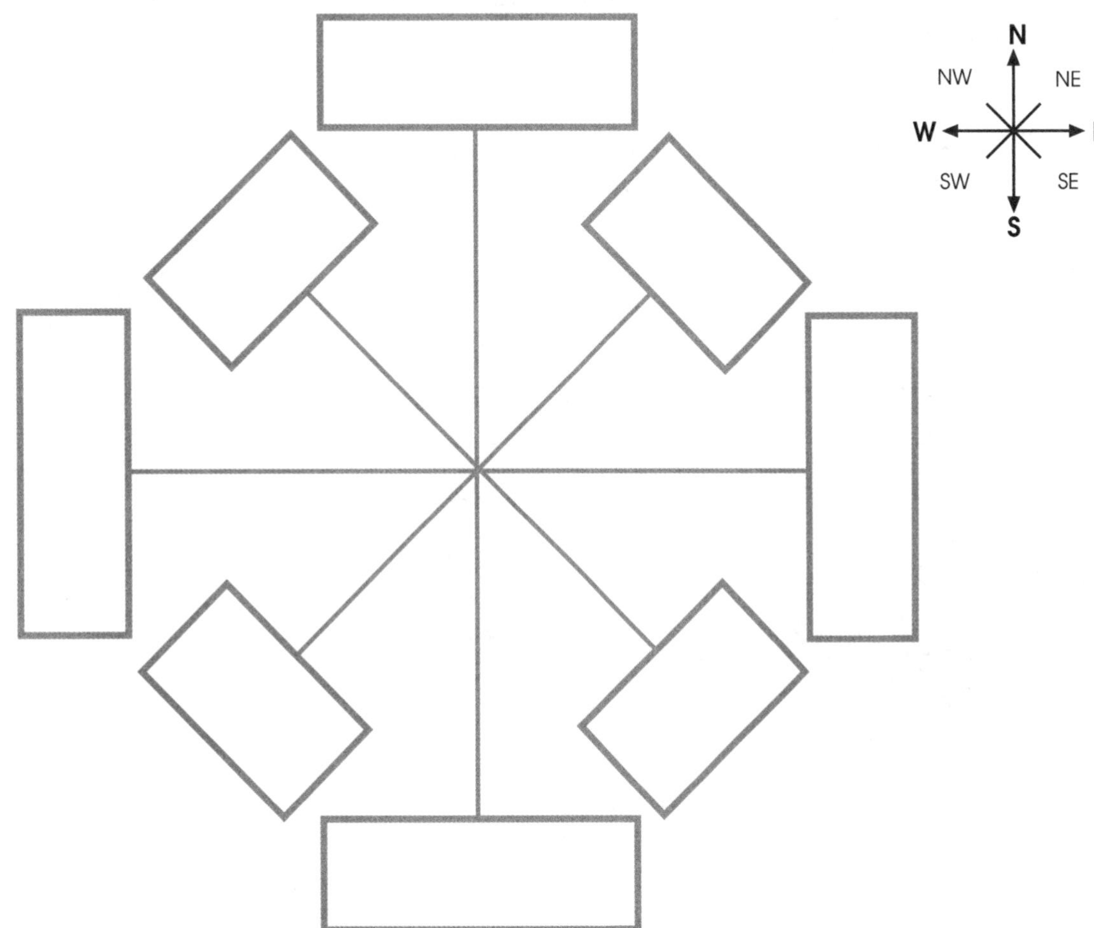

1. Draw red and black stripes in the **SW** box.
2. Draw 3 green triangles in the **N** box.
3. Make the **E** box red and blue plaid.
4. Draw purple polka dots in the **NW** box.
5. Make orange wavy lines in the **SE** box.
6. Draw two red squares in the **S** box.
7. Draw green diagonal lines in the **W** box.
8. Make two yellow smiling faces in the **NE** box.

Name________________________________

Which Way is Up?

Label the direction each arrow is pointing on the matching line. Use N, E, S, W, NE, SE, NW, SW. Then, color the arrows as directed in the Color Code Box.

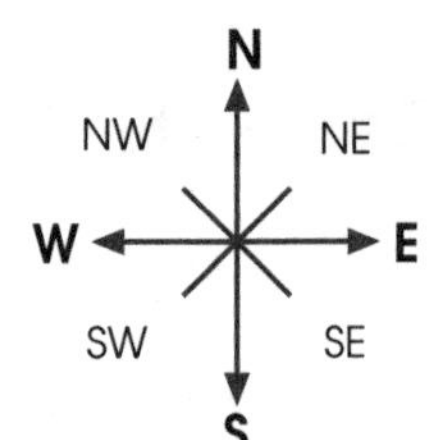

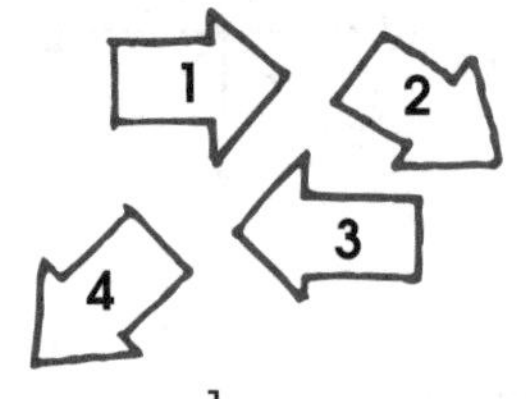

1. ________
2. ________
3. ________
4. ________

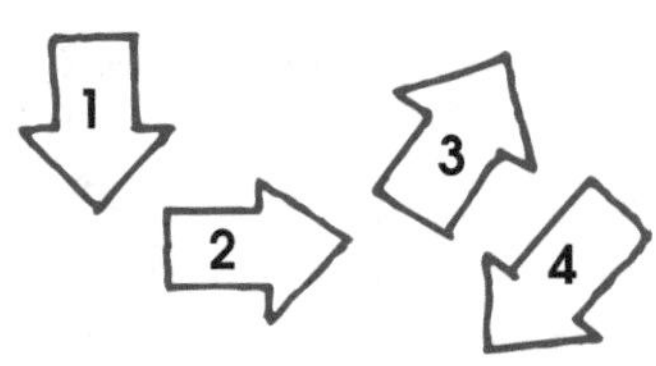

1. ________
2. ________
3. ________
4. ________

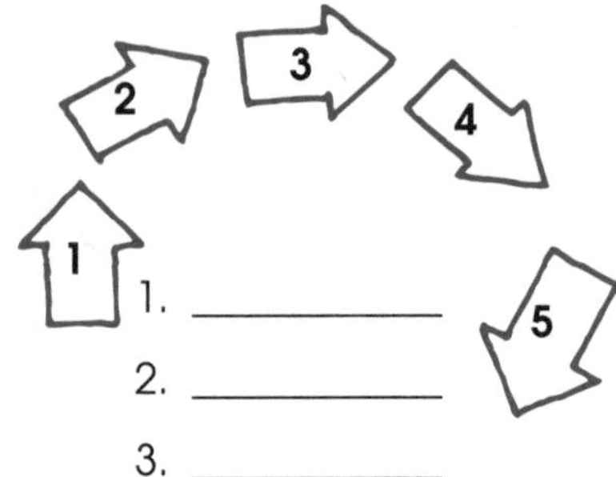

1. ________
2. ________
3. ________
4. ________
5. ________

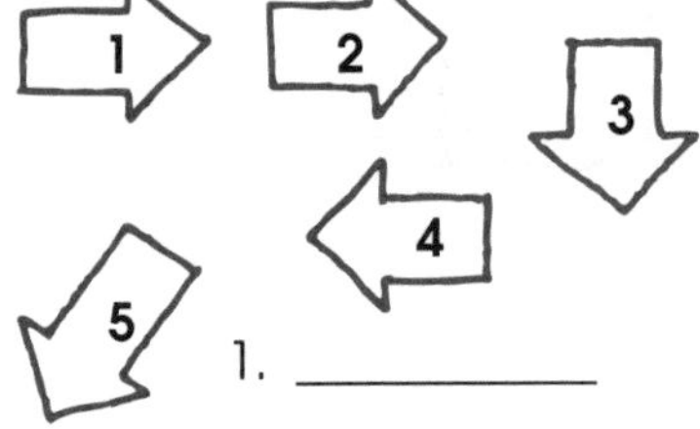

1. ________
2. ________
3. ________
4. ________
5. ________

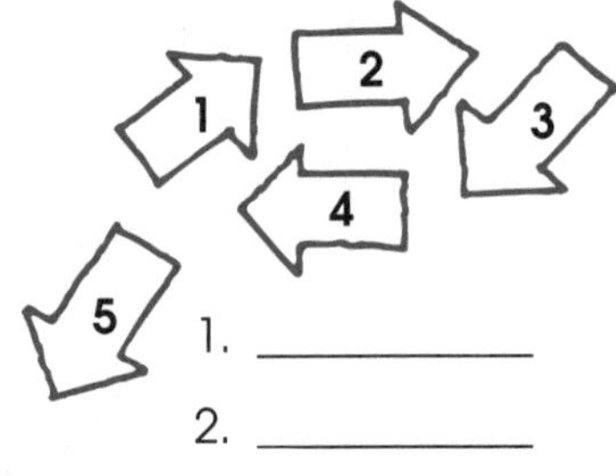

1. ________
2. ________
3. ________
4. ________
5. ________

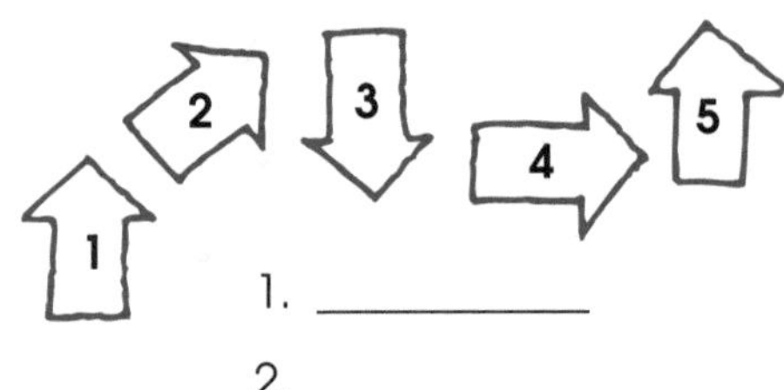

1. ________
2. ________
3. ________
4. ________
5. ________

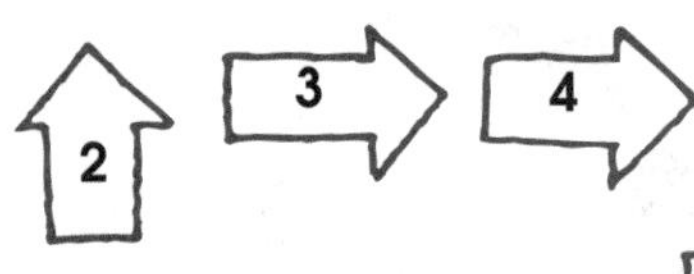

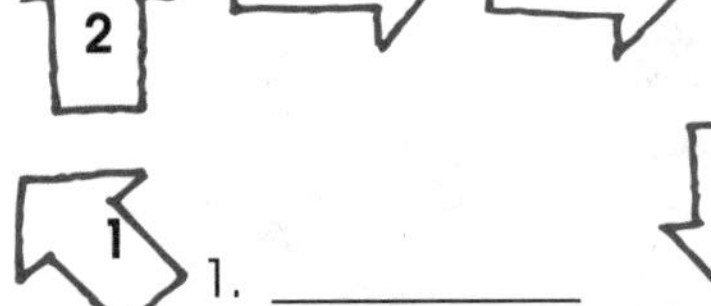

1. ________
2. ________
3. ________
4. ________
5. ________
6. ________

1. ________
2. ________
3. ________
4. ________
5. ________
6. ________

Color Code Box

N	red	**W**	brown
NE	blue	**NW**	orange
S	green	**SW**	yellow
SE	pink	**E**	purple

Name ______________________________

Space Ship Search

Gus Galactic needs help in identifying these alien spaceships. Write a ship's letter in each blank to solve these riddles.

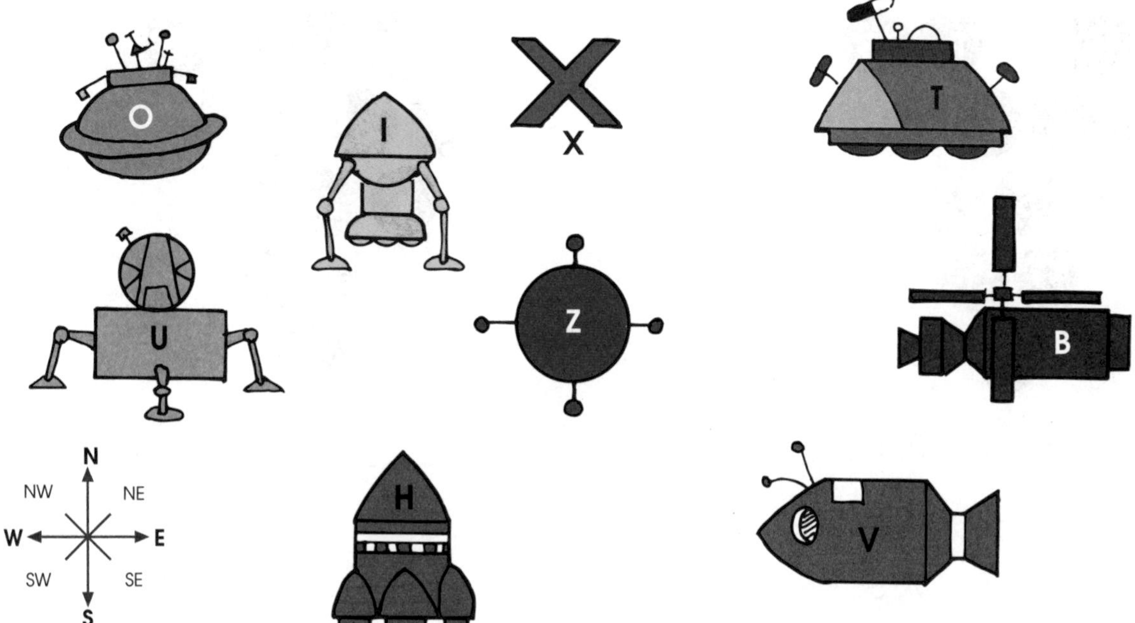

1. I am **N** of Ship **H**. __________
2. I am **E** of Ship **Z**. __________
3. I am **SE** of Ship **Z**. __________
4. I am **S** of Ship **O**. __________
5. I am **NW** of Ship **Z**. __________
6. I am **SW** of Ship **B**. __________
7. I am **NE** of Ship **Z**. __________
8. I am **NE** of Ship **I**. __________
9. I am **SE** of Ship **U**. __________
10. I am **NW** of Ship **B**. __________

Cosmic Challenge

Start at Ship H. Travel in the orbit given. Which ship will you dock with?

1. Go **NW** to Ship ______________.
2. Go **NE** to Ship ______________.
3. Go **NE** to Ship ______________.
4. Go **S** to Ship ______________.
5. Go **SE** to Ship ______________.
6. Go **NE** to Ship ______________.
7. Go **NW** to Ship ______________.

This is your docking station. Congratulations!

Name____________________________________

Compass Rose Pool

Chalk your cue! Start with the numbered ball given. Follow the directions to find the mystery ball.

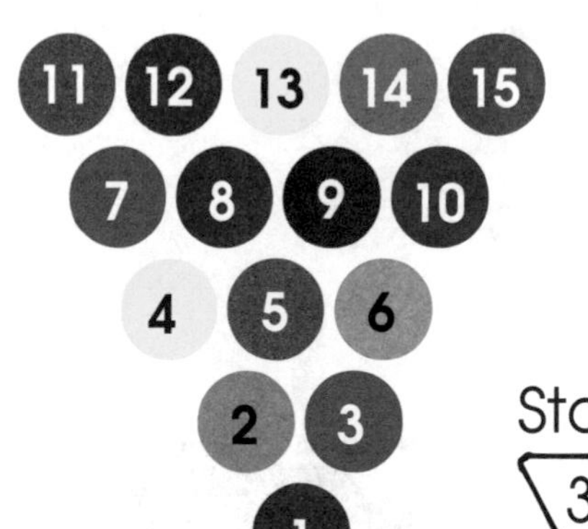

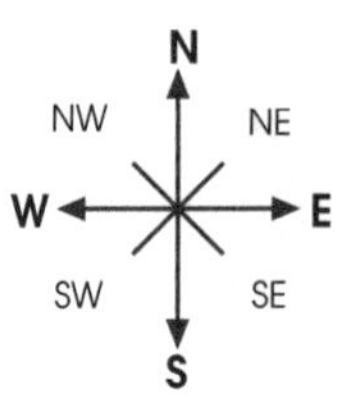

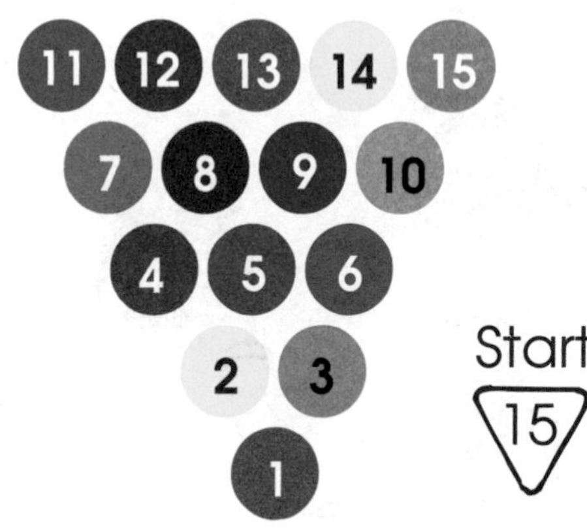

1. NW ______
2. NE ______
3. W ______
4. W ______
5. NW ______
6. E ______
7. SE ______
8. NE ______

1. W ______
2. SW ______
3. SW ______
4. E ______
5. NE ______
6. W ______
7. SW ______
8. SW ______

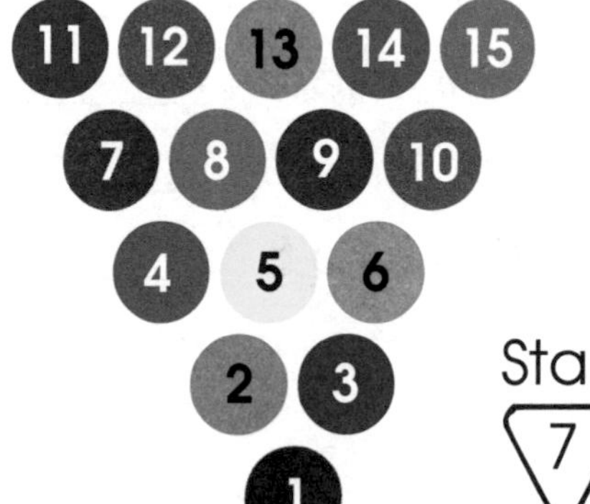

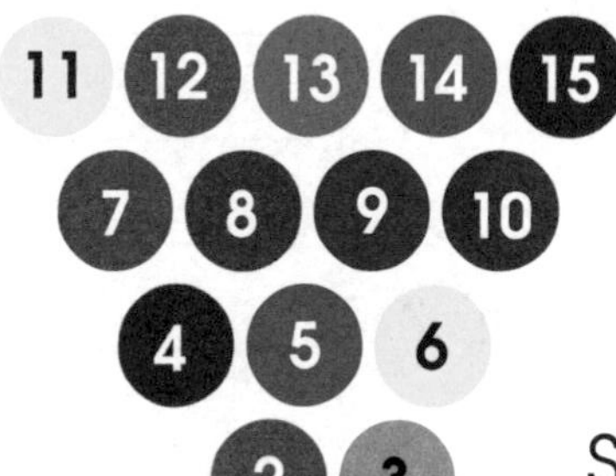

1. E ______
2. E ______
3. SW ______
4. SW ______
5. E ______
6. NE ______
7. NW ______
8. NE ______

1. NE ______
2. NE ______
3. W ______
4. NE ______
5. E ______
6. NE ______
7. W ______
8. SW ______

Name ______________________________

The Sleuth Pooch

Help the Sleuth Pooch find his missing collar. Trace over only the arrows given in order on his notepad. Then, color the Sleuth Pooch's collar.

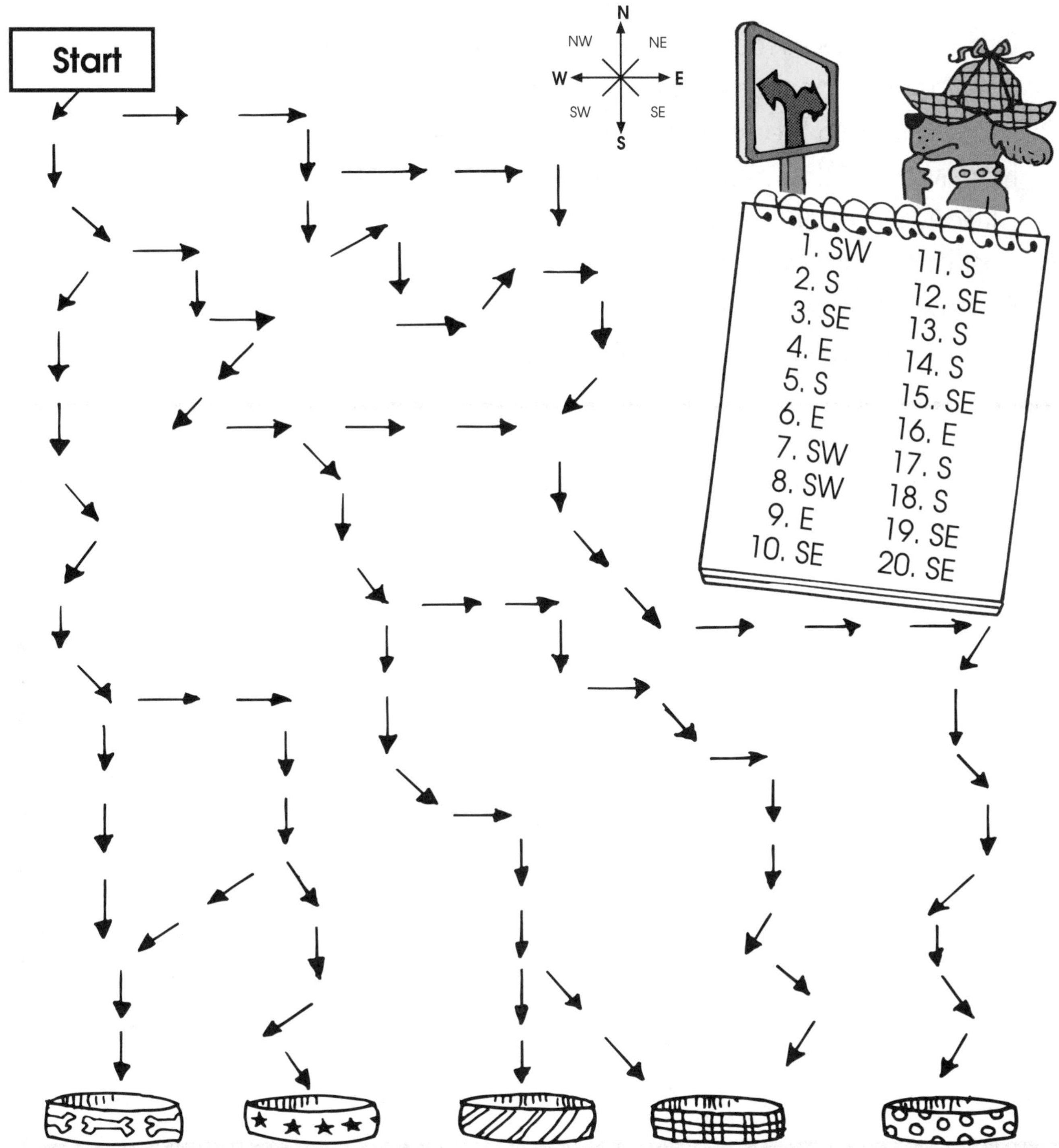

Name________________________________

Draw Your Own Map

A cartographer makes maps. Try your hand at being a cartographer and make your own map by following these directions. Read all directions before you begin.

1. Draw a compass rose using both cardinal and intermediate directions in the bottom right-hand corner of the map.
2. Draw a lake in the center of the map.
3. Northwest of the lake, draw some ducks in flight.
4. Directly south of the lake, draw six trees.
5. East of the ducks, draw the sun.
6. Southwest of the lake, draw a playground area.
7. East of the lake, draw a picnic area.

Name ______________________________

Acorn Park

Write the names of the intermediate directions correctly on the lines below.

NW is ____________________. NE is ____________________.

SW is ____________________. SE is ____________________.

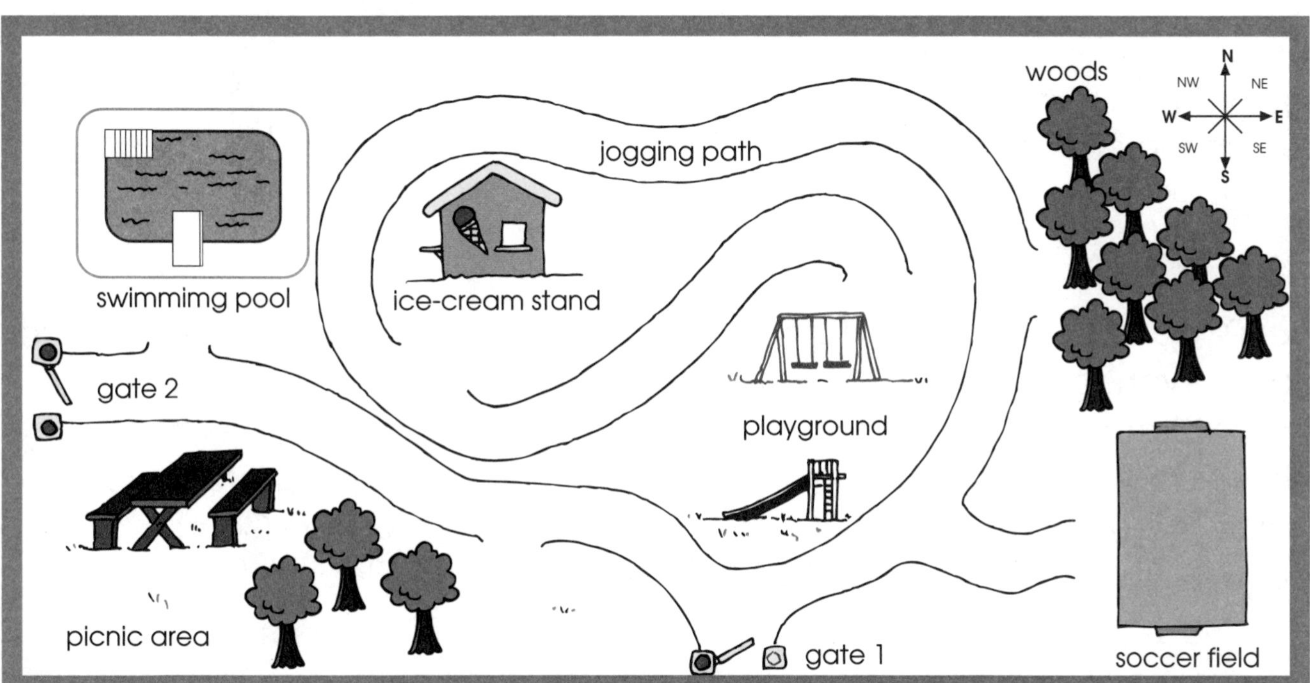

Directions: Use the names of cardinal and intermediate directions to complete these sentences about the map of Acorn Park.

1. The swimming pool is ____________________ of the playground.
2. The ice-cream stand is ____________________ of the picnic area.
3. The soccer field is ____________________ of the swimming pool.
4. The playground is ____________________ of the picnic area.
5. The woods are ____________________ of the playground.
6. Gate 2 is on the ____________________ side of Acorn Park.
7. The swimming pool is ____________________ of the picnic area.
8. Gate 1 is in the ____________________ part of Acorn Park.
9. The woods are ____________________ of gate 1.

Name____

Street Names

How did your street get its name? Was it named after a famous explorer like Columbus? Maybe it's named after a state, like Michigan Avenue. Perhaps it's named after a tree (Oak Street) or a food (Apple Avenue).

Read through the street signs below. Decide how they got their names. Write the name of each street in the correct category.

River Road
Lincoln Avenue
Church Street
Willow Road
Mexico Avenue
Dolphin Court
Flamingo Road
Market Avenue
Hill Street
Ohio Street
Tulip Lane
Jefferson Street
Pennsylvania Avenue
Oak Street
College Avenue
Lake Shore Drive
Edison Court
Elephant Avenue

Famous People	Places	Trees and Plants
____________	____________	____________
____________	____________	____________
____________	____________	____________

Land and Water Features	Human Institutions	Animals
____________	____________	____________
____________	____________	____________
____________	____________	____________

Name________________________________

City Streets

Every town has some interesting street names. Streets can get their names in many different ways. They are often named after presidents, states, trees and flowers. What are some of the interesting street names in your town?

People's Names	Places	Funny Names
Human Institutions	Natural Features	Animals
Plants and Trees	Directions	Other

Name ____

Near School

Geographers can tell us how places are the same and how they are different. Where you live is different from where your friend lives. Maybe you live southwest of school while your friend lives north of the school.

Directions: Write the names and draw pictures of landmarks that are found near your school. Place each one on the chart in its correct location relative to your school.

Northwest	North	Northeast
West	School  ELEMENTARY SCHOOL	East
Southwest	South	Southeast

Name ______________________

A Walk Around Town

Let's take a walk around the town of Forest Grove. Use a marker or crayon to trace your route.

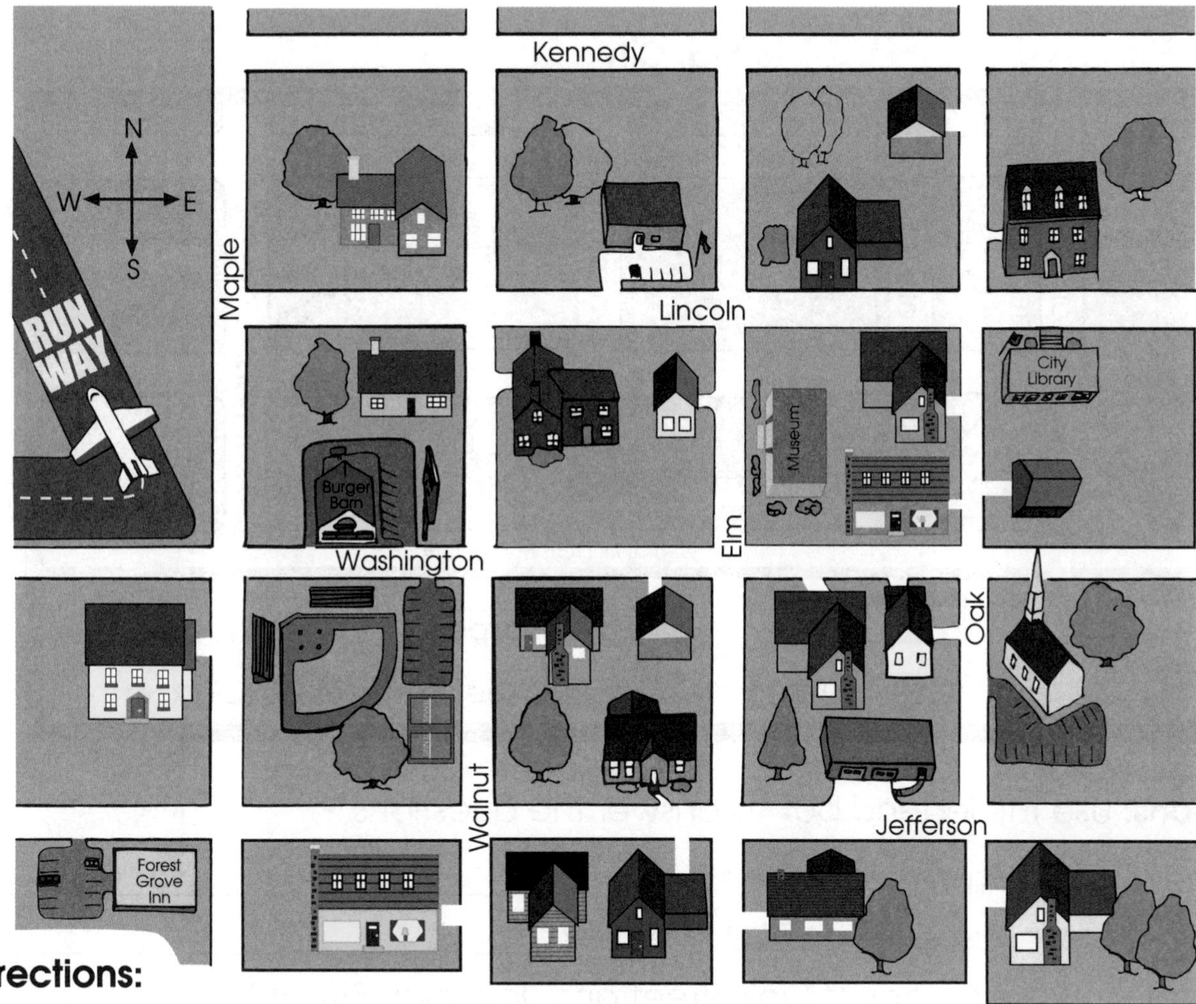

Directions:

1. Begin your walking tour at Forest Grove Inn.
2. Walk two blocks east to Elm Street.
3. Turn north on Elm Street. Walk to the Museum.
4. Go one-half block north to the corner of Elm and Lincoln.
5. Turn east on Lincoln. Walk until you come to the City Library.
6. Go south on Oak Street until you reach Washington Street.
7. Turn west on Washington and walk two and one-half blocks to the Burger Barn.
8. Lunch is over. Take the shortest way back to Forest Grove Inn.

Name ____________________________________

Legends Help You Read Maps

A legend is another word for a key. A map legend explains the symbols found in a map.

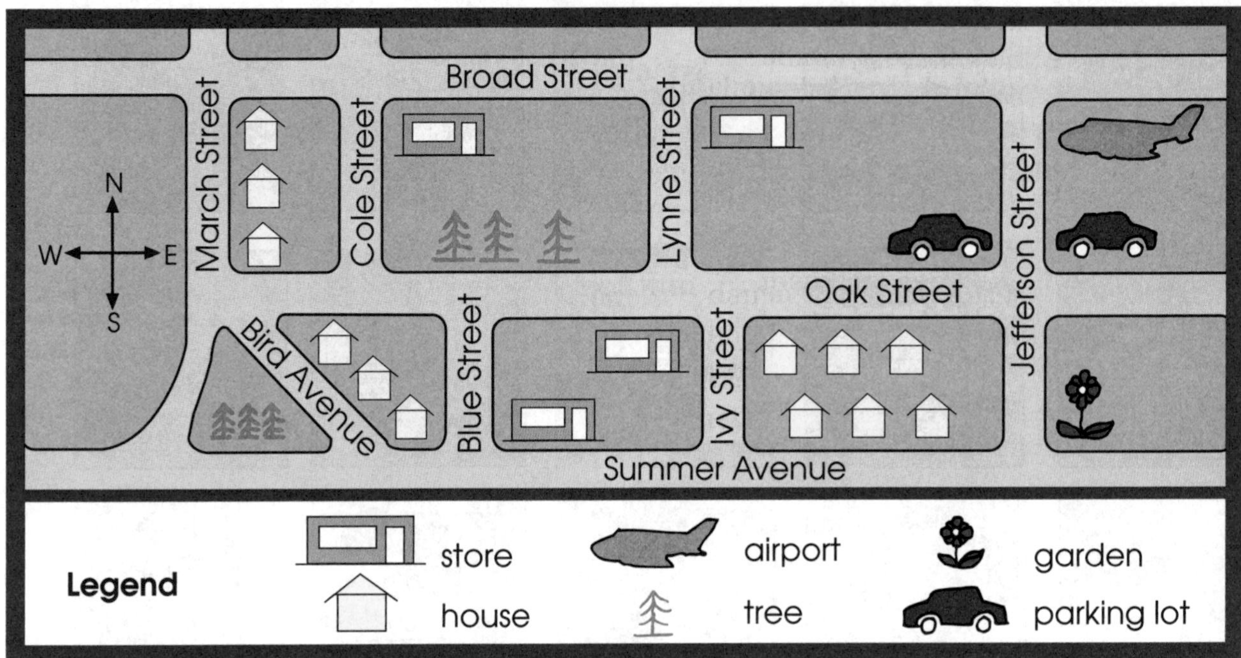

Directions: Use the legend box to answer the questions.

1. Does Star City have an airport? ____________________
2. How many houses are on Bird Avenue? ____________________
3. What is on the corner of Oak Street and Jefferson Street? ____________
4. The garden is on the corner of Jefferson Street and ____________.
5. How many stores are in Star City? ____________________
6. What direction is Summer Avenue from Oak Street? ____________
7. Which street is directly west of Ivy Street? ____________________
8. How many trees are north of Oak Street? ____________________
9. How many houses are between Ivy Street and Jefferson Street? ________
10. How many stores are north of Summer Avenue? ____________

Name______________________________________

Cartographers Use Symbols

Directions: On another sheet of paper, draw a map using the symbols and directions given below.

1. Draw a compass rose in the lower right-hand corner of the page.
2. Draw a [road] in the center of your paper from west to east.
3. Draw 6 [house] in the southwest corner of the map.
4. Draw 4 [tree] east of the [house].
5. Draw a [grocery store] north of the [road].
6. Draw a [clothing store] west of the [grocery store].
7. Draw a [movie theater] south of the [road].
8. Draw a [clothing store] north of the [house].

On another sheet of paper, draw another map using the symbols and directions given below.

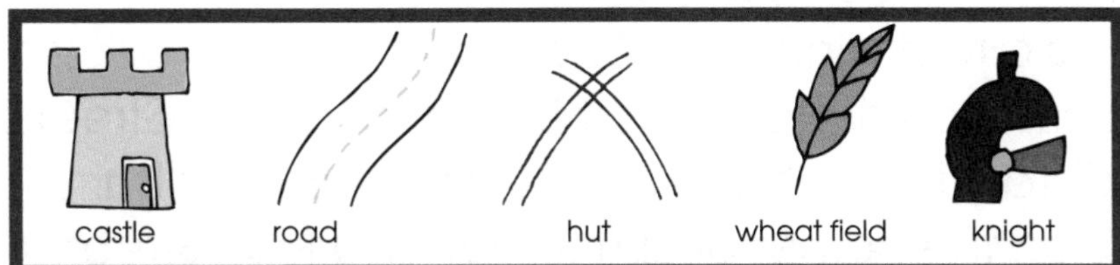

1. Draw a compass rose in the lower right-hand corner of the page.
2. Draw a castle in the center of the page.
3. Draw a road from the castle door southeast to the bottom of the page.
4. Draw 4 huts west of the castle.
5. Draw a knight on the east and west sides of the castle door.
6. Draw a wheat field east of the castle.
7. Draw a road east from the huts to the castle road.

Name______________________________________

Welcome to Crystal River

Crystal River is a great small town to live in. It has stores, parks, churches, schools, libraries, etc.

Complete the map of Crystal River on page 69. Use the directions below to draw the buildings and parks, and to write the names of the streets and businesses on the map where they belong.

When you finish your map, share it with a friend. How are your maps alike? How are they different?

Directions:

1. Bridge Street crosses the Crystal River.
2. Diamond Avenue runs east and west. It is south of the Crystal River.
3. North Street is one block north of Park Street.
4. Elm Street runs directly into Park Street.
5. The Burger Barn is on the corner of Bridge and Park Streets.
6. The Crystal Library is a half block west of the Burger Barn.
7. Elm School is on the corner of Elm Street and Park Street.
8. Crystal Church is west of Elm School.
9. There are stores on the remainder of the north side of Park Street.
10. Bob's Bait Shop is on Bridge Street near the river.
11. The only buildings on North Street are houses.
12. The Crystal River flows through the middle of the city park.
13. The Crystal Airport is on the south edge of town.
14. Memorial Hospital is south of the river.
15. The fire station is on Bridge Street.

Name________________________________

Welcome to Crystal River

Use the directions from page 68 to complete the map of Crystal River.

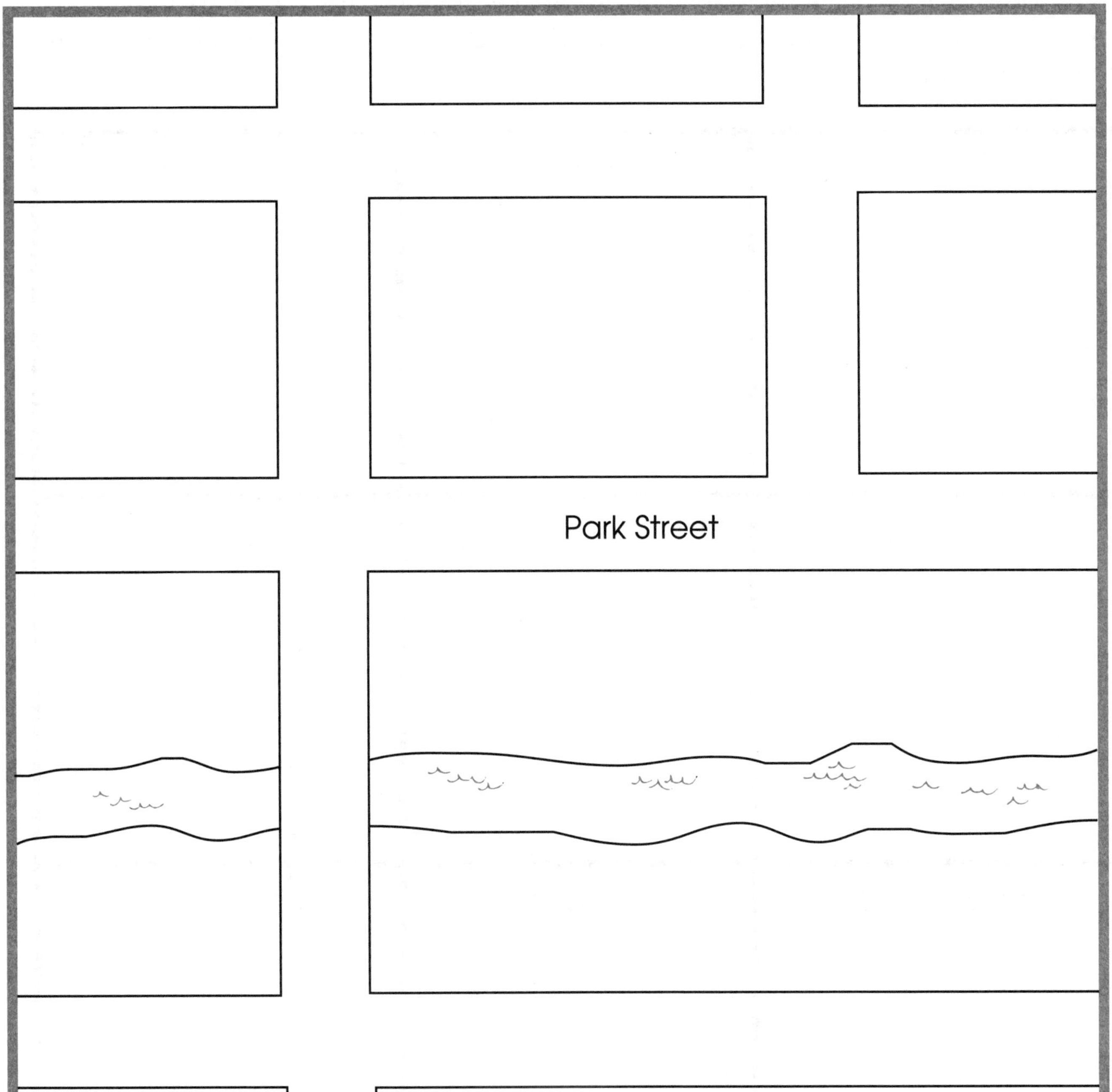

Park Street

N
W E
S

Name____

Near My Community

Use a state map to locate your community. Then, write the names of other communities, cities, towns, lakes, places to visit and other well-known landmarks on the chart below. Write each one in its correct location relative to your community.

Northwest	North	Northeast
West	My Community	East
Southwest	South	Southeast

Name ________________________________

Tourist Map of Oldtown

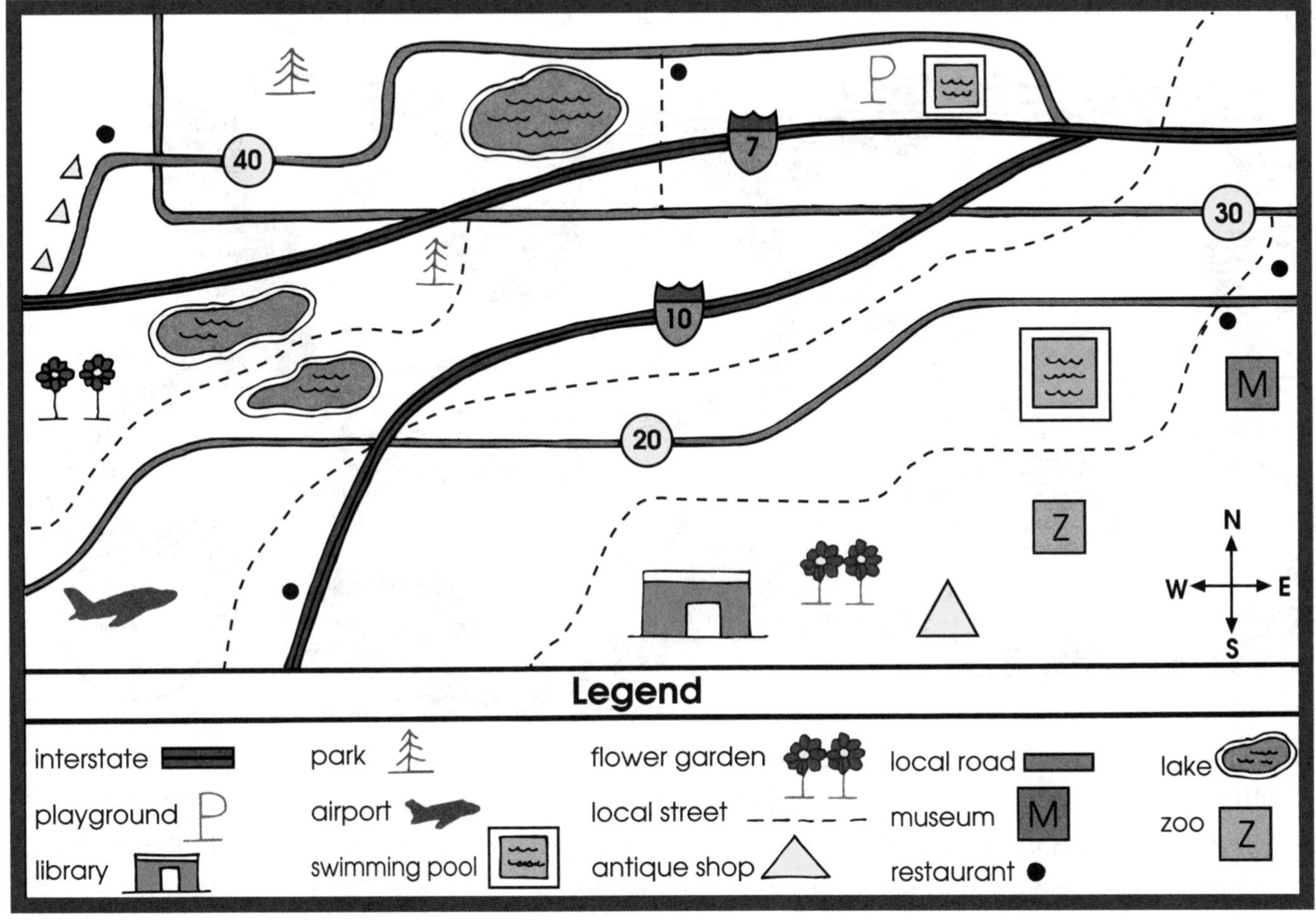

1. The airport is located between interstate ________ and local road ________________.
2. What attractions are north of interstate 7? ________________________________
____
3. Could you take a local street from the airport to the library? ________________
4. How many lakes are in Oldtown? ________________________________
5. On which side of town is the museum located? ________________________
6. What is located at the point where local road 30 crosses interstate 7? ____________
7. Name the road that runs north of the playground. ________________________
8. How many swimming pools are in Oldtown? ________________________
9. How many antique shops are in the town? ________________________
10. Is there a local street between the zoo and the swimming pool? ________________

Name____________________________________

Is It North, South, East or West?

Direction words can help you locate places quickly on a map.

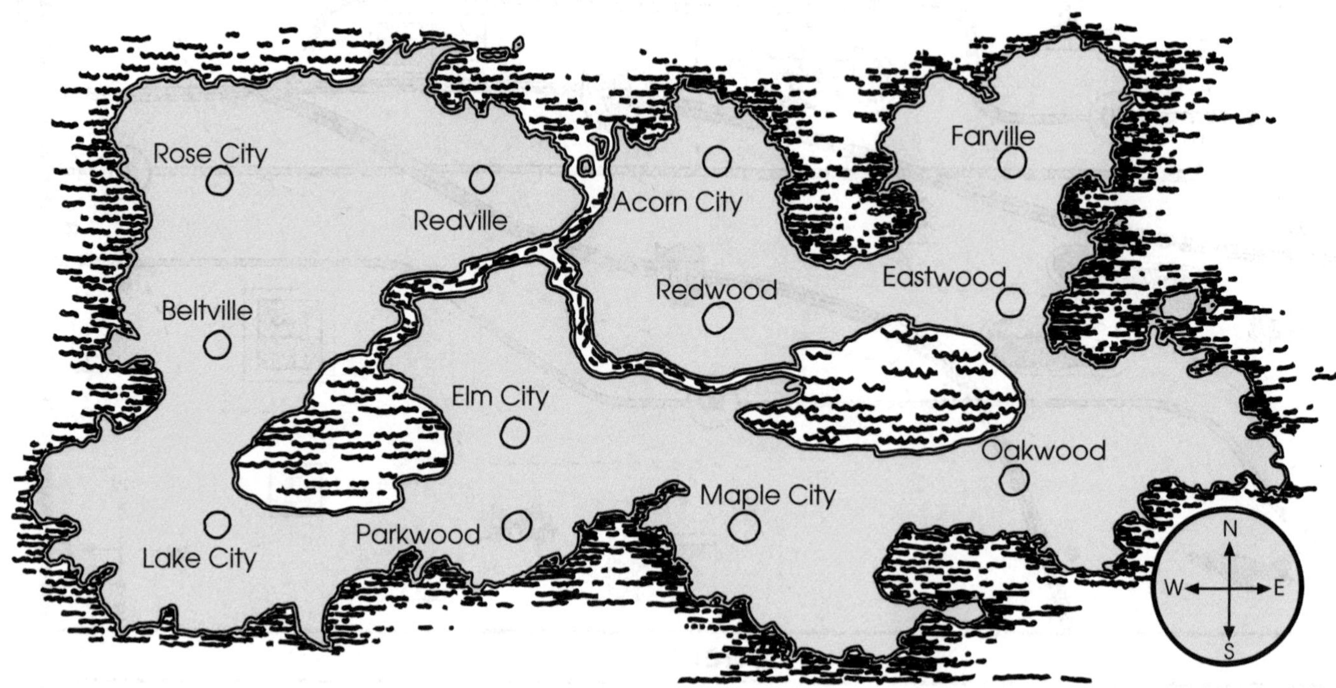

Directions: Circle the correct answer.

1. What city is south of Acorn City?	Rose City	Redwood	Farville
2. What city is north of Beltville?	Rose City	Redwood	Lake City
3. What city is east of Rose City?	Beltville	Lake City	Redville
4. What city is west of Maple City?	Redwood	Acorn City	Parkwood
5. What city is south of Farville?	Acorn City	Eastwood	Redville
6. What city is west of Redwood?	Eastwood	Maple City	Beltville
7. What city is north of Lake City?	Beltville	Maple City	Oakwood
8. What city is west of Farville?	Acorn City	Oakwood	Eastwood

Use crayons or markers to follow these directions.

1. Draw a line south from Farville to Eastwood.
2. Draw a line north from Maple City to Redwood.
3. Draw a line east from Beltville to Redwood.
4. Draw a line west from Redville to Rose City.
5. Place an A on the city directly south of Eastwood.
6. Place a B on the city east of Acorn City.

Name ___________________________

North, South, East and West

You are flying in an airplane with the wind blowing sharply in your face. You are flying from Chicago to Nashville. In what direction are you traveling?

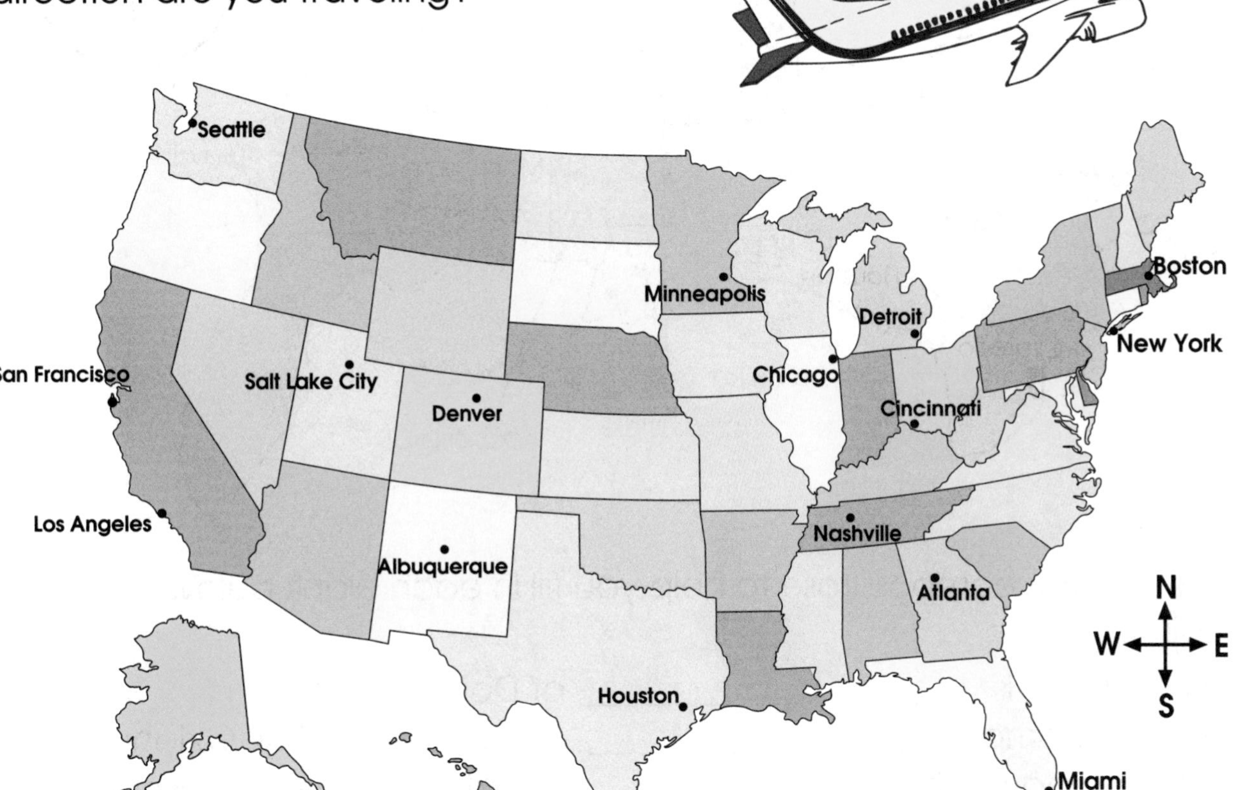

If you said "south" to the above question, you are correct!

Write the direction you would be traveling for each set of cities. Use the four cardinal directions—north, south, east and west.

Atlanta to Los Angeles ______________

Seattle to Los Angeles ______________

San Francisco to Nashville ______________

Denver to Salt Lake City ______________

Cincinnati to Detroit ______________

Chicago to Boston ______________

Houston to Minneapolis ______________

Miami to New York ______________

Detroit to New York ______________

Boston to Minneapolis ______________

Atlanta to Albuquerque ______________

Nashville to Miami ______________

Name____

Locating Cities

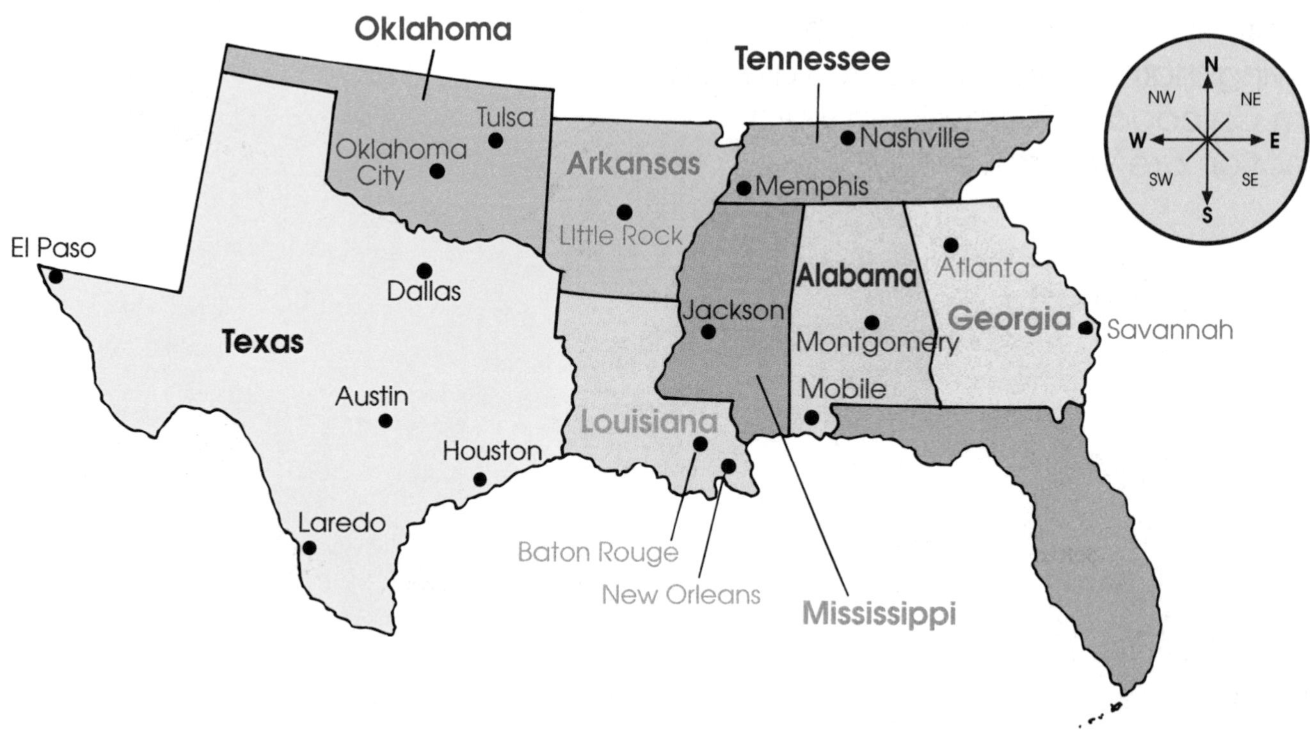

Directions: Use the compass rose to help you fill in each blank below with the correct direction.

1. El Paso, Texas, is ________________ of Dallas, Texas.
2. Tulsa, Oklahoma, is ________________ of Oklahoma City, Oklahoma.
3. Mobile, Alabama, is ________________ of Baton Rouge, Louisiana.
4. Little Rock, Arkansas, is ________________ of Nashville, Tennessee.
5. Houston, Texas, is ________________ of New Orleans, Louisiana.
6. Jackson, Mississippi, is ________________ of Memphis, Tennessee.
7. Dallas, Texas, is ________________ of Austin, Texas.
8. The state of Louisiana is ________________ of Arkansas.
9. The state of Alabama is ________________ of Texas.
10. The state of Oklahoma is ________________ of Tennessee.
11. The state of Georgia is ________________ of Texas.
12. Atlanta, Georgia, is ________________ of Savannah, Georgia.
13. The state of Tennessee is ________________ of Arkansas.
14. Dallas, Texas, is ________________ of Little Rock, Arkansas.
15. Mobile, Alabama, is ________________ of Atlanta, Georgia.

Name ____________________

Scale is Fun!

Scale measures distance on a map. Use the scale given to measure distances in this winter wonderland. Cut out the ruler. Use it to measure from ❄ to ❄ to answer the questions below.

1. On the scale, how many feet equal one inch? ________
2. How far is it from the shovel to the sleigh? ________
3. How many feet is the snow angel from the snowman? ________
4. How far is the igloo from the sleigh? ________
5. How many feet is it from the snowmobile to the skis and poles? ______
6. How many feet is the snow fort from the shovel? ________
7. It is ________feet from the sledding hill to the shovel.
8. It is ________feet from the skis and pole to the sleigh.
9. It is ________feet from the skis and pole to the igloo.

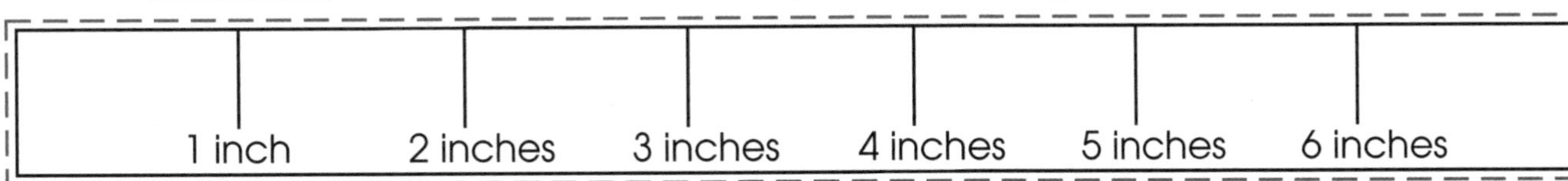

Page is blank for cutting exercise on previous page.

Name____________________________________

Go the Distance

This map shows the route for the yearly Pedalville Bike-a-thon. At the bottom of the map is a scale.

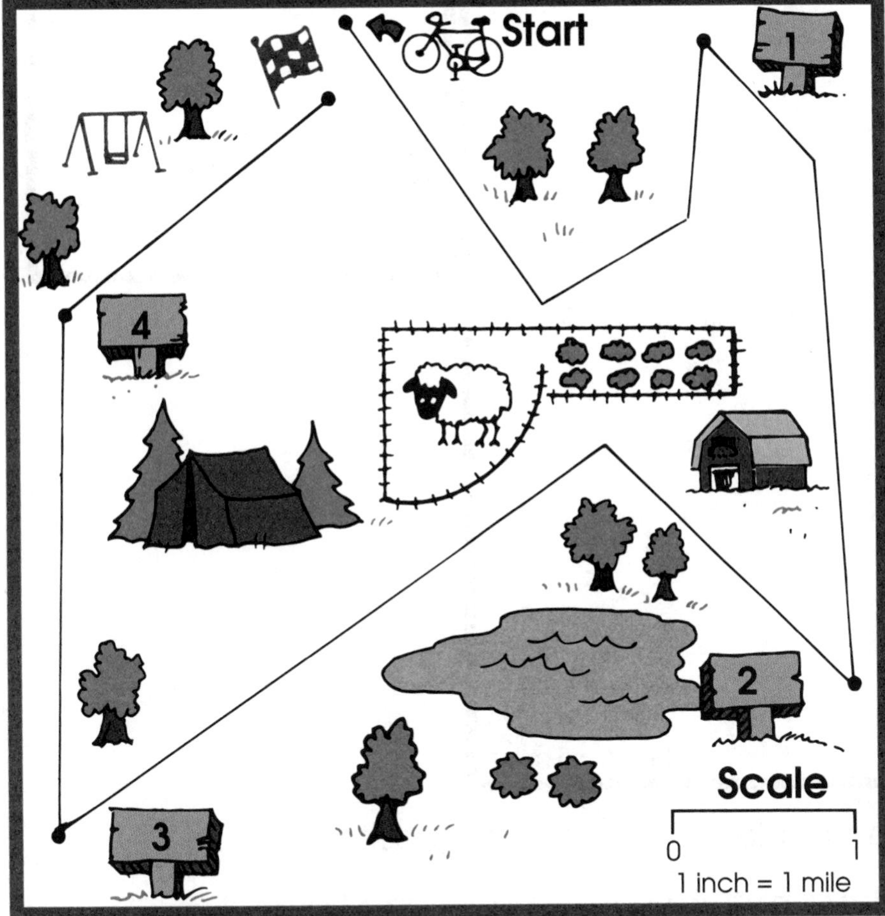

Directions: Use a ruler and the scale to measure the distances on the map.

1. How many miles are between "race start" and checkpoint 1? ______
2. How many miles are between checkpoint 1 and checkpoint 2? ______
3. How many miles are between checkpoint 2 and checkpoint 3? ______
4. How many miles are between checkpoint 3 and checkpoint 4? ______
5. How many miles are between checkpoint 4 and "race end"? ______

Name________________________________

Are We There Yet?

Calvin is going on a vacation to Getaway Campground.

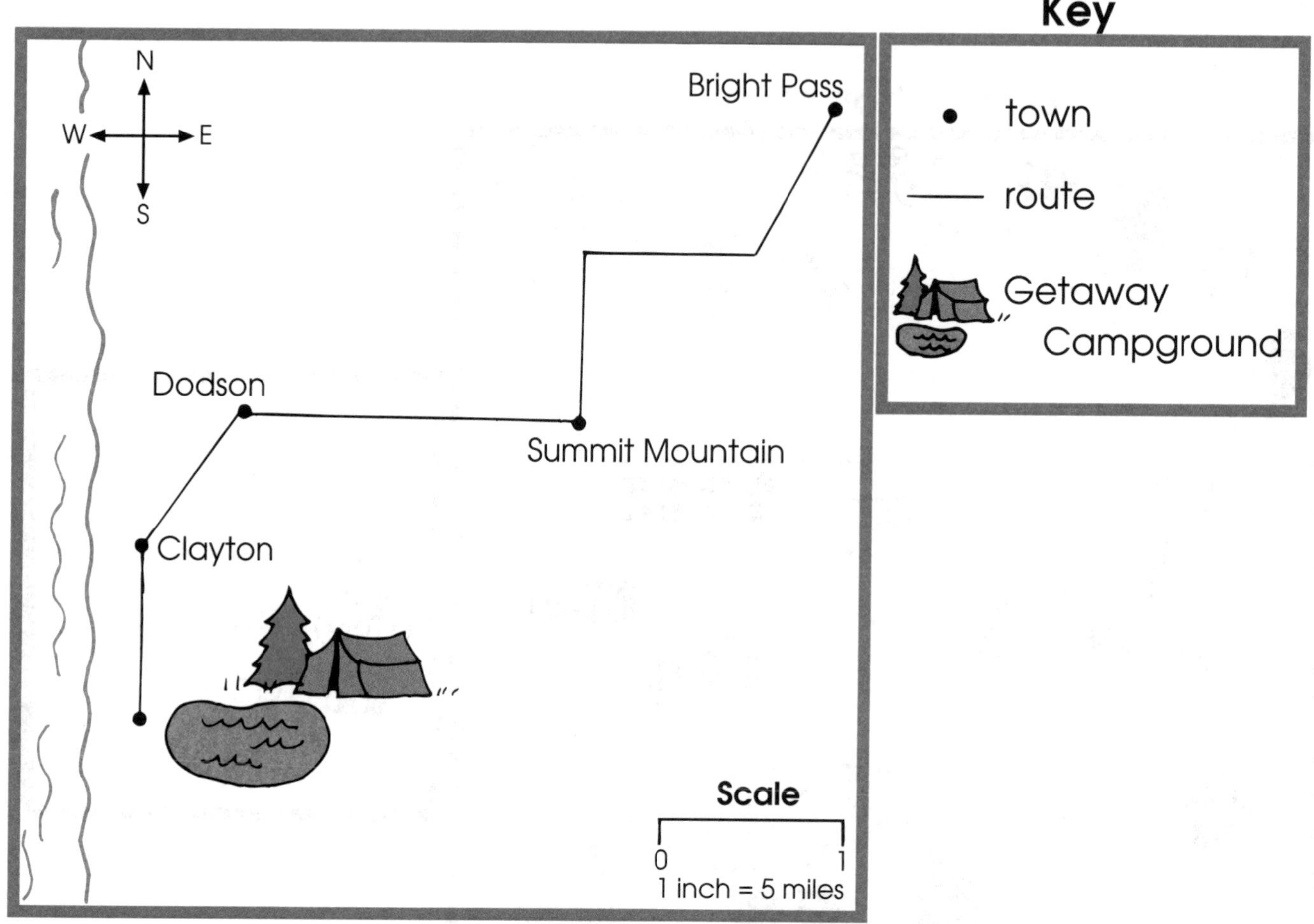

Directions: Use the scale and a ruler to answer the questions below.

1. How many miles are there between Bright Pass and Summit Mountain?____________
2. How far is it from Summit Mountain to Dodson? ____________________
3. How many miles are there between Dodson and Clayton? _________
4. How far is it from Clayton to Getaway Campground? ____________
5. How many miles in all are there between Bright Pass and Getaway Campground?____________

Name ______________________________

How Far Is It?

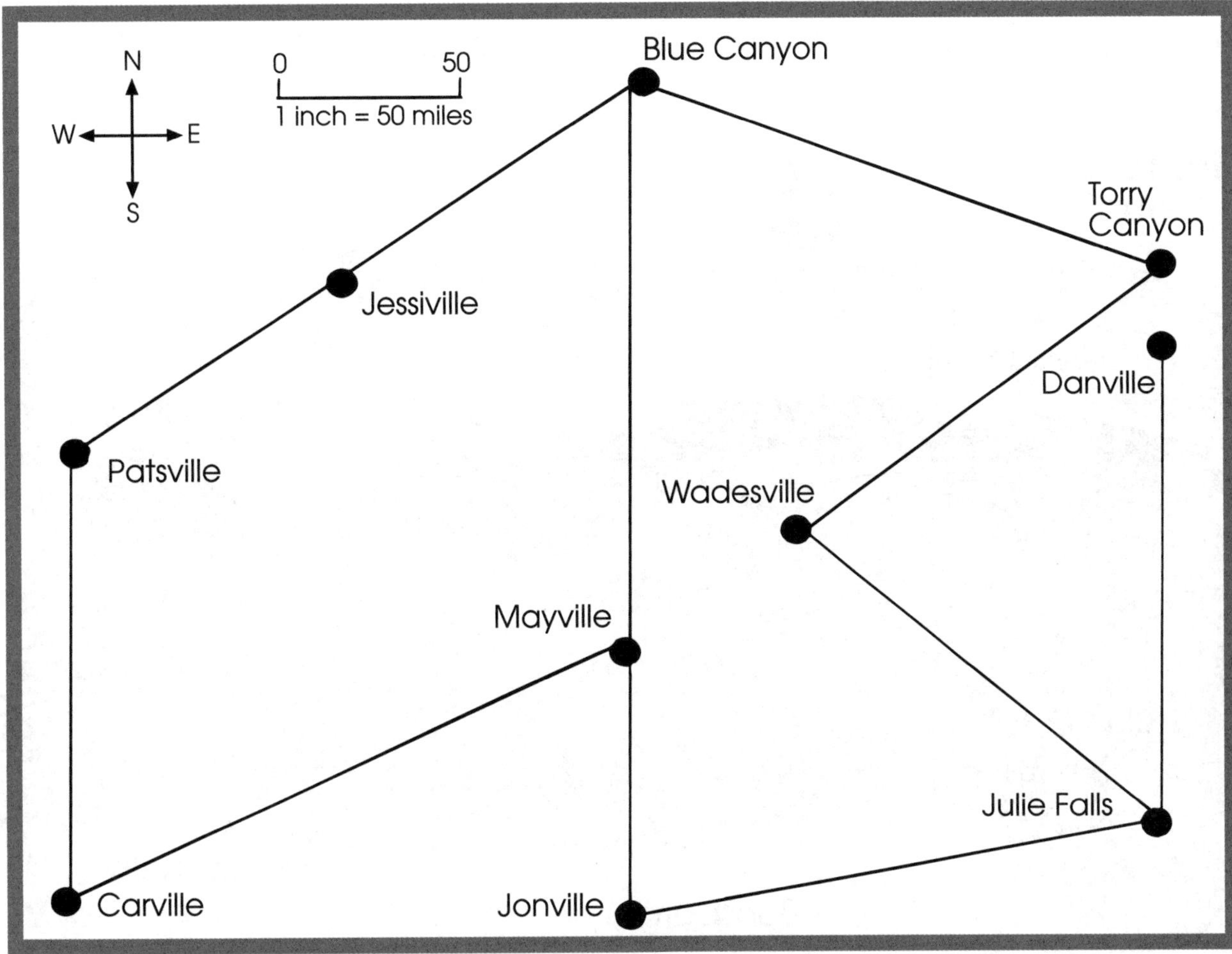

Directions: Measure these distances and answer the questions below.

1. How far is it from Carville to Mayville? ______________________________
2. How far is it from Wadesville to Torry Canyon? ______________________________
3. If you travel from Blue Canyon to Jonville, how far will you travel? ______________
4. What town is between Patsville and Blue Canyon? ______________________________
5. If you go through Wadesville, how far is it from Torry Canyon to Julie Falls? __________
6. Which is longer—going from Carville to Patsville, or Carville to Mayville?

____

Name________________________________

Hamburg Haven

Welcome to the mouth-watering county of Hamburg Haven! Use a ruler and the map scale to figure approximate distances around this "burg."

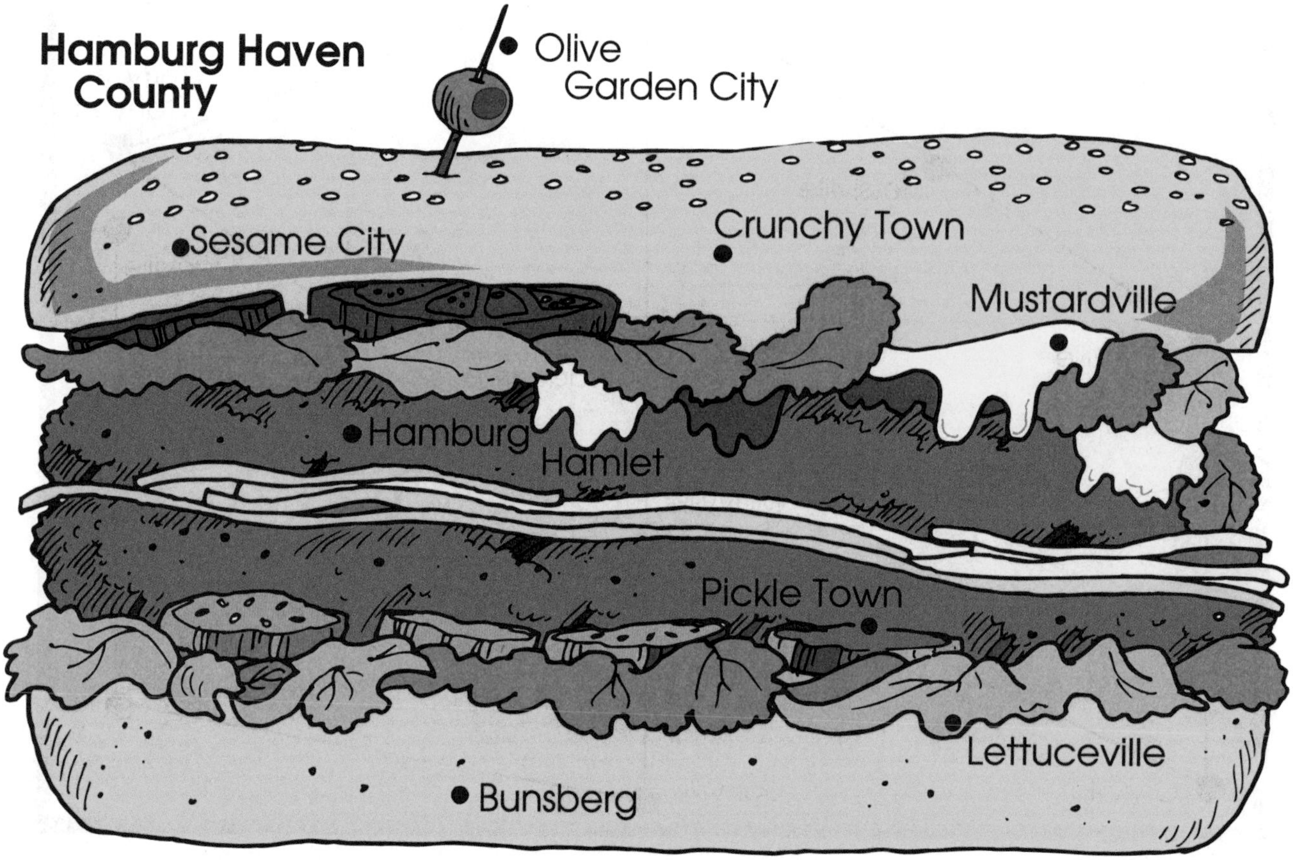

Hamburg Haven County

Olive Garden City

Sesame City

Crunchy Town

Mustardville

Hamburg Hamlet

Pickle Town

Lettuceville

Bunsberg

About how many miles? (Hint: Measure from dot to dot.)

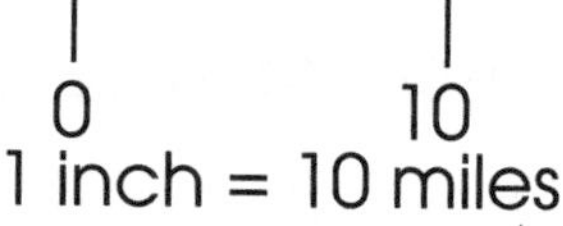

1. From Olive Garden City to Pickle Town? __________
2. From Bunsberg to Lettuceville? __________________
3. From Crunchy Town to Mustardville?______________
4. From Mustardville to Pickle Town? _____________
5. From Bunsberg to Sesame City? ______________
6. From Hamburg Hamlet to Lettuceville? __________
7. From Crunchy Town to Bunsberg? _____________

Name ______________________________

Camping in Nature Park

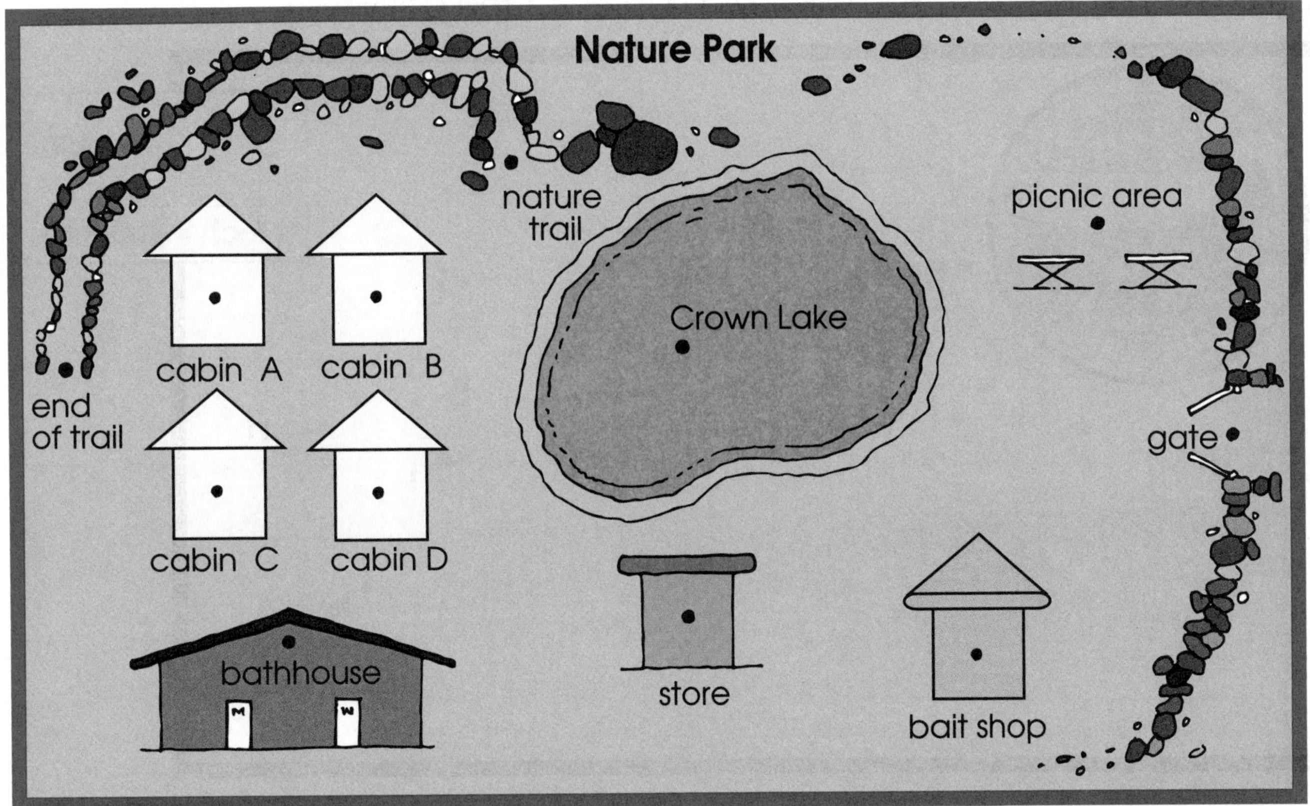

0 1
1 inch = 1 miles

Directions: Use a ruler to help you answer these questions.

1. How far is it from the center of Crown Lake to the bait shop? __________
2. How far is it from the picnic area to Crown Lake? __________
3. How far must you travel from cabin C to the bathhouse? __________
4. What is the distance from the nature trail to Crown Lake? __________
5. Your family is staying in cabin A. How far must you travel from the gate to the cabin? __________
6. What is the approximate distance in miles from the beginning to the end of the nature trail? __________
7. How far must your family travel to the store if you are staying in cabin D?

   ____
8. How far is it from the store to cabin B? __________
9. The end of the nature trail is how far from the picnic area? __________
10. How far is the bathhouse from cabin A? __________

Name________________________________

Flying from Place to Place

You are an airline pilot. You will need a ruler for this activity.

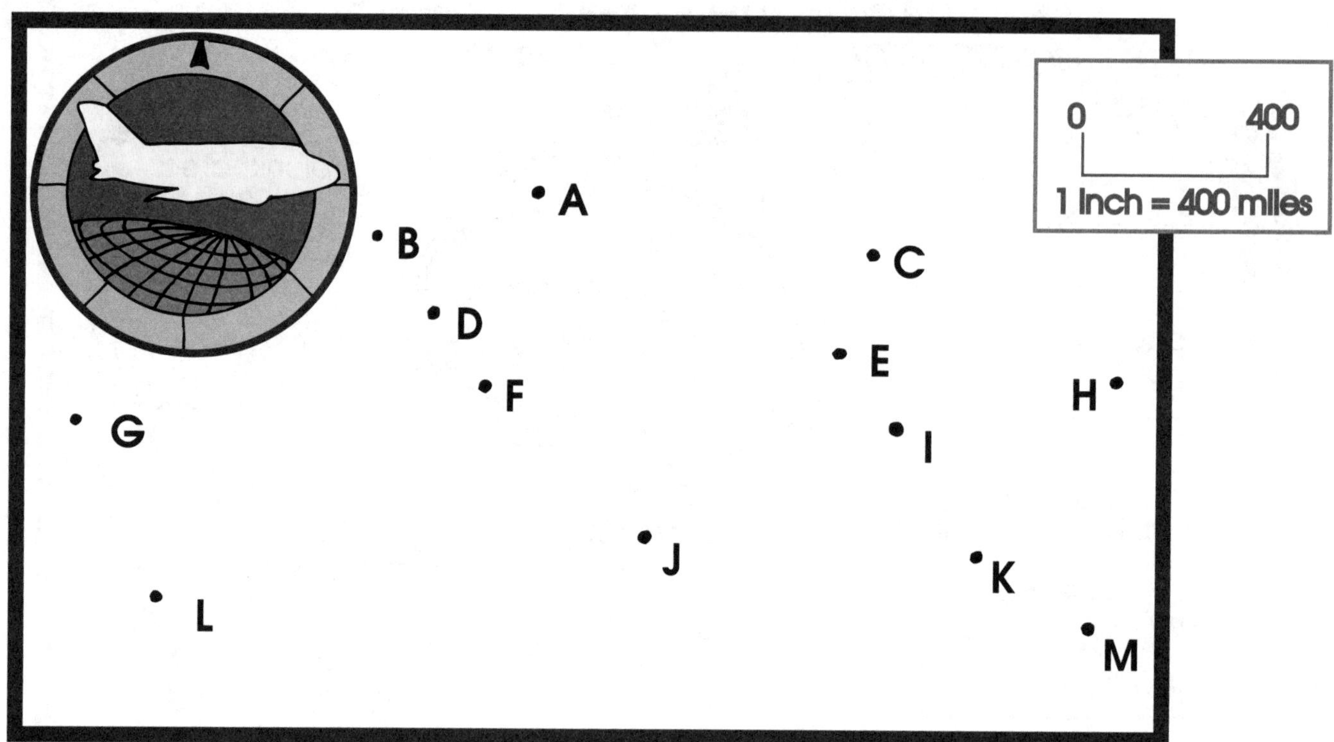

1. You need to file a flight plan from city **J** to city **C**. How far will the plane travel? ______________________
2. You must fly from city **D** to city **F** to city **E**. How many miles will you travel?______________________
3. How far is it from city **H** to city **C**? ______________________
4. Is it closer to fly from city **I** to city **M** or from city **I** to city **A**? __________
5. If your plane holds enough fuel to fly 500 miles, can you fly from city **L** to city **G** without refueling? ______________________
6. With fuel for 500 miles, can you fly from city **A** to city **J**? __________
7. About how many miles is it from city **C** to city **M**? __________
8. What direction must you fly from city **H** to city **F**?__________
9. What direction must you fly from city **J** to city **K**?__________

Name ____________________

Amazing Arizona

Get to know Arizona, the 48th state. Below is a map showing the largest Indian reservations and cities located in or near them in Arizona. Use the scale to answer the questions.

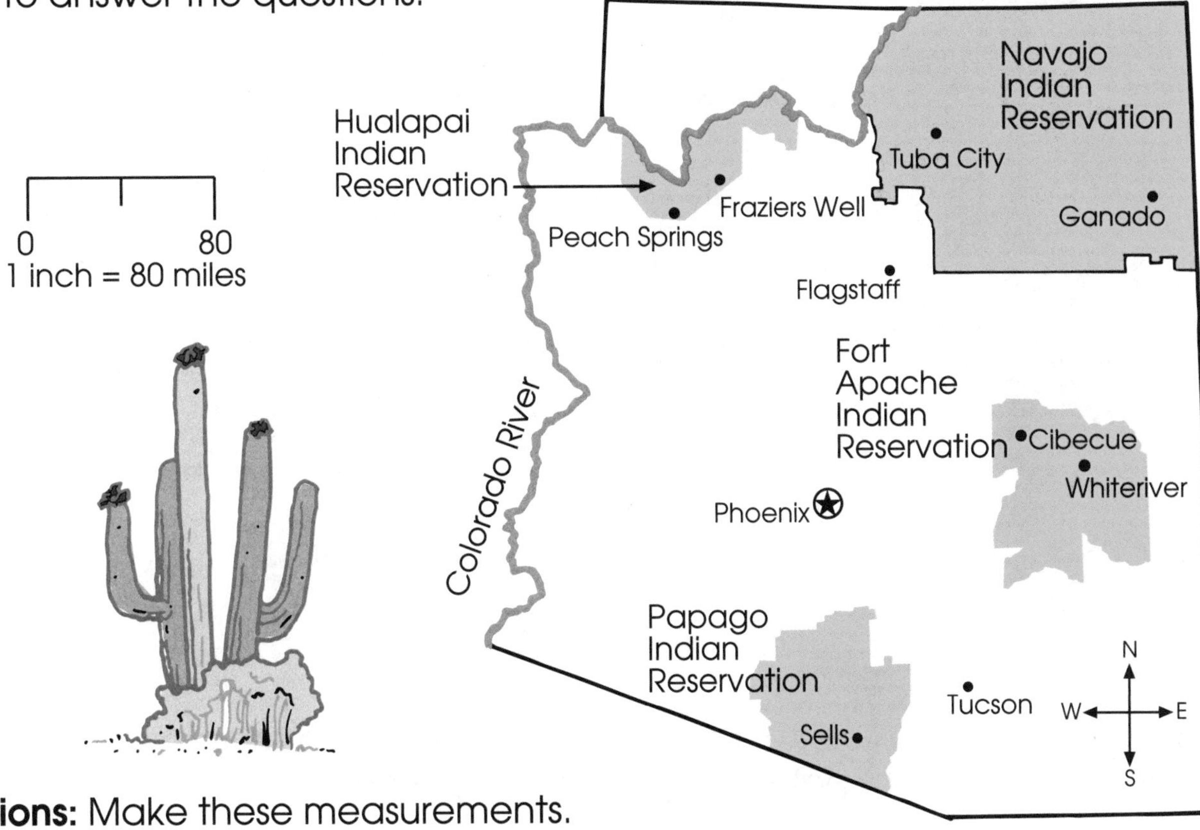

Directions: Make these measurements.

1. About how many miles from Phoenix to Peach Springs? ____________________
2. About how many miles from north to south on its eastern border? ____________________
3. About how many miles from Flagstaff to Ganado? __________
4. From Tucson to Flagstaff? ______
5. From Whiteriver to Ganado? ____________________
6. From Tuba City to Tucson? ____________________
7. From Peach Springs to Sells? ____________________
8. From Cibecue to Sells? __________
9. The Fort Apache Indian Reservation from north to south at its greatest distance. ________
10. The Navajo Indian Reservation from east to west at its greatest distance. ____________

Name____

Flight Path Frenzy

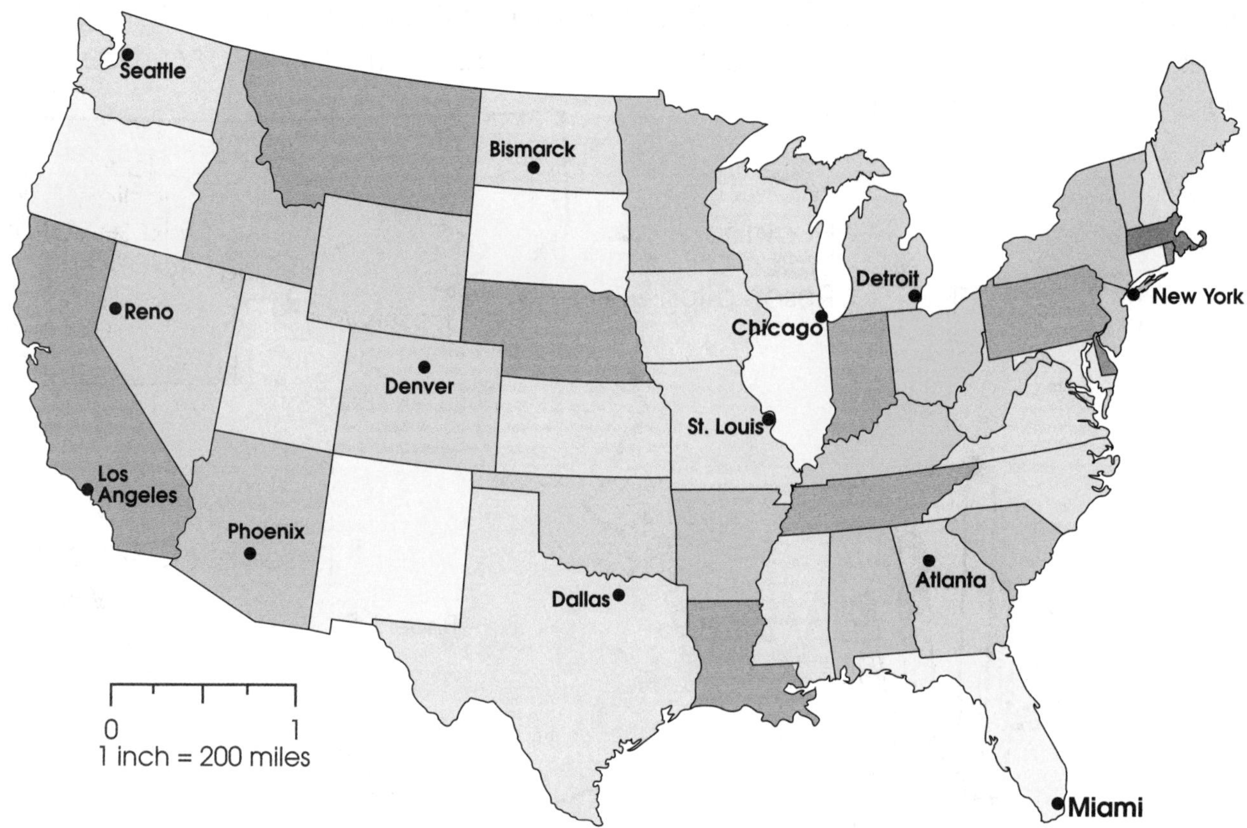

Directions: Use the scale to measure the approximate distance of these flights. Draw the flight paths using the colors stated.

From:

1. Atlanta to Dallas______miles (orange)
2. Denver to Chicago ______miles (purple)
3. Los Angeles to Phoenix______miles (yellow)
4. Seattle to Dallas ______miles (green)

5. St. Louis to New York______miles (brown)
6. Denver to Miami ______miles (red)
7. Reno to Detroit ______miles (dark blue)
8. Los Angeles to New York______miles (pink)
9. Seattle to St. Louis______miles (black)
10. Chicago to Miami______miles (light blue)

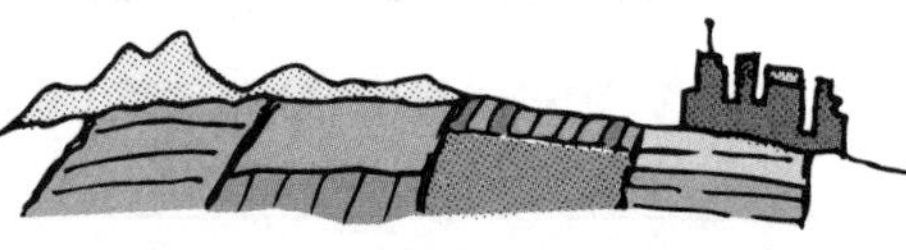

Name ________________________________

Traveling on Different Roads

Use a ruler to measure distances on this map and answer the questions below. Don't forget to use the compass rose and the legend.

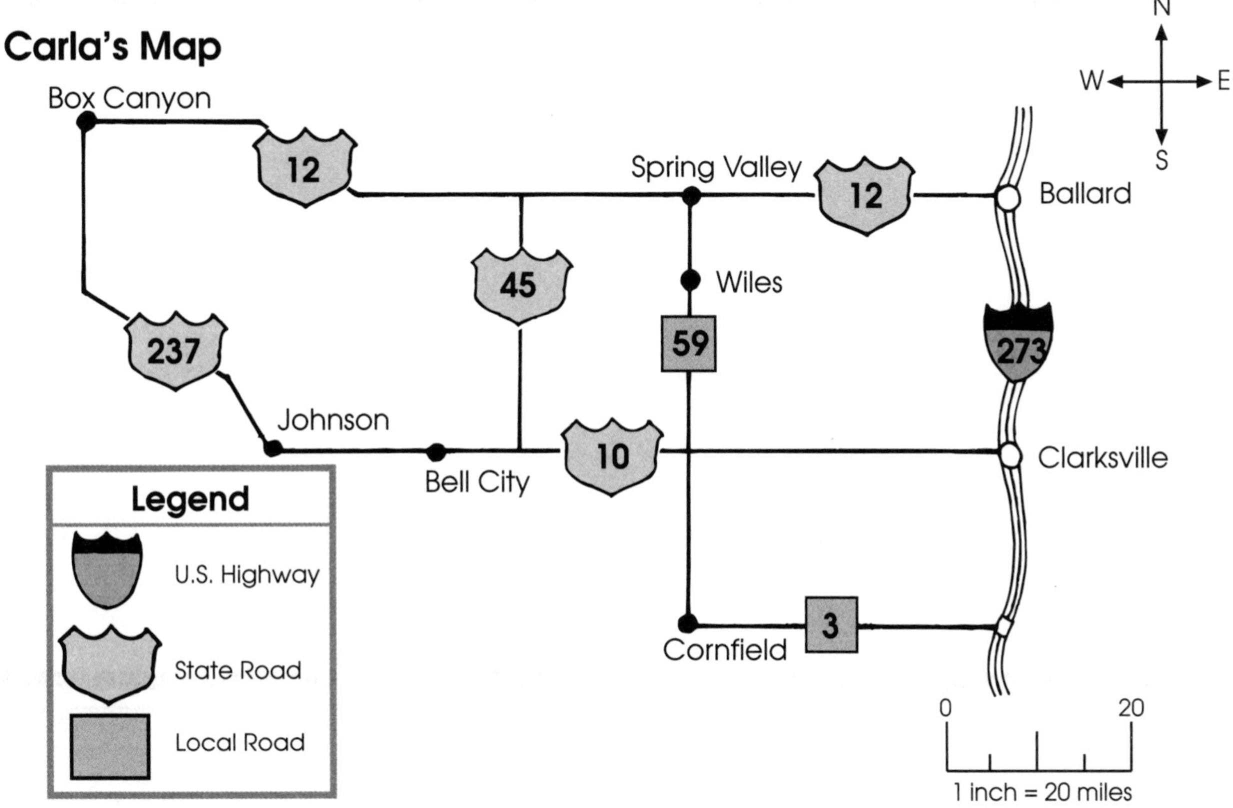

1. What U. S. highway would you travel on from Clarksville to Ballard? _______
2. If Carla travels from Bell City to Clarksville, what state road will she use?

   ____

3. How far is it from Johnson to Bell City? ________________________________
4. Do you take a state or local road to travel from Wiles to Spring Valley? _____

   ____

5. Cornfield is located at the junction of which two local roads? _________

   ____

6. What direction is Johnson from Bell City? ________________________________
7. If you plan a trip from Clarksville to Ballard, what direction will you be traveling? ________________________________

Name________________________________

Map Scales

Recreation Location

You are the planner for a new recreation center. Use the map scale to measure and draw its features, following the directions below.

0 20
1 inch = 20 feet

Directions:

1. Draw a 20 ft. square in the SE corner of the map.
2. Draw a rectangle N of the square 25 ft. wide by 45 ft. long.
3. Draw a rectangle in the SW corner, measuring 60 ft. long by 25 ft. wide.
4. Draw a 20 ft. square in the NW corner of the map.

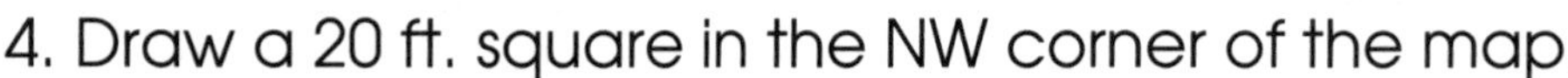

5. Draw another 20 ft. square east of the square you drew in #4.

N
W E
S

Add details to your shapes to transform the shapes into . . .

1. a racquetball court.
2. a basketball court.
3. a swimming pool.
4. a golf driving range.
5. a baseball batting cage.

Write a name for the recreation center in the middle.

Name ____________________

How Many People?

This map uses symbols to show how many people live in each town. Use this map and the legend to answer the questions below.

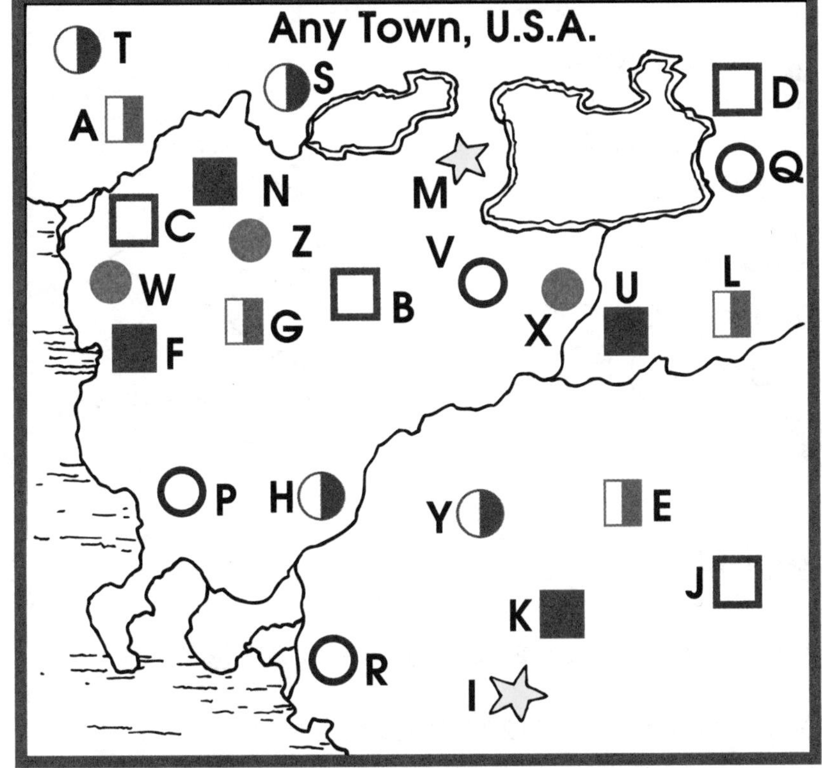

Legend

Symbol	People
☐	0-500
◧	500-1,000
■	1,000-5,000
○	5,000-25,000
◑	25,000-50,000
●	50,000-100,000
☆	over 100,000

1. How many people live in a town that has this symbol ■ ?____________
2. What does ☆ mean on the map? ____________
3. Name the four towns with 0-500 people. ____________
4. How many towns have 1,000-5,000 people? ____________
5. How many people live in town G? ____________
6. Circle the town with the most people. A B I
7. Circle the town with the fewest people. L K J
8. Name the towns with 1,000-5,000 people. ____________
9. How many towns have over 100,000 people? ____________
10. Name the towns with 50,000-100,000 people. ____________
11. Draw a circle around the towns with 500-1,000 people.
12. Draw a large **X** on the towns with 25,000-50,000 people.

Name____________________________________

What Is the Population?

Use this map of an imaginary state to answer the following questions.

Population Map

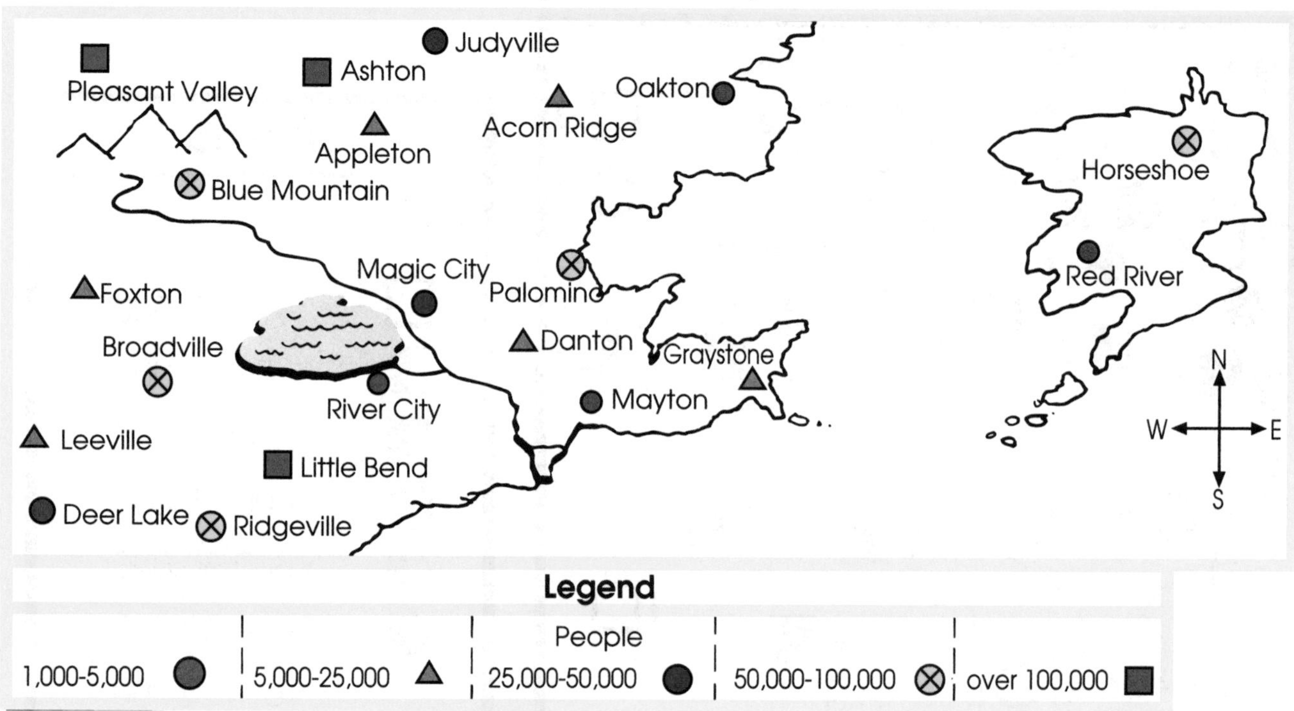

1. Name the five cities with a population of 50,000-100,000.

____

2. Would you choose Foxton or Ashton for a baseball stadium which seats 50,000 people? _______________________

3. Name the three towns with a population over 100,000. __________

____

4. Which is bigger—Pleasant Valley or Mayton? __________

5. Which town has more people—River City or Magic City? __________

6. Which town has more people—Judyville or Danton? __________

7. Which is larger—Little Bend or Ridgeville? __________

8. Which city is smaller—Blue Mountain or Deer Lake?__________

9. How many towns have 1,000-5,000 people?__________

10. How many towns have 5,000-25,000 people? __________

Section 2

United States Geography

This page has been
intentionally left blank.

Name ____________________

What a Great Country!

The United States is a country. It is made up of many states. Make your own map of the United States. Cut out this page and page 93 along the outer dotted (- - - -) lines. Glue the tab to the back of the map on page 93.

United States Map

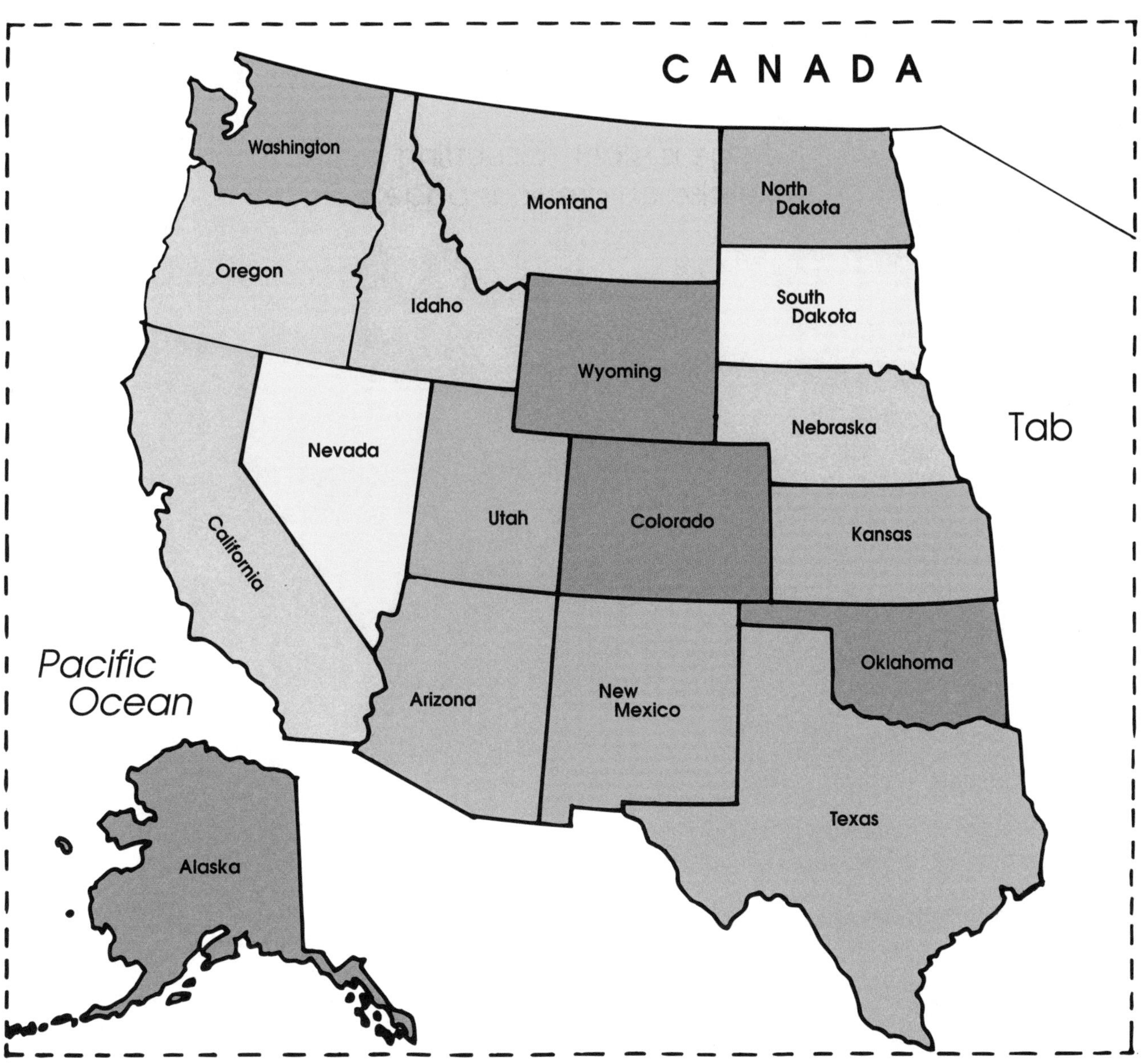

Page is blank for cutting
exercise on previous page.

Name________________________________

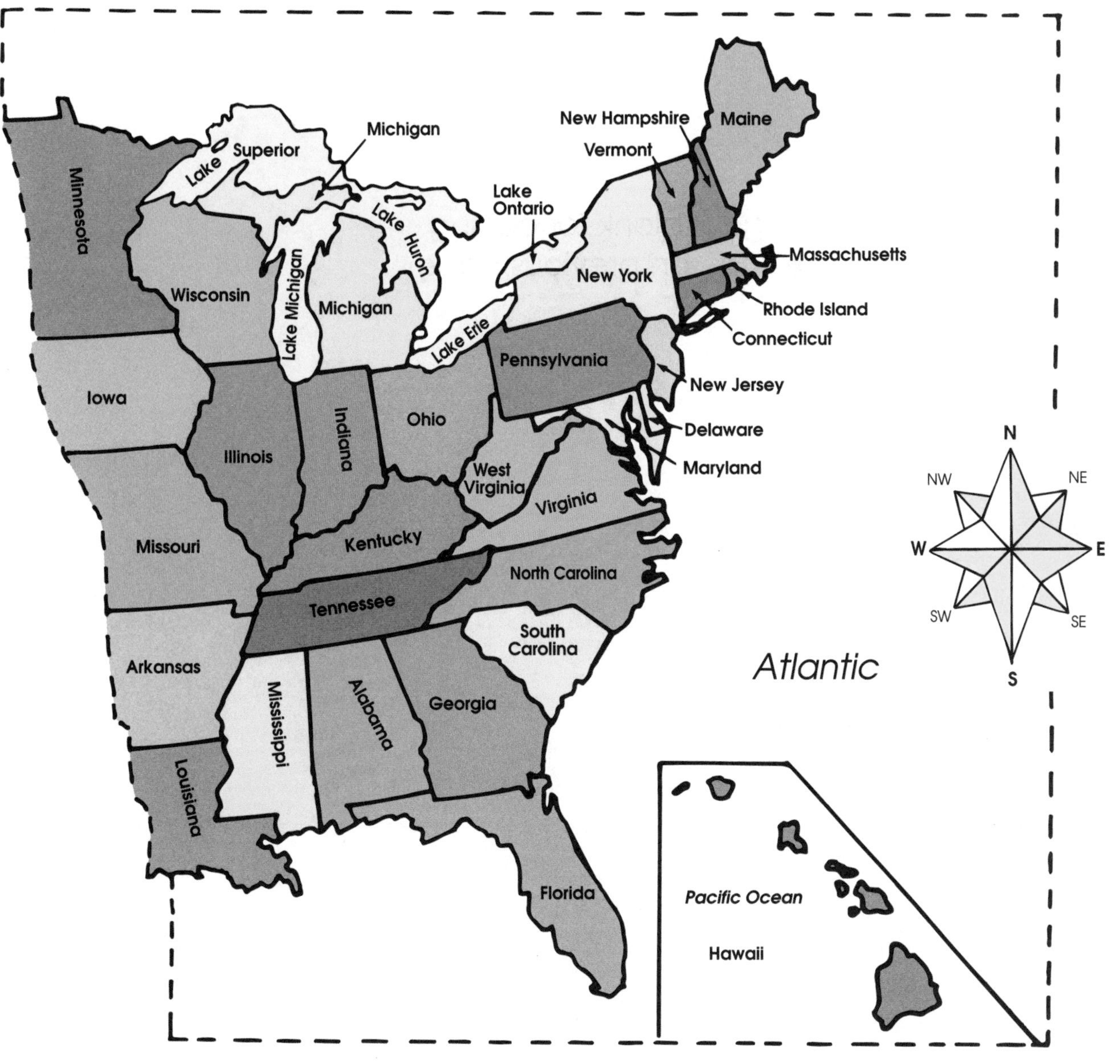

Minnesota
Lake Superior
Michigan
New Hampshire
Maine
Vermont
Lake Huron
Lake Ontario
Massachusetts
Wisconsin
Lake Michigan
Michigan
New York
Rhode Island
Lake Erie
Connecticut
Pennsylvania
Iowa
New Jersey
Illinois
Indiana
Ohio
Delaware
Maryland
West Virginia
Virginia
Missouri
Kentucky
North Carolina
Tennessee
South Carolina
Arkansas
Mississippi
Alabama
Georgia
Atlantic
Louisiana
Florida
Pacific Ocean
Hawaii
N
NE
E
SE
S
SW
W
NW

Page is blank for cutting
exercise on previous page.

Name ______________________

Crossing the States

Use the map of the United States on pages 91 and 93 and the compass rose to fill in the puzzle.

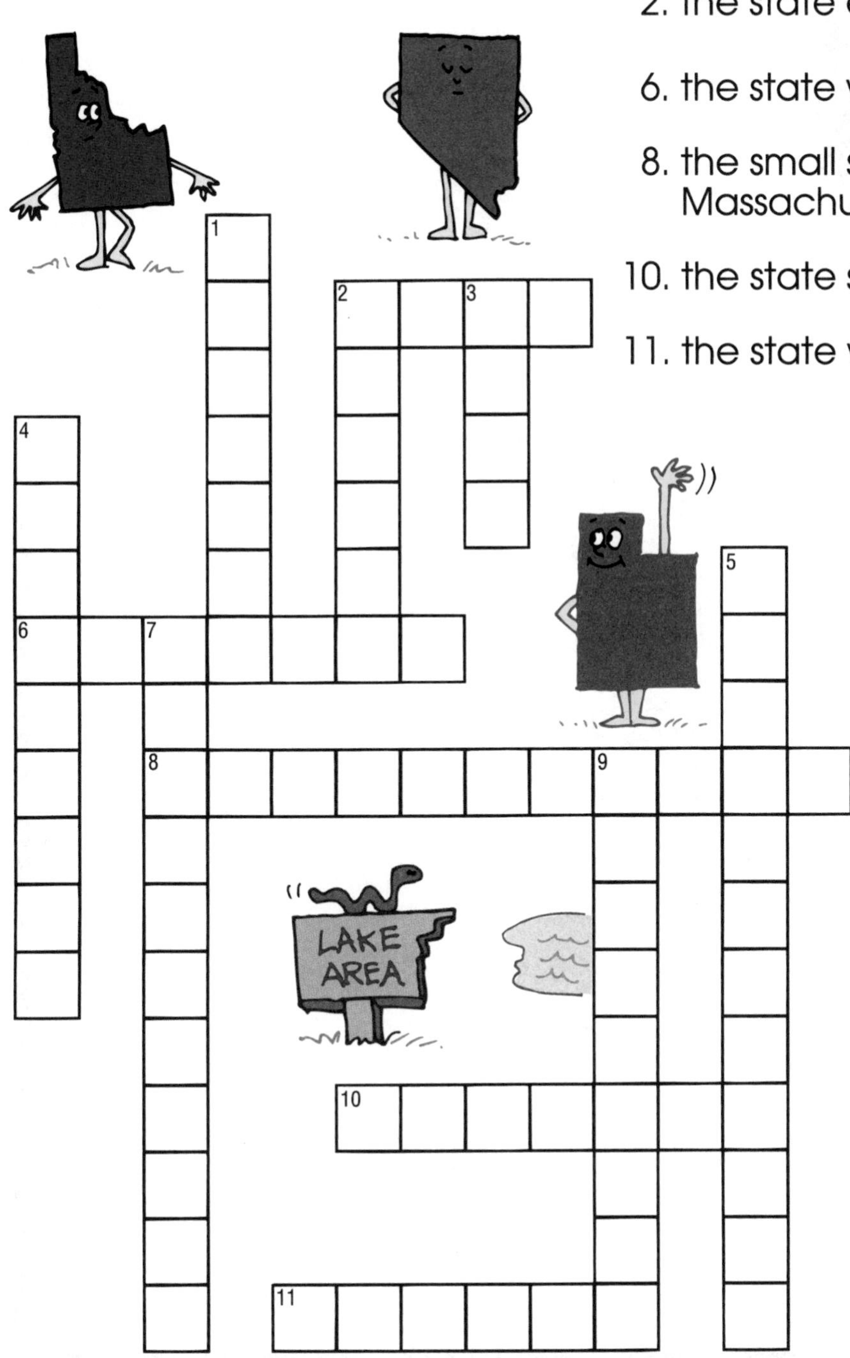

Across:

2. the state east of Indiana
6. the state west of North Dakota
8. the small state south of Massachusetts
10. the state south of Georgia
11. the state west of Utah

Down:

1. the state west of New Hampshire
2. the state south of Washington
3. the state north of Missouri
4. the state east of Arizona
5. the larger state south of New York
7. the state north of South Dakota
9. the state south of Arkansas

Name______________________________

Postcard Geography

Use this postcard to tell a friend about a place within the states where you are vacationing. Design your own stamp and write in your friend's address.

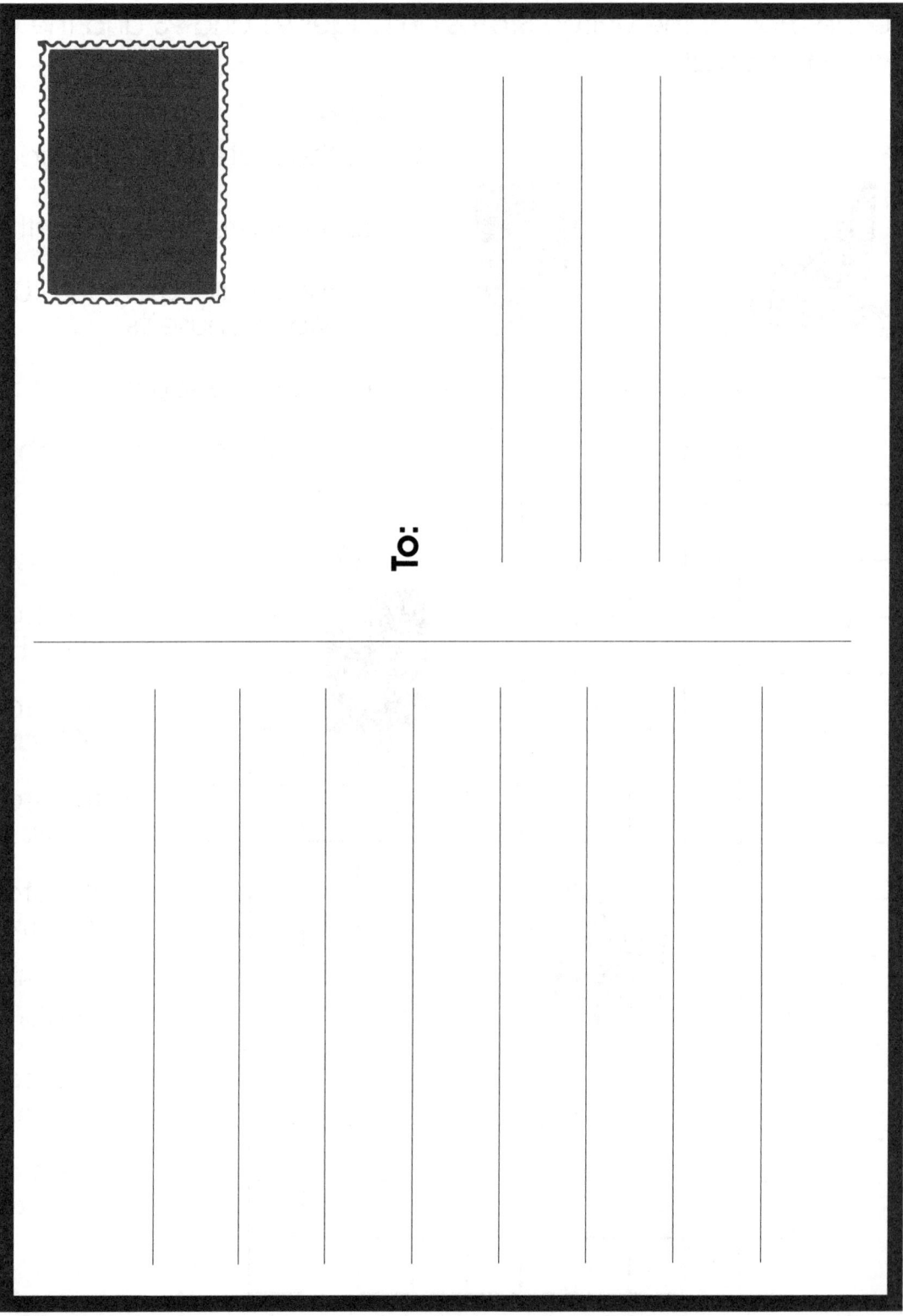

Name____________________________________

See the States

Use the map of the United States that you made with pages 91 and 93. Color the van at the bottom of this page. Cut out along the outer line of the oval. Use a piece of tape to attach it to your pencil.

Now your van is packed and you are ready to start your trip. Read the sentences below. Move your pencil where the directions lead you to find answers to the questions below.

Directions:

1. Start in Ohio.
2. Go west to Iowa. Which states did you pass through?

   ____

3. Go south to Louisiana. Which states did you pass through?

   ____

4. Go west to California. Which states did you pass through?

   ____

   ____

5. Turn and go north to Washington. What state did you pass through?

   ____

6. It's time to head home to Ohio. In which direction will you travel?

   ____

Name____

What a Vacation!

This is a map of the United States. It shows where four children went for a vacation. Use this map and the key on page 99 to find out where each child went.

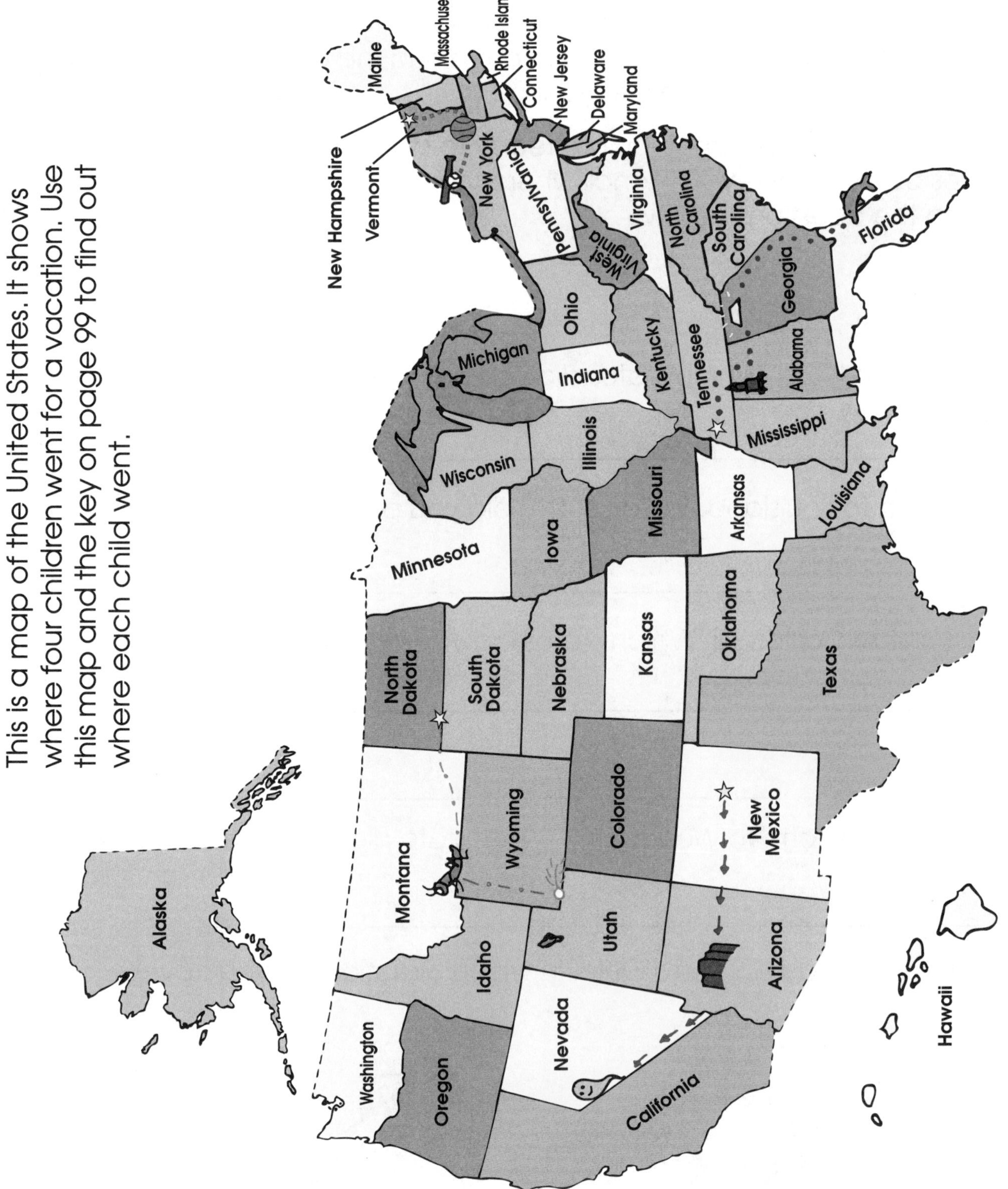

Name____

What a Vacation!

Key

→ → →	David's trip
• • • • •	Becky's trip
········	Adam's trip
— · — · —	Sheila's trip
☆	home
	National Baseball Hall of Fame and Museum
	Fossil Butte National Monument
	Dahlonega Gold Museum
	Sea World
	Grand Canyon
	U.S. Space and Rocket Center
	Grasshopper Glacier
	Basketball Hall of Fame
	Virginia City (old mining town)

1. Use a yellow crayon to trace David's route.

2. Use a blue crayon to trace Becky's route.

3. Use a red crayon to trace Adam's route.

4. Use a green crayon to trace Sheila's route.

6. Which person traveled the farthest west? ____________________

5. Which person probably likes sports? ____________________

7. Which person traveled the farthest south? ____________________

8. Write the names of the places Sheila went to see on her vacation.

____

____

9. Where did Becky go in Florida? ____________________

Name ____________________________

Flying Cross-Country

Pretend you are on an airplane that is flying cross-country. Name the states that you would fly over if you flew in a straight line from the first city to the second.

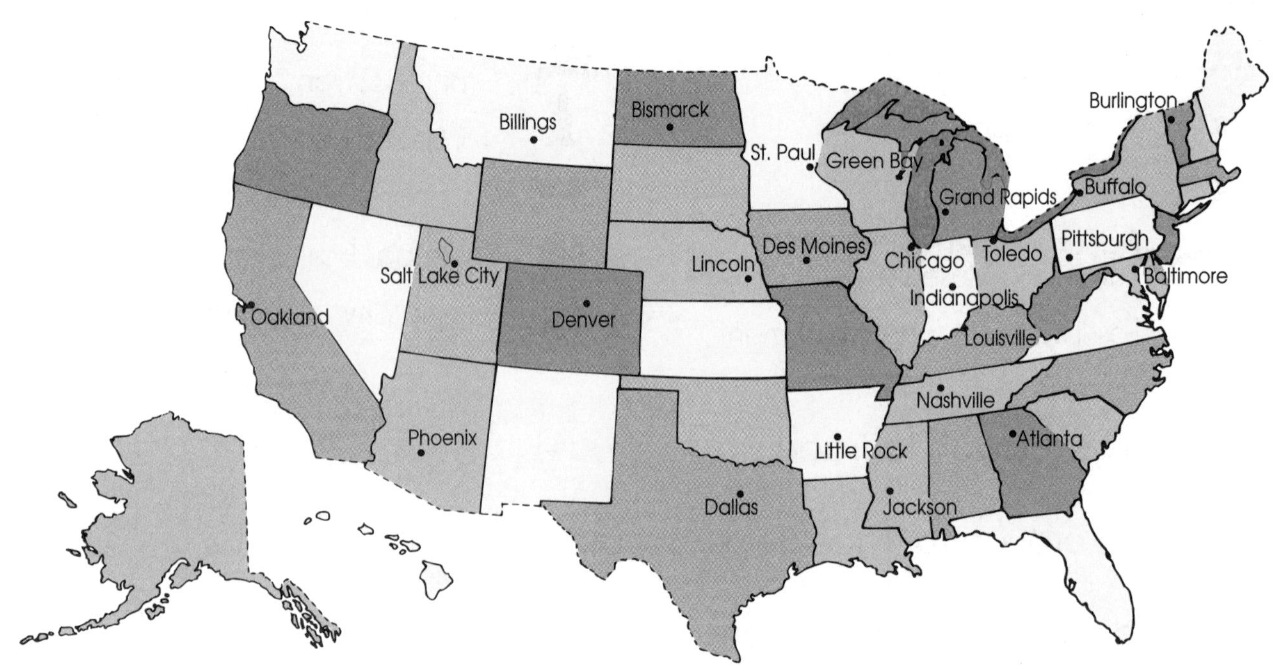

Atlanta, Georgia to Jackson, Mississippi ____________________

Grand Rapids, Michigan to St. Paul, Minnesota ____________________

Bismarck, North Dakota to Lincoln, Nebraska ____________________

Oakland, California to Salt Lake City, Utah ____________________

Phoenix, Arizona to Dallas, Texas ____________________

Little Rock, Arkansas to Chicago, Illinois ____________________

Toledo, Ohio to Green Bay, Wisconsin ____________________

Pittsburgh, Pennsylvania to Burlington, Vermont ____________________

Denver, Colorado to Billings, Montana ____________________

Nashville, Tennessee to Indianapolis, Indiana ____________________

Des Moines, Iowa to Louisville, Kentucky ____________________

Baltimore, Maryland to Buffalo, New York ____________________

Name ______________________________

State Snatcher

The State Snatcher has stolen some of the abbreviations of the states. Write in the missing abbreviations. Use another U.S. map to help you.

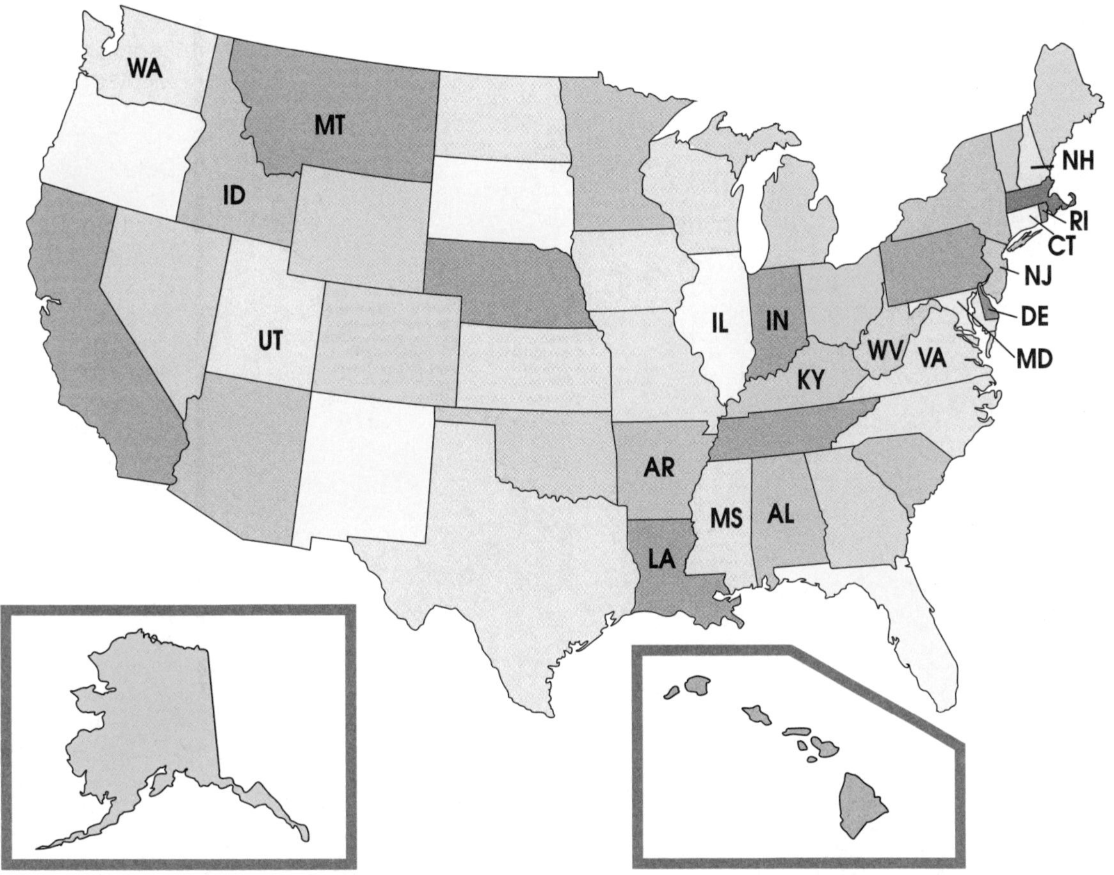

Postal Abbreviations Chart

Alabama	AL	Indiana	IN	Nebraska	NE	South Carolina	SC
Alaska	AK	Iowa	IA	Nevada	NV	South Dakota	SD
Arizona	AZ	Kansas	KS	New Hampshire	NH	Tennessee	TN
Arkansas	AR	Kentucky	KY	New Jersey	NJ	Texas	TX
California	CA	Louisiana	LA	New Mexico	NM	Utah	UT
Colorado	CO	Maine	ME	New York	NY	Vermont	VT
Connecticut	CT	Maryland	MD	North Carolina	NC	Virginia	VA
Delaware	DE	Massachusetts	MA	North Dakota	ND	Washington	WA
Florida	FL	Michigan	MI	Ohio	OH	West Virginia	WV
Georgia	GA	Minnesota	MN	Oklahoma	OK	Wisconsin	WI
Hawaii	HI	Mississippi	MS	Oregon	OR	Wyoming	WY
Idaho	ID	Missouri	MO	Pennsylvania	PA		
Illinois	IL	Montana	MT	Rhode Island	RI		

Name____

Super Cities

Write the name of each city in the blank by its number. Then, write each state's two-letter state abbreviation.

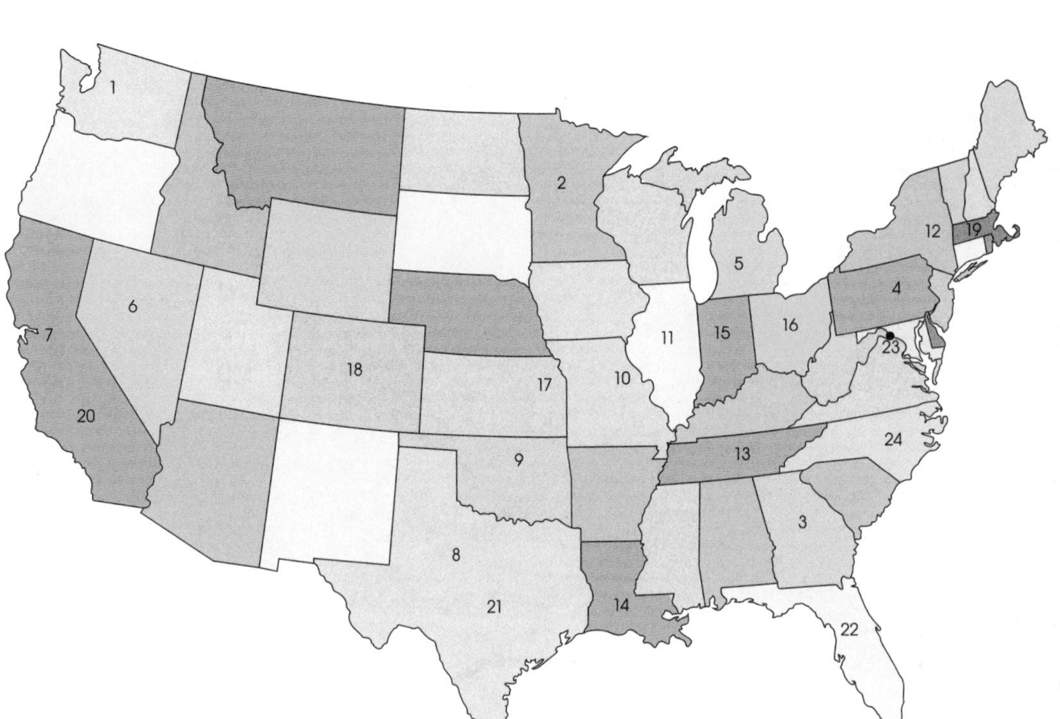

Cities

Seattle
Minneapolis
Atlanta
Philadelphia
Detroit
Las Vegas
San Francisco
Dallas
Tulsa
St. Louis
Chicago
New York City
Memphis
New Orleans
Indianapolis
Columbus
Kansas City
Denver
Boston
Los Angeles
San Antonio
Miami
Washington, D.C.
Charlotte

	City	State		City	State
1.	____________	______	13.	____________	______
2.	____________	______	14.	____________	______
3.	____________	______	15.	____________	______
4.	____________	______	16.	____________	______
5.	____________	______	17.	____________	______
6.	____________	______	18.	____________	______
7.	____________	______	19.	____________	______
8.	____________	______	20.	____________	______
9.	____________	______	21.	____________	______
10.	____________	______	22.	____________	______
11.	____________	______	23.	____________	______
12.	____________	______	24.	____________	______

Name ______________________

Play Ball!

In the spring, you can hear the umpire shout, "Play Ball!" In North America, there are 30 Major League baseball teams. Most of the teams are named after the city in which they play, but four teams are named after their states. One of the teams is in Canada.

Write the name of the state/province where each team plays. You get bonus points if you can give the team name. Then, complete the map on page 104.

American League

City	State/Province	Team name
Baltimore		
Boston		
Los Angeles	California	
Chicago		
Cleveland	Ohio	
Detroit		
Kansas City		
Minneapolis	Minnesota	
New York		
Oakland		
Seattle		
Arlington	Texas	
Tampa Bay		
Toronto		

National League

City	State/Province	Team name
Chicago		
Cincinnati		
Denver	Colorado	
Miami	Florida	
Houston		
Los Angeles		
Milwaukee		
Washington		
New York		
Philadelphia		
Phoenix	Arizona	
Pittsburgh		
San Diego		
San Francisco		
St. Louis		
Atlanta		

Name____

Play Ball!

Label the cities where the Major League baseball teams play. Label the American League cities red and the National League cities blue.

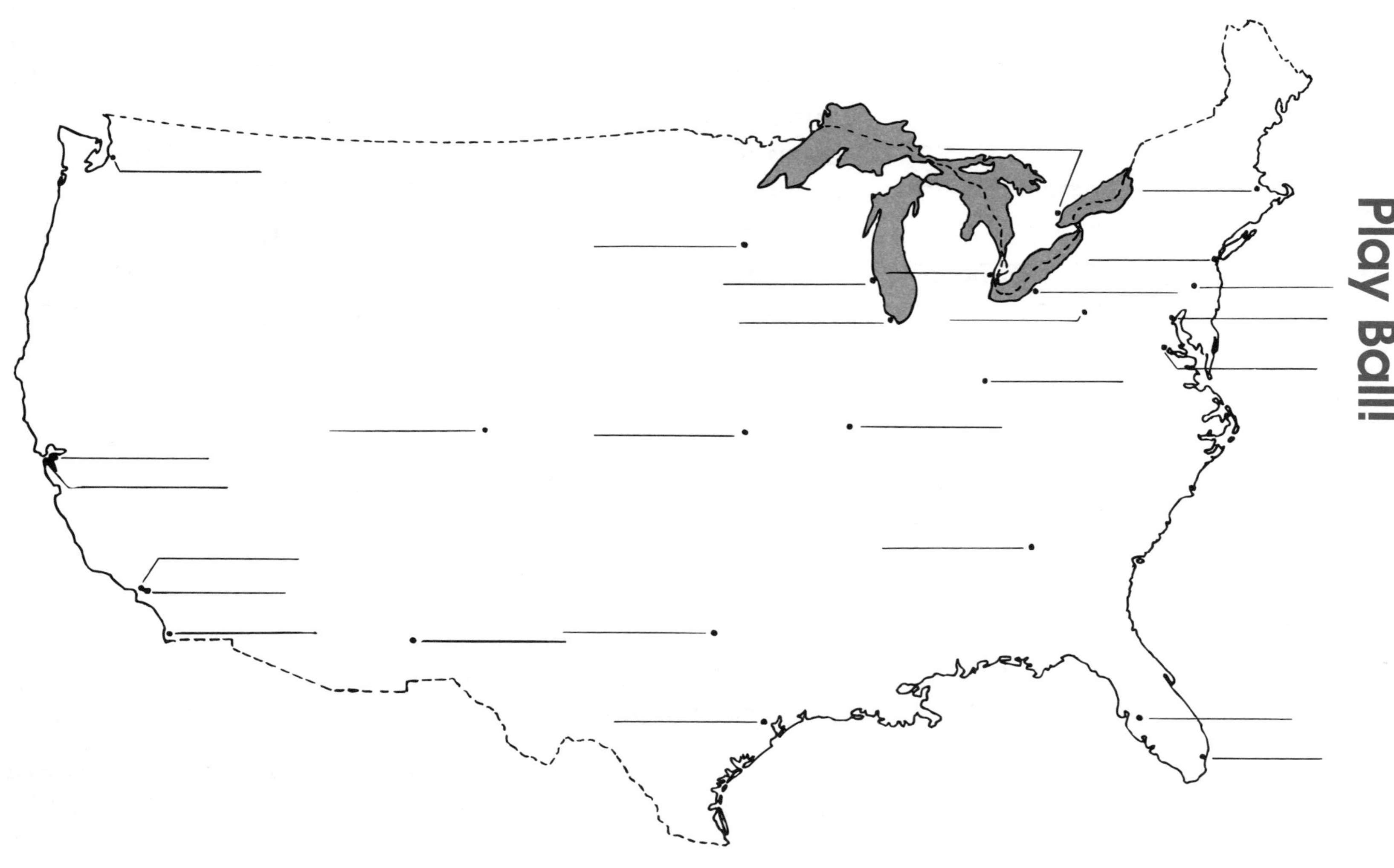

Name ______________________

Mystery States I

Can you identify these state shapes? Use a U.S. map to help you. Write the name of each state and its capital city ☆.

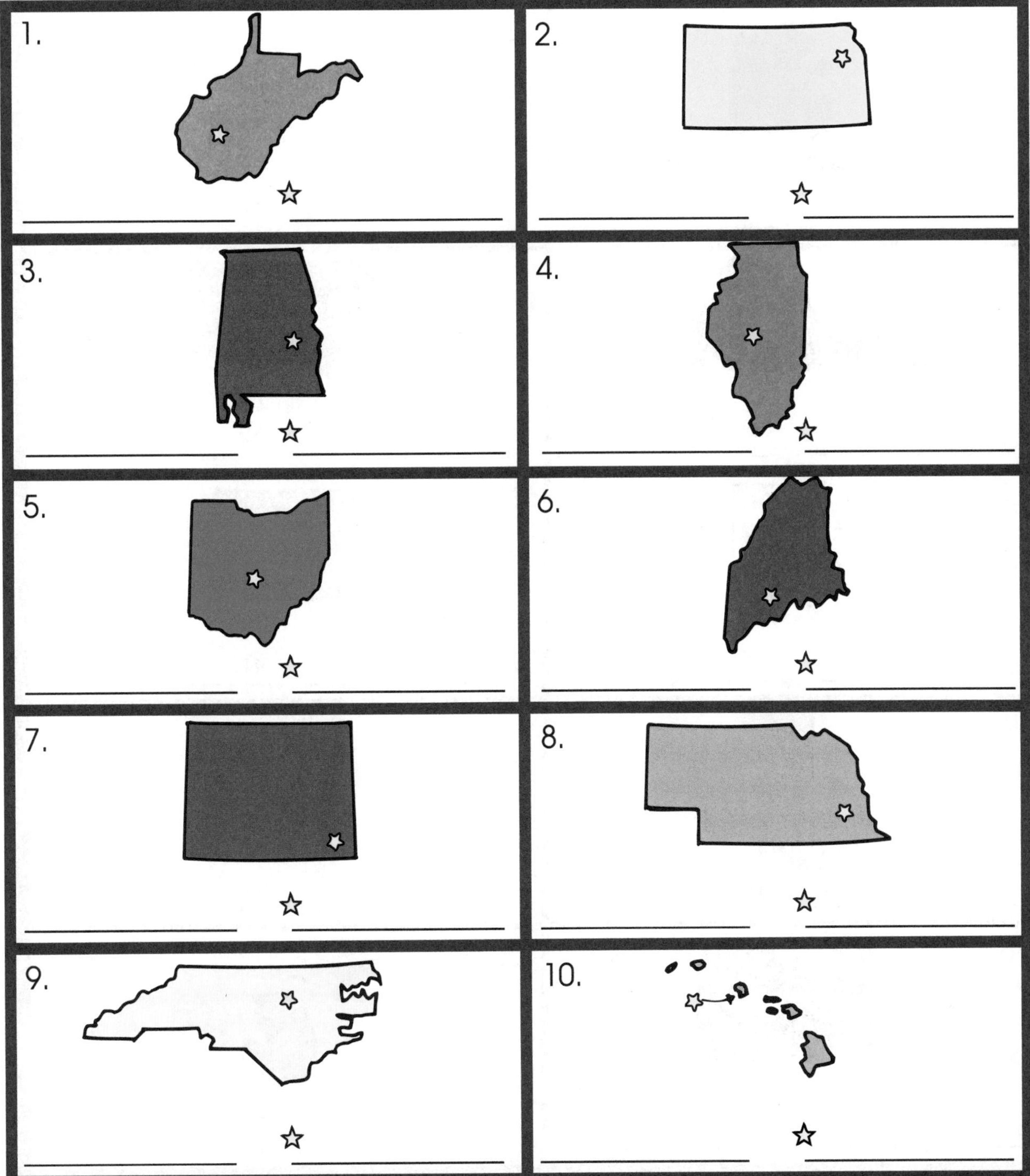

Name____

Mystery States II

Can you identify these state shapes? Use a U.S. map to help you. Write the name of each state and its capital city☆.

1. ______________ ☆______________	2. ______________ ☆______________
3. ______________ ☆______________	4. ______________ ☆______________
5. ______________ ☆______________	6. ______________ ☆______________
7. ______________ ☆______________	8. ______________ ☆______________
9. ______________ ☆______________	10. ______________ ☆______________

Name ____________________

Mystery States III

Can you identify these state shapes? Use a U.S. map to help you. Write the name of each state and its capital city ☆.

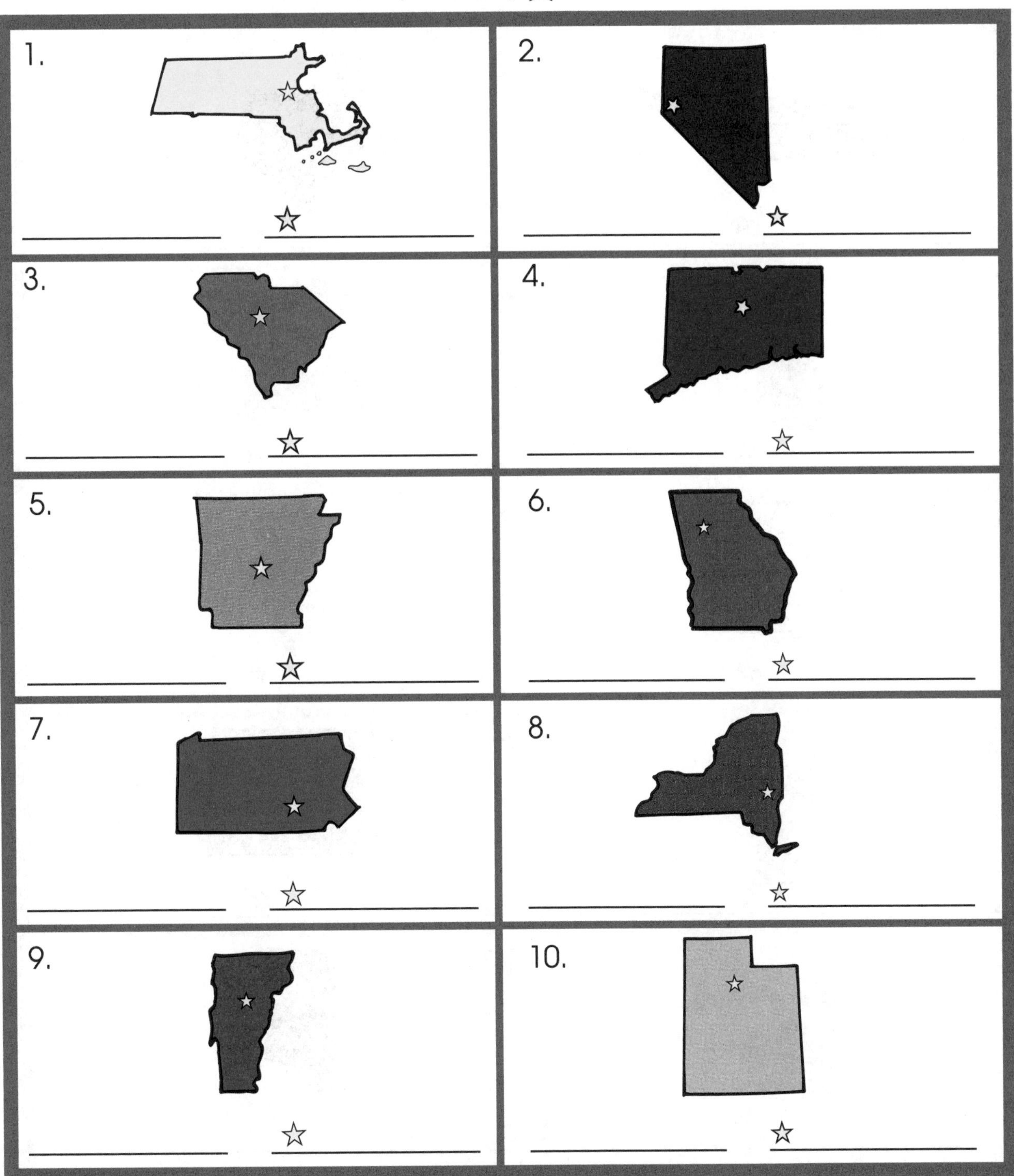

Name________________________________

Mystery States IV

Can you identify these state shapes? Use a U.S. map to help you. Write the name of each state and its capital city ☆.

Name ________________________________

Mystery States V

Can you identify these state shapes? Use a U.S. map to help you. Write the name of each state and its capital city ☆.

1. ______________ ☆ ______________

2. ______________ ☆ ______________

3. ______________ ☆ ______________

4. ______________ ☆ ______________

5. ______________ ☆ ______________

6. ______________ ☆ ______________

7. ______________ ☆ ______________

8. ______________ ☆ ______________

9. ______________ ☆ ______________

10. ______________ ☆ ______________

Name ____

My Hometown

Find and color your state on the United States map. Then, draw an outline map of your state in the space below. Label your hometown, capital and any other important cities, rivers and bodies of water.

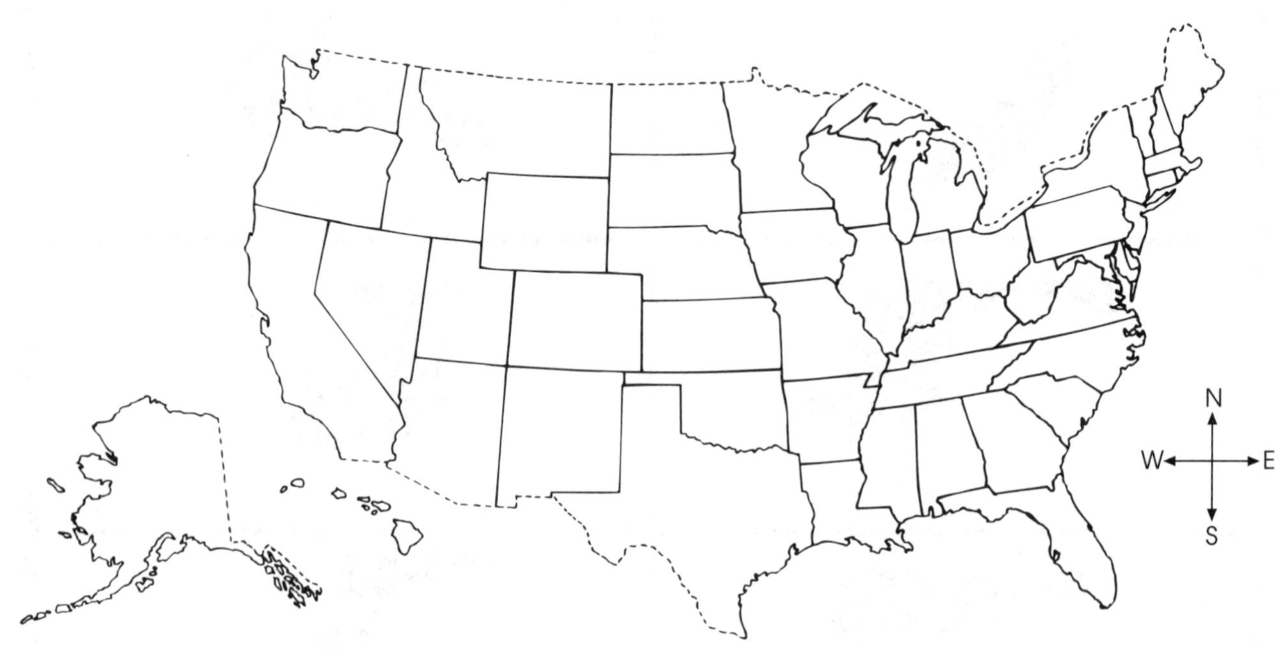

____
My State

Key

Home Town

☆ Capital

● Important Cities

N
W
E
S

Name________________________________

Near My State

Use a map of the United States to locate your state. Write the names of the bordering states/countries and/or bodies of water on the chart below. Write each one in its correct location relative to your state.

Northwest	North	Northeast
West	**My State** Draw an outline of your state.	**East**
Southwest	**South**	**Southeast**

Name____

"We're Going Places" Mileage Chart

Let's take a trip around your state. On the left side of the chart, fill in the names of five cities in your state. The first one should be your hometown. Then, write the names of five additional cities or places to visit in your state across the top. Use a state highway map or other source to find the number of miles between each place. Complete the chart.

Places to Visit in My State

Cities in My State

my hometown					

Name ______________________

Boundary Bonanza

Directions: Use the map on page 114 to answer these questions about boundaries.

1. Which state is made of islands? ______________
2. Which state is S of Utah? ______________
3. Which state is NE of Idaho? ______________
4. Which states are E of Ohio? ______________
5. Which state is W of Arkansas? ______________
6. Which state lies between Colorado and Missouri? ______________
7. Which two states are just S of Michigan? ______________
8. Which states touch New York on its eastern border? ______________

   ______________, ______________.
9. Which state is in the NE corner of the U.S.A.? ______________
10. Which state is S of Oklahoma? ______________
11. Which states border the Gulf of Mexico? ______________, ______________,

    ______________, ______________, ______________.
12. The only state that borders Maine is ______________.
13. Four states that border Texas are ______________, ______________,

    ______________ and ______________.
14. The state S of North Dakota is ______________.
15. The state SW of Nebraska is ______________.

Name____

Boundaries and Rivers

Across the Line

This is a map of the United States. The lines show the boundaries (lines that separate one state from another) of each state. Use this page with pages 113 and 115.

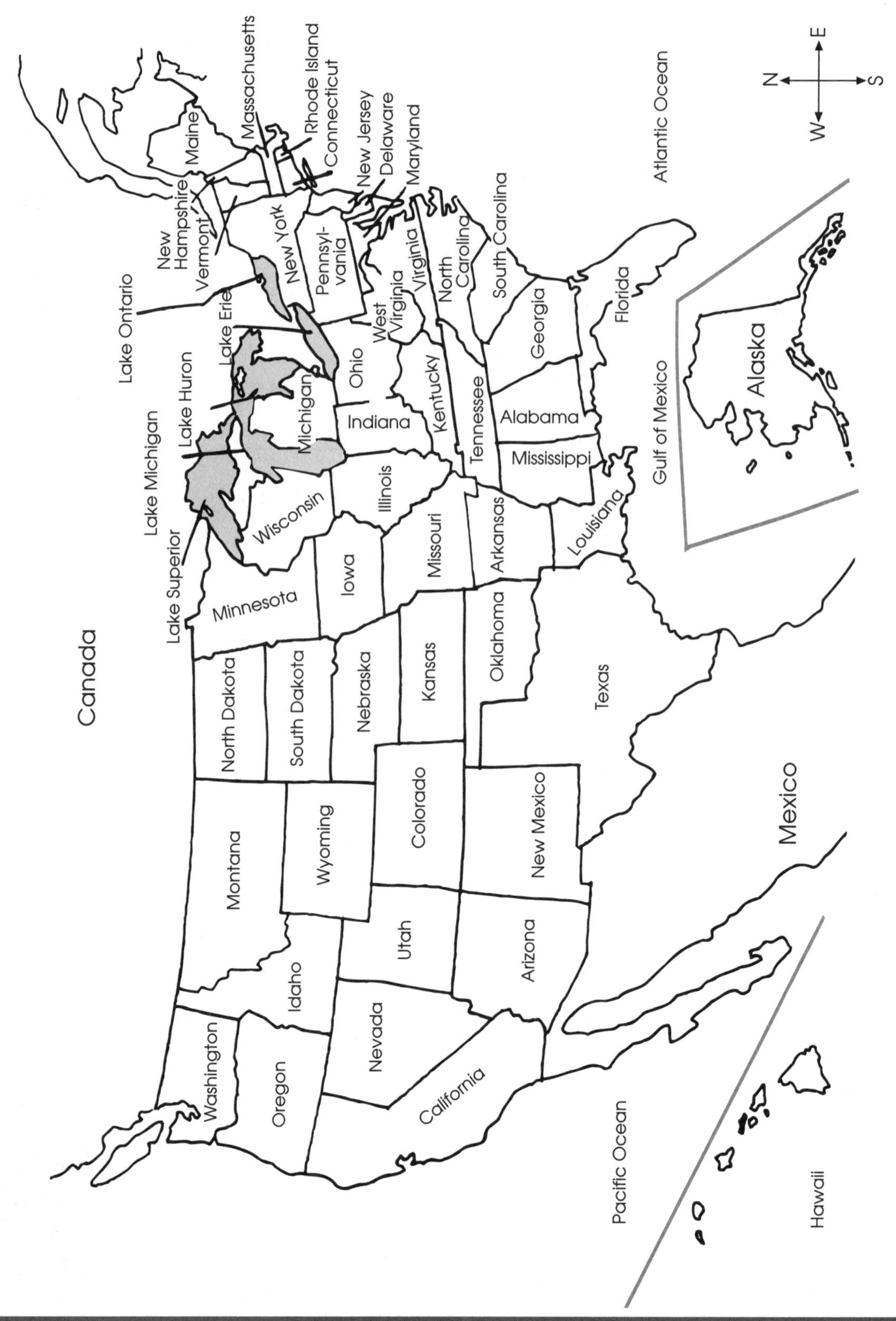

Name____

Across the Line

Directions: Use the United States map on page 114 to complete the following.

1. What is the name of the state in which you live? ____________________

2. Draw a blue line along the boundary lines of the state where you live.

3. What country is north of the United States? _________________________

4. Draw a green line along the boundary between the United States and Canada.

5. What country is south of the United States? _________________________

6. Draw an orange line along the southern boundary of the United States.

7. Find the state, country or body of water that is the . . .

   a. northern boundary of your state. Color it green.

   b. eastern boundary of your state. Color it blue.

   c. southern boundary of your state. Color it yellow.

   d. western boundary of your state. Color it red.

Name________________________________

Water Watch

Some of the largest lakes are shown on the map. Find and color them blue. Then, go on to page 117.

Name___________________________________

Water Watch

Directions: Use the maps on page 116 and 118 to find the answers to the questions.

1. The lakes along the northern border of the United States are called the Great Lakes. Write the names of these five lakes.

____

____

2. Which river flows along the border between Canada and Minnesota?

____

3. What two rivers flow through Utah? ______________________

4. Which river flows along the border between Washington and Oregon?

____

5. Circle the name of the river that flows along the border between Mexico and the United States.

   Mississippi River   Rio Grande River   Yukon River   Missouri River

6. Circle the name of the river that flows through the state of Alaska.

   Mississippi River   Rio Grande River   Yukon River   Missouri River

7. How many states does the Mississippi River flow through or past?

____

Name____

Rivers Run Through It

Trace the contiguous U. S. A.'s major rivers in blue. Then, use the map to answer the river riddles on page 119.

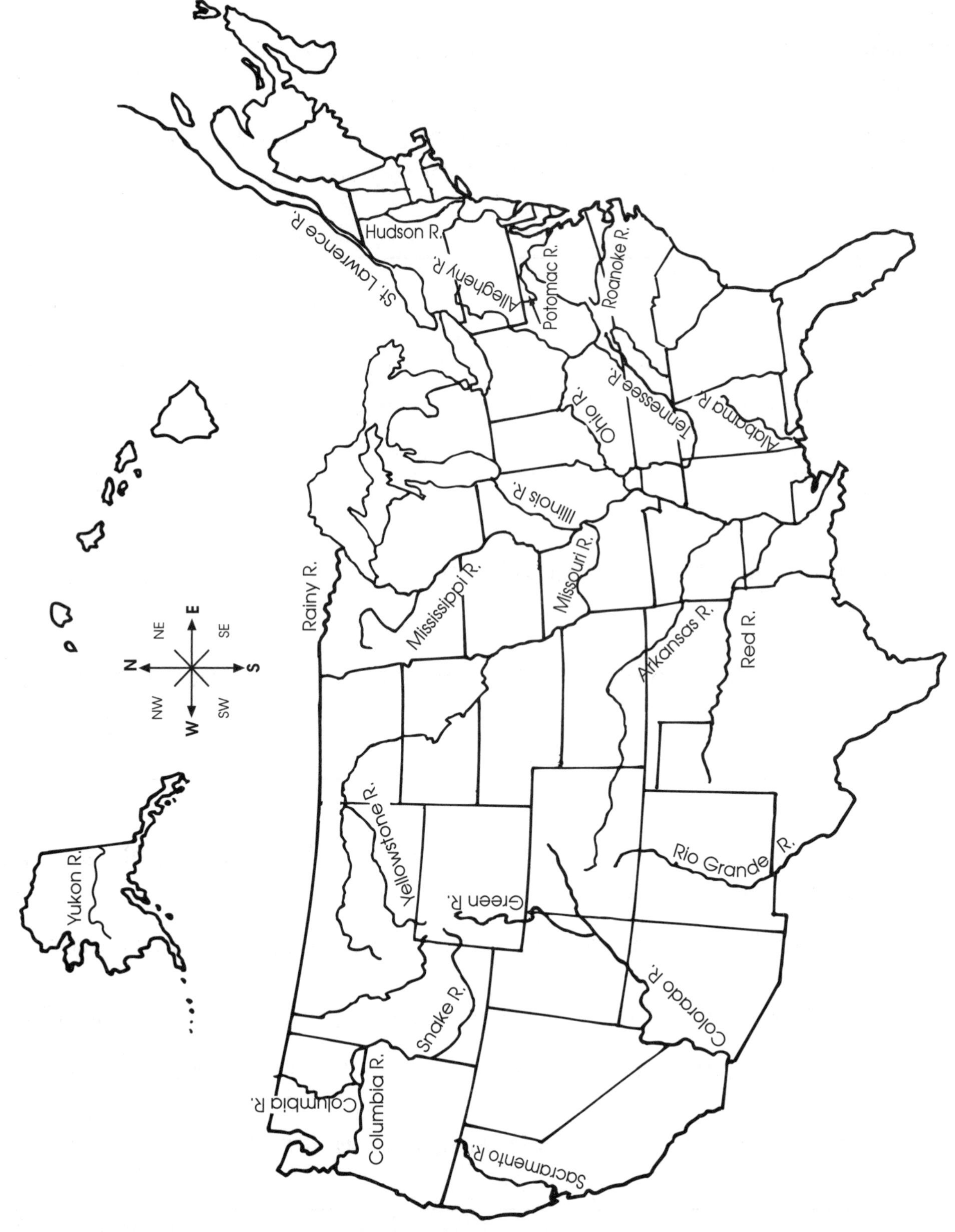

Name ______________________________

Rivers Run Through It

Directions: Use with page 118.

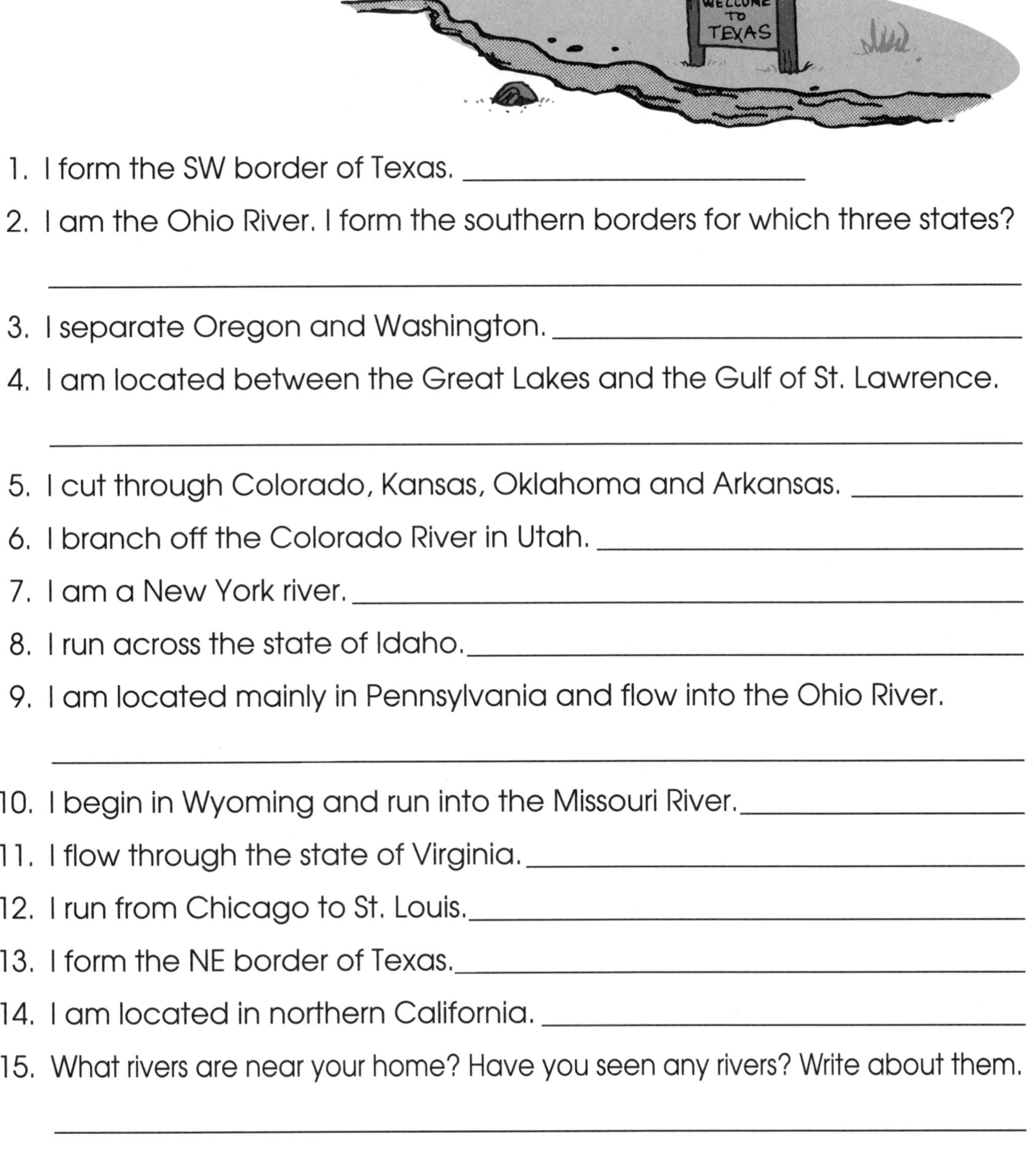

1. I form the SW border of Texas. ____________________
2. I am the Ohio River. I form the southern borders for which three states?

   ____

3. I separate Oregon and Washington. ____________________
4. I am located between the Great Lakes and the Gulf of St. Lawrence.

   ____

5. I cut through Colorado, Kansas, Oklahoma and Arkansas. __________
6. I branch off the Colorado River in Utah. ____________________
7. I am a New York river. ____________________
8. I run across the state of Idaho. ____________________
9. I am located mainly in Pennsylvania and flow into the Ohio River.

   ____

10. I begin in Wyoming and run into the Missouri River. ______________
11. I flow through the state of Virginia. ____________________
12. I run from Chicago to St. Louis. ____________________
13. I form the NE border of Texas. ____________________
14. I am located in northern California. ____________________
15. What rivers are near your home? Have you seen any rivers? Write about them.

    ____

    ____

Name ____________________________________

River Boundaries

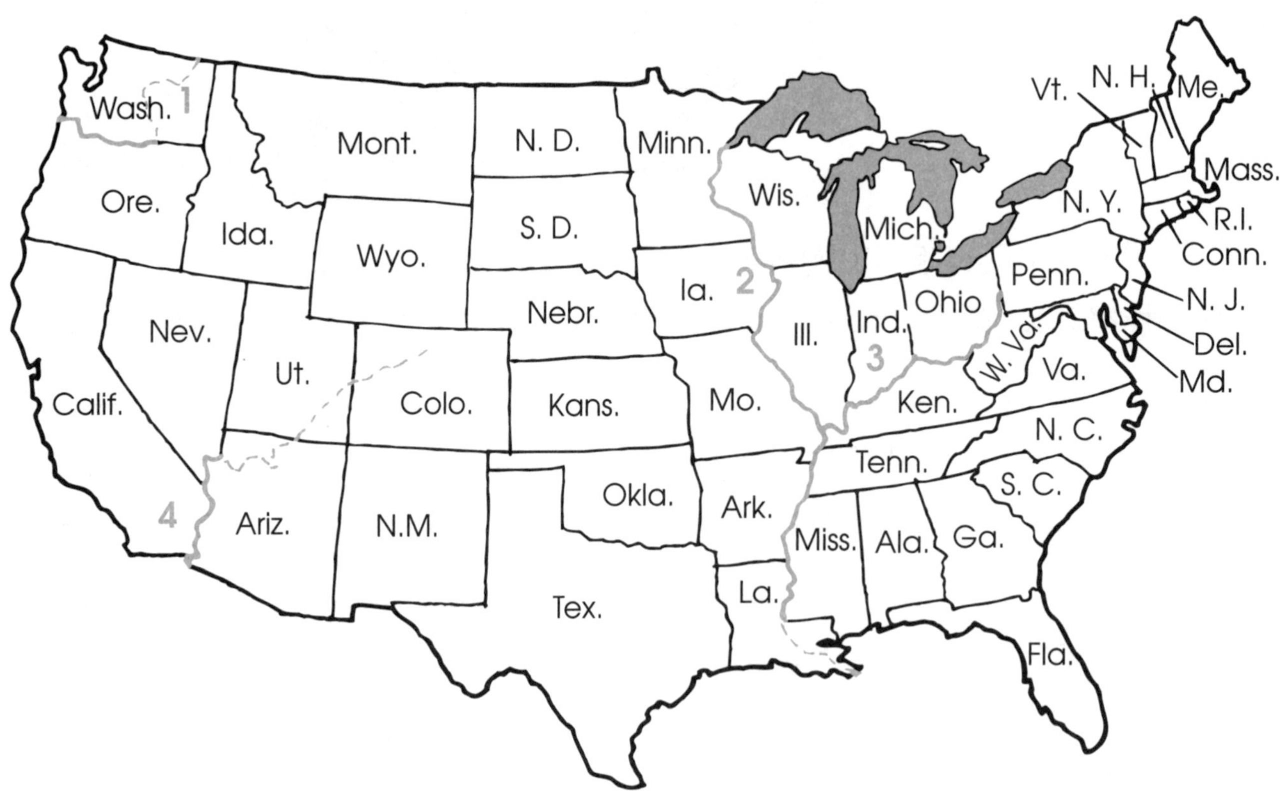

Directions: Write the number from the map by the name of each river. Refer to the map on page 29 to help you.

_____ Colorado River _____Mississippi River _____Columbia River _____Ohio River

Use the map above to answer these questions.

1. The Columbia River forms a natural boundary between these states: ____________________ and ________________________.

2. The Mississippi River forms all or part of the eastern borders of these states:___________, ___________, ___________, ___________ and _________.

3. The Ohio River forms the southern borders of these states: ___________ ____ and____________________.

4. The Colorado River forms a short border between ____________________ and____.

Name ____________________

Up the Lazy River

"The steamboat is coming!" was a cry heard in the many small river towns in the 1800s. Steamboats carried people and packages along the waterways before the faster railroads were developed.

The shipping tags below tell where each package is beginning and ending its journey. Use a map, atlas or other reference book to find the river on which the steamboat will be traveling. Some steamboats may have to travel on more than one river.

Directions: Write the name of the river route(s) on each shipping tag.

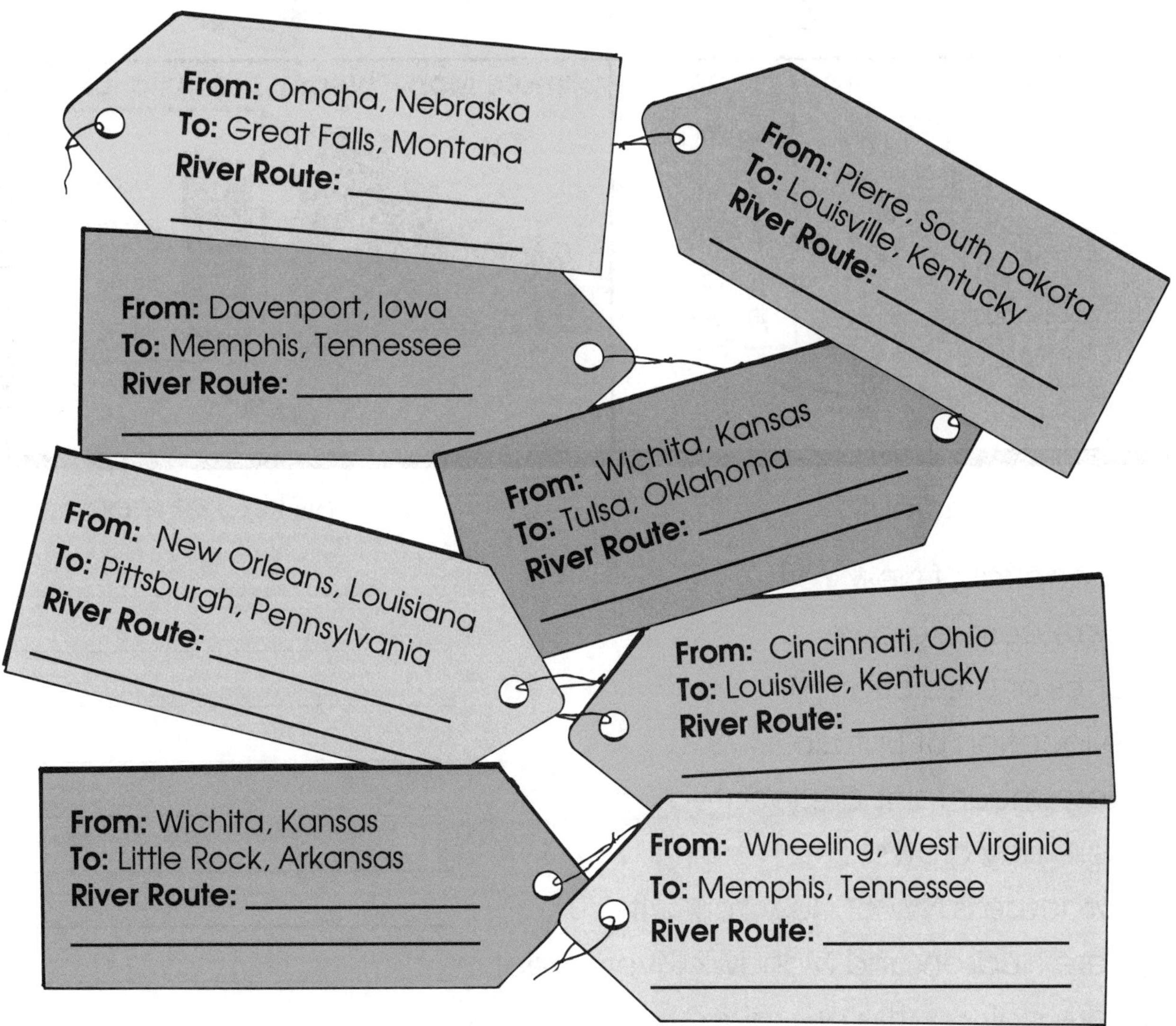

Name________________________________

Focusing on Four

Shown are four kinds of maps.

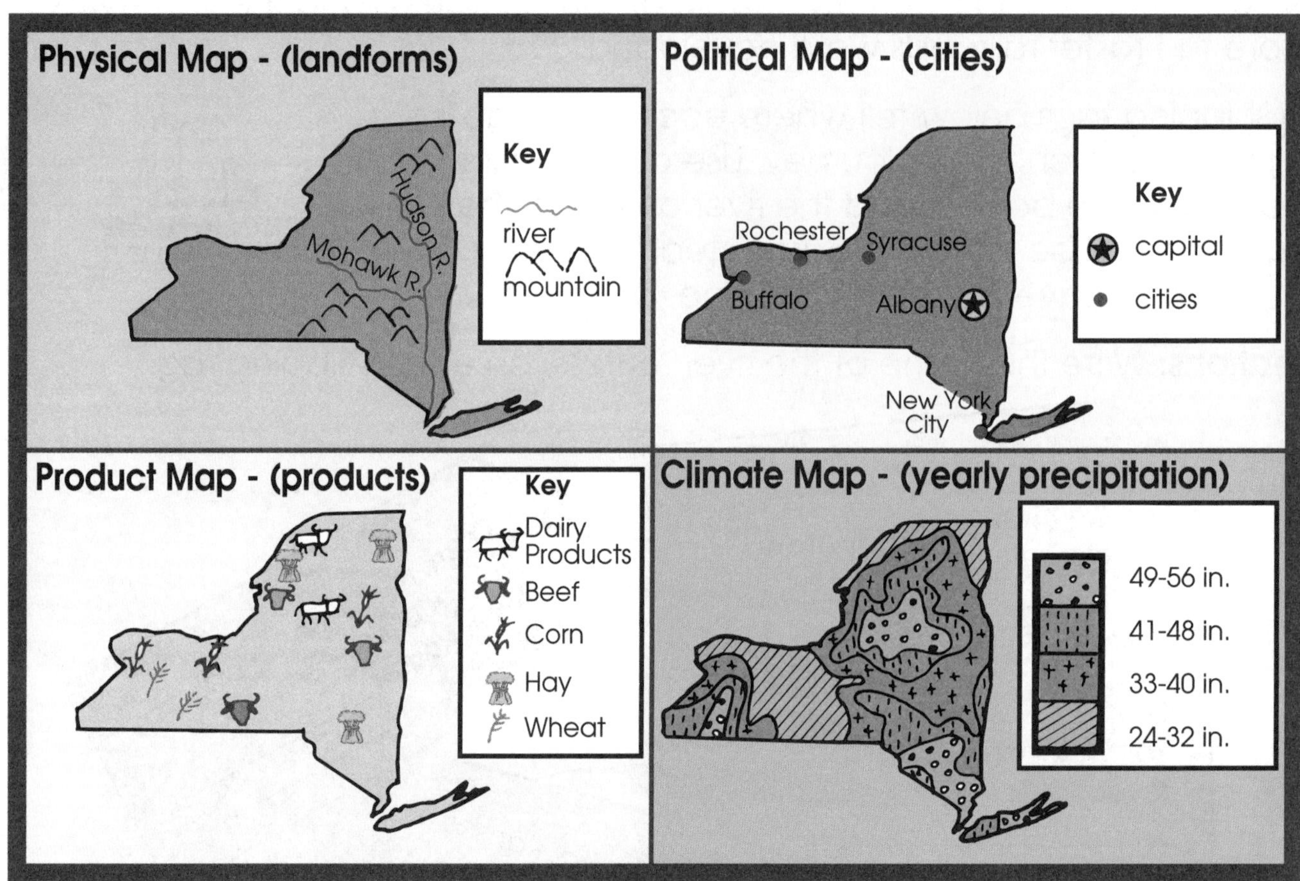

To find out . . .	Use this kind of map . . .
1. the capital of New York	______________
2. where corn is grown	______________
3. inches of precipitation	______________
4. the location of Buffalo	______________
5. where mountains are located	______________
6. where hay grows	______________
7. if Syracuse is NW of New York City	______________
8. where Hudson and Mohawk Rivers meet	______________
9. where dairy cattle are raised	______________

Name________________________________

Political Maps

Political maps not only show where cities are located, they also show boundary lines between states and between countries.

Key

State boundary_____
International boundary - - - -
Cities •
State Capitals ★

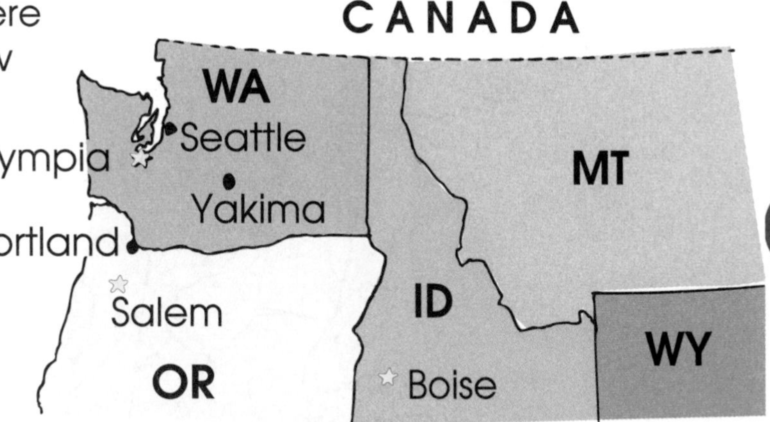

Use a map, atlas or other resource to help you label the names of the states and cities on the political map of the United States on page 124. Use the states' postal abbreviations. As you complete the map, cross off each state in the list below.

States

Alabama	AL	Louisiana	LA	Ohio	OH
Alaska	AK	Maine	ME	Oklahoma	OK
Arizona	AZ	Maryland	MD	Oregon	OR
Arkansas	AR	Massachusetts	MA	Pennsylvania	PA
California	CA	Michigan	MI	Rhode Island	RI
Colorado	CO	Minnesota	MN	South Carolina	SC
Connecticut	CT	Mississippi	MS	South Dakota	SD
Delaware	DE	Missouri	MO	Tennessee	TN
Florida	FL	Montana	MT	Texas	TX
Georgia	GA	Nebraska	NE	Utah	UT
Hawaii	HI	Nevada	NV	Vermont	VT
Idaho	ID	New Hampshire	NH	Virginia	VA
Illinois	IL	New Jersey	NJ	Washington	WA
Indiana	IN	New Mexico	NM	West Virginia	WV
Iowa	IA	New York	NY	Wisconsin	WI
Kansas	KS	North Carolina	NC	Wyoming	WY
Kentucky	KY	North Dakota	ND		

Cities

Chicago, Illinois	New York, New York	Philadelphia, Pennsylvania
Los Angeles, California	Miami, Florida	Detroit, Michigan
Atlanta, Georgia	Washington D.C.	Denver, Colorado
Seattle, Washington	Boston, Massachusetts	St. Louis, Missouri

Name ______________________________

Kinds of Maps: Political

United States Map

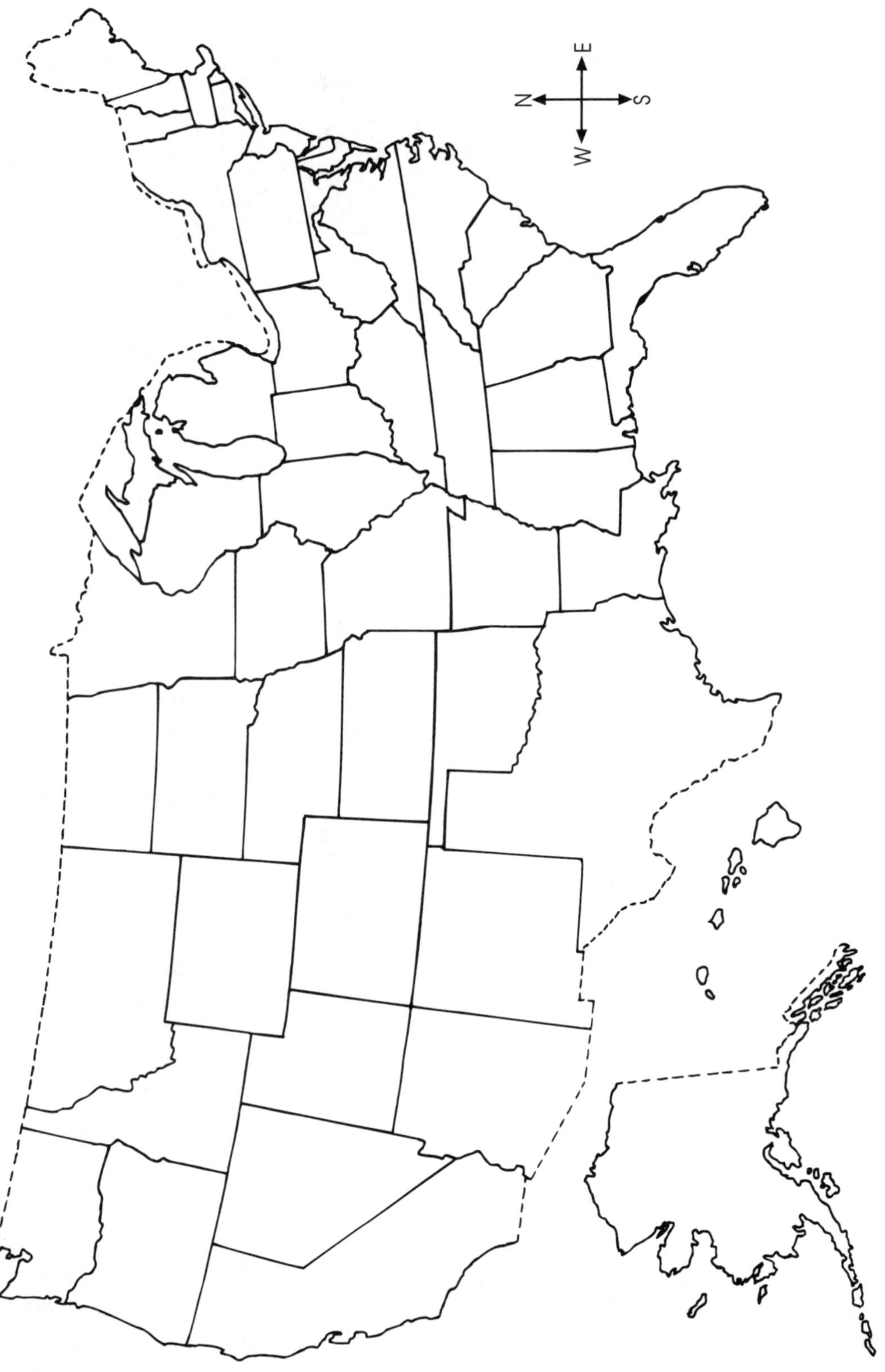

Name ____________________

State Smart

Use this map of some of the states to answer the questions below.

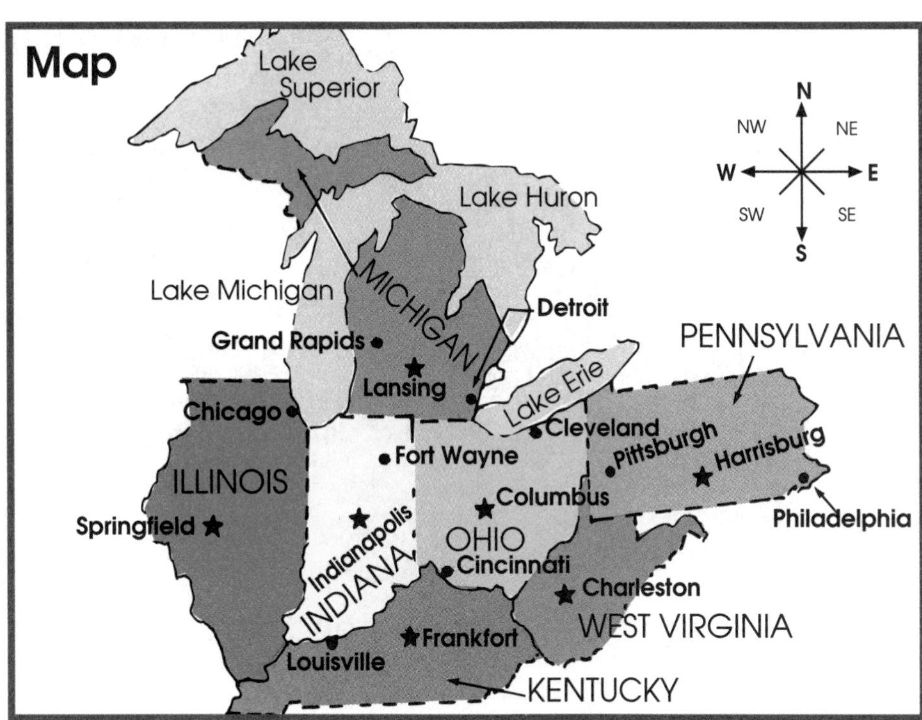

Key
- ★ state capital
- • city
- ∼∼ river
- - - - state

1. What state is west of Ohio? ____________________
2. The capital of West Virginia is ____________________.
3. Pittsburgh is a city in the state of ____________________.
4. What Ohio city is on the Ohio River? ____________________
5. Which state is southwest of Michigan? ____________________
6. What lake is west of Michigan? ____________________
7. Frankfort is the capital of ____________________.
8. What is the capital of Indiana? ____________________
9. Springfield is the capital of ____________________.
10. Chicago is ____________________ of Springfield, Illinois.
11. What Ohio city is northeast of Columbus? ____________________
12. Grand Rapids is ____________________ of Lansing, Michigan.
13. What state is east of Illinois? ____________________
14. What lake forms the northern border of Ohio? ____________________

Name ______________________________

What is a Political Map?

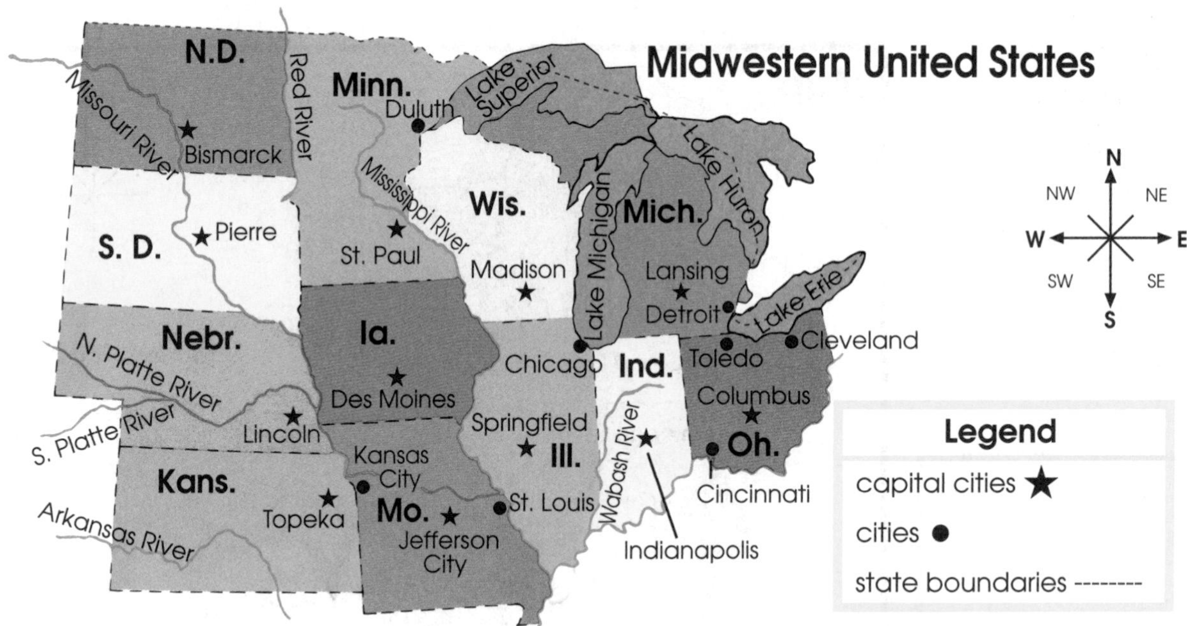

1. What do these three symbols stand for on this map?
   A. ★ ____________________ B ● ______________________________
   C. - - - - - ______________________________
2. The________________ forms the boundary between Missouri and Illinois.
3. ______________ forms the boundary between Wisconsin and Michigan.
4. The eastern boundary of North Dakota is formed by the ____________.
5. Ohio's western boundary is formed by the state of________________.
6. The southern part of Iowa is bordered by the state of ______________.
7. What are the capital cities of these states?
   A. Kansas ________________ D. North Dokota ________________
   B. Indiana ________________ E. Michigan________________
   C. Wisconsin ______________ F. Illinois ________________
8. The ____________________________ River is north of Indianapolis.
9. Name the four lakes shown on this map. ________________________

   ____
10. Name the river which cuts South Dakota in half. ________________
11. The northeastern border of Michigan is formed by Lake______________.
12. Chicago is on the coast of Lake ______________________________.

Name ____________________

Counties in Arizona

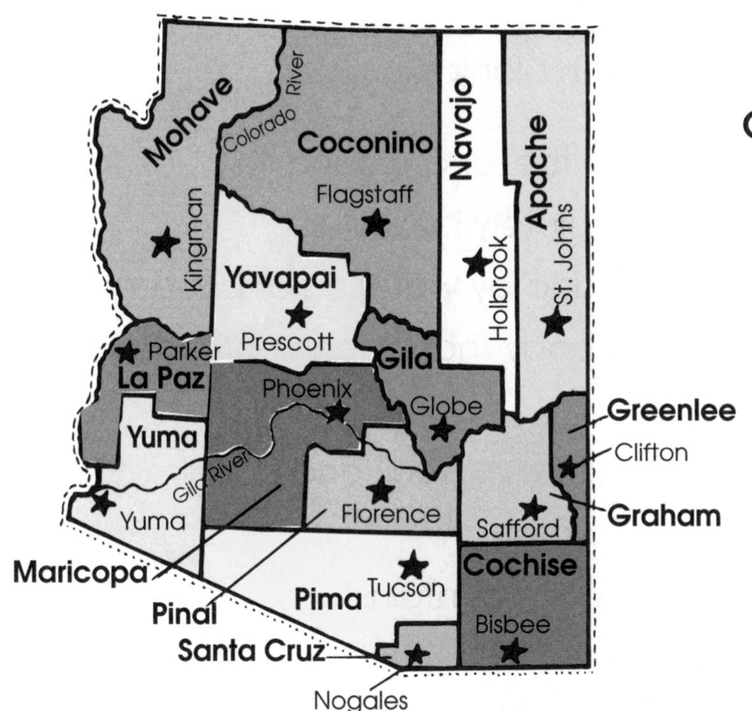

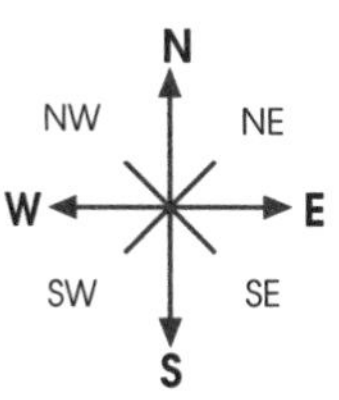

Legend
county seats ★
county lines ——

1. What do these symbols stand for on the map?
   A. ★ ____________________ B. ▬ ____________________
2. What county is located in the southwest corner of the state?__________
3. Is Pima in the northern or southern part of Arizona? __________
4. Name the county seat for each county listed.
   A. Cochise ____________ D. Yuma ____________
   B. Mohave ____________ E. Coconino ____________
   C. Greenlee____________ F. Navajo ____________
5. Is Cochise east or west of Pima County?__________
6. The county directly north of Yuma is __________.
7. What is the county seat for Santa Cruz? __________
8. Name the county which is south of Graham. __________
9. What is the smallest county in Arizona? __________
10. Name the river which flows through Yuma. __________
11. The county seat of Pinal is __________.
12. Which county and county seat have the same name?__________

Name____

Natural Wonders

Earth's physical features are its natural formations. Match each formation with its definition by writing a number in each blank.

______	river	1. land rising high above the land around it
______	bay	2. land surrounded completely by water
______	island	3. piece of land surrounded by water on all but one side
______	gulf	4. inlet of a large water body that extends into the land; smaller than a gulf
______	mountain	5. Earth opening that spills lava, rock and gases
______	plain	6. large inland body of water
______	lake	7. lowland between hills or mountains
______	peninsula	8. long, narrow body of water
______	valley	9. large area of flat grasslands
______	volcano	10. vast body of salt water
______	ocean	11. large area of a sea or ocean partially enclosed by land

Directions: Now, write each feature's number on the map.

Features Map

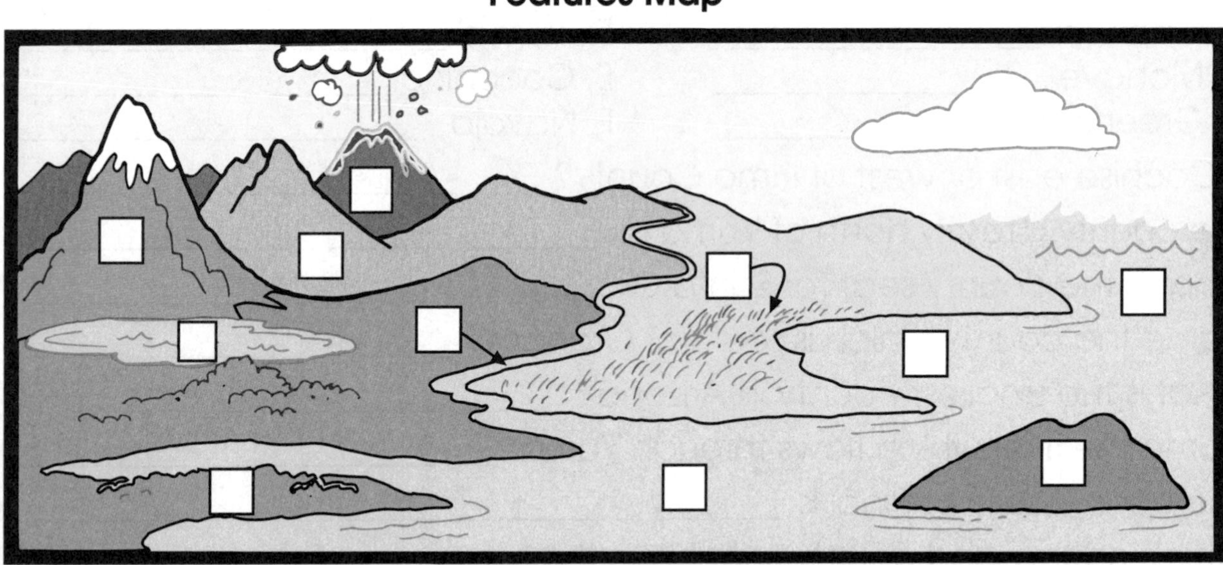

Name ____________________

Landforms and Physical Features

Notice different landforms and physical features found in the picture.

Label the ten landforms on the picture. Then, write the name of each one next to its definition below.

mountain	lake	peninsula	basin	canyon
plain	plateau	hill	island	river

- a large area of flat or gently sloping land ____________
- a body of land completely surrounded by water ____________
- a deep valley with steep sides ____________
- a body of land surrounded by water on three sides ____________
- an area of flat land that is higher than the surrounding land ____________
- a low region surrounded by higher land ____________
- a large stream of water that flows into a larger body of water ____________
- a natural elevation smaller than a mountain ____________
- a body of water that is completely surrounded by land ____________
- a very high hill ____________

Name___________________________________

Land Regions

Physical maps show natural features of the earth such as water, mountains, deserts and high and low regions. Finish the map as directed.

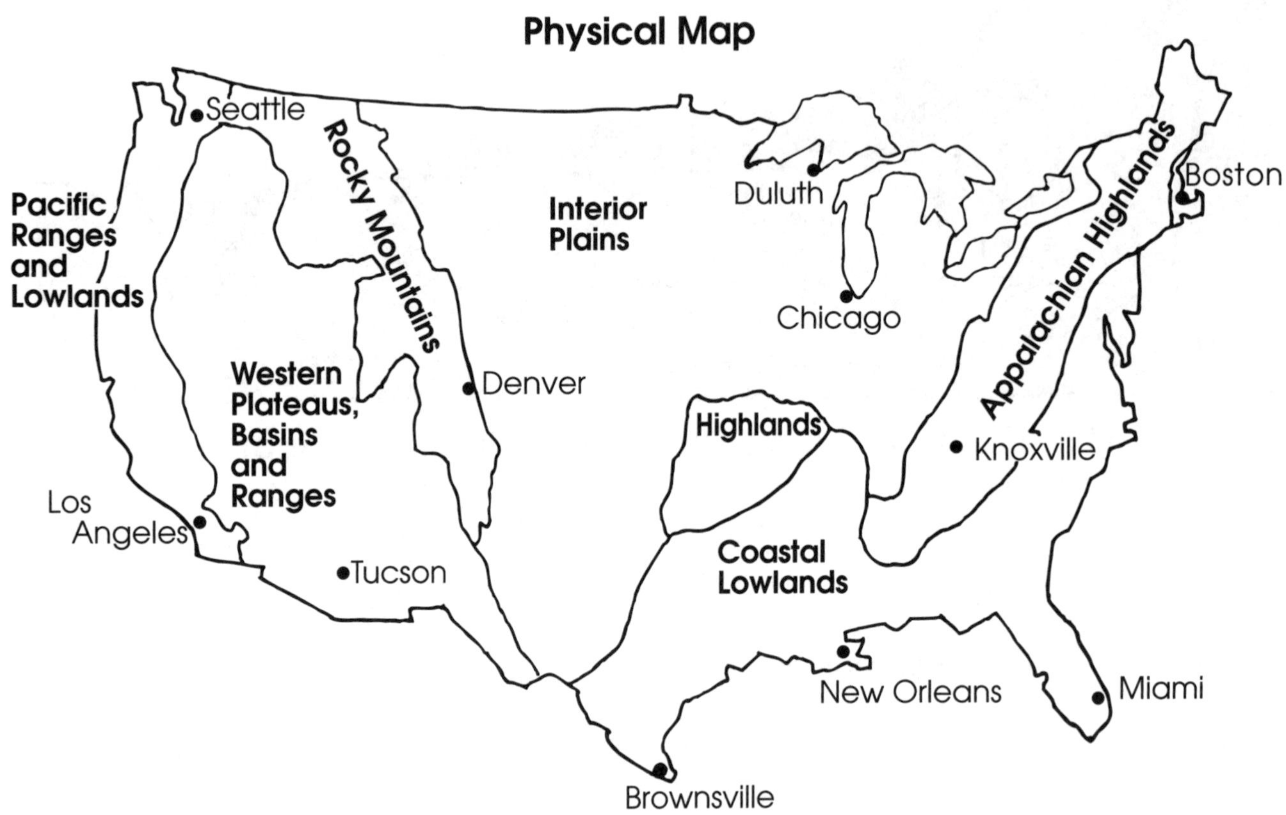

1. Draw brown ⋀⋀ in the mountain and highland regions.
2. Draw orange ╌╌ on the Pacific Ranges and Lowlands.
3. Color the 5 Great Lakes blue.
4. Draw green ⌄⌄⌄ on the Coastal Lowlands.
5. Draw red ////////// in the Western Plateaus, Basins and Ranges.
6. Color the Interior Plains yellow.
7. Name one city found in the mountains. ____________________________
8. Name one city found in the Coastal Lowlands. ______________________

Name________________________________

Physical Features of the United States

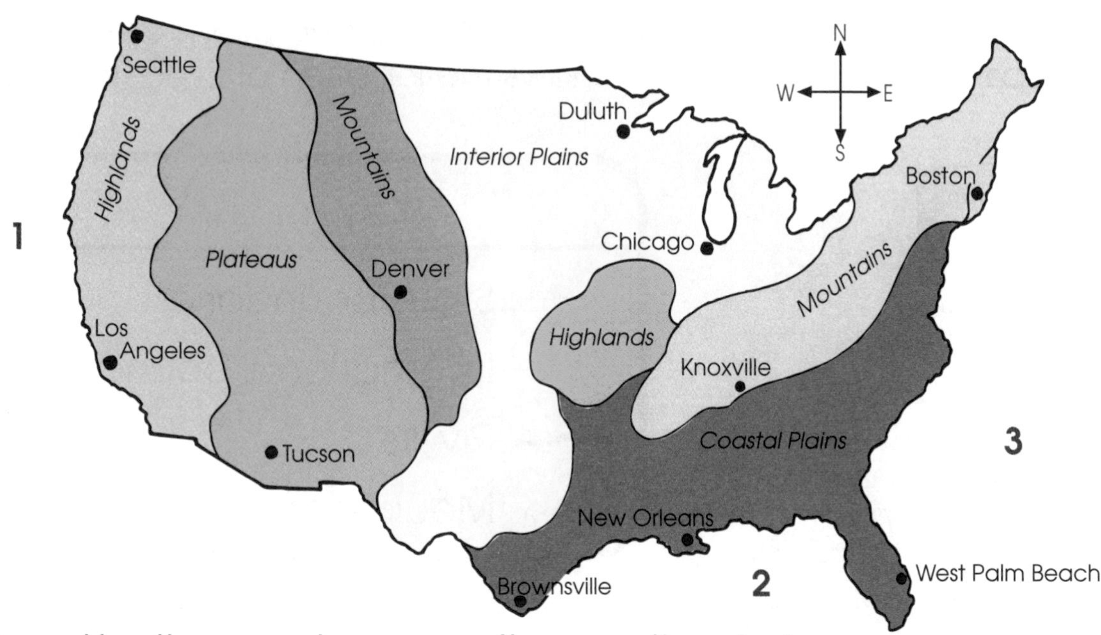

Directions: Use the map to answer the questions below.

1. Name the two cities on the map found in mountain areas.

 ____

2. Name the three cities found on coastal plains.

 ____

3. Seattle and Los Angeles are found on which coast—east or west?_____

 ____

4. Name the two cities located on the interior plains. ______________

 ____

5. Your home state is located on which type of land? ______________

Use a map of North America and the map above to answer these questions.

1. Identify the bodies of water marked with numbers on the map above.

 (1) ______________ (2) ______________ (3) ______________

2. The mountains on the eastern side of the United States are the ________

 ____.

3. The ____________ Mountains are in the western part of the United States.

Name____

Physical Maps

Maps that show landforms like mountains, deserts, and plains are called physical maps. A physical map also shows the location of rivers, lakes and oceans.

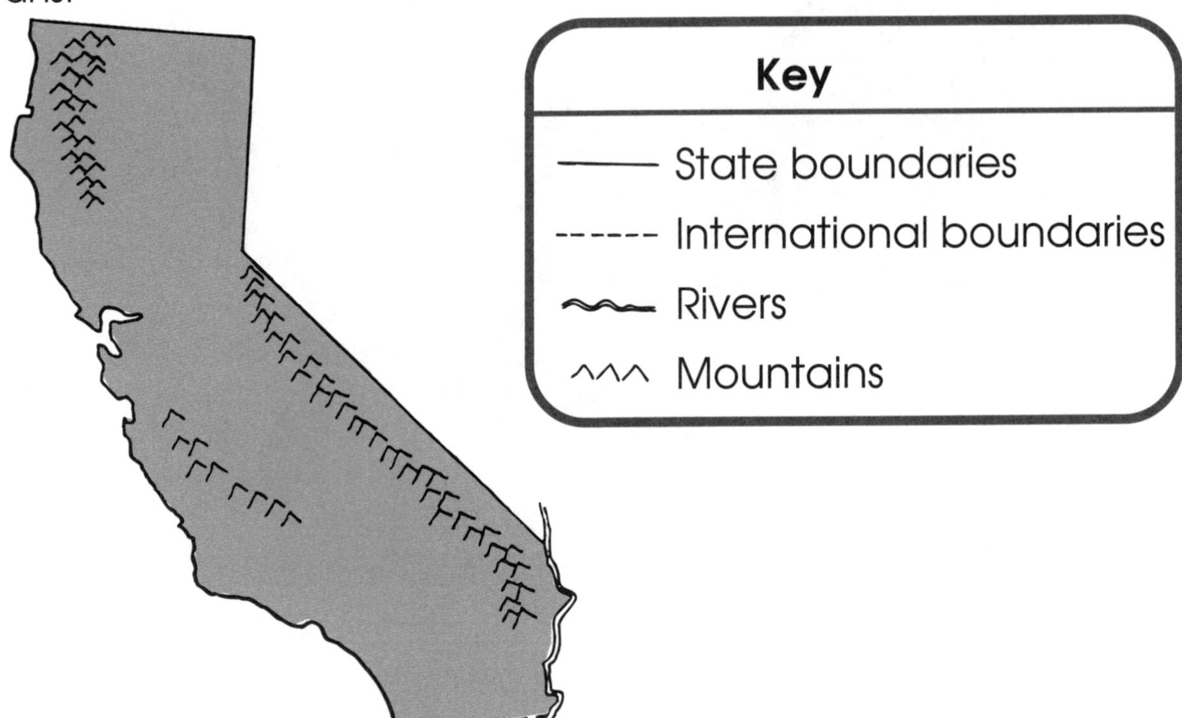

Use a map, atlas or other resource to help you locate the physical features listed below. Label them on the Physical Map of the United States on page 130.

Rivers
Mississippi River
Missouri River
Colorado River
Ohio River
Hudson River
Arkansas River

Mountains
Sierra Nevada Mountains
Cascade Mountains

Lakes
Great Salt Lake
Lake Michigan
Lake Superior
Lake Huron
Lake Erie
Lake Ontario

Land Regions
Great Plains
Mojave Desert
Great Basin

Oceans and Sea
Pacific Ocean
Atlantic Ocean
Gulf of Mexico

Name ______________________________

Types of Land

Directions: Use this map of the United States and a large wall map to answer the questions.

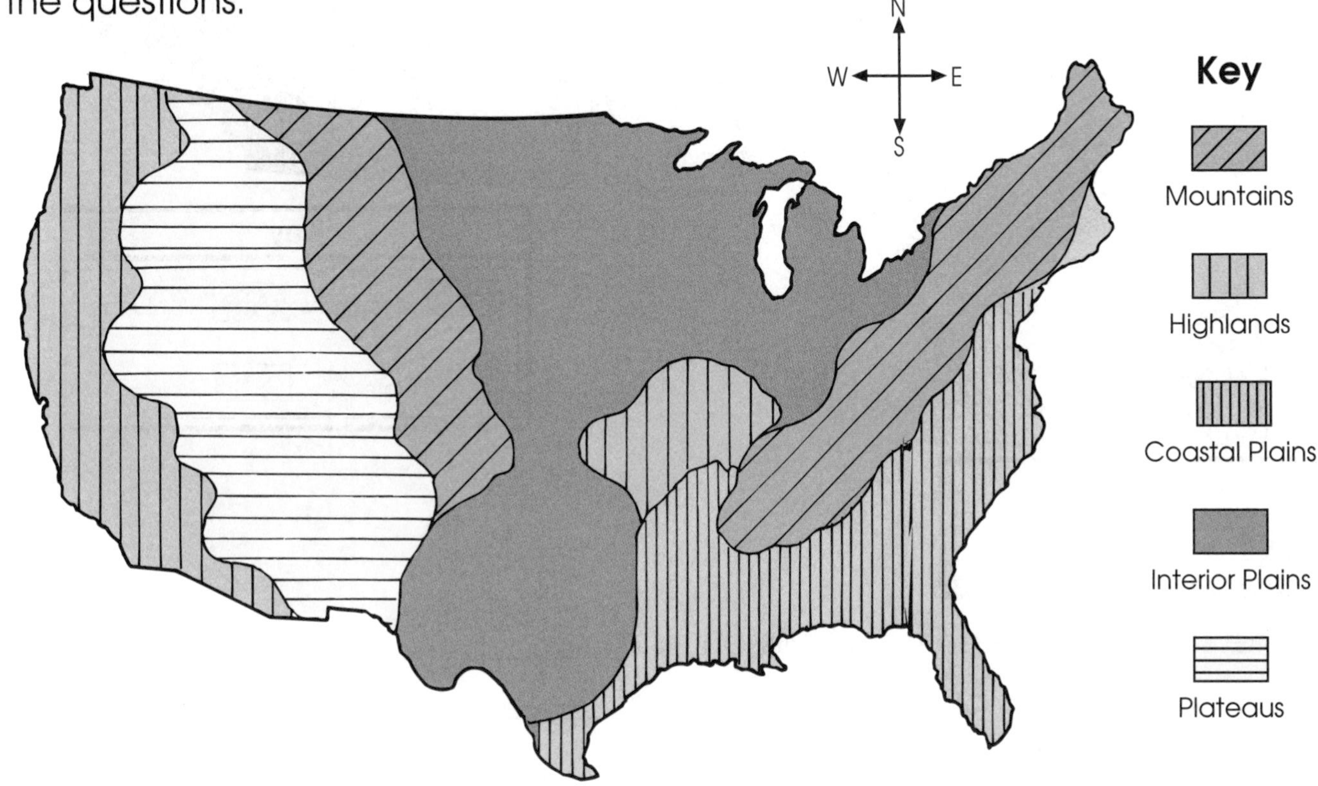

1. The western coast of the United States is composed of ______________.
2. The central part of the United States is ______________________________.
3. The northeastern part of the United States has______________________.
4. What does the symbol [plateaus symbol] stand for on the map? ______________
5. In which part of the United States will you find coastal plains?__________
6. The state of California is mostly ______________________________.
7. Florida is composed of ______________________________________.
8. The southern part of Texas is _________________________________.
9. What symbol is used to show mountains? ______________________

Name ________________________________

Comparing Two States

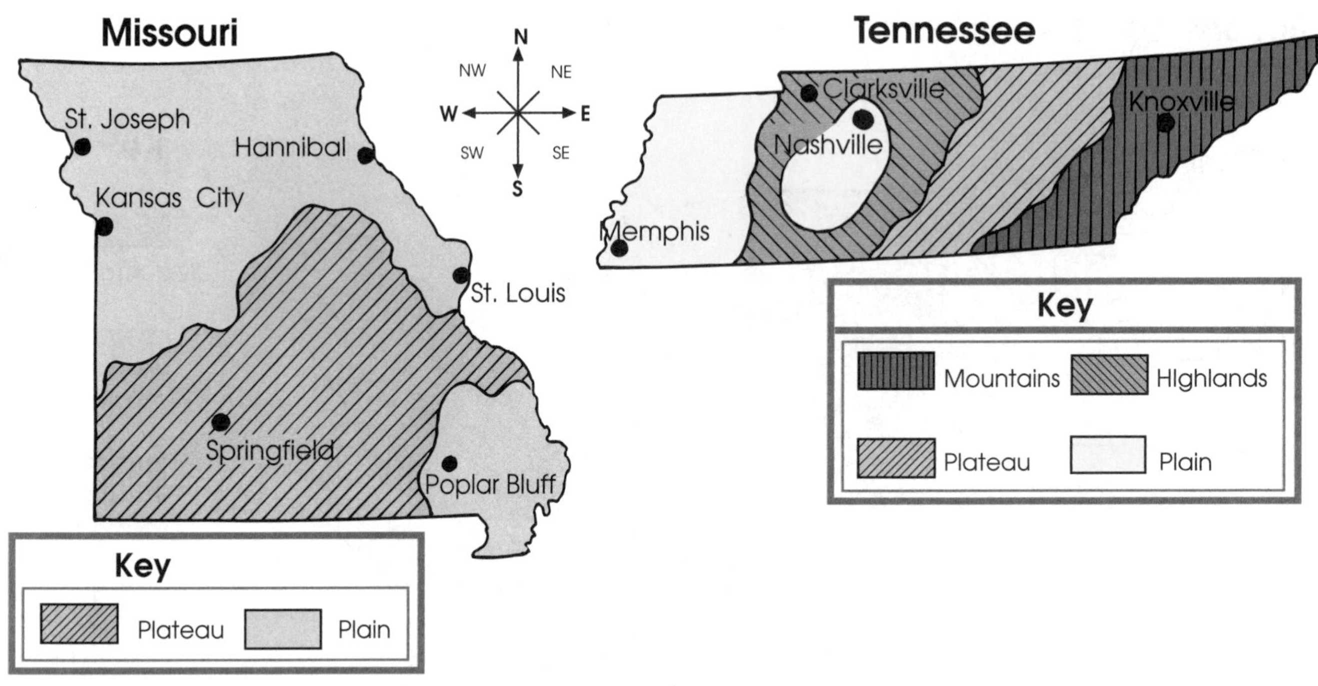

1. The southeastern corner of Missouri is a ________________________.
2. The northern part of Missouri is a ________________________.
3. Most of southern Missouri is a ________________________.
4. What type of land is between Kansas City and Hannibal? __________
5. On a trip from St. Joseph to Poplar Bluff, what type of land will you travel over? ________________________
6. The eastern half of Tennessee is covered by ______________ and ________________________.
7. Memphis is located on a ________________________.
8. What two features do Tennessee and Missouri share? __________ and ________________________
9. The central part of Tennessee is mostly ________________________.
10. What types of land will you cross between Memphis and Knoxville?

 ________________________.
11. Which of the states is almost half plateau? ________________________

Name ______________________________

Alaska and New York

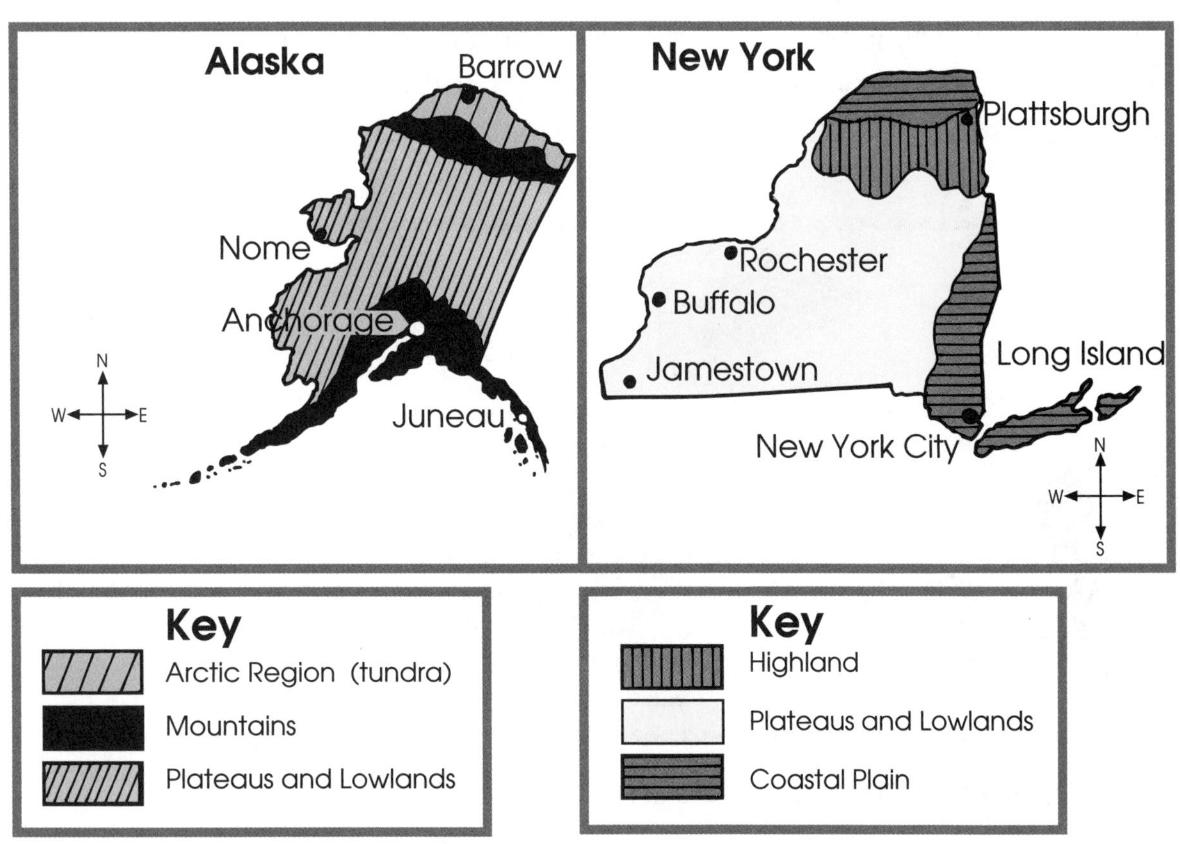

1. Barrow is part of the ______________________________ Region.
2. Most of Alaska is covered with ______________________________.
3. The southern part of Alaska is ______________________________.
4. What type of land would you travel over from Barrow to Juneau?

   ____

5. The northeastern part of New York is mostly ______________________.
6. Both New York and Alaska have ____________________ and lowlands.
7. Plattsburgh, New York, is located in which part of the state—southwest or northeast? ______________________________
8. The western half of New York is composed of ______________________.
9. The extreme northern part of New York is a ______________________.
10. Is Nome on the eastern or western coast of Alaska? ________________

Name____

Poetic Forms

Just as there are many kinds of landforms and physical features, there are also many forms of poetry. Let's use what you know about landforms and physical features to write a diamanté poem. Look at the sample below.

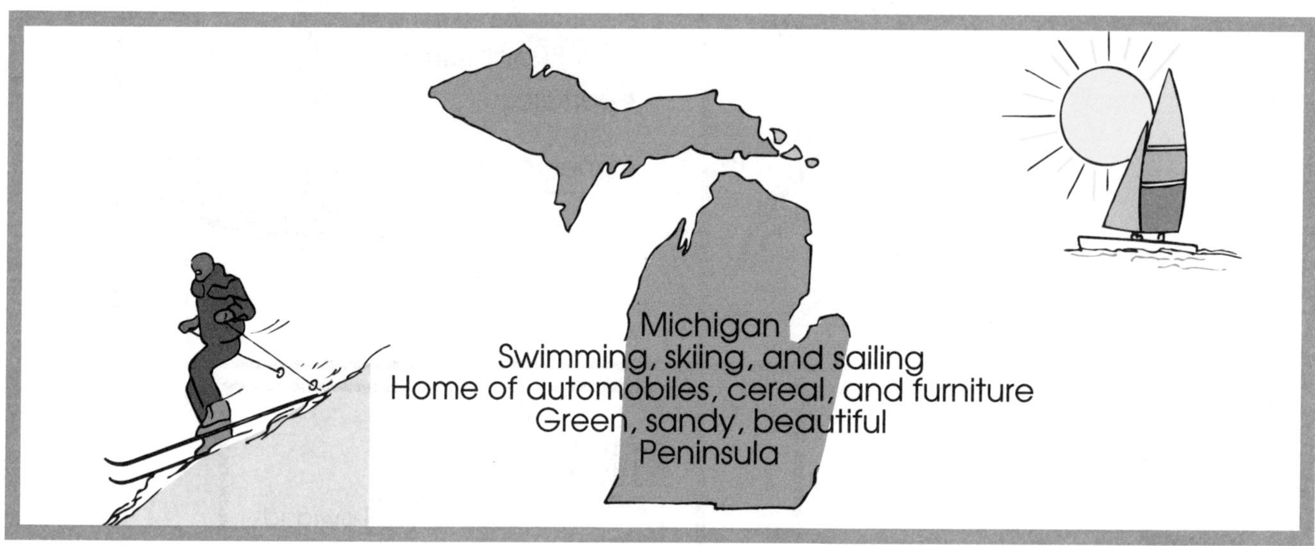

Michigan
Swimming, skiing, and sailing
Home of automobiles, cereal, and furniture
Green, sandy, beautiful
Peninsula

This is how you write a diamanté poem about a place:

line one ______________________________ place name

line two ______________________________ 2 or 3 things to do there

line three ____________________________ 3 or 4 words telling what it is known for

line four _____________________________ 2 or 3 adjectives describing it

line five _____________________________ landform or physical feature

Now it's your turn to write a diamanté. Choose a place with a special landform or physical feature. It might have a cape, island, peninsula, mountain, canyon or desert, among others.

____

____

____

____

____

Name____

Natural Wonders of the U.S.

Listed below are ten natural physical features found in the United States. Use an encyclopedia, atlas or other source to complete the chart. Write the number of each feature on a copy of the U.S. Products and Natural Resources Map on page 138.

Natural Feature	State	Description
1. Devil's Tower		
2. Grand Canyon		
3. Mount McKinley		
4. Everglades		
5. Mount St. Helens		
6. Kilauea		
7. Carlsbad Caverns		
8. Cape Cod		
9. Badlands National Park		
10. Mojave Desert		

Name____

Kinds of Maps: Product

U.S. Products and Natural Resources

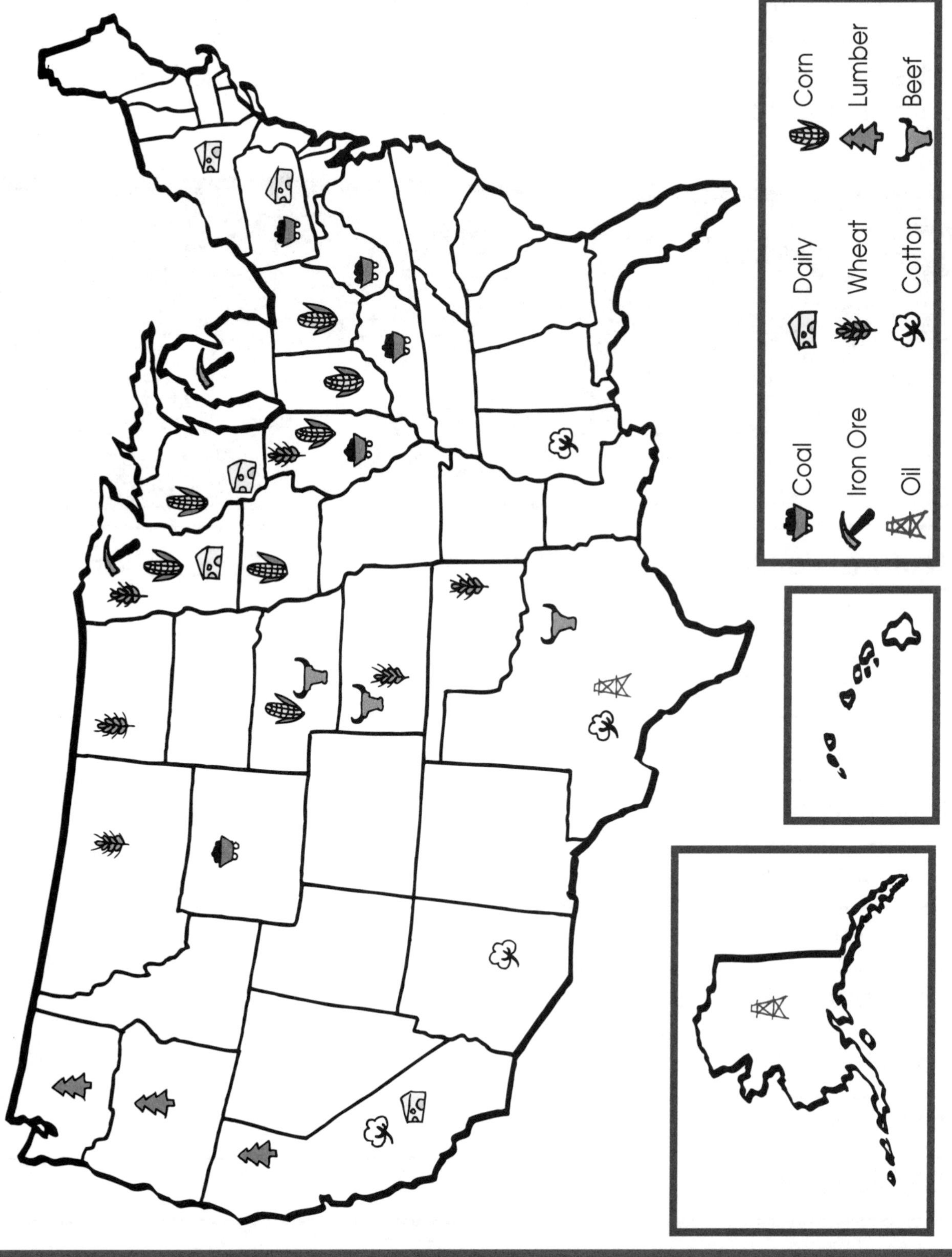

Use with pages 137 and page 139.

Name ____________________

U.S. Products and Natural Resources

The United States is one of the world's largest producers of manufactured goods because it is very rich in natural resources.

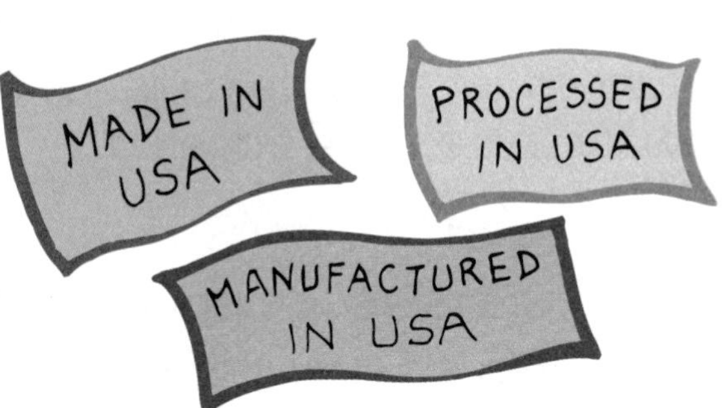

A study of the U.S. Products and Natural Resources map will indicate which states are the chief suppliers of certain products and natural resources.

Directions: For each product and natural resource listed below, use the map on page 138 to name the states that are major suppliers.

Coal
____
____
____
____
____

Iron Ore
____
____
____
____
____

Oil
____
____
____
____
____

Corn
____
____
____
____
____

Wheat
____
____
____
____
____

Cotton
____
____
____
____
____

Dairy
____
____
____
____
____

Lumber
____
____
____
____
____

Beef
____
____
____
____
____

Name_______________________________________

Grocery Store Geography

Since many foods are shipped long distances, let's create a display showing how far some have traveled.

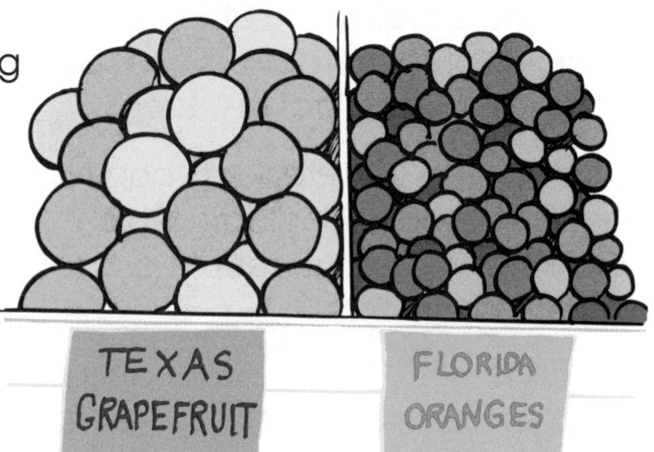

You will need:

Grocery Store Geography (page 141)
a map of the United States
a large piece of posterboard or paper
markers or crayons
glue

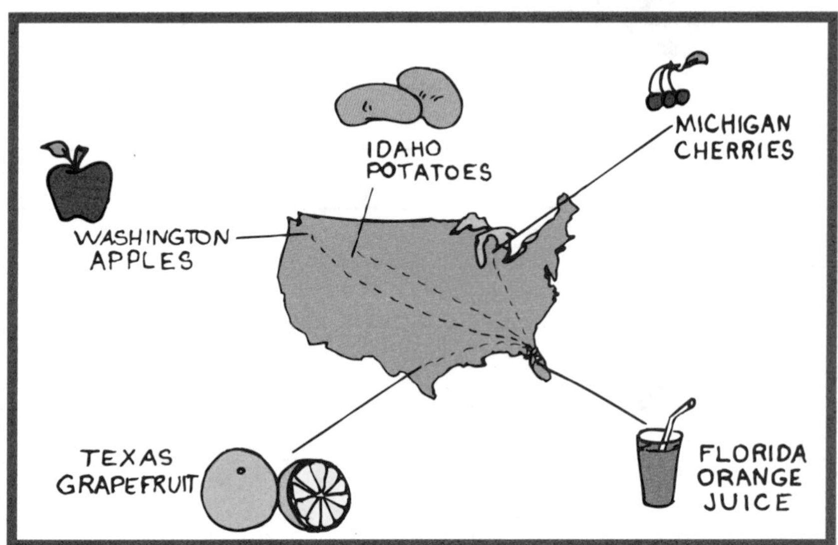

Directions:

1. Glue the outline map of the United States in the middle of your posterboard.
2. Label and color the states where each type of food on your food chart comes from.
3. Draw a picture of each food or cut out pictures from a magazine to glue around the border of the poster. Draw a line from the food to where it is grown.
4. Label your community on the map with a star.
5. Draw a dotted line from the product source to your community.

Name ___________________________________

Grocery Store Geography

Many foods that we eat are not grown in our own community. While some foods come from neighboring states, others come from countries halfway around the world.

Check some of the foods in your cupboard and refrigerator at home. Check the labels to find out where they came from. Then, go to a grocery store and look at the labels on some other foods. Where did they come from? Look at the fruits and vegetables in the produce area. Many of them probably came from far away. Ask the grocer or produce manager where some of the fruits and vegetables are from.

Directions: Complete the chart.

Food	Where It Was Grown	Kind of Transportation Used to Ship the Product

On a map, locate where these foods were grown.

Which was shipped the greatest distance? ___________________________

How far did it have to travel to reach your grocery store? _______________

Name____

Tilling the Soil

Use this map to answer the questions on page 143.

Agriculture Map

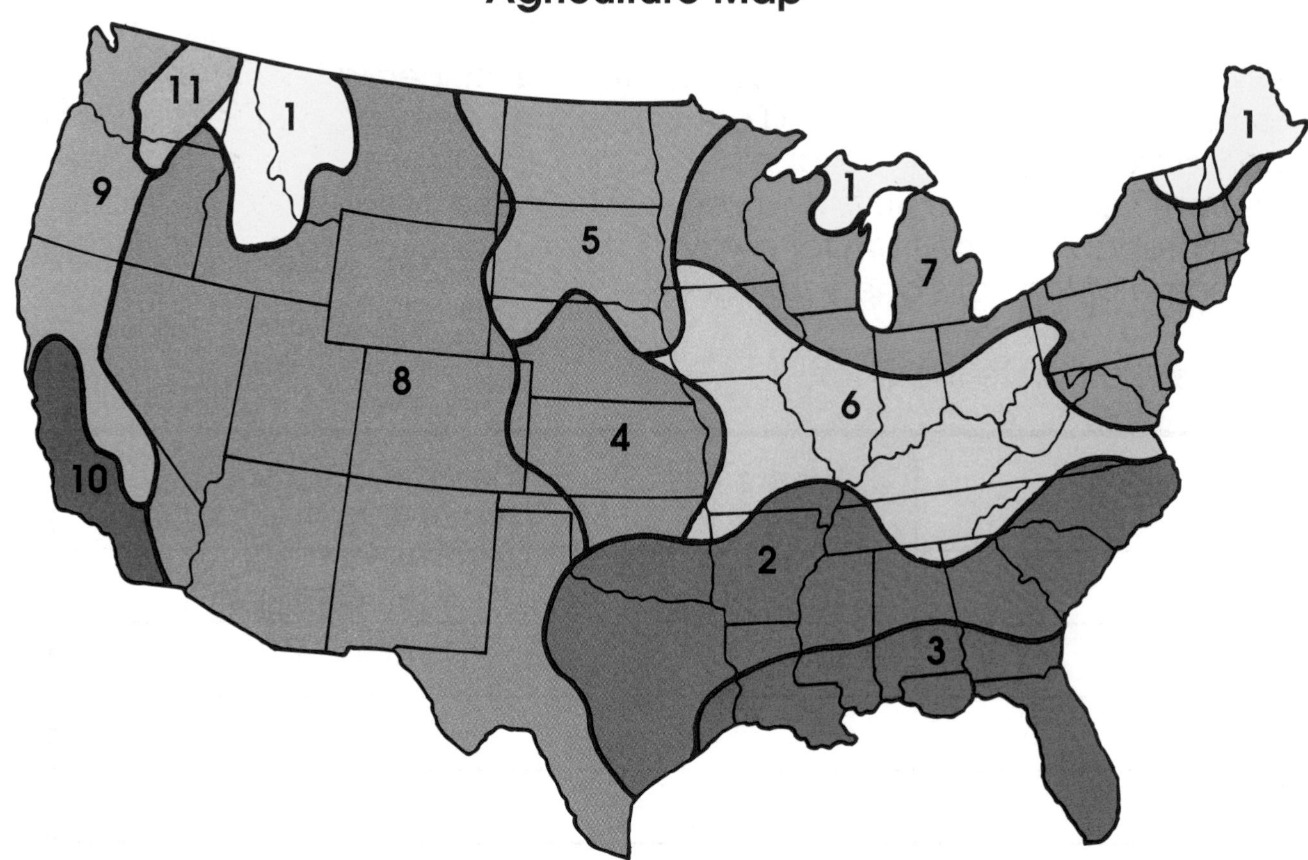

Legend

1. Timber
2. Cotton
3. Sub-tropical fruits, vegetables
4. Winter wheat
5. Spring wheat
6. Corn and Livestock
7. Dairy, hardy crops
8. Livestock ranching
9. Pacific hay, pasture and timber
10. Pacific fruits and vegetables
11. Wheat

Name______________________________

Tilling the Soil

Directions: Use the map on page 142 to answer the questions below.

1. The northeastern corner of the United States has ________________.
2. What types of crops are found on the Pacific coast?

   ____

3. What is a common crop grown in many southern states? __________
4. What two types of wheat are grown in 4 and 5? _______________

   ____

5. Much of the land in the western part of the United States is used for

   ____.

6. What is most of the land in your state used for? _______________

   ____

Use the map on page 142 and a political map of the United States to help you answer the questions below.

1. What crops are grown in Florida? ____________________

   ____

2. Name the states where cotton is a major crop. ______________

   ____

   ____

3. The major crop in Kansas is _______________________.
4. The eastern part of Washington grows __________________.
5. Southwestern California grows ______________________.
6. North and South Dakota are major producers of ____________.
7. Which of these states is a major producer of corn—Maine, Illinois or California? ____________________________
8. What is done in western Texas? ______________________
9. Michigan and Wisconsin produce _____________________.
10. Most of Nebraska produces winter ____________________.
11. Hay, pasture and timber are produced in ____________California.

Name_______________________________________

Natural Resource Riddles

U.S. Products and Natural Resources—Leading States

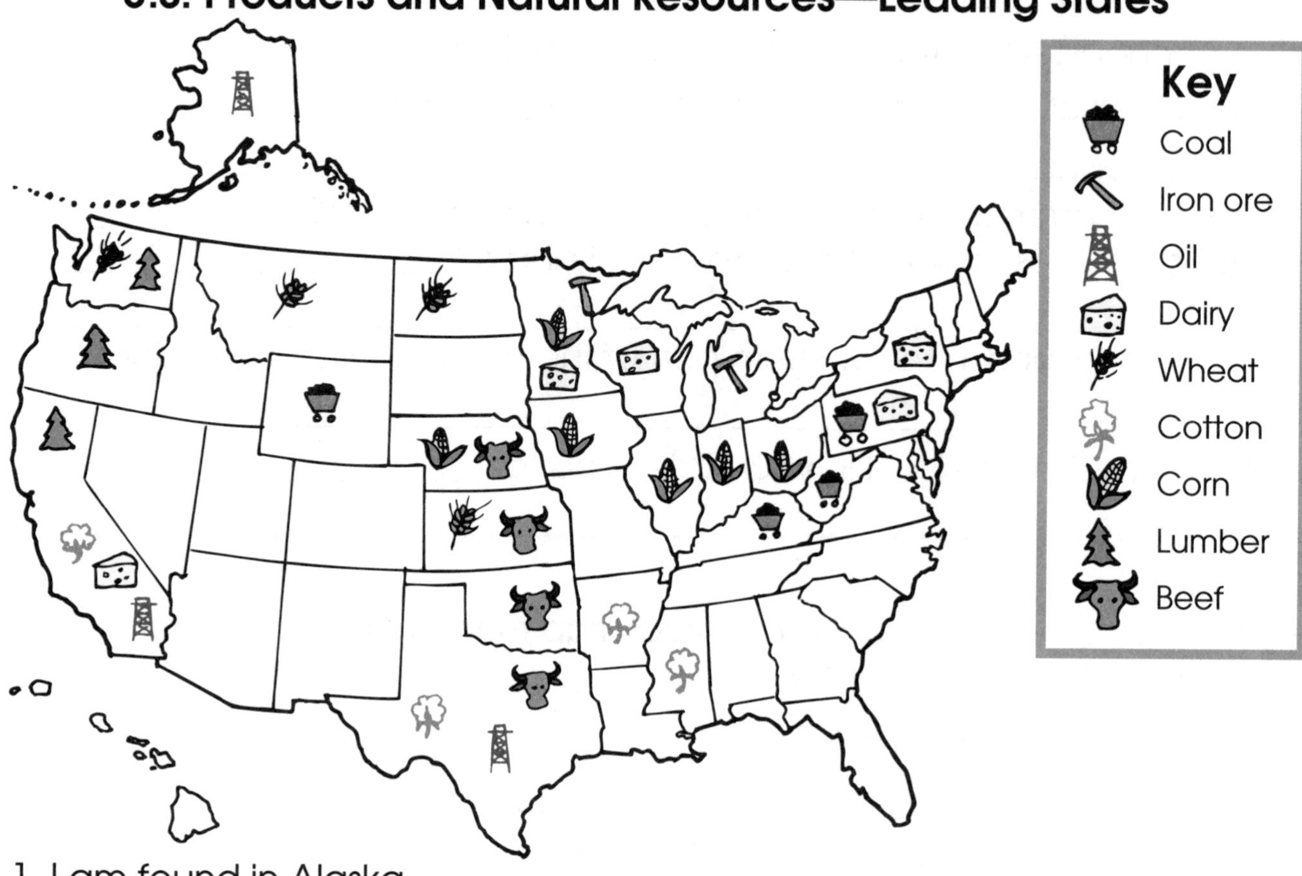

1. I am found in Alaska. ______________________________
2. Montana is a leading producer of me. ______________________________
3. New York produces me. ______________________________
4. Illinois, Indiana and Ohio are all leading producers of me. ______________
5. My name is lumber. Which states are leading suppliers of me? __________

____

6. Michigan is a leading supplier of me. ______________________________
7. I am Texas. Name the products I produce. ______________________________

____

8. I am Nebraska. Name my products. ______________________________

Name ______________________________

Products in California

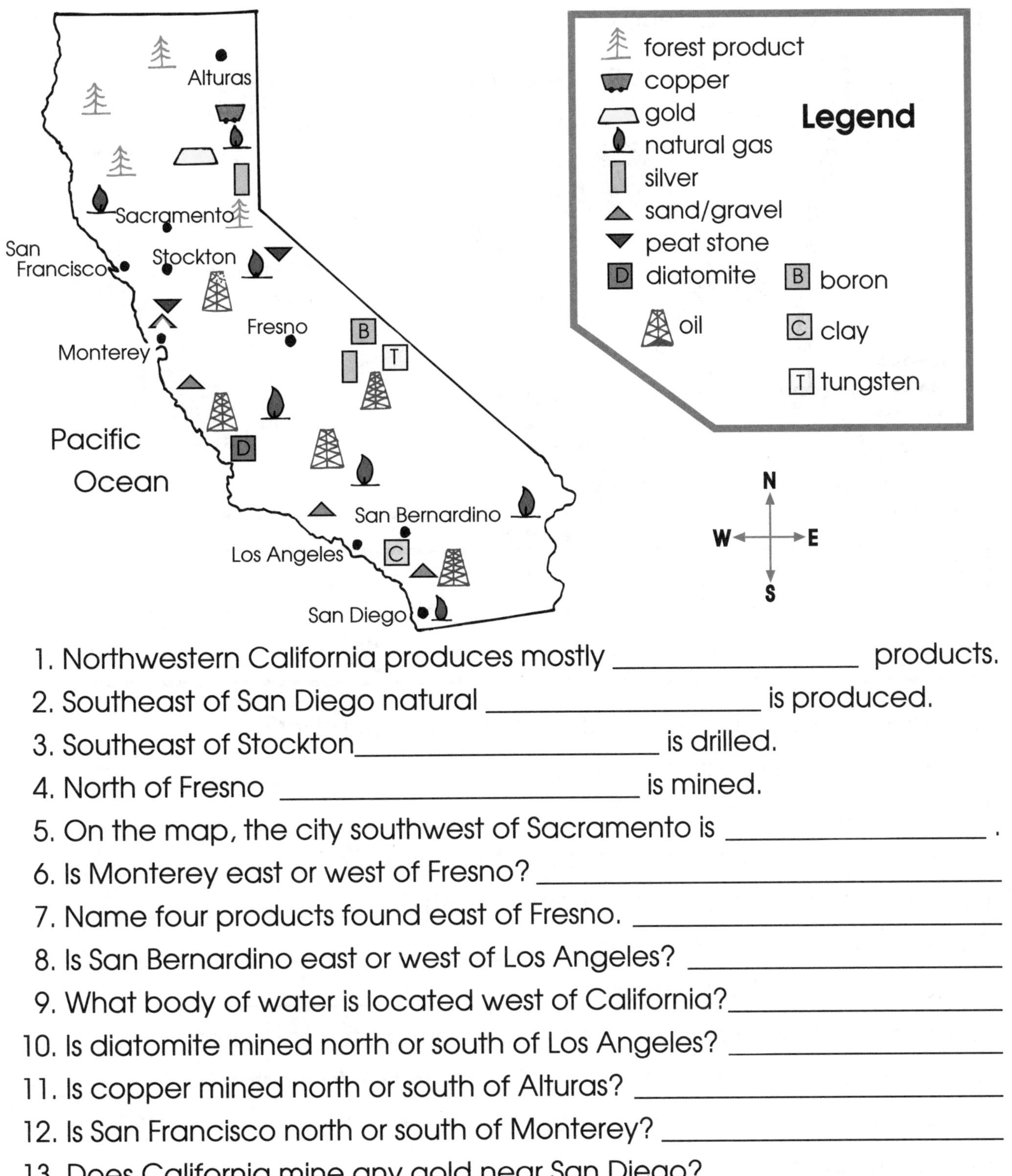

1. Northwestern California produces mostly ________________ products.
2. Southeast of San Diego natural ________________ is produced.
3. Southeast of Stockton ________________ is drilled.
4. North of Fresno ________________ is mined.
5. On the map, the city southwest of Sacramento is ________________ .
6. Is Monterey east or west of Fresno? ________________
7. Name four products found east of Fresno. ________________
8. Is San Bernardino east or west of Los Angeles? ________________
9. What body of water is located west of California? ________________
10. Is diatomite mined north or south of Los Angeles? ________________
11. Is copper mined north or south of Alturas? ________________
12. Is San Francisco north or south of Monterey? ________________
13. Does California mine any gold near San Diego? ________________

Name ____

How Much Revenue?

Directions: Use the product map of this imaginary state to answer the questions.

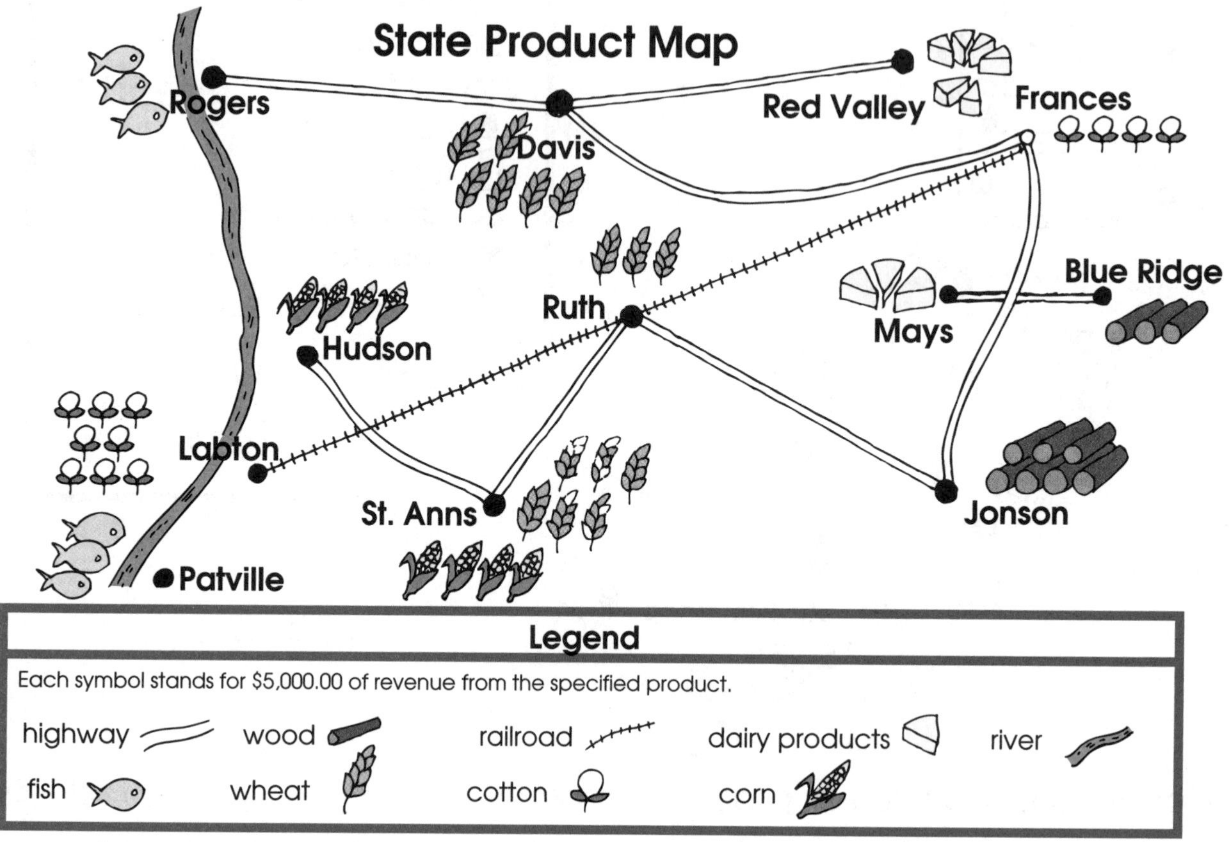

1. How much money, or revenue, does each symbol stand for? ____________
2. How much does the state make from corn? ____________
3. What product is grown near Jonson? ____________
4. Does this state get more money from cotton or wood? ____________
5. How much money does the state earn from fish? ____________
6. Patville earns money by catching ____________.
7. The town of Red Valley produces ____________ products.
8. What is the shortest way to transport cotton from Labton to Rogers? ____________
9. How much money does the corn grown at Hudson produce for the state? ____________
10. How much money does wheat produce for the state? ____________
11. What is grown near Ruth? ____________

Name ___________________________

Products in the United States

Directions: Use the map and the legend to answer the questions below.

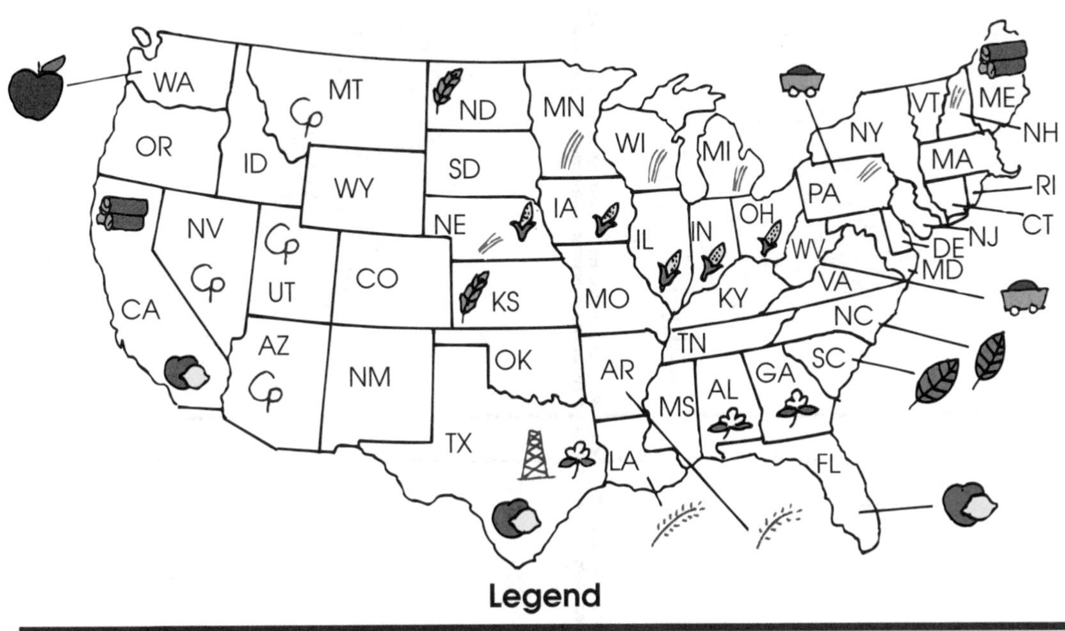

Legend

1. Which state grows apples? ___________________________
2. How many states on this map grow oranges and lemons? ___________
3. Both Arkansas and Louisiana grow ___________________________.
4. Wheat and barley are grown in ___________________________.
5. North and South Carolina both grow ___________________________.
6. ___________________________ is produced in Maine.
7. Name the product grown in Alabama and Georgia. ___________
8. Coal is mined in the states of ___________________________.
9. Name the states which grow corn. ___________________________

   ____
10. Name the products produced in California. ___________________________

Name______________________________________

How Much Did It Rain?

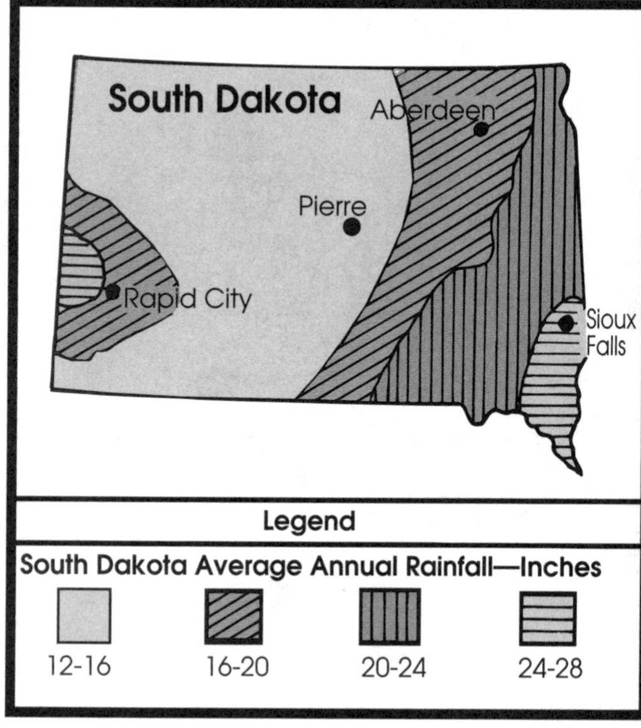

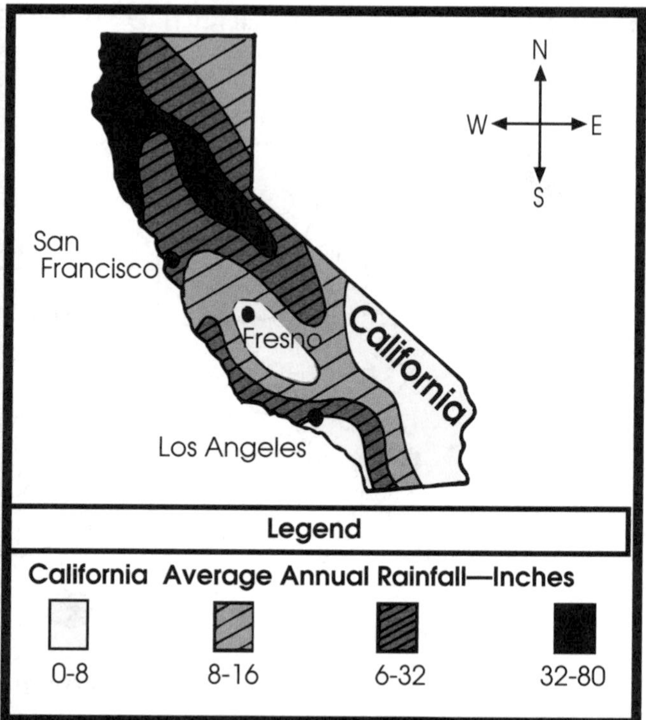

1. Aberdeen, South Dakota receives ______________inches of rain a year.
2. Which city receives more rain—Sioux Falls or Rapid City? ____________
3. Northwestern South Dakota receives ___________ inches of rain a year.
4. How much rain does Pierre, South Dakota usually receive? ___________
5. The southeastern corner of South Dakota receives _____inches of rain.
6. What does the symbol □ mean on the map of California? ___________
7. Southeastern California receives________________inches of rain a year.
8. Los Angeles, California, receives an average of _______ inches of rain a year.
9. The northeastern part of California receives ____________inches or rain.
10. What does this symbol ■ mean on the map of California? __________
11. Fresno, California, receives an average of _____________inches of rain.
12. Which city receives more rain—Sioux Falls, South Dakota or Fresno, California?____
13. The extreme northwestern corner of California receives _______inches of rain a year.

Name ______________________________

Temperature Ranges

What is the average January temperature where you live? The average monthly temperature is figured using the daily temperatures for the whole month. This information can be found in most almanacs and encyclopedias. Why would it be helpful to know the average temperature of a city? __________

____

Directions: Use an almanac or encyclopedia fo find the average high and low temperatures for the cities listed below for January and July.

State	City	Average Monthly Temperatures (F°)			
		January		July	
		High	Low	High	Low
Alaska	Nome				
California	Los Angeles				
Colorado	Denver				
Florida	Tampa				
Iowa	Des Moines				
Michigan	Detroit				
New York	Syracuse				
North Dakota	Fargo				
South Carolina	Columbia				
Texas	Dallas				
Wisconsin	Madison				
State of your choice:					

Circle the highest temperature in each "high" column and the lowest temperature in each "low" column.

Name____

U.S. Climate Zones

The word climate is used to describe the weather in a particular place over a long period of time. Because the United States covers such a large area, it has a number of different climate zones. Some areas have long, cold winters and short, cool summers, while other areas are always warm in both the summer and the winter.

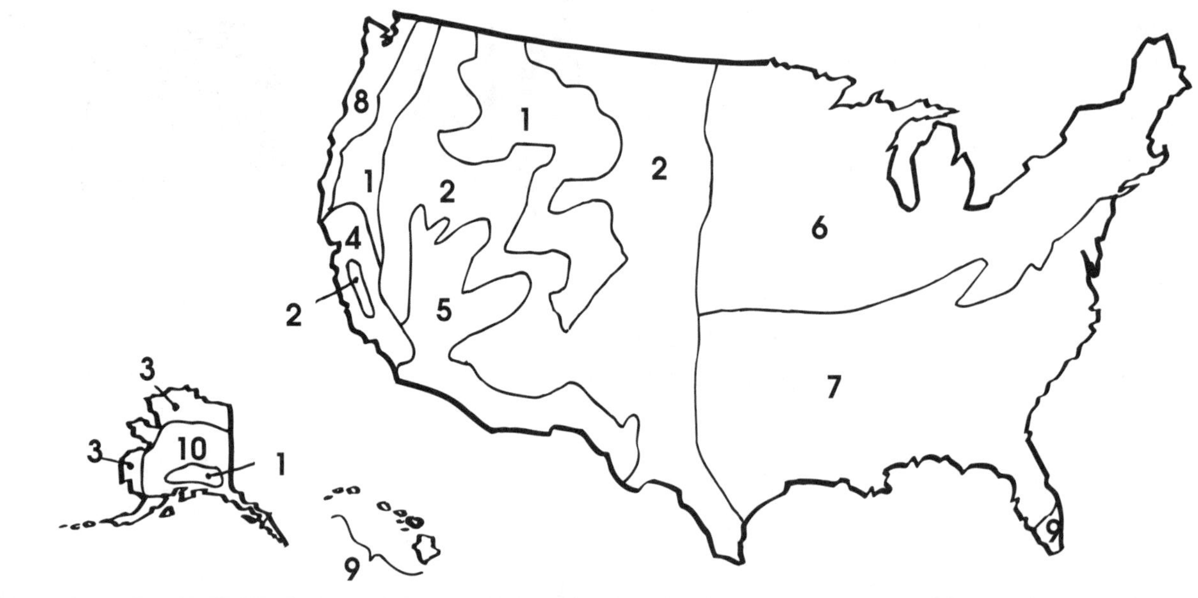

Key

1	☐	alpine	4	☐	mediterranean					
2	☐	steppe	5	☐	desert	7	☐	subtropical	9	☐ tropical
3	☐	tundra	6	☐	continental	8	☐	marine	10	☐ subarctic

Directions: Choose colors to color-code the key and the climate zone map. Then, determine the . . .

- climate zone in which you live ________________________
- climate zone of the northeast ________________________
- climate zones of the Rocky Mountains ____________________
- three climate zones found in Alaska ____________________
- climate zones found in Texas ________________________
- climate zones of Florida ___________________________
- climate zone of Michigan __________________________

Section 3

United States Regions

Name________________________________

The Pacific States

The Pacific States is a region with majestic mountains, beautiful beaches and coastlines, thick green forests and hot, dry deserts.

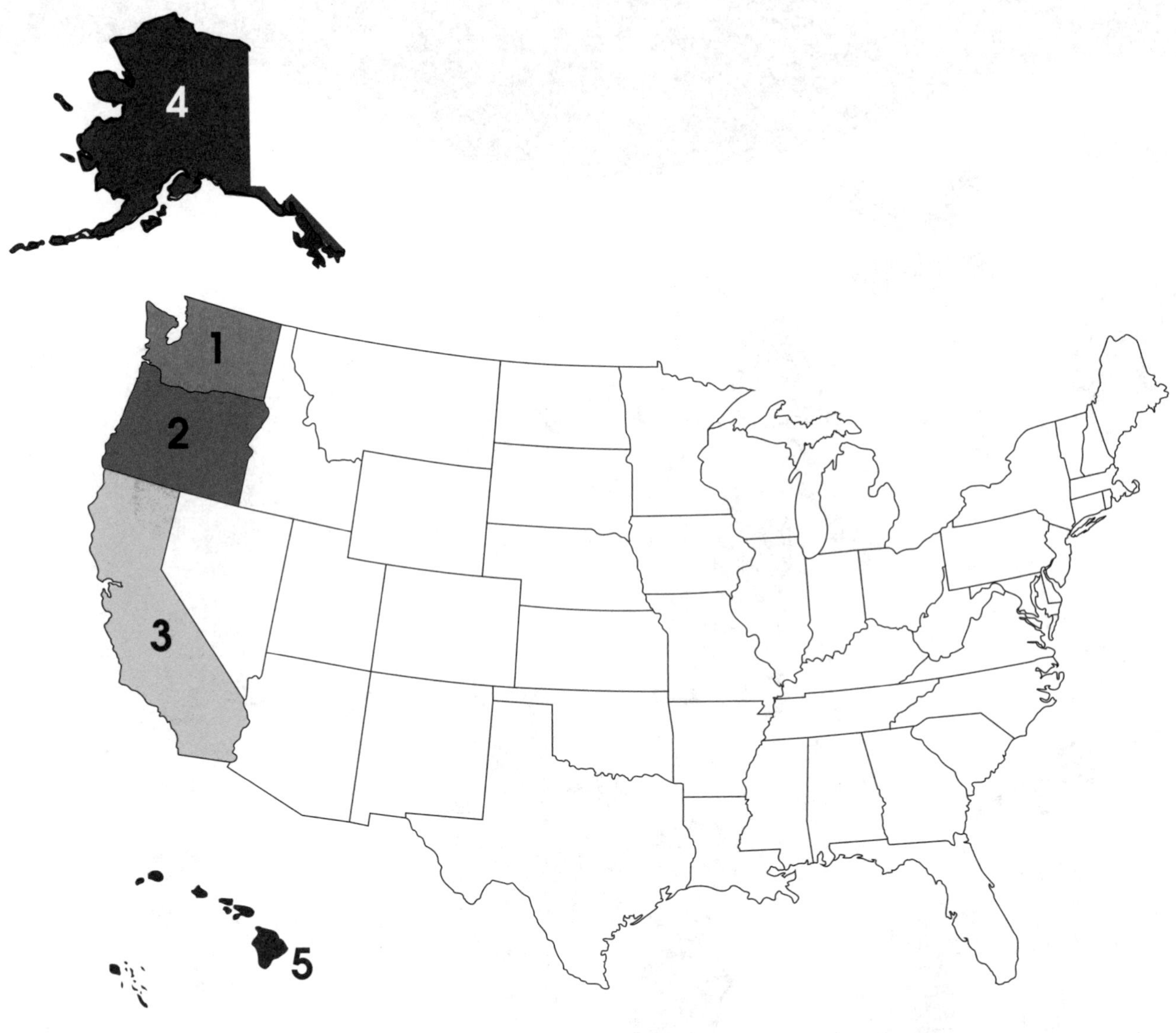

1. Washington
2. Oregon
3. California
4. Alaska
5. Hawaii

Name________________________________

Fill in the "Five Fundamental Themes of Geography" for each state. After "discovering" a state, fill in all the columns of the chart except **Regions**. When you have finished with all of the states in a section, fill in **Regions**.

Five Fundamental Themes of Geography

Name of State	**Location** (Where is it?)	**Place** (What is it like?)	**People and Environment** (What do the people do?)	**Movement** (How do people, goods and ideas move?)	**Regions** (What are some of the common features?)

Name____

Pacific States

Washington

The Evergreen State

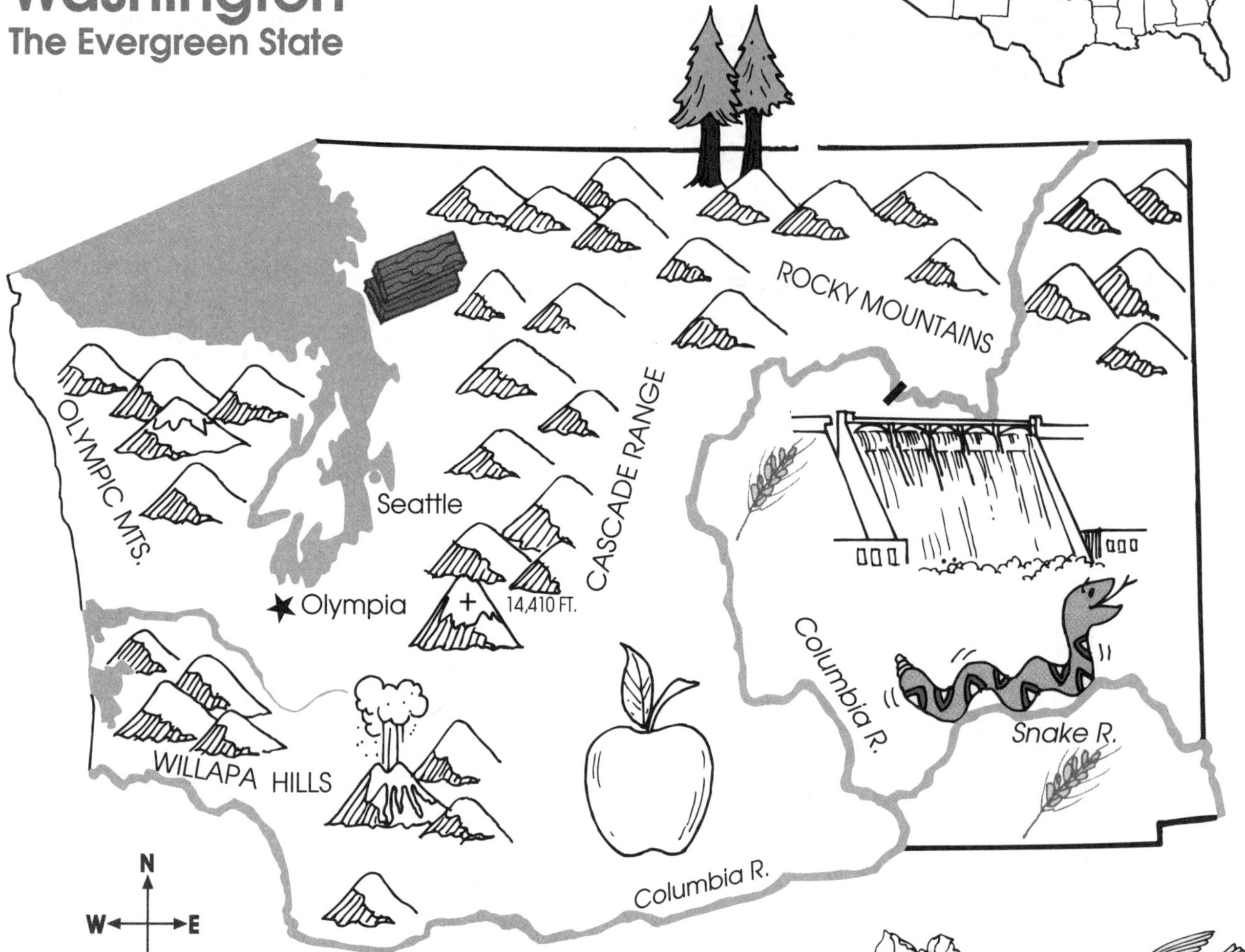

ROCKY MOUNTAINS

OLYMPIC MTS.

CASCADE RANGE

Seattle

Olympia

14,410 FT.

WILLAPA HILLS

Columbia R.

Snake R.

Columbia R.

N

W E

S

Coast Rhododendron
State Flower

Willow Goldfinch
State Bird

- named for the first president—George Washington
- nicknamed the Evergreen State for the abundance of evergreen trees

Mount Rainier—14,410 ft.

Mt. St. Helens—erupted on May 18, 1980

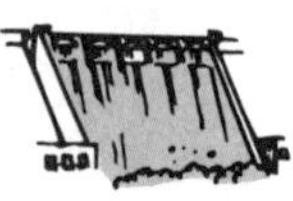

Grand Coulee Dam—largest concrete dam in United States

Apples—leads the states in apple production

Circle the capital city. Locate the landmarks found in the above key. Color them on the map.

Name________________________________

Oregon

The Beaver State

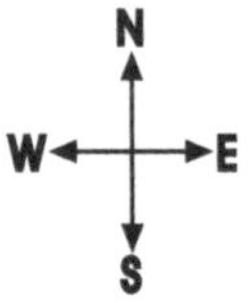

N
W E
S

Columbia R.
Portland
11,239 FT.
Salem
Snake R.
Blue Mountains
Willamette R.
Range
Coastal Range
Cascade Range

Oregon Grape
State Flower

Western Meadowlark
State Bird

- name originated from the French word *ouragan*, meaning *hurricane*
- nicknamed the Beaver State because the area supplied thousands of beaver skins during early fur trading

Mount Hood—11,239 ft.

Pendleton Round-Up

Sea Lion Caves

Oregon Caverns

Crater Lake—deepest lake in the United States

Circle the capital city. Locate the landmarks found in the above key. Color them on the map.

Name______________________________________

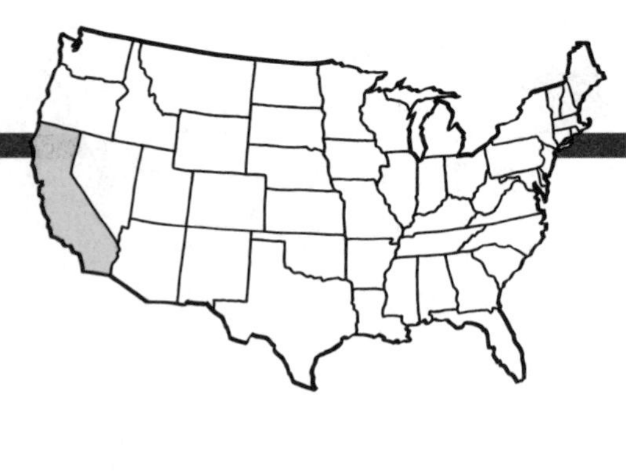

Pacific States

California

The Golden State

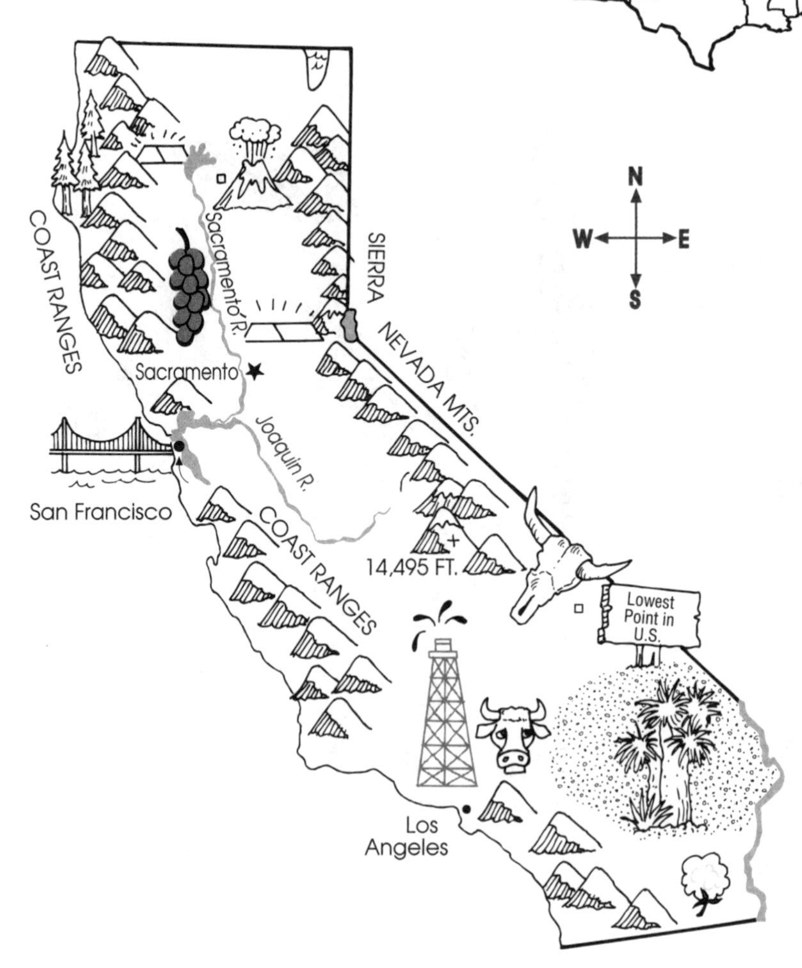

California Valley Quail
State Bird

Golden Poppy
State Flower

- named by early explorers, possibly referring to a treasure island in a Spanish story
- nicknamed the Golden State, possibly for its gold fields, its golden pastures and its sunshine

 Mount Whitney—the highest point in the contiguous United States—14,495 ft.

 Golden Gate Bridge

 Lassen Volcanic Park

 Joshua Tree National Monument

Death Valley National Monument

 Redwood National Park—contains world's tallest known tree

Circle the capital city. Locate the landmarks found in the above key. Color them on the map.

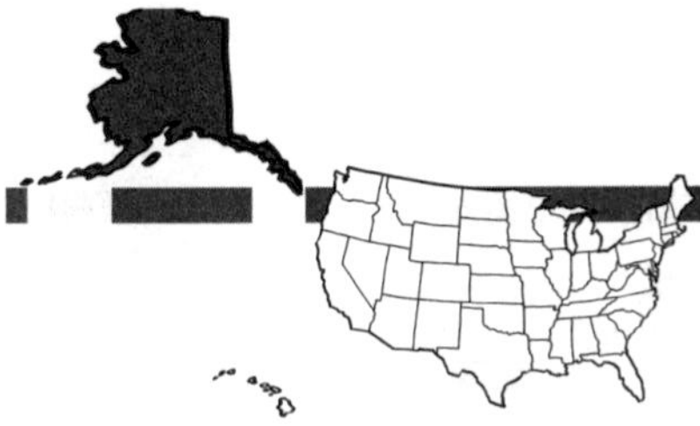

Name ____________________

Alaska

The Last Frontier

Point Barrow

N W E S

Yukon R.

Kuskokwim R.

Milk

Mt. McKinley 20,320 FT.

Anchorage

Haines

Juneau

Kenai

Kodiak

Pribilof Islands

ALEUTIAN ISLANDS

Saxman

Ketchikan

Forget-Me-Not
State Flower

Willow Ptarmigan
State Bird

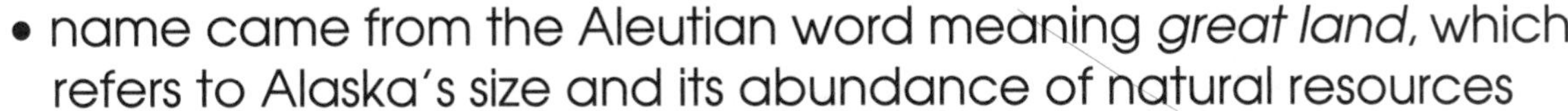

- name came from the Aleutian word meaning *great land,* which refers to Alaska's size and its abundance of natural resources
- nickname the Last Frontier reflects the fact that much of the region is as yet unsettled

Point Barrow—northernmost point of the United States

Saxman—world's largest collection of totem poles

Malaspina—North America's largest glacier

Kenai and Kodiak—major salmon processing areas

Kodiak and Aleutian Islands—known for their catches of Alaskan King Crab

Pribilof Islands—colonies of puffins and world's largest herd of northern fur seals

Green Creek Mine—largest silver mine in the United States

Mount McKinley—20,320 ft.

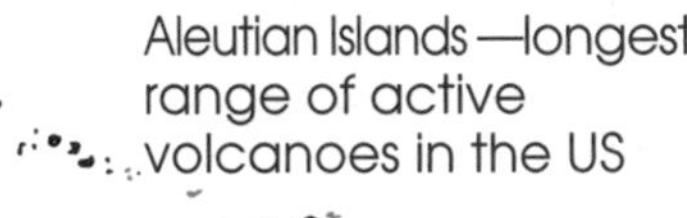

Aleutian Islands—longest range of active volcanoes in the US

Bald Eagles—greater number of bald eagles gather north of Haines than any other place in the world

Circle the capital city. Locate the landmarks found in the above key. Color them on the map.

Name______________________________________

Pacific States

Hawaii

The Aloha State

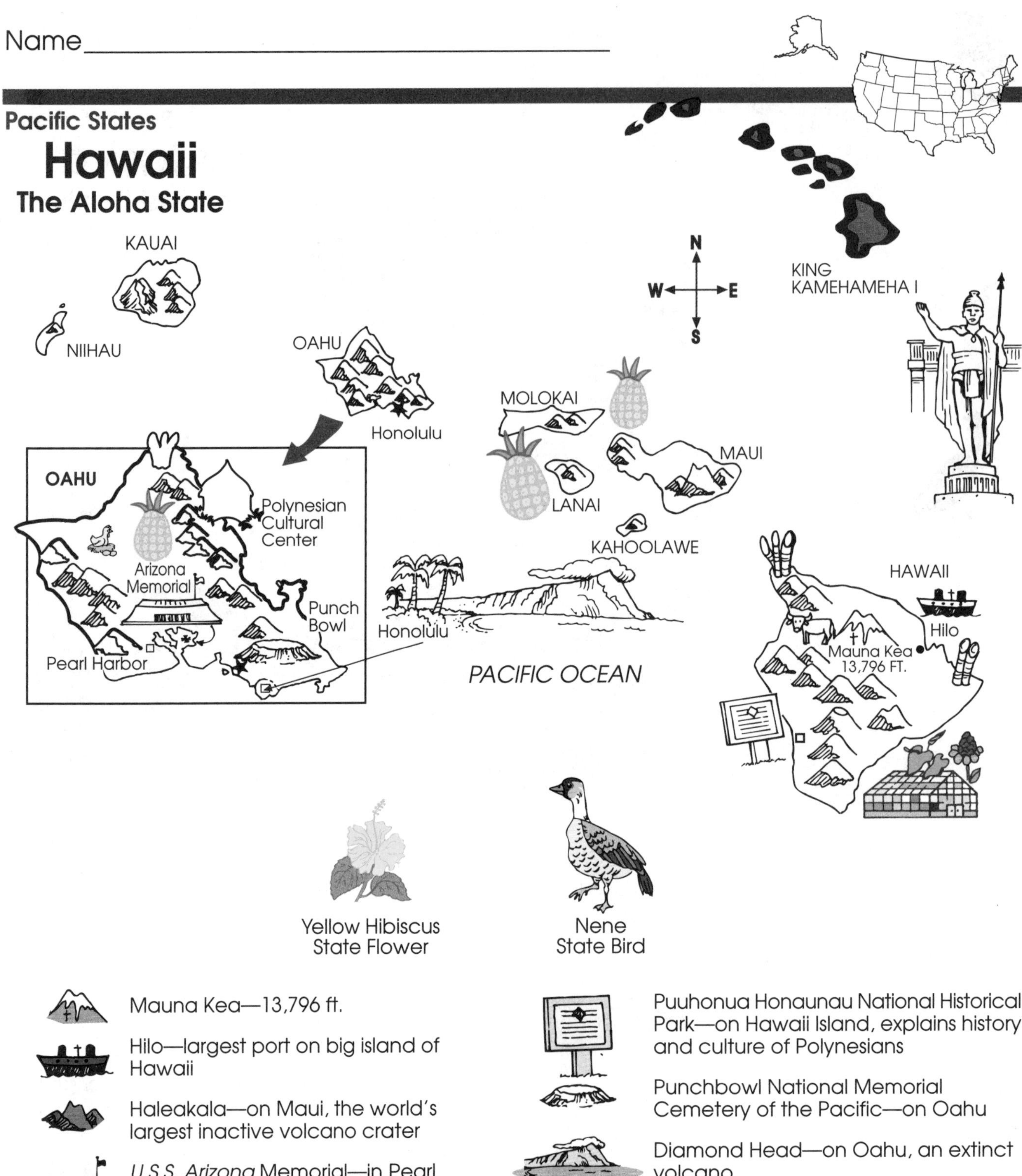

Yellow Hibiscus
State Flower

Nene
State Bird

- Mauna Kea—13,796 ft.
- Hilo—largest port on big island of Hawaii
- Haleakala—on Maui, the world's largest inactive volcano crater
- *U.S.S. Arizona* Memorial—in Pearl Harbor, honors those who died aboard the *U.S.S. Arizona* when Japanese attacked on December 7, 1941
- King Kamehameha—statue of Hawaii's greatest ruler
- Puuhonua Honaunau National Historical Park—on Hawaii Island, explains history and culture of Polynesians
- Punchbowl National Memorial Cemetery of the Pacific—on Oahu
- Diamond Head—on Oahu, an extinct volcano
- Polynesian Cultural Center on Oahu
- Waimea Canyon—on Kauai, gorges of many beautiful colors

Circle the capital city. Locate the landmarks found in the above key. Color them on the map.

Name________________________________

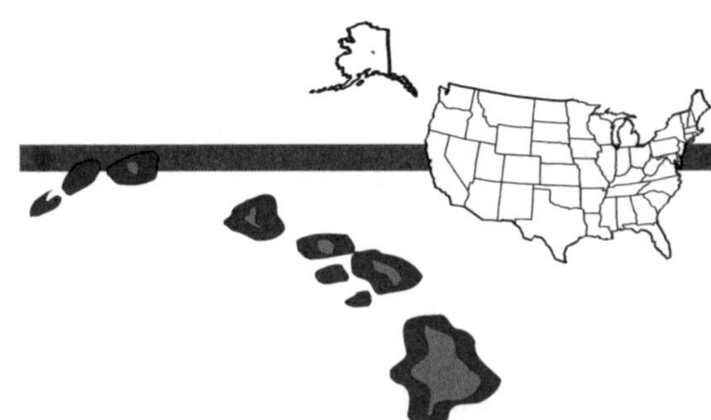

Pacific States

Hawaii

The Aloha State

- name believed to come from Hawaiian word *Havaiki,* which was the name of a Pacific Island on which the Hawaiian people had resided earlier
- nickname the Aloha State refers to the Hawaiian word *aloha,* which means *love* and is used for greetings of *hello, welcome* or *goodbye*

Islands—Hawaii consists of 132 islands, of which there are 8 main islands

1. Hawaii—nickname the Big Island refers to it being the largest island
2. Lanai—nickname the Pineapple Island refers to the island being one large pineapple plantation
3. Kahoolawe—smallest of the main islands and is uninhabited
4. Molokai—nickname the Friendly Island refers to how graciously the people welcome visitors
5. Kauai—nickname the Garden Island refers to its beautiful gardens and numerous green plants
6. Oahu—nickname the Gathering Place refers to it being the residence of 80% of the population
7. Maui—nickname the Valley Island refers to the canyons cut into the two volcanoes which form the island
8. Niihau—nicknamed the Forbidden Island because no one can visit the island without the owner's permission

Name____

The Mountain States

The Mountain States' major feature is the majestic Rocky Mountains that stretch from north to south in this region. The Mountain States are known for their high plateaus, deep canyons and desert regions.

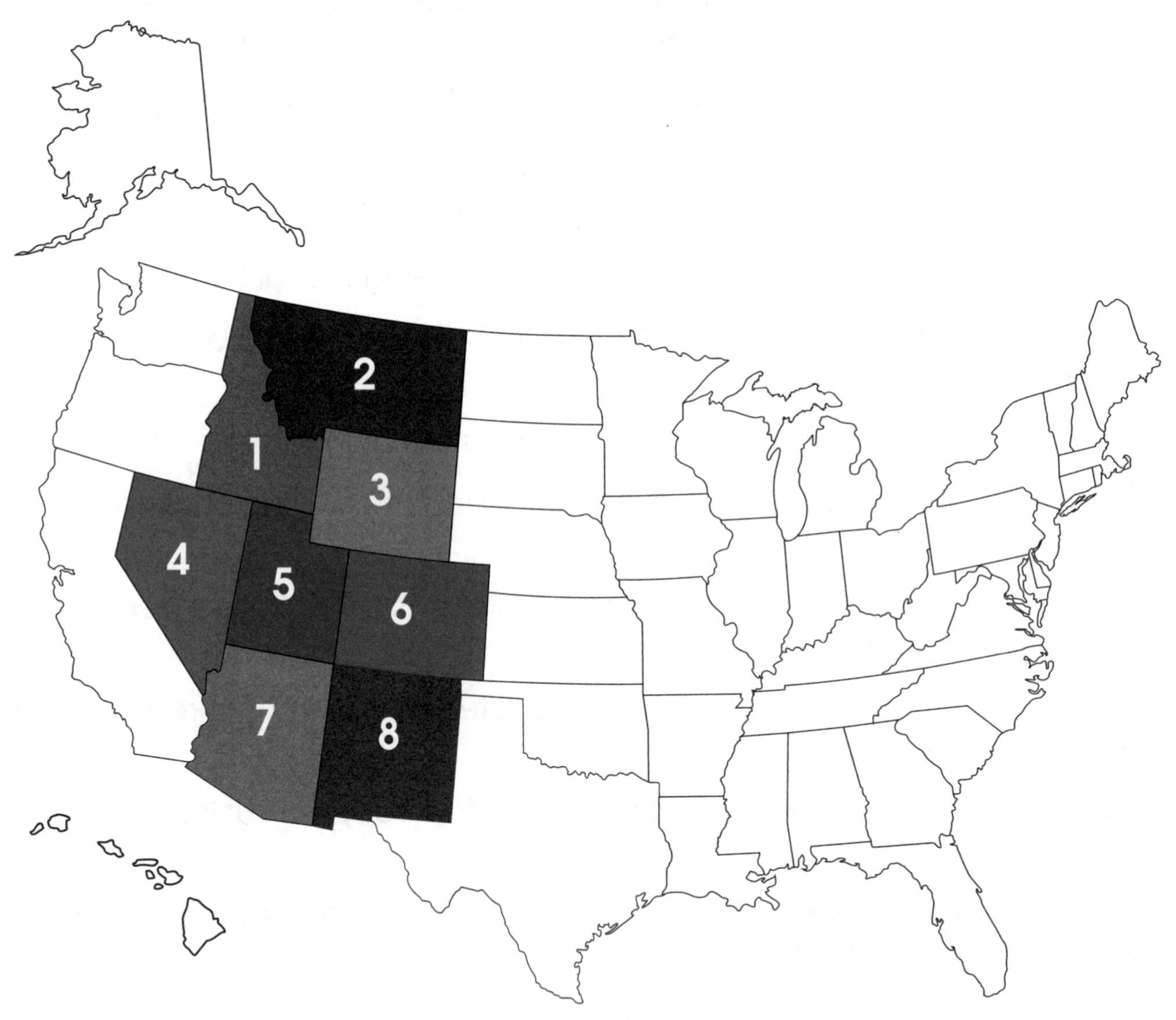

1. Idaho
2. Montana
3. Wyoming
4. Nevada
5. Utah
6. Colorado
7. Arizona
8. New Mexico

048113111 Zeeland, MI U.S.A.

Name________________________________

Fill in the "Five Fundamental Themes of Geography" for each state. After "discovering" a state, fill in all the columns of the chart except **Regions**. When you have finished with all of the states in a section, fill in **Regions**.

Five Fundamental Themes of Geography					
Name of State	**Location** (Where is it?)	**Place** (What is it like?)	**People and Environment** (What do the people do?)	**Movement** (How do people, goods and ideas move?)	**Regions** (What are some of the common features?)

Name________________________________

Mountain States

Fill in the "Five Fundamental Themes of Geography" for each state. After "discovering" a state, fill in all the columns of the chart except **Regions**. When you have finished with all of the states in a section, fill in **Regions**.

Five Fundamental Themes of Geography					
Name of State	**Location** (Where is it?)	**Place** (What is it like?)	**People and Environment** (What do the people do?)	**Movement** (How do people, goods and ideas move?)	**Regions** (What are some of the common features?)

Name______________________________

Idaho

The Gem State

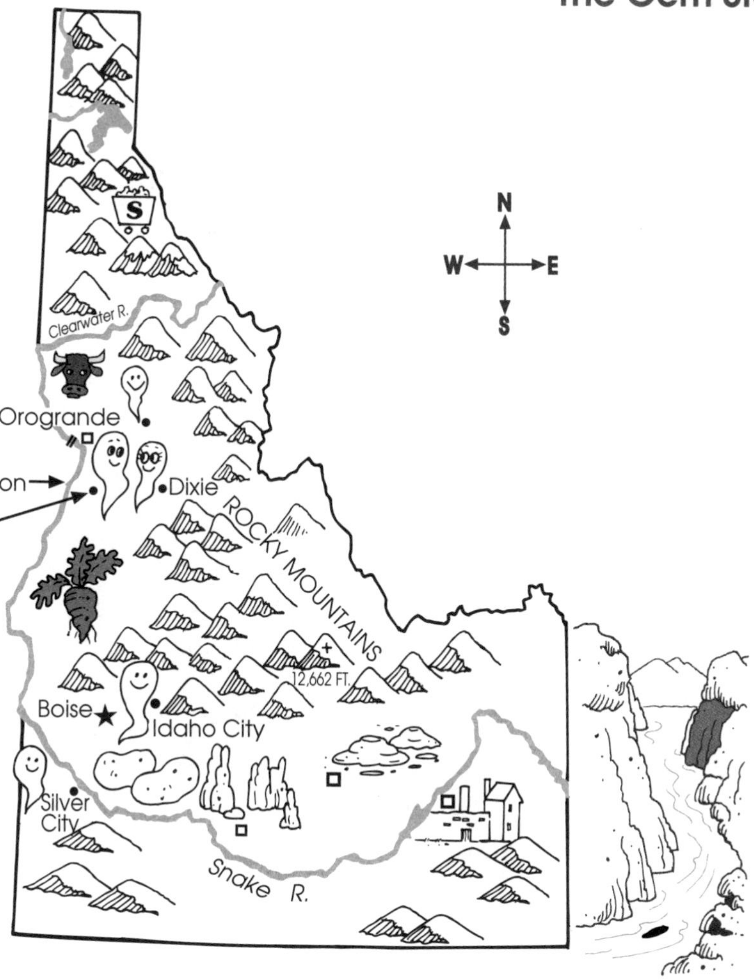

N
W E
S

Clearwater R.
Orogrande
Hells Canyon
Dixie
Florence
ROCKY MOUNTAINS
12,662 FT.
Boise
Idaho City
Silver City
Snake R.

Syringa
State Flower

Mountain Bluebird
State Bird

- name originated from the Shoshone Indian word *ee-dah-how*, which means *sun coming down the mountain* or *daybreak*
- nicknamed the Gem State for the gold, silver and other minerals in the area that brought a mining boom

Borah Peak—12,662 ft.

Craters of the Moon National Monument

Cities of Rock

Ghost Towns—Silver City, Florence, Idaho City, Dixie and Orogrande

Pocatello—contains Old Fort Hall, a reconstruction of a trading post on the Oregon Trail

Hells Canyon—the nation's deepest canyon

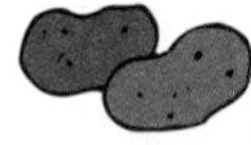
Potatoes—grows more than any other state

Circle the capital city. Locate the landmarks found in the above key. Color them on the map.

Name____

Montana

The Treasure State

BEAR PAW MTS.

Fort Peck Dam

Missouri R.

Great Falls

ROCKY

MOUNTAINS

Missoula

Helena

Whitehall

Yellowstone R.

Bighorn R.

12,799 FT.

Virginia City

N

W E

S

Western Meadowlark
State Bird

Bitterroot
State Flower

- named from the Spanish word that means *mountainous*
- nicknamed the Treasure State for the vast amounts of gold and silver found in its mountains

Granite Peak—12,799 ft.

Blackfoot Indian Reservation

Grasshopper Glacier—swarms of grasshoppers trapped in a glacier

Little Bighorn National Monument

National Bison Range

● Virginia City—site of one of richest gold deposits in 1862

Circle the capital city. Locate the landmarks found in the above key. Color them on the map.

Name ______________________________

Mountain States

Wyoming

The Equality State

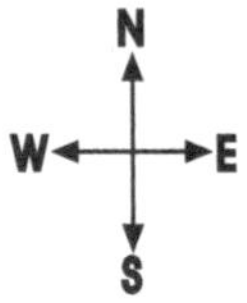

Indian Paintbrush
State Flower

Meadowlark
State Bird

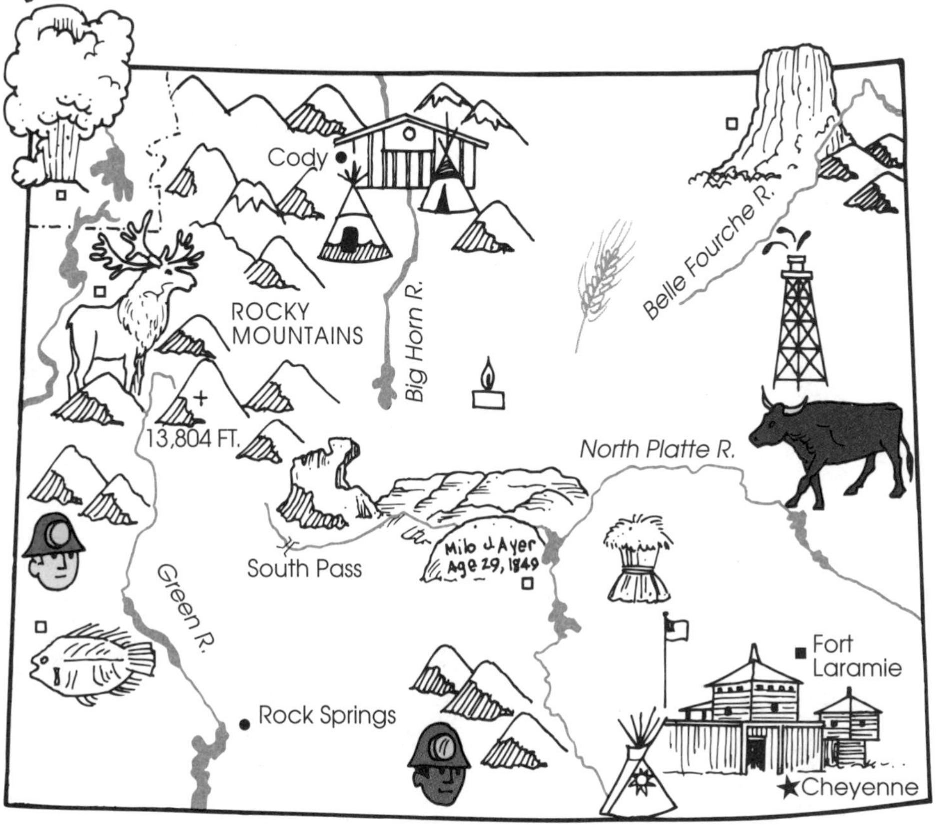

- named for the Delaware Indian word which means *upon the great plain*
- nickname the Equality State refers to being the first state in which women could vote, hold a position in public office and serve on a jury

Gannett Peak—13,804 ft.

Old Faithful Geyser in Yellowstone National Park—world's 1st national park

Fossil Butte National Monument

Independence Rock—more than 5,000 pioneers carved their names here

National Elk Refuge

Fort Laramie—restored fur trading center

Buffalo Bill Historical Center

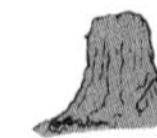

Devil's Tower—United States' first monument

Circle the capital city. Locate the landmarks found in the above key. Color them on the map.

Name____

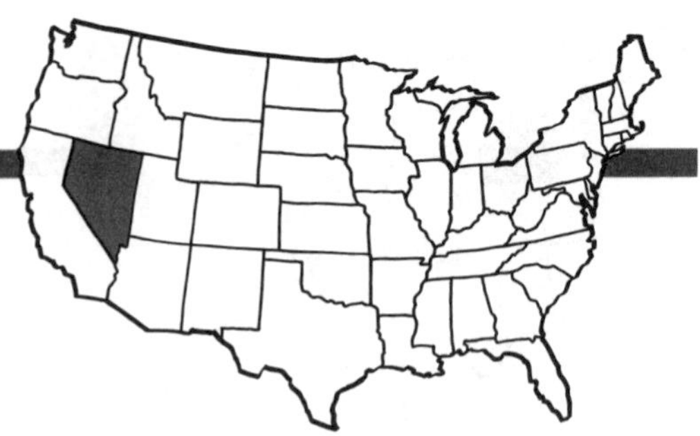

Mountain States

Nevada

The Silver State

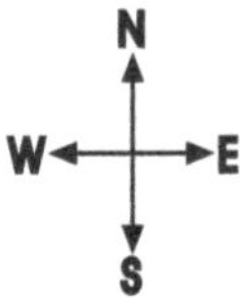

N
W E
S

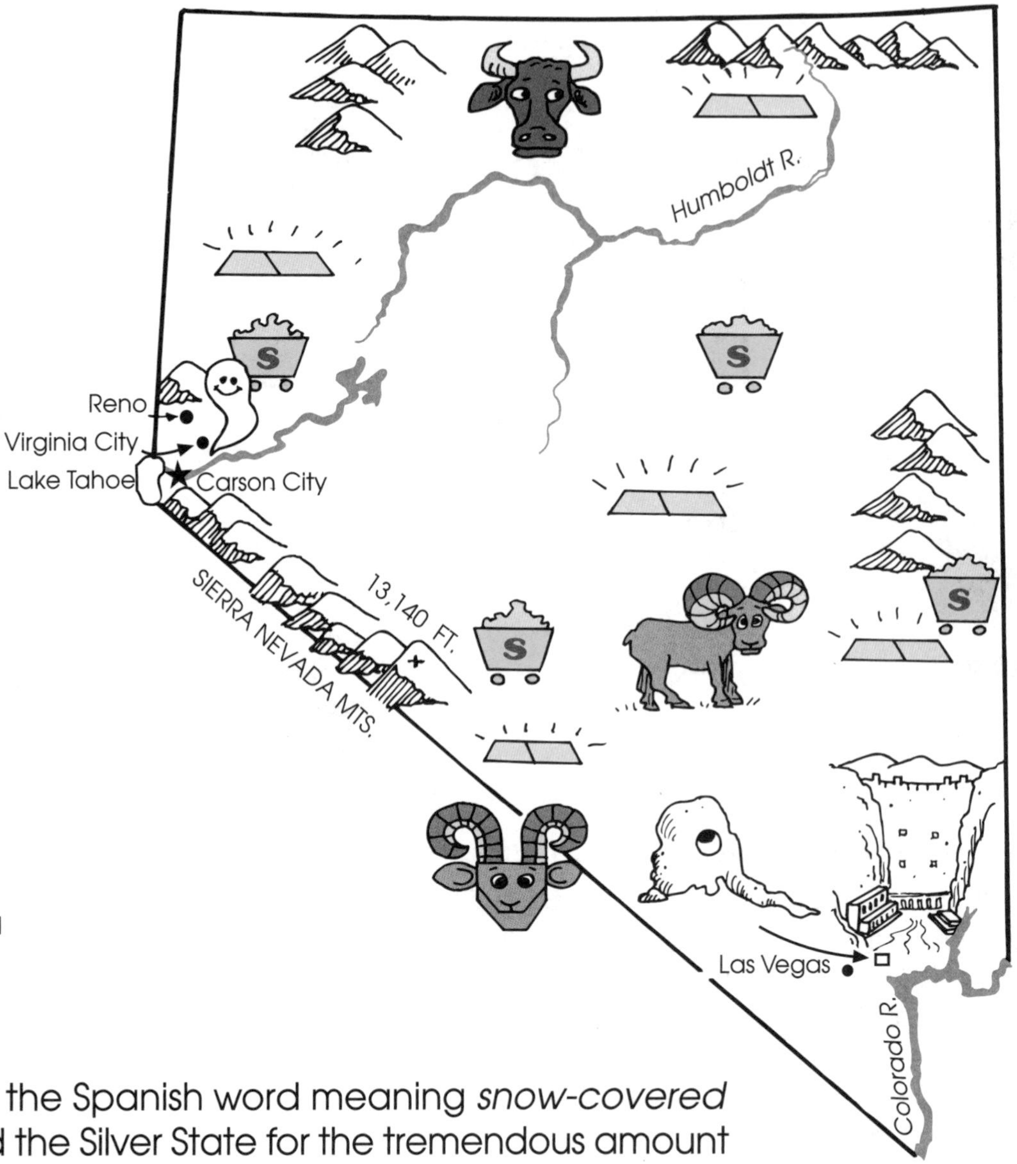

Reno
Virginia City
Lake Tahoe
Carson City
Humboldt R.
13,140 FT.
SIERRA NEVADA MTS.
Las Vegas
Colorado R.

Sagebrush
State Flower

Mountain Bluebird
State Bird

- named for the Spanish word meaning *snow-covered*
- nicknamed the Silver State for the tremendous amount of silver that was mined

 Boundary Peak—13,140 ft.

 Valley of Fire State Park—contains Elephant Rock, formed by the weather

 Hoover Dam—one of the world's largest concrete dams

 Lake Tahoe

Circle the capital city. Locate the landmarks found in the above key. Color them on the map.

Name ______________________________

Mountain States

Utah

The Beehive State

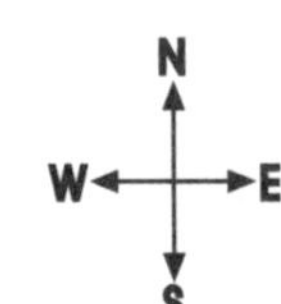

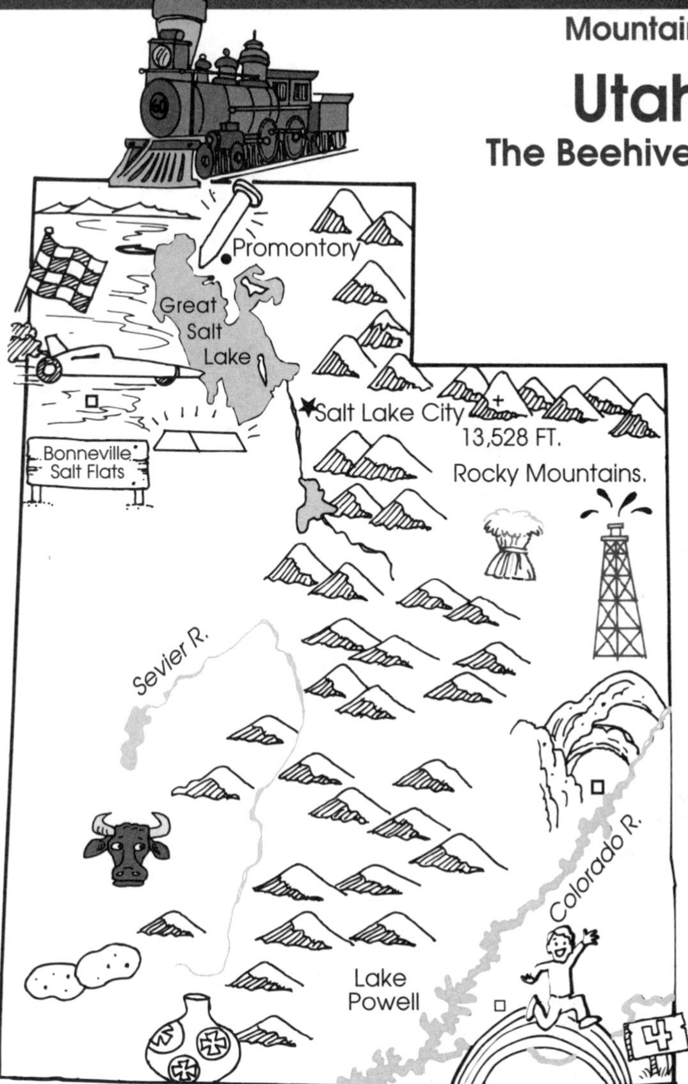

Sego Lily
State Flower

Sea Gull
State Bird

- named for the Ute Indians
- nicknamed the Beehive State because pioneers called the region *Deseret*—Mormon for *honeybee*

King's Peak—13,528 ft.

Indian Cliff Dwelling Ruins—housed Anasazi about A.D. 1000-1300

International Speedway—cars race on flat salt beds

Promontory—first transcontinental railroad completed in 1869

Four Corners—where Utah, Arizona, New Mexico and Colorado meet

Bonneville Salt Flats

Arches National Park

Rainbow Bridge National Monument—world's largest natural stone bridge

Circle the capital city. Locate the landmarks found in the above key. Color them on the map.

Name____________________________________

Mountain States

Colorado

The Centennial State

Dinosaur National Park

South Platte R.

Colorado R.

Denver

Grand Junction

Aspen

Leadville

Rocky Mountain Columbine State Flower

14,433 FT.

Colorado Springs

Gunnison R.

Arkansas R.

Lark Bunting State Bird

Rio Grande R.

- named for the Colorado River, whose name is Spanish for *colored red*
- nicknamed the Centennial State for becoming a state in 1876, which was the centennial of the Declaration of Independence

Mount Elbert—14,433 ft.

Mesa Verde National Park—1,000-year-old-cliff dwellings

Four Corners—place where four states meet

Garden of the Gods—giant formations of red sandstone

Royal Gorge Bridge

U.S. Mint—millions of coins made yearly

Circle the capital city. Locate the landmarks found in the above key. Color them on the map.

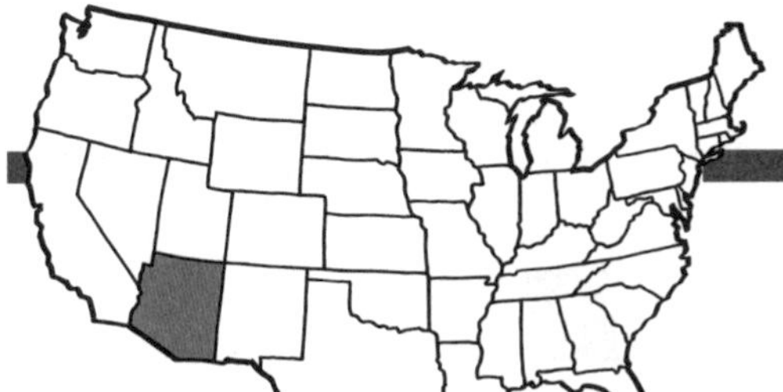

Name______________________________

Arizona

The Grand Canyon State

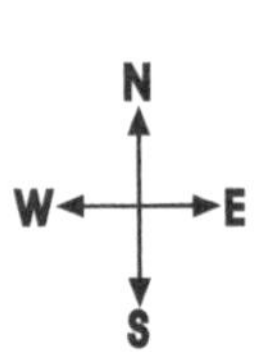

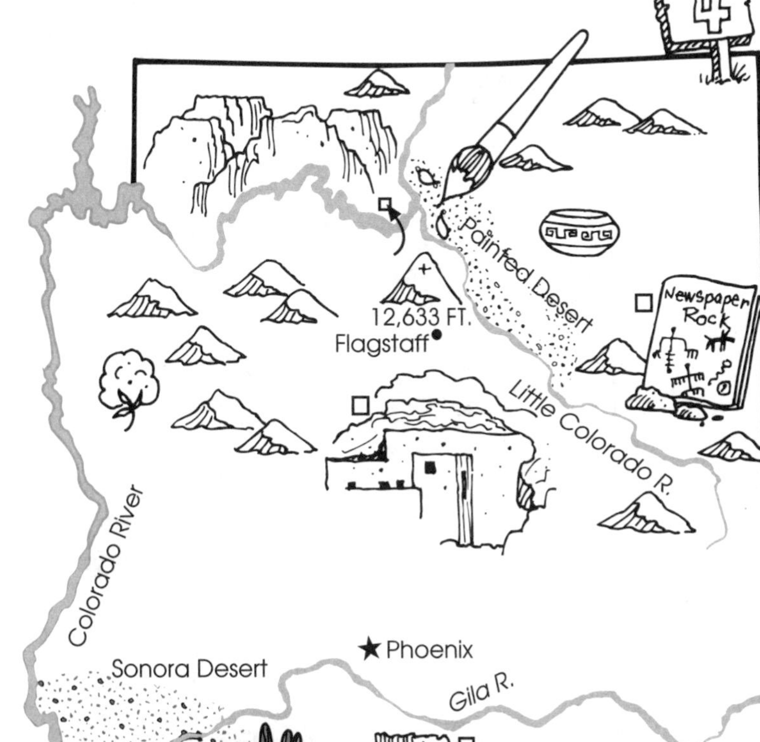

Saguaro
State Flower

Cactus Wren
State Bird

- name derived from the Native American word *arizonac*, which possibly means *small spring*
- nicknamed the Grand Canyon State for the Grand Canyon, which is located in the northwest corner of the state

 Humphreys Peak—12, 633 ft.

Petrified Forest Park—location of Newspaper Rock

 Four Corners—place where Arizona, Colorado, New Mexico and Utah meet

 Monument Valley Navajo Tribal Park

 Painted Desert—colorful rock and sand

 Montezuma Castle National Monument—five-story cliff-dwelling ruin

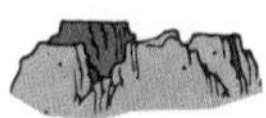 Grand Canyon National Park—one of the U.S.'s most famous scenic wonders

 Casa Grande Tower—built by Hohokum Indians about A.D. 1350

Circle the capital city. Locate the landmarks found in the above key. Color them on the map.

Name____

Mountain States

New Mexico

Land of Enchantment

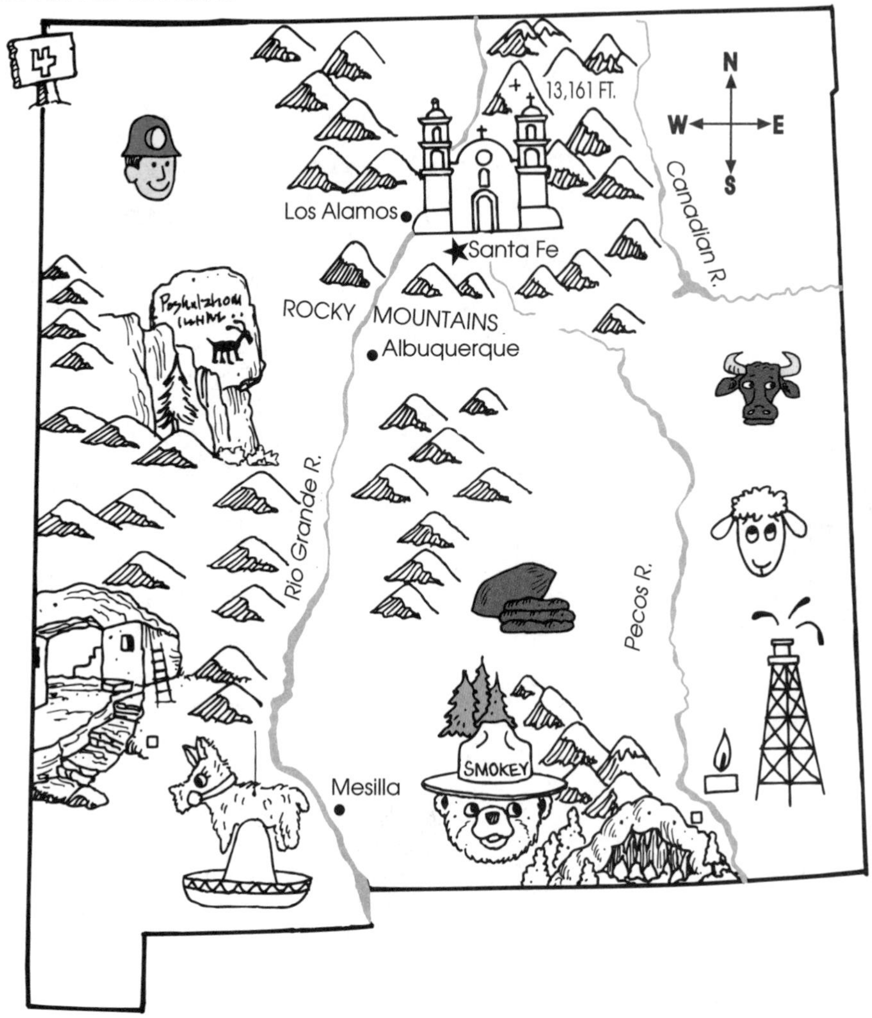

13,161 FT.

N
W
E
S

Canadian R.

Los Alamos

Santa Fe

ROCKY MOUNTAINS

Albuquerque

Rio Grande R.

Pecos R.

Mesilla

SMOKEY

Yucca Flower
State Flower

Roadrunner
State Bird

- named after Mexico, which was named after Mexitli, an Aztec Indian war god
- nicknamed the Land of Enchantment for its beautiful scenery and rich, history

Wheeler Peak—13,161 ft.

Four Corners

San Miguel Mission

Carlsbad Caverns—one of the world's great natural wonders

Gila Cliff Dwellings National Monument

Historic Mesilla

Inscription Rock National Monument—has petroglyphs never deciphered

Smokey the Bear Historical Park

Circle the capital city. Locate the landmarks found in the above key. Color them on the map.

Name____

The North Central States

Look around the North Central states and you will see why they are also called the Plains states. The plains have rich soil that makes this area famous for growing wheat and corn.

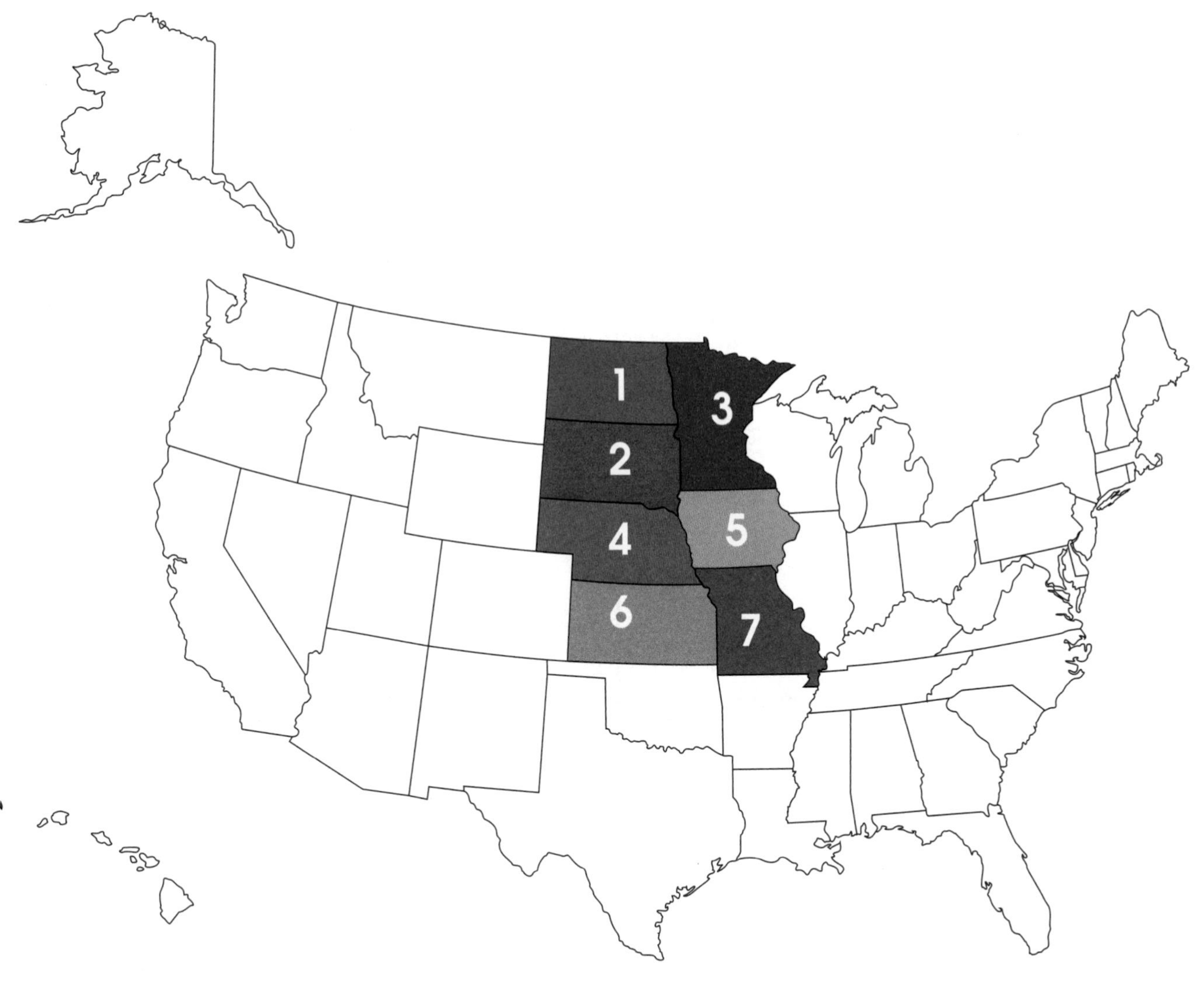

1. North Dakota
2. South Dakota
3. Minnesota
4. Nebraska
5. Iowa
6. Kansas
7. Missouri

Name____________________________________

North Central States

Fill in the "Five Fundamental Themes of Geography" for each state. After "discovering" a state, fill in all the columns of the chart except **Regions**. When you have finished with all of the states in a section, fill in **Regions**.

Five Fundamental Themes of Geography					
Name of State	**Location** (Where is it?)	**Place** (What is it like?)	**People and Environment** (What do the people do?)	**Movement** (How do people, goods and ideas move?)	**Regions** (What are some of the common features?)

Name______________________________

Fill in the "Five Fundamental Themes of Geography" for each state. After "discovering" a state, fill in all the columns of the chart except **Regions**. When you have finished with all of the states in a section, fill in **Regions**.

Five Fundamental Themes of Geography					
Name of State	**Location** (Where is it?)	**Place** (What is it like?)	**People and Environment** (What do the people do?)	**Movement** (How do people, goods and ideas move?)	**Regions** (What are some of the common features?)

Name____

North Central States

North Dakota

Peace Garden State

N
W E
S

Wild Prairie Rose
State Flower

Western
Meadowlark
State Bird

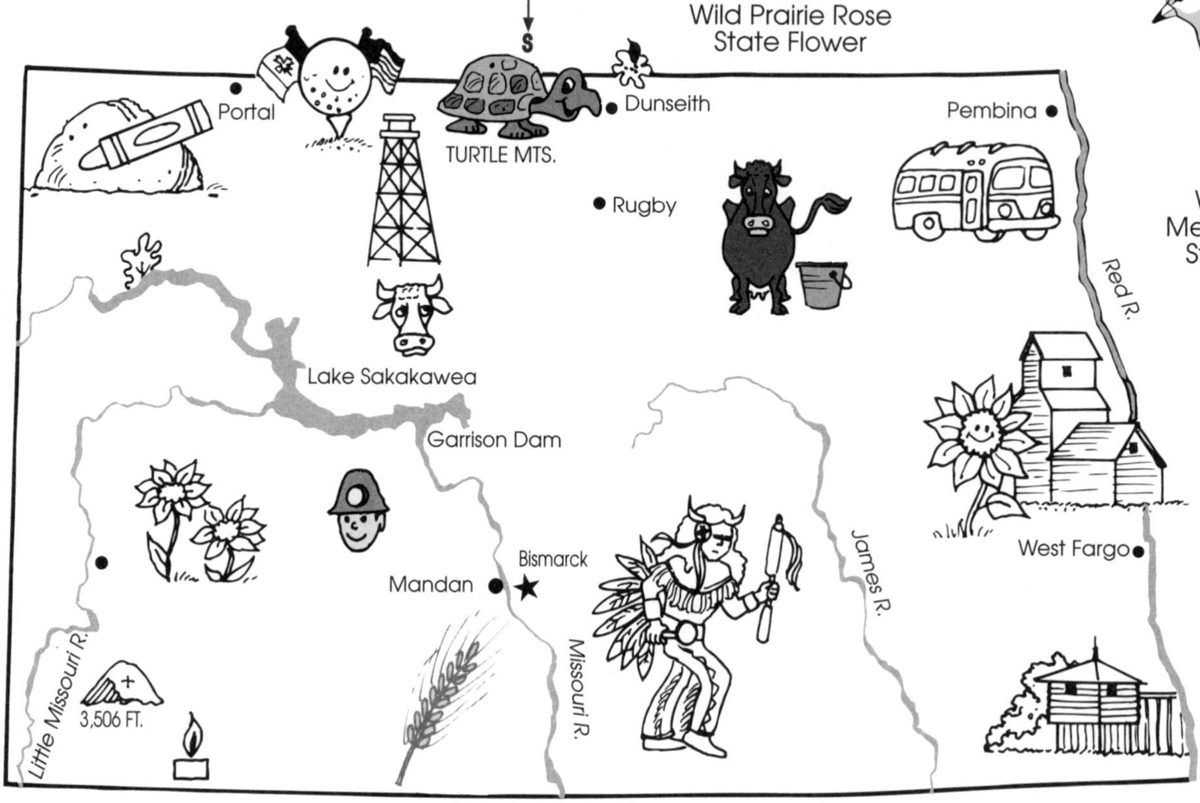

Portal
TURTLE MTS.
Dunseith
Pembina
Rugby
Red R.
Lake Sakakawea
Garrison Dam
Bismarck
Mandan
West Fargo
James R.
Missouri R.
Little Missouri R.
3,506 FT.

- named for Sioux Indians who called themselves Dakota or Lakota, which means *allies* or *friends*
- nicknamed the Peace Garden State

White Butte—3,506 ft.

Sunflowers—top producer of seeds

Bonanzaville—preserved pioneer village

United Tribes Powwow

Pembina—nations' largest bus plant

International Peace Garden—symbolizes friendship between U.S. and Canada

Writing Rock—boulder with ancient Indian picture writing

International Golf Course—spans two countries; tee for the 9th hole in Canada and cup in the U.S.

Fort Abercrombie—1st U.S. military post in North Dakota

• Rugby—geographic center of North America

Circle the capital city. Locate the landmarks found in the above key. Color them on the map.

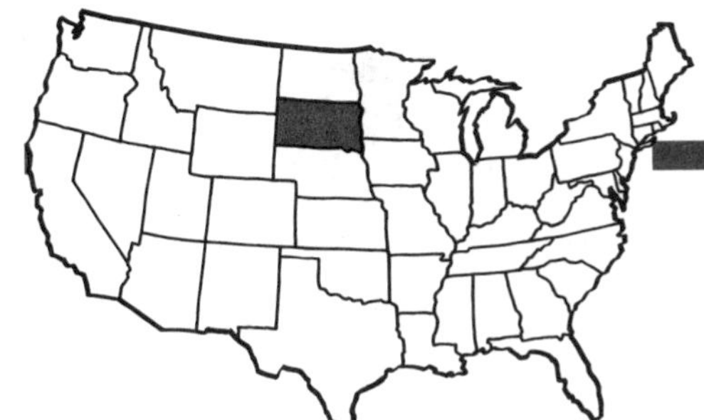

Name________________________________

South Dakota

Mount Rushmore State

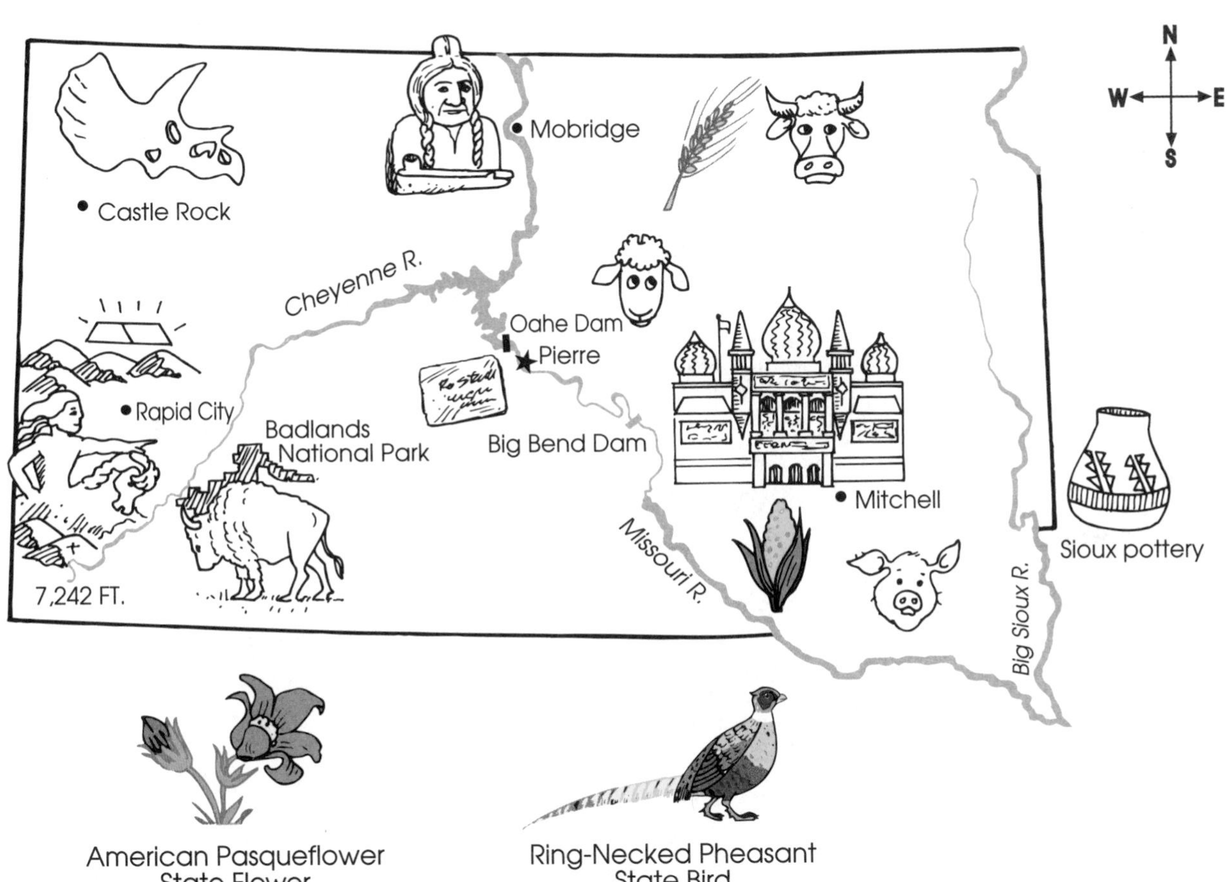

American Pasqueflower
State Flower

Ring-Necked Pheasant
State Bird

- named for Sioux Indians who called themselves Dakota or Lakota, which means *allies* or *friends*
- nicknamed the Mount Rushmore State

Harney Peak—7,242 ft.

Mobridge—sculpture marking the gravesite of Sioux leader Sitting Bull

Triceratops Fossil—found in 1927 in Harding County and now on display

Custer State Park

Castle Rock—geographic center of the 50 United States

Lead Plate—buried by the La Vérendrye brothers in 1743—discovered in 1913

Circle the capital city. Locate the landmarks found in the above key. Color them on the map.

Name____

Minnesota

The Gopher State

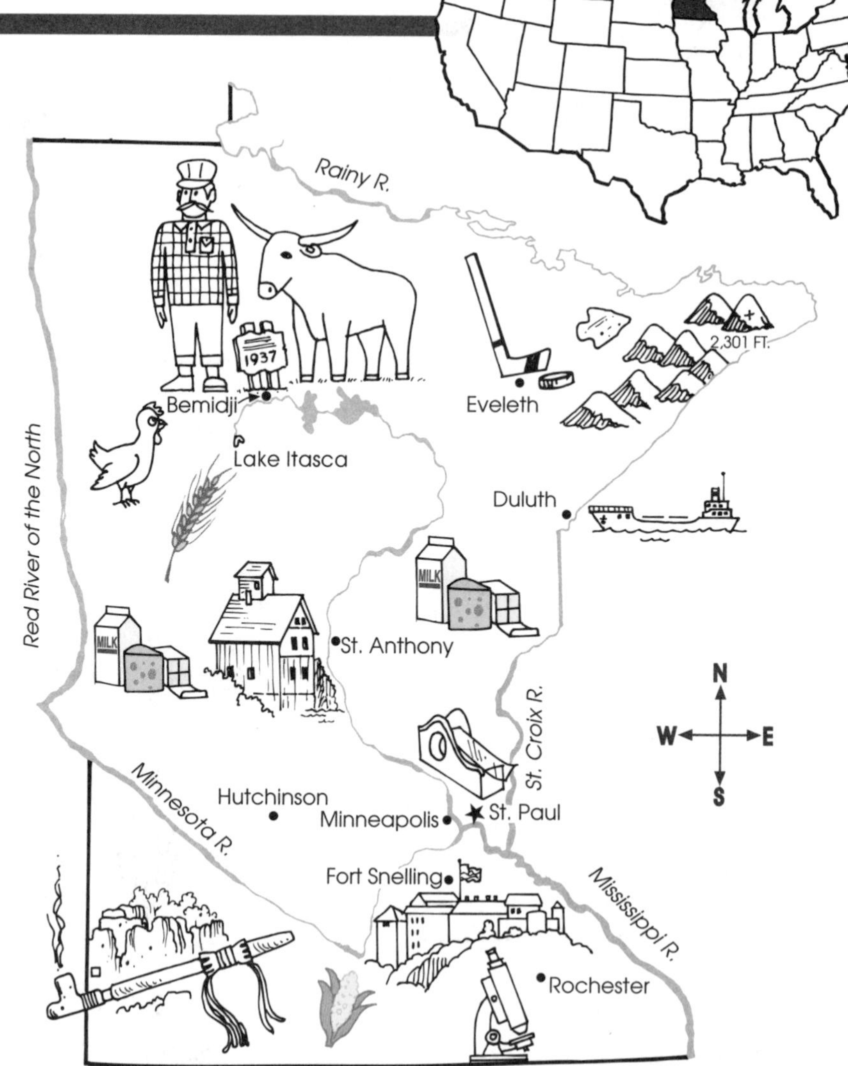

Pink and White Lady's Slipper State Flower

Common Loon State Bird

- name derived from the Sioux Indian words *mini sota,* meaning *sky-tinted water*
- nicknamed the Gopher State for the vast numbers of gophers that inhabited its prairie

Eagle Mountain—2,301 ft.

Arrowhead Country—northeastern tip shaped like an arrowhead

Bemidji—Paul Bunyan and Babe

St. Paul—where cellophane tape was invented

Fort Snelling—1819 restored military post

Lake Itasca—beginning of the Mississippi River

Mayo Clinic—one of the world's most famous medical centers

U.S. Hockey Hall of Fame

Falls of St. Anthony—first flour mill in Minnesota, in 1823

Duluth—farthest inland port in U.S.

Pipestone National Monument—Indians used red pipestone found here to make peace pipes

Circle the capital city. Locate the landmarks found in the above key. Color them on the map.

Name________________________________

Nebraska

The Cornhusker's State

N
W E
S

Niobrara R.
Missouri R.
Carhenge
SAND HILLS
Platte R.
Omaha
Grand Island
5,426 FT.
Wellfleet
Kearney
Lincoln
Nebraska City

Western Meadowlark
State Bird

Goldenrod
State Flower

- named for the Oto Indian word *nebrathka*, meaning *flat water*, which was the Indian name for the Platte River
- nicknamed the Cornhusker State for the state's leading crop of corn and for the cornhusking contests that used to be held in the fall

Toadstool Park—in the Badlands, has rock formations resembling toadstools

Wellfleet—largest mammoth fossil ever found

National Museum of Roller Skating

Arbor Lodge—home of Julius Sterling Morton, founder of Arbor Day

Chimney Rock National Historic Site

Carhenge—replica of Stonehenge made of cars

Cranes—about 500,000 stop along the Platte River every spring as they migrate north

Buffalo Bill's home

Homestead National Monument of America—site of the first piece of land claimed under the Homestead Act

Circle the capital city. Locate the landmarks found in the above key. Color them on the map.

Name____

North Central States

Iowa

The Hawkeye State

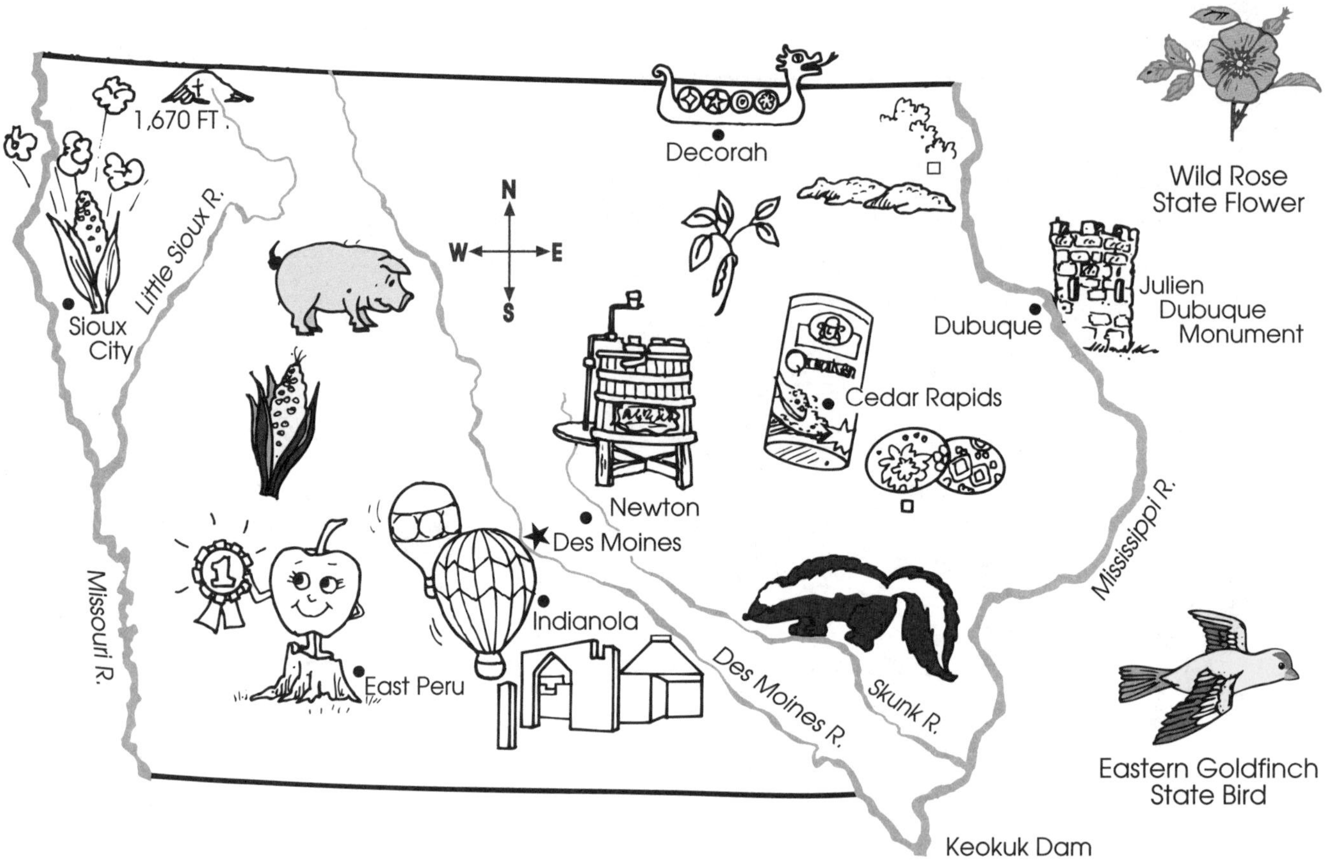

1,670 FT.
Decorah
N
W
E
S
Little Sioux R.
Sioux City
Wild Rose
State Flower
Julien
Dubuque
Monument
Dubuque
Cedar Rapids
Newton
Des Moines
Indianola
East Peru
Missouri R.
Mississippi R.
Des Moines R.
Skunk R.
Eastern Goldfinch
State Bird
Keokuk Dam

- named after the Sioux Indian tribe Ayuhwa whose name means *beautiful land* or *sleepy ones*
- nicknamed the Hawkeye State in honor of Chief Black Hawk, a Sauk and Fox Indian leader

Vesterheim Museum—Norwegian culture exhibits

Julien Dubuque Monument—gravesite of the first permanent white settler in Iowa

Indianola—National Balloon Museum

Cedar Rapids—one of the largest cereal mills in the U.S.

East Peru—red delicious apple was developed here in the1880s

Newton—washing machine capital of the world

Sioux City—largest popcorn processing plants in U.S.

Effigy Mounds—earthen mounds shaped like animals, built by prehistoric Indians

Circle the capital city. Locate the landmarks found in the above key. Color them on the map.

Name ____________________

Kansas

The Sunflower State

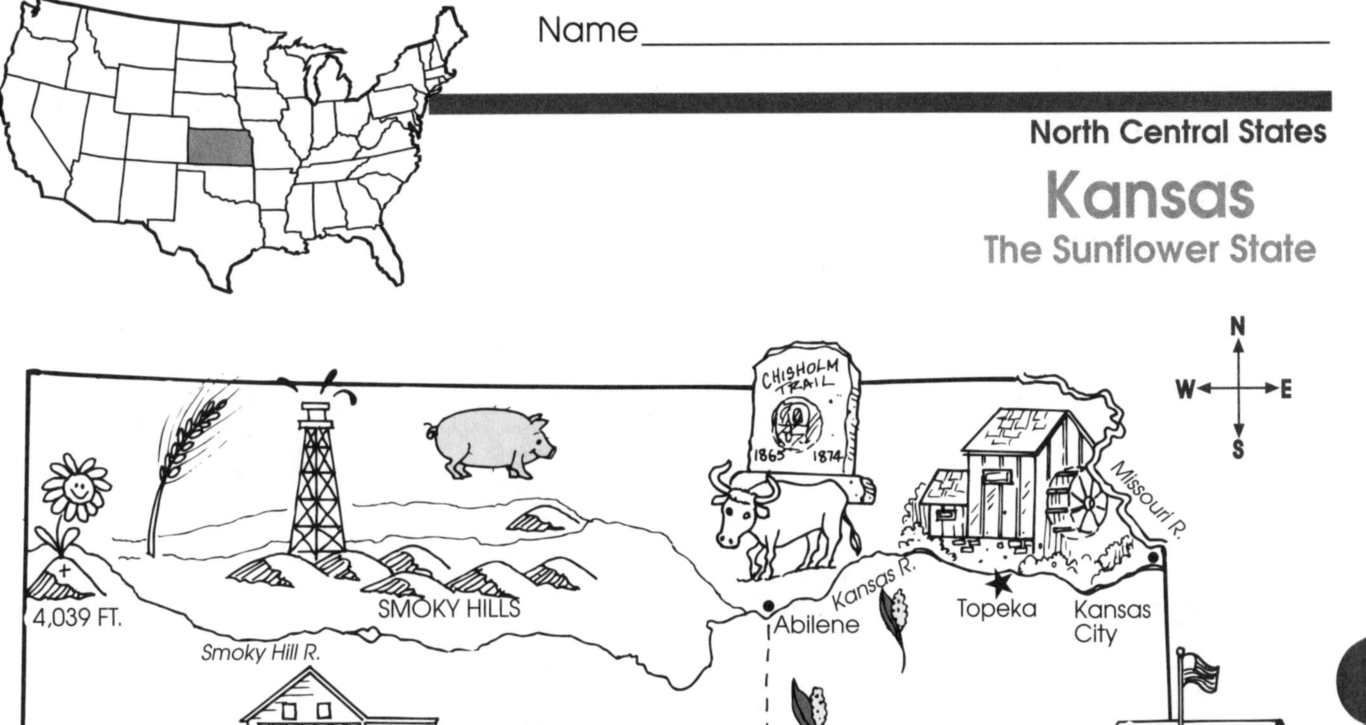

Sunflower
State Flower

Western Meadowlark
State Bird

- named for the Kansa, or Kaw, Indians, whose name means *people of the south wind*
- nicknamed the Sunflower State for the abundance of sunflowers

Mount Sunflower—4,039 ft.

Liberal—home of the original model of Dorothy's house from the 1939 film *The Wizard of Oz*

Old flour mill—represents the many flour mills in Topeka today

Cowboy Capital of the World

Chisholm Trail—used for herding cattle from Texas to Abilene for shipment to the East

Fort Scott—restored 1840's cavalry post

Circle the capital city. Locate the landmarks found in the above key. Color them on the map.

Name____

North Central States

Missouri

The Show Me State

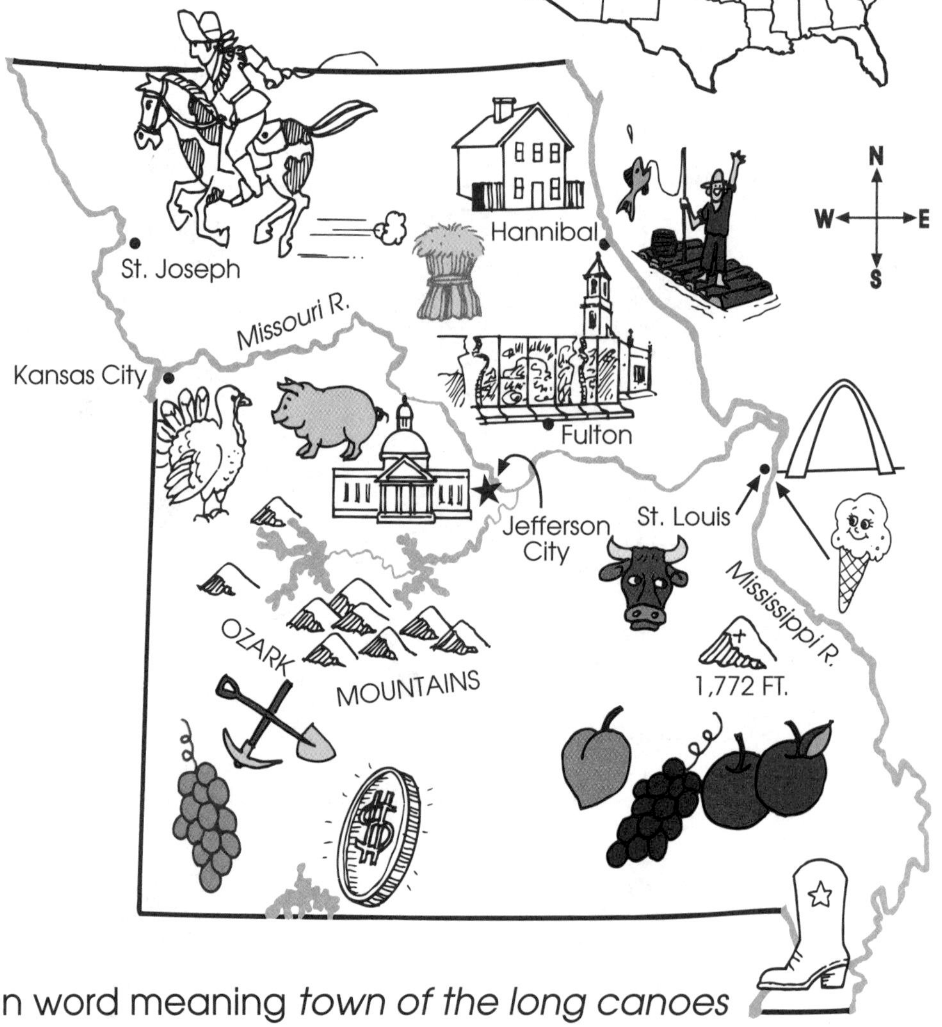

St. Joseph
Hannibal
Missouri R.
Kansas City
Fulton
Jefferson City
St. Louis
Mississippi R.
OZARK MOUNTAINS
1,772 FT.
N
W
E
S

Bluebird
State Bird

Hawthorn
State Flower

- named for an Indian word meaning *town of the long canoes*
- nickname the Show Me State related to an 1899 speech by Congressman Vandiver in which he indicated he was unimpressed with speeches and wanted to be shown results

Taum Sauk Mountain—1,772 ft.

Pony Express—carried mail from St. Joseph, Missouri to Sacramento, California from 1860 to 1861

Hannibal—contains the home and museum of Mark Twain, who wrote *Tom Sawyer*

Fulton—has a 1990 sculpture using eight Berlin Wall sections

Gateway Arch—tallest monument in U.S.

Boot Heel Country—named because the shape resembles a boot heel

Silver Dollar City—reconstructed 1880s mining town

First ice-cream cone—at Louisiana Purchase Centennial Expo in St. Louis in 1904

Circle the capital city. Locate the landmarks found in the above key. Color them on the map.

Name________________________________

The South Central States

The South Central states is a region with large areas of flat land good for raising cattle and growing cotton. This region is also known for its rich deposits of oil that are found beneath the surface of the land and ocean floor.

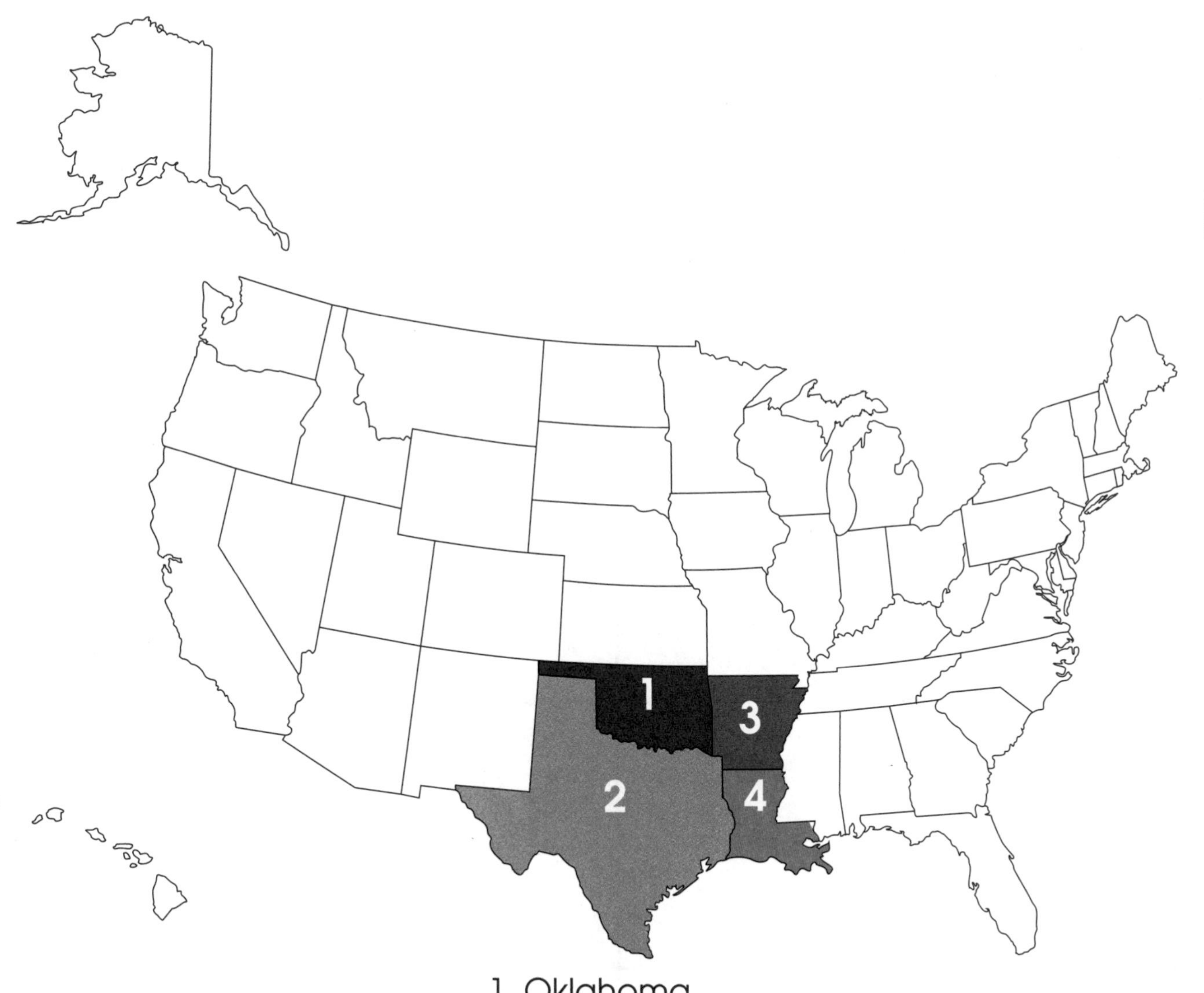

1. Oklahoma

2. Texas

3. Arkansas

4. Louisiana

Name________________________________

South Central States

Fill in the "Five Fundamental Themes of Geography" for each state. After "discovering" a state, fill in all the columns of the chart except **Regions**. When you have finished with all of the states in a section, fill in **Regions**.

Five Fundamental Themes of Geography					
Name of State	**Location** (Where is it?)	**Place** (What is it like?)	**People and Environment** (What do the people do?)	**Movement** (How do people, goods and ideas move?)	**Regions** (What are some of the common features?)

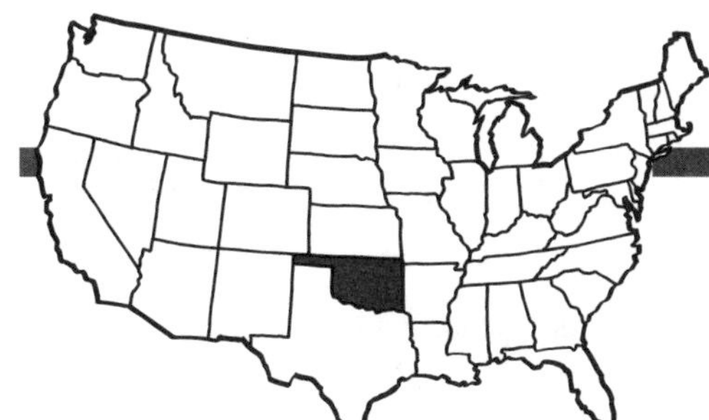

Name________________________________

Oklahoma

The Sooner State

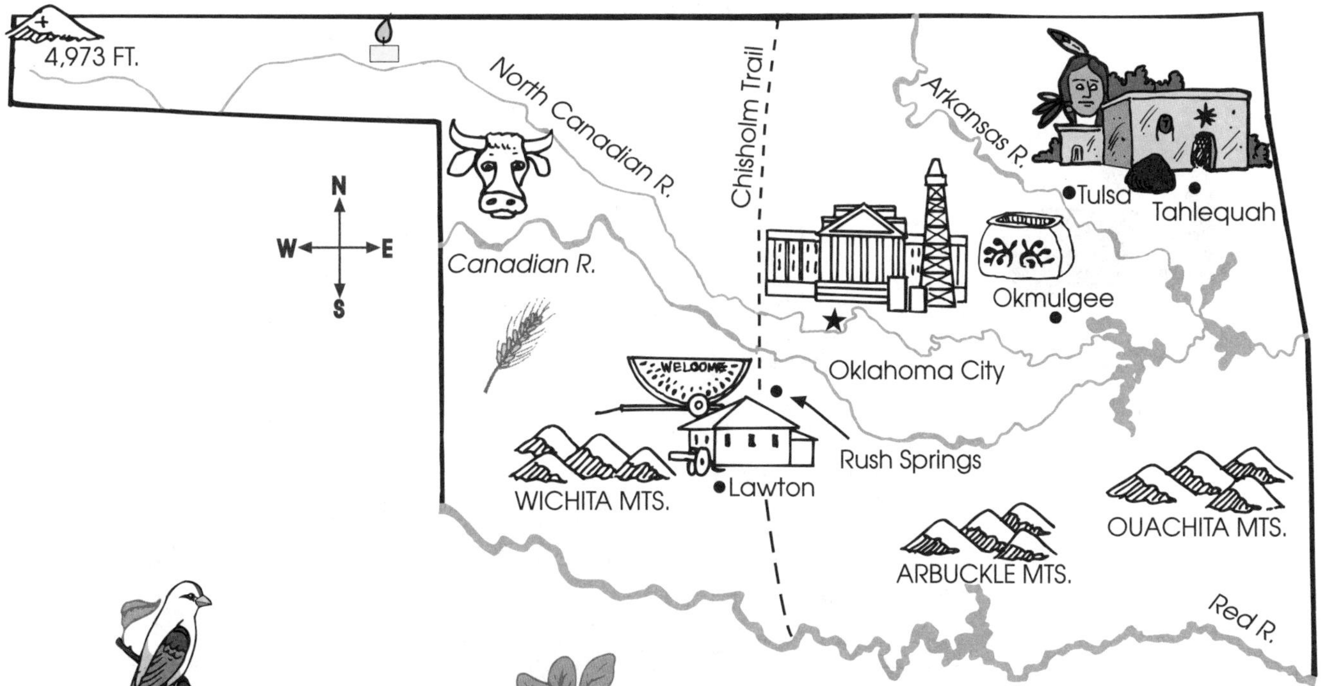

4,973 FT.
North Canadian R.
Chisholm Trail
Arkansas R.
N
W
E
S
Canadian R.
Tulsa
Tahlequah
Okmulgee
Oklahoma City
Rush Springs
Lawton
WICHITA MTS.
ARBUCKLE MTS.
OUACHITA MTS.
Red R.

Scissor-Tailed Flycatcher
State Bird

Mistletoe
State Flower

- name derived from the Chocotaw Indian words *okla,* meaning *people,* and *homma,* meaning *red*
- nicknamed the Sooner State for the settlers who arrived before the land was opened for settlement

Black Mesa—4,973 ft.

Oklahoma City—only state capital with working oil well on its site

Fort Sill—historical site built in 1869

Rush Springs—Watermelon Capital of the World

Circle the capital city. Locate the landmarks found in the above key. Color them on the map.

Name____

South Central States

Texas

The Lone Star State

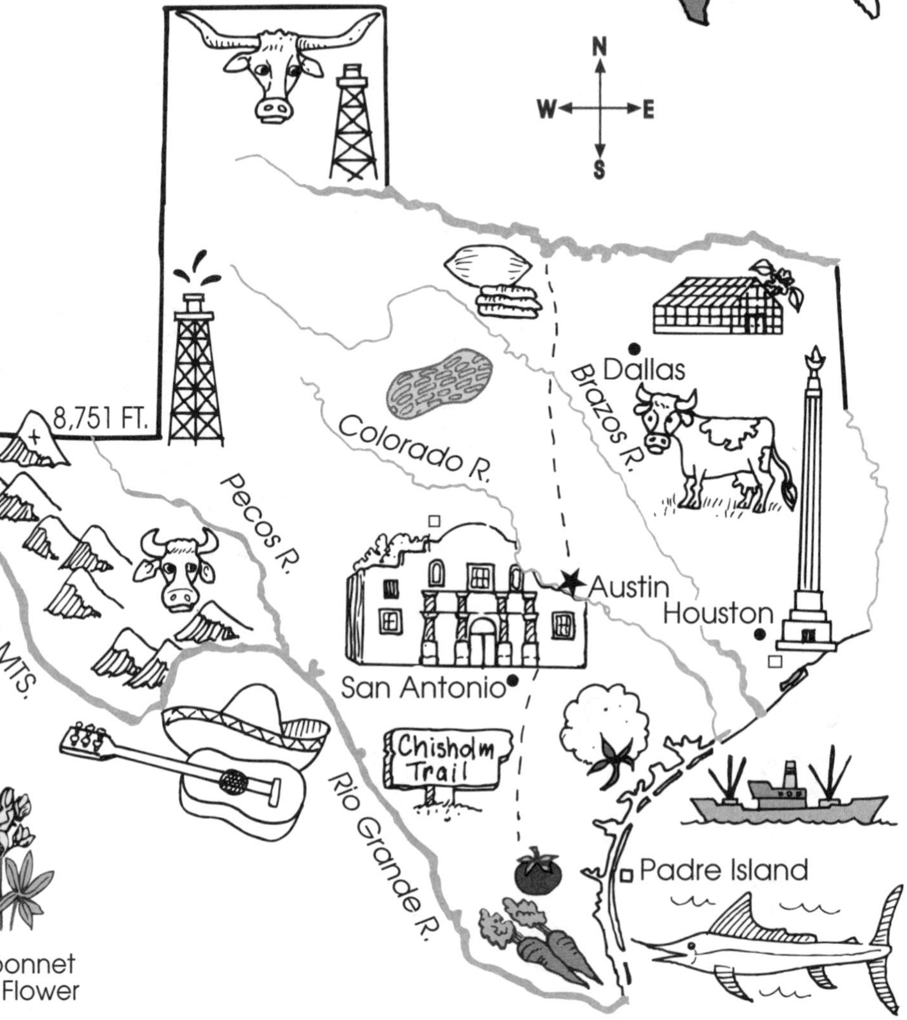

Mockingbird
State Bird

Bluebonnet
State Flower

- name comes from the Spanish pronunciation of the Indian word *Tejas,* which means *allies* or *friends*
- nickname the Lone Star State comes from having only one star on its state flag

Guadalupe Peak—8,751 ft.

San Jacinto Monument—honors Texans who fought and won the battle for independence from Mexico

The Alamo—a famous San Antonio battle site

Chisholm Trail—begins here

Padre Island—national seashore

Mexican culture and influence seen throughout the state

Circle the capital city. Locate the landmarks found in the above key. Color them on the map.

Name ____________________

Arkansas

The Land of Opportunity

Bull Shoals Lake
Eureka Springs
White R.
Mountain View
Arkansas R.
2,753 FT.
Little Rock
Hot Springs
OUACHITA MTS.
Mississippi R.
Murfreesboro
Texarkana
TEXAS
STATE LINE
ARKANSAS
Red R.
N
W
E
S

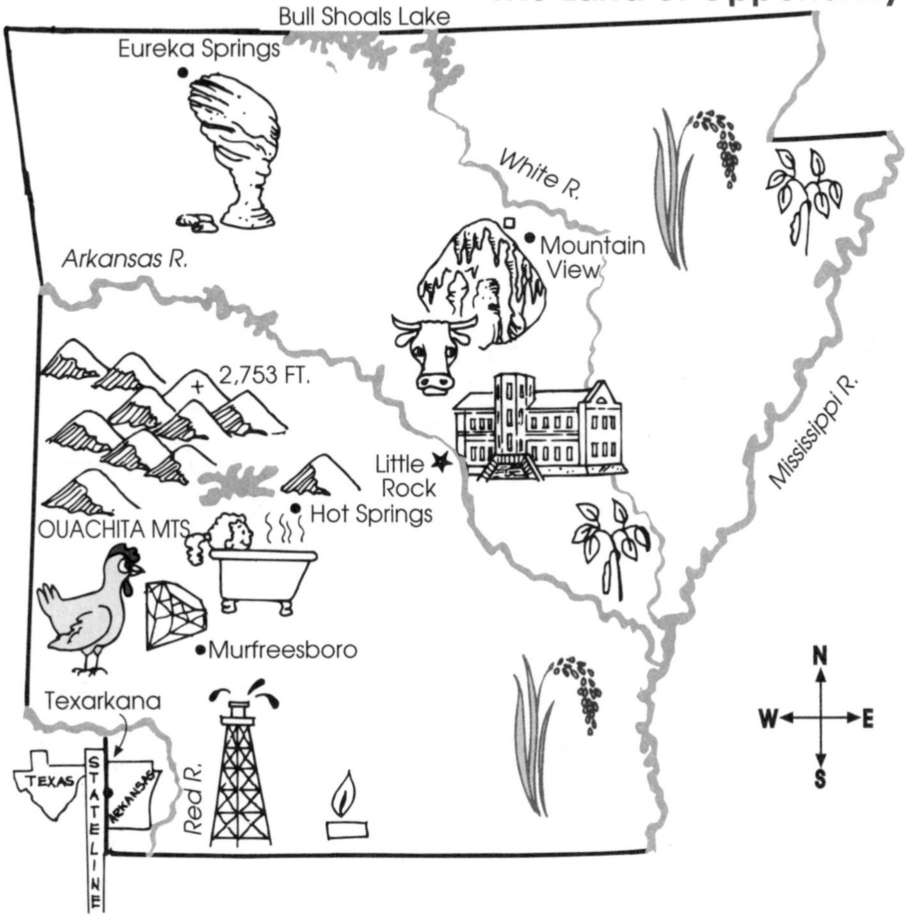

Apple Blossom
State Flower

Mockingbird
State Bird

- named for a Sioux Indian tribe named Arkansa, which means *downstream people*
- nickname the Land of Opportunity relates to the abundance of varied natural resources which provide excellent opportunities for mining, factories and farming

Magazine Mountain—2,753 ft.

Pivot Rock—balances on a small base

MacArthur Park—honors military commander, Douglas MacArthur

Crater of Diamonds State Park—diamond mine which tourists can visit

Hot Springs National Park—minerals and hot springs believed to be helpful for certain illnesses

Blanchard Spring Caverns

Texarkana—town on the border between Texas and Arkansas

Circle the capital city. Locate the landmarks found in the above key. Color them on the map.

Name______________________________________

South Central States

Louisiana

The Pelican State

Epps
535 FT.
Red R.
Mississippi R.
Sabine R.
Lafayette
Baton Rouge
Pearl R.
New Orleans
N
W
E
S

Magnolia
State Flower

Brown Pelican
State Bird

- named for the French King, Louis XIV
- nicknamed the Pelican State for the many brown pelicans that reside along the coast

Driskill Mountain—535 ft.

Poverty Point National Monument—ancient Indian ceremonial mounds built between 1700 and 700 B.C.

Avery Island—chili peppers grown here to make Tabasco sauce

Egrets—three of the world's largest egret sanctuaries

Preservation Hall—famous for its jazz bands

Bald cypress swamps

Jean Lafitte National Historical Park & Preserve—area where pirate Jean Lafitte fought with Andrew Jackson in the Battle of New Orleans

Acadian Village—features Cajun food and culture

Mardi Gras—features dancing, parties and parades

Circle the capital city. Locate the landmarks found in the above key. Color them on the map.

Name ____________________

The Midwest States

The Midwest States is a region with beautiful freshwater lakes, deep green forests and fertile farmland.

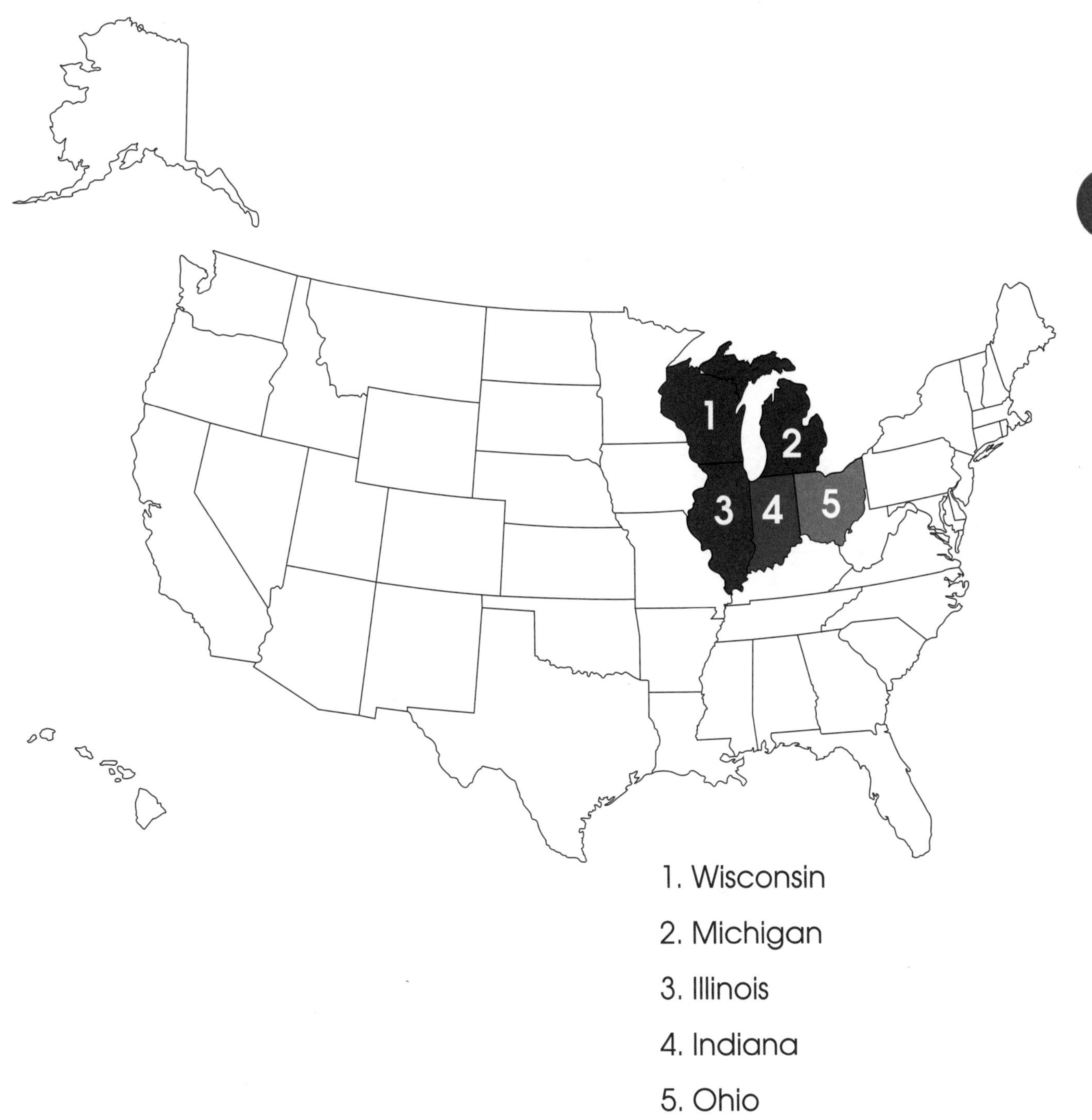

1. Wisconsin
2. Michigan
3. Illinois
4. Indiana
5. Ohio

Name____

Midwest States

Fill in the "Five Fundamental Themes of Geography" for each state. After "discovering" a state, fill in all the columns of the chart except **Regions**. When you have finished with all of the states in a section, fill in **Regions**.

Five Fundamental Themes of Geography					
Name of State	**Location** (Where is it?)	**Place** (What is it like?)	**People and Environment** (What do the people do?)	**Movement** (How do people, goods and ideas move?)	**Regions** (What are some of the common features?)

Name________________________________

Midwest States

Wisconsin

The Badger State

N
W E
S

Hayward
Brule R.
Menominee R.
1,952 FT.
St. Croix R.
MILK
TISSUE
Green Bay
NFL
Neenah
Mississippi R.
Wisconsin R.
Baraboo
Madison
Mt. Horeb
Milwaukee
Racine

Wood Violet
State Flower

Robin
State Bird

- name comes from the Chippewa Indian word *ouisconsin*, meaning *gathering of waters*
- nickname the Badger State used to describe the lead miners of the 1820s who lived in caves dug into the hillsides

Timms Hill—1,952 ft.

Circus World Museum

Racine—malted milk invented here in 1887

Green Bay Packer Hall of Fame

Neenah—facial tissue invented here in the early 1900s

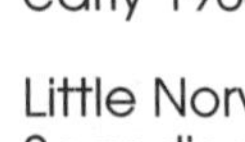

Little Norway—built in 1926, shows Scandinavian pioneer houses

National Freshwater Fishing Hall of Fame

Circle the capital city. Locate the landmarks found in the above key. Color them on the map.

Name____

Michigan

The Wolverine State

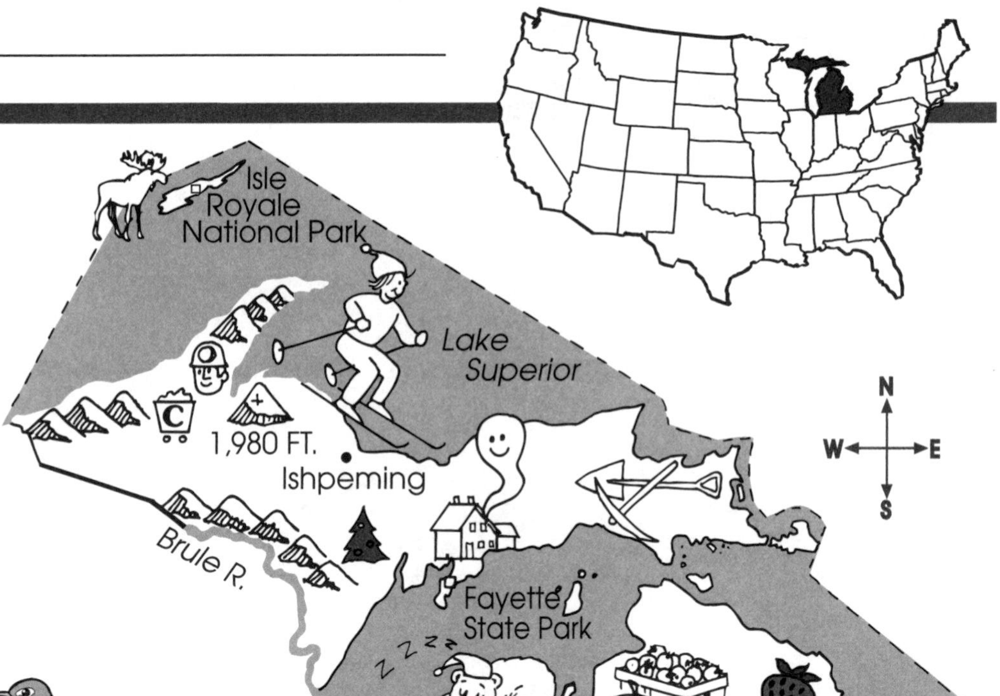

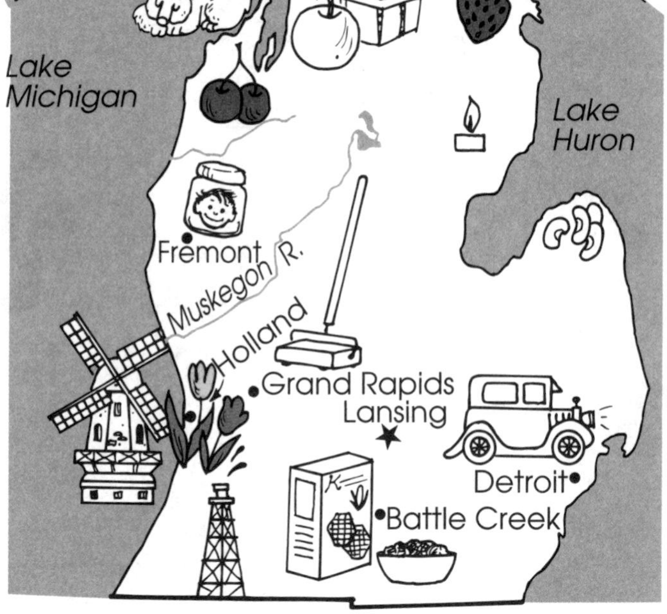

Apple Blossom
State Flower

Robin
State Bird

- named for the Indian word for Lake Michigan, *Michigama,* meaning *great lake*
- nicknamed the Wolverine State for the once-abundant wolverines that were trapped by fur traders and sold at trading posts

Mount Curwood—1,980 ft.

United States Ski Hall of Fame

Gerber—largest baby food plant in the U.S.

Fayette State Park—iron-ore smelting village from 1866 to 1890

Isle Royale—has one of the largest herds of moose in the United States

Grand Rapids—first carpet sweeper invented here in 1876 by M.R. Bissel

Battle Creek—produces the most breakfast cereal in the world

Sleeping Bear Dunes National Lakeshore—features sand dune shaped like a sleeping bear

Keweenaw Peninsula—one of the world's few sources of pure copper

Windmill Island Municipal Park—has the only authentic and operational Dutch windmill in the U.S.

Detroit—nicknamed Motor City for its large concentration of car and truck production

Circle the capital city. Locate the landmarks found in the above key. Color them on the map.

Name ____________________

Illinois

The Land of Lincoln

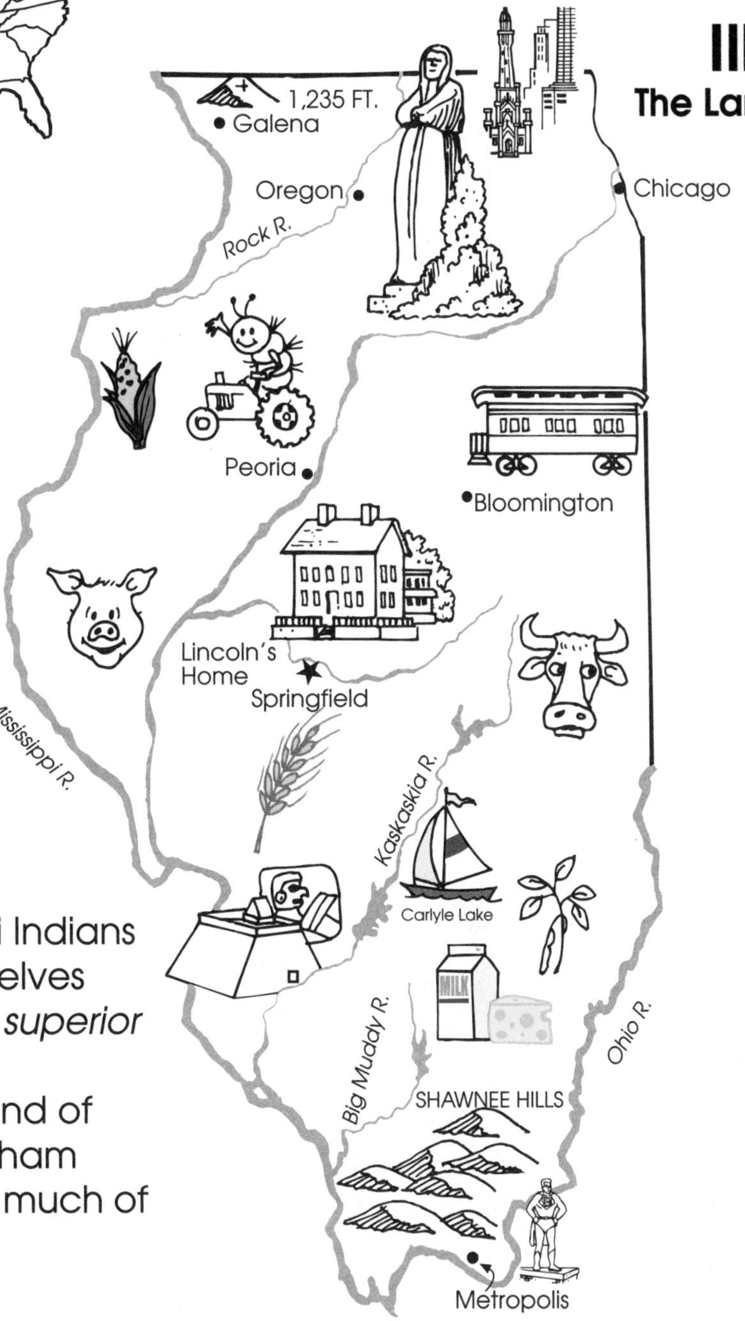

1,235 FT.
Galena
Oregon
Rock R.
Chicago
Peoria
Bloomington
Lincoln's Home
Springfield
Mississippi R.
Kaskaskia R.
Carlyle Lake
Big Muddy R.
Ohio R.
SHAWNEE HILLS
Metropolis
N
W
E
S

Native Violet
State Flower

Cardinal
State Bird

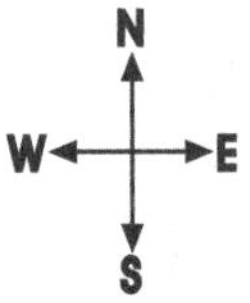

- named for the Illini Indians who called themselves *Illiniwek*, meaning *superior men*
- nicknamed the Land of Lincoln after Abraham Lincoln, who lived much of his life in the state

Charles Mound—1,235 ft.

Cahokia Mounds—65 earthen mounds made by Mississippian Indians

Peoria—headquarters of Caterpillar Co.

Lowden Memorial State Park—statue of Black Hawk honors the area's Indians

Metropolis—town centered around Superman

The Old Water Tower—survived the Great Chicago Fire in 1871

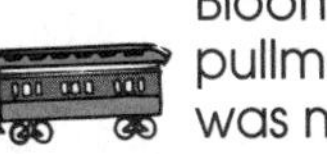

Bloomington—the first pullman sleeping car was made here in 1858

Circle the capital city. Locate the landmarks found in the above key. Color them on the map.

Name ____

Midwest States

Indiana

The Hoosier State

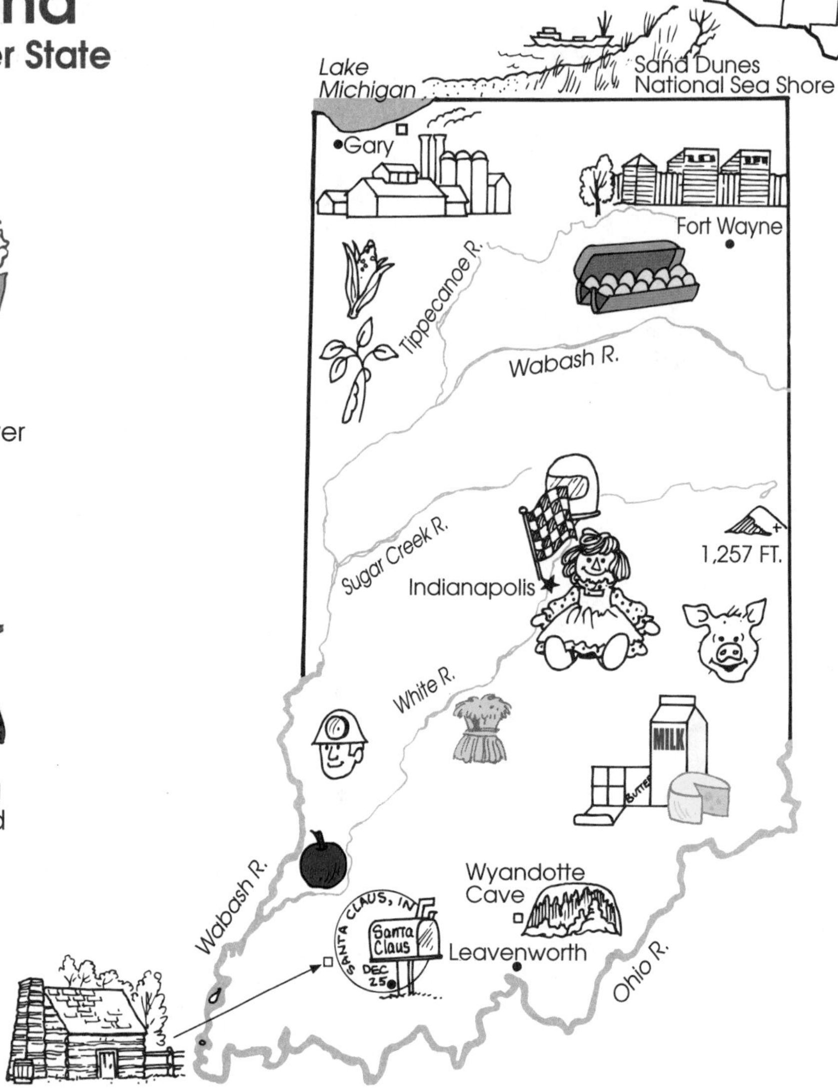

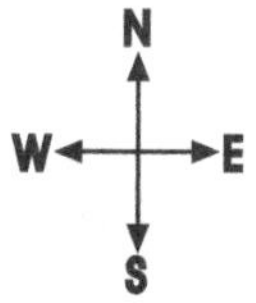

Peony
State Flower

Cardinal
State Bird

N
W E
S

Lake Michigan
Sand Dunes National Sea Shore
Gary
Fort Wayne
Tippecanoe R.
Wabash R.
Sugar Creek R.
Indianapolis
1,257 FT.
White R.
MILK
Wabash R.
Wyandotte Cave
Santa Claus
Leavenworth
Ohio R.

- name taken from the Indians living there in the 1700s - 1800s
- nickname the Hoosier State may have come from a pioneer's greeting of "*Who's here?*"

Indianapolis 500—car race

Indianapolis—Raggedy Ann doll created here in 1914

Santa Claus—remails many letters with its postmark at Christmas time

Wyandotte Cave—one of the largest caverns in the U.S.

Historic Fort Wayne—reconstructed 1816 American Army fort

Gary—has some of nation's largest steel mills

Lincoln Boyhood National Memorial—original cabin where Abraham Lincoln lived from age 7-21

Circle the capital city. Locate the landmarks found in the above key. Color them on the map.

Name________________________________

Ohio

The Buckeye State

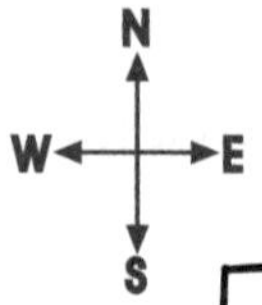

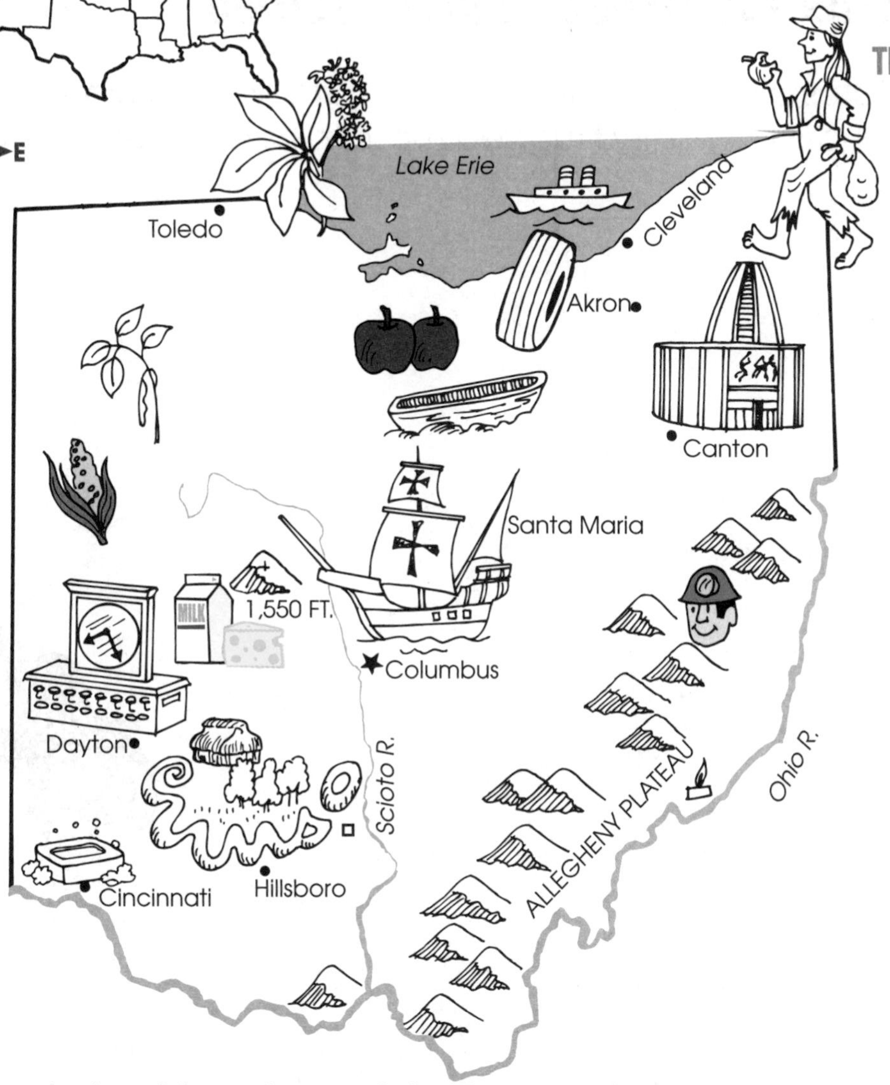

Lake Erie

Toledo

Cleveland

Akron

Canton

Santa Maria

1,550 FT.

Columbus

Dayton

Scioto R.

ALLEGHENY PLATEAU

Ohio R.

Cincinnati

Hillsboro

Cardinal
State Bird

Scarlet Carnation
State Flower

- name derived from Iroquois Indian word meaning *something great*
- nicknamed the Buckeye State for its abundance of buckeye trees

Campbell Hill—1,550 ft.

Dayton—first cash register invented here in 1879

Great Serpent Mound—prehistoric Indian burial mound, resembles a snake

Ancient Dugout Canoe—from about 1600 B.C.; discovered in Ashland County, 1977, oldest known watercraft in North America

Cincinnati—contains the largest soap factory in the U.S.

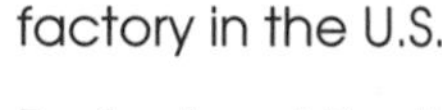

Professional Football Hall of Fame

Cleveland—shipping port

Johnny Appleseed—traveled through state, planting orchards

Akron—for many years, the largest producer of tires

Circle the capital city. Locate the landmarks found in the above key. Color them on the map.

Name____

The Northeastern States

The Northeastern States is a region with many natural harbors along the Atlantic Ocean. Inland, you will find rugged mountains and dense forests.

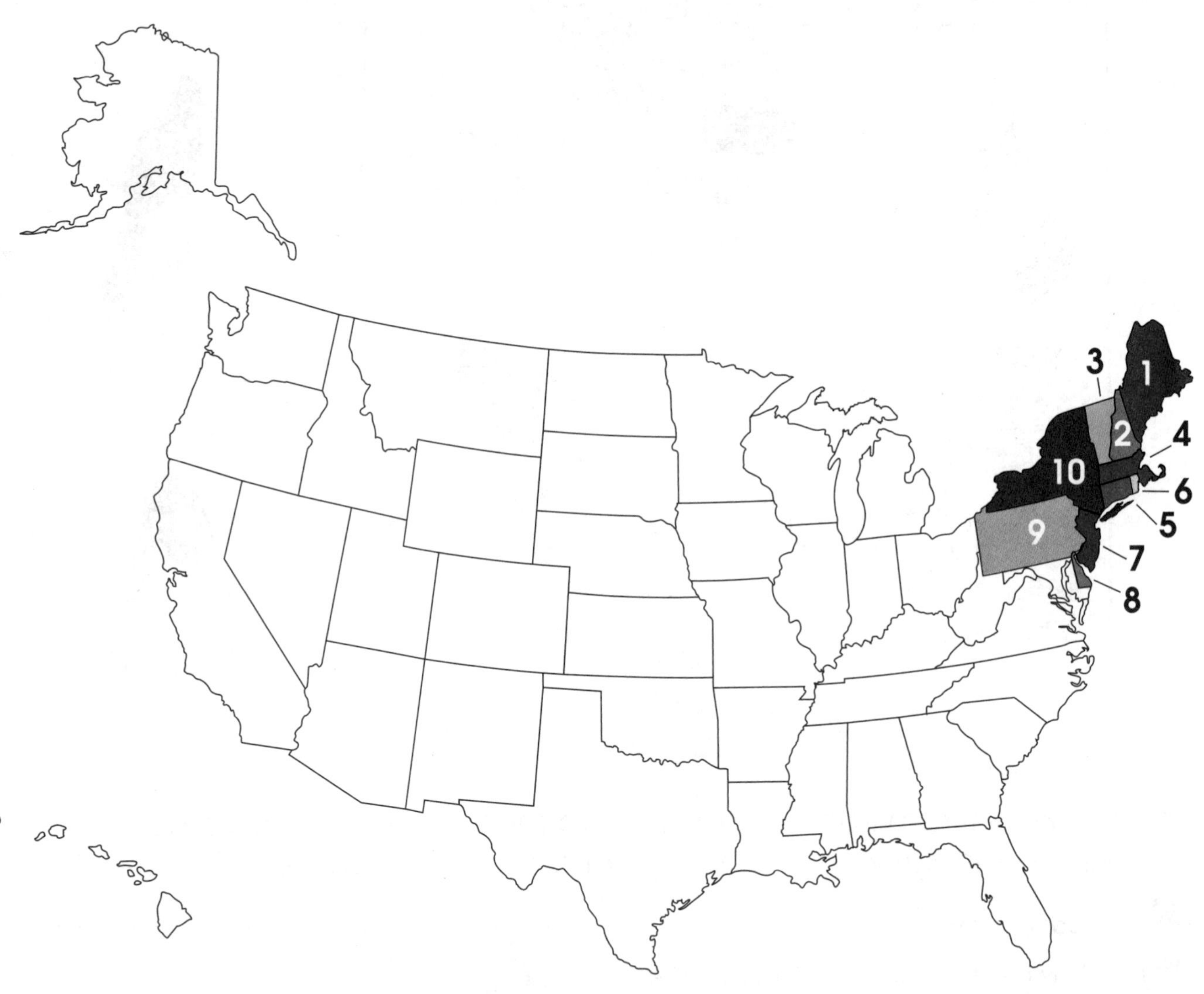

1. Maine
2. New Hampshire
3. Vermont
4. Massachusetts
5. Connecticut
6. Rhode Island
7. New Jersey
8. Delaware
9. Pennsylvania
10. New York

Name________________________________

Fill in the "Five Fundamental Themes of Geography" for each state. After "discovering" a state, fill in all the columns of the chart except **Regions**. When you have finished with all of the states in a section, fill in **Regions**.

Five Fundamental Themes of Geography					
Name of State	**Location** (Where is it?)	**Place** (What is it like?)	**People and Environment** (What do the people do?)	**Movement** (How do people, goods and ideas move?)	**Regions** (What are some of the common features?)

Name______________________________________

Northeastern States

Fill in the "Five Fundamental Themes of Geography" for each state. After "discovering" a state, fill in all the columns of the chart except **Regions**. When you have finished with all of the states in a section, fill in **Regions**.

Five Fundamental Themes of Geography					
Name of State	**Location** (Where is it?)	**Place** (What is it like?)	**People and Environment** (What do the people do?)	**Movement** (How do people, goods and ideas move?)	**Regions** (What are some of the common features?)

Name ____________________

Maine

The Pine Tree State

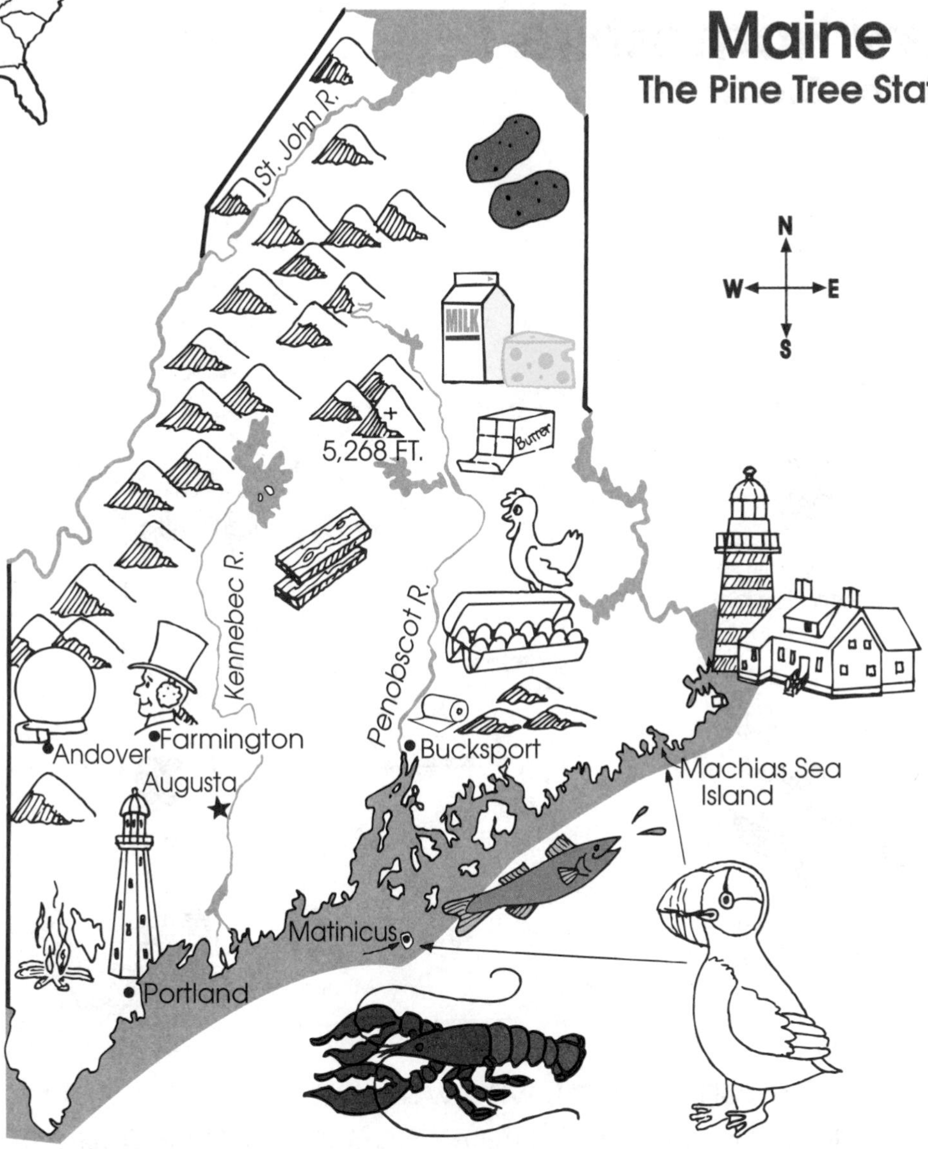

St. John R.
5,268 FT.
MILK
Butter
Kennebec R.
Penobscot R.
Andover
Farmington
Augusta
Bucksport
Machias Sea Island
Matinicus
Portland

N
W
E
S

Chickadee
State Bird

White Pine
cone and tassel
State Flower

- name believed to have originated from the English explorers who used the term *main* to refer to the *mainland,* as opposed to the islands
- nicknamed the Pine Tree State for the abundance of pine tree forests

Mount Katahdin—5,268 ft.

Matinicus—sanctuary for puffins

Satellite Earth Station—sends and receives orbiting satellites' signals

Sebago Lake—Camp Fire Girls originated here in 1910

Farmington—Earmuff Capital of the World—first earmuffs patented here in 1873

West Quoddy Head Light—located on land that is the most easterly point of U.S.

Portland Head Light—among the best known lighthouses in the U.S.

Circle the capital city. Locate the landmarks found in the above key. Color them on the map.

Name____

Northeastern States

New Hampshire

The Granite State

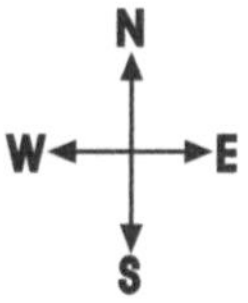

N
W E
S

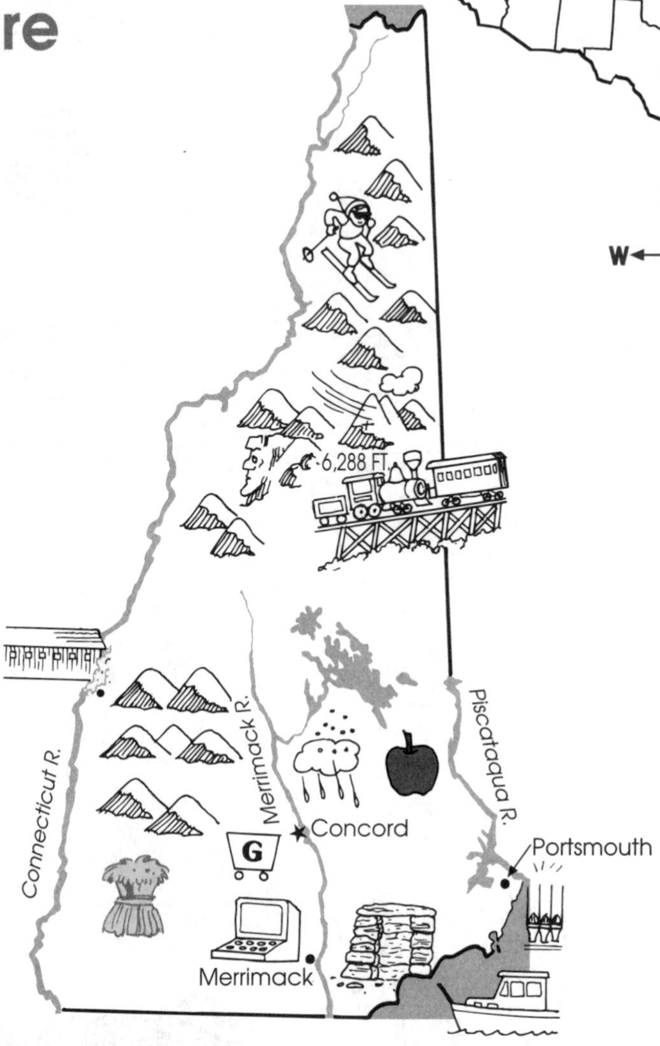

6,288 FT.

Piscataqua R.

Merrimack R.

Connecticut R.

Concord

Portsmouth

Merrimack

Purple Lilac
State Flower

Purple Finch
State Bird

- named by John Mason, who was from the county of Hampshire in England
- nickname the Granite State reflects the vast deposits of granite in the state

Mount Washington—6,288 ft.

Waterville Valley—World Cup skiing competitions

Mount Washington—first cog railway in the United States

Merrimack—one of the largest computer companies in the U.S. located here

Concord—first place artificial rain was used to fight a forest fire

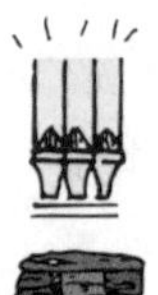

Brattle Organ—in St. John's Episcopal Church, the oldest pipe organ in the U.S.

America's Stonehenge—one of the largest and possibly oldest man-made stone constructions in the U.S.

Windsor-Cornish Covered Bridge—one of the longest covered bridges in the world

Old Man of the Mountain—natural formation of granite

Circle the capital city. Locate the landmarks found in the above key. Color them on the map.

Name____

Vermont

The Green Mountain State

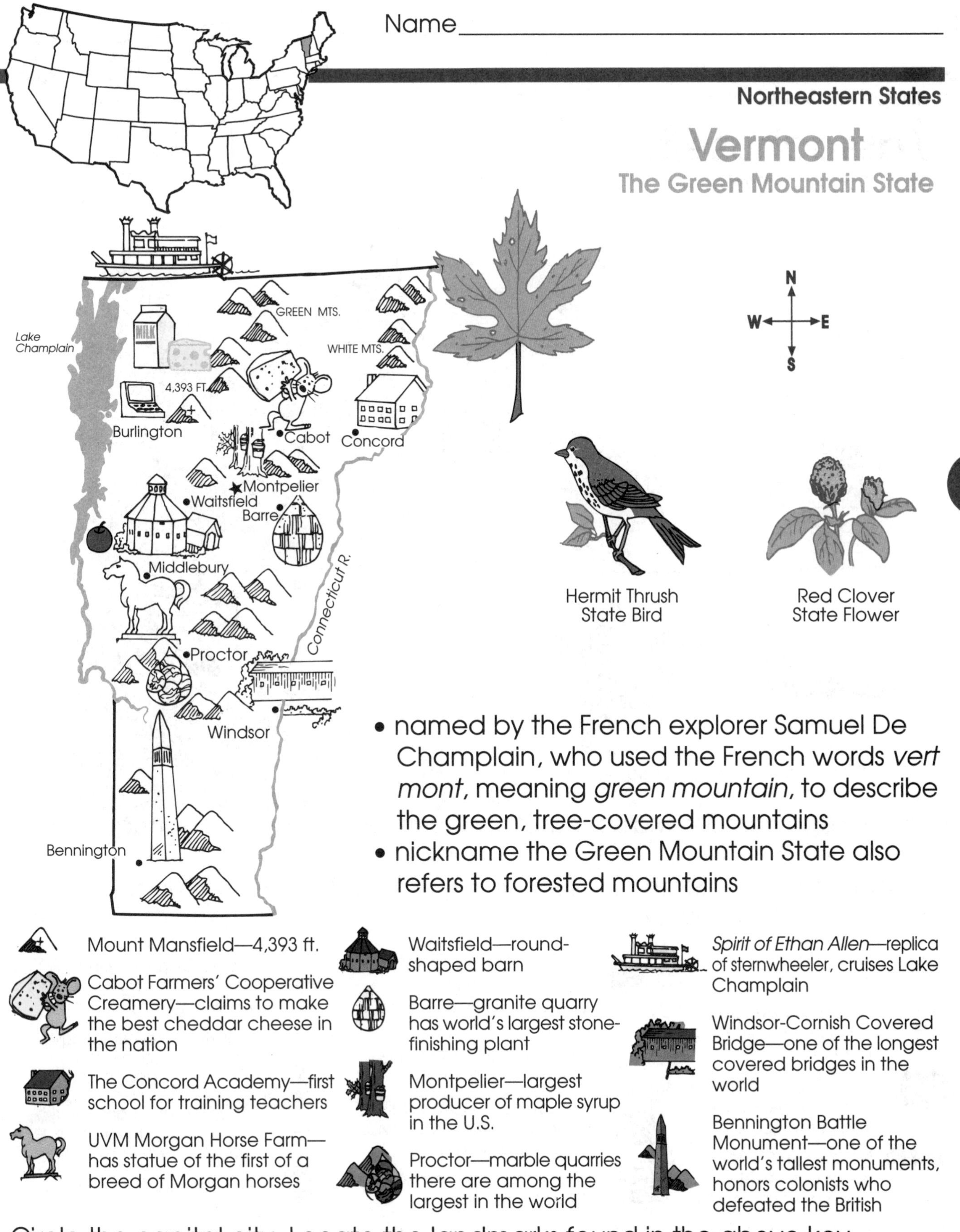

Hermit Thrush
State Bird

Red Clover
State Flower

- named by the French explorer Samuel De Champlain, who used the French words *vert mont*, meaning *green mountain*, to describe the green, tree-covered mountains
- nickname the Green Mountain State also refers to forested mountains

Mount Mansfield—4,393 ft.

Cabot Farmers' Cooperative Creamery—claims to make the best cheddar cheese in the nation

The Concord Academy—first school for training teachers

UVM Morgan Horse Farm—has statue of the first of a breed of Morgan horses

Waitsfield—round-shaped barn

Barre—granite quarry has world's largest stone-finishing plant

Montpelier—largest producer of maple syrup in the U.S.

Proctor—marble quarries there are among the largest in the world

Spirit of Ethan Allen—replica of sternwheeler, cruises Lake Champlain

Windsor-Cornish Covered Bridge—one of the longest covered bridges in the world

Bennington Battle Monument—one of the world's tallest monuments, honors colonists who defeated the British

Circle the capital city. Locate the landmarks found in the above key. Color them on the map.

Name____

Northeastern States

Massachusetts

The Bay State

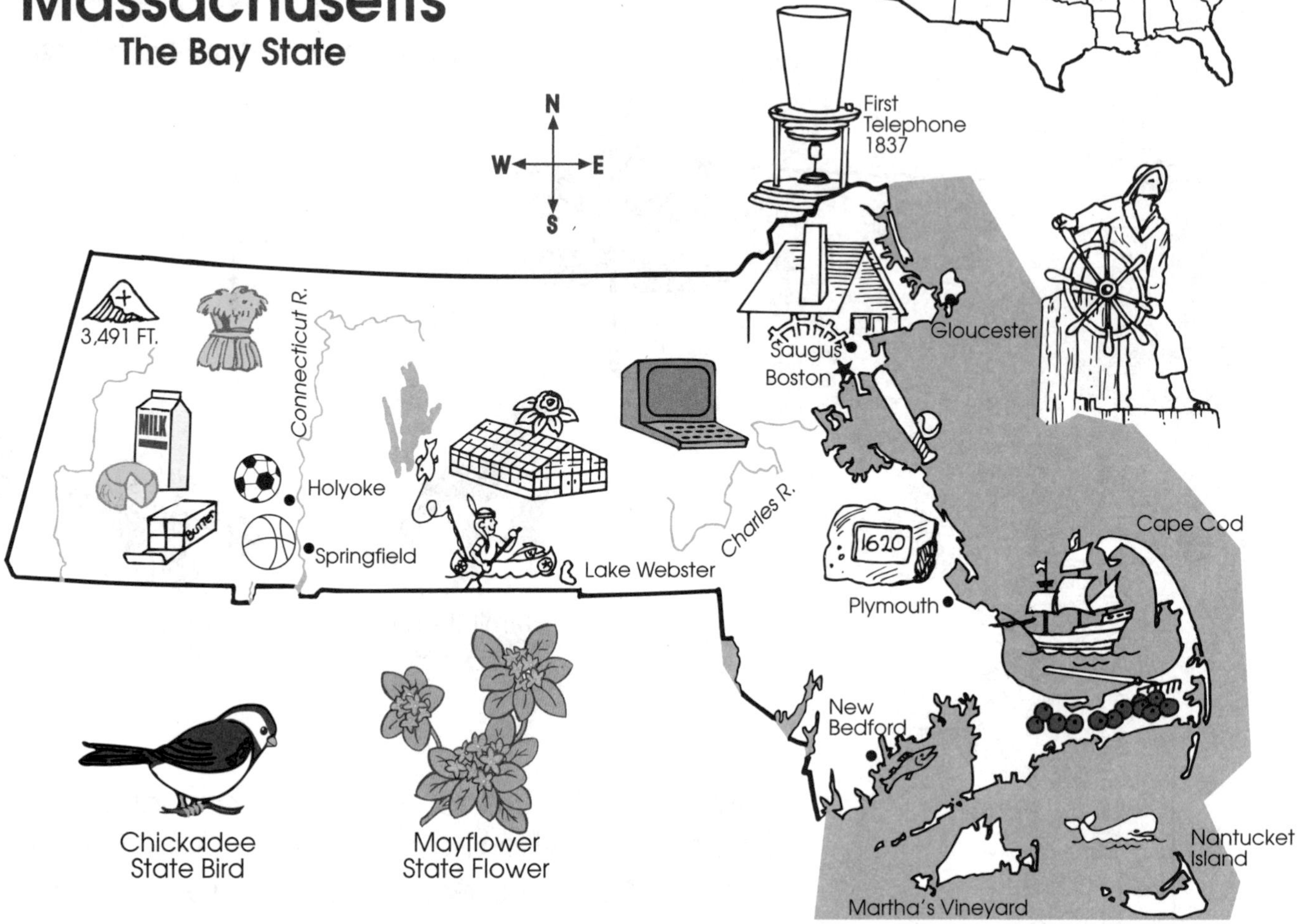

N
W E
S

First Telephone 1837

3,491 FT.

Connecticut R.

Holyoke

Springfield

Lake Webster

Charles R.

Saugus

Boston

Gloucester

Cape Cod

1620

Plymouth

New Bedford

Nantucket Island

Martha's Vineyard

Chickadee
State Bird

Mayflower
State Flower

- name taken from the Massachusetts Indian tribe, whose name means *near the great hill*
- nickname the Bay State refers to Massachusetts Bay, where Puritans established their colony

Mount Greylock—3,491 ft.

Holyoke—volleyball was developed here in 1895

Saugus Iron Works—made and exported iron in the 1600s

Nantucket Island—resort area that was once a whaling port

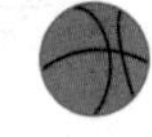

Springfield—basketball invented here in 1891, contains Basketball Hall Of Fame

Boston—first World Series played here in 1903

Gloucester—statue built to honor all its fishermen who have died at sea

Plymouth Rock—marks where the Pilgrims landed

Cape Cod—Pilgrims landed here before going on to Plymouth

Webster Lake—Algonquian Indians called this lake *Chargoggagoggmanchau-gagoggchaubunagungam-gaug,*which means *You fish on your side, I fish on my side, nobody fish in the middle*

First Telephone—1876 in Boston

Circle the capital city. Locate the landmarks found in the above key. Color them on the map.

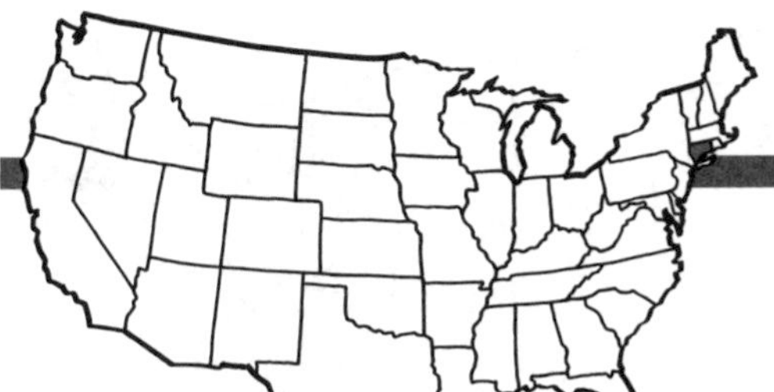

Name ________________________________

Connecticut

The Constitution State

2,380 FT.

Naugatuck R.

Connecticut R.

Hartford

Bristol

Housatonic R.

Hadlyme

Groton

Shelton

East Haven

Stratford

Bridgeport

Norwalk

N

W E

S

Robin
State Bird

Mountain Laurel
State Flower

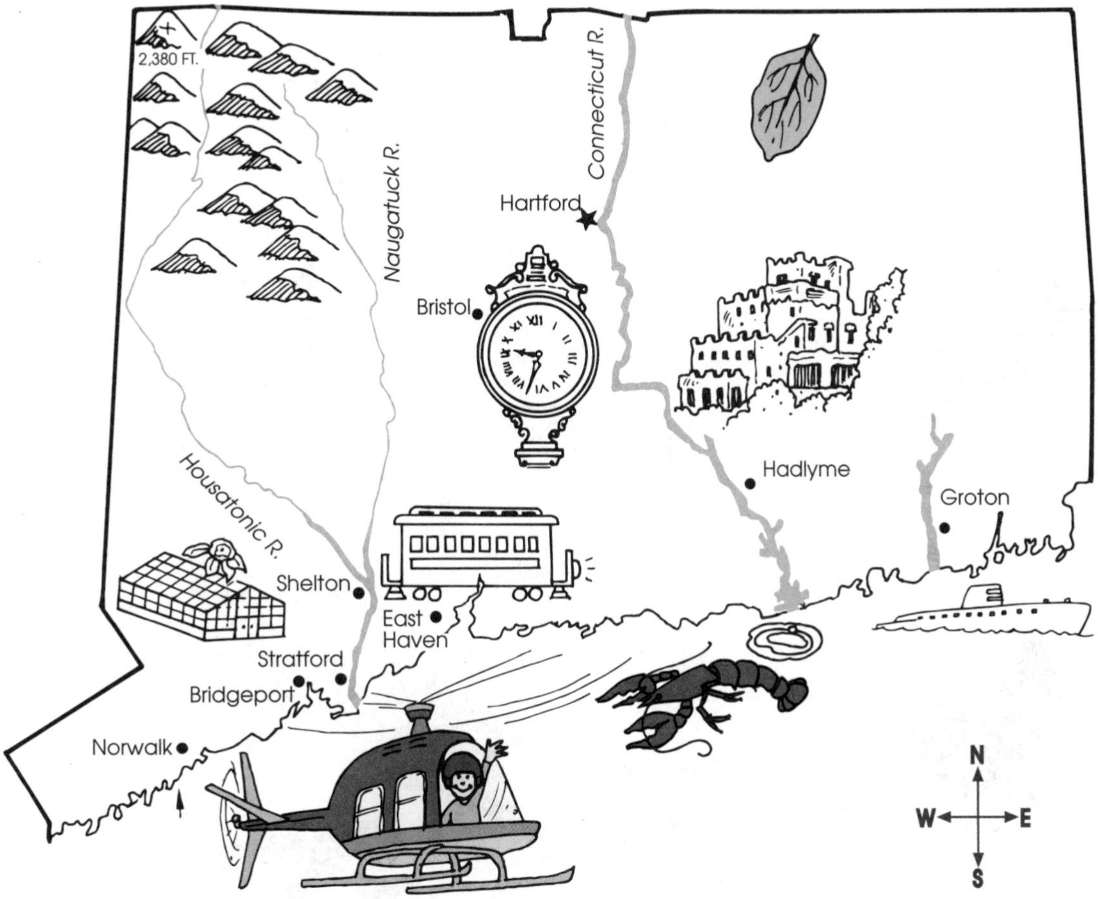

- name came from the Mohican Indian word *Quinnehtukqet,* meaning *on the long tidal river,* which referred to where they lived in relation to the Connecticut River
- nickname the Constitution State refers to Connecticut's colonial laws being used as one of the models for the Constitution of the United States

Mount Frissel—2,380 ft.

Gillette Castlle

Great American Clock and Watch Museum

Groton—United States Naval Submarine Base

Circle the capital city. Locate the landmarks found in the above key. Color them on the map.

Name________________________________

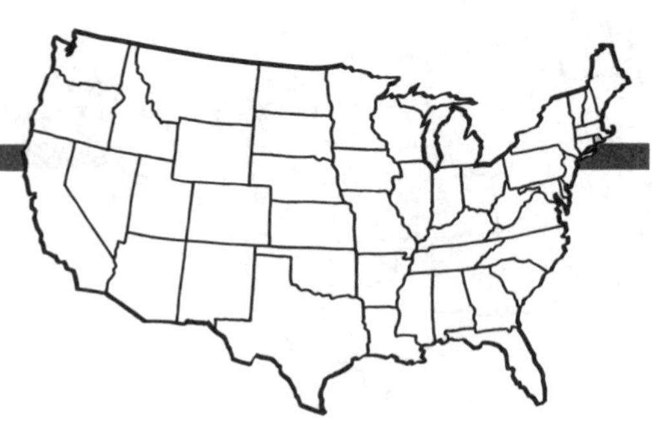

Northeastern States

Rhode Island

The Ocean State

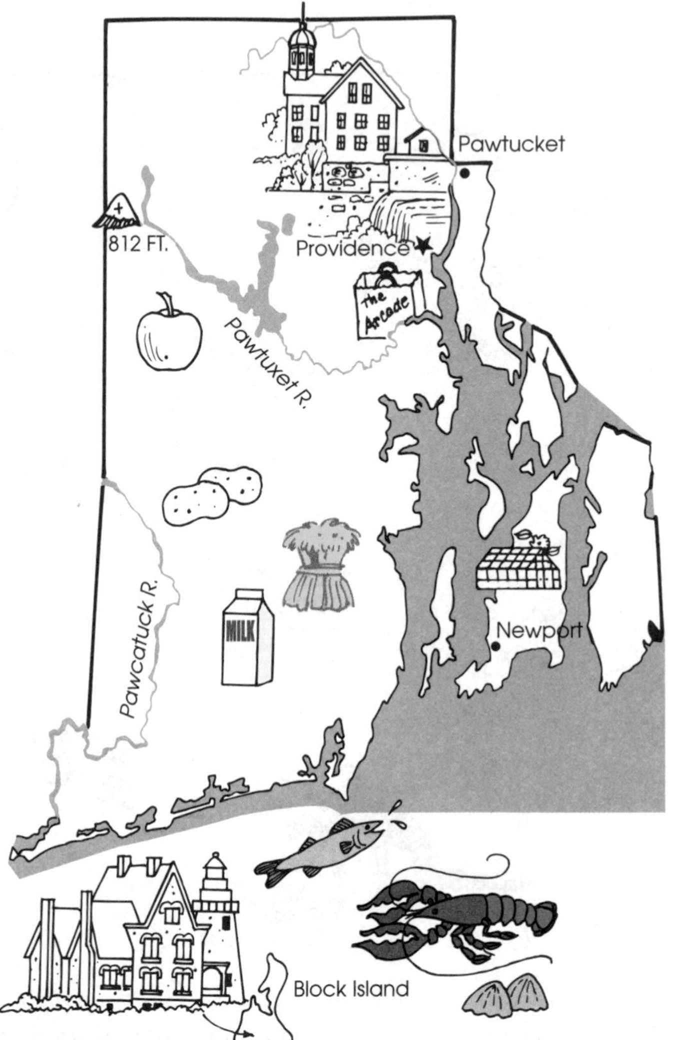

Violet
State Flower

Rhode Island Red
State Bird

- name is officially the State of Rhode Island and Providence Plantations, the largest of the state's islands being called Rhode Island and the towns on the mainland being called Providence Plantations
- nicknamed the Ocean State

Jerimoth Hill—812 ft.

Slater Mill Historic Site—one of the first textile mills in North America

Southeast Lighthouse

The Arcade—oldest indoor shopping mall in the U.S., built in 1828

Circle the capital city. Locate the landmarks found in the above key. Color them on the map.

Name ____________________

New Jersey

The Garden State

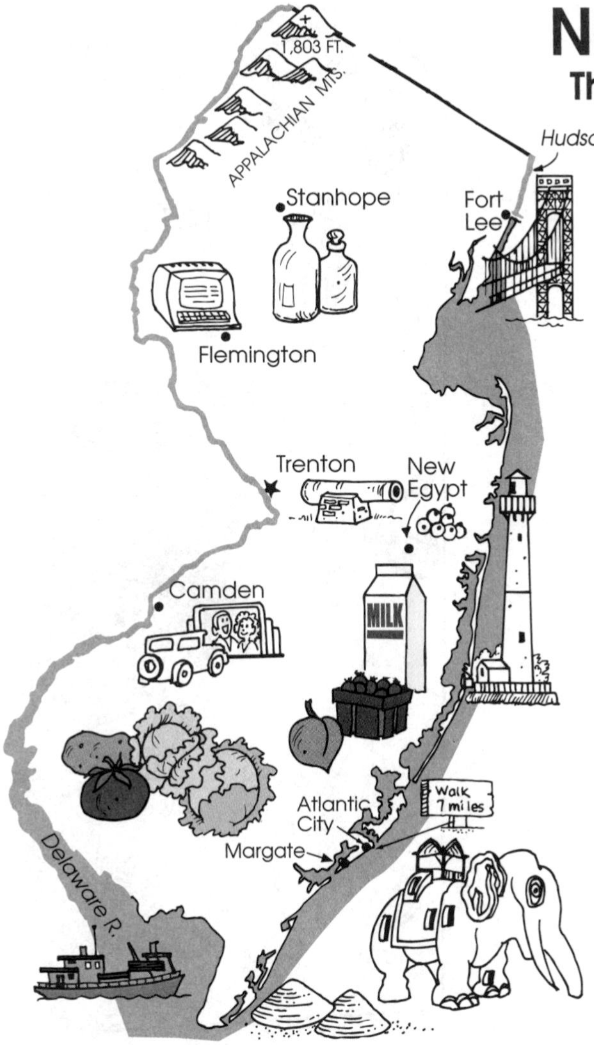

Hudson R.

1,803 FT.

APPALACHIAN MTS.

Stanhope

Fort Lee

Flemington

Trenton

New Egypt

Camden

MILK

Atlantic City

Walk 7 miles

Margate

Delaware R.

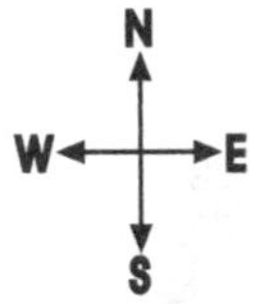

N

W E

S

Eastern Goldfinch
State Bird

Purple Violet
State Flower

- named in 1664 by Sir George Carteret after the Isle of Jersey in England
- nicknamed the Garden State for its numerous truck farms, flower gardens and orchards

 High Point—1,803 ft.

 Margate—a 100-year-old house shaped like an elephant, now a museum

 Flemington—leader in machinery and computer assembly

 George Washington Bridge—thousands use this to commute from New Jersey to New York City

 Old Barracks—British soldiers used these barracks during the French and Indian Wars

 Camden—first drive-in theater opened here on June 6, 1933

 New Egypt—Ocean Spray first made

Atlantic City—7-mile boardwalk and casinos make this popular for tourists

 Waterloo Village—a restored town of the 1700s

Circle the capital city. Locate the landmarks found in the above key. Color them on the map.

Name____

Northeastern States

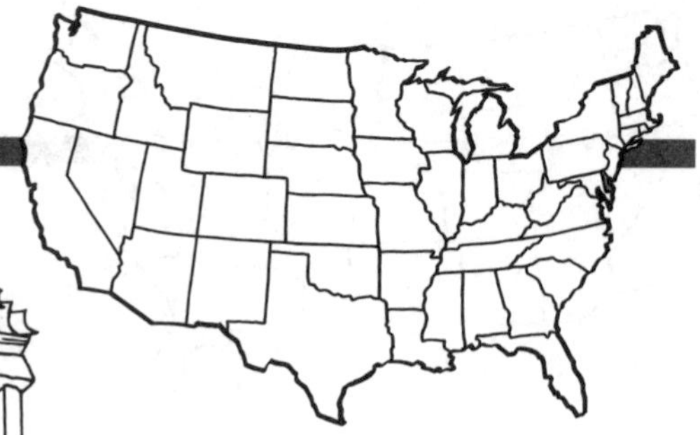

Delaware

The First State

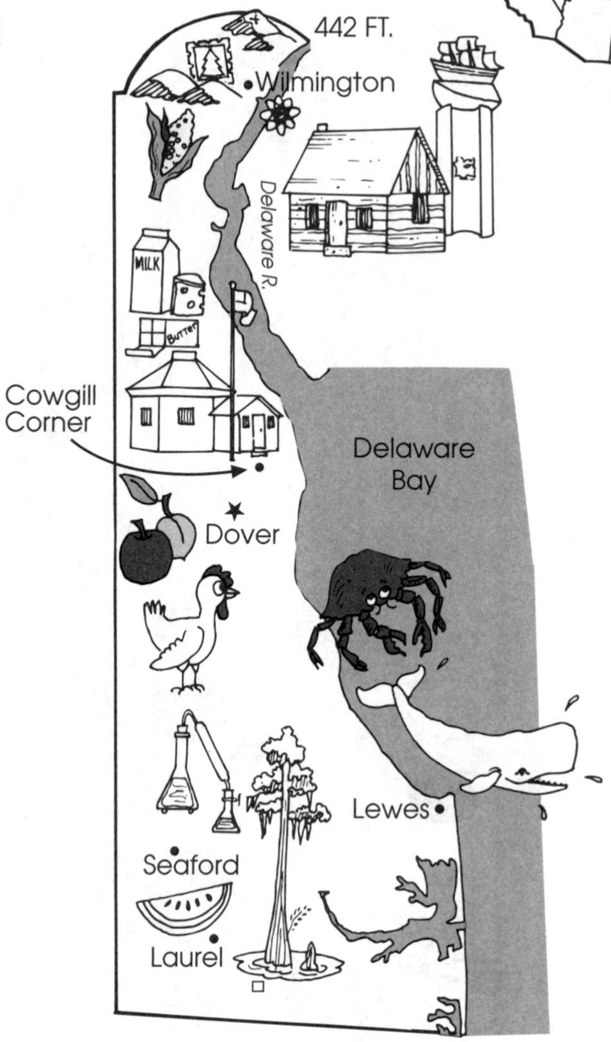

442 FT.
Wilmington
Delaware R.
MILK
BUTTER
Cowgill
Corner
Delaware
Bay
Dover
Lewes
Seaford
Laurel

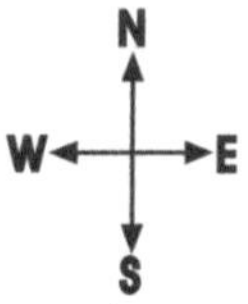

N
W
E
S

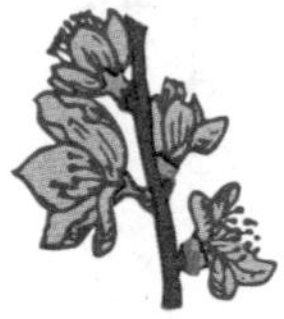

Peach Blossom
State Flower

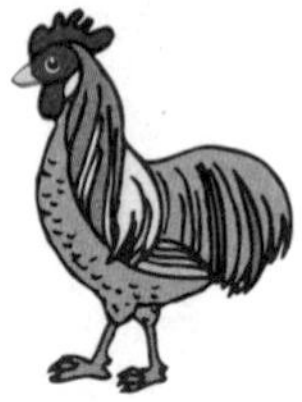

Blue Hen Chicken
State Bird

- named for the governor of Virginia, Lord De La Warr
- nickname the First State resulted from being the first state to approve the United States Constitution

 Wilmington—Chemical Capital of the World

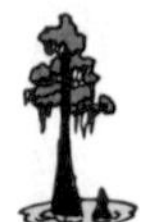

 Great Cypress Swamp—contains the most bald cypress trees found in U.S.

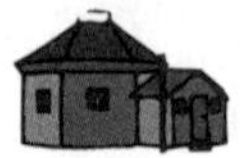

 The Octagonal School

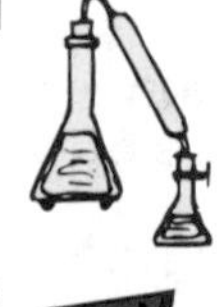

 Seaford-Nylon Capital of the World—nylon first made by Du Pont Company in 1939

 Annual Watermelon Festival

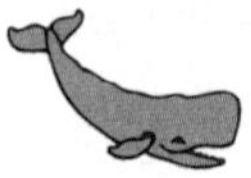

 Lewes—whaling colony settled by the Dutch in 1631

 First Christmas Seals—sold in Wilmington Post Office in 1907

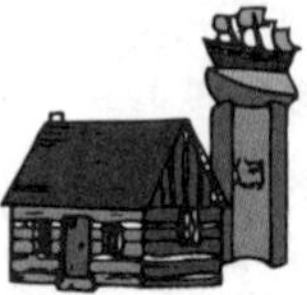

 Fort Christina—site of the first permanent settlement of Swedes and Finns in Delaware

Circle the capital city. Locate the landmarks found in the above key. Color them on the map.

Name ________________________________

Pennsylvania

The Keystone State

Mountain Laurel
State Flower

Ruffed Grouse
State Bird

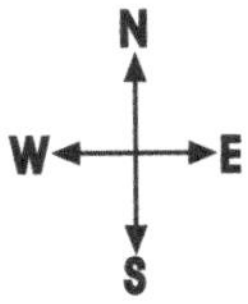

N
W E
S

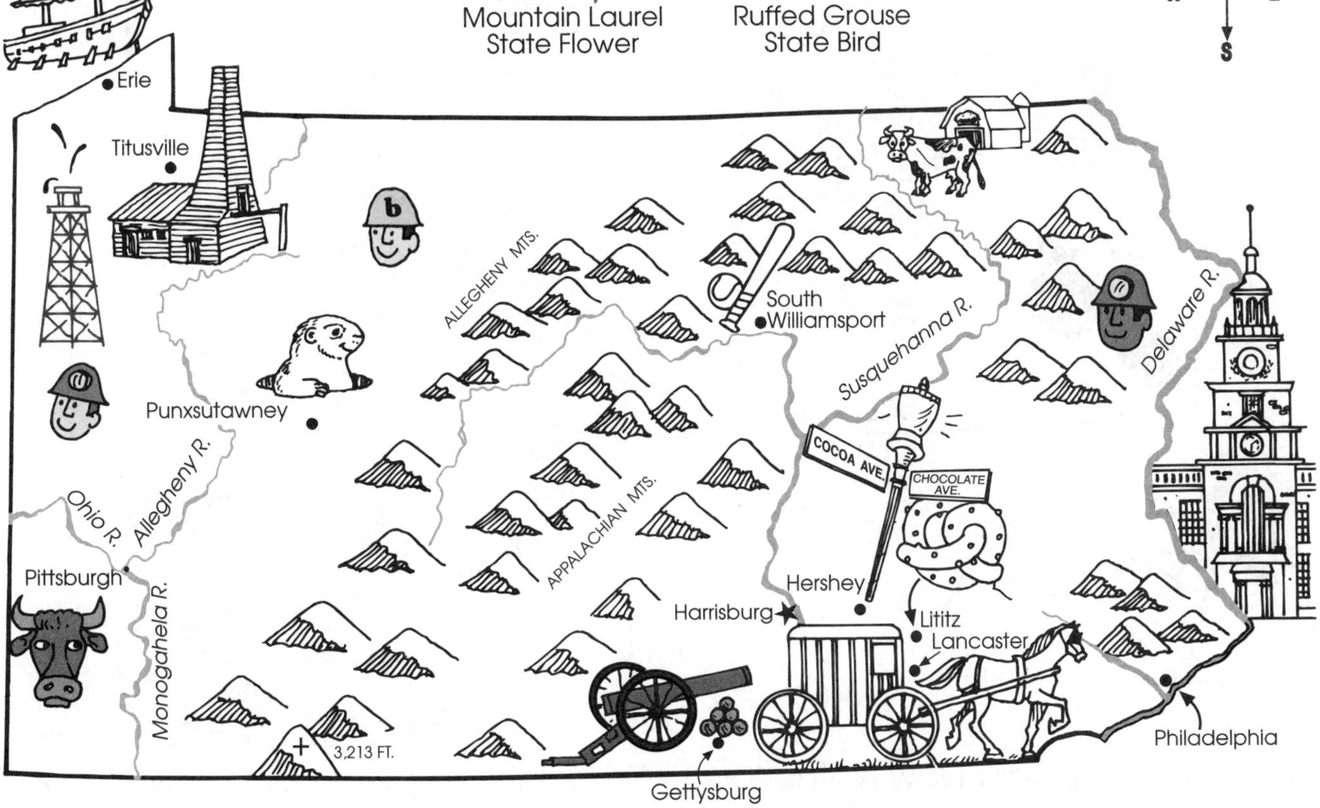

Niagara
Erie
Titusville
Punxsutawney
Pittsburgh
Ohio R.
Allegheny R.
Monogahela R.
ALLEGHENY MTS.
APPALACHIAN MTS.
South Williamsport
Susquehanna R.
Delaware R.
COCOA AVE.
CHOCOLATE AVE.
Hershey
Harrisburg
Lititz
Lancaster
Philadelphia
Gettysburg
3,213 FT.

- named in 1681 for William Penn, means *Penn's Woods*
- nicknamed the Keystone State because of its location in the center of the thirteen original colonies

Mount Davis—3,213 ft.

Flagship Niagara—used by Oliver Perry to defeat the British in War of 1812

Lititz—first pretzel bakery opened in 1861

Hershey—world's largest chocolate and cocoa factory, established in 1905

Little League Baseball World Series

Drake's Well Museum—site of the first commercial oil well in America

Ground Hog Day Festivities

Pennsylvania Farm Museum of Landis Valley

Independence Hall—Declaration of Independence signed here in 1776

Circle the capital city. Locate the landmarks found in the above key. Color them on the map.

Name ____

Northeastern States

New York

The Empire State

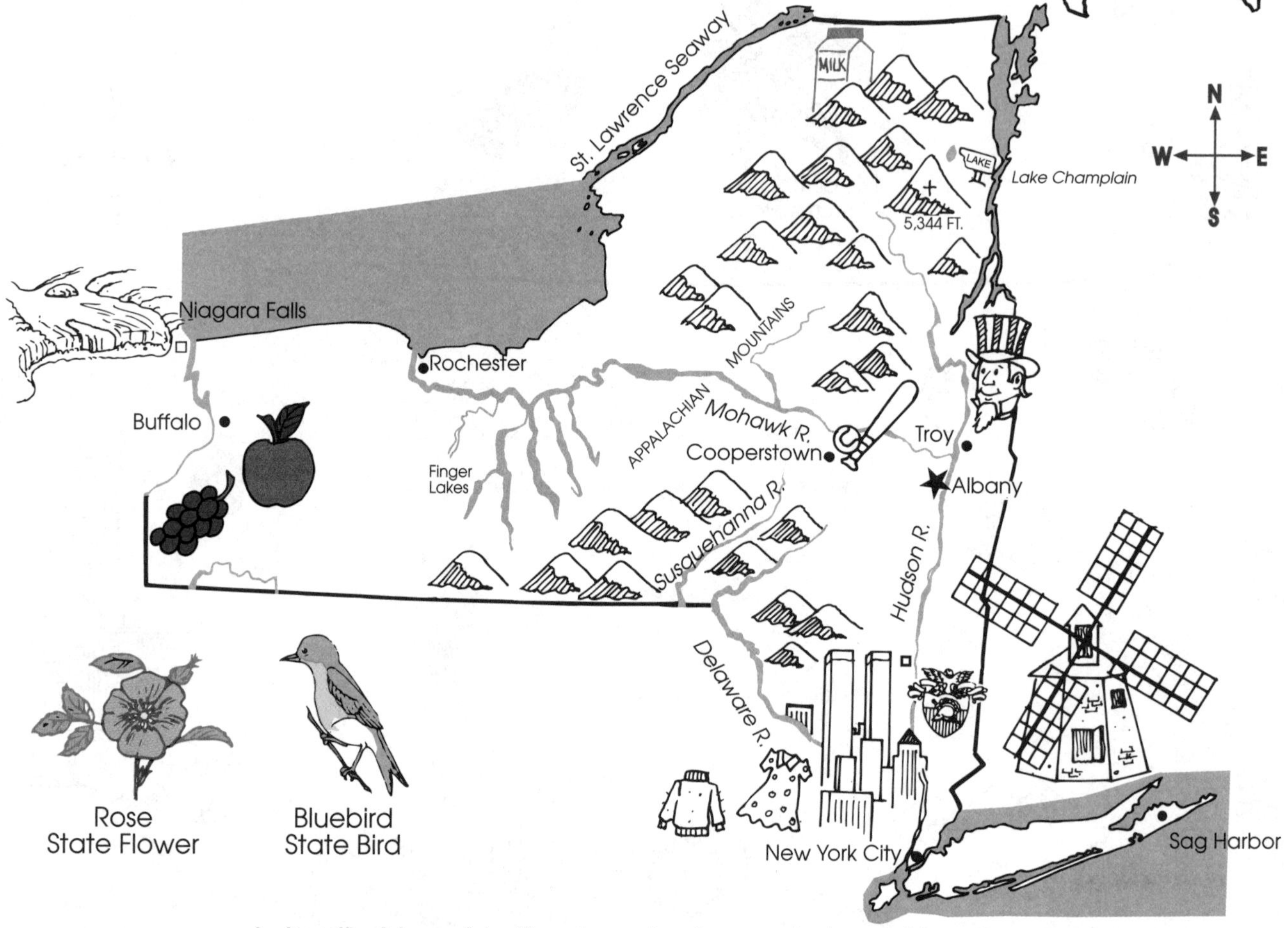

St. Lawrence Seaway
MILK
Lake Champlain
LAKE
5,344 FT.
N
W
E
S
Niagara Falls
Rochester
Buffalo
MOUNTAINS
APPALACHIAN
Mohawk R.
Troy
Cooperstown
Albany
Finger Lakes
Susquehanna R.
Hudson R.
Delaware R.
New York City
Sag Harbor

Rose
State Flower

Bluebird
State Bird

- name was originally New Netherland when claimed by the Dutch; was then claimed by the English and the name was changed to New York to honor the Duke of York
- nickname the Empire State possibly related to a comment made by George Washington in 1783 when he anticipated that New York would become the core of a new empire

Mount Marcy—5,344 ft.

New York City—center of publishing industry and leads women's clothing production in the United States

West Point—U.S. Military Academy

Niagara Falls—most famous waterfall in the world

Lake Placid—world famous resort with a glacial lake

National Baseball Hall of Fame

Sag Harbor—windmill once used here as a major source of energy

Uncle Sam—symbol originated in Troy

Circle the capital city. Locate the landmarks found in the above key. Color them on the map.

Name_______________________________________

The Southeastern States

The Southeastern States is a region with many different kinds of land formations. It has long jagged coastlines, rugged mountains, deep pine forests, steep valleys and beautiful rivers.

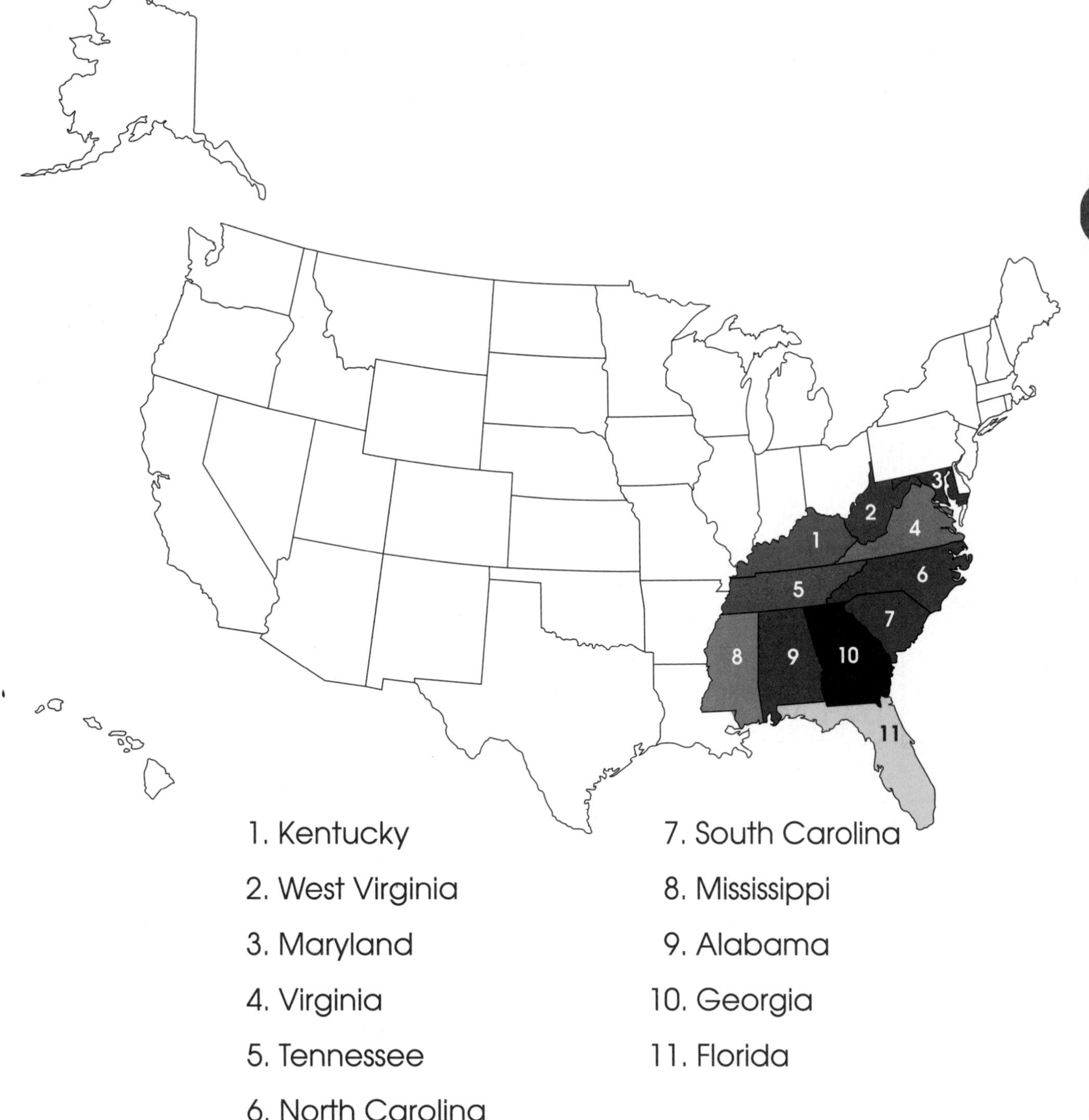

1. Kentucky
2. West Virginia
3. Maryland
4. Virginia
5. Tennessee
6. North Carolina
7. South Carolina
8. Mississippi
9. Alabama
10. Georgia
11. Florida

Name____

Southeastern States

Fill in the "Five Fundamental Themes of Geography" for each state. After "discovering" a state, fill in all the columns of the chart except **Regions**. When you have finished with all of the states in a section, fill in **Regions**.

Five Fundamental Themes of Geography					
Name of State	**Location** (Where is it?)	**Place** (What is it like?)	**People and Environment** (What do the people do?)	**Movement** (How do people, goods and ideas move?)	**Regions** (What are some of the common features?)

Name ______________________________

Five Fundamental Themes of Geography

Name of State	Location (Where is it?)	Place (What is it like?)	People and Environment (What do the people do?)	Movement (How do people, goods and ideas move?)	Regions (What are some of the common features?)

Name____

Southeastern States

Kentucky

The Bluegrass State

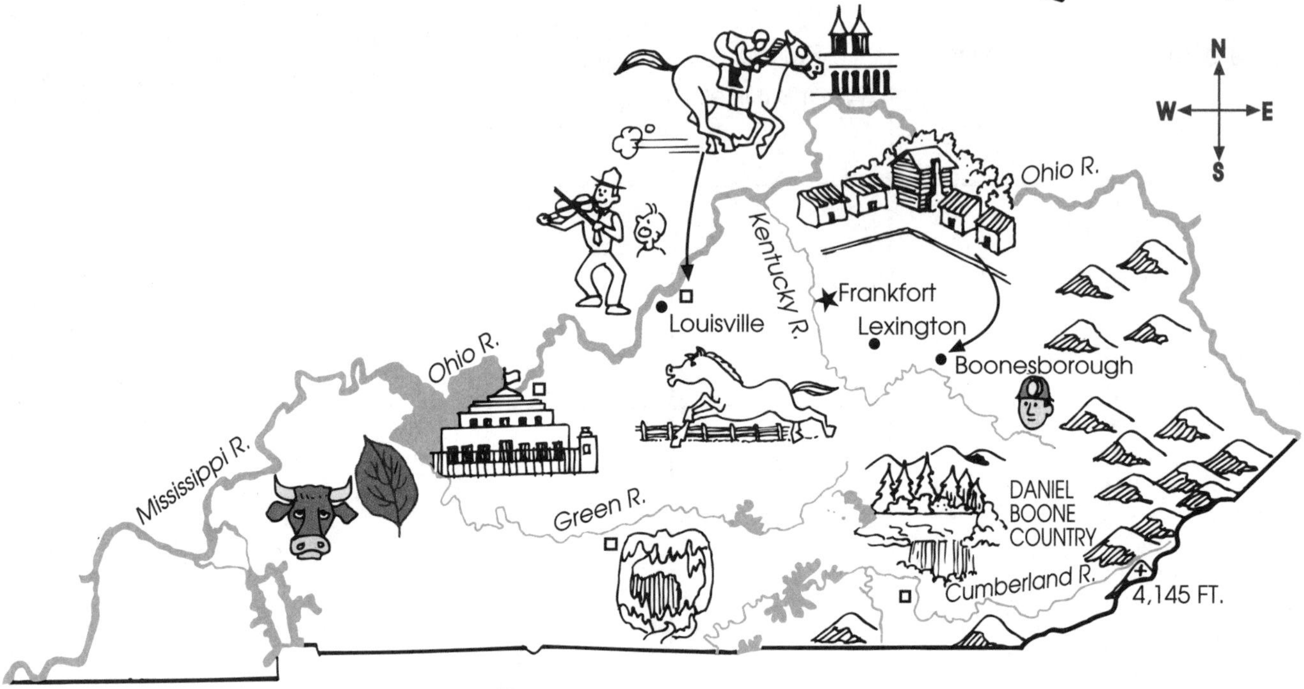

N
W E
S
Ohio R.
Kentucky R.
Frankfort
Louisville
Lexington
Boonesborough
Ohio R.
Mississippi R.
Green R.
DANIEL
BOONE
COUNTRY
Cumberland R.
4,145 FT.

Goldenrod
State Flower

Cardinal
State Bird

- name derived from the Cherokee Indian word *kentake,* which means *meadow* or *pasture*
- nicknamed the Bluegrass State for the blue blossoms on the grass of this region

Black Mountain—4,145 ft.

Fort Boonesborough State Park—reconstructed fort founded by Daniel Boone

Fort Knox Gold Vault—nation's gold depository

Kentucky Derby—at Churchill Downs Race Track; oldest horse racing event in U.S.

Mammoth Cave National Park—world's longest continuous cave system

Louisville American Bluegrass Music Fest

Lexington—thousands of thoroughbred horses raised on horse farms here

Cumberland Falls—nicknamed Niagara of the South

Circle the capital city. Locate the landmarks found in the above key. Color them on the map.

Name ____________________

West Virginia

The Mountain State

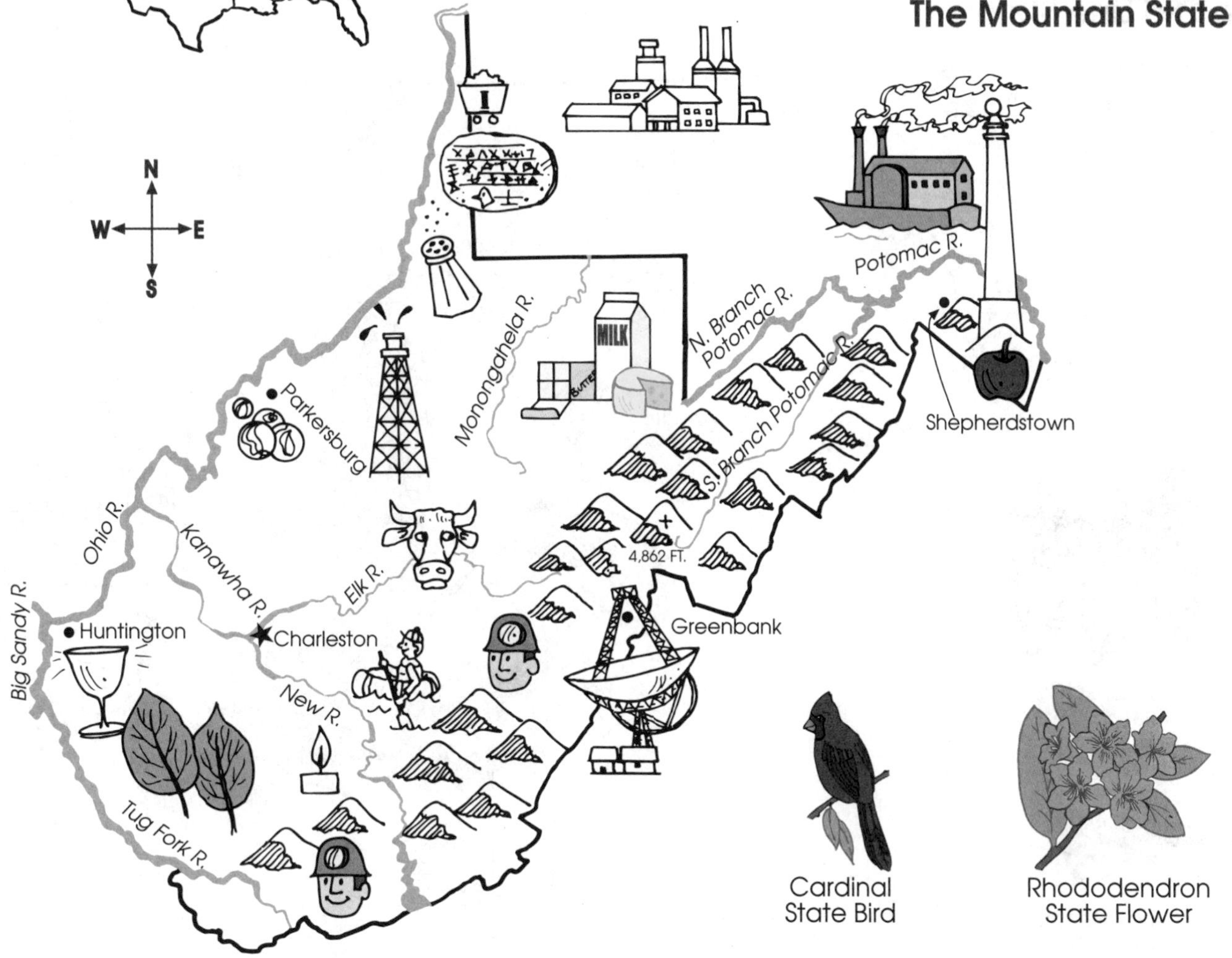

Potomac R.
N. Branch Potomac R.
S. Branch Potomac R.
Monongahela R.
Shepherdstown
Parkersburg
Ohio R.
Kanawha R.
Elk R.
4,862 FT.
Greenbank
Big Sandy R.
Huntington
Charleston
New R.
Tug Fork R.

Cardinal
State Bird

Rhododendron
State Flower

- named when northwestern counties separated from Virginia during the Civil War and sided with the North
- nicknamed the Mountain State for its rugged mountains, steep hills and narrow valleys

Spruce Knob—4,862 ft.

Grave Creek Mounds—largest conical burial mound, built 2,000 years ago

Marshall County—underground salt mines

Huntington—famous for its glassware and pottery

Shepherdstown—monument to James Rumsey, inventor of the steamboat

Parkersburg—glass marble manufacturing center of U.S.

National Radio Astronomy Observatory

Circle the capital city. Locate the landmarks found in the above key. Color them on the map.

Name ____________________________________

Maryland

The Old Line State

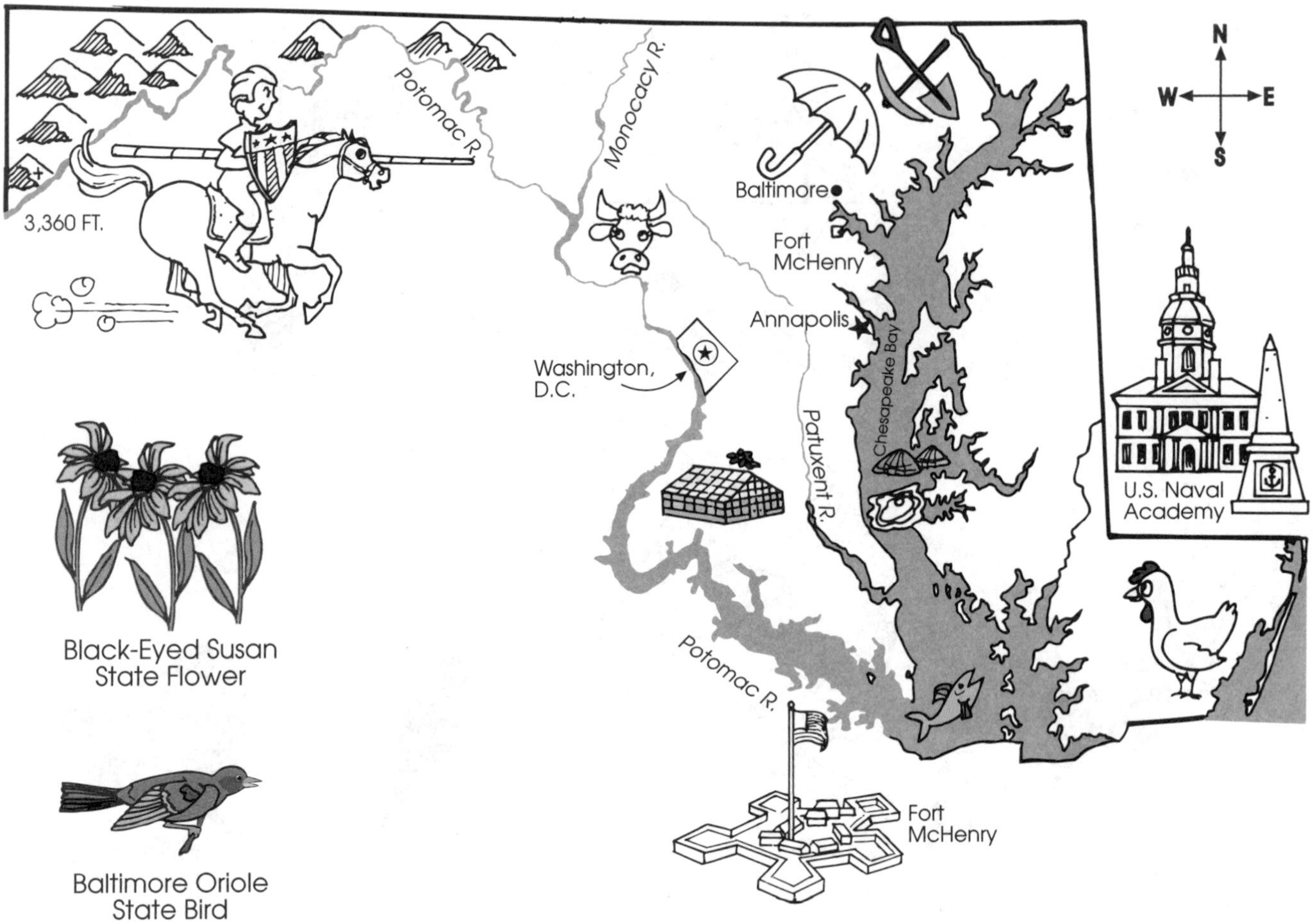

3,360 FT.
Potomac R.
Monocacy R.
Baltimore
Fort McHenry
Annapolis
Washington, D.C.
Chesapeake Bay
Patuxent R.
Potomac R.
U.S. Naval Academy
Fort McHenry
N
W
E
S

Black-Eyed Susan
State Flower

Baltimore Oriole
State Bird

- named in 1632 for Queen Henrietta Maria, the wife of England's King Charles I
- nicknamed the Old Line State in honor of the troops from Maryland who fought so bravely on the line during the Revolutionary War

Backbone Mountain—3,360 ft.

Fort McHenry National Monument and Shrine—Frances Scott Key wrote the "Star-Spangled Banner" here during the War of 1812

State Jousting Championships—held each year

Baltimore—first umbrella factory in the U.S., established in 1828

Washington, D.C.—George Washington chose this spot for the U.S. capital

U.S. Naval Academy

Circle the capital city. Locate the landmarks found in the above key. Color them on the map.

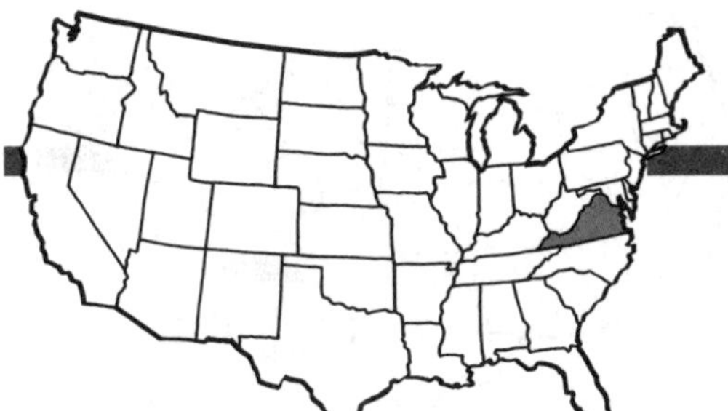

Name________________________________

Virginia

Old Dominion

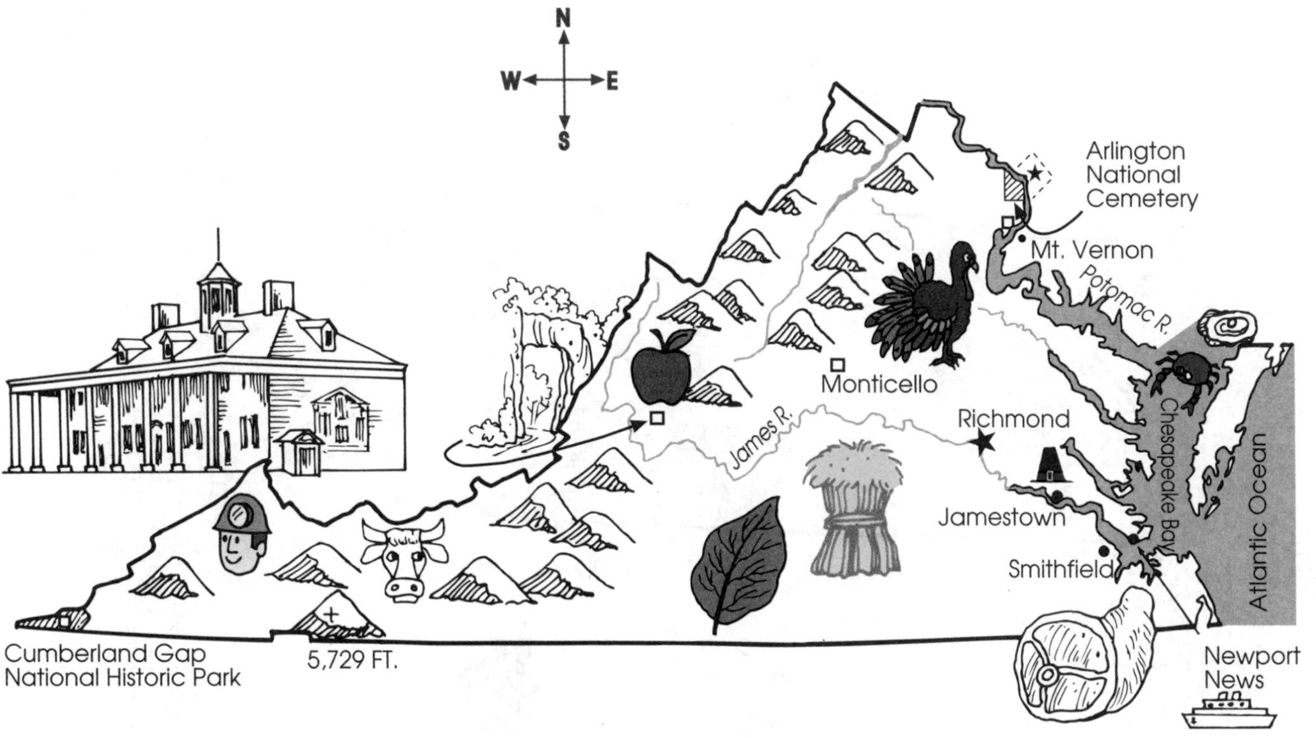

Cardinal
State Bird

American Dogwood
State Flower

- named for England's Queen Elizabeth I, who was called the Virgin Queen because she never married
- nicknamed Old Dominion by Charles II because Virginia was loyal to the crown during the English Civil War

Mount Rogers—5,729 ft.

Washington, D.C.—nation's capital

Arlington National Cemetery—Tomb of the Unknown Soldier

Smithfield—famous for its hams

Circle the capital city. Locate the landmarks found in the above key. Color them on the map.

Name____

Southeastern States

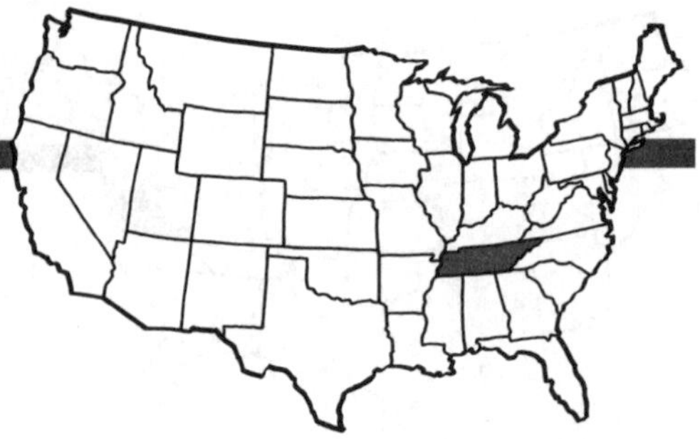

Tennessee

The Volunteer State

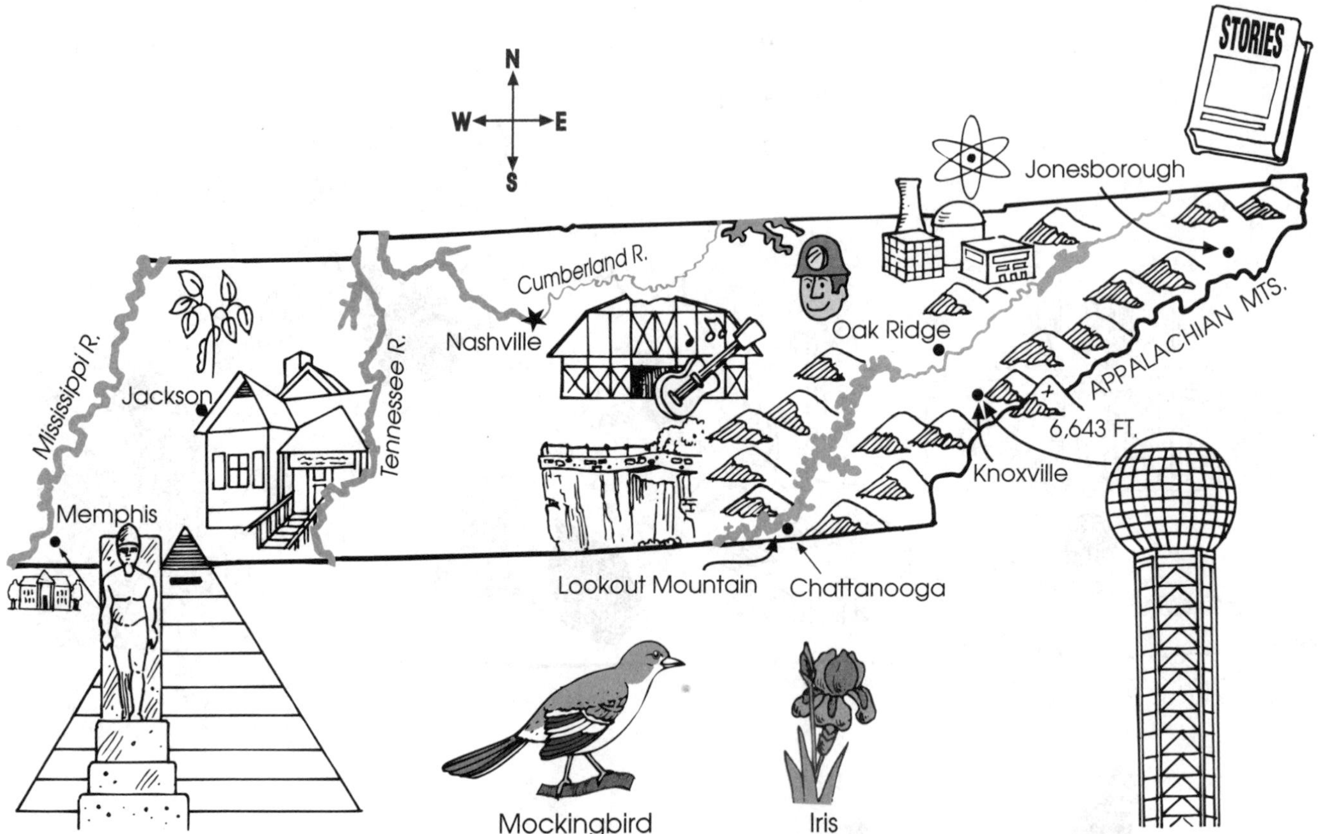

STORIES
N
W
E
S
Jonesborough
Cumberland R.
Nashville
Oak Ridge
APPALACHIAN MTS.
Mississippi R.
Jackson
Tennessee R.
6,643 FT.
Knoxville
Memphis
Lookout Mountain
Chattanooga

Mockingbird
State Bird

Iris
State Flower

- named for a Cherokee village, *Tanasie*
- nickname the Volunteer State refers to the large number of men who unhesitatingly volunteered for military service during the War of 1812 and the Mexican War

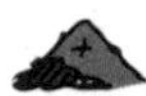

 Clingmans Dome—6,643 ft.

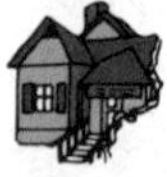

 Casey Jones Home and Railroad Museum

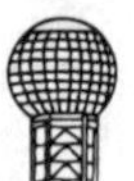

 Sunsphere—266-foot tower built for 1982 World's Fair

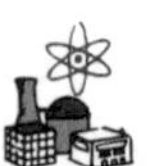

 American Museum of Science and Energy

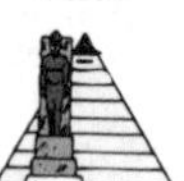

 The Pyramid—32-story stainless steel sports and entertainment facility

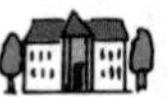

 Graceland—estate of Elvis Presley

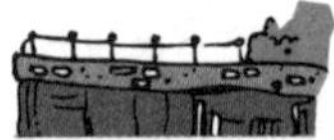

 Lookout Mountain

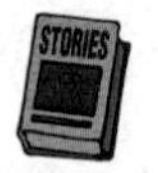

STORIES
National Storytelling Festival

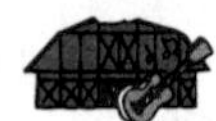

 Grand Ole Opry

Circle the capital city. Locate the landmarks found in the above key. Color them on the map.

Name ____________________

North Carolina

The Tarheel State

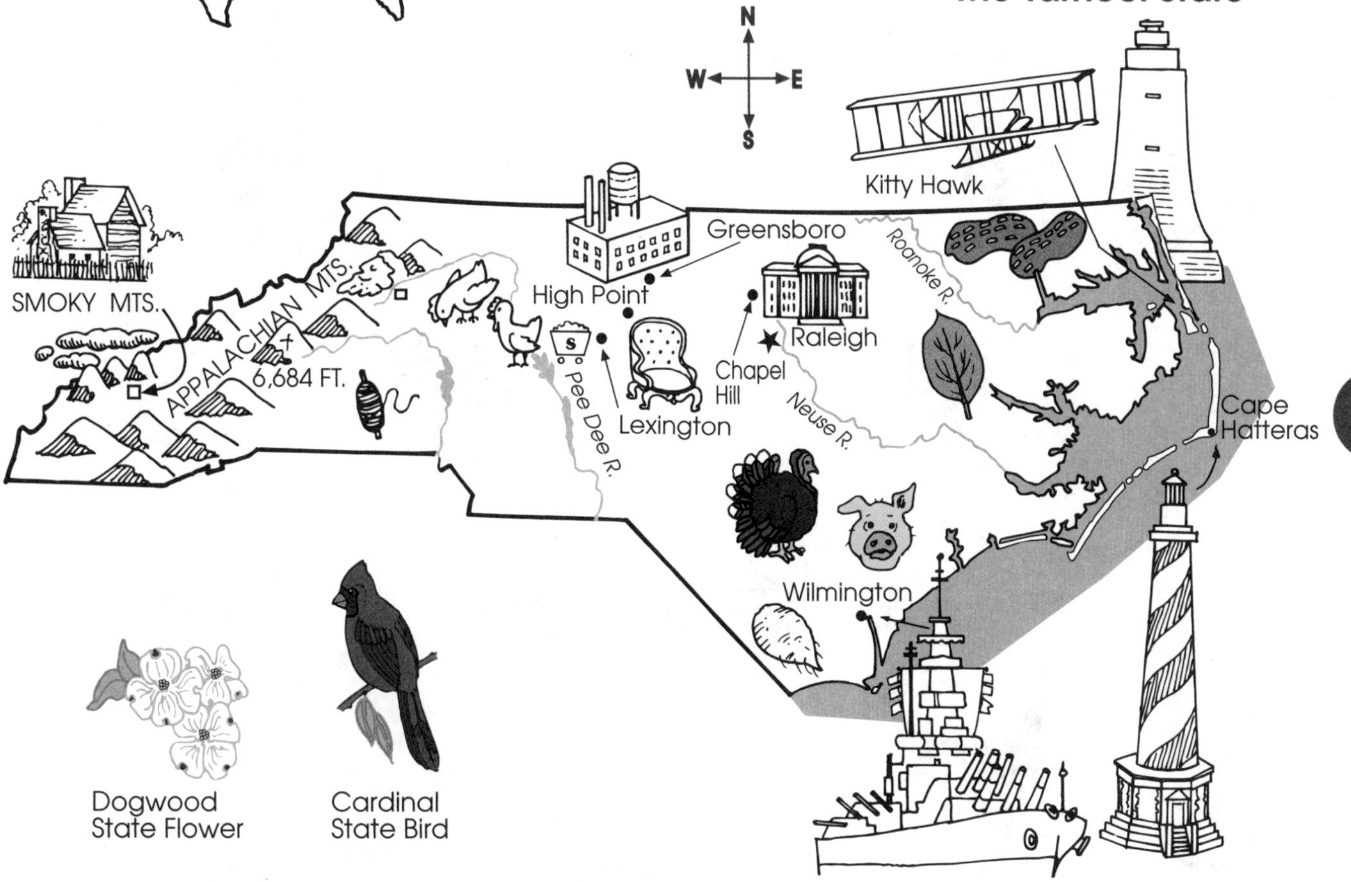

N
W E
S

Kitty Hawk
SMOKY MTS.
APPALACHIAN MTS.
6,684 FT.
Greensboro
High Point
Roanoke R.
Raleigh
Chapel Hill
Lexington
Pee Dee R.
Neuse R.
Cape Hatteras
Wilmington

Dogwood
State Flower

Cardinal
State Bird

- named for King Charles I of England
- nickname the Tarheel State refers to the large amount of tar produced which made North Carolina the leading colony in the naval store industry

Mount Mitchell—6,684 ft.

Morehead Planetarium

High Point—often called the Furniture Capital of America

Lexington—location of first silver mine in the U.S.

Gaston County—spins more yarn than any other U.S. county

Greensboro—largest denim-weaving mill in the world

Cape Hatteras Lighthouse—guards the Graveyard of the Atlantic

Wright Brothers National Memorial

Cherokee Indian Reservation—has replica of a 1700 Indian village

Grandfather Mountain—resembles an old man sleeping

U.S.S. North Carolina—took part in every major Pacific Ocean battle in WWII

Circle the capital city. Locate the landmarks found in the above key. Color them on the map.

Name____

South Carolina

The Palmetto State

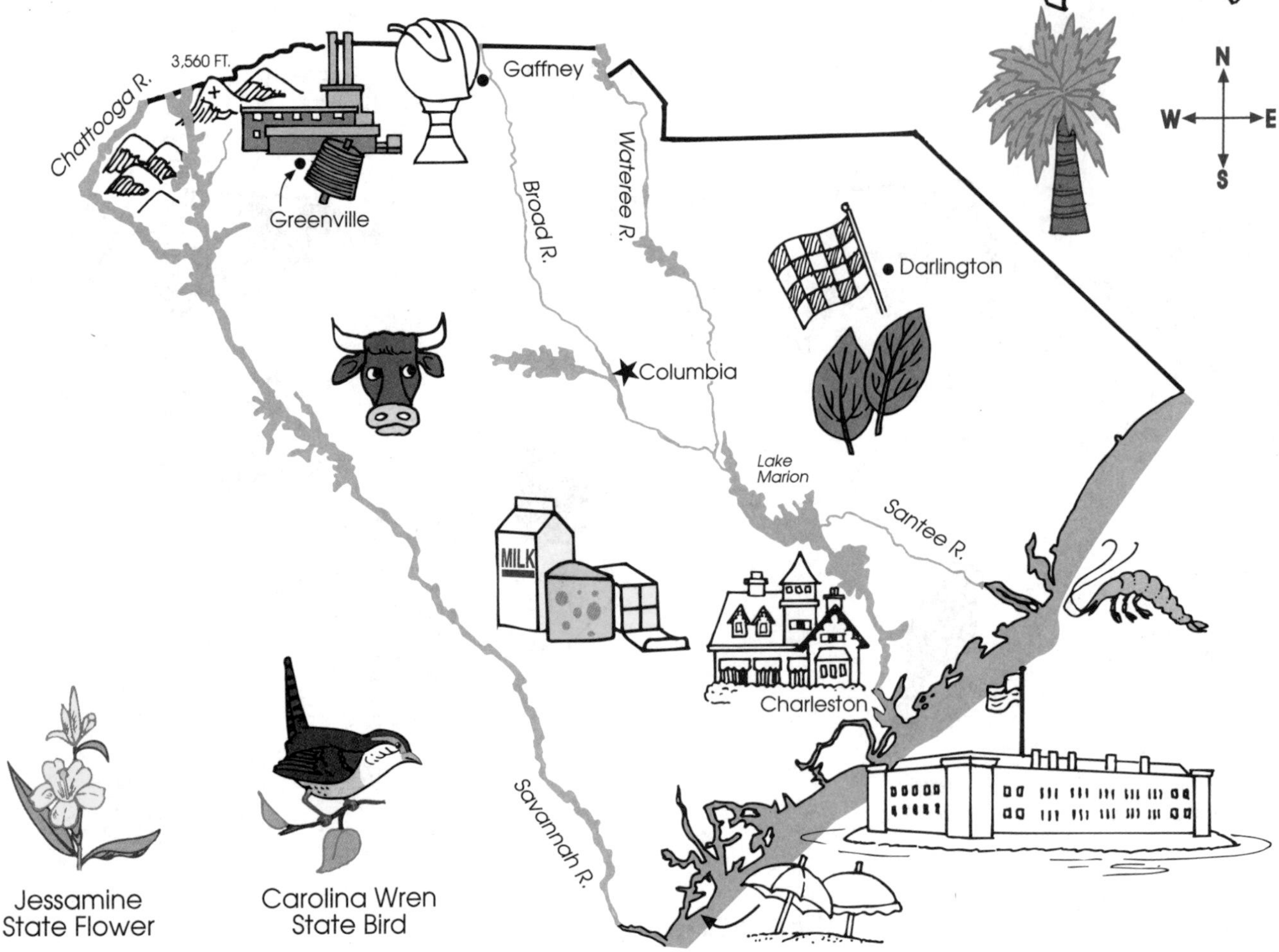

3,560 FT.
Chattooga R.
Greenville
Gaffney
Broad R.
Wateree R.
Darlington
Columbia
Lake Marion
Santee R.
MILK
Charleston
Savannah R.
N
W
E
S

Jessamine
State Flower

Carolina Wren
State Bird

- named for King Charles I of England; "South" was added when the Carolinas separated
- nickname the Palmetto State may be the result of an incident during the Revolutionary War where smoke from a burning British ship resembled the state's palmetto tree

 Sassafras Mountain—3,560 ft.

 The Peachoid—a tank holding one million gallons of water

 Fort Sumter National Monument—site of the beginning of the Civil War

 Southern 500—stock car race

 Middleton Place—one of Charleston's finest plantations

 Hilton Head Island—popular vacation resort

Circle the capital city. Locate the landmarks found in the above key. Color them on the map.

Name ______________________________

Mississippi

The Magnolia State

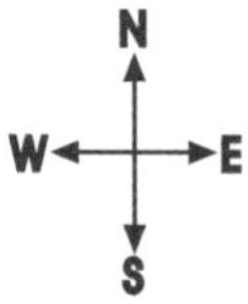

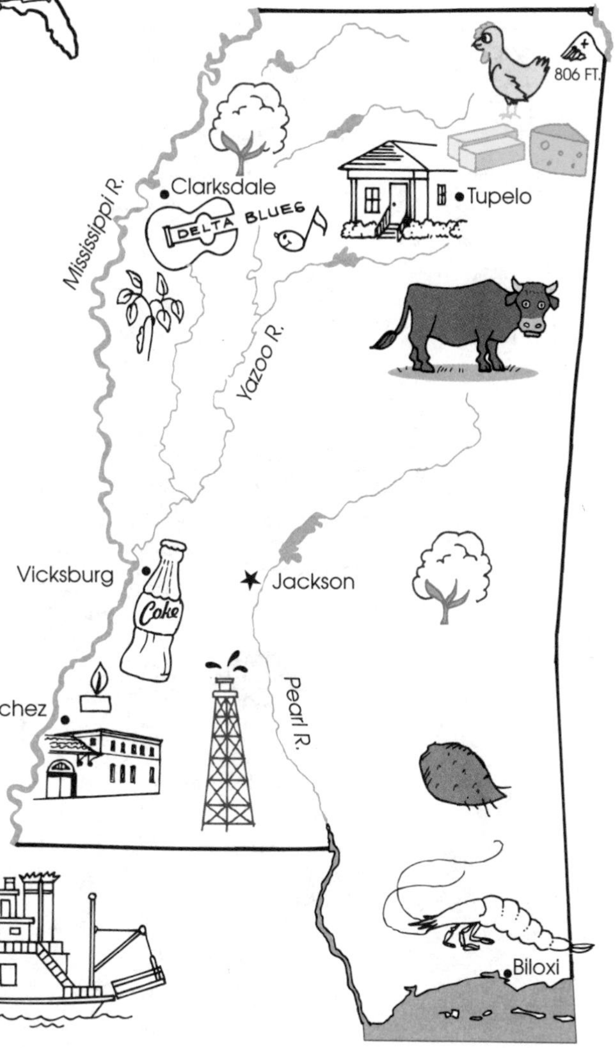

Mockingbird
State Bird

Magnolia
State Flower

- name taken from two Indian words, *misi* and *sipi* meaning *big river* or *great water*
- nickname the Magnolia State refers to the many magnolia trees that grow in the state

Woodall Mountain—806 ft.

Delta Blues Museum—dedicated to blues musicians and music

Shrimp Festival—chief shrimp-packing port

Elvis Presley Park—site of famous rock 'n' roll singer's birthplace

Vicksburg—site where Coca-Cola was first bottled in 1894

Delta Queen—built in 1926, tours the Mississippi River

Natchez—oldest town on the Mississippi River

Circle the capital city. Locate the landmarks found in the above key. Color them on the map.

Name____

Alabama

The Heart of Dixie

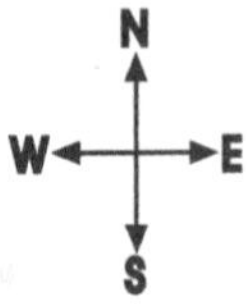

N
W E
S

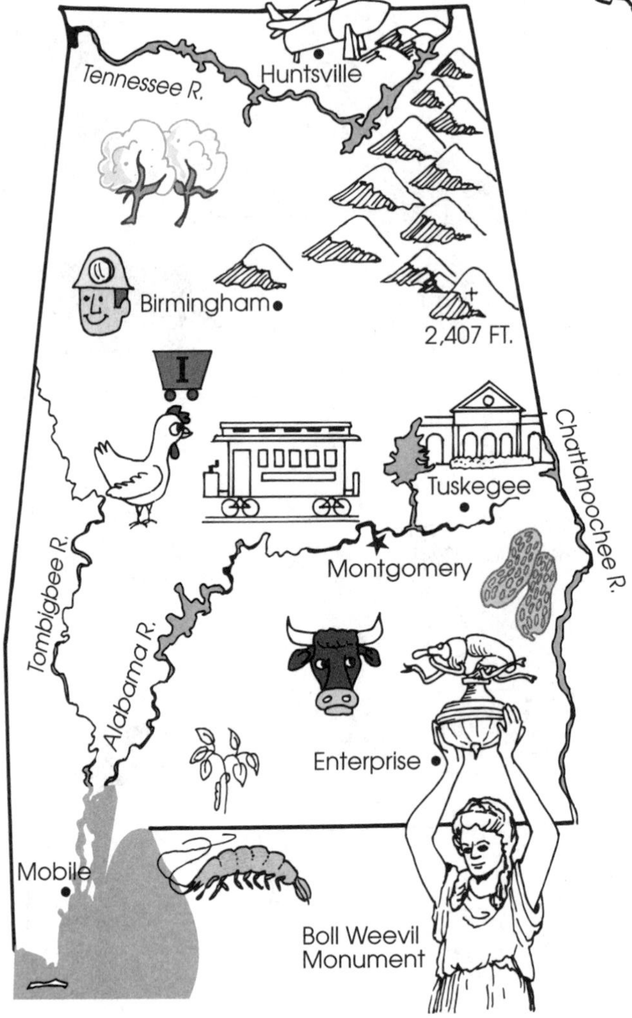

Tennessee R.
Huntsville
Birmingham
2,407 FT.
Tuskegee
Chattahoochee R.
Montgomery
Tombigbee R.
Alabama R.
Enterprise
Mobile
Boll Weevil Monument

Yellow Hammer
State Bird

Camellia
State Flower

- named for a Creek Indian tribe, the Alibamu, whose name means *clearers of the thickets*
- nickname the Heart of Dixie refers to the importance the state had during the Civil War

Cheaha Mountain—2,407 ft.

U.S. Space and Rocket Center

Boll Weevil Monument

Montgomery—first electric trolley car in the U.S. began operating here in 1866

George Washington Carver Museum—honors Carver's discovery of over 300 uses for peanuts and over 100 uses for sweet potatoes

Circle the capital city. Locate the landmarks found in the above key. Color them on the map.

Name ______________________________

Georgia
The Peach State

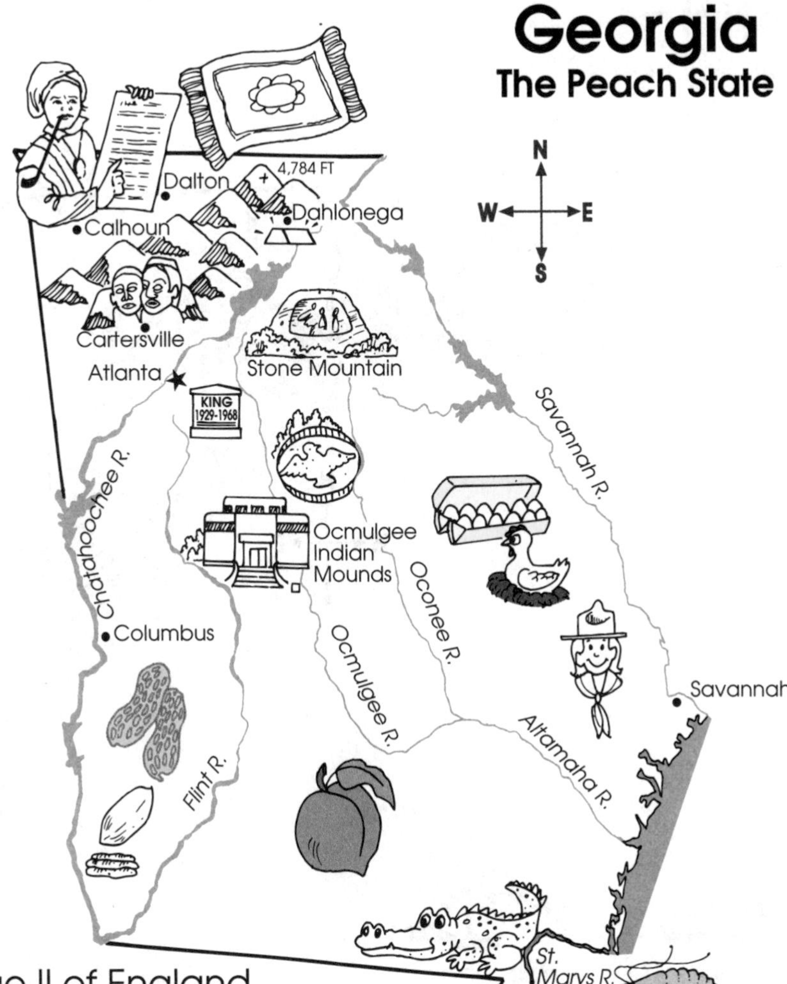

Cherokee Rose
State Flower

Brown Thrasher
State Bird

- named for King George II of England
- nickname the Peach State

Brasstown Bald Mountain—4,784 ft.

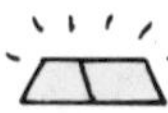
Dahlonega Gold Museum—located at the site of the first gold rush in the U.S.

Etowah Mounds—built by prehistoric Indians

Savannah—Juliet Gordon Lowe, founder of the Girl Scouts of the U.S.A., lived here

Calhoun—statue honors Sequoya, who developed Cherokee alphabet

Ocmulgee National Monument—contains remains of Indian mounds

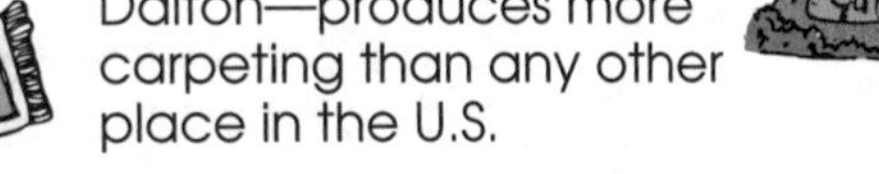
Dalton—produces more carpeting than any other place in the U.S.

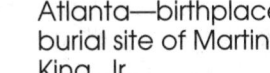

Atlanta—birthplace and burial site of Martin Luther King, Jr.

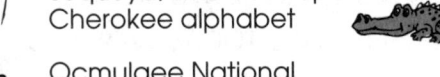

Okefenokee Swamp—national wildlife refuge, which is known as America's greatest botanical garden

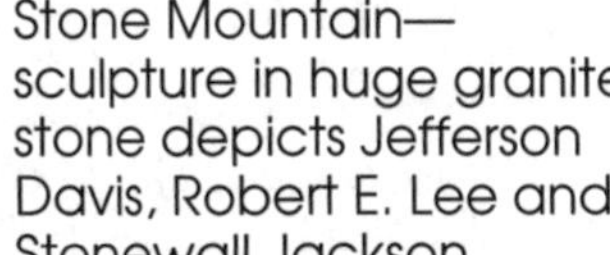
Stone Mountain—sculpture in huge granite stone depicts Jefferson Davis, Robert E. Lee and Stonewall Jackson

Rock Eagle Effigy—6,000-year-old monument made by ancient Indians

Circle the capital city. Locate the landmarks found in the above key. Color them on the map.

Name____

Southeastern States

Florida

The Sunshine State

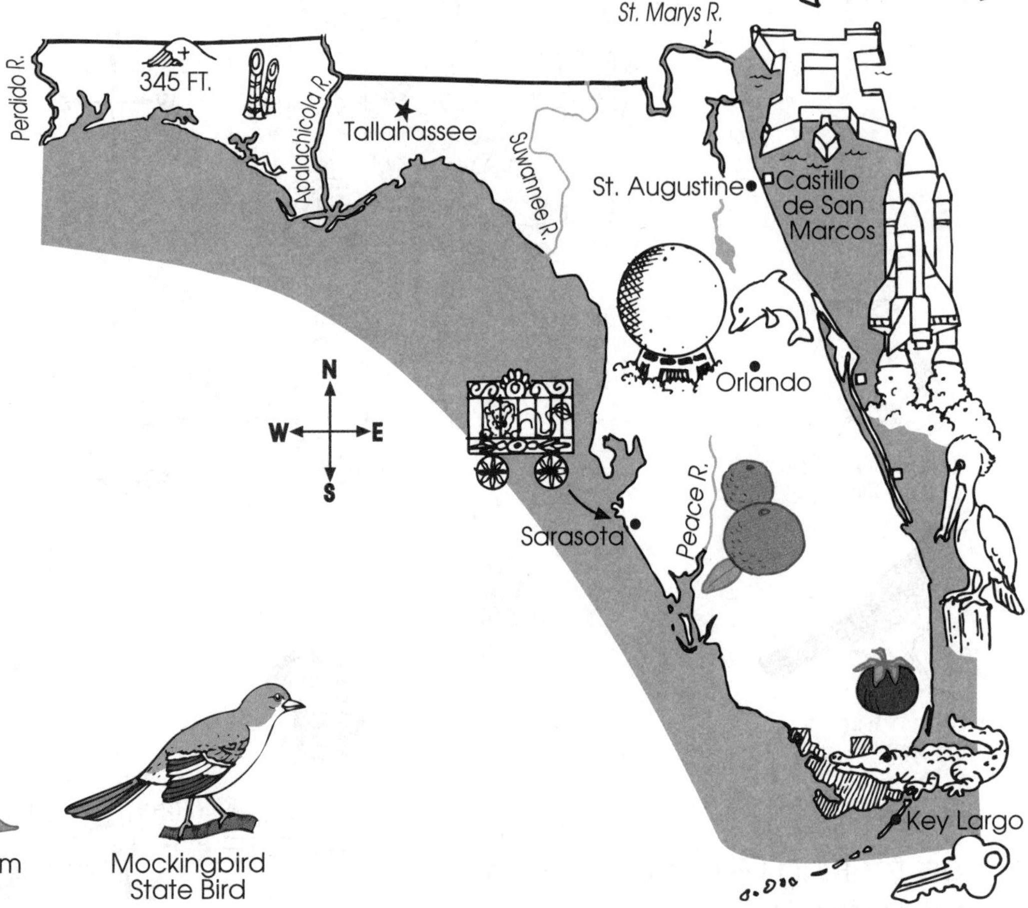

St. Marys R.
Perdido R.
345 FT.
Apalachicola R.
Tallahassee
Suwannee R.
St. Augustine
Castillo de San Marcos
Orlando
N
W
E
S
Sarasota
Peace R.
Key Largo

Orange Blossom
State Flower

Mockingbird
State Bird

- name comes from the Spanish word *florida,* meaning *flowery,* which may refer to the many flowers given by Spanish explorer Juan Ponce de León
- nicknamed the Sunshine State for its warm and sunny climate

Sea World—a popular tourist attraction featuring killer whales and dolphins

Pelican Island National Wildlife Refuge—first federal wildlife refuge

EPCOT Center—displays future technology

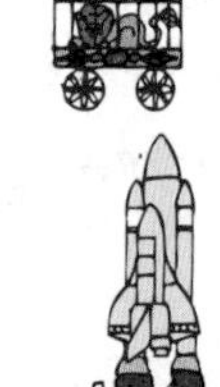
John and Mable Ringling Museum—Museum of Art and Circus Galleries

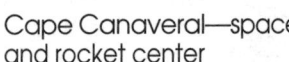

Cape Canaveral—space and rocket center

Everglades National Park—largest subtropical wilderness in U.S.

Castillo de San Marcos National Monument—oldest permanent European settlement in the United States

John Pennekamp Coral Reef State Park—first underseas park in the continental United States

Circle the capital city. Locate the landmarks found in the above key. Color them on the map.

Section 4

North & South America

Name________________________________

Introduction: North and South America

What Is Where in North and South America?

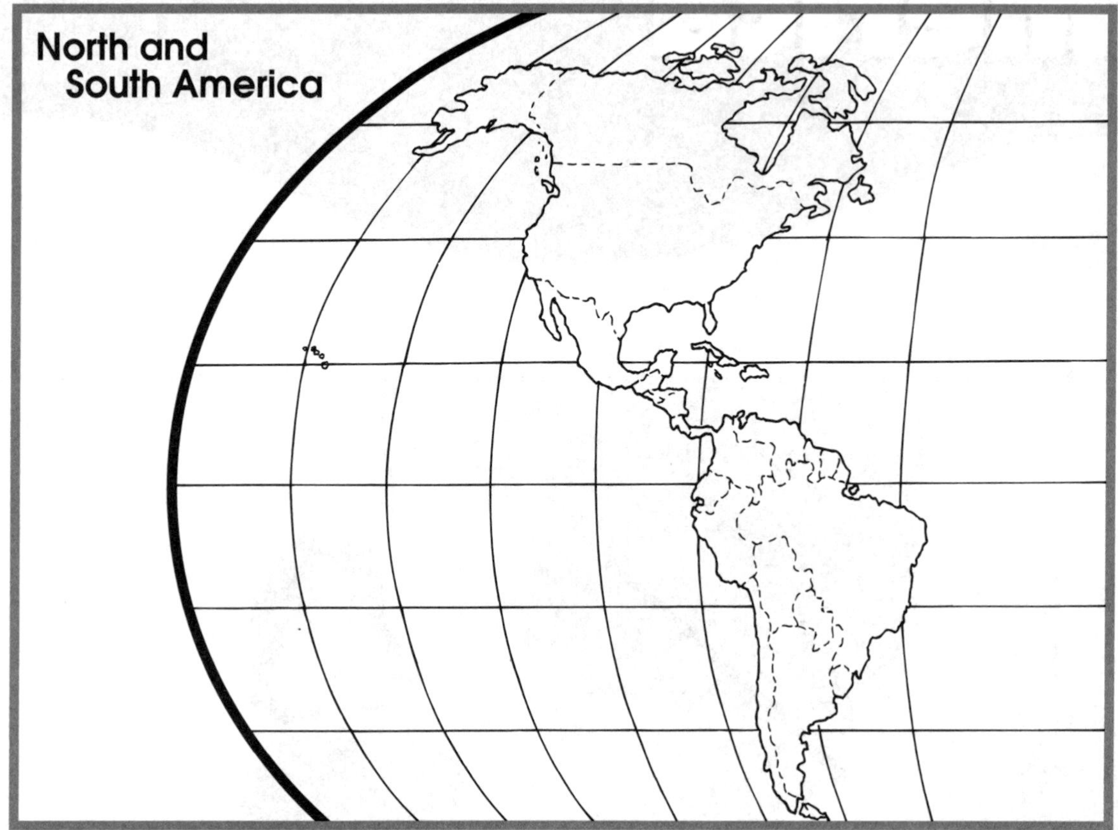

Directions: Follow these directions to complete the map. You may also use a political map of North and South America.

1. Outline Canada in red.
2. Outline the United States in black. (Remember Alaska and Hawaii.)
3. Outline Mexico in orange.
4. Outline Brazil in brown.
5. Outline Chile in red.
6. Outline Argentina in orange.
7. Outline Paraguay in yellow.
8. Outline Colombia in black.
9. Outline Bolivia in red.
10. Color Peru yellow.
11. Color Ecuador orange.
12. Color Uruguay brown.
13. Color Venezuela purple.
14. Color Guyana pink.
15. Color Suriname orange.
16. Color French Guiana yellow.
17. Color the Gulf of Mexico green.
18. Color the Arctic Ocean blue.
19. Color the Pacific Ocean grey.
20. Color the Atlantic Ocean purple.

Name________________________________

Neighboring Countries

Use a map of North America to locate your country. In the direction boxes write the names of all the countries and/or bodies of water surrounding your country.

Northwest	North	Northeast
West	My Country Draw an outline map of your country.	East
Southwest	South	Southeast

Name________________________________

Within Continents

A continent is a large area of land.

This map shows two continents, North America and South America, and two oceans, the Atlantic Ocean and Pacific Ocean. It also shows the countries that are on each continent. A solid line (——) shows the boundaries of each country. Use this map to answer the questions on page 225.

Name______________________________

Within Continents

1. Write the names of the continents shown on the map.

____

____

2. Find the United States on the map. Color it green.
3. Find Alaska and Hawaii. They are part of the country of the United States. Color them green.
4. What country is north of the United States? Color it orange.

____

5. What large country is south of the United States? Color it red.

____

6. Which South American country is the biggest? ________________
7. What long, skinny country is on the west coast of South America?

____

8. Which ocean is to the west of the continents of North America and South America? ____________________
9. In which direction would you go to travel from Canada to Chile?

____

Name______________________________________

O Canada!

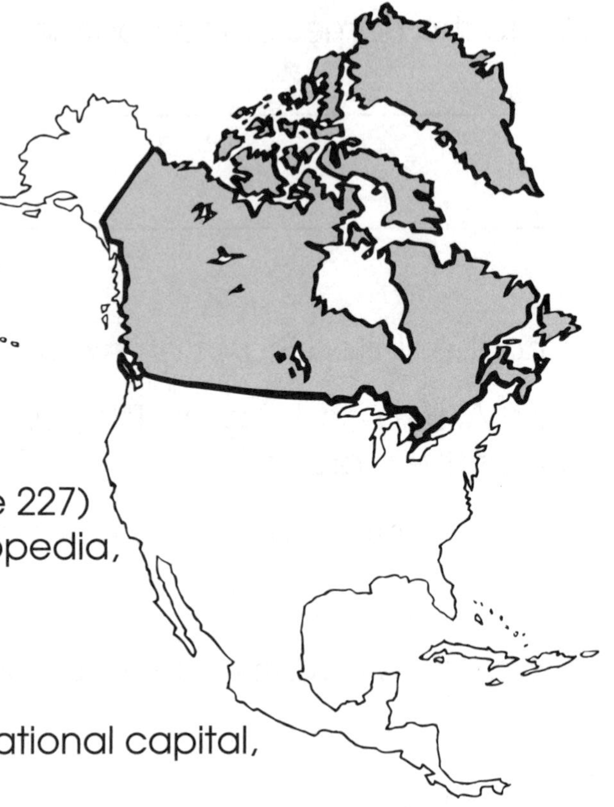

Canada, the largest country in area in the Western Hemisphere, stretches across the North American Continent with its shores touching three oceans.

Canada has 10 provinces and 2 territories. A province is a political area that is very similar to a state.

You will need:

copy of Political Map of Canada (page 227)
physical Canada map, atlas or encyclopedia,
colored pencils, crayons or markers

Directions:

1. Complete a key with symbols for the national capital, province/territory capitals and cities.
2. Label each of the ten provinces and two territories using upper-case letters.
3. Label the national capital and the capitals of each province and territory.
4. Label these major cities:
   Calgary   Saskatoon   Windsor   Montreal   Vancouver
5. Label these bodies of water:
   Atlantic Ocean   Pacific Ocean   Arctic Ocean   Hudson Bay
   Labrador Sea   Baffin Bay
6. Color each province and territory a different color.
7. Color the bodies of water blue.
8. Color the United States one color.

Name ______________________________

Political Map of Canada

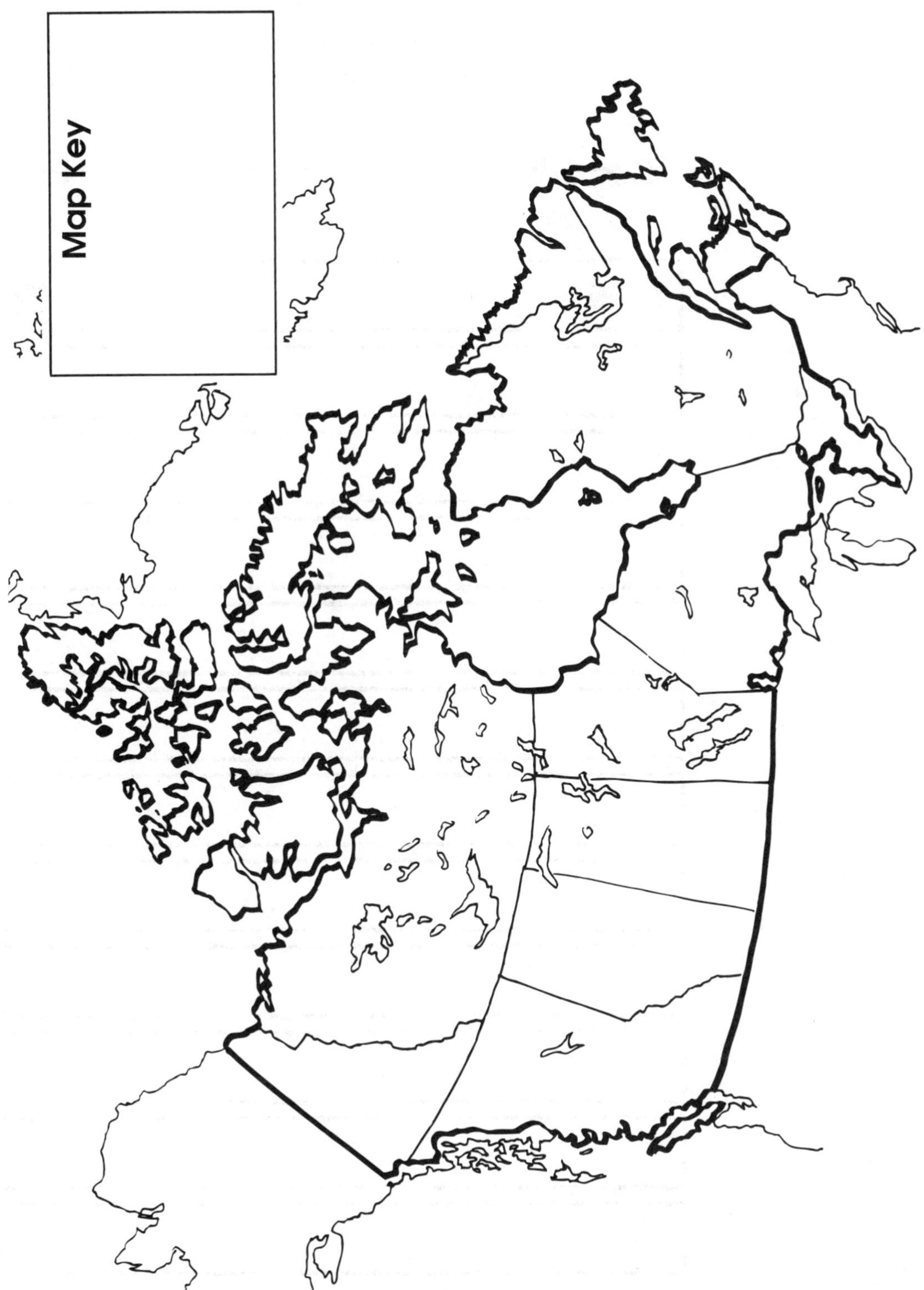

Use with page 226.

Name____________________________________

Products and Natural Resources

Canada is rich in natural resources. Study the Products and Natural Resources map (page 229). Determine which natural resources or products are available in each of the provinces and territories. Draw the symbol for each product or natural resource on the graph. The Province of Alberta has been done for you as an example.

Canadian Natural Resources and Products

	Moderate Producer → Major Producer
Alberta	
British Columbia	
Manitoba	
New Brunswick	
Newfoundland	
Northwest Territory	
Nova Scotia	
Ontario	
Prince Edward Island	
Quebec	
Saskatchewan	
Yukon Territory	

Name______________________________

Products and Natural Resources

Use with page 228.

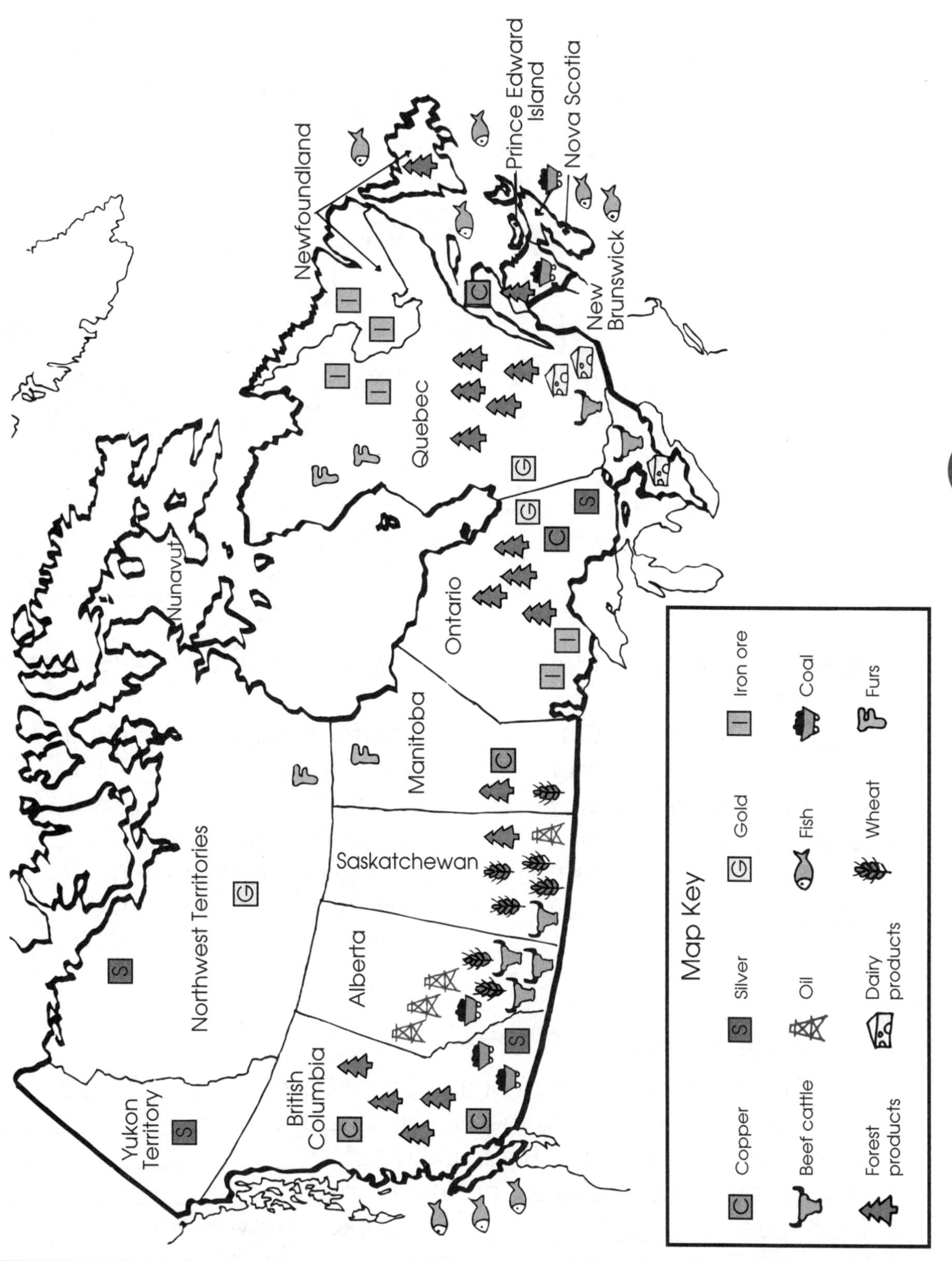

Name________________________________

Canada

Northern Neighbors

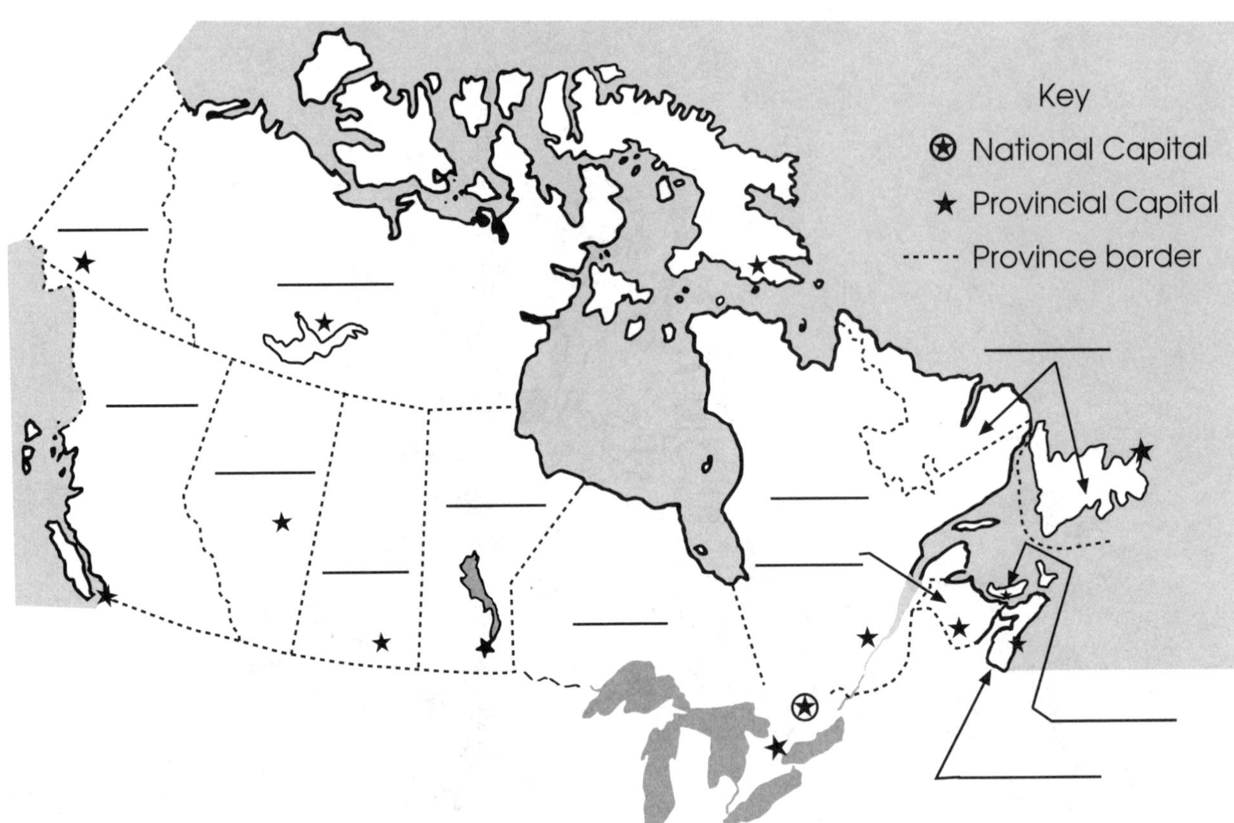

Write each province or territory name abbreviation by the correct number on the map.

1. British Columbia	(B.C.)	7. Newfoundland	(Nfld.)
2. Alberta	(Alta.)	8. New Brunswick	(N.B.)
3. Saskatchewan	(Sask.)	9. Nova Scotia	(N.S.)
4. Manitoba	(Man.)	10. Prince Edward Island	(P.E.I.)
5. Ontario	(Ont.)	11. Northwest Territories	(N.W.T.)
6. Quebec	(Que.)	12. Yukon Territory	(Y.T.)
		13. Nunavut	(N.U.)

Answer these questions.

1. Which provinces are north of the Great Lakes? ____________________
2. Which province contains the national capital? ____________________
3. What province is east of British Columbia? ____________________
4. What province is southeast of New Brunswick? ____________________
5. Manitoba is ________________ of Saskatchewan.

Name____

Mexico

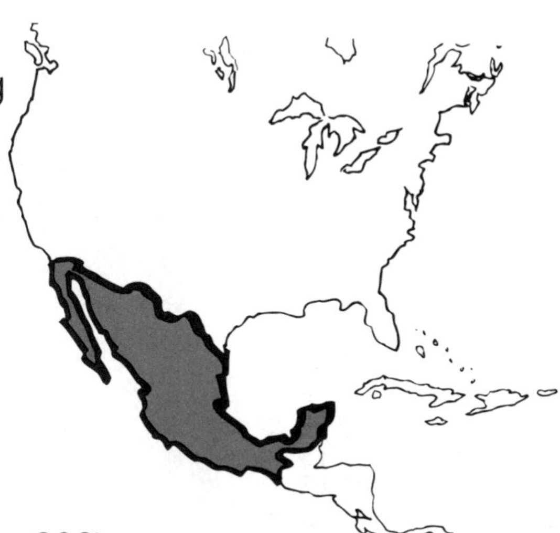

Mexico is the United States' neighbor to the south. The two countries share a 2,000-mile long border. Mexico is the third most populated country in the Western Hemisphere; only the United States and Brazil have more people.

Mexico is home to one of the largest cities in the world, Mexico City.

You will need:

copy of Mexico Physical-Political Map (page 232)
physical map of Mexico, atlas or encyclopedia
colored pencils, markers or crayons

Directions:

1. Label and color-code the map key, and color Mexico's six main land regions:

Pacific Northwest	Plateau of Mexico	Gulf Coastal Plain
Southern Uplands	Chiapas Highlands	Yucatan Peninsula

2. Draw and label the following mountain ranges. Use ΛΛΛ as symbols for mountains.

Sierra Madre Oriental	Sierra Madre del Sur	Sierra Madre Occidental

3. Label these large cities:

Mexico City	Monterrery	Guadalajara
Puebla	Chihuahua	Juarez
Tijuana	Acapulco	Tampico

4. Label these bodies of water:

Gulf of Mexico	Pacific Ocean	Gulf of California

Name____________________________________

Physical/Political Map

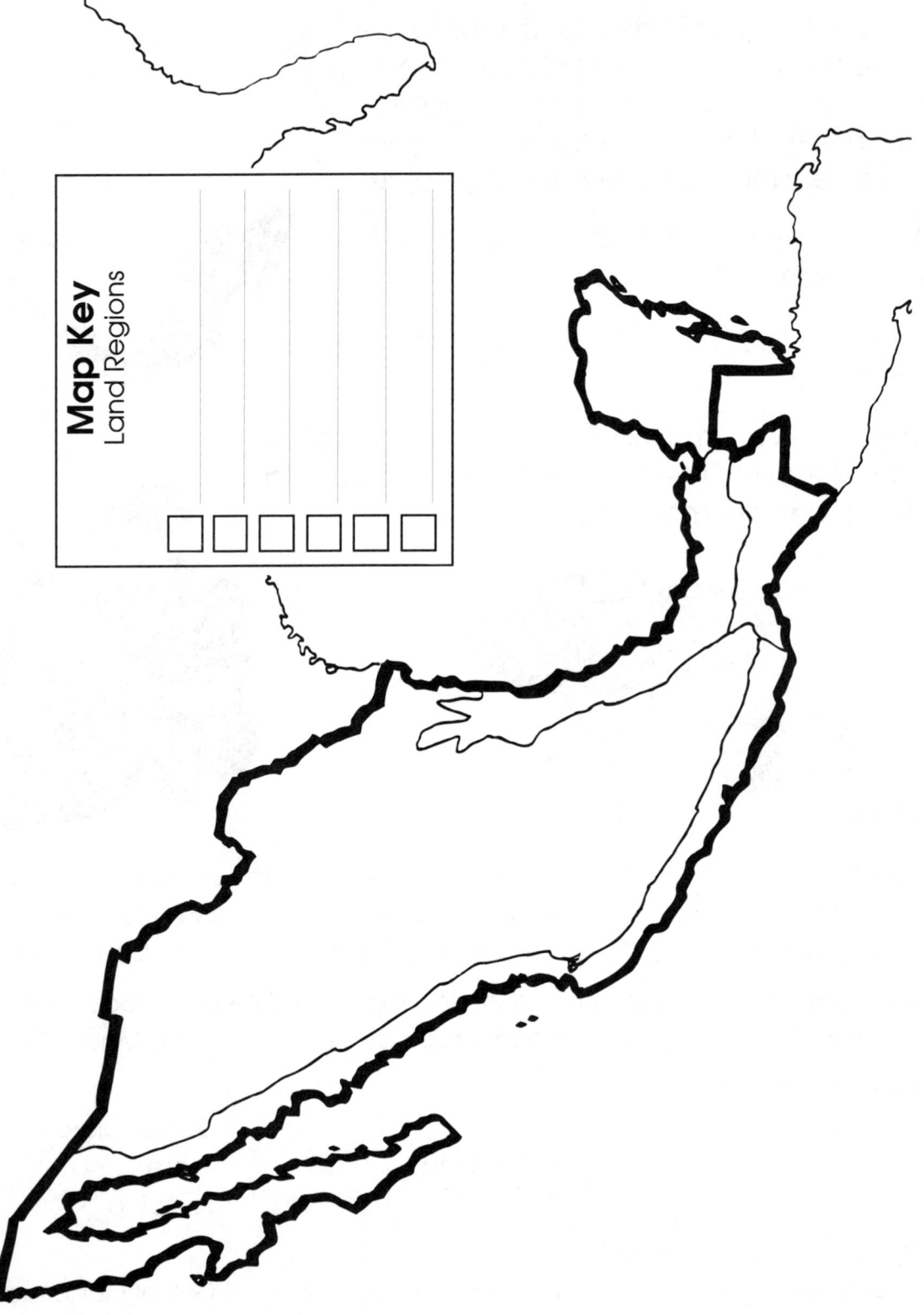

Map Key
Land Regions

Use with page 231.

Name ____________________________

Mexico

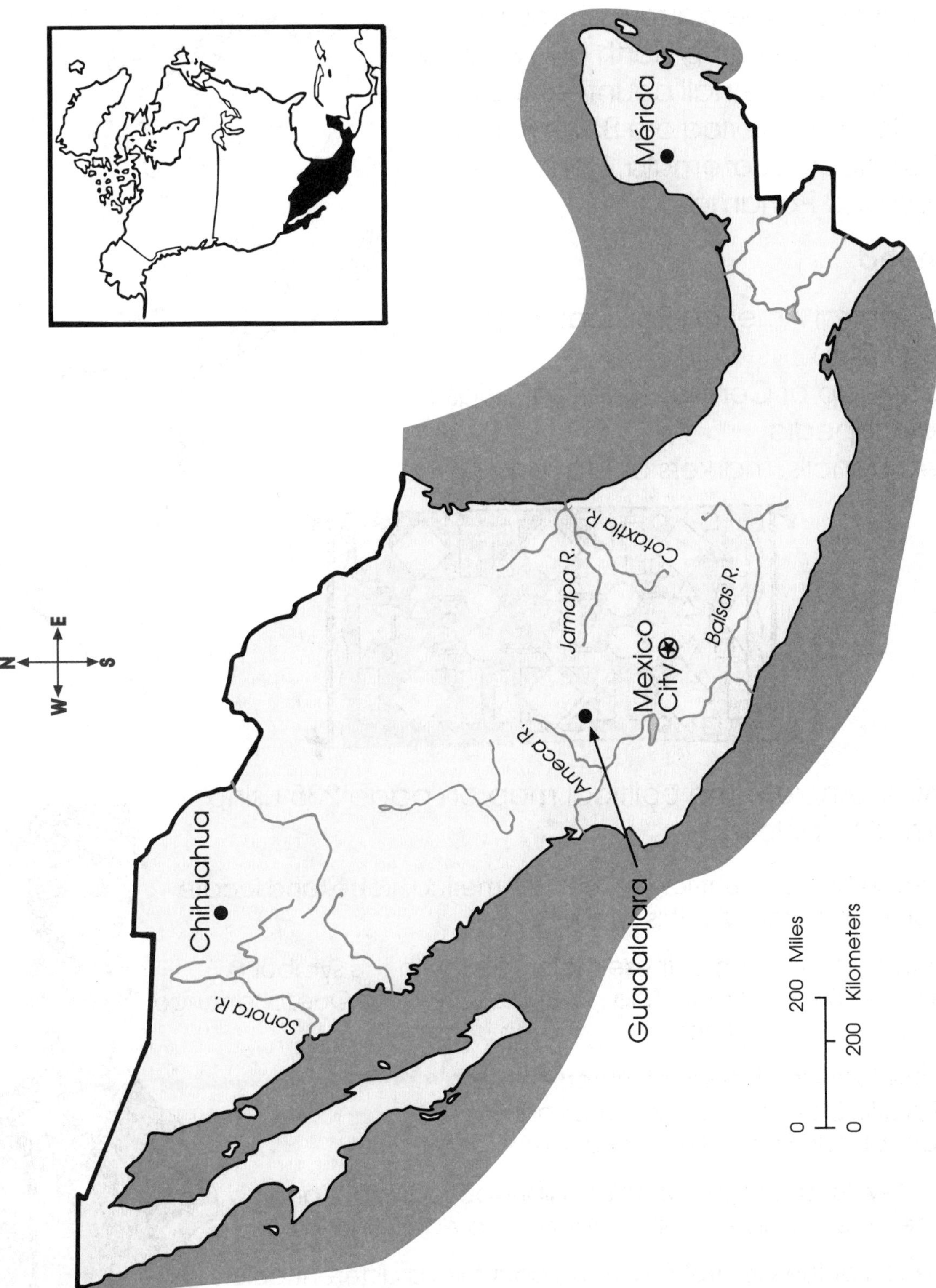

Area: 756,067 sq. mi.

Name____

Central America

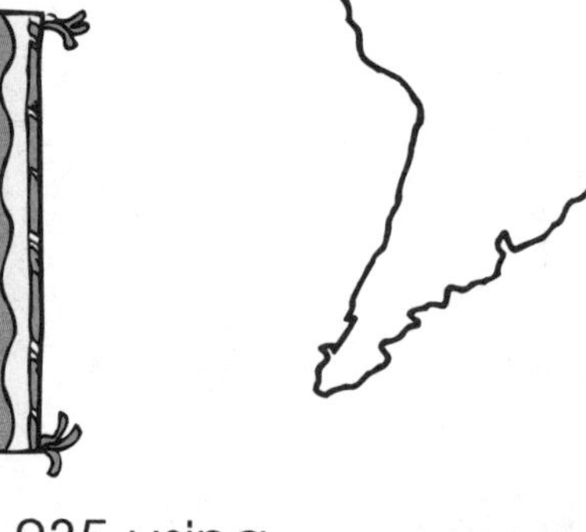

Central America is the narrow isthmus, or ridge of land, connecting North and South America. The seven small countries that make up Central America are Belize, Costa Rica, El Salvador, Guatemala, Honduras, Nicaragua and Panama.

You will need:

blank Central America Political map (page 235)
physical map of Central America, atlas or encyclopedia
colored pencils, markers or crayons

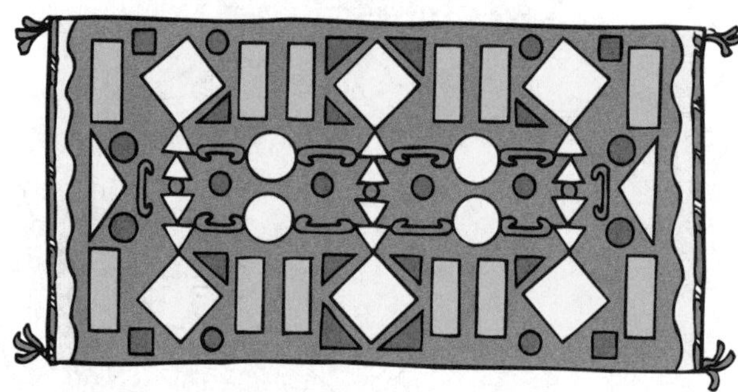

Directions: Complete the political map on page 235 using the information below.

1. Label each of the countries of Central America. Label and locate each of the capitals with this symbol ✪.
2. Label and locate each of these major cities with this symbol ●.

San Pedro Sula	Santa Ana	Belize City	Quezaltenango
Colon	Limón	León	

3. Label the following bodies of water:

Pacific Ocean	Panama Canal
Caribbean Sea	Gulf of Panama

4. On the Key, list all of the capitals in alphabetical order and write the letter-number coordinates behind each one.
5. Color each of the Central American countries a different color.

Name____

Political Map

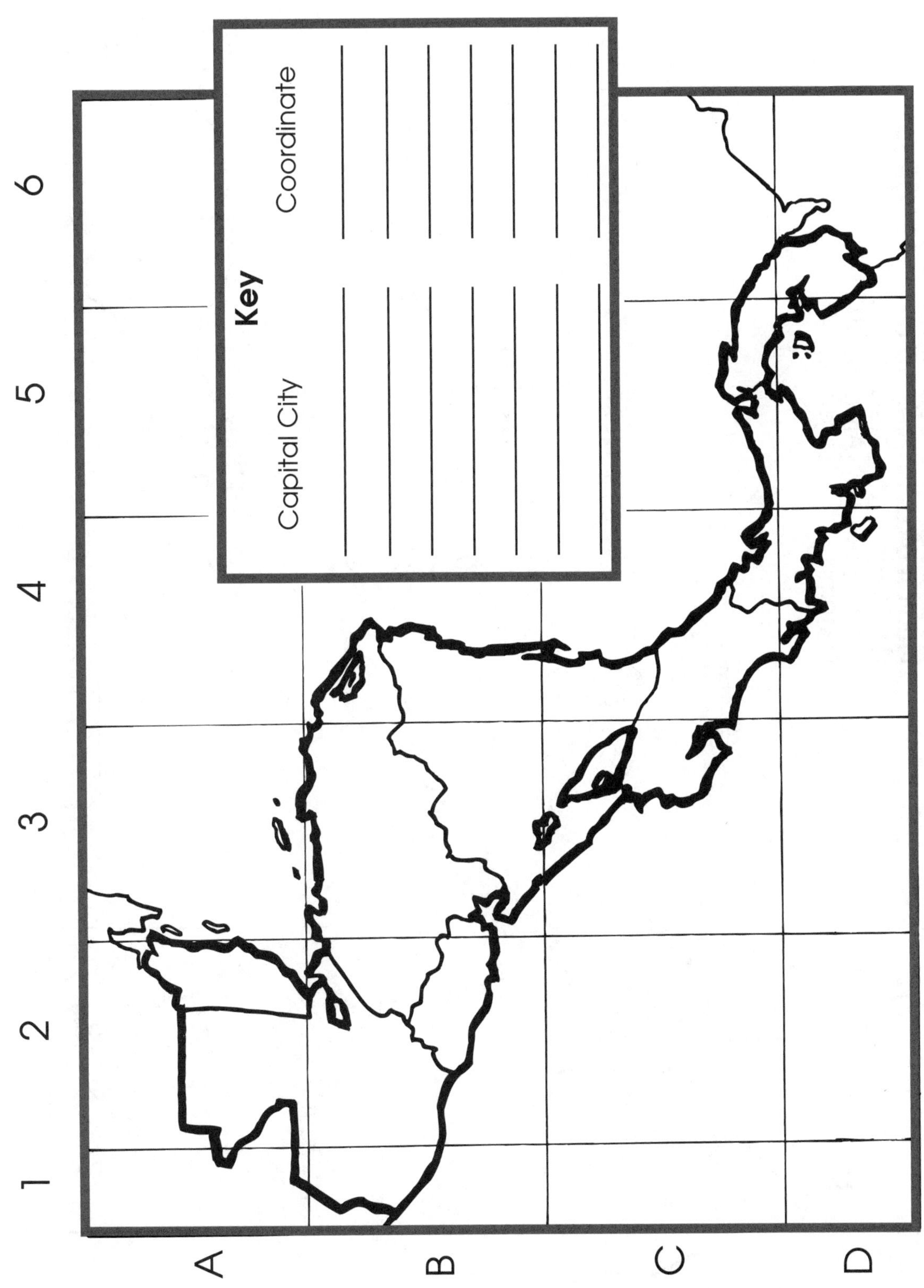

Use with page 234.

Name____

Central America

Central America	Area: Approx. 202,000 sq. mi.
Belize	Area: 8,867 sq. mi.
Costa Rica	Area: 19,730
El Salvador	Area: 8,124
Guatemala	Area: 42,042
Honduras	Area: 43,277
Nicaragua	Area: 50,193
Panama	Area: 29,856

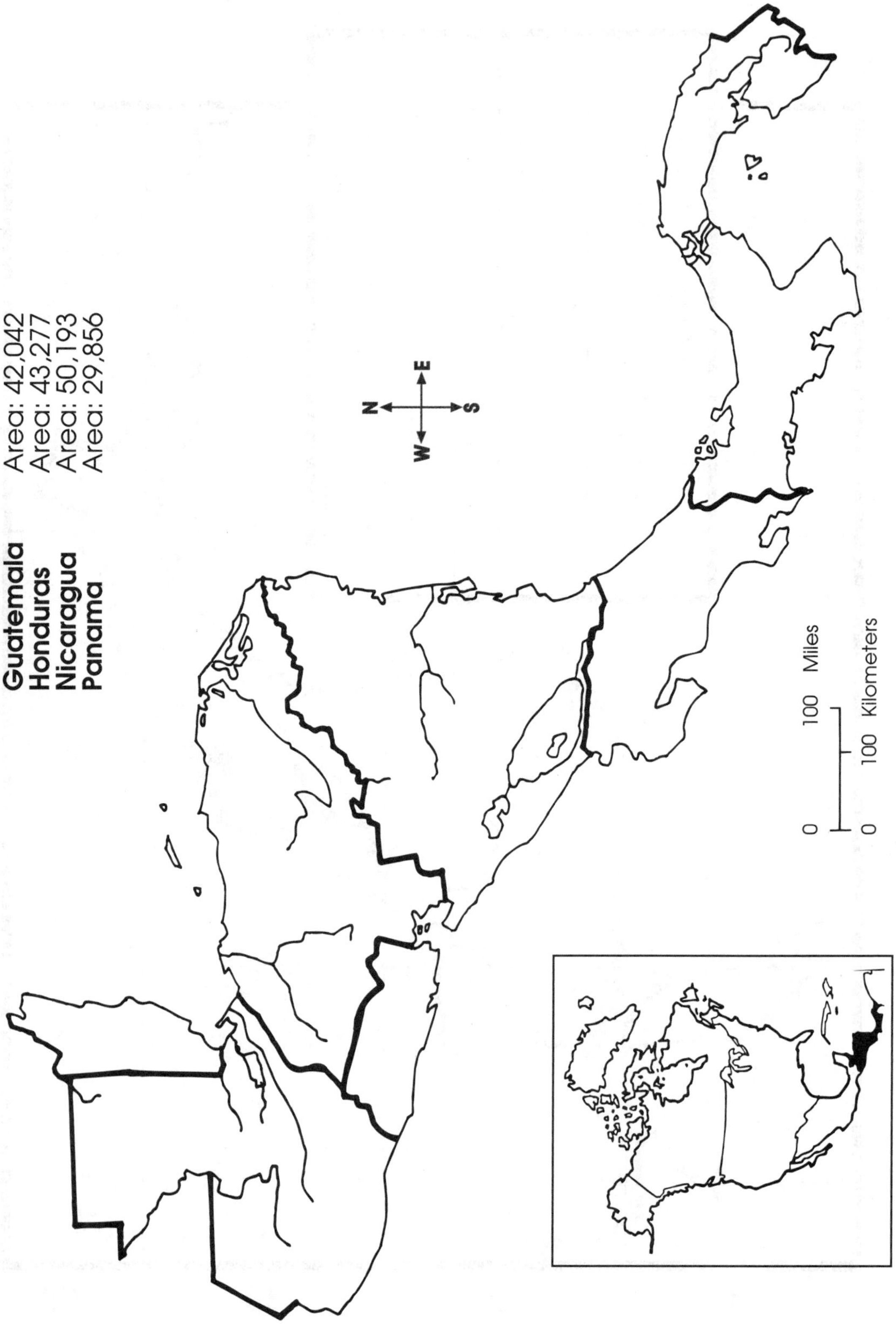

N E S W

0 100 Miles

0 100 Kilometers

Name ____________________

South America

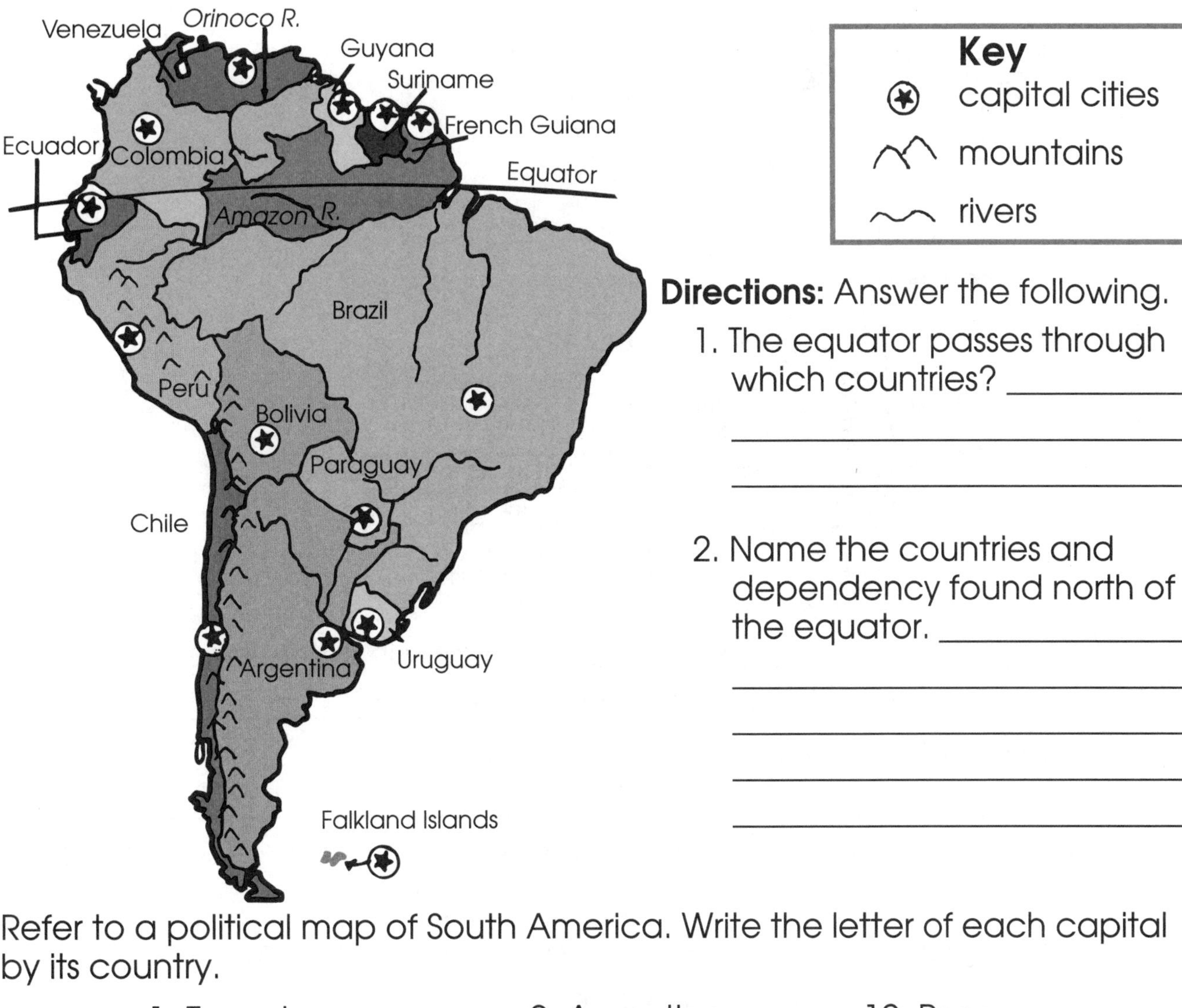

Directions: Answer the following.

1. The equator passes through which countries? ____________________

2. Name the countries and dependency found north of the equator. ____________________

Refer to a political map of South America. Write the letter of each capital by its country.

_____ 1. Ecuador
_____ 2. Colombia
_____ 3. Venezuela
_____ 4. Guyana
_____ 5. Suriname
_____ 6. French Guiana
_____ 7. Brazil
_____ 8. Uruguay
_____ 9. Argentina
_____ 10. Chile
_____ 11. Bolivia
_____ 12. Peru
_____ 13. Paraguay
_____ 14. Falkland Islands

A.	Buenos Aires	H.	Lima
B.	Sucre	I.	Paramaribo
C.	Brasília	J.	Montevideo
D.	Bogotá	K.	Caracas
E.	Quito	L.	Santiago
F.	Georgetown	M.	Cayenne
G.	Asunción	N.	Stanley

Name ______________________________

Countries and Cities in South America

1. ______________________ is the largest country in South America.
2. Which country forms Argentina's western border? ______________
3. List three countries which share a border with Brazil.

   ______________ ______________ ______________
4. Name the two countries which form the southern border of Colombia.

   ______________ ______________
5. Name the country between Guyana and French Guiana. __________
6. ______________ is the capital of Venezuela.
7. Uruguay is between the countries of Argentina and ______________.
8. The capital of Bolivia is ______________.
9. ______________ forms Peru's northwest border.
10. The capital of Paraguay is ______________.
11. Cayenne is the capital of ______________.
12. Name the country west of Guyana. ______________
13. Name the three countries which share a border with Chile.

    ______________ ______________ ______________

Name ______________________________

Where Is It Raining?

South America—Precipitation Map

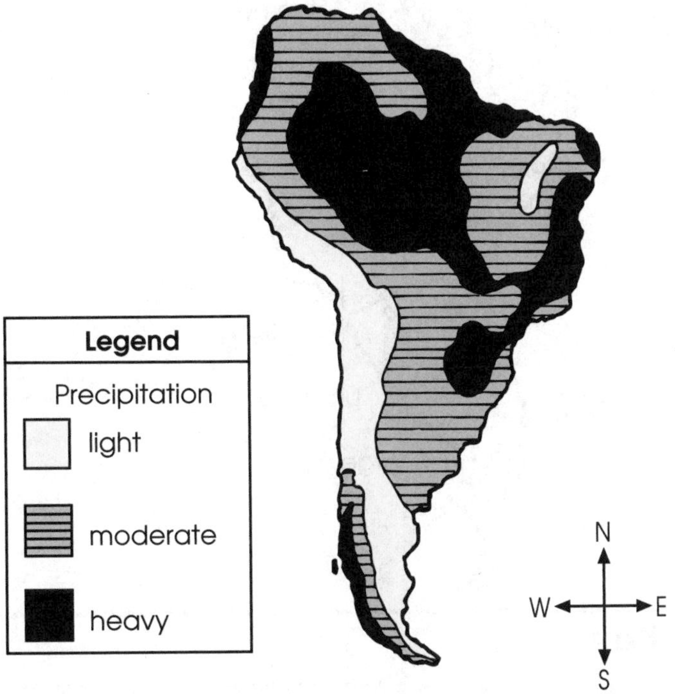

Legend

Precipitation

light

moderate

heavy

N
W E
S

South America—Political Map

Venezuela
Guyana
Suriname
French Guiana
Colombia
Ecuador
Brazil
Peru
Bolivia
Paraguay
Uruguay
Chile
Argentina

Directions: Use both maps to answer these questions about South America.

1. What do these symbols stand for on the precipitation map?

   A. ______________ B. ________________ C. ______________

2. The lightest precipitation falls mainly on the ______________ part of South America.
3. The heaviest precipitation falls mainly in the ______________ part of South America.
4. The majority of Argentina receives ______________ precipitation.
5. The majority of South America receives ______________ precipitation.
6. Most of Chile receives ______________ precipitation.
7. The northwestern tip of Colombia receives ______________ precipitation.
8. The western half of Ecuador receives ______________ precipitation.
9. Most of Brazil receives ______________ precipitation.

Name ____________________

Land in South America

Key

Brazilian Highlands	Guiana Highlands	Andes Mountains	Pampas

1. Over half of the continent is covered by ____________________.
2. The ____________________ Mountains run from north to south on the western half of the continent.
3. In what part of the country are the Guiana Highlands located? ________
4. In the eastern part of South America is an area called the ____________ ____________________ Highlands.
5. Most of Argentina is covered by ____________________.
6. The eastern part of Brazil is the ____________________ Highlands.
7. Which country is covered completely by pampas—Uruguay or Venezuela? ____________________
8. Colombia's northeast border is formed by the country of ____________.
9. Name the country which borders Argentina to the west. ____________
10. Which country does not contain the Andes Mountains within its borders—Chile, Peru or Uruguay? ____________________

Section 5

Grid Maps

Name ________________________________

Numbers and Letters on a Map

This is a map of Red Falls.

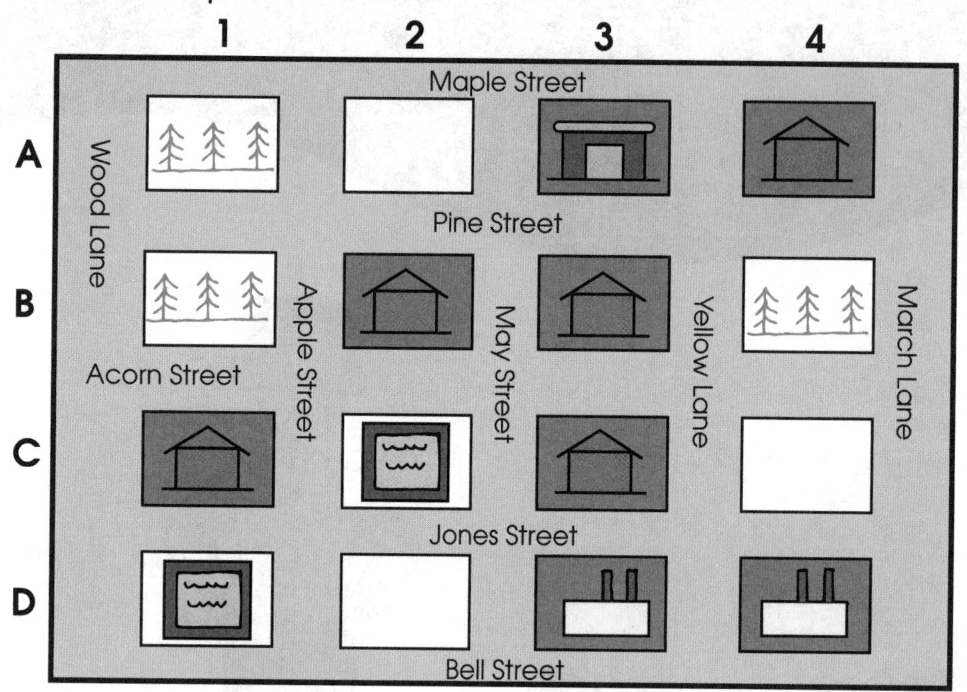

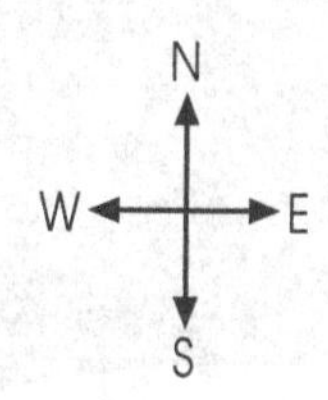

Directions: Use the numbers and letters to help you answer the questions below.

1. Locate the blocks. Write down what you see in each block.
   "A 1" ________________ "C 1" ________________
   "D 4" ________________ "D 1" ________________
2. Name the blocks with swimming pools. ________________
3. Name the blocks with houses. ________________
4. Name the blocks with woods. ________________
5. Tell what is located in the first block south of "A 3." ________________
6. What is in the block south of "C 1"? ________________
7. How many houses are in "B 2"? ________________
8. What is in the block east of "B 3"? ________________
9. What is in the block west of "D 4"? ________________
10. Draw a swimming pool in "A 2."
11. Draw a house in "D 2."
12. Draw a factory in "C 4."

Name____________________________________

Using a Grid

A map grid helps people locate places easily.

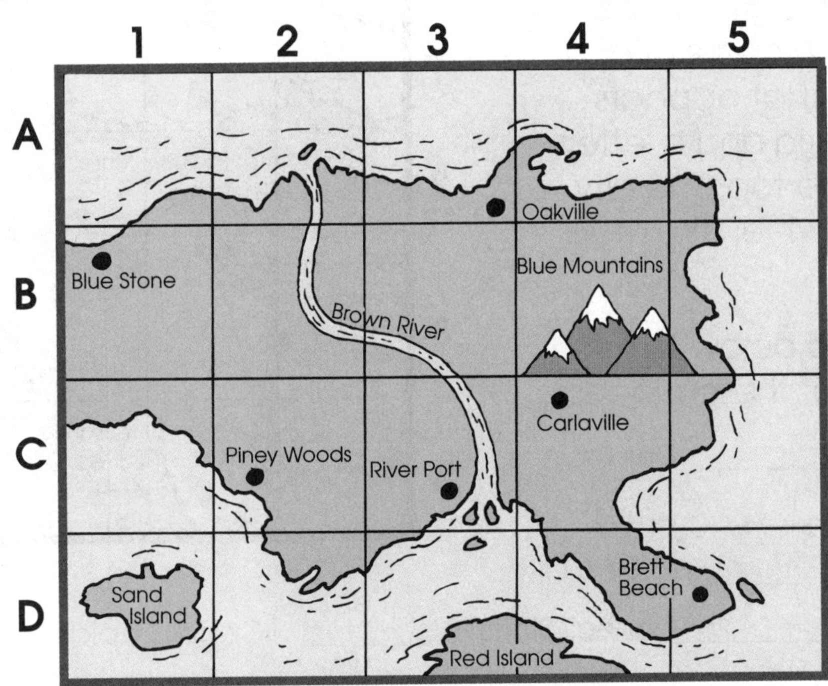

Directions: Use the numbers and letters to help you answer the questions bel

1. In which block is Brett Beach? ____________________
2. In which block is Blue Stone? ____________________
3. In which block is Piney Woods? ____________________
4. In which two blocks is Red Island? ____________________
5. In which four blocks is the Brown River? ____________________
6. In which block is Carlaville? ____________________
7. In which two blocks are the Blue Mountains? ____________________
8. Name the town located in "A 3." ____________________
9. Name the two islands found on the map. ____________________
10. In "C 5," add a town to the map.
11. In "B 2," add some trees.
12. In "A 5," add an island and name the island.

Name ______________________________________

A Little Gridwork

A grid makes it easier to find places on a map. The lines of a grid divide the map into imaginary squares. Each square has a number that appears along the side of the grid and a letter that appears along the top. The city of Detroit is found at "D 4" on the map at the right.

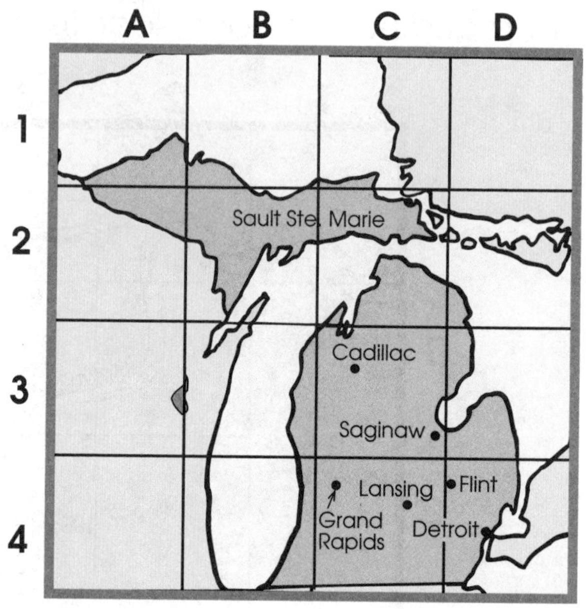

Directions: Use the grid below to find the location of each of these places.

_________ Sioux City _________ Des Moines

_________ Davenport _________ Ames

_________ Dubuque _________ Mason City

_________ Waterloo _________ Council Bluffs _________ Cedar Rapids

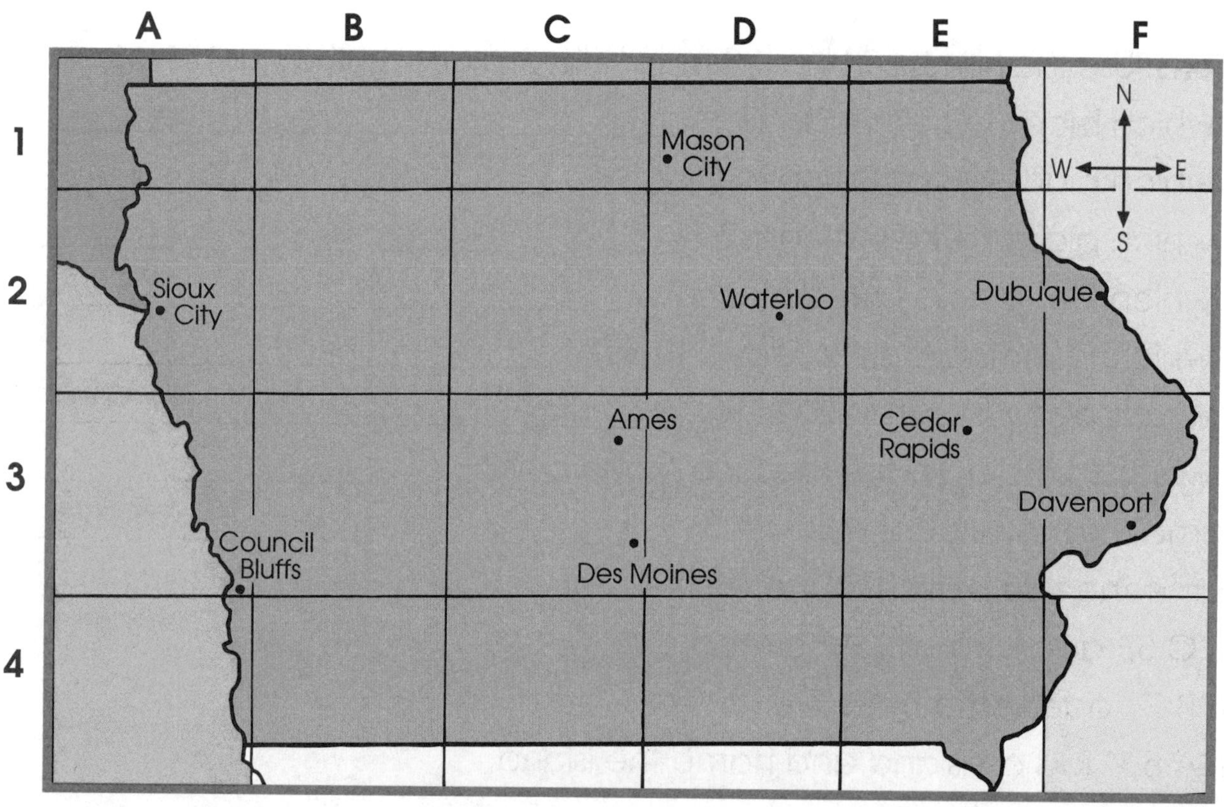

Name ______________________________

Getting to Pirates' Island

You are a pirate captain on your way home to Pirates' Island.

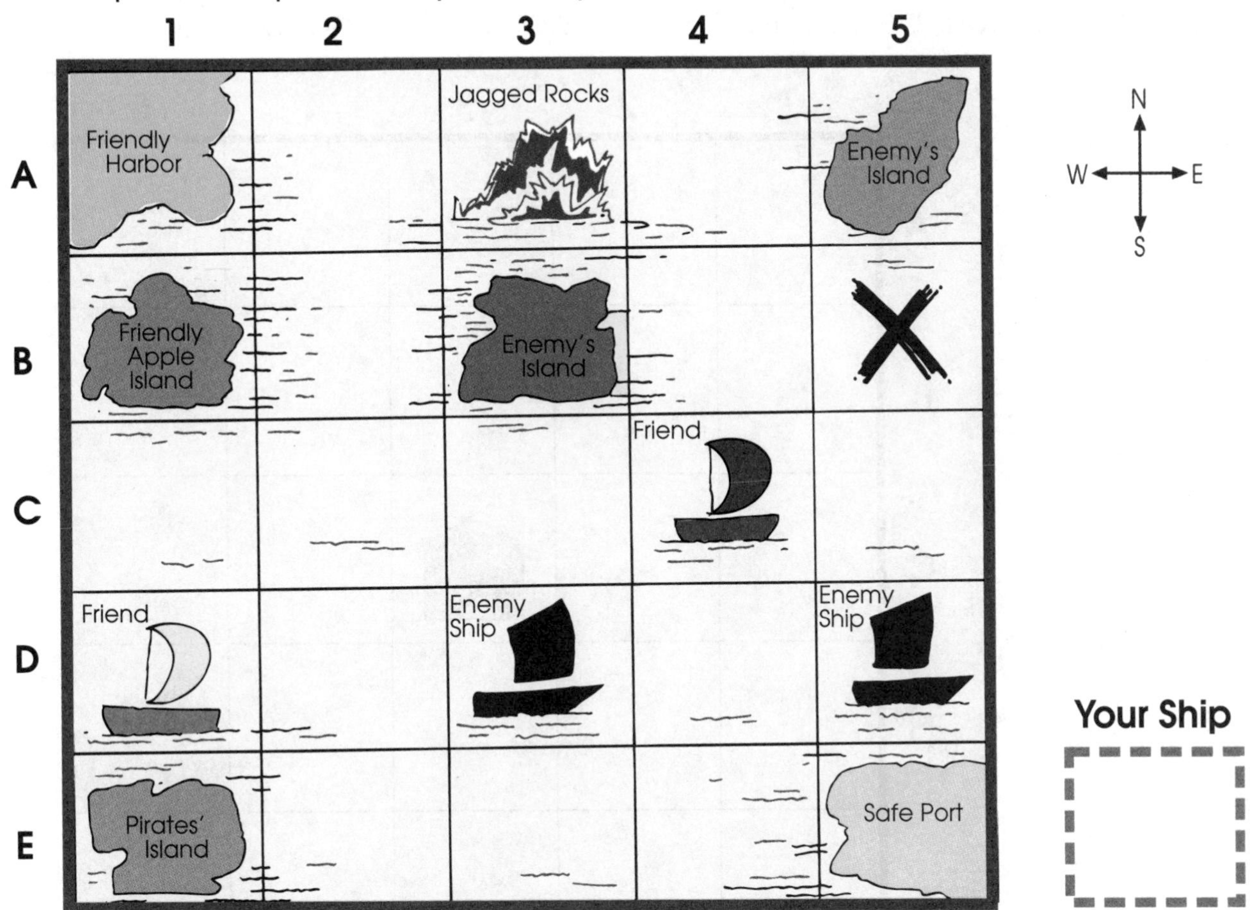

Directions: Draw a picture of your ship in the box and cut it out. Place the ship on the large **X**.

1. In which space is your ship located? ______________________
2. If you move your ship west two spaces, will you be safe? ____________
3. Name another space where your ship will not be safe. ______________
4. Move your ship from "B 5" to "B 2." Are you in a safe place? __________
5. Move your ship south three spaces from "B 2." What is your location?

   ____

6. If you move your ship from "E 2" to "E 1," where will you be? __________
7. Give the location for both enemy ships. ______________________
8. Can you safely move two spaces east of Friendly Apple Island? ______

Name____

Creating Your Own Grid Map

Create your own symbols for each object listed in the legend below. Then, follow the directions below. The first one is already done for you.

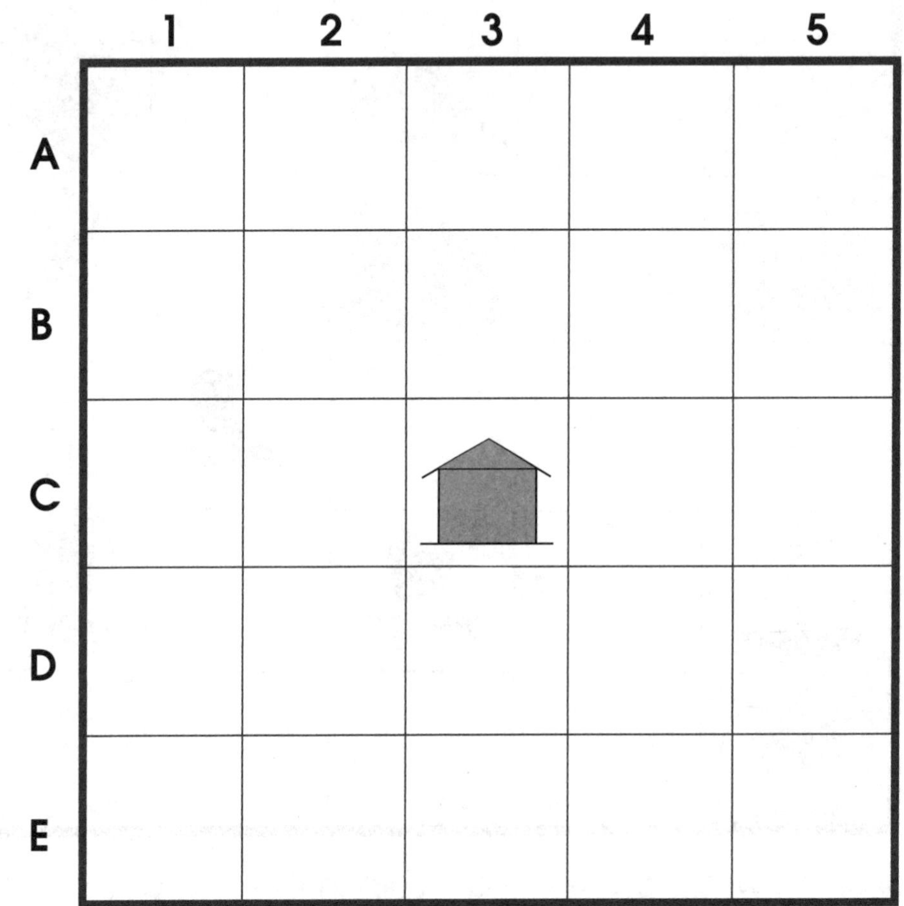

Legend

house	tree	flower
pond	bird	swing set

1. Draw a house in "C 3."
2. Draw a pond in "D 5" and "E 5."
3. Draw two birds in "A 2."
4. Draw one bird in "A 4."
5. Draw a tree in "C 1" and "B 1."
6. Draw a swing set in "E 3" and "E 4."
7. Draw two flowers in "D 2."
8. Draw a tree in "B 5" and "C 5."

Name____________________________________

Jumbo Gym

A new gym has been built in your city. Use the coordinates to name the location of the fitness features. The first one has been done for you.

Gym Grid Map

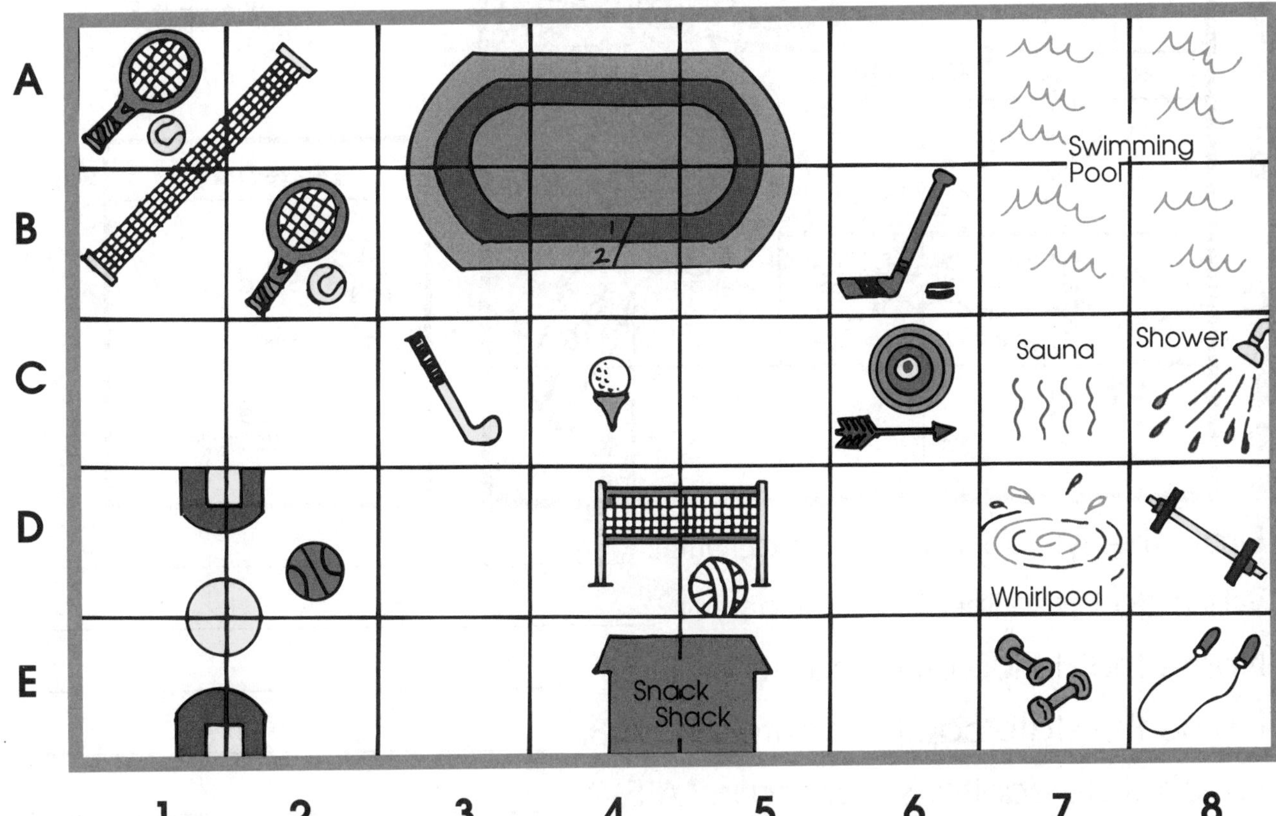

1. Archery ___C6___
2. Whirlpool__________
3. Swimming pool________ ,________ ,
________ ,________
4. Golf driving range ________,
____
5. Floor hockey__________
6. Small weights room ________
7. Basketball court ________, ________,
________, ________
8. Track ________, ________, ________,
________, ________, ________
9. Snack Shack ________, ________
10. Volleyball court ________, ________
11. Weightlifting ________
12. Shower ________
13. Sauna________
14. Rope jumping ________
15. Tennis courts ________, ________,
________, ________

Name ______________________________

The Southern States

Directions: Use the grid to help you locate places of the southern United States on this map.

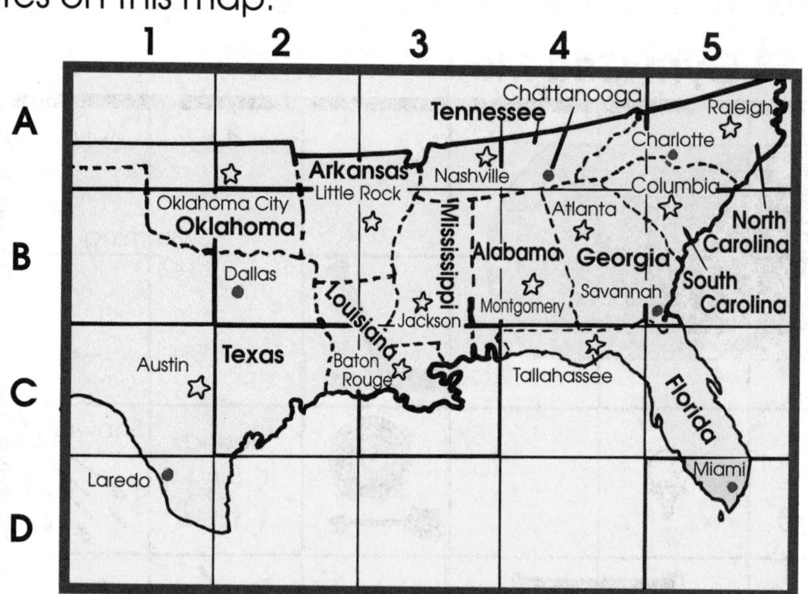

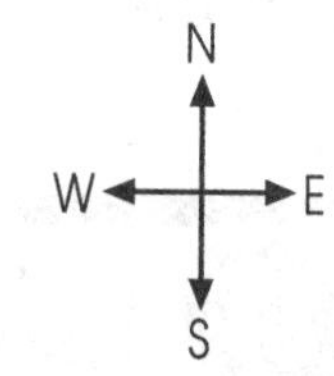

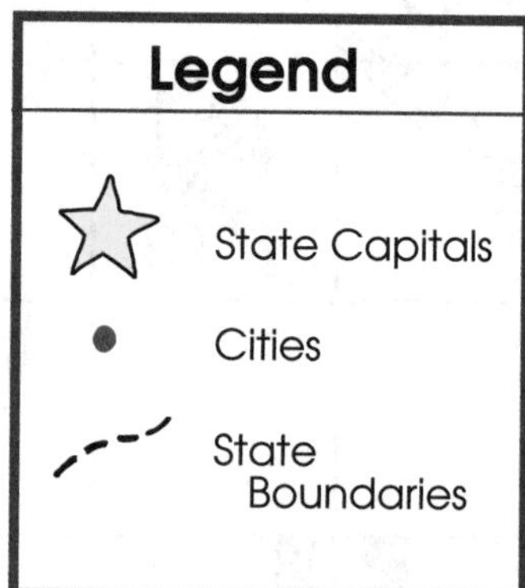

1. Draw the symbol for a state capital. ______________________
2. What do these lines - - - - stand for? ______________________
3. Name the Florida city located in "D 5." ______________________
4. Name the state capital located in "A 3." ______________________
5. Which state capital is located in "A 5"? ______________________
6. What is the location of Atlanta, Georgia? ______________________
7. Name the state capital located in "C 3." ______________________
8. Give the location of Jackson, Mississippi. ______________________
9. What state capital is located in "A 2"? ______________________
10. Give the location of Austin, Texas. ______________________
11. Name the cities located in "B 4." ______________________
12. Name the state located in "A 4" and "A 5." ______________________
13. Name the Tennessee city found in "A 4." ______________________
14. Name the two North Carolina cities located in "A 5." ______________________

Name ______________________________

We're Going Places

Directions: Draw an outline map of your state on the grid below. Label places or cities that are familiar to you. List them at the bottom of the page using the number and letter coordinates.

	A	B	C	D
1				
2				
3				
4				
5				

City or Place	Location	City or Place	Location
______	______	______	______
______	______	______	______
______	______	______	______
______	______	______	______
______	______	______	______

Name____

Grid Maps

Picture This!

Directions: Make a dot at each coordinate on the graph. Draw lines to connect the dots in order to make a picture. Add details and color the fuzzy fellow you drew on the graph.

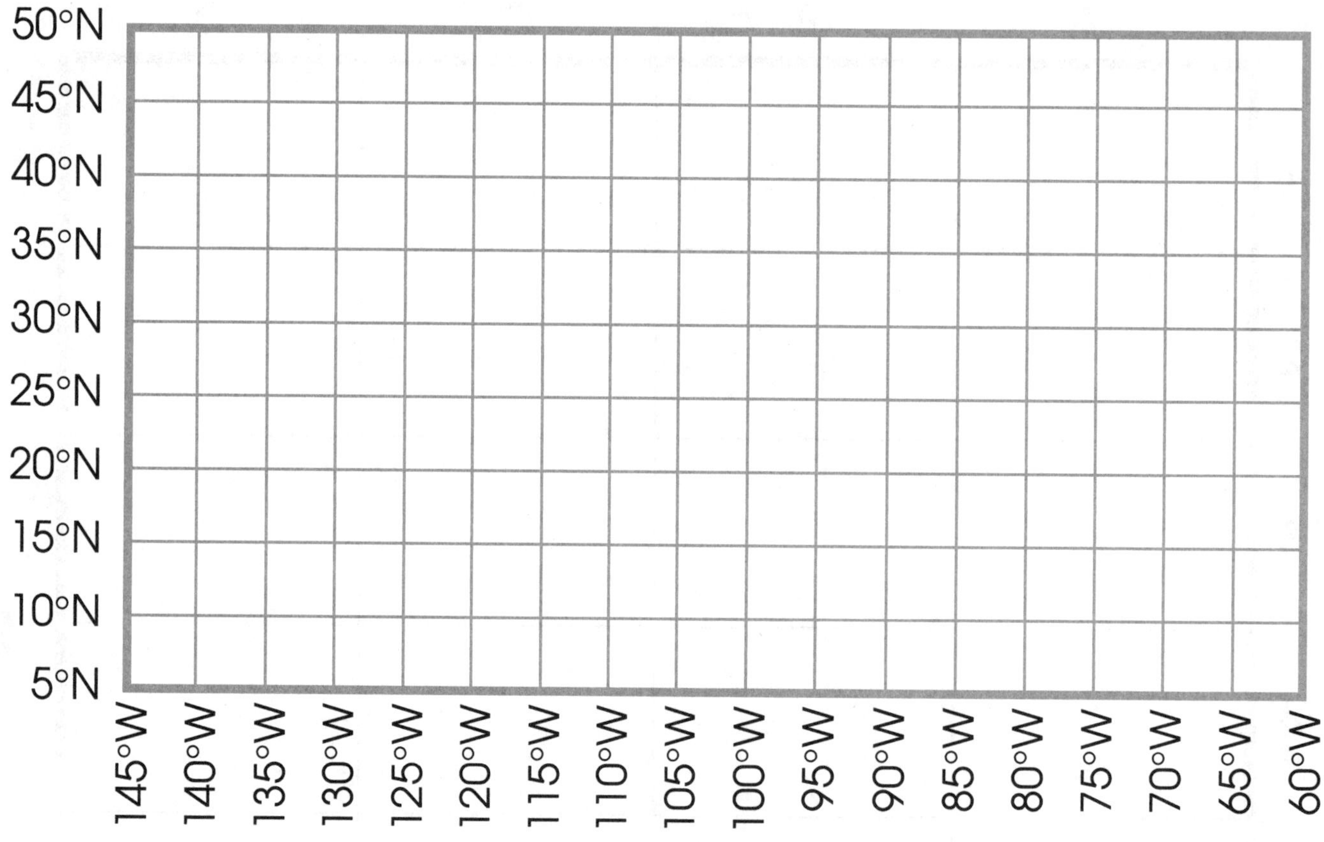

1. 5°N / 135°W
2. 15°N / 135°W
3. 15°N / 125°W
4. 25°N / 125°W
5. 25°N / 130°W
6. 35°N / 130°W
7. 35°N / 120°W
8. 45°N / 120°W
9. 45°N / 125°W
10. 50°N / 125°W
11. 50°N / 120°W
12. 45°N / 120°W
13. 45°N / 105°W
14. 50°N / 105°W
15. 50°N / 100°W
16. 45°N / 100°W
17. 45°N / 105°W
18. 35°N / 105°W
19. 35°N / 95°W
20. 25°N / 95°W
21. 25°N / 100°W
22. 15°N / 100°W
23. 15°N / 90°W
24. 5°N / 90°W
25. 5°N / 135°W

Section 6

Global Geography

Name____

The Globe

Imagine you are flying around in space. You look down and see a big round ball. It is the earth.

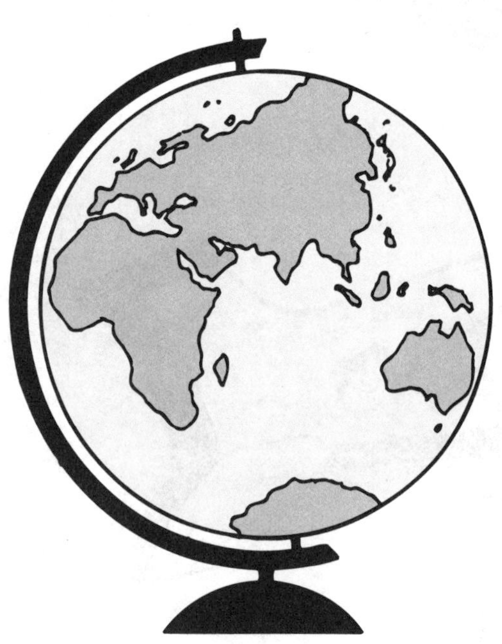

A model of the earth is called a globe. It is a round map that shows land and water. It uses colors to show which is the land and which is the water.

Directions: Unscramble the letters below to find out the colors that are used on the globe.

Land is ____________________. e r g e n

Water is____________________. l u b e

Color the land on the globe green.

Color the water on the globe blue.

Name________________________________

It's a Round World

Use these maps with pages 254 and 255.

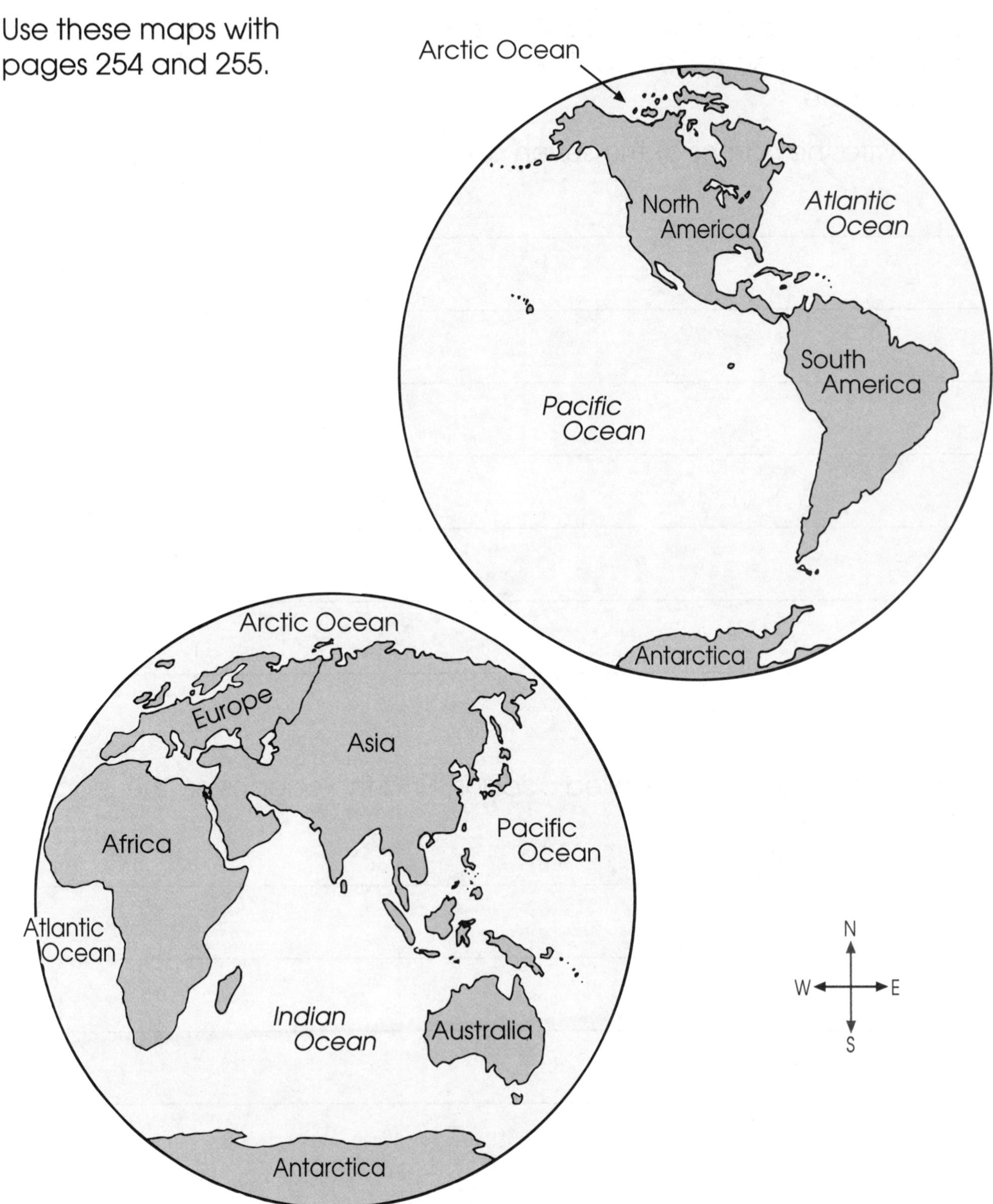

Name________________________________

It's a Round World

The picture of the globe on page 253 shows both halves of the world. It shows the large pieces of land called continents. There are seven continents. Find them on the globe.

Directions: Write the names of the seven continents.

1. ________________________________

2. ________________________________

3. ________________________________

4. ________________________________

5. ________________________________

6. ________________________________

7. ________________________________

There are four bodies of water called oceans. Find the oceans on the globe. Write the names below.

1. ________________________________

2. ________________________________

3. ________________________________

4. ________________________________

Name ______________________________

A Global Guide

Use the globe on page 253. Read the clues below. Write the answers on the lines. Then, use the numbered letters to solve the riddle at the bottom of the page.

1. This direction points up. ___ ___ ___ ___ ___ (1, 2, 22, 3)

2. This direction points down. ___ ___ ___ ___ ___ (4, 5, 6)

3. This direction points right. ___ ___ ___ ___ (7, 8)

4. This direction points left. ___ ___ ___ ___ (9, 10)

5. This ocean is west of North America. ___ ___ ___ ___ ___ ___ ___ (11, 12) ___ ___ ___ ___ ___ (13, 14)

6. This ocean is south of Asia. ___ ___ ___ ___ ___ ___ (15, 16, 17) ___ ___ ___ ___ ___

7. This ocean is east of South America. ___ ___ ___ ___ ___ ___ ___ ___ (18, 19) ___ ___ ___ ___ ___ (20, 21)

Riddle: What does a globe do?

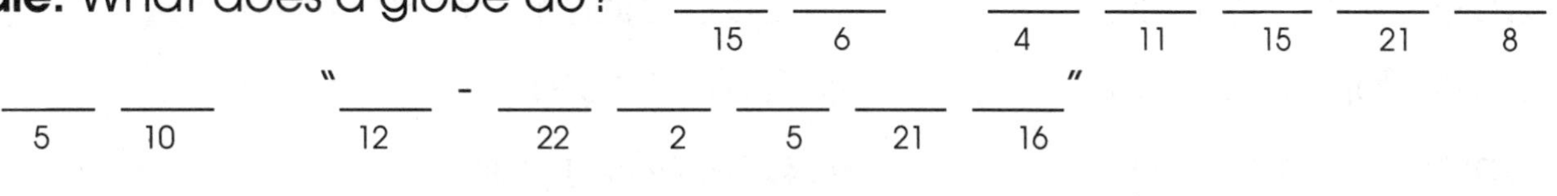

Name________________________________

Land and Water

Directions: Use the map below plus a wall map to do this activity.

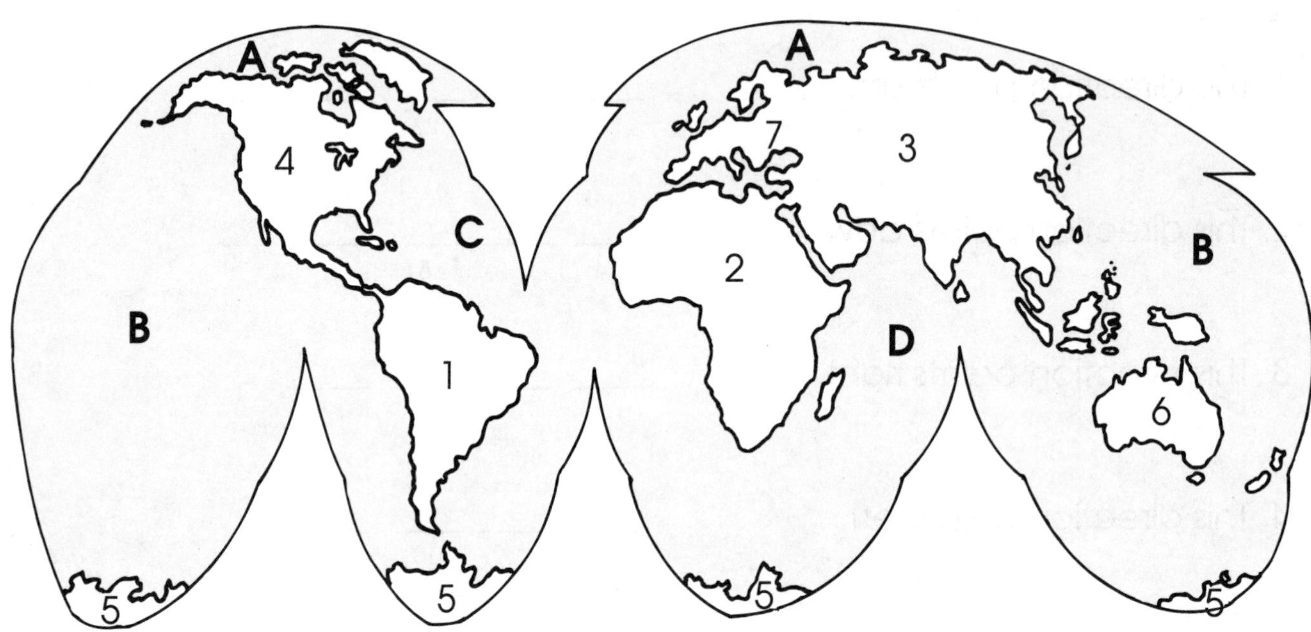

Write the name of each continent in the correct blank.

1. ________________ 5. ________________
2. ________________ 6. ________________
3. ________________ 7. ________________
4. ________________

Write the name of each ocean in the correct blank.

A. ________________ C. ________________

B. ________________ D. ________________

Use crayons or markers to follow these directions.

1. Color Australia green.
2. Color Europe yellow.
3. Color Africa orange.
4. Color Antarctica blue.
5. Color North America red.
6. Color South America brown.
7. Color Asia purple.

Name____________________

Color My World

Is it a city, state, country, continent or body of water? Color each box according to the Color Key. Use an atlas for help.

Color Key

city—orange state—green country—yellow
water—blue continent—purple

Atlantic Ocean	India	Colorado	Miami
Peru	Antarctica	Lake Michigan	Hawaii
New Orleans	Spain	Europe	Gulf of Mexico
Vermont	Phoenix	Japan	Paris
East China Sea	Egypt	Wyoming	Sweden
Africa	London	Hudson Bay	Connecticut
Greece	Minnesota	South America	Dallas
Oakland	Great Salt Lake	Argentina	Arctic Ocean
North America	Canada	Chicago	Arkansas
Lake Victoria	Iowa	Asia	Venezuela
Lima	Persian Gulf	Mexico	Moscow
Pacific Ocean	Maryland	Cincinnati	Brazil

Name____________________________________

Where in the World Is. . .

What is your global address? It's more than your street, city, state and ZIP code.

What would your address be if you wanted to get a letter from a friend living in outer space?

Use an atlas, encyclopedia, science book or other source to complete your global address.

Inter-Galactic Address Book

Name ____________________

Street ____________________

County or Parish ____________________

State or Province ____________________

Country ____________________

Continent ____________________

Hemisphere ____________________

Planet ____________________

Galaxy ____________________

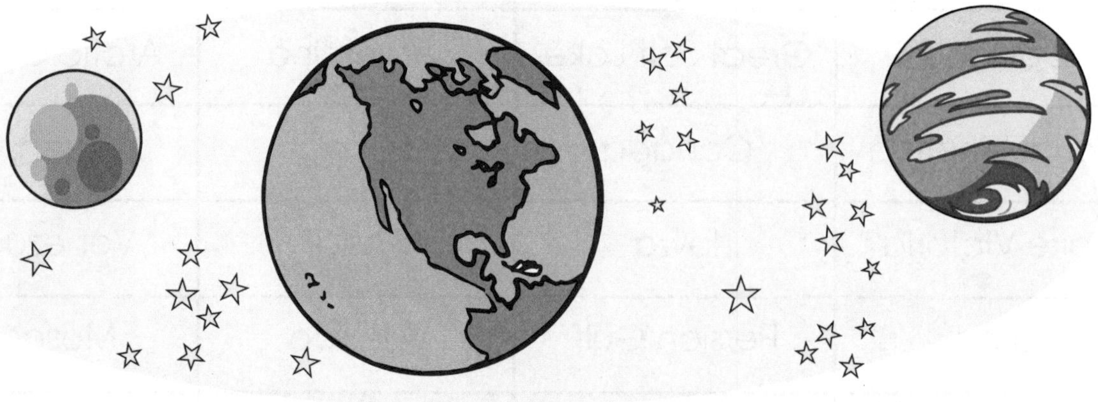

Draw an **X** to mark the approximate place where you live.

Name______________________________________

Where in the World?

Refer to the globe on page 253, a real globe or a world map. Find the seven continents and four oceans. Now, you are ready to make your own globe using this page and pages 261 and 263.

Directions:

1. Cut out all the continent and ocean labels.
2. Glue them where they belong in the boxes on the maps on pages 261 and 263.
3. Cut out all of the map circles along the outer lines.
4. Fold each circle in half along the dotted line. Keep the map side on the inside.
5. Be sure to keep the numbers on the circles at the top. Glue the back of the right half of circle **1** to the back of the left half of circle **2**.
6. Glue the back of the right half of circle **2** to the back of the left half of circle **3**.
7. Glue the back of the right half of circle **3** to the back of the left half of circle **4**.
8. Complete the globe by gluing the back of the right half of circle **4** to the back of the left half of circle **1**.

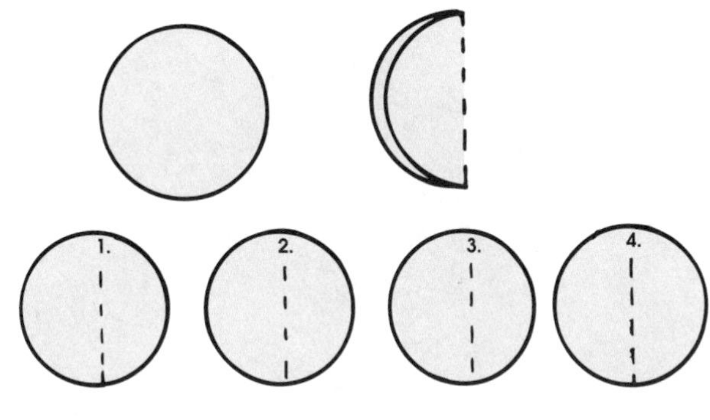

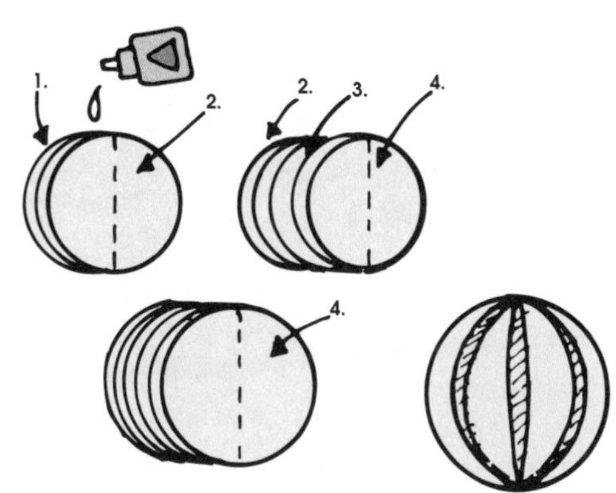

This page has been intentionally left blank.

Name ______________________________

Where in the World?

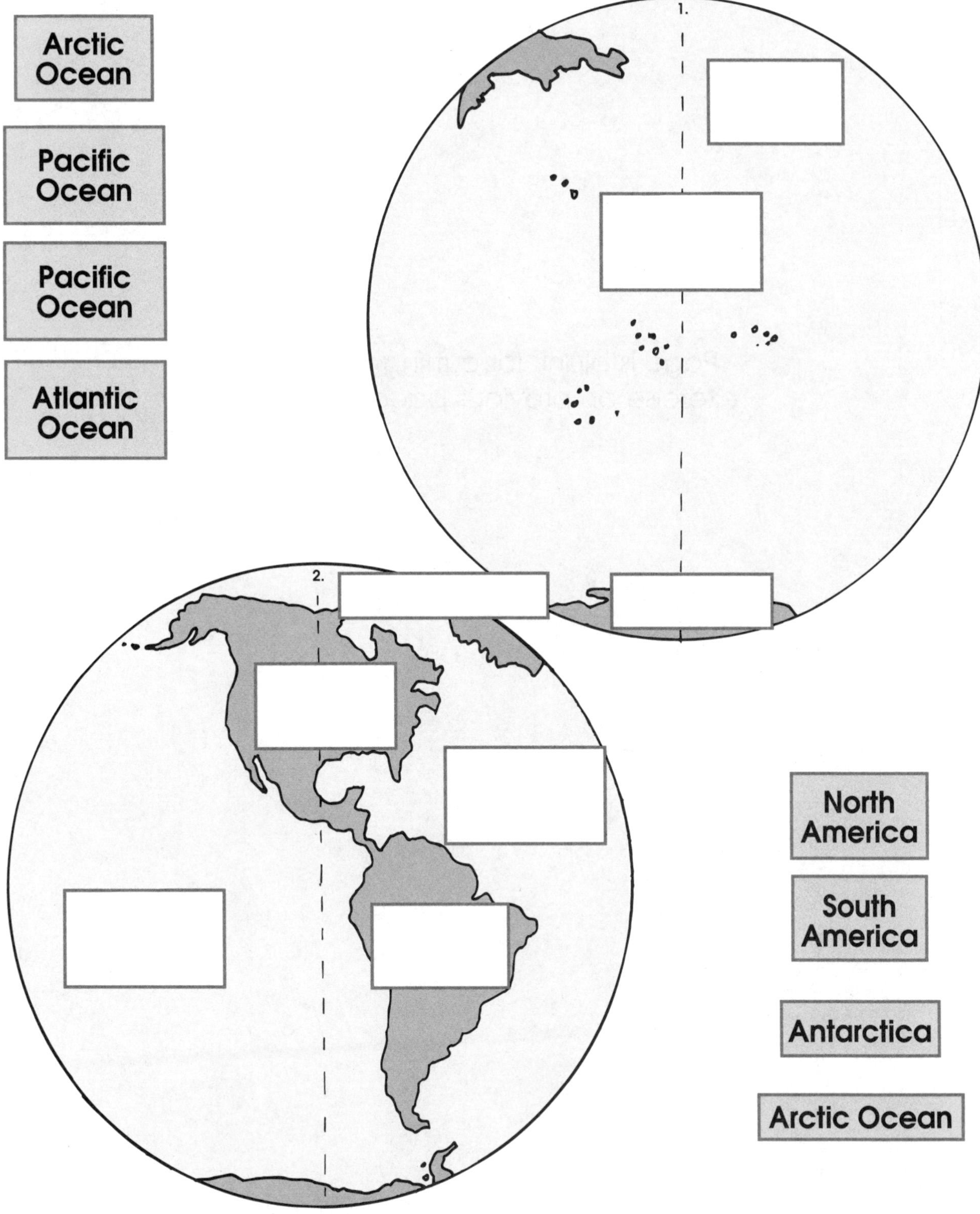

Page is blank for cutting exercise on previous page.

Name ____________________

Where in the World

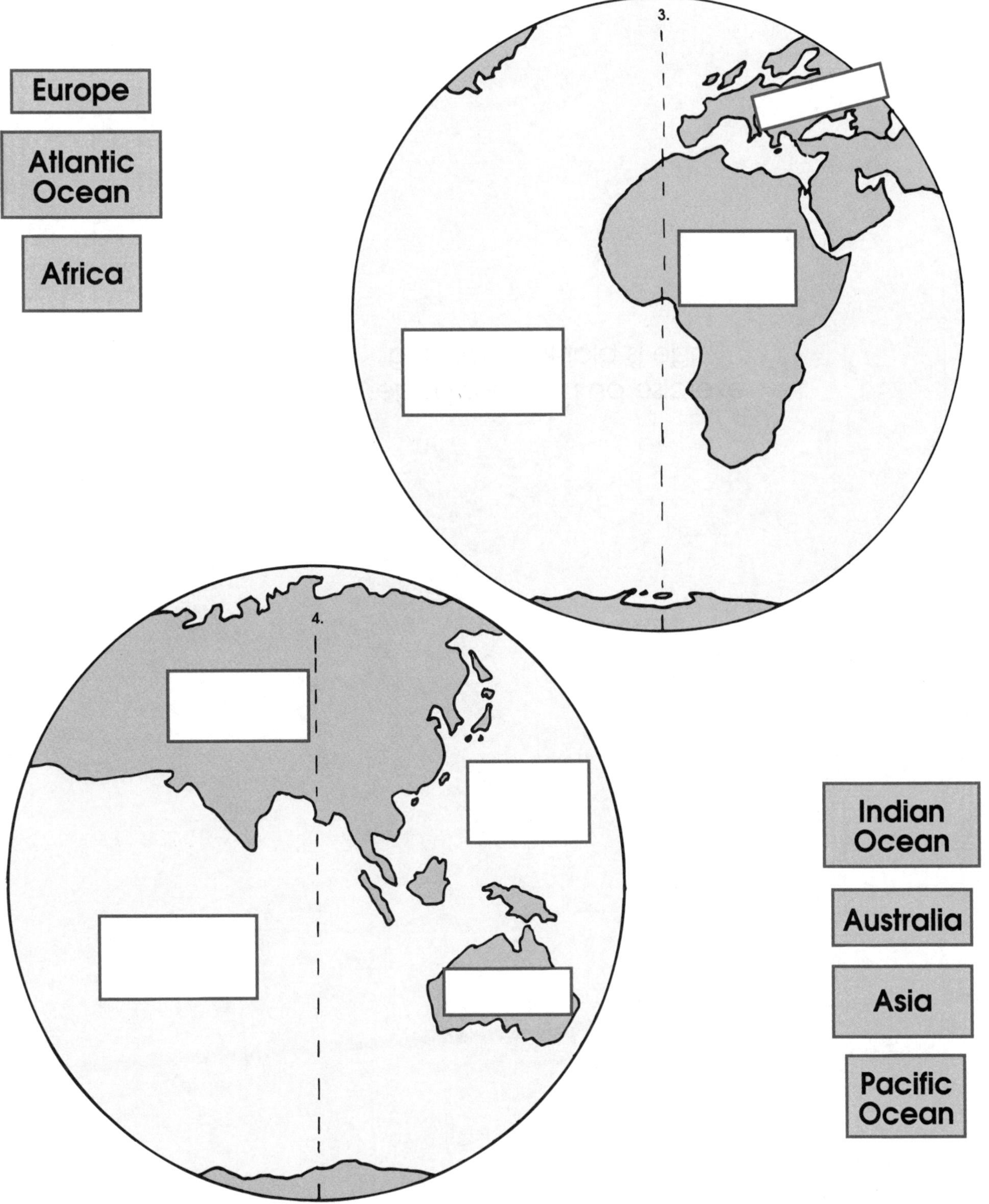

Page is blank for cutting exercise on previous page.

Name____________________

Near and Far

Below is a map of the world. It shows the seven continents. Around the map are pictures of animals that are native to the continents. The continent on which each animal can be found is written below the name of the animal.

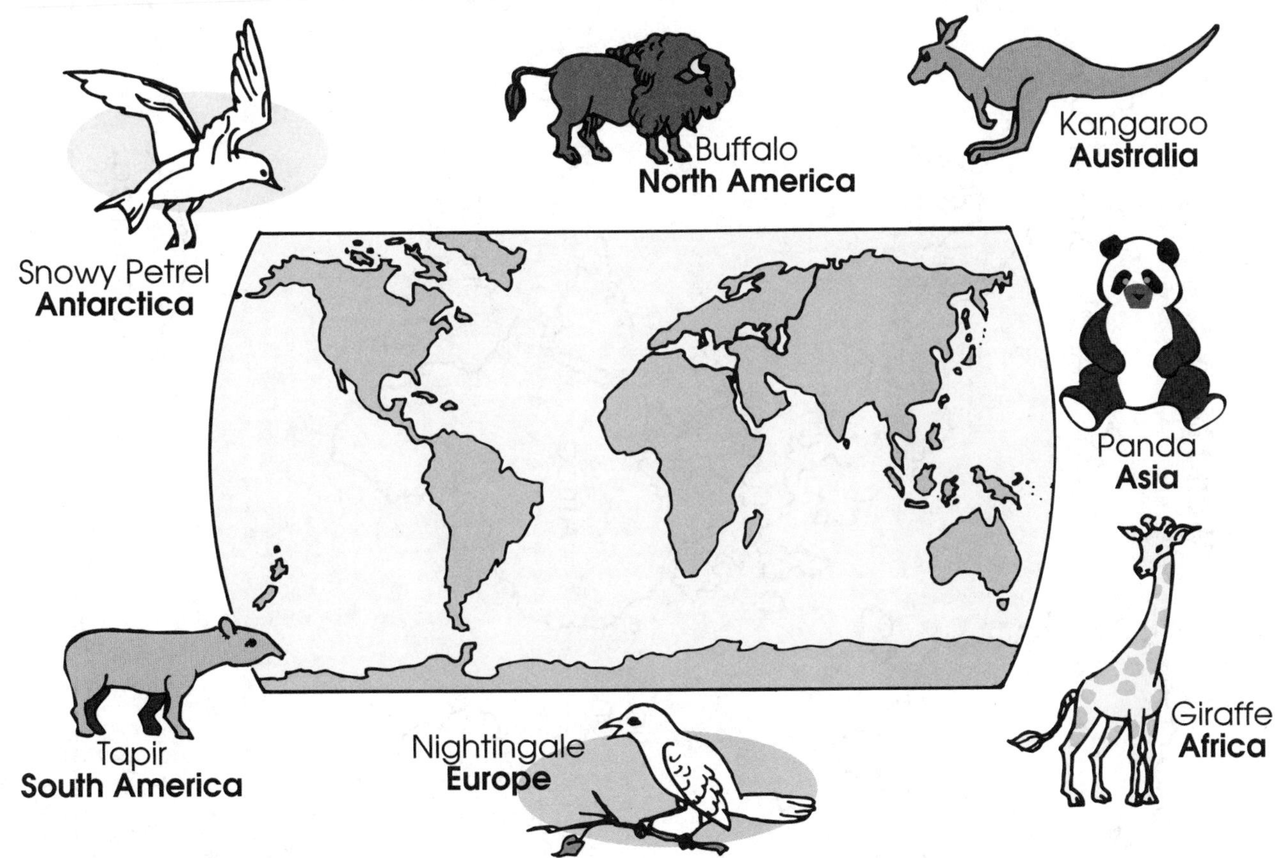

Directions: Use a globe or world map to locate each continent. Draw a line from the picture of the animal to the continent where it is found.

1. Find the continent where you live.
2. Which animal lives on your continent? ____________________
3. Which animal lives on a continent far from you? ____________________

Name____

Let's Travel the Earth

World Map

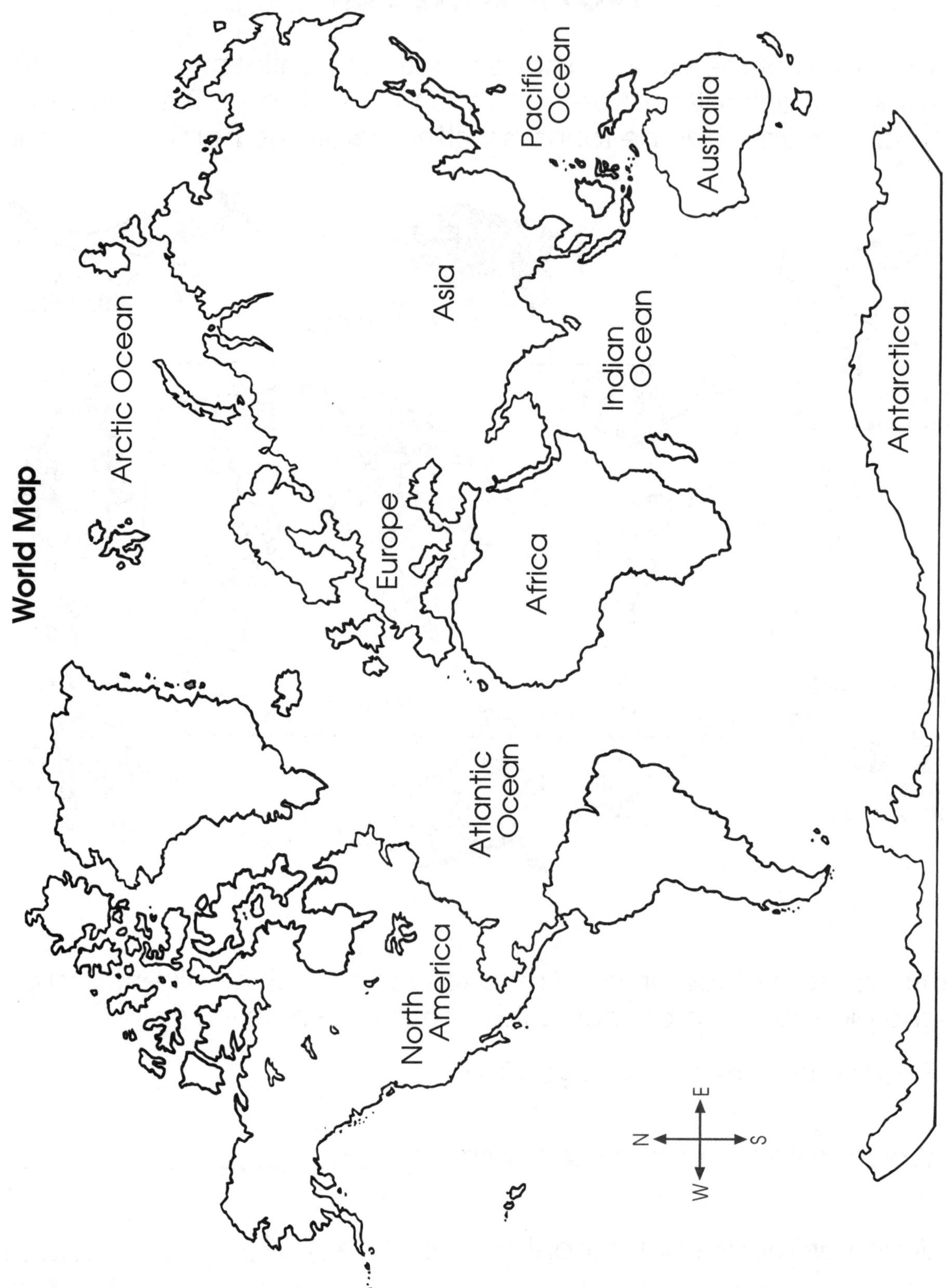

Use with page 267.

Name ______________________________

Let's Travel the Earth

Directions: Use the map on page 266 to answer the questions below.

Circle the word that correctly completes each statement.

1. If you sail from North America to Antarctica, you will be on the . . .
   Arctic Ocean   Atlantic Ocean   Indian Ocean
2. If you fly from Africa to Australia, you will fly over the . . .
   Indian Ocean   Pacific Ocean   Atlantic Ocean
3. To sail from Europe to South America, you will sail on the . . .
   Pacific Ocean   Arctic Ocean   Atlantic Ocean
4. To sail from North America to Europe, you will sail on the . . .
   Indian Ocean   Atlantic Ocean   Pacific Ocean
5. To travel from Europe to Asia, you must cross . . .
   the Pacific Ocean   the Indian Ocean   land

Fill in the blanks with the correct word.

1. The continent north of South America is ______________________.
2. The ocean directly south of Asia is the ______________________.
3. The ocean directly north of Asia is the ______________________.
4. The continent directly south of Europe is ______________________.
5. The continent directly south of Australia is ______________________.

Use a crayon or marker to follow these directions.

1. Draw a red line from North America to Africa.
2. Draw a green line from Asia to Antarctica.
3. Draw an orange line from Australia to Africa.
4. Draw a black line from Europe to South America.
5. Circle the names of all four oceans with blue.
6. Color North America green.
7. Draw a black dotted line (- - - - - -) around South America.

Name____

Hemispheres

The earth is a sphere. When the earth is cut in half horizontally along an imaginary line called the **equator**, the **Northern** and **Southern Hemispheres** of the earth are created.

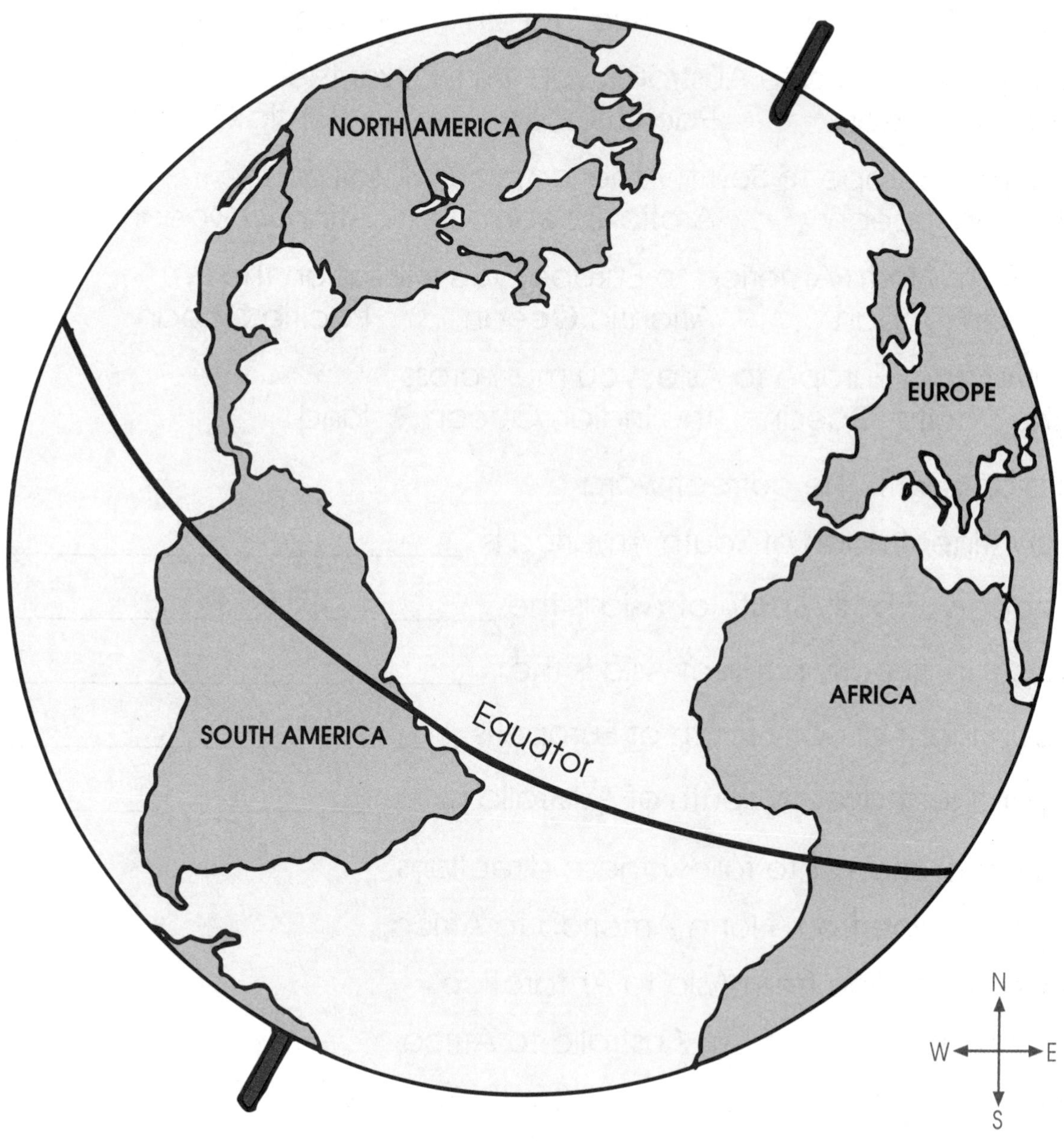

Trace the equator in orange.

Label the two hemispheres on the globe above.

Name_______________________________________

Hemispheres

When the earth is cut in half vertically along an imaginary line called the **prime meridian**, the **Eastern** and **Western Hemispheres** of the earth are created.

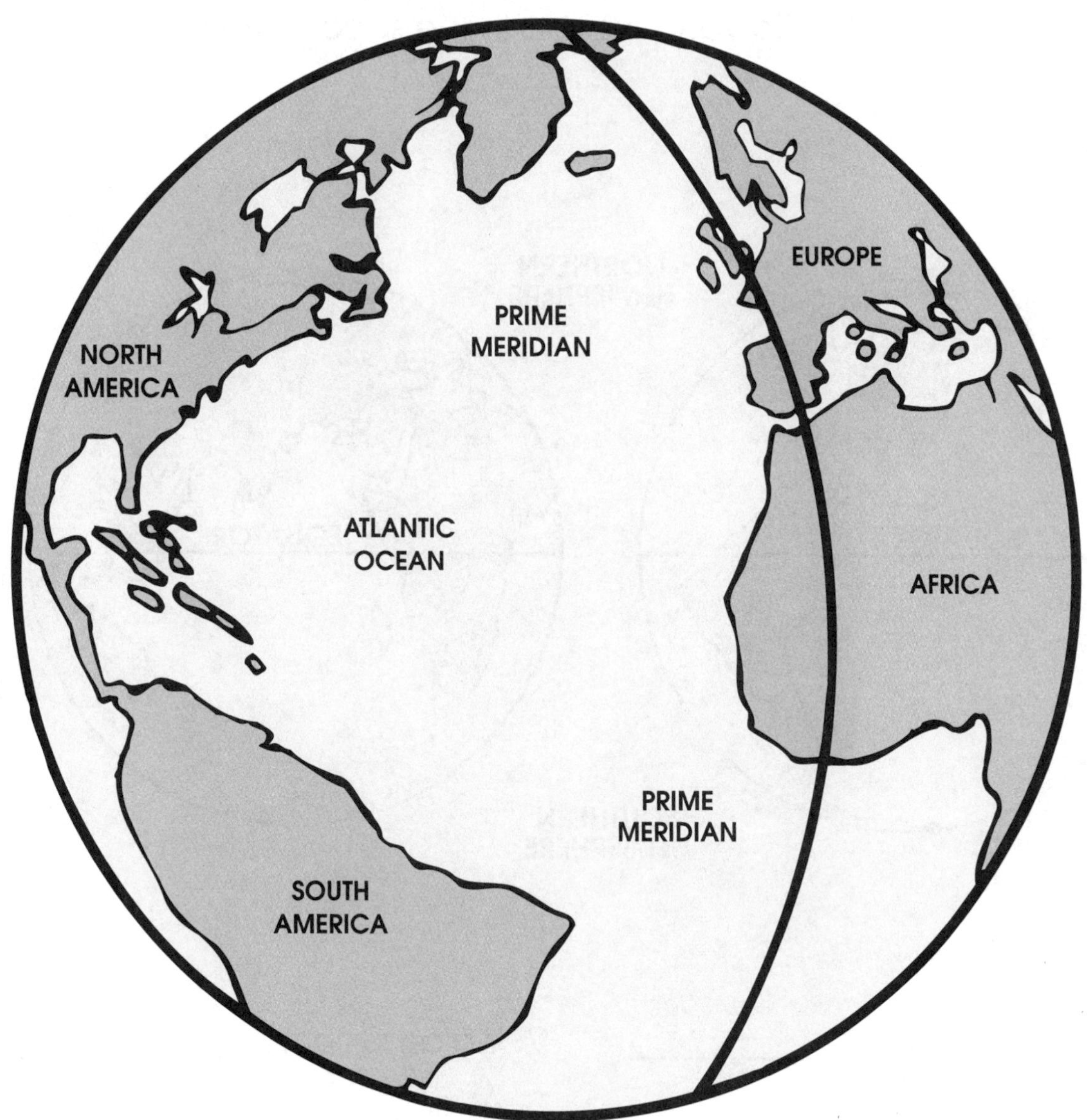

Trace the prime meridian in blue.

Label the two hemispheres on the globe above.

Color the axis, or poles, red.

Name____________________________________

Hemispheres

Directions: Examine the illustration below. Decide in which two hemispheres (Eastern or Western and Northern or Southern) each of the following continents or oceans is located. (Example: The United States is in the Northern and Western Hemispheres.) Write your answers in the space provided.

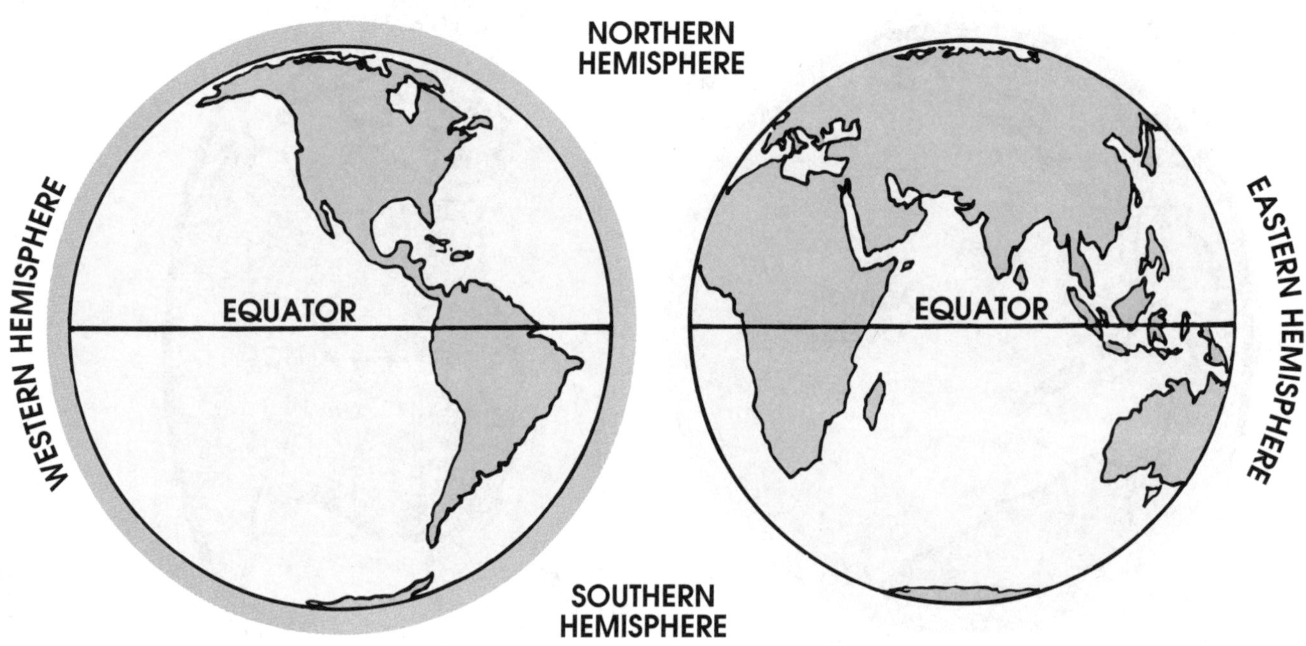

1. North America ______________
2. Europe ______________
3. South America ______________
4. Pacific Ocean ______________
5. Australia ______________
6. Atlantic Ocean ______________
7. Indian Ocean ______________
8. Asia ______________
9. Africa ______________
10. Antarctica ______________
11. Arctic Ocean ______________

Name________________________________

Locating the Continents and Oceans

Directions: Use these maps plus wall maps to complete this page. **Note**: Some continents belong to more than one hemisphere.

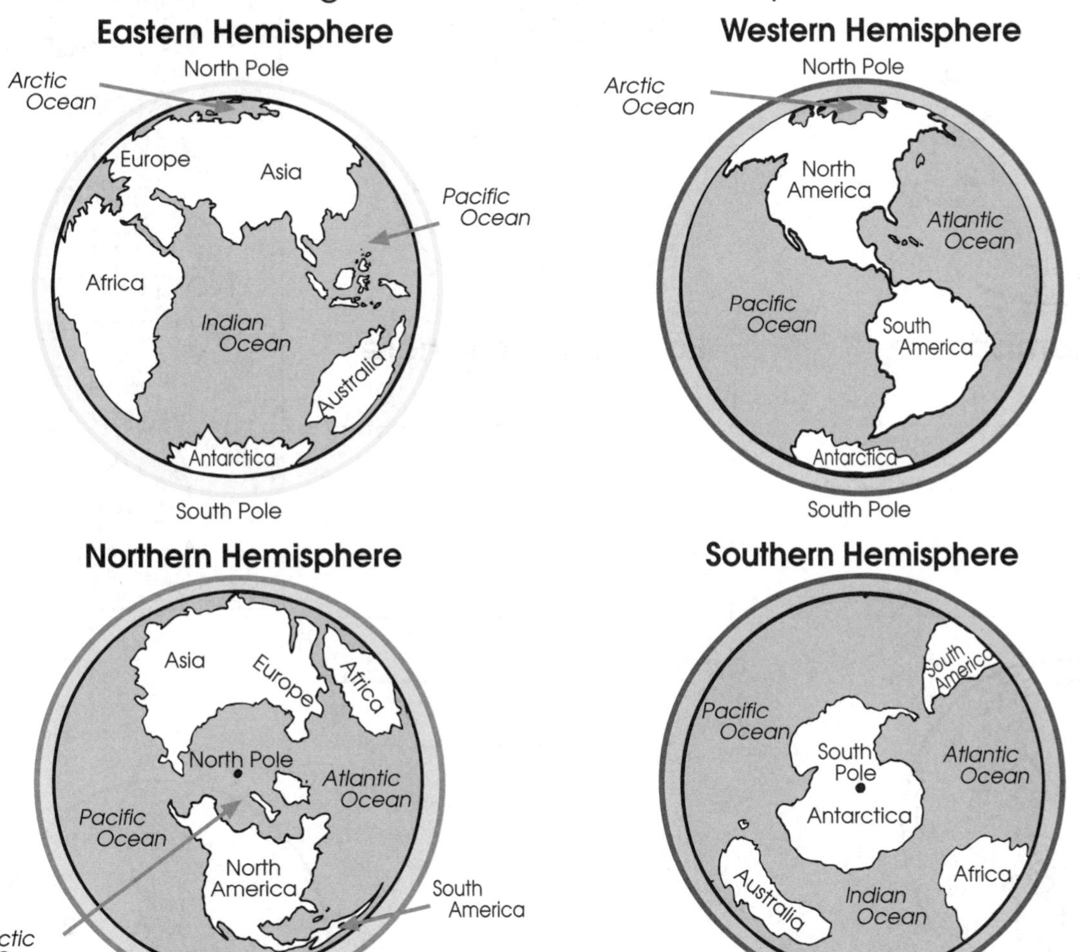

1. Which continent is found in both the Eastern and Western Hemispheres?

____

2. Which map does not show any part of Antarctica?

____

3. Which hemisphere does not include any part of Africa?

____

4. Color the continent located entirely in the Western and Northern Hemispheres red.
5. Color the continent located entirely in the Eastern and Southern Hemispheres green.

Name______________________________

Happy Hemispheres

Write the name of each continent and ocean next to its number.

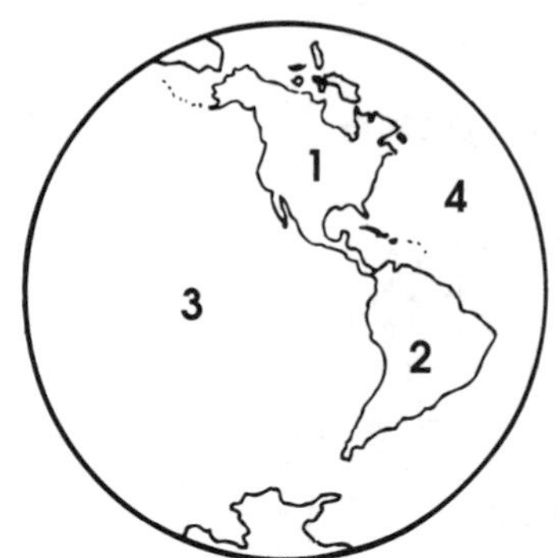

Word Bank

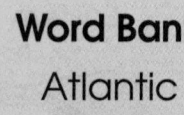

Atlantic
Pacific
Indian
Arctic
North America
South America
Europe
Australia
Asia
Africa
Antarctica

Western Hemisphere

1. ______________
2. ______________
3. ______________
4. ______________

Eastern Hemisphere

1. ______________
2. ______________
3. ______________
4. ______________
5. ______________
6. ______________

Northern Hemisphere

1. ______________
2. ______________
3. ______________
4. ______________
5. ______________
6. ______________

Southern Hemisphere

1. ______________
2. ______________
3. ______________
4. ______________
5. ______________
6. ______________
7. ______________

Name ______________________________

North to South

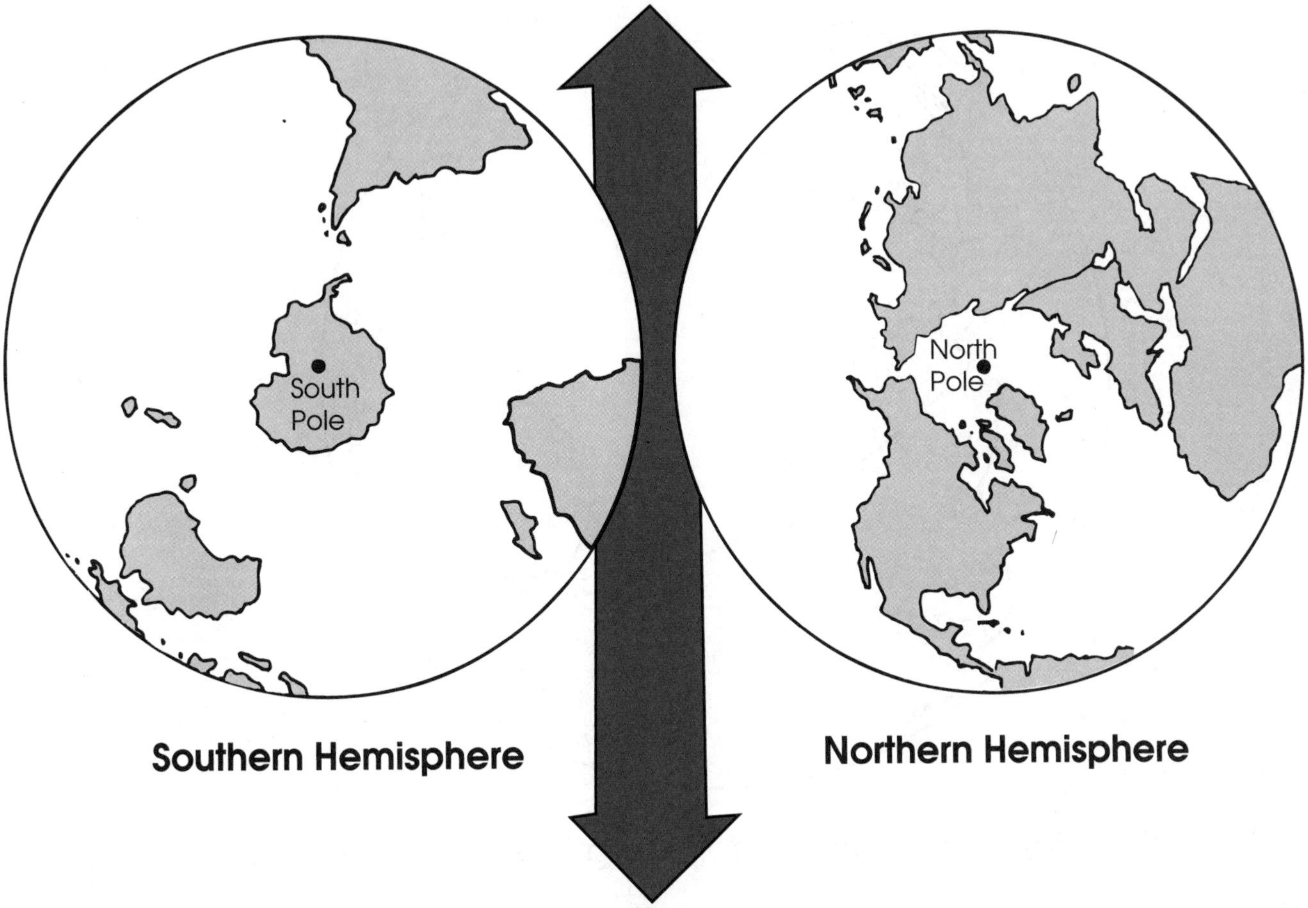

South Pole

North Pole

Southern Hemisphere

Northern Hemisphere

Directions: Label the continents on each hemisphere. Use the abbreviations below.

N.A.	=	North America	**Ant.**	=	Antarctica
S.A.	=	South America	**Aust.**	=	Australia
Eur.	=	Europe	**Afr.**	=	Africa
As.	=	Asia			

Color the oceans in each hemisphere using the colors and designs below.

(purple) 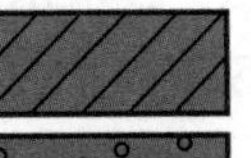 Indian Ocean

(green) 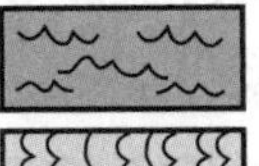 Atlantic Ocean

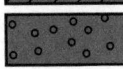

(blue) Pacific Ocean

(lt. green) 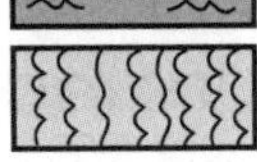 Arctic Ocean

Name____

Global Fun

Directions: Complete the globe by following the directions below.

1. Draw a whale in the Southern Hemisphere of the Pacific Ocean.
2. Trace the equator in orange.
3. Draw a shark in the Arctic Ocean.
4. Draw a smiling face near Antarctica.
5. Draw an ocean liner in the Northern Hemisphere of the Atlantic Ocean.
6. Color the axis poles red.
7. In North America, color Mexico yellow, Canada green and the U.S.A. red.
8. Draw a yellow **X** in the Northern Hemisphere of Africa.
9. Color Europe purple.
10. Draw rainbow-colored diagonal stripes on South America.
11. Draw an orange circle on the Southern Hemisphere of Africa.

Name____

From East to West

Directions: Label the continents using the abbreviations below. Cut out the continents. Glue them onto the correct hemisphere in the proper places. Include Antarctica on each hemisphere.

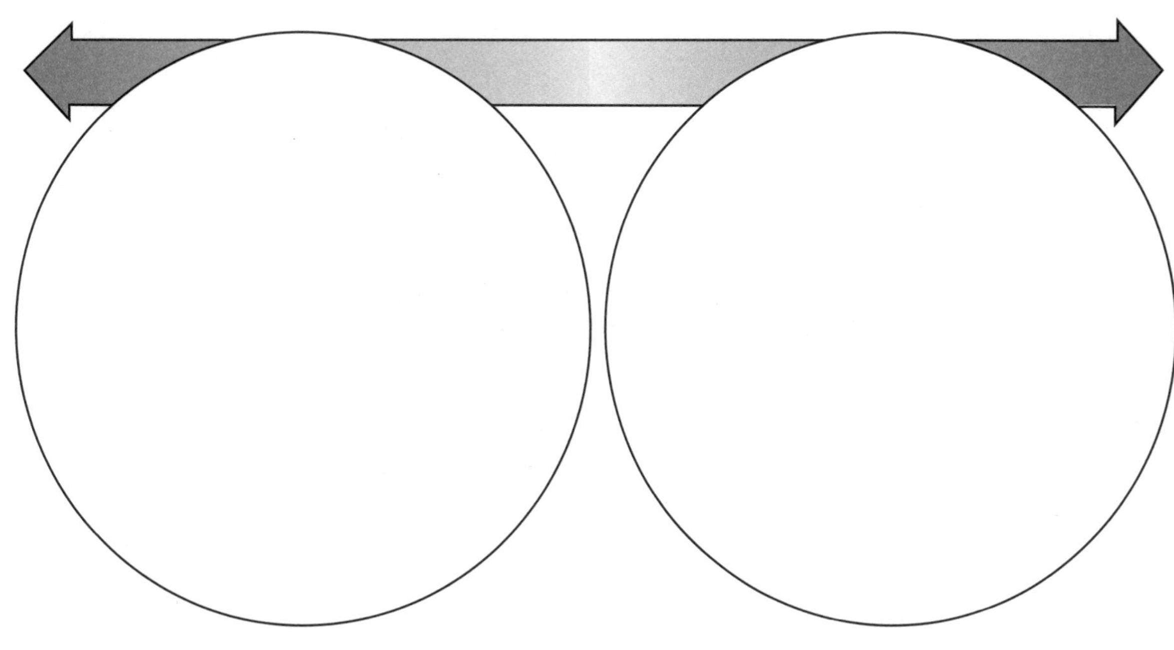

Western Hemisphere **Eastern Hemisphere**

Abbreviations

N.A.	=	North America
Eur.	=	Europe
Aust.	=	Australia
S.A.	=	South America
As.	=	Asia
Afr.	=	Africa
Ant.	=	Antarctica

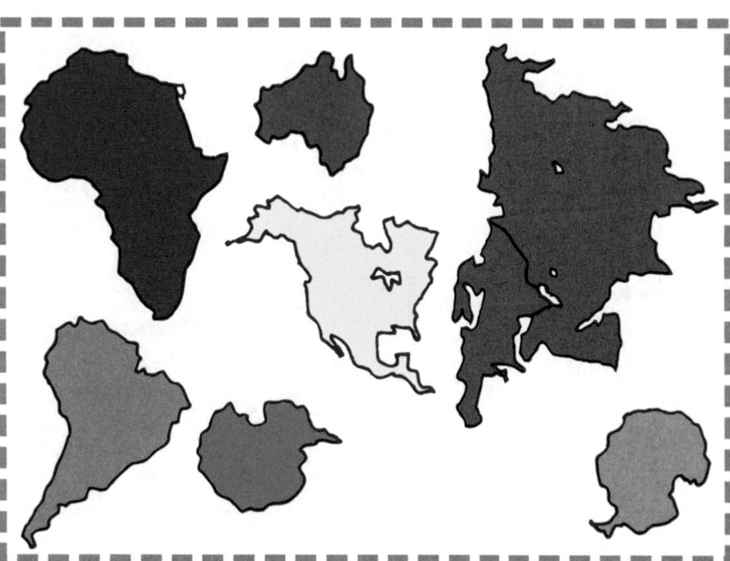

Page is blank for cutting exercise on previous page.

Name ______________________________

The Long Lines

Lines of longitude on a globe run north and south. They are sometimes called **meridians**. Zero degrees longitude (0°) is an imaginary line called the **prime meridian**. It passes through Greenwich, England. Half of the lines of longitude are west of the prime meridian, and half are east of it.

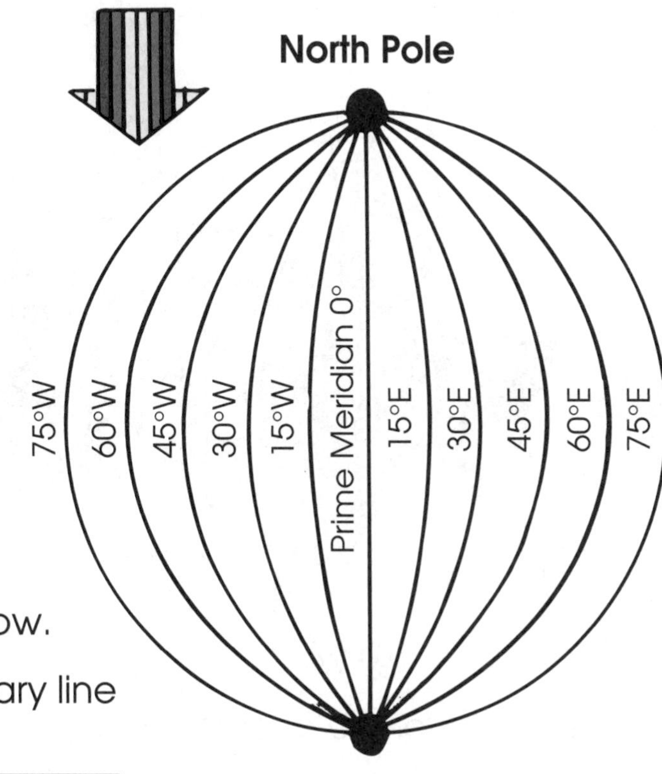

Directions: Answer the questions below.

1. What is the name for the imaginary line at 0° longitude? ____________________
2. Lines to the left of the prime meridian are which direction? ____________________
3. Lines to the right of the prime meridian are which direction? __________
4. Where do lines of longitude come together?
   ______________________ and _________________________
5. Where does the prime meridian pass through?
   ____
6. Lines of longitude run in which directions?
   ______________________ and _________________________
7. Color the prime meridian red.
8. Color the other meridians blue.

Name_______________________________________

Merry Meridians

Shown on the map are the lines of longitude west of the prime meridian.

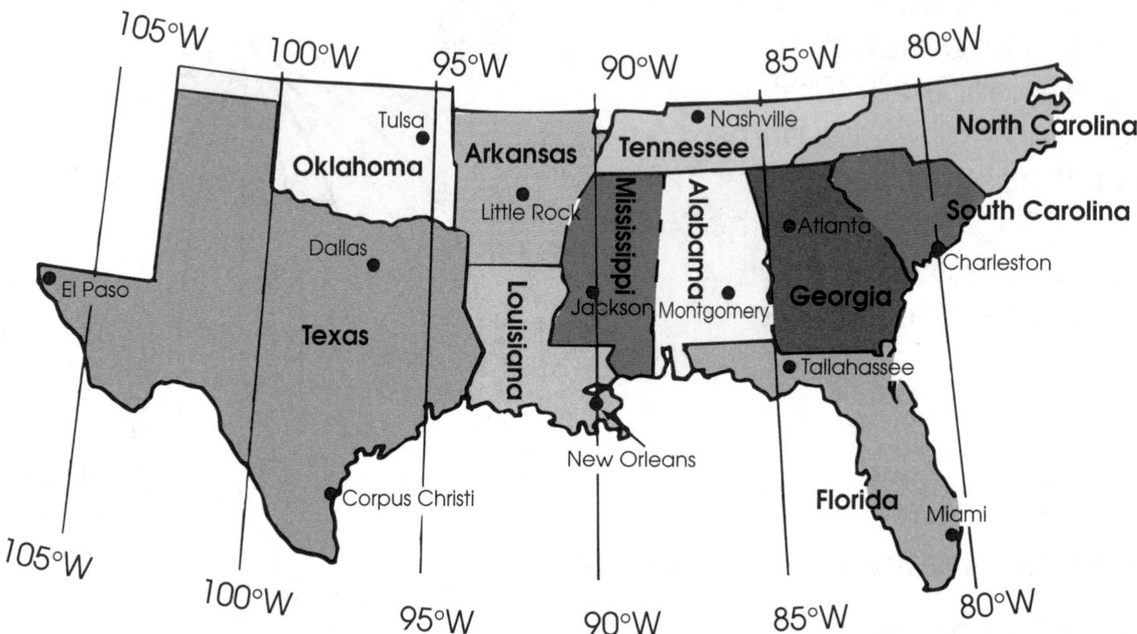

Directions: Answer the questions about these southeastern states.

1. Which two cities lie closest to 90°W?

   ____________________, ______________________,
2. To which longitude line is Miami, Florida, closest? ______________________
3. Which cities lie between 80°W and 85°W? ______________________,

   ____________________, ______________________, ______________________,
4. Which city is closest to 95°W? ______________________
5. El Paso, Texas, is closest to which meridian? ______________________
6. Which two cities are closest to 85°W?______________, ______________
7. Little Rock is between which two meridians? ______________________and

   ____
8. Parts of which states lie between 85°W and 90°W?______________________,

   ____________________, ______________________, ______________________,

   ____________________, ______________________, ______________________,
9. Most of Florida lies between which meridians? ______________________
10. Corpus Christi lies between which meridians? ______________________
    and ______________________

Name____

Where Is the Prime Meridian?

Meridians of longitude help people locate places east and west of the prime meridian and are measured in units called degrees (°).

Directions: Complete this page and page 280.

1. What do the letters N, S, E and W stand for?

   ____

2. The ______________________ is 0° longitude.

3. Meridians of longitude are measured ________________ and ________________ of the prime meridian.

4. Where do all the meridians meet?________

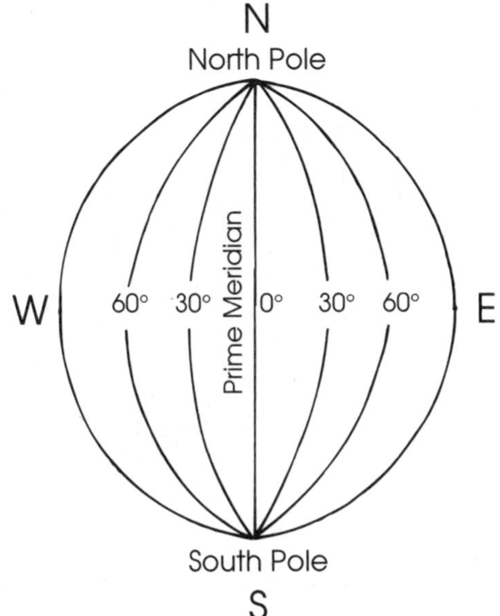

5. Meridians of longitude are measured in units called

   ____.

Do the following to complete this map.

Hint: The map above will help you.

A. Label the four cardinal directions.

B. Draw a meridian at 30°E and 30°W.

C. Draw a meridian at 60°E and 60°W.

D. Label the North and South Poles.

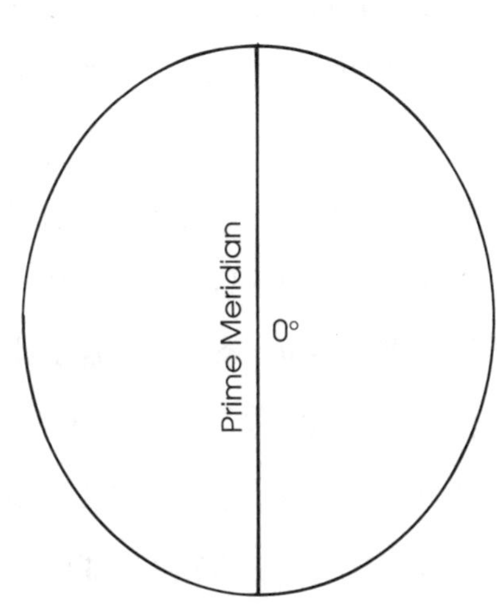

Name ____________________

Meridians of Longitude

Where Is the Prime Meridian?

Use with page 279.

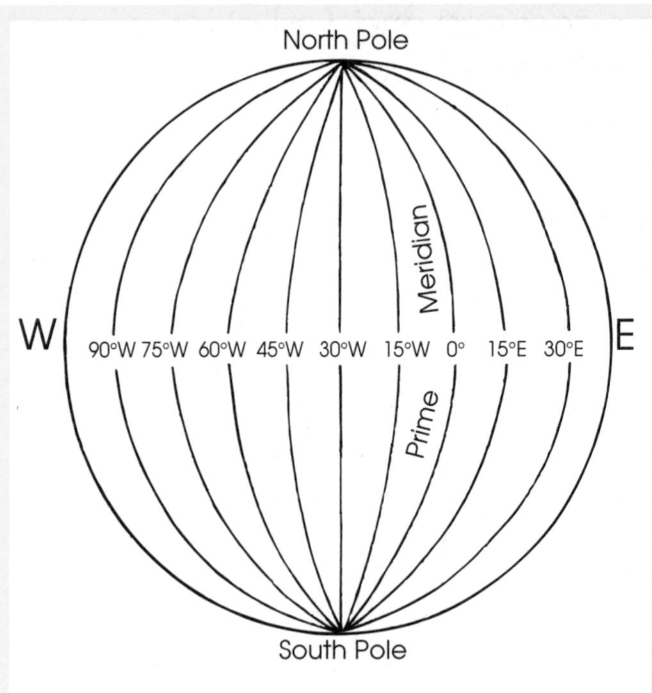

1. Is 15°E or 30°W farther from the prime meridian? ____________
2. Is 60°W or 15°E closer to the prime meridian? ____________
3. Name the two meridians east of the prime meridian on this map.

____

4. How many meridians are west of the prime meridian on this map? ____
5. On this map, what meridian is located between 15°W and 15°E?

____

6. Is 30°W or 15°E closer to the prime meridian? ____________
7. Is 75°W or 90°W closer to the prime meridian? ____________
8. Is 90°W or 15°E closer to 15°W? ____________
9. Is 90°W or 75°W closer to the prime meridian? ____________
10. Is 45°W or 30°E closer to the prime meridian? ____________
11. Name the meridian west of 75°W. ____________
12. Name the meridian east of 15°E. ____________

Name ____________________

Lines of Longitude

Directions: Use the meridians shown in the globe below to answer the questions.

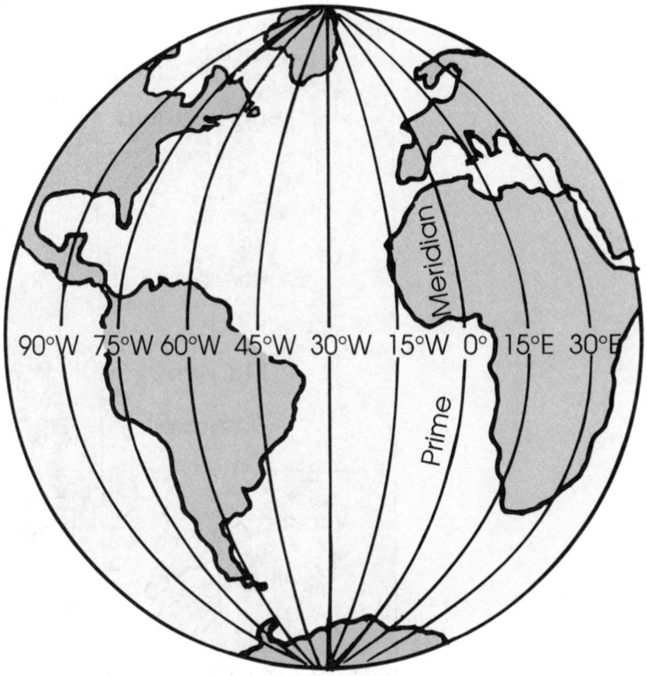

90°W 75°W 60°W 45°W 30°W 15°W 0° 15°E 30°E
Prime Meridian

1. Lines of longitude are called ____________________.
2. They run in which directions? __________ and __________
3. 0° longitude passes through ____________________.
4. 0° longitude is called the ____________________.
5. Degrees to the right of the prime meridian are which direction? ____________________
6. What meridian is west of 75°W? ____________________
7. Degrees to the left of the prime meridian are which direction? __________
8. Name the meridians east of 0° on this globe. __________ __________
9. What meridian is east of 15°W? __________
10. Which meridians shown on this map pass through the continent of Africa? ____________________
11. What meridian is west of 45°W? __________
12. Trace the prime meridian orange.
13. Trace the other meridians yellow.

Name_______________________________________

Meridians of Longitude

Locating Cities

This map shows part of the northeastern United States. All longitude meridians on this map are west.

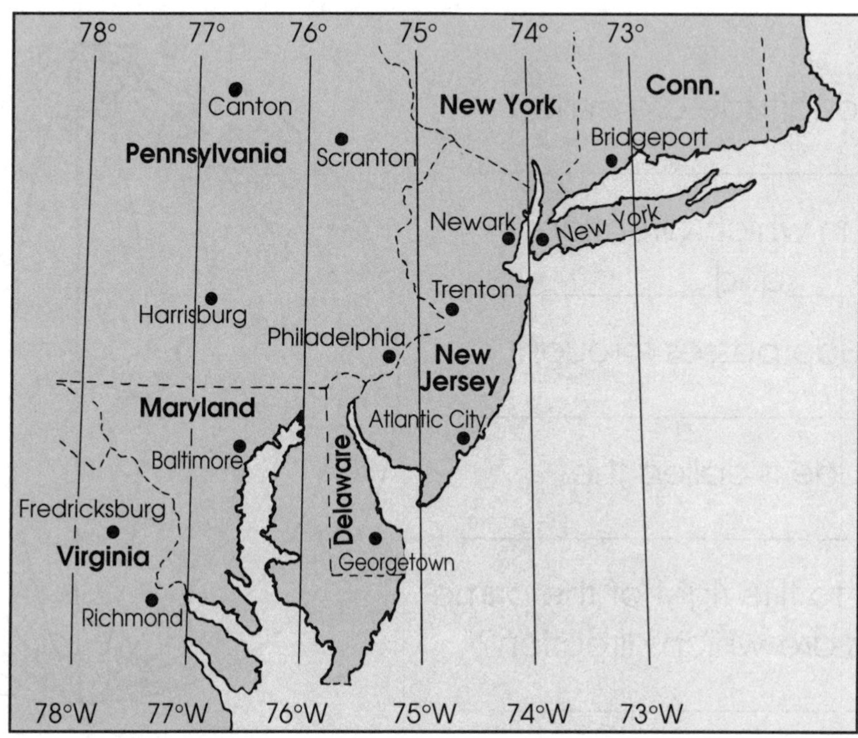

Directions: Use the longitude meridians above to answer the questions below.

1. Bridgeport, Connecticut, is closest to which meridian? ______________
2. Trenton, New Jersey is closest to which meridian? ________________
3. Name the meridians closest to these cities:

   Philadelphia _________ Georgetown __________

   Scranton _________ Newark ___________
4. Name the seven states shown on this map. ________________________

   __________________ ___________________ ____________________

   __________________ ___________________ ____________________
5. Atlantic City is between ___________ and _________ longitude.
6. Harrisburg is closest to which meridian? ___________________________
7. Which is farther west—Harrisburg or Philadelphia? ___________________
8. Richmond is closest to __________________longitude.

Name ______________________________

North and South Dakota

Directions: Use this map to answer the questions. All longitude meridians will be west.

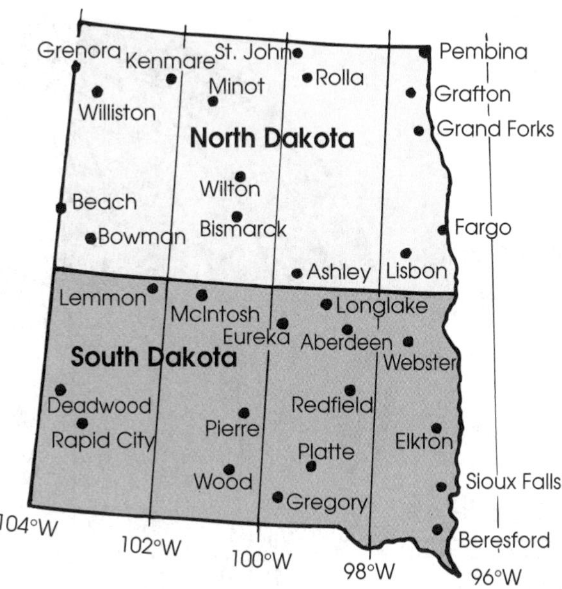

1. Which meridian is closest to Eureka, South Dakota? ____________
2. Which town is closer to 98°W—Platte, South Dakota or Lisbon, North Dakota? ____________
3. Grenora, North Dakota is located almost exactly on the ______ meridian.
4. Is Deadwood, South Dakota north or south of Rapid City? ____________
5. Which town is closer to 104°W—Bowman, North Dakota or Lemmon, South Dakota? ____________
6. If you were traveling east from Rapid City, which meridian would you arrive at first? ____________
7. Which meridian would you reach first when traveling east from Sioux Falls, South Dakota? ____________
8. Bismarck is in the state of ____________.
9. Lemmon, South Dakota is closest to the ____________ meridian.
10. Name the North Dakota cities located east of 98°W longitude.

____

____

____

Name ________________________________

Lines of Longitude

Remember... The lines of longitude tell how far east or west of the **prime meridian** (0°) you are.

All lines of longitude are measured from the prime meridian in degrees. Everything west of the prime meridian is labeled **W** for **west**, and everything east of the prime meridian is labeled **E** for **east**.

Directions: Use a globe or map to find the longitude for each of the following cities. Remember to indicate both the number of degrees and whether it is east or west of the prime meridian.

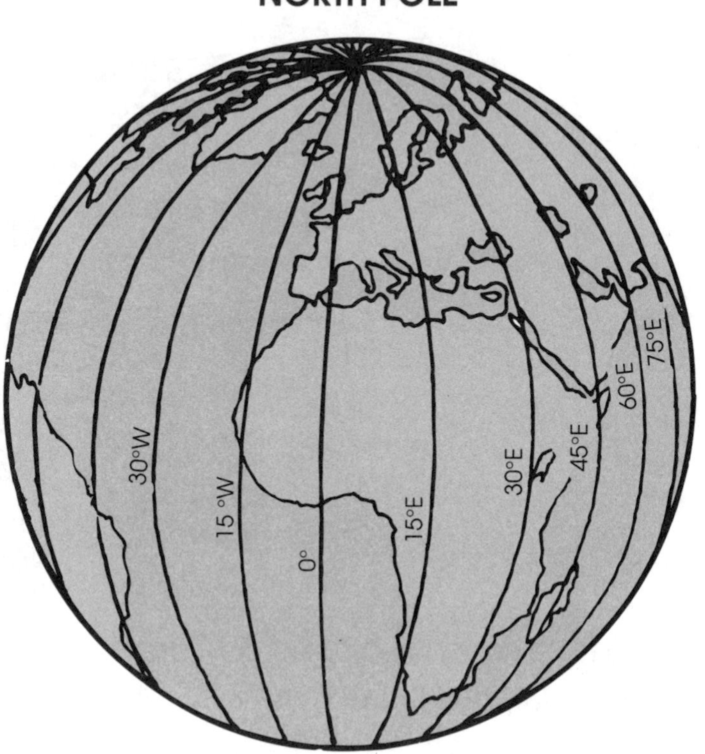

1. Los Angeles, U.S.A. ____________
2. London, England ____________
3. Wellington, New Zealand ____________
4. Tokyo, Japan ____________
5. Bangkok, Thailand ____________
6. Santiago, Chile ____________
7. Nairobi, Kenya ____________
8. Tehran, Iran ____________
9. Paris, France ____________
10. Glasgow, Scotland ____________
11. Rome, Italy ____________
12. Buenos Aires, Argentina ____________
13. Anchorage, Alaska ____________
14. Calcutta, India ____________
15. Cairo, Egypt ____________
16. Shanghai, China ____________

Name ____________________

Locating Cities in Europe

Directions: Use this map to answer the questions. Pay particular attention to the location of the prime meridian.

1. On the map label each longitude meridian either east or west.
2. Rome, Italy, is located between the __________ and __________ meridians.
3. Which meridian passes through the western edge of Ireland? __________
4. Portugal is located between the __________ and __________ meridians.
5. Between which two meridians is Switzerland located? __________
6. Explain how you would decide which of the 5° meridians is east and which is west. __________
7. Warsaw is closest to the __________ meridian.
8. Marseille, France, is which direction from the 5°E meridian? __________
9. Gdansk is in the country of __________.
10. Prague is __________ of 15°E longitude.
11. Hamburg is on the __________ meridian.
12. Marseille is almost on the __________ meridian of longitude.

Name____

Lines of Latitude

Lines of latitude on a globe are called parallels. They run east and west. The equator is at 0° latitude. Use the map below to answer the questions.

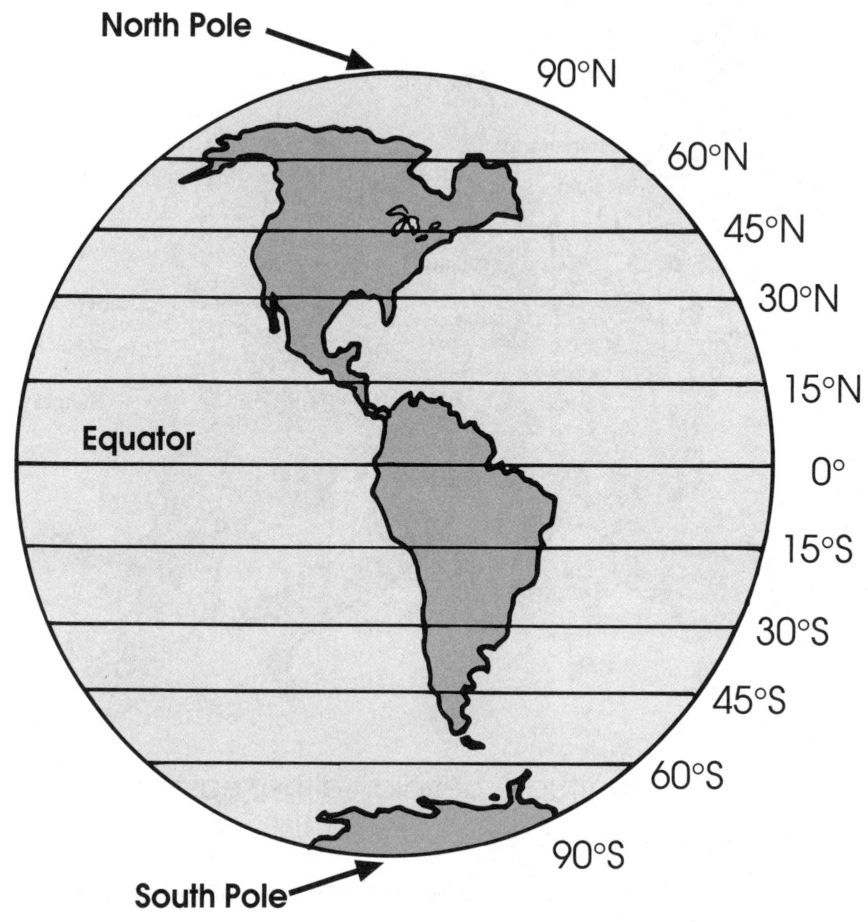

1. 0° latitude is called the ____________________________.
2. Lines of latitude are called ____________________________.
3. Parallels run which directions? _________________ and _________________
4. The latitude of the North Pole is ____________________________.
5. Which parallel runs through Florida? ___________________________
6. What is located at 90°S latitude? ___________________________
7. Which parallel runs through Canada? ___________________________
8. Lines of latitude above the equator are which direction?______________
9. Below the equator, the parallels are which direction? _________________

Name ____________________

Lateral Movement

Parallels measure the distance north or south from the equator. Zero degrees latitude (0°) is at the equator. Half of the parallels are north of the equator and half are south of it. The lines do not meet.

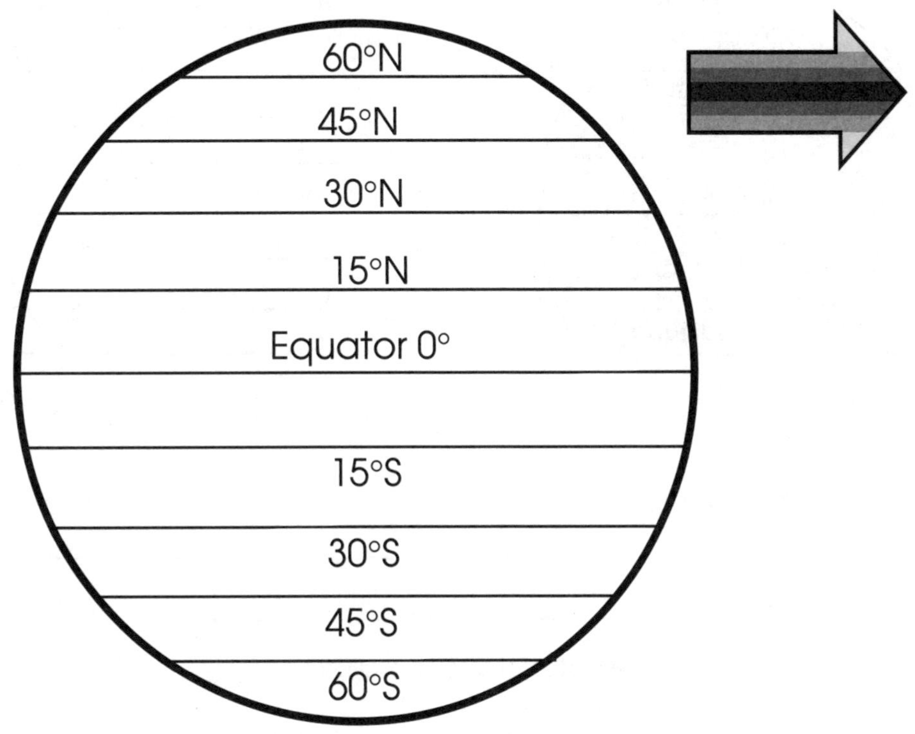

1. What is the symbol for degrees? ____________
2. Latitude lines run ____________ and ____________.
3. Latitude lines are called ________________.
4. Give the latitude of the equator. ________________
5. The parallels above the equator are which direction? ______________
6. The parallels below the equator are which direction? ______________
7. Color the equator parallel orange.
8. Color 15°N and 15°S green.
9. Color 30°N and 30°S blue.
10. Color 45°N and 45°S red.
11. Color 60°N and 60°S purple.

Name ____________________________________

Imaginary Lines

Directions: Answer the questions below using these maps.

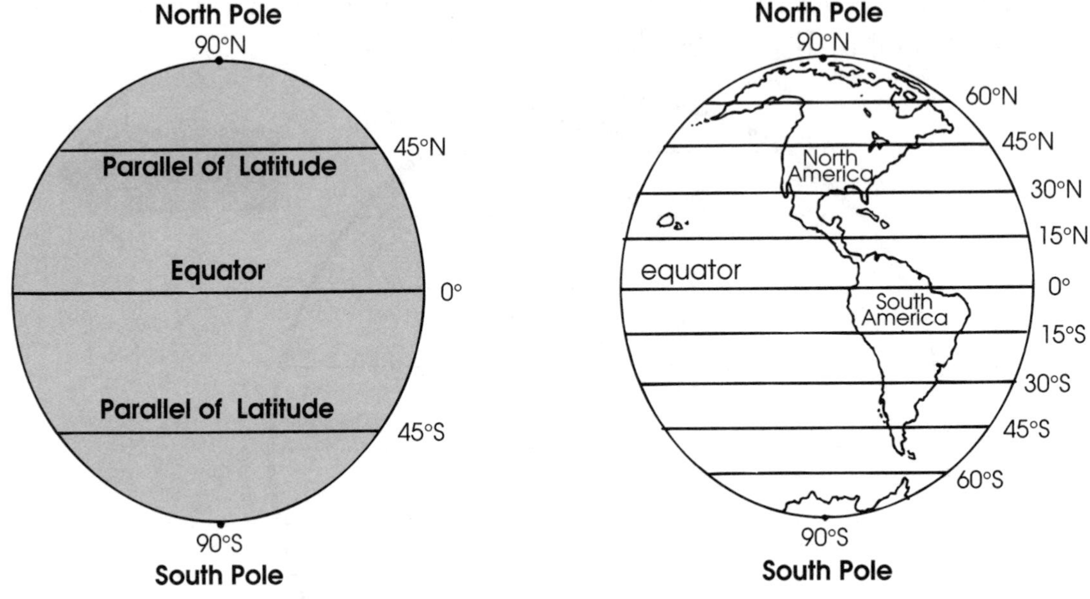

1. The ________________________________ is 0° latitude.
2. The North Pole is ________________________ degrees north latitude.
4. Lines north and south of the equator are called ____________________.
5. The ________________________________ is 90°S latitude.
6. Which line is closer to the equator—30°N or 15°S? ____________________
7. Which is closer to the South Pole—45°S or 30°S? ____________________
8. At what degree is the South Pole? ____________________
9. If you wanted to find a city located at 45°N, would you look above or below the equator? ____________________
10. Which continent on the map is entirely north of the equator? ______________
11. South America lies between the parallels of latitude ______________°N and 60°S.
12. The equator runs through the northern part of the continent of ______________.
13. Color all the land north of the equator red.
14. Color all of the land south of the equator green.

Name ______________________________

What's My Line?

There are several important lines of latitude on the globe which have special names.

Directions: Use a map, globe or other resource to identify the special lines on the illustration of the globe below.

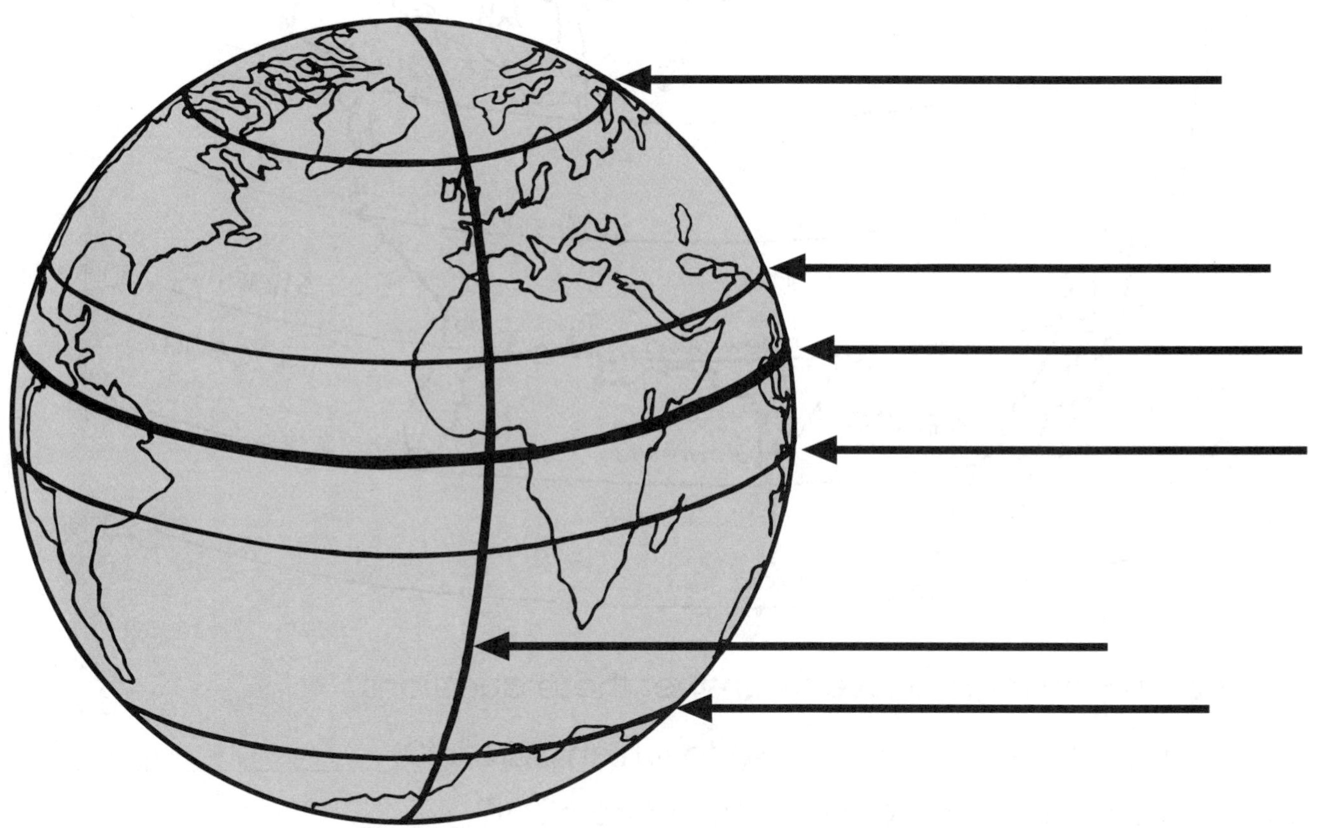

Name the imaginary line that . . .

passes through Mexico. ______________________

is 0° latitude. ________________________

passes through Alaska. ______________________

is 0° longitude. ________________________

divides the Northern and Southern hemispheres. __________________

passes through Botswana. ____________________

Name ______________________________

Lines of Latitude

Across the U.S.A.

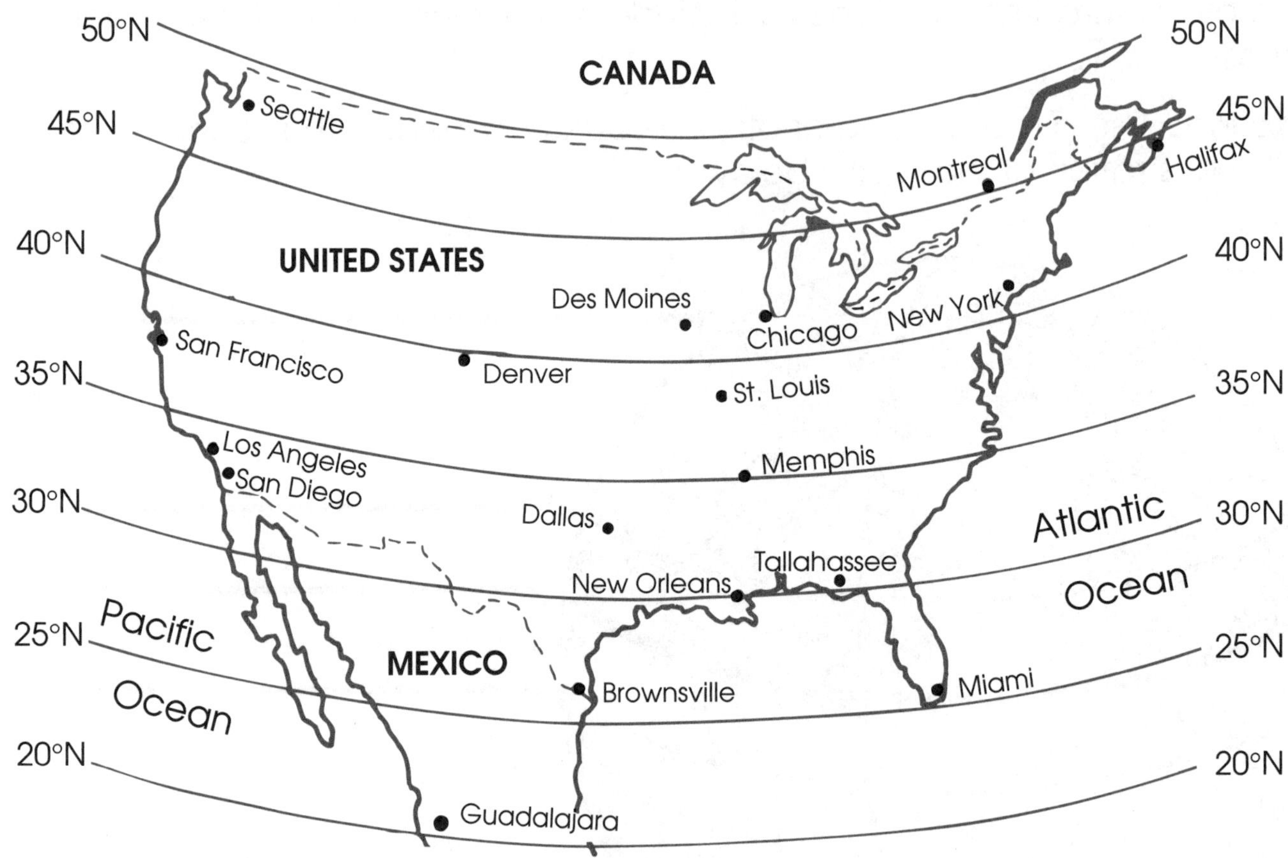

Directions: Use the map above to answer these questions.

1. Denver and New York are close to which parallel? ______________
2. Which two cities are between 45°N and 50°N? ______________
3. Los Angeles and Memphis are near which parallel? ______________
4. Tallahassee is closest to which parallel? ______________
5. St. Louis is between which parallels? __________ and __________
6. Which city is farthest north? ______________ It is between which parallels? ______________ and ______________
7. Which city is farthest south? ______________ It is between which parallels? ______________ and ______________
8. San Francisco is halfway between __________ and __________.

Name ______________________________

Latitude in North America.

Use with page 292.

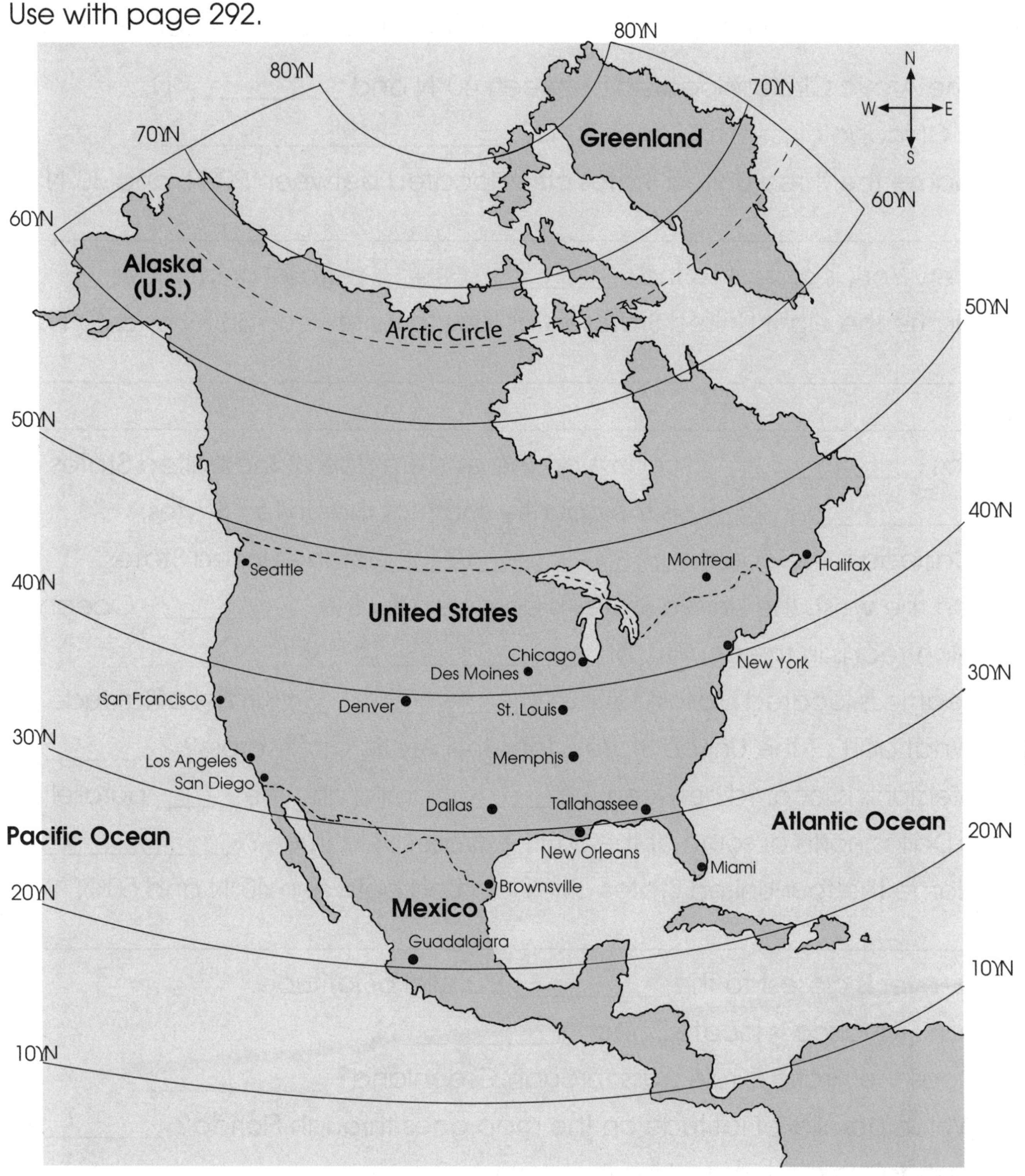

Name______________________________________

Latitude in North America

Directions: Use the map on page 291 to answer the questions below.

1. The Arctic Circle is located between 60°N and __________ °N.
2. Is Chicago closer to 40°N or 50°N?________________________
3. Name the three United States cities located between 20°N and 30°N.

   ____________________ ____________________ ____________________

4. New York is closest to the ________________ parallel of latitude.
5. Name the eight United States cities located between 30° N and 40°N.

   ______________ ______________ ______________ ______________

   ______________ ______________ ______________ ______________

6. The ______________ Ocean is on the eastern side of the United States.
7. ____________________ is the country south of the United States.
8. Canada is the country ____________________ of the United States.
9. On the west, the United States is bordered by the ___________ Ocean.
10. Montreal is in the country of ______________________.
11. Seattle is located closest to the _________________ parallel of latitude.
12. What part of the United States does the Arctic Circle cross?__________
13. Memphis is located between the ______ parallel and the _____ parallel.
14. Is Dallas north or south of the 30°N parallel of latitude? ____________
15. Name the four United States cities located between 40°N and 50°N.

    ______________ ______________ ______________ ______________

16. Denver is closest to the __________ parallel of latitude.
17. San Francisco is located near __________ °N.
18. Does the Arctic Circle pass through Greenland? _____________
19. Which parallel of latitude on the map goes through Florida? ________
20. Guadalajara is located in what country? _________________________

Name ______________________________

Parallels Help With Location

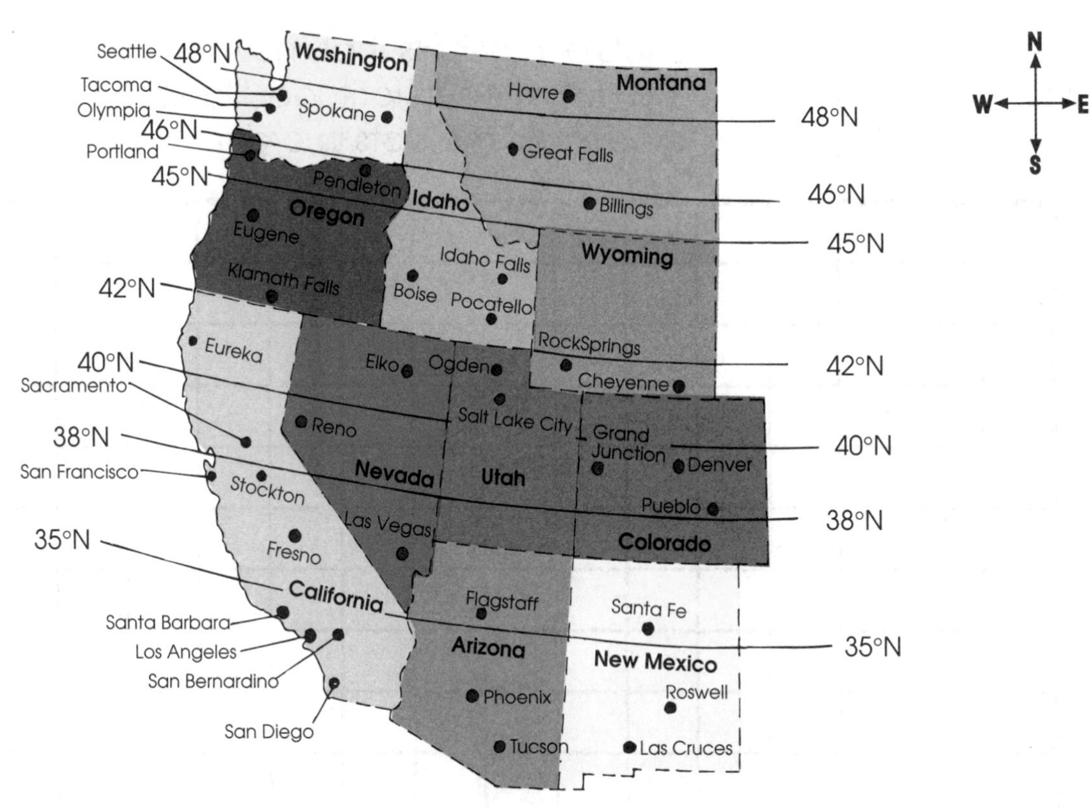

1. Billings, Montana is which direction from the 46°N parallel? ____________
2. Pueblo, Colorado is almost directly on the ____________ parallel of latitude.
3. The boundary between Oregon and California is formed by the ____ parallel.
4. The state of Wyoming is located between 41°N parallel and ______ parallel.
5. Name three cities in Idaho south of the 45°N parallel of latitude.

   ____________________ ____________________ ____________________

6. Which of these cities is south of the 35°N parallel—Flagstaff, Arizona or Roswell, New Mexico? ______________________________
7. Name the three California cities located between the 35°N and 38°N parallels.

   ____________________ ____________________ ____________________

8. All of the cities shown in Washington are between the parallels of ____________ and ____________.
9. Which two Nevada cities are north of the 38°N parallel? ______________ and ______________
10. Klamath Falls, Oregon is almost directly on the ____________ parallel.

Name____

Picture It!

Directions: Coordinates are sets of numbers that show where lines of latitude and longitude meet. Place a dot at each latitude / longitude coordinate on the graph. Draw lines to connect the dots in order.

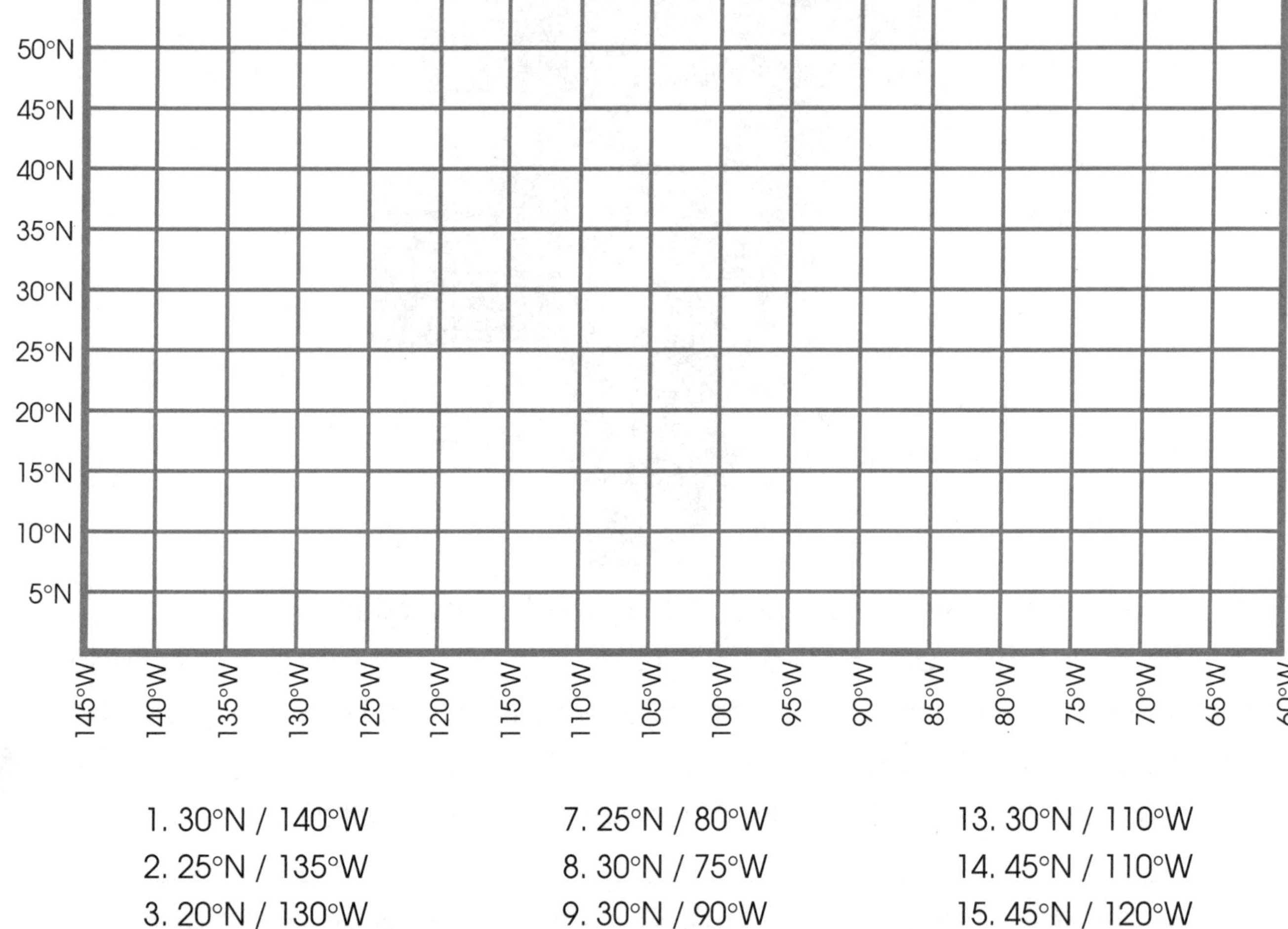

1. 30°N / 140°W
2. 25°N / 135°W
3. 20°N / 130°W
4. 15°N / 125°W
5. 15°N / 90°W
6. 20°N / 85°W
7. 25°N / 80°W
8. 30°N / 75°W
9. 30°N / 90°W
10. 45°N / 90°W
11. 45°N / 100°W
12. 30°N / 100°W
13. 30°N / 110°W
14. 45°N / 110°W
15. 45°N / 120°W
16. 30°N / 120°W
17. 30°N / 140°W

Now place a yellow **X** at each coordinate below. Do not connect the **X**s.

1. 45°N / 140°W
2. 35°N / 135°W
3. 45°N / 130°W
4. 40°N / 80°W
5. 45°N / 70°W
6. 35°N / 65°W

Color the rest of the picture.

Name________________________________

What Will They Be?

Directions: Place a dot at each of these latitude and longitude points on the graph.

1. 45°N / 105°W
2. 40°N / 110°W
3. 35°N / 115°W
4. 30°N / 120°W
5. 25°N / 125°W
6. 20°N / 120°N
7. 15°N / 115°W
8. 10°N / 110°W
9. 5°N / 105°W
10. 10°N / 100°W
11. 15°N / 95°W
12. 20°N / 90°W
13. 25°N / 85°W
14. 30°N / 90°W
15. 35°N / 95°W
16. 40°N / 100°W

Draw a line to connect the dots in order. What have you drawn?__________

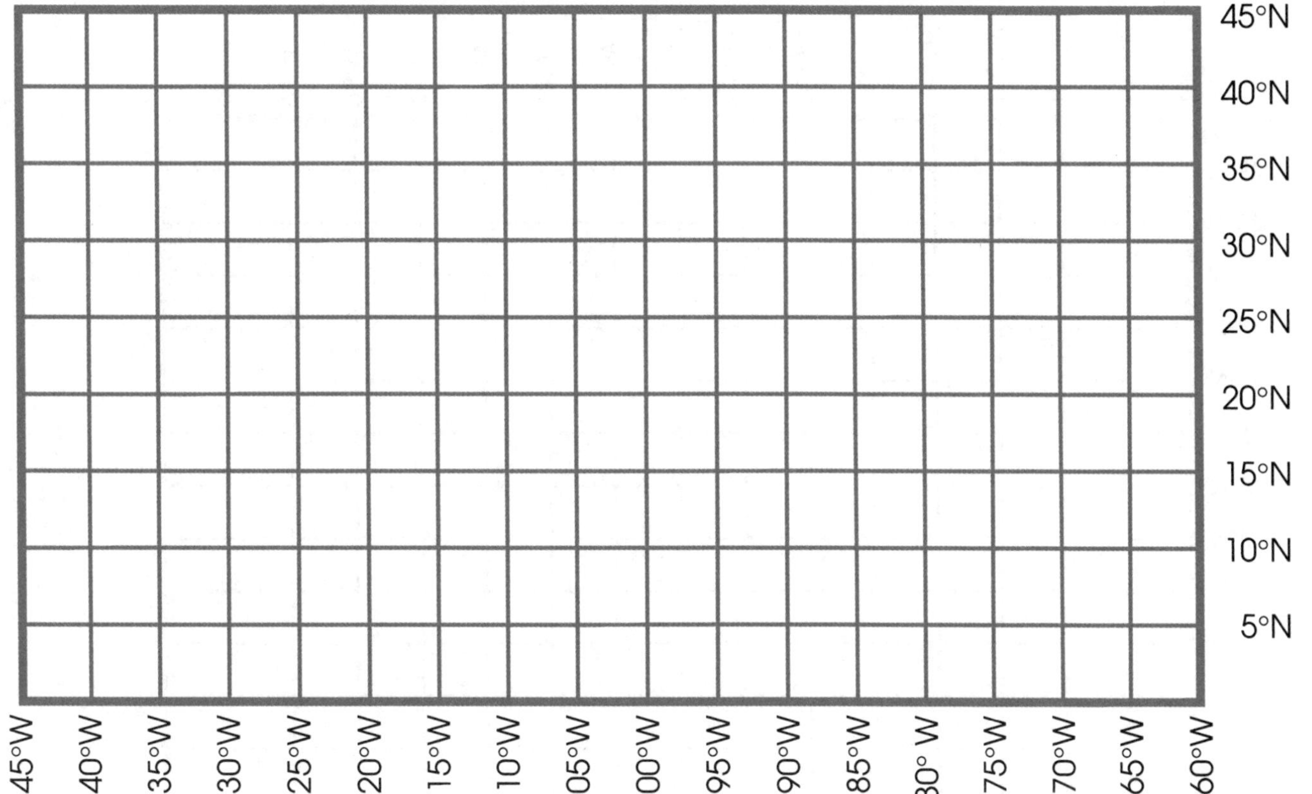

Now with a different color, place a dot at each of these latitude and longitude points.

1. 45°N / 85°W
2. 35°N / 85°W
3. 35°N / 65°W
4. 45°N / 65°W

Connect the dots. What have you drawn? ______________________________

Name____

Latitude and Longitude

Using Lines to Draw a State

Directions: Place a dot on the grid for each point given. The first two have been done for you.

1. 38°N / 99°W
2. 38° N / 102°W
3. 36°N / 102°W
4. 34°N / 102°W
5. 34°N / 104°W
6. 34°N / 106°W
7. 33°N / 105 1/2°W
8. 32 1/2°N / 105°W
9. 32°N / 104 1/2°W
10. 31°N / 104°W
11. 30°N / 104°W
12. 29 1/2°N / 103°W
13. 30°N / 102°W
14. 30°N / 101°W
15. 29°N / 101°W
16. 28°N / 100°W
17. 27 1/2°N / 99°W
18. 26 1/2°N / 97 1/2°W
19. 28°N / 97 1/2°W
20. 29°N / 96 1/2°W
21. 30°N / 95°W
22. 31°N / 94°W
23. 33°N / 94°W
24. 35°N / 94°W
25. 35°N / 96°W
26. 35°N / 99°W
27. 37°N / 99°W

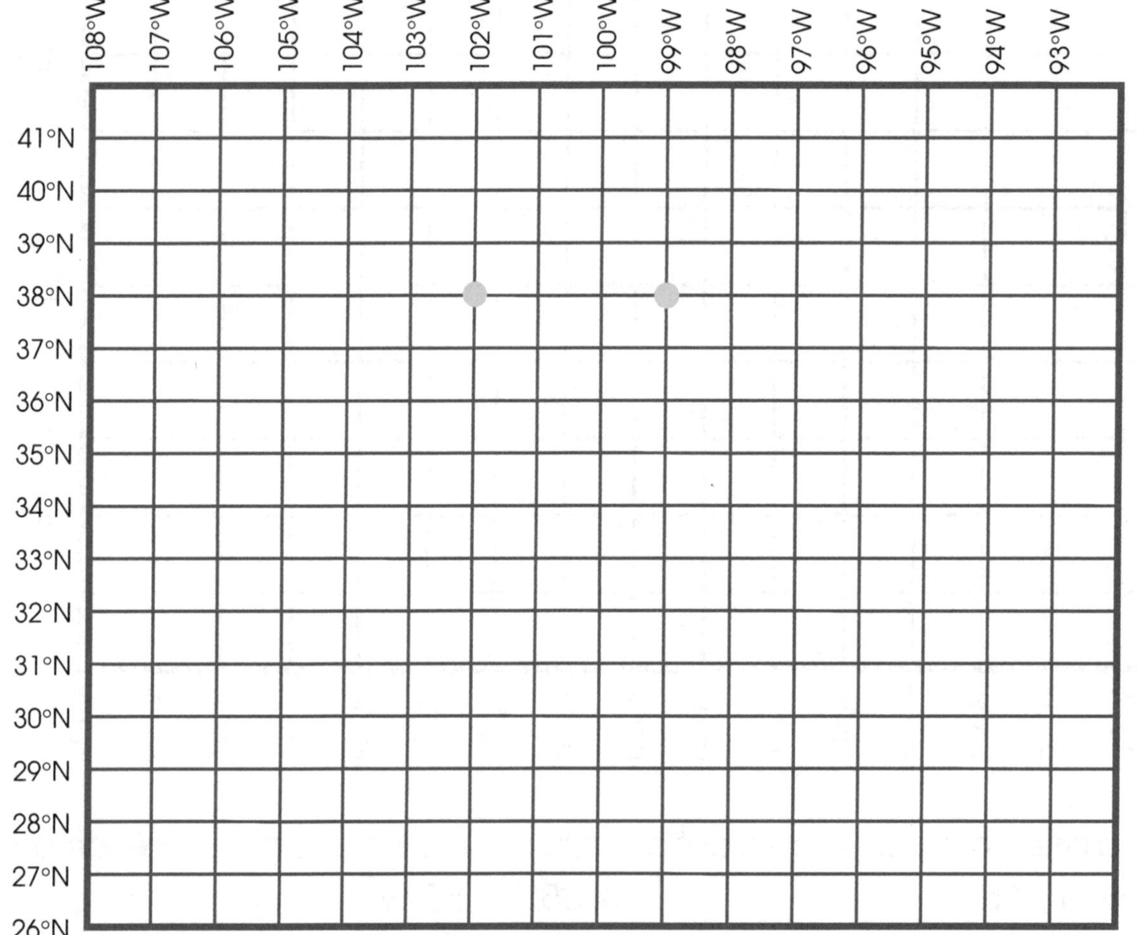

Draw a line to connect all of the dots in order. What state did you draw?

Name ____________________

Casey's Island

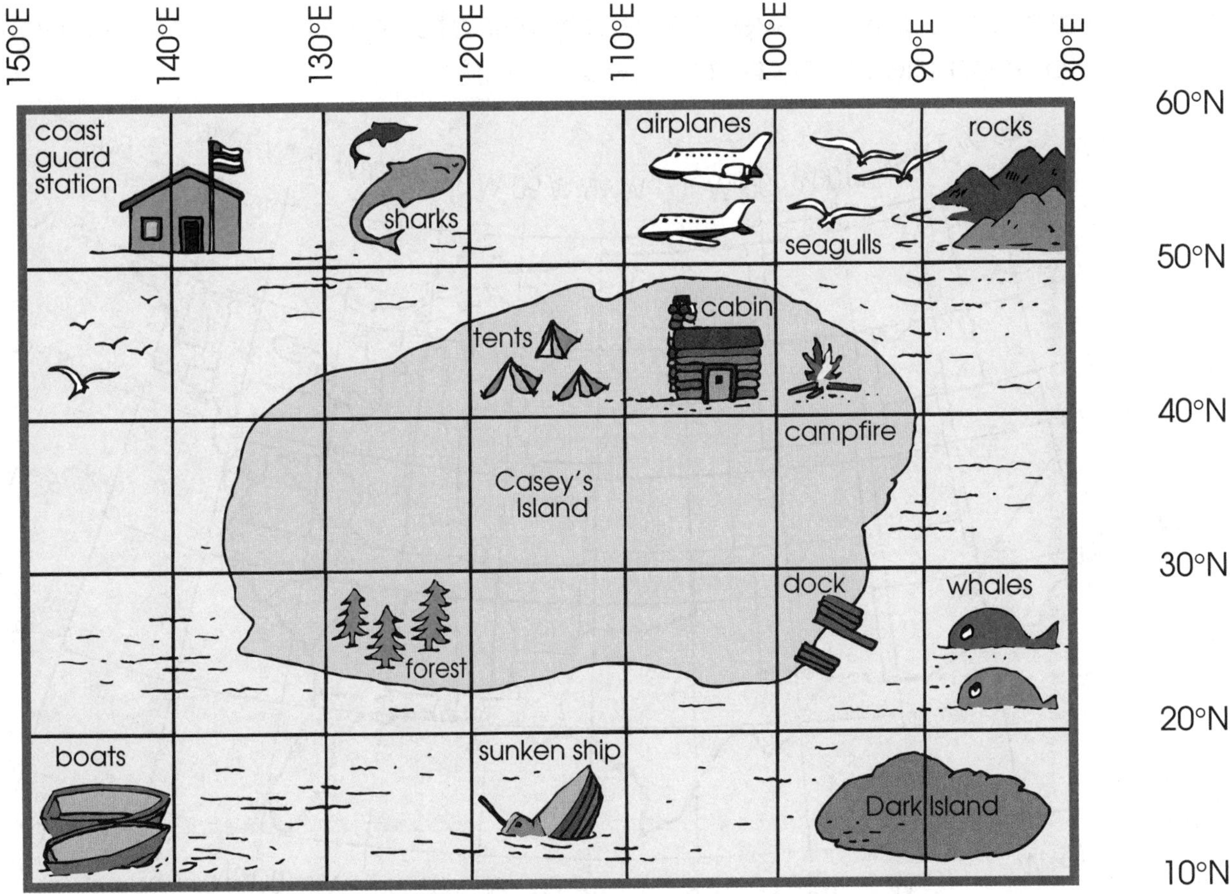

Directions: Use the map above to answer the questions below.

1. The whales are between which two latitude lines? ____________
2. The coast guard station is located between which longitude lines? ______
3. If the whales go north to 55°N latitude, what will they hit? ____________
4. The boats must cross what longitude lines to get to the sunken ship? _____
____
5. If you draw a latitude line at 35°N, what will you cross? ____________
6. If the whales cross 90°E longitude, what will they reach? ____________
7. Name the items crossed by the 55°N latitude line. ____________
____
8. Which longitude lines cross Casey's Island? ____________

Name____

State Search

Which state is roughly between the coordinates given? After locating the state, color it on the map as directed.

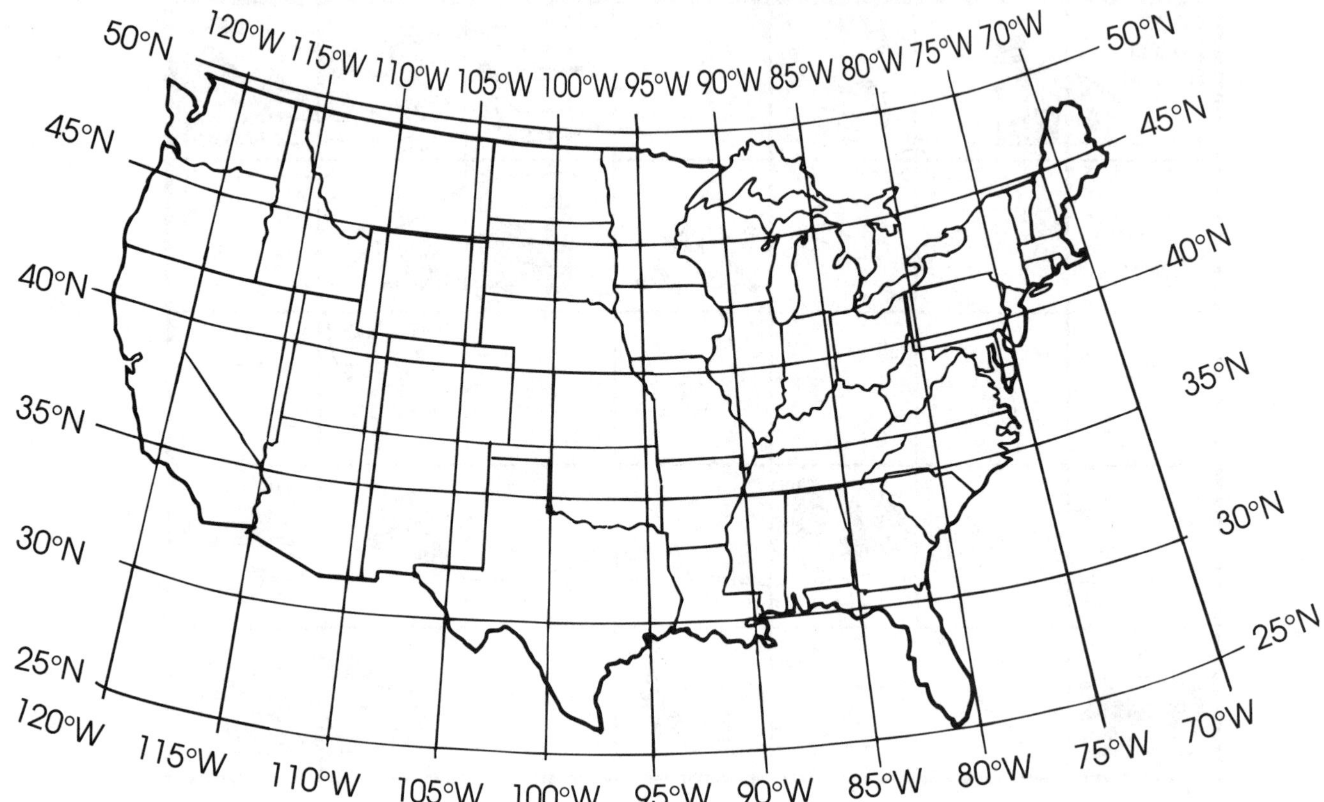

	Latitude	Longitude	State	Color
1.	45°N / 50°N	105°W / 115°W	____________	orange
2.	40°N / 45°N	75°W / 80°W	____________	tan
3.	44°N / 50°N	67°W / 70°W	____________	red
4.	25°N / 30°N	80°W / 85°W	____________	yellow
5.	40°N / 45°N	90°W / 95°W	____________	gray
6.	30°N / 35°N	85°W / 90°W	____________	green
7.	43°N / 47°N	87°W / 93°W	____________	blue
8.	31°N / 36°N	104°W / 109°W	____________	pink
9.	36°N / 38°N	82°W / 89°W	____________	lt. green
10.	36°N / 39°N	76°W / 84°W	____________	gold
11.	26°N / 34°N	94°W / 107°W	____________	purple
12.	41°N / 45°N	104°W / 111°W	____________	lt. blue
13.	36°N / 41°N	90°W / 95°W	____________	brown

Name____________________________

See the U.S.A.

Use the coordinates to plan a trip across the U.S.A.

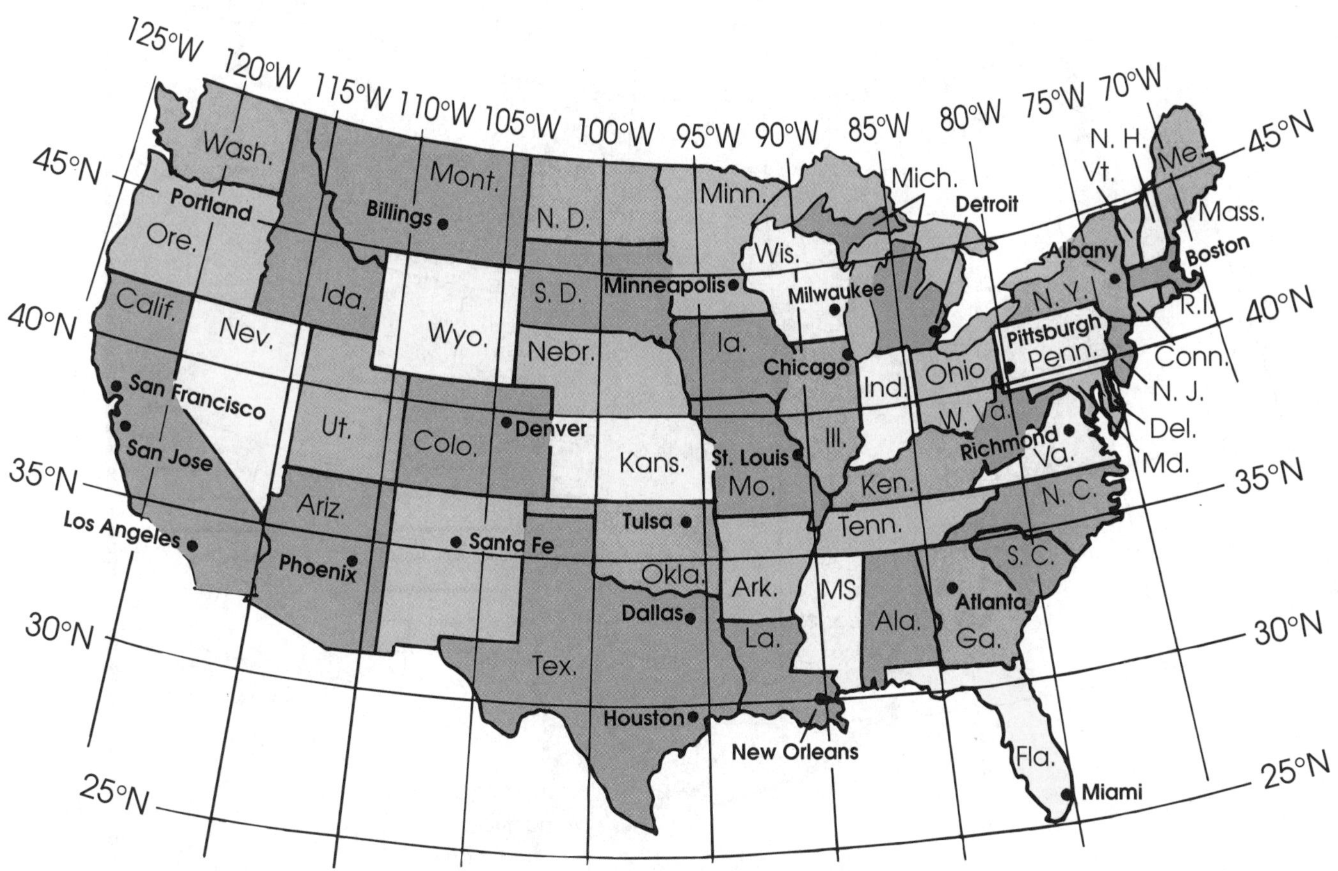

Directions: Write the name of the city closest to the intersection.

1. Your trip begins at 40°N / 105°W, the Mile-High City. ____________
2. You fly over the Rocky Mountains to 45°N / 125°W. ____________
3. Now, to 35°N / 105°W in New Mexico. ____________
4. Next, stop is Texas, the city of . . . 30°N / 95°W. ____________
5. It's Mardi Gras time at 30°N / 90°W. ____________
6. Then, fun in the sun and the Atlantic Ocean 25°N / 80°W. ____________
7. To the Gateway Arch in the city of . . 40°N / 90°W. ____________
8. The Steelers play football here—40°N / 80°W. ____________
9. Next, to the capital of New York—40°N / 75°W. ____________

Name____

Plotting North American Cities

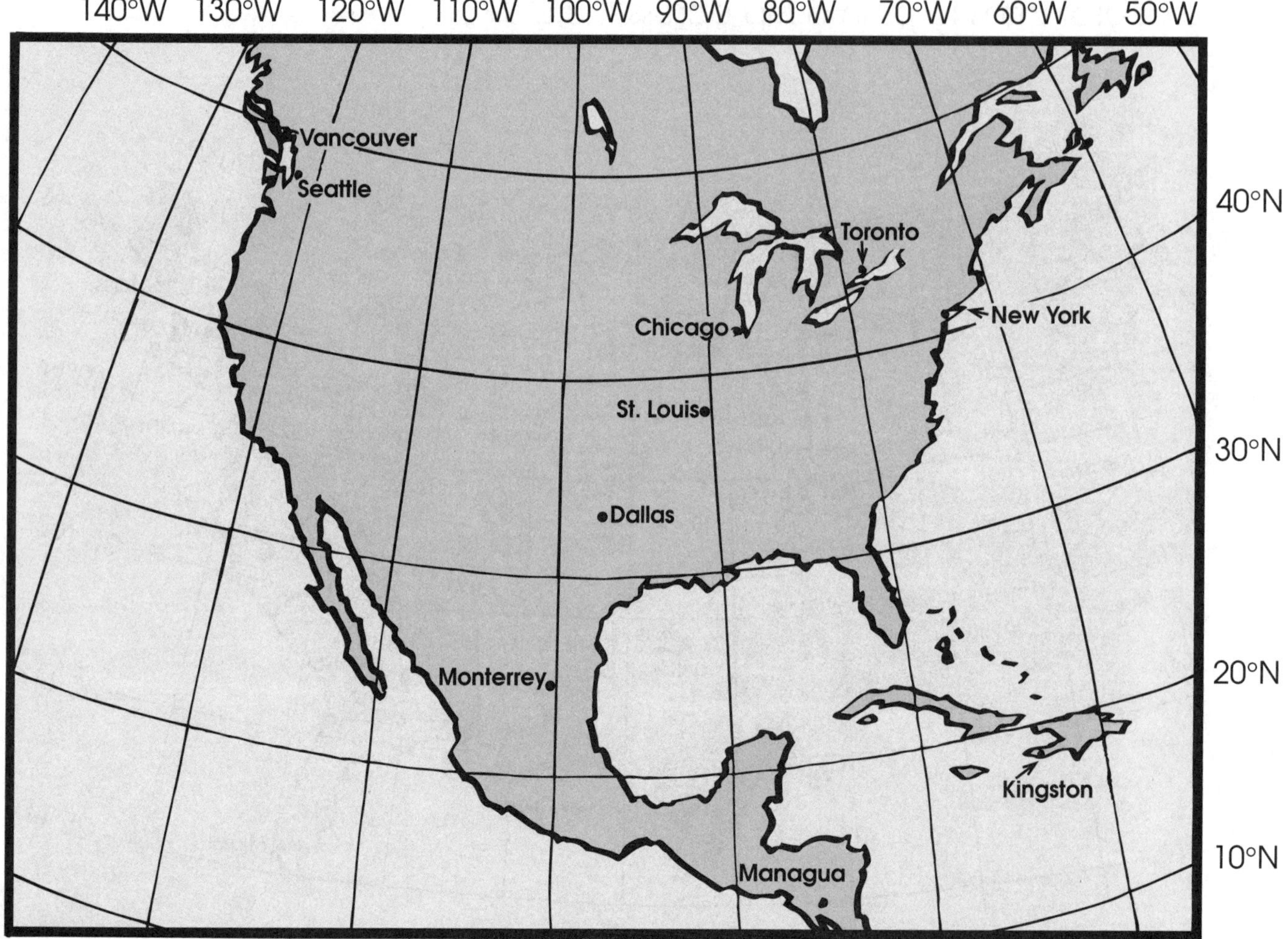

Directions: Use the lines of latitude and longitude to determine the approximate coordinates of the North American cities on the map above. Write the coordinates for each city in the blanks.

	Latitude	Longitude		Latitude	Longitude
1. Seattle	________	________	6. St. Louis	________	________
2. Kingston	________	________	7. Toronto	________	________
3. Dallas	________	________	8. New York	________	________
4. Vancouver	________	________	9. Monterrey	________	________
5. Managua	________	________	10. Chicago	________	________

Name ____________________

Batter Up!

Directions: Use the coordinates below and the map on page 302 to locate these cities. Then, unscramble the words to find out the baseball teams which call these cities "home base."

	Latitude	Longitude	City	State	Baseball Team Names		
1.	41°N	74°W	______	______	(yeesank) or (tmes)	=	______
2.	40°N	105°W	______	______	(ocrkeis)	=	______
3.	34°N	84°W	______	______	(sebarv)	=	______
4.	29°N	96°W	______	______	(satosr)	=	______
5.	39°N	84°W	______	______	(dser)	=	______
6.	38°N	123°W	______	______	(ginsta)	=	______
7.	42°N	88°W	______	______	(cbus) or (twihe xso)	=	______
8.	47°N	122°W	______	______	(raimnesr)	=	______
9.	39°N	90°W	______	______	(rdcailnas)	=	______
10.	42°N	82°W	______	______	(nidaisn)	=	______
11.	43°N	71°W	______	______	(der sxo)	=	______
12.	34°N	117°W	______	______	(ddogesr)	=	______
13.	39°N	76°W	______	______	(rioolse)	=	______

Word Bank

Orioles, Indians, Cardinals, Dodgers, Giants, Rockies, Cubs, White Sox, Yankees, Astros, Mets, Braves, Reds, Mariners, Red Sox

Name____

Latitude and Longitude

Batter Up!

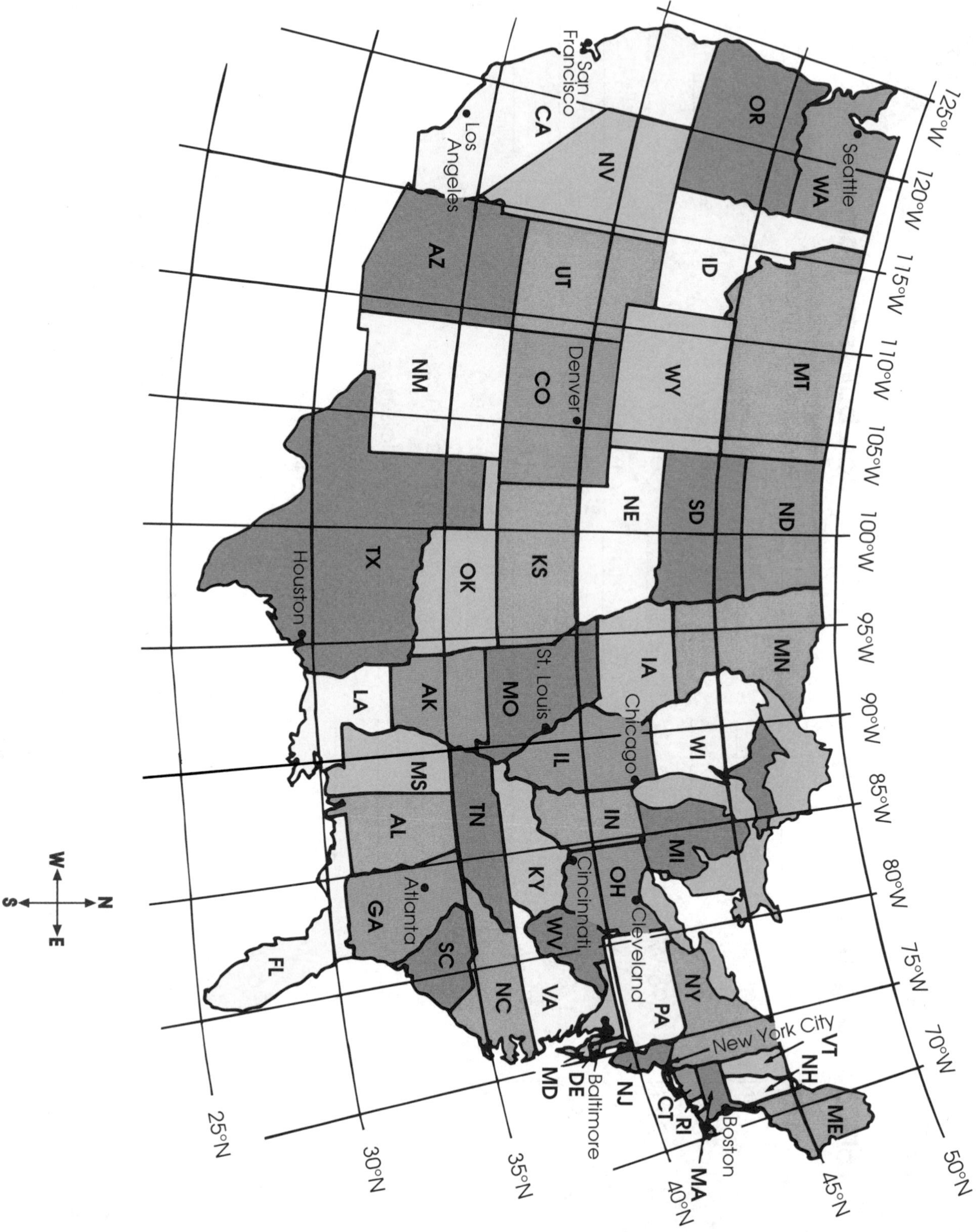

Name________________________________

Four States

Directions: Use this map to fill in the charts on page 304. Two answers have been filled in for you.

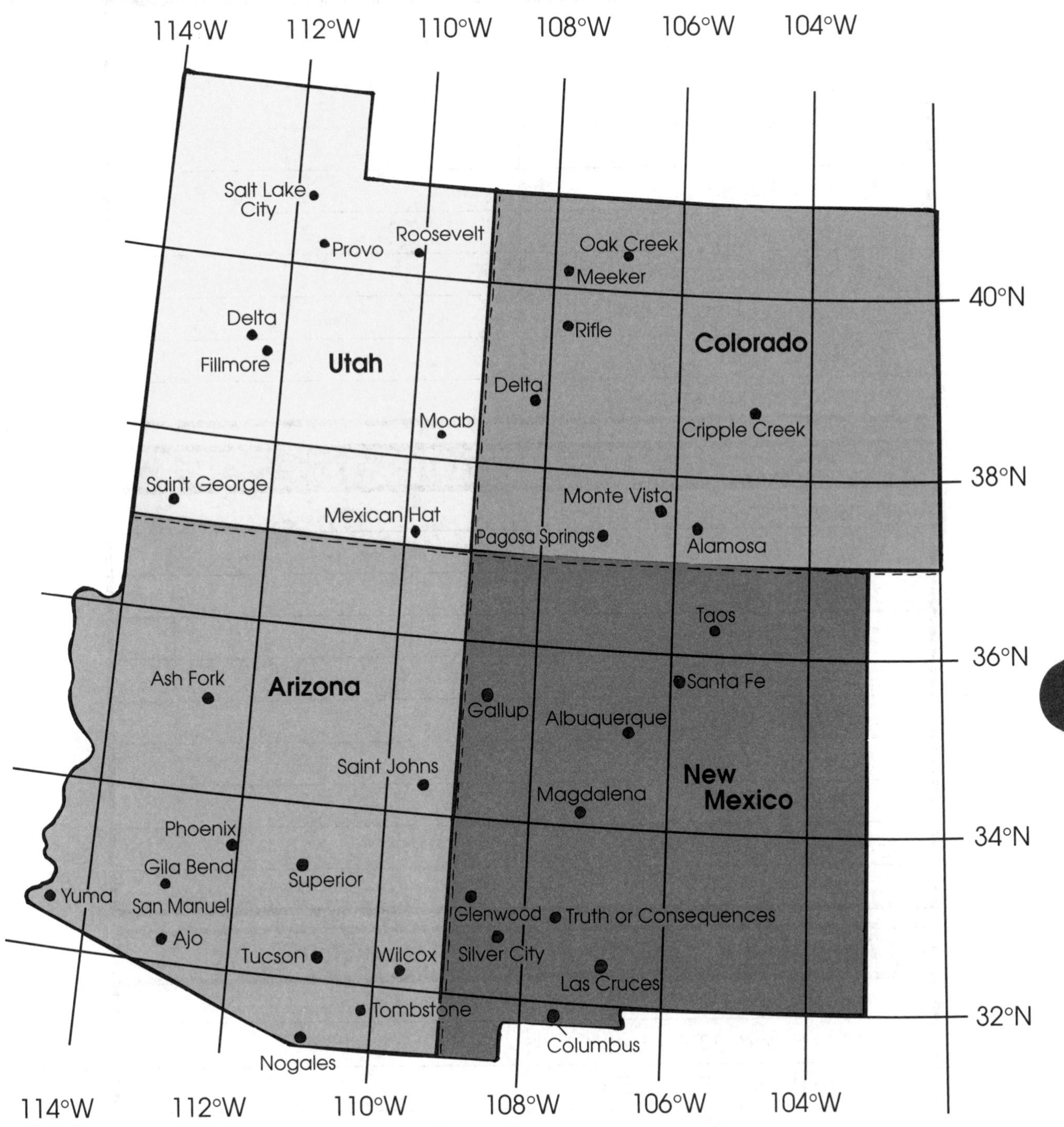

Name________________________________

Four States

Use with page 303.

City	Coordinates
1. Salt Lake City, Utah	41°N / 112°W
2. Tucson, Arizona	
3. Santa Fe, New Mexico	
4. Oak Creek, Colorado	
5. Wilcox, Arizona	
6. Cripple Creek, Colorado	
7. Las Cruces, New Mexico	
8. Albuquerque, New Mexico	
9. Meeker, Colorado	
10. Saint George, Utah	

Coordinates	City
1. 33°N / 109°W	Glenwood
2. 41°N / 112°W	
3. 39°N / 108°W	
4. 31°N / 111°W	
5. 37°N / 110°W	
6. 40 1/2°N / 110°W	
7. 33 1/2°N / 107°W	
8. 39°N / 112 1/2°W	
9. 35 1/2°N / 108 1/2°W	
10. 33°N / 111°W	

Approximate Coordinates	State
32°N / 36°N and 110°W / 114°W	
36°N / 40°N and 110°W / 114°W	
32°N / 36°N and 104°W / 108°W	
36°N / 40°N and 104°W / 108°W	

Name ____________________

Name the City

Directions: Use the coordinates given below to locate each of the cities. The first one has been done for you.

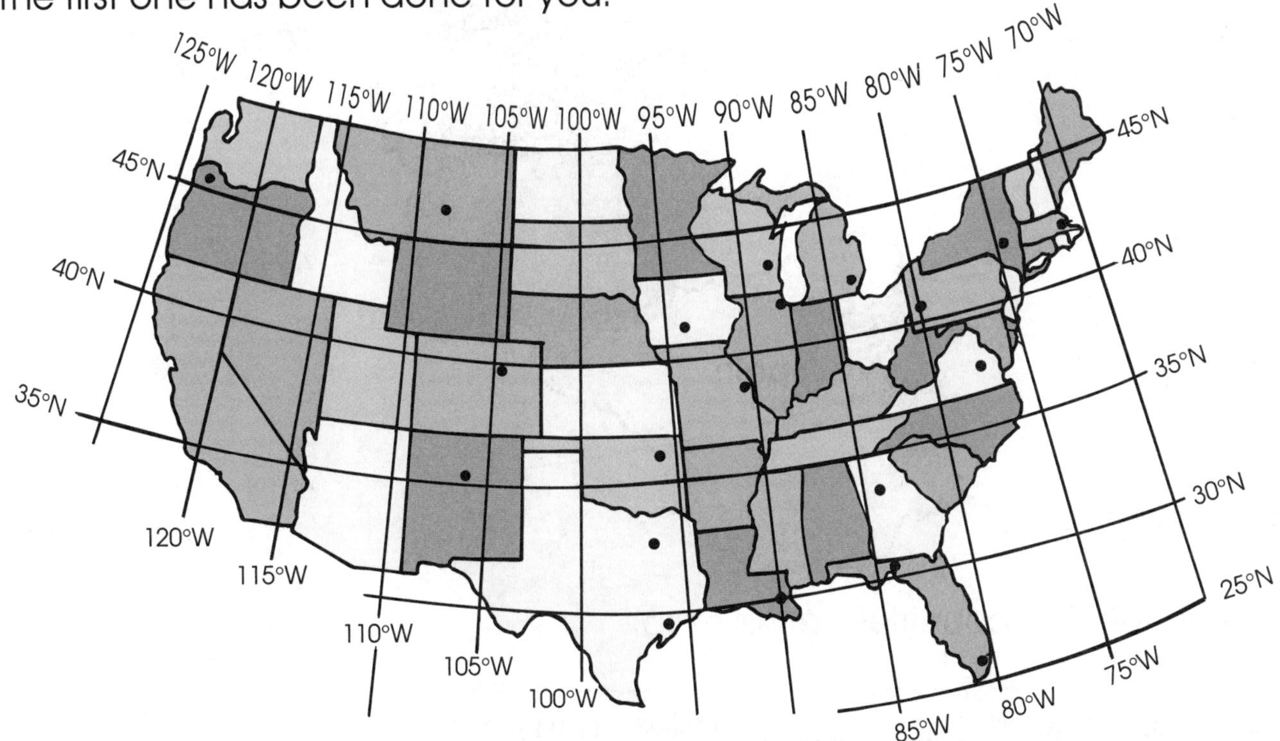

Latitude	Longitude	City
1. 34°N	84°W	Atlanta
2. 26°N	80°W	
3. 40°N	80°W	
4. 36°N	96°W	
5. 37°N	122°W	
6. 33°N	112°W	
7. 39°N	90°W	
8. 46°N	108°W	
9. 43°N	88°W	
10. 42°N	94°W	
11. 43°N	74°W	
12. 45°N	93°W	
13. 33°N	97°W	
14. 30°N	95°W	

Name ____________________________________

Locating Places in Western Europe

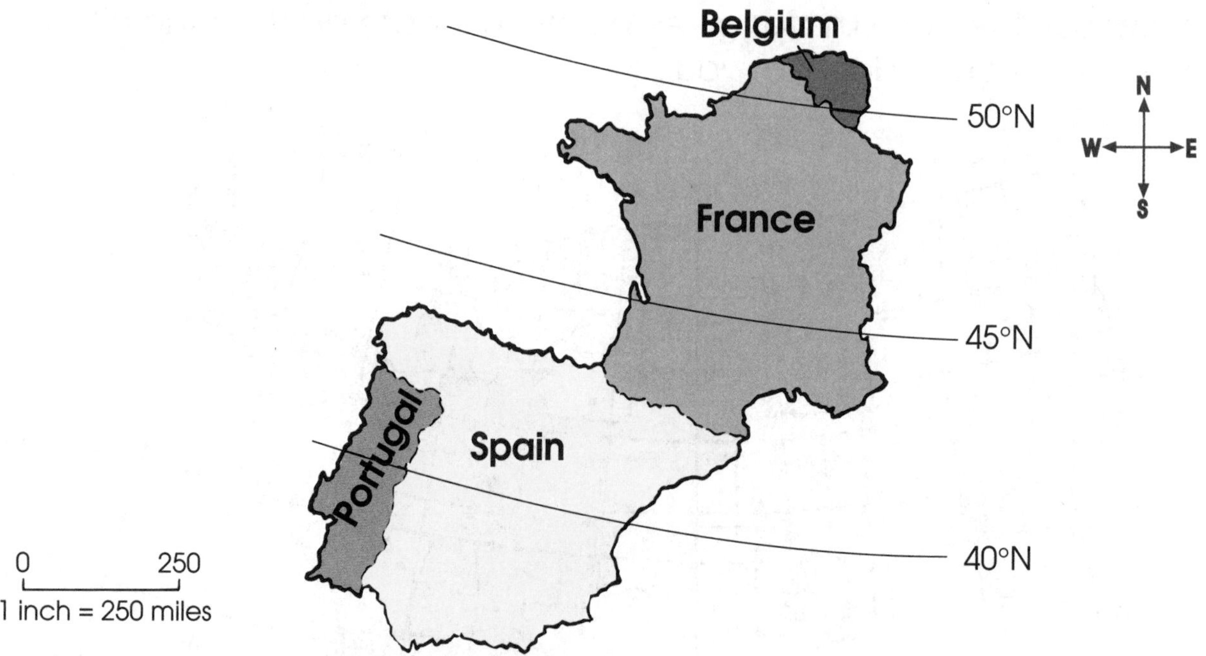

1. Name the four countries on this map.

   ______________ ______________ ______________ ______________

2. One inch equals ______________ miles on the map.
3. Which parallel line crosses both Portugal and Spain? ______________
4. Which two parallel lines cross France? ______________ ______________
5. Name the country directly north of France. ______________
6. Place the city of Barcelona on the northeastern coast of Spain about 225 miles south of the 45°N parallel.
7. Place the city of Paris in the north-central part of France about 75 miles south of the 50°N parallel.
8. Place Lisbon on the western coast of Portugal about 75 miles south of the 40°N parallel.
9. Place Madrid in the center of Spain about 50 miles north of the 40°N parallel.
10. Place Brussels near the northcentral part of Belgium about 50 miles north of the 50°N parallel line.
11. Place Toulouse in the southwestern part of France 100 miles south of the 45°N parallel.

Name____________________

Where in Europe?

Use with page 308.

Name________________________________

Where in Europe?

Directions: Estimate and write the coordinates and countries for these European cities using the map on page 307. The first one has been done for you.

City	Latitude	Longitude	Country
1. London	52°N	0°	United Kingdom
2. Belgrade			
3. Warsaw			
4. Stockholm			
5. Athens			
6. Helsinki			
7. Paris			
8. Munich			
9. Copenhagen			
10. Oslo			
11. Glasgow			
12. Prague			
13. Bern			
14. Hamburg			
15. Dresden			
16. Dublin			
17. Rome			
18. Budapest			
19. Vienna			
20. Amsterdam			

Name ____________________

Latitude and Longitude Lines

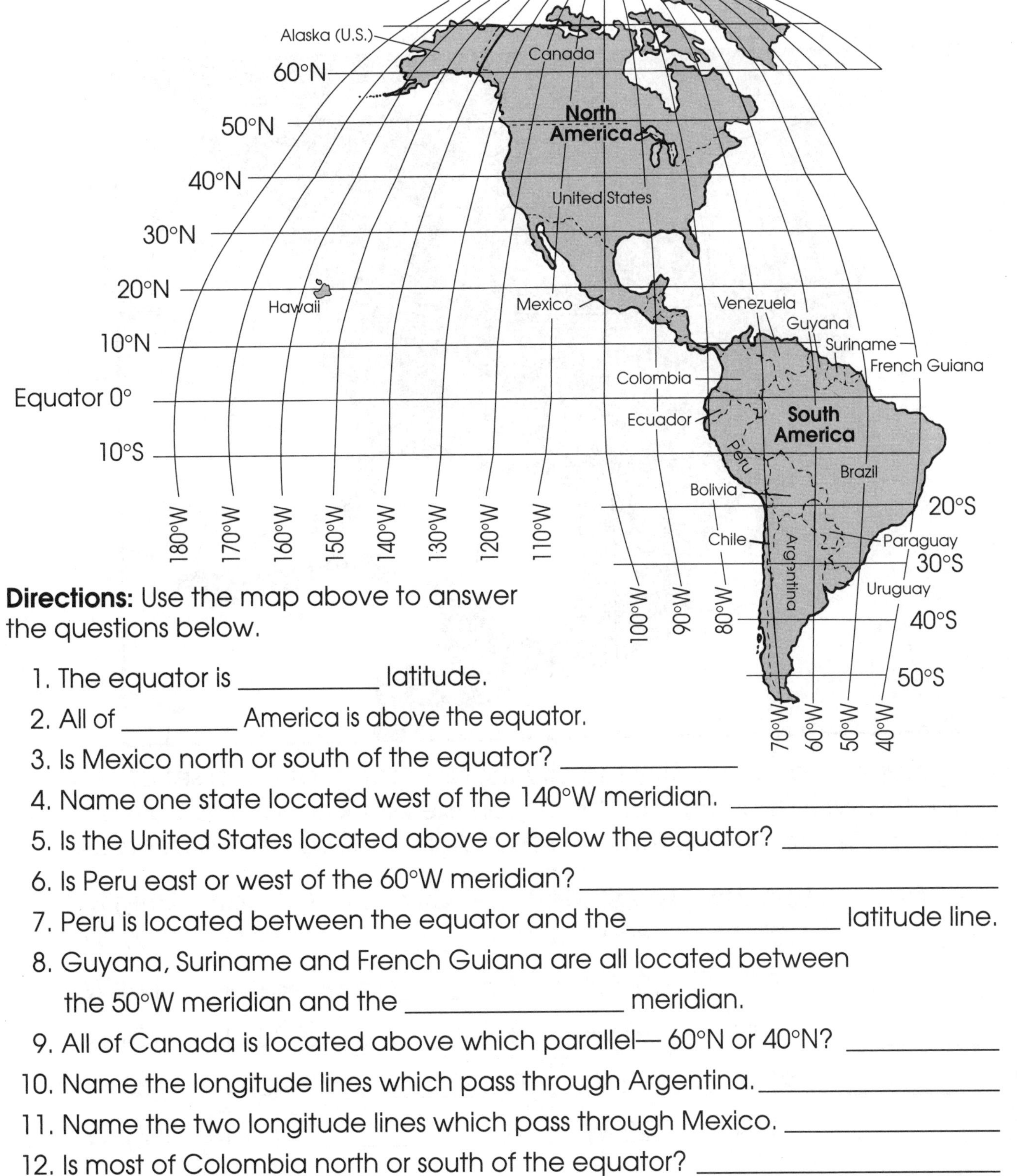

Directions: Use the map above to answer the questions below.

1. The equator is __________ latitude.
2. All of __________ America is above the equator.
3. Is Mexico north or south of the equator? __________
4. Name one state located west of the 140°W meridian. __________
5. Is the United States located above or below the equator? __________
6. Is Peru east or west of the 60°W meridian? __________
7. Peru is located between the equator and the __________ latitude line.
8. Guyana, Suriname and French Guiana are all located between the 50°W meridian and the __________ meridian.
9. All of Canada is located above which parallel— 60°N or 40°N? __________
10. Name the longitude lines which pass through Argentina. __________
11. Name the two longitude lines which pass through Mexico. __________
12. Is most of Colombia north or south of the equator? __________

Name____

Pinpointing North American Cities

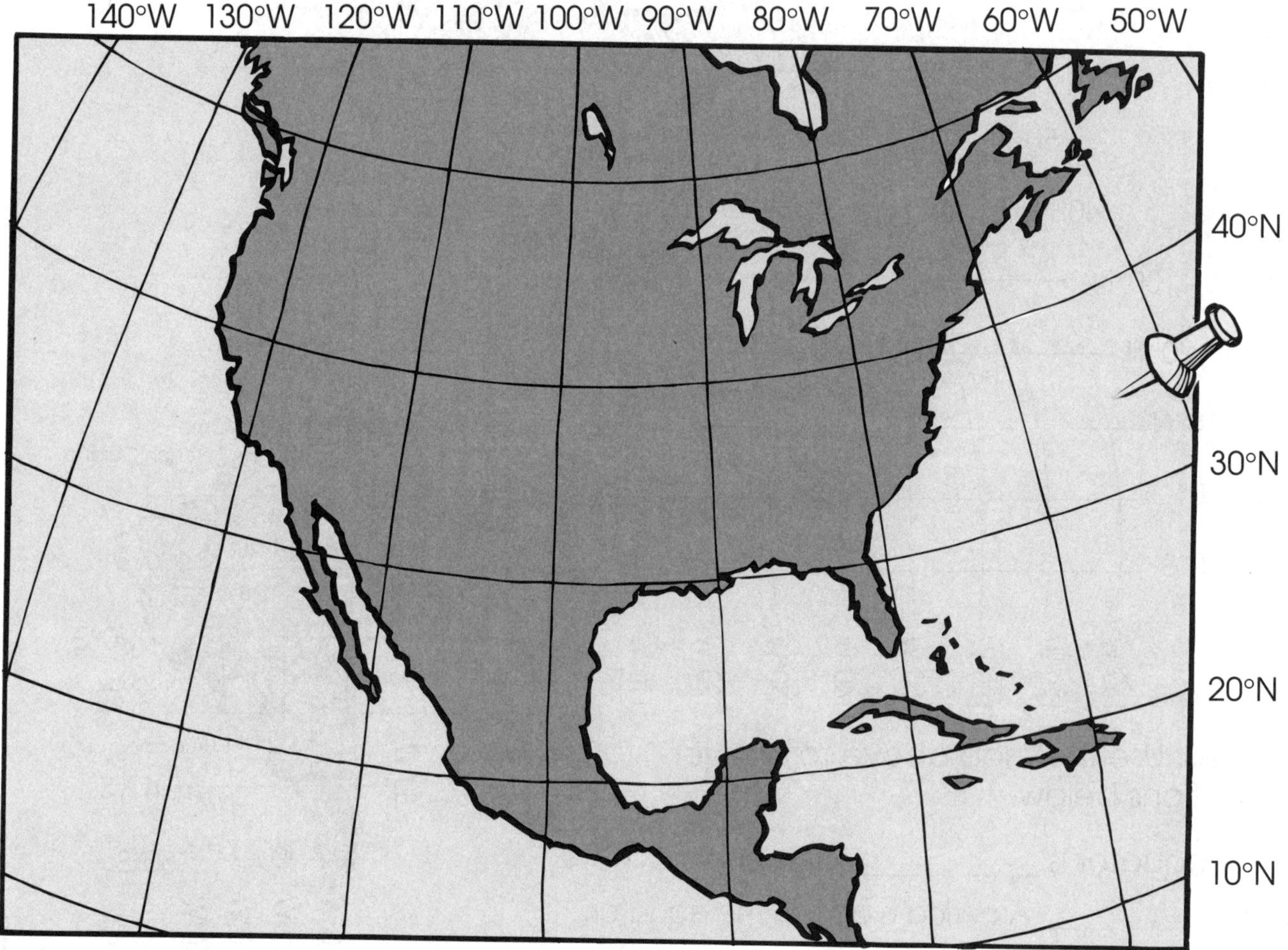

Use a globe or map to identify the city that is located at each set of coordinates. Write the name of the city on the blank and in the correct location on the map. There may be some slight variance in the degrees.

	City	Latitude	Longitude		City	Latitude	Longitude
1.	____________	25°N	80°W	6.	____________	19°N	99°W
2.	____________	39°N	104°W	7.	____________	51°N	114°W
3.	____________	50°N	97°W	8.	____________	33°N	84°W
4.	____________	23°N	82°W	9.	____________	42°N	83°W
5.	____________	37°N	122°W	10.	____________	46°N	71°W

Name________________________________

Night and Day Difference

What causes the daily change from daylight to darkness? Day turns into night because the earth rotates, or spins, on its axis. The earth's axis is an imaginary line that cuts through the earth from the North Pole to the South Pole. The earth spins in a counter-clockwise direction.

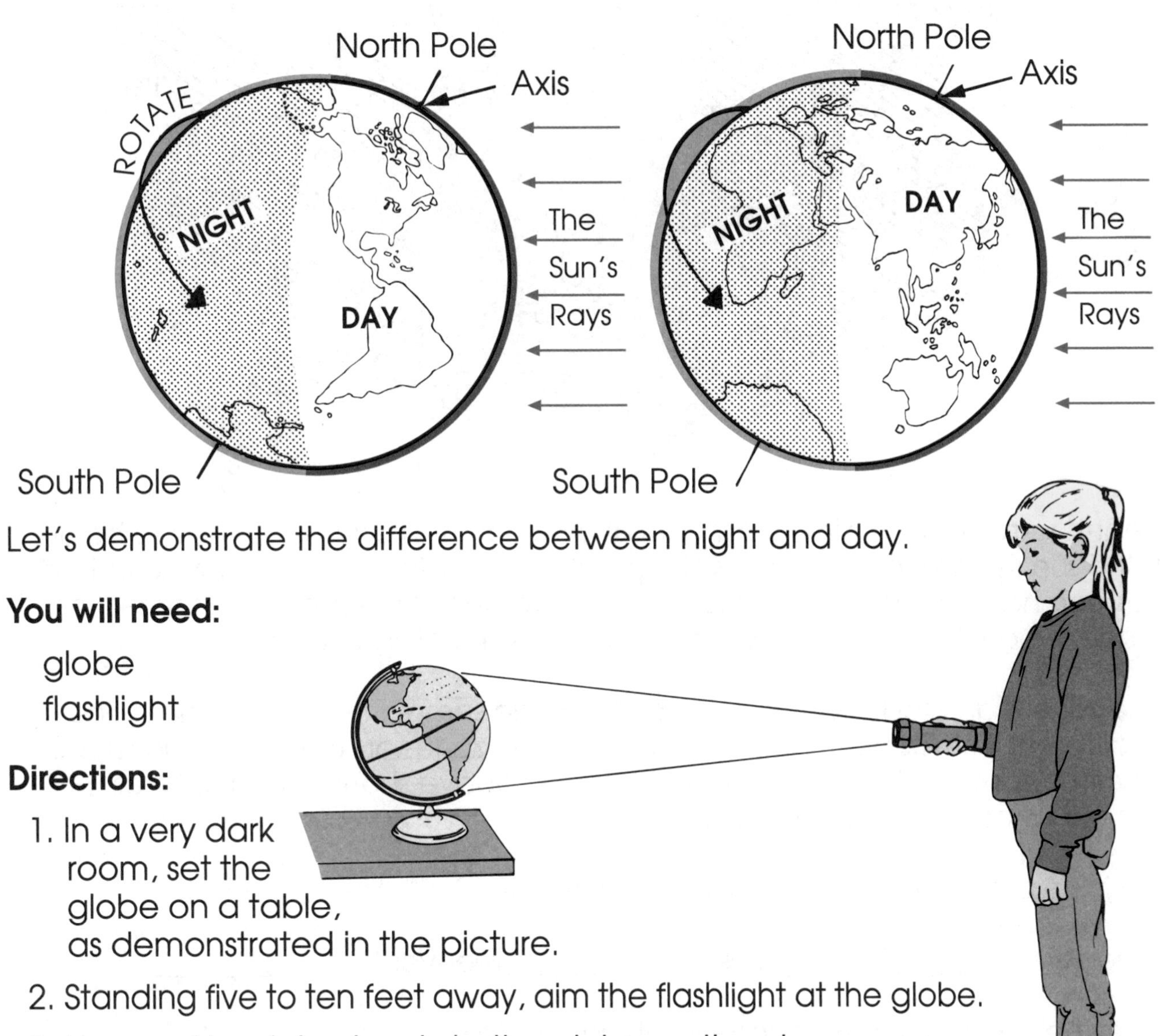

Let's demonstrate the difference between night and day.

You will need:

globe
flashlight

Directions:

1. In a very dark room, set the globe on a table, as demonstrated in the picture.
2. Standing five to ten feet away, aim the flashlight at the globe.
3. Have a friend slowly rotate the globe on its axis.
4. Discover what parts of the world are sleeping when it is daytime in your community.

Name___________________________________

Do You Have the Time?

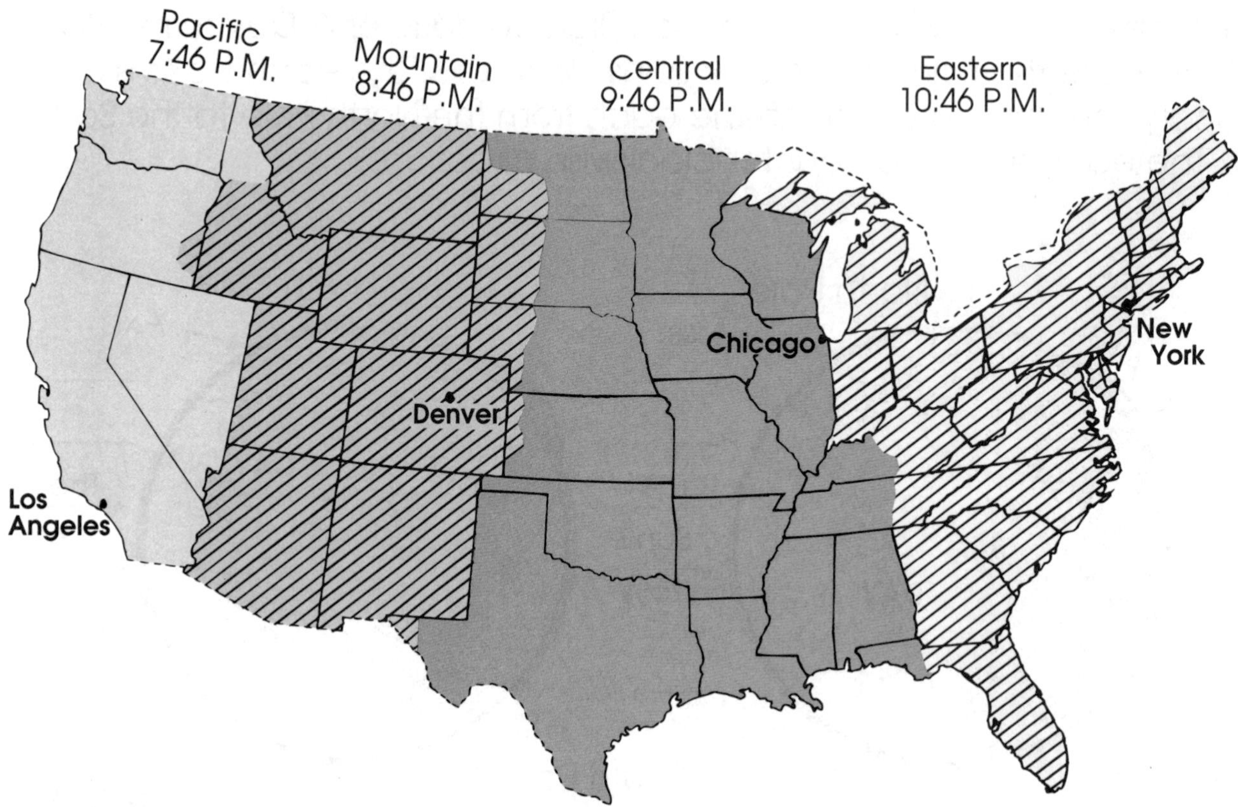

The earth spins on its axis in a west to east direction. This causes our day to begin with the sun rising in the east and setting in the west. Different areas of the United States can have different amounts of daylight at the same moment in time. For instance, when the sun is rising in New York, it is still dark in California.

A **time zone** is an area in which everyone has the same time. Every zone is one hour different from its neighbor. There are 24 time zones around the world. There are six time zones in the United States. The map above shows the four zones that cover the 48 contiguous, or touching, states.

When it is 6 o'clock in New York, what time is it in . . .

Chicago?__________ Los Angeles?____________ Denver?______________

What is the name of the time zone in which you live? ________________

Name three other states in your time zone.

____________________ ____________________ ____________________

Name____________________________________

World Time Zones

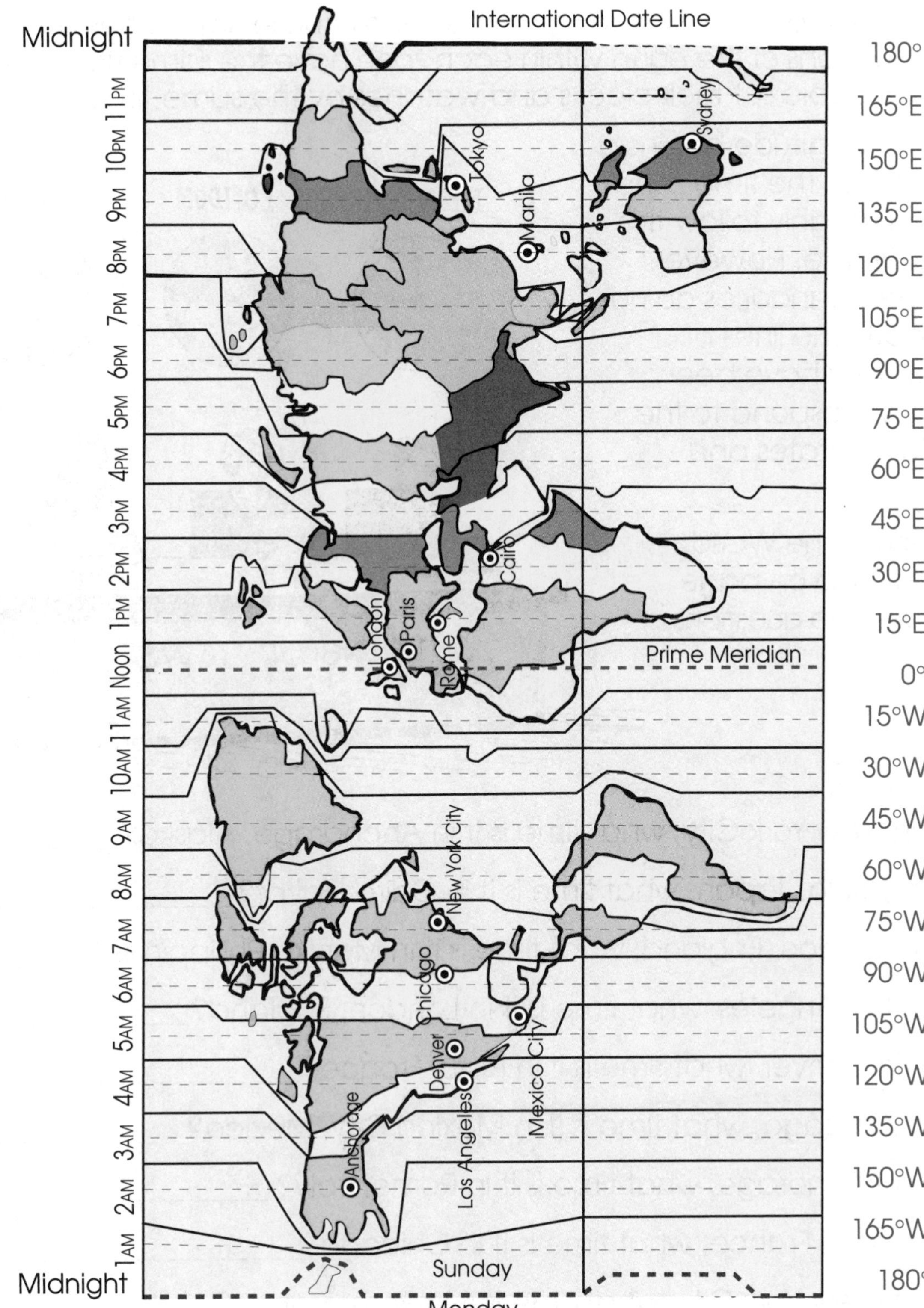
International Date Line
Midnight
11PM
10PM
9PM
8PM
7PM
6PM
5PM
4PM
3PM
2PM
1PM
Noon
11AM
10AM
9AM
8AM
7AM
6AM
5AM
4AM
3AM
2AM
1AM
Midnight
180°
165°E
150°E
135°E
120°E
105°E
90°E
75°E
60°E
45°E
30°E
15°E
Prime Meridian
0°
15°W
30°W
45°W
60°W
75°W
90°W
105°W
120°W
135°W
150°W
165°W
180°
Sydney
Tokyo
Manila
Cairo
London
Paris
Rome
New York City
Chicago
Mexico City
Denver
Los Angeles
Anchorage
Sunday
Monday

Use with page 314.

Name ______________________________

24-Hour Globe

The earth is divided into 24 standard time zones. These time zones are set so that large sections of the earth within each zone have the same time. In each time zone, people set their clocks and watches by the same time.

Every 15° of longitude begins a new time zone. The time zone boundaries roughly follow the lines of longitude. However, many of the boundaries do not follow exactly the lines of longitude. They have been altered to correspond to the boundaries of states and countries.

Directions: Use the World Time Zones map on page 313 to answer the questions below.

If it is . . .

3 A.M. in New York City, what time is it in Anchorage, Alaska? __________

4 P.M. in Tokyo, Japan, what time is it in Cairo, Egypt? __________

1 P.M. in London, England, what time is it in Manila, Philippines? __________

3 P.M. in Los Angeles, what time is it in London, England? __________

10 A.M. in Denver, what time is it in Paris, France? __________

9 P.M. in Chicago, what time is it in Mexico City, Mexico? __________

4 A.M. in Anchorage, what time is it in Rome, Italy? __________

1 P.M. in Paris, France, what time is it in Chicago? __________

11 P.M. in New York City, what time is it in Paris, France? __________

Name ____________________

Changing Times

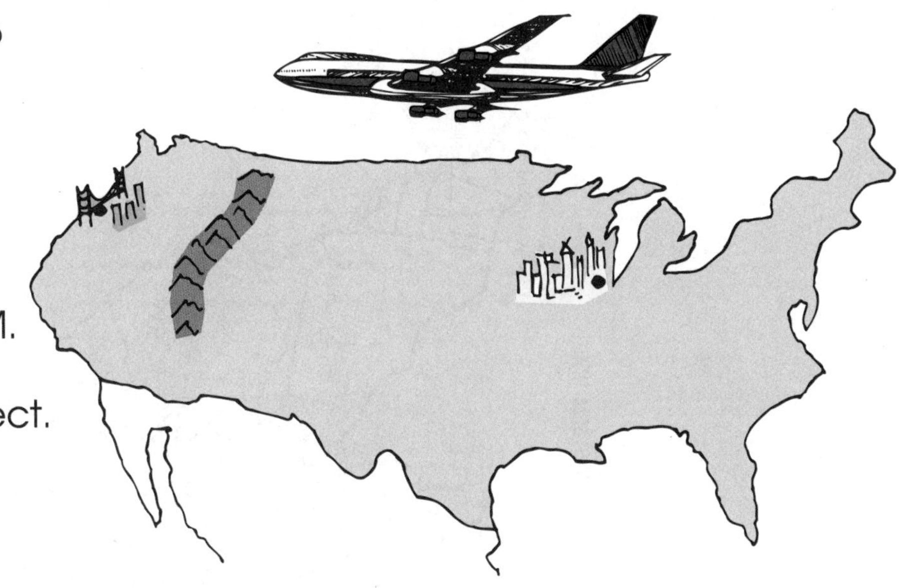

A plane leaves Chicago at 5:30 P.M. heading for San Francisco. The flight takes 3 hours. At what time will it arrive in San Francisco?

If you answered 8:30 P.M. to the above question, you are only partly correct. It would be 8:30 P.M. "Chicago time" but it would be 6:30 P.M. in San Francisco because the plane crossed two time zones.

Examine the time zones of the United States on the map on page 316. Notice that the time-zone boundaries do not always follow the state boundaries. Some states are in more than one time zone.

Directions: Use the United States Time Zones map (page 316) to answer the following questions.

1. How many time zones are there in the United States? ____________
2. How many time zones are there in the 48 contiguous (touching) states? ____________
3. Name the time zones in all 50 states. ____________________
4. If it is 3:30 P.M. in your state, what time is it in . . .
   California? ____________ Iowa? ____________
   New York? ____________ Colorado? ____________
5. What time is it right now in . . .
   Miami, Florida? ____________ Portland, Oregon? ____________
   Grand Rapids, Michigan? ____________ Dallas, Texas? ____________
   Cody, Wyoming? ____________ Richmond, Virginia? ____________

Name______________________________________

United States Time Zones

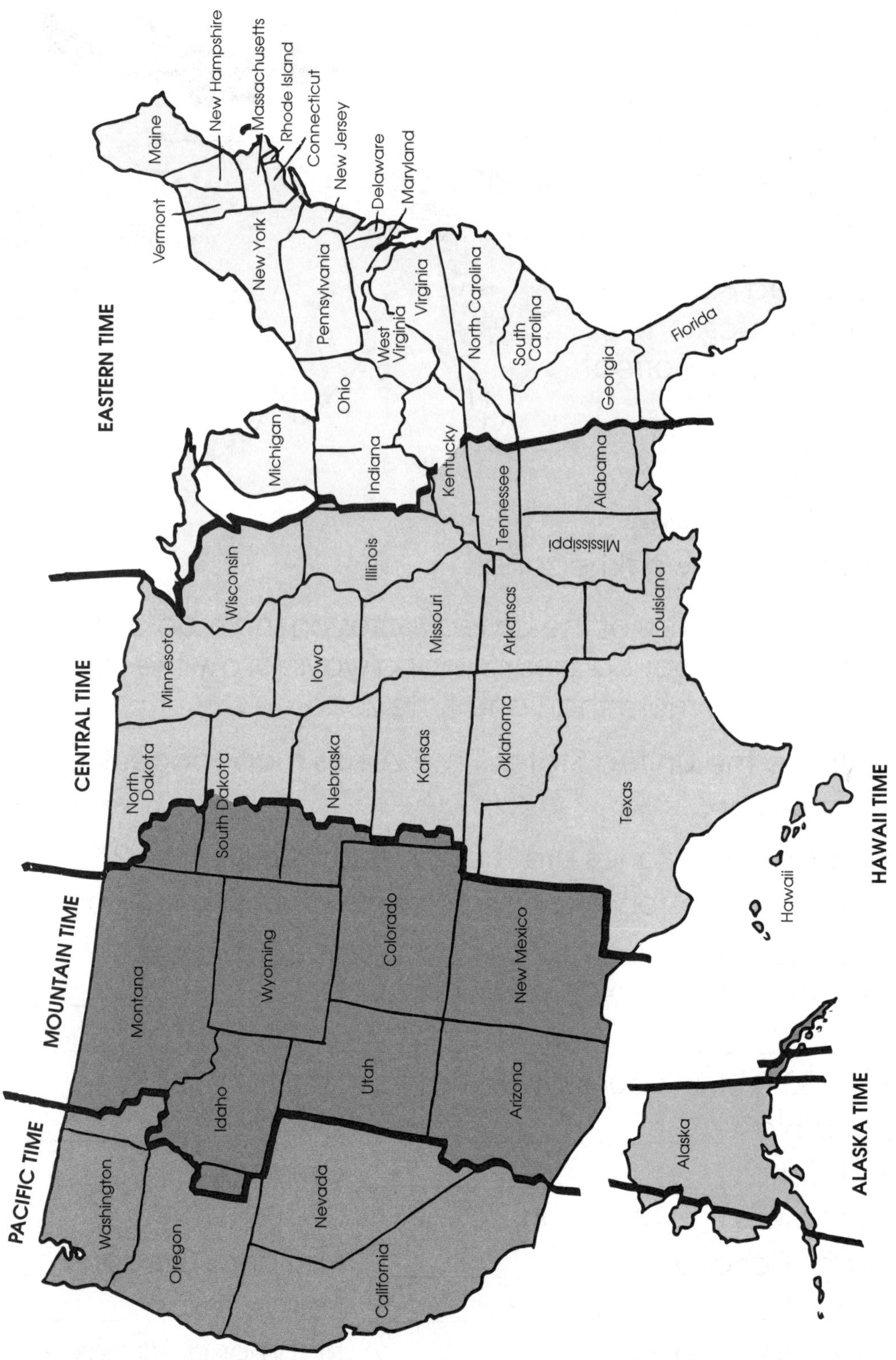

Use with page 315.

Name______________________________________

Map Skills Check-Up

Directions: Fill in the blanks below to show what you know about map skills.

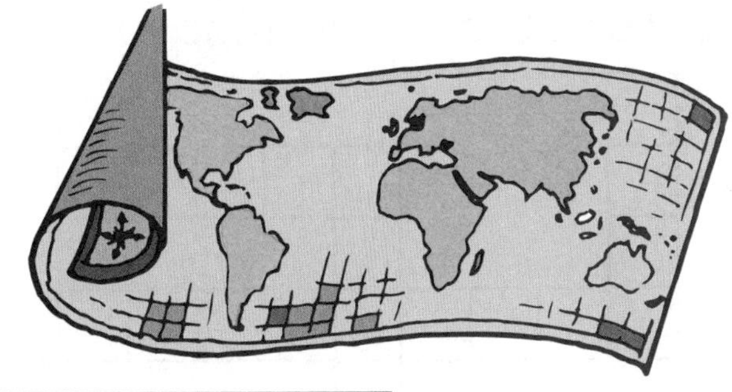

1. Sets of numbers that show where lines of latitude and longitude meet are called________________.
2. What are meridians? ______________________________
3. What is another name for 0° latitude? ____________________________
4. 0° longitude is called ________________________ and passes through ____________________________________.
5. Map symbols are shown in a box called a ______________________.
6. Which kind of map shows capitals, cities and boundaries? __________
7. Which kind of map shows rivers, mountains and plateaus? __________
8. Distance on a map is measured with a ______________________.
9. The earth spins on its ________________ in an west to east direction.
10. A ________ ________ is an area in which everyone has the same time.
11. Name the 7 continents. ______________ ____________ ____________ ______________ ______________ ______________ ______________
12. What is a peninsula?____
13. Name the 4 oceans. ____________________ ______________________ ______________________ ______________________
14. One-half of the earth is called a ____________________.
15. Label this compass rose.

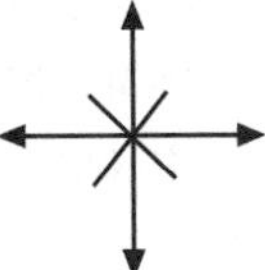

Name____

Globe Puzzle

Directions: Use a world map to solve this puzzle.

Europe
Australia
Africa
Asia
Pacific
Indian
Atlantic
Arctic
equator
axis
north
south
continents
North America
South America
Antarctica

Across:

2. U.S.A.'s continent
3. southernmost continent
5. opposite north
6. continent west of Asia
8. divides the earth into northern and southern hemispheres
9. island continent
11. earth "spins" on it
12. largest ocean
13. ocean east of Africa

Down:

1. large continent northeast of Africa
2. direction of the North Pole from the equator
4. continent between the Atlantic and Indian Oceans
5. Brazil's continent
7. land masses of earth
10. ocean east of North America
11. northernmost ocean

Name______________________________

Carnac the Cartographer

A cartographer is a person who makes maps. Carnac the Cartographer was recently fired from his profession. Can you detect the errors he made on the map on page 320? Place a red **X** on all the mistakes that you see on the map. Then, list corrections in the appropriate sections.

Continents

Mistake	It should be...

Oceans/Seas

Mistake	It should be...

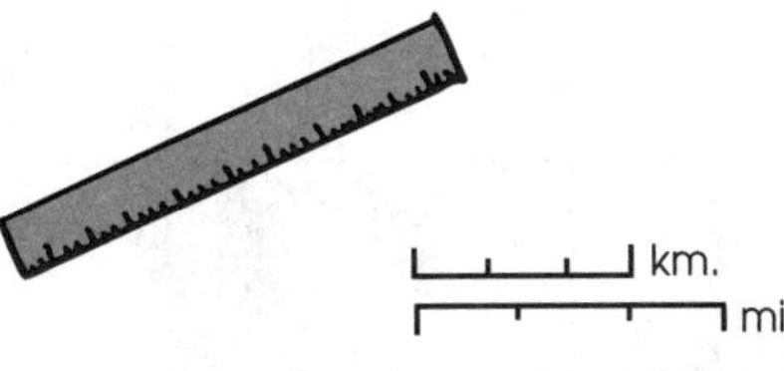

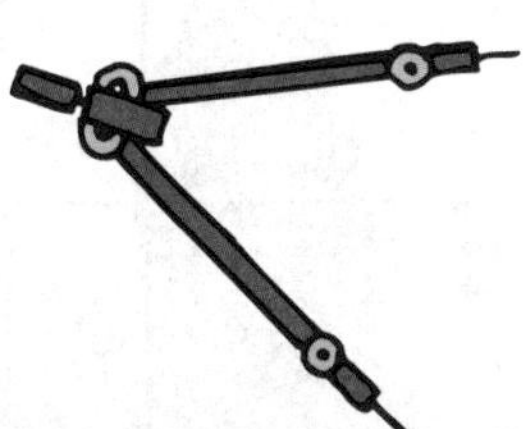

Latitude /Longitude

Mistake	It should be...

Direction Finder

Mistake	It should be . . .

Name____

Carnac the Cartographer

Mixed-Up World Map

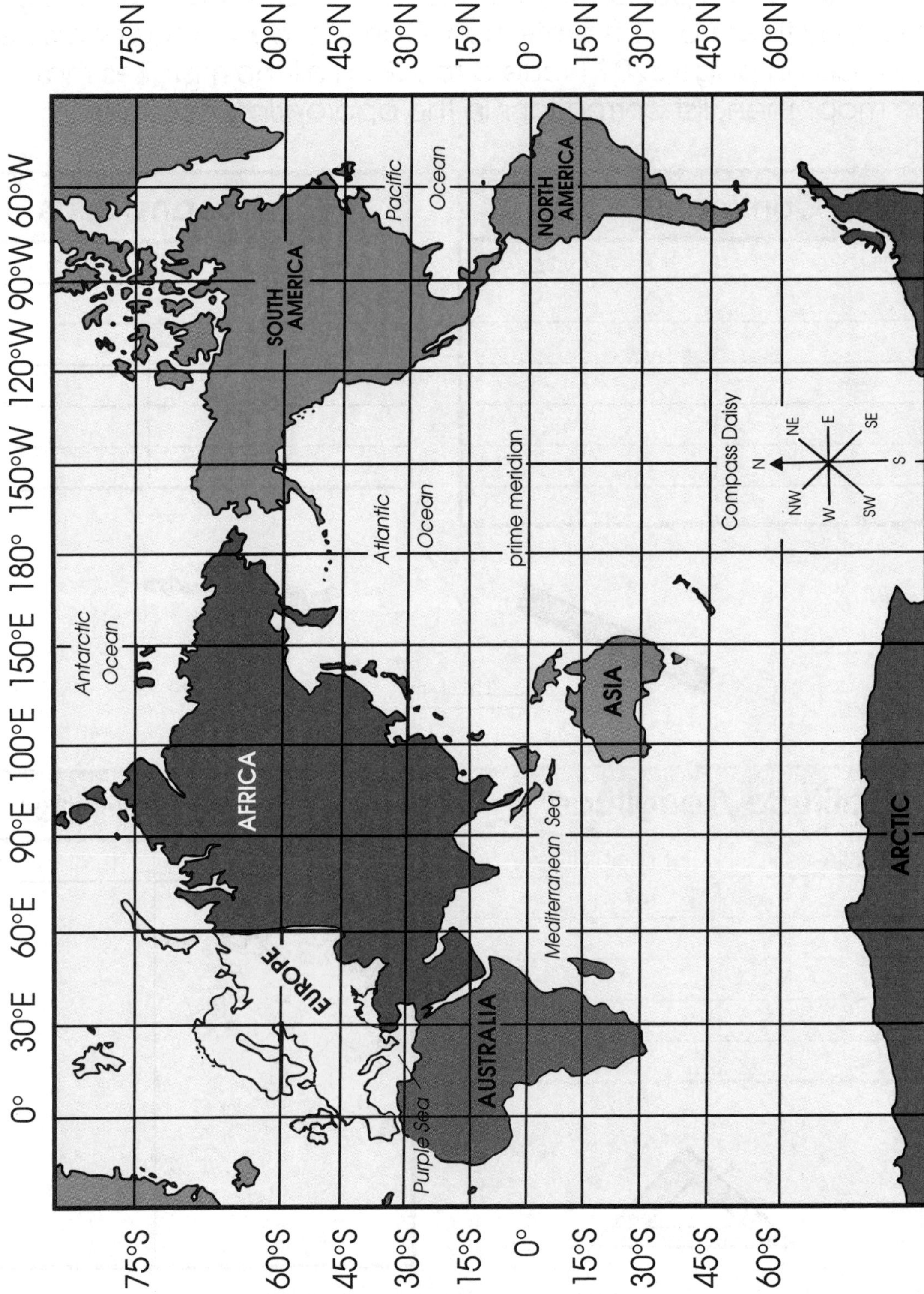

Name ______________________________

Map Skills Check-Up

How well do you understand map concepts? Test yourself!

1. Name the 7 continents. ____________, ______________, ____________,

 ____________, ______________, ____________, ______________

2. Circle what is usually the map symbol for a national capital.

3. Lines of latitude are called ______________.
4. Circle the globe which shows lines of latitude.
5. 0° latitude is called the ______________.

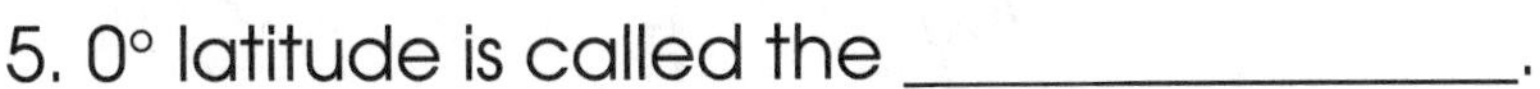

6. Name the 4 oceans. ________________, ________________

 ________________, ________________.

7. Lines of longitude are called ________________________.
8. 0° longitude is called the________________________.
9. Draw meridians on this circle. Will they be lines of latitude or longitude?

 ____

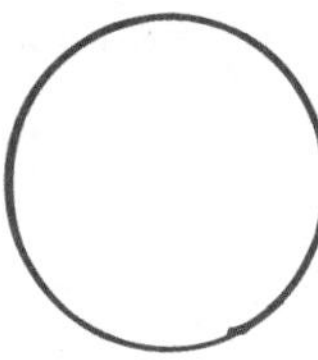

10. What is used on a map to measure distance? ____________
11. A spherical map of the earth is called a ___________.
12. Draw the symbol for degrees. ___________
13. Label the points of the compass rose.

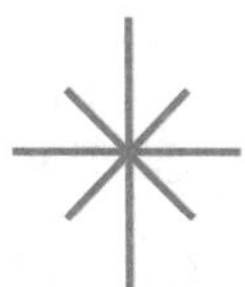

Name____

World Map

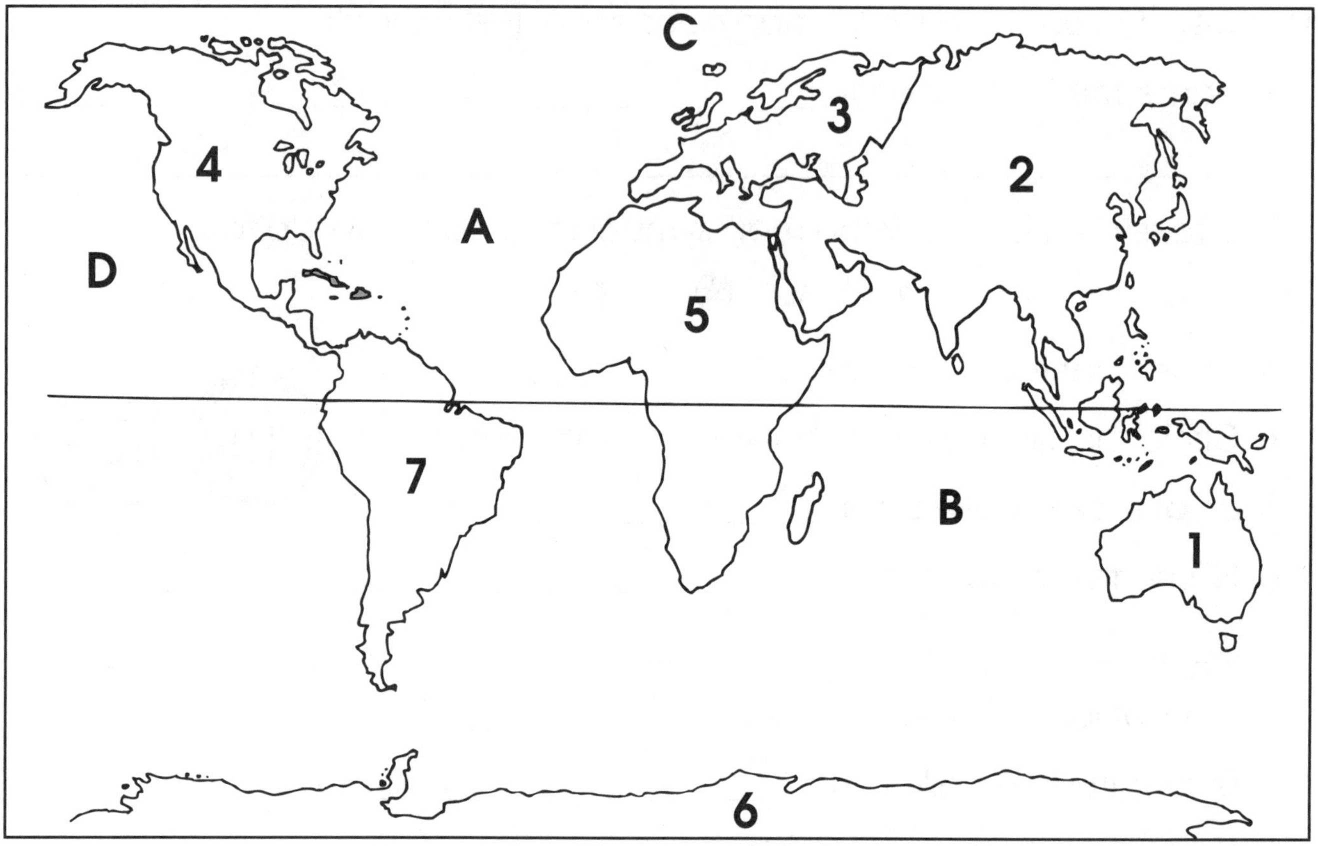

Name the continents as numbered on the map.

1. ______________________________
2. ______________________________
3. ______________________________
4. ______________________________
5. ______________________________
6. ______________________________
7. ______________________________

Outline all of the continents in green.

Draw one blue fish in each ocean.

Name the oceans as lettered on the map.

A. ______________________________

B. ______________________________

C. ______________________________

D. ______________________________

Color the equator red.

The Complete Book of Maps & Geography
Grades 3-6

ANSWER KEY

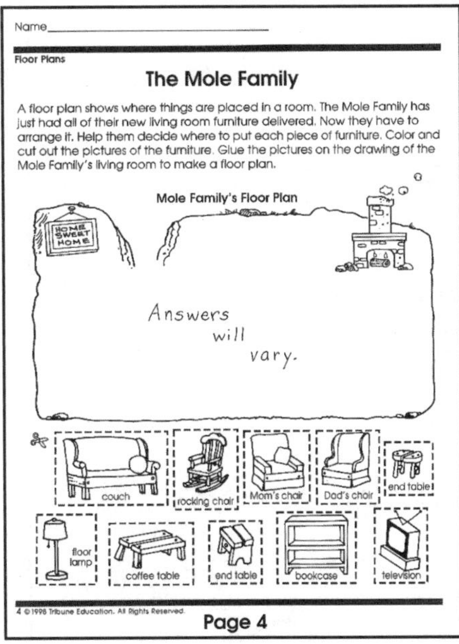
Name________________

Floor Plans

The Mole Family

A floor plan shows where things are placed in a room. The Mole Family has just had all of their new living room furniture delivered. Now they have to arrange it. Help them decide where to put each piece of furniture. Color and cut out the pictures of the furniture. Glue the pictures on the drawing of the Mole Family's living room to make a floor plan.

Mole Family's Floor Plan

HOME SWEET HOME

Answers will vary.

couch | rocking chair | Mom's chair | Dad's chair | end table | floor lamp | coffee table | end table | bookcase | television

4 ©1998 Tribune Education. All Rights Reserved.

Page 4

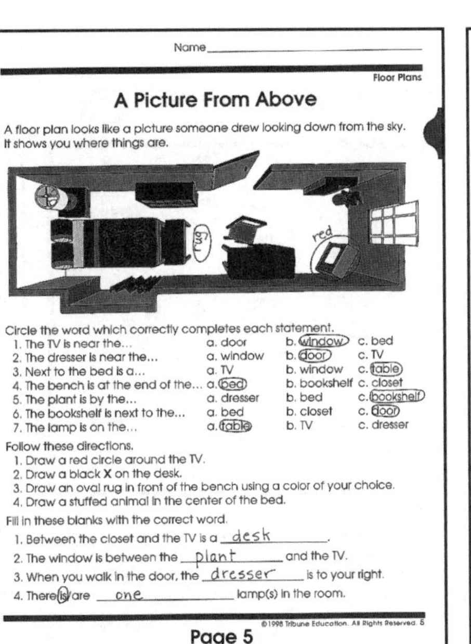
Name________________

Floor Plans

A Picture From Above

A floor plan looks like a picture someone drew looking down from the sky. It shows you where things are.

red

Circle the word which correctly completes each statement.

1. The TV is near the... a. door b. (window) c. bed
2. The dresser is near the... a. window b. (door) c. TV
3. Next to the bed is a... a. TV b. window c. (table)
4. The bench is at the end of the... a. (bed) b. bookshelf c. closet
5. The plant is by the... a. dresser b. bed c. (bookshelf)
6. The bookshelf is next to the... a. bed b. closet c. (door)
7. The lamp is on the... a. (table) b. TV c. dresser

Follow these directions.

1. Draw a red circle around the TV.
2. Draw a black X on the desk.
3. Draw an oval rug in front of the bench using a color of your choice.
4. Draw a stuffed animal in the center of the bed.

Fill in these blanks with the correct word.

1. Between the closet and the TV is a desk.
2. The window is between the plant and the TV.
3. When you walk in the door, the dresser is to your right.
4. There (is)/are one lamp(s) in the room.

©1998 Tribune Education. All Rights Reserved. 5

Page 5

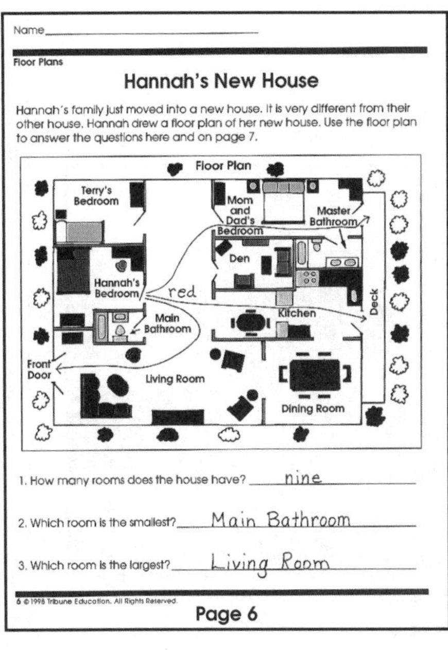
Name________________

Floor Plans

Hannah's New House

Hannah's family just moved into a new house. It is very different from their other house. Hannah drew a floor plan of her new house. Use the floor plan to answer the questions here and on page 7.

1. How many rooms does the house have? nine
2. Which room is the smallest? Main Bathroom
3. Which room is the largest? Living Room

6 ©1998 Tribune Education. All Rights Reserved.

Page 6

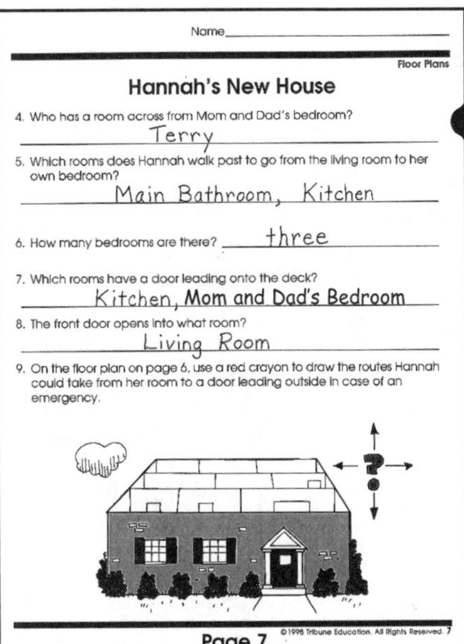
Name________________

Floor Plans

Hannah's New House

4. Who has a room across from Mom and Dad's bedroom? Terry
5. Which rooms does Hannah walk past to go from the living room to her own bedroom? Main Bathroom, Kitchen
6. How many bedrooms are there? three
7. Which rooms have a door leading onto the deck? Kitchen, Mom and Dad's Bedroom
8. The front door opens into what room? Living Room
9. On the floor plan on page 6, use a red crayon to draw the routes Hannah could take from her room to a door leading outside in case of an emergency.

©1998 Tribune Education. All Rights Reserved. 7

Page 7

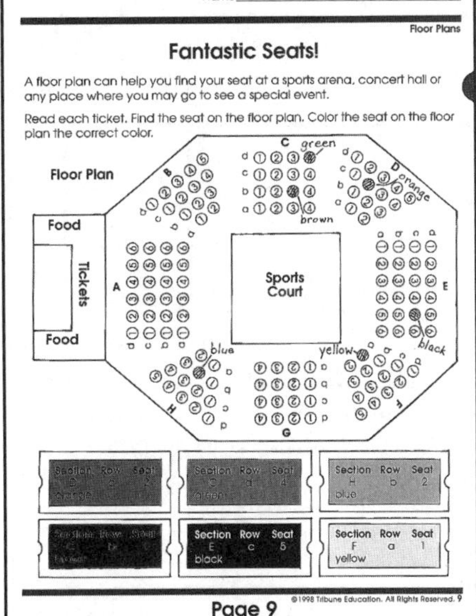
Name________________

Floor Plans

Fantastic Seats!

A floor plan can help you find your seat at a sports arena, concert hall or any place where you may go to see a special event.

Read each ticket. Find the seat on the floor plan. Color the seat on the floor plan the correct color.

Section	Row	Seat
H	b	2
blue		

Section	Row	Seat
E	c	5
black		

Section	Row	Seat
F	a	1
yellow		

©1998 Tribune Education. All Rights Reserved. 9

Page 9

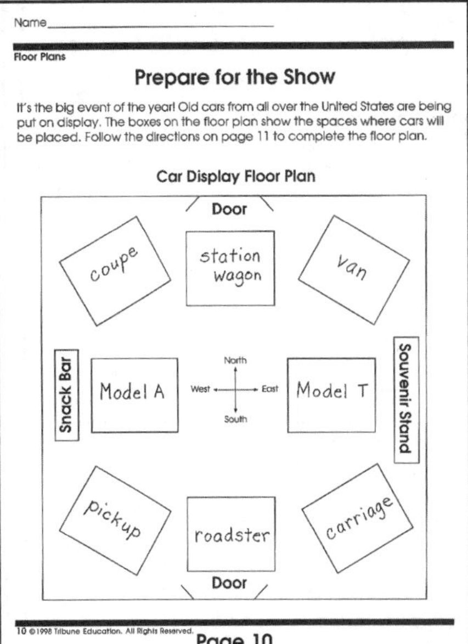
Name________________

Floor Plans

Prepare for the Show

It's the big event of the year! Old cars from all over the United States are being put on display. The boxes on the floor plan show the spaces where cars will be placed. Follow the directions on page 11 to complete the floor plan.

Car Display Floor Plan

10 ©1998 Tribune Education. All Rights Reserved.

Page 10

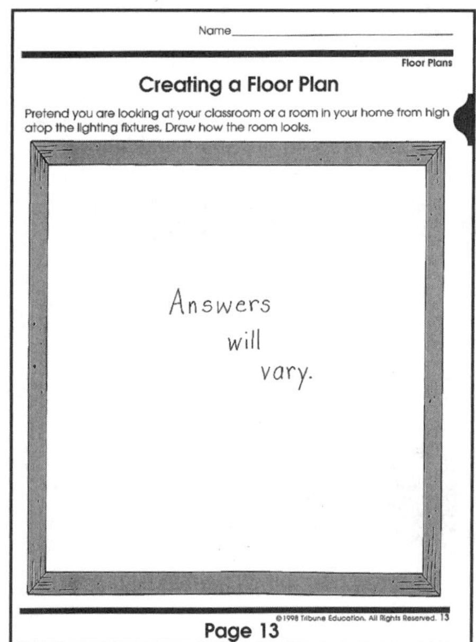

Name________________________

Floor Plans

Creating a Floor Plan

Pretend you are looking at your classroom or a room in your home from high atop the lighting fixtures. Draw how the room looks.

Answers will vary.

 13

Page 13

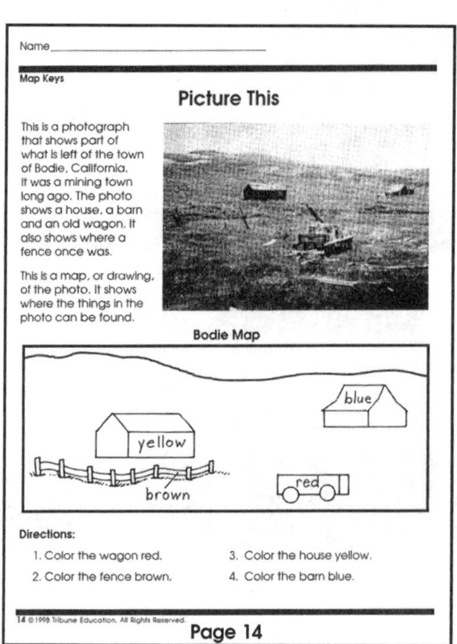

Name________________________

Map Keys

Picture This

This is a photograph that shows part of what is left of the town of Bodie, California. It was a mining town long ago. The photo shows a house, a barn and an old wagon. It also shows where a fence once was.

This is a map, or drawing, of the photo. It shows where the things in the photo can be found.

Bodie Map

Directions:

1. Color the wagon red.
2. Color the fence brown.
3. Color the house yellow.
4. Color the barn blue.

14

Page 14

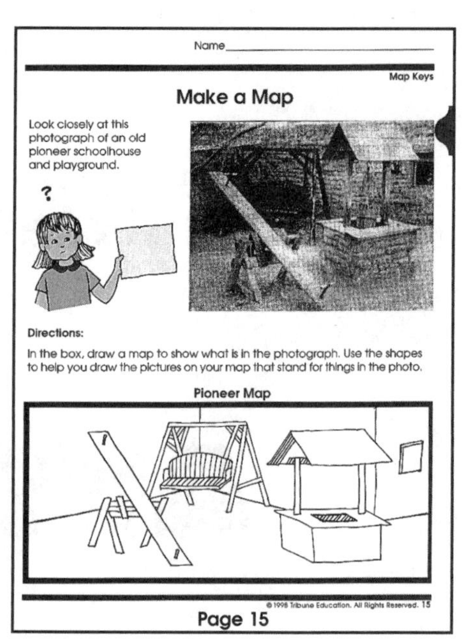

Name________________________

Map Keys

Make a Map

Look closely at this photograph of an old pioneer schoolhouse and playground.

Directions:

In the box, draw a map to show what is in the photograph. Use the shapes to help you draw the pictures on your map that stand for things in the photo.

Pioneer Map

 15

Page 15

Name________________________

Map Keys

Symbols on Maps

A symbol is a picture that stands for something that is shown on a map. Symbols used in a map are shown in the Map Key. Look at the symbols. Draw a line from each symbol to what it stands for in the drawing below.

16

Page 16

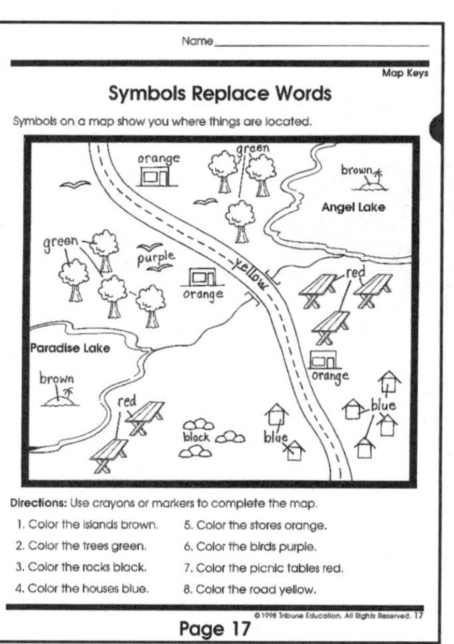

Name________________________

Map Keys

Symbols Replace Words

Symbols on a map show you where things are located.

Directions: Use crayons or markers to complete the map.

1. Color the islands brown.
2. Color the trees green.
3. Color the rocks black.
4. Color the houses blue.
5. Color the stores orange.
6. Color the birds purple.
7. Color the picnic tables red.
8. Color the road yellow.

 17

Page 17

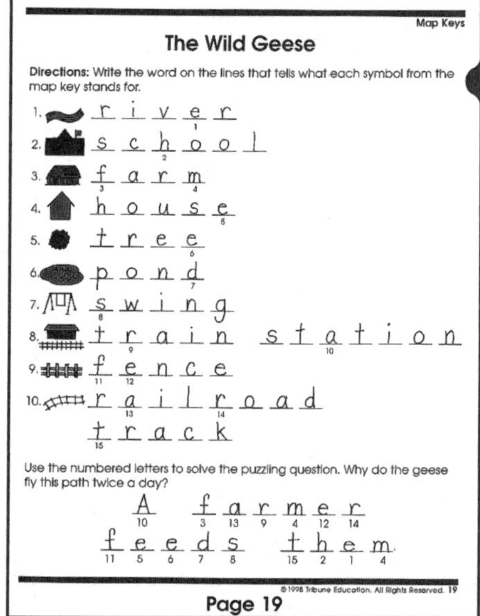

Name________________________

Map Keys

The Wild Geese

Directions: Write the word on the lines that tells what each symbol from the map key stands for.

1. river
2. school
3. farm
4. house
5. tree
6. pond
7. swing
8. train station
9. fence
10. railroad track

Use the numbered letters to solve the puzzling question. Why do the geese fly this path twice a day?

A farmer feeds them.

 19

Page 19

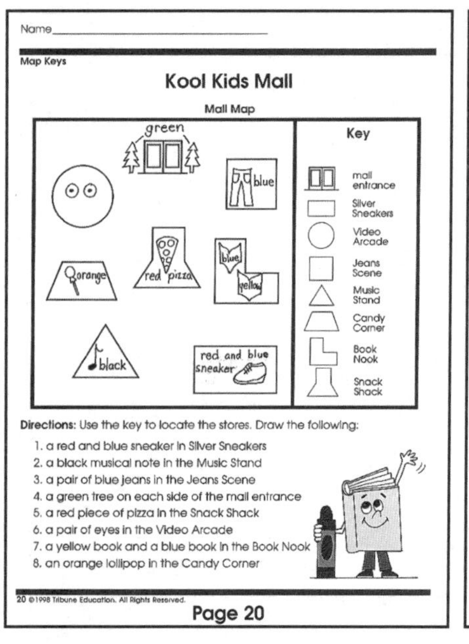

Name________________________

Map Keys

Kool Kids Mall

Mall Map

Directions: Use the key to locate the stores. Draw the following:

1. a red and blue sneaker in Silver Sneakers
2. a black musical note in the Music Stand
3. a pair of blue jeans in the Jeans Scene
4. a green tree on each side of the mall entrance
5. a red piece of pizza in the Snack Shack
6. a pair of eyes in the Video Arcade
7. a yellow book and a blue book in the Book Nook
8. an orange lollipop in the Candy Corner

20

Page 20

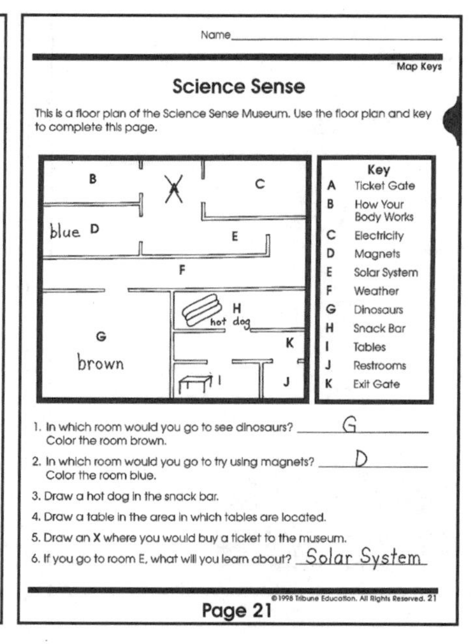

Name________________________

Map Keys

Science Sense

This is a floor plan of the Science Sense Museum. Use the floor plan and key to complete this page.

Key	
A	Ticket Gate
B	How Your Body Works
C	Electricity
D	Magnets
E	Solar System
F	Weather
G	Dinosaurs
H	Snack Bar
I	Tables
J	Restrooms
K	Exit Gate

1. In which room would you go to see dinosaurs? G
   Color the room brown.
2. In which room would you go to try using magnets? D
   Color the room blue.
3. Draw a hot dog in the snack bar.
4. Draw a table in the area in which tables are located.
5. Draw an X where you would buy a ticket to the museum.
6. If you go to room E, what will you learn about? Solar System

 21

Page 21

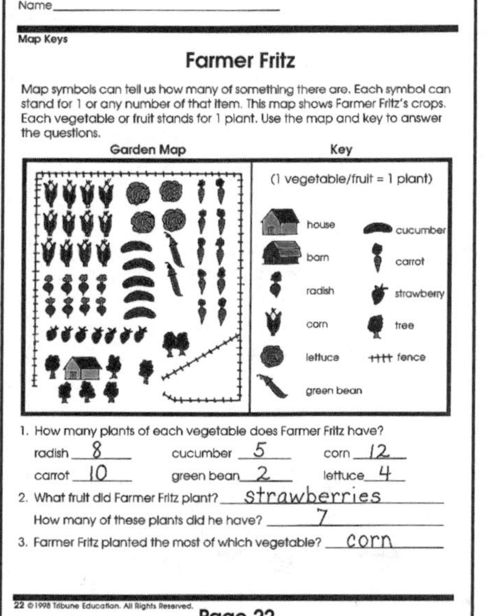

Name________________________

Map Keys

Farmer Fritz

Map symbols can tell us how many of something there are. Each symbol can stand for 1 or any number of that item. This map shows Farmer Fritz's crops. Each vegetable or fruit stands for 1 plant. Use the map and key to answer the questions.

Garden Map

1. How many plants of each vegetable does Farmer Fritz have?
   radish 8 cucumber 5 corn 12
   carrot 10 green bean 2 lettuce 4
2. What fruit did Farmer Fritz plant? strawberries
   How many of these plants did he have? 7
3. Farmer Fritz planted the most of which vegetable? corn

22

Page 22

Name________________________

Map Keys

Carmella's Candy

Carmella made a map of her candy store so that her customers could easily find their favorite candy. Use the map and key to answer the questions.

Candy Store Map

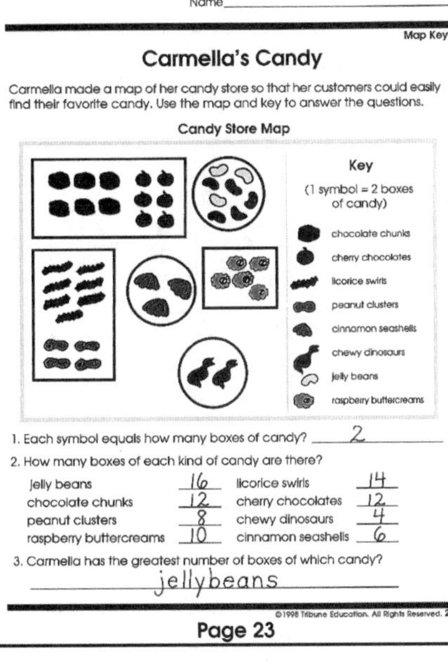

1. Each symbol equals how many boxes of candy? 2
2. How many boxes of each kind of candy are there?

jelly beans	16	licorice swirls	14
chocolate chunks	12	cherry chocolates	12
peanut clusters	8	chewy dinosaurs	4
raspberry buttercreams	10	cinnamon seashells	6

3. Carmella has the greatest number of boxes of which candy? jellybeans

 23

Page 23

Name________________________

Map Keys

Mixed-Up Map Maker

Mattie Map Maker goofed when creating a map of the state of Oopsylvania. Circle her mistakes and put a number by each one. Then, describe each error on the line with the matching number. (Hint: The key shows the correct map symbols.)

Oopsylvania Map

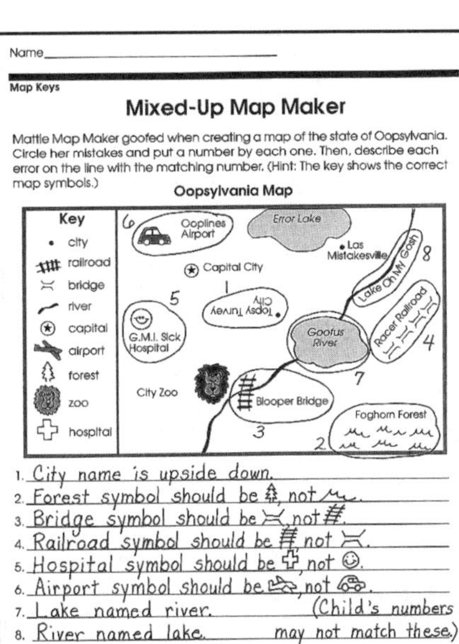

1. City name is upside down.
2. Forest symbol should be [tree symbol], not [grass symbol].
3. Bridge symbol should be [bridge symbol], not [railroad symbol].
4. Railroad symbol should be [railroad symbol], not [bridge symbol].
5. Hospital symbol should be [cross symbol], not [smiley symbol].
6. Airport symbol should be [plane symbol], not [car symbol].
7. Lake named river. (Child's numbers
8. River named lake. may not match these.)

24

Page 24

Name________________________

Map Routes

Time to Go Home

This map shows routes the dinosaur can take to get to its cave. Use the key to find each symbol on the map. Then, follow the directions.

Dinosaur Cave Map

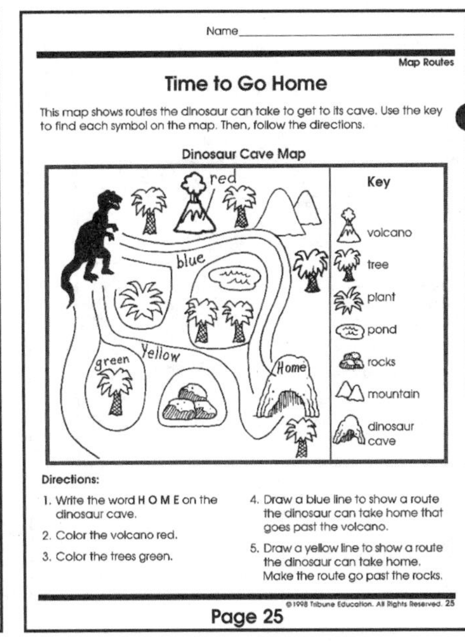

Directions:

1. Write the word H O M E on the dinosaur cave.
2. Color the volcano red.
3. Color the trees green.
4. Draw a blue line to show a route the dinosaur can take home that goes past the volcano.
5. Draw a yellow line to show a route the dinosaur can take home. Make the route go past the rocks.

 25

Page 25

Name________________________

Map Routes

Seeing the Wildlife

Martin and Norma are excited about visiting the Wildlife Safari. It is different from a zoo. Here they drive slowly along a road to see the animals run freely in large fenced areas. They stop at the gate to buy tickets and to get a map. They will use the map so that they will be sure to see all the animals.

Safari Map

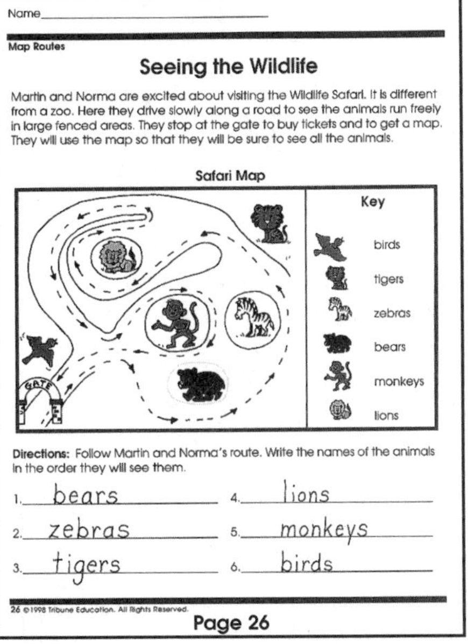

Directions: Follow Martin and Norma's route. Write the names of the animals in the order they will see them.

1. bears
2. zebras
3. tigers
4. lions
5. monkeys
6. birds

26

Page 26

Name________________________

Map Routes

Take a Hike

This is a map showing three hiking trails.

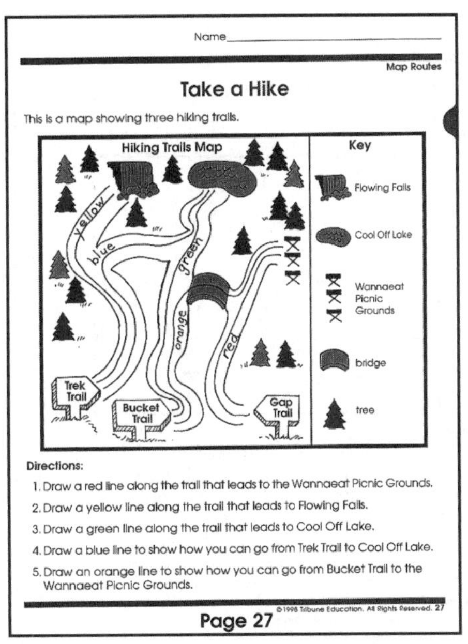

Directions:

1. Draw a red line along the trail that leads to the Wannaeat Picnic Grounds.
2. Draw a yellow line along the trail that leads to Flowing Falls.
3. Draw a green line along the trail that leads to Cool Off Lake.
4. Draw a blue line to show how you can go from Trek Trail to Cool Off Lake.
5. Draw an orange line to show how you can go from Bucket Trail to the Wannaeat Picnic Grounds.

 27

Page 27

Name________________________

Map Routes

Waiting at the Airport

Jenny and Carl went to the airport to pick up their grandparents. Dad let Mom and the kids out in front of the airport doors while he went to park the van. The dotted line (- - -) shows where they had to walk to go to the correct gate to meet their grandparents.

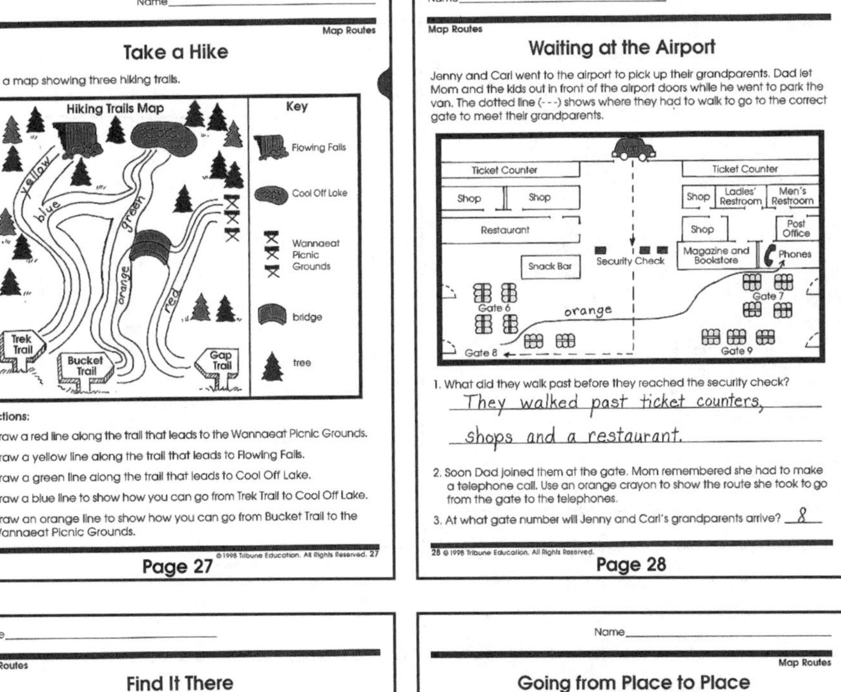

1. What did they walk past before they reached the security check? They walked past ticket counters, shops and a restaurant.
2. Soon Dad joined them at the gate. Mom remembered she had to make a telephone call. Use an orange crayon to show the route she took to go from the gate to the telephones.
3. At what gate number will Jenny and Carl's grandparents arrive? 8

28

Page 28

Name________________________

Map Routes

A Real "Moose-tery"

Horrible Harvey Hunter has disappeared somewhere in the Mysterious Moosehead Mansion. Detective Dimwitt is trying to find him. Use the key to identify rooms in the mansion. Then, use a pencil to trace the route Detective Dimwitt took to locate the hapless Harvey.

Moosehead Mansion Map

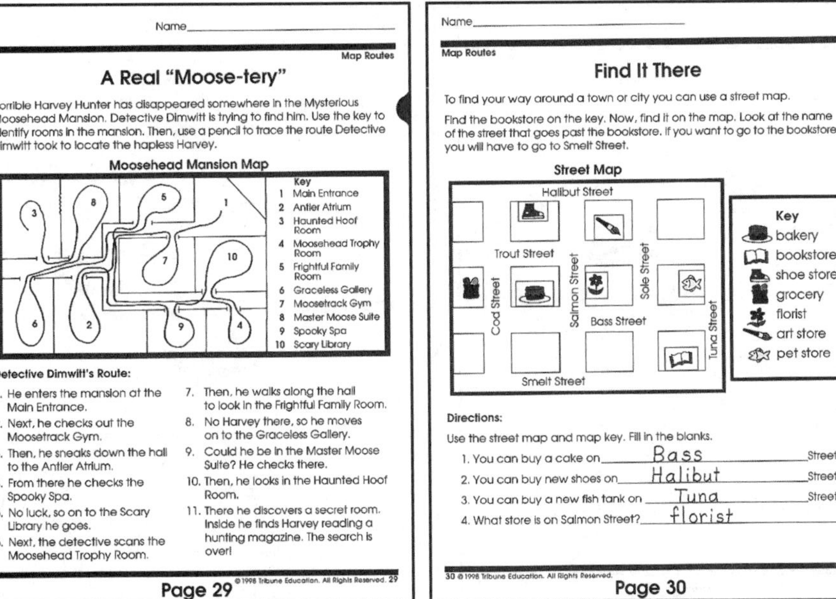

Key
1 Main Entrance
2 Antler Atrium
3 Haunted Hoof Room
4 Moosehead Trophy Room
5 Frightful Family Room
6 Graceless Gallery
7 Moosetrack Gym
8 Master Moose Suite
9 Spooky Spa
10 Scary Library

Detective Dimwitt's Route:

1. He enters the mansion at the Main Entrance.
2. Next, he checks out the Moosetrack Gym.
3. Then, he sneaks down the hall to the Antler Atrium.
4. From there he checks the Spooky Spa.
5. No luck, so on to the Scary Library he goes.
6. Next, the detective scans the Moosehead Trophy Room.
7. Then, he walks along the hall to look in the Frightful Family Room.
8. No Harvey there, so he moves on to the Graceless Gallery.
9. Could he be in the Master Moose Suite? He checks there.
10. Then, he looks in the Haunted Hoof Room.
11. There he discovers a secret room. Inside he finds Harvey reading a hunting magazine. The search is over!

 29

Page 29

Name________________________

Map Routes

Find It There

To find your way around a town or city you can use a street map.

Find the bookstore on the key. Now, find it on the map. Look at the name of the street that goes past the bookstore. If you want to go to the bookstore, you will have to go to Smelt Street.

Street Map

Key
bakery
bookstore
shoe store
grocery
florist
art store
pet store

Directions:

Use the street map and map key. Fill in the blanks.

1. You can buy a cake on Bass Street.
2. You can buy new shoes on Halibut Street.
3. You can buy a new fish tank on Tuna Street.
4. What store is on Salmon Street? florist

30

Page 30

Name________________________

Map Routes

Going from Place to Place

Some maps show you where places are located in a town.

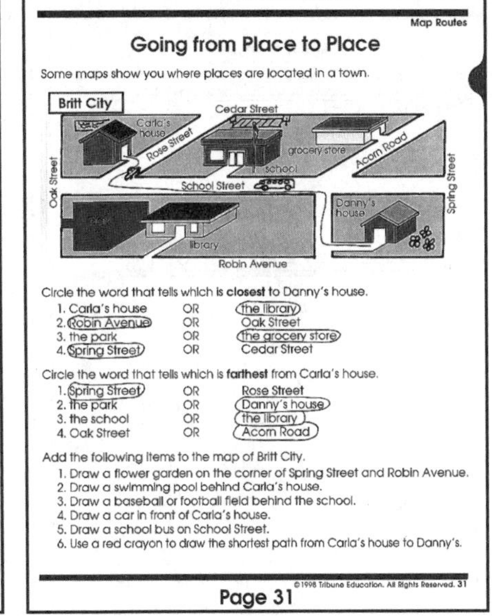

Circle the word that tells which is **closest** to Danny's house.

1. Carla's house	OR	(the library)
2. (Robin Avenue)	OR	Oak Street
3. the park	OR	(the grocery store)
4. (Spring Street)	OR	Cedar Street

Circle the word that tells which is **farthest** from Carla's house.

1. (Spring Street)	OR	Rose Street
2. the park	OR	(Danny's house)
3. the school	OR	(the library)
4. Oak Street	OR	(Acorn Road)

Add the following items to the map of Britt City.

1. Draw a flower garden on the corner of Spring Street and Robin Avenue.
2. Draw a swimming pool behind Carla's house.
3. Draw a baseball or football field behind the school.
4. Draw a car in front of Carla's house.
5. Draw a school bus on School Street.
6. Use a red crayon to draw the shortest path from Carla's house to Danny's.

 31

Page 31

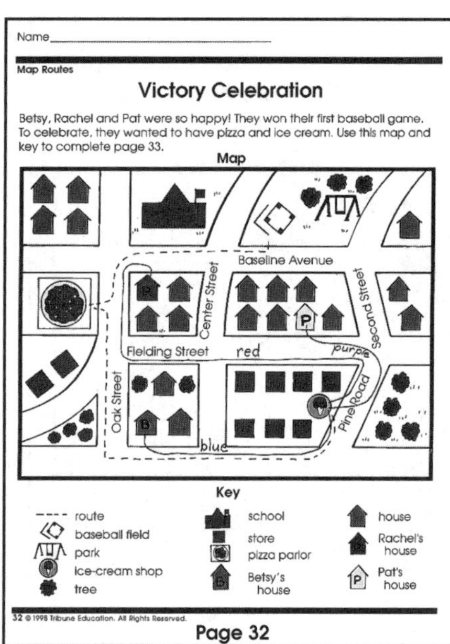
Name____________________

Map Routes

Victory Celebration

Betsy, Rachel and Pat were so happy! They won their first baseball game. To celebrate, they wanted to have pizza and ice cream. Use this map and key to complete page 33.

Map

Key

- route
- baseball field
- park
- ice-cream shop
- tree
- school
- store
- pizza parlor
- Betsy's house
- house
- Rachel's house
- Pat's house

Page 32

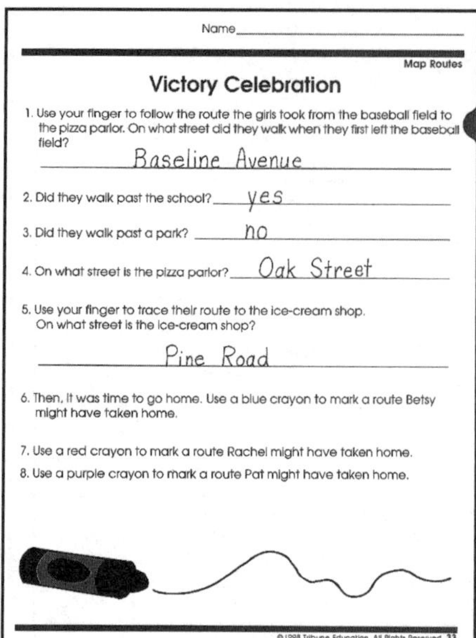
Name____________________

Map Routes

Victory Celebration

1. Use your finger to follow the route the girls took from the baseball field to the pizza parlor. On what street did they walk when they first left the baseball field? Baseline Avenue
2. Did they walk past the school? yes
3. Did they walk past a park? no
4. On what street is the pizza parlor? Oak Street
5. Use your finger to trace their route to the ice-cream shop. On what street is the ice-cream shop? Pine Road
6. Then, it was time to go home. Use a blue crayon to mark a route Betsy might have taken home.
7. Use a red crayon to mark a route Rachel might have taken home.
8. Use a purple crayon to mark a route Pat might have taken home.

Page 33

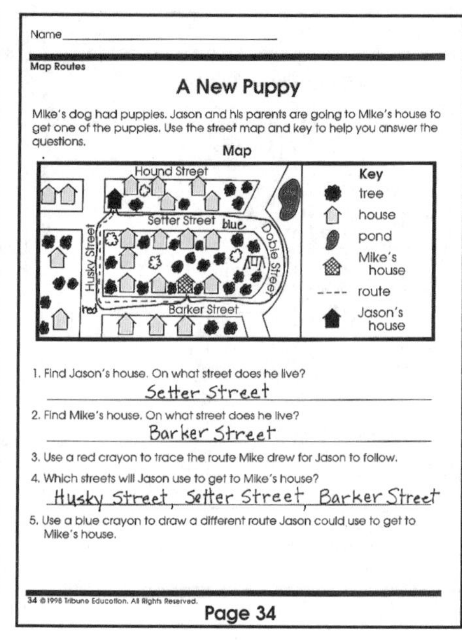
Name____________________

Map Routes

A New Puppy

Mike's dog had puppies. Jason and his parents are going to Mike's house to get one of the puppies. Use the street map and key to help you answer the questions.

Map

Key

- tree
- house
- pond
- Mike's house
- route
- Jason's house

1. Find Jason's house. On what street does he live? Setter Street
2. Find Mike's house. On what street does he live? Barker Street
3. Use a red crayon to trace the route Mike drew for Jason to follow.
4. Which streets will Jason use to get to Mike's house? Husky Street, Setter Street, Barker Street
5. Use a blue crayon to draw a different route Jason could use to get to Mike's house.

Page 34

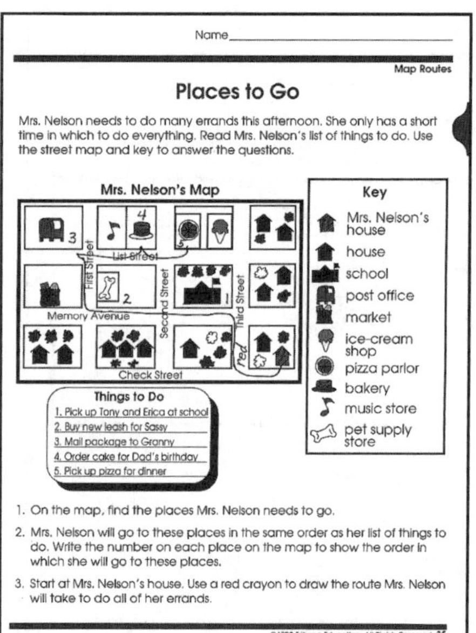
Name____________________

Map Routes

Places to Go

Mrs. Nelson needs to do many errands this afternoon. She only has a short time in which to do everything. Read Mrs. Nelson's list of things to do. Use the street map and key to answer the questions.

Mrs. Nelson's Map

Key

- Mrs. Nelson's house
- house
- school
- post office
- market
- ice-cream shop
- pizza parlor
- bakery
- music store
- pet supply store

Things to Do

1. Pick up Tony and Erica at school
2. Buy new leash for Sassy
3. Mail package to Granny
4. Order cake for Dad's birthday
5. Pick up pizza for dinner

1. On the map, find the places Mrs. Nelson needs to go.
2. Mrs. Nelson will go to these places in the same order as her list of things to do. Write the number on each place on the map to show the order in which she will go to these places.
3. Start at Mrs. Nelson's house. Use a red crayon to draw the route Mrs. Nelson will take to do all of her errands.

Page 35

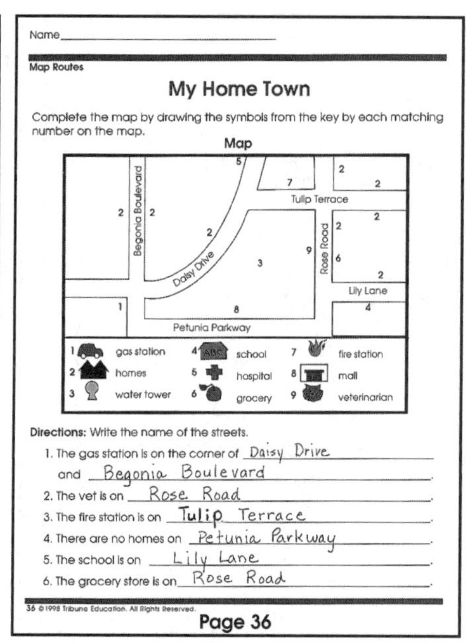
Name____________________

Map Routes

My Home Town

Complete the map by drawing the symbols from the key by each matching number on the map.

Map

1 gas station	4 school	7 fire station
2 homes	5 hospital	8 mall
3 water tower	6 grocery	9 veterinarian

Directions: Write the name of the streets.

1. The gas station is on the corner of Daisy Drive and Begonia Boulevard.
2. The vet is on Rose Road.
3. The fire station is on Tulip Terrace.
4. There are no homes on Petunia Parkway.
5. The school is on Lily Lane.
6. The grocery store is on Rose Road.

Page 36

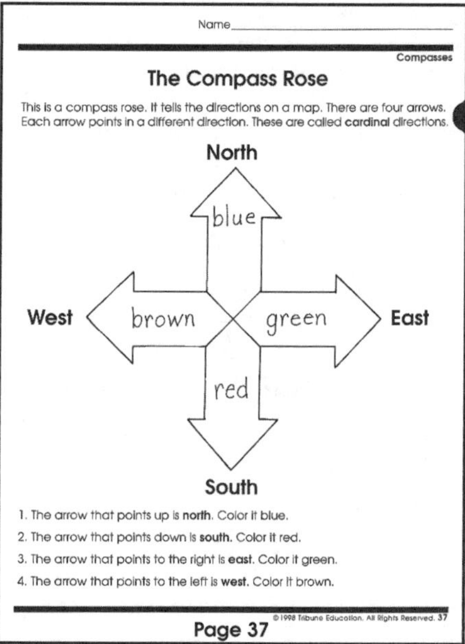
Name____________________

Compasses

The Compass Rose

This is a compass rose. It tells the directions on a map. There are four arrows. Each arrow points in a different direction. These are called **cardinal** directions.

1. The arrow that points up is **north**. Color it blue.
2. The arrow that points down is **south**. Color it red.
3. The arrow that points to the right is **east**. Color it green.
4. The arrow that points to the left is **west**. Color it brown.

Page 37

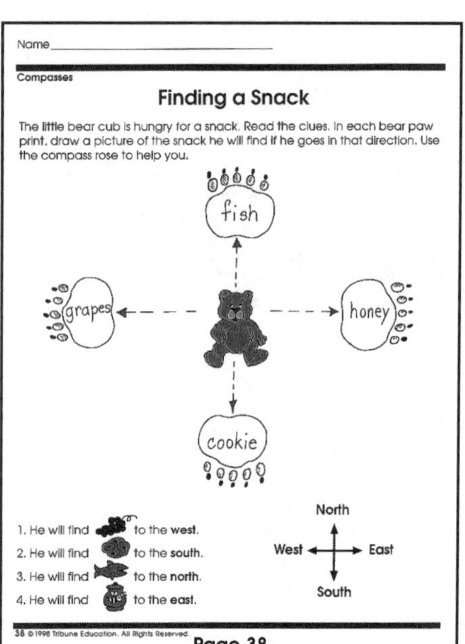
Name____________________

Compasses

Finding a Snack

The little bear cub is hungry for a snack. Read the clues. In each bear paw print, draw a picture of the snack he will find if he goes in that direction. Use the compass rose to help you.

1. He will find [grapes] to the **west**.
2. He will find [cookie] to the **south**.
3. He will find [fish] to the **north**.
4. He will find [honey] to the **east**.

Page 38

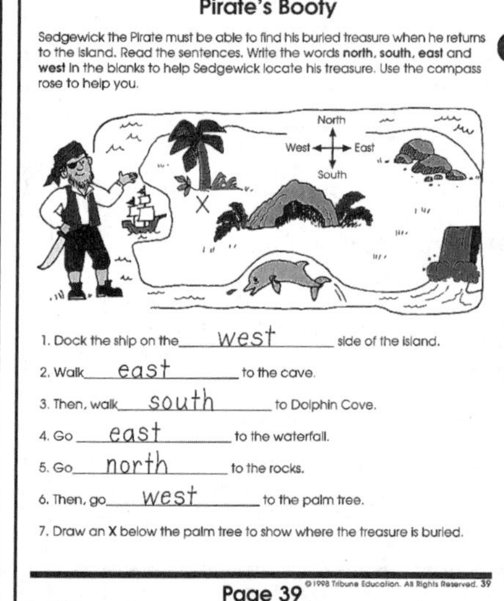
Name____________________

Compasses

Pirate's Booty

Sedgewick the Pirate must be able to find his buried treasure when he returns to the island. Read the sentences. Write the words **north, south, east** and **west** in the blanks to help Sedgewick locate his treasure. Use the compass rose to help you.

1. Dock the ship on the west side of the island.
2. Walk east to the cave.
3. Then, walk south to Dolphin Cove.
4. Go east to the waterfall.
5. Go north to the rocks.
6. Then, go west to the palm tree.
7. Draw an X below the palm tree to show where the treasure is buried.

Page 39

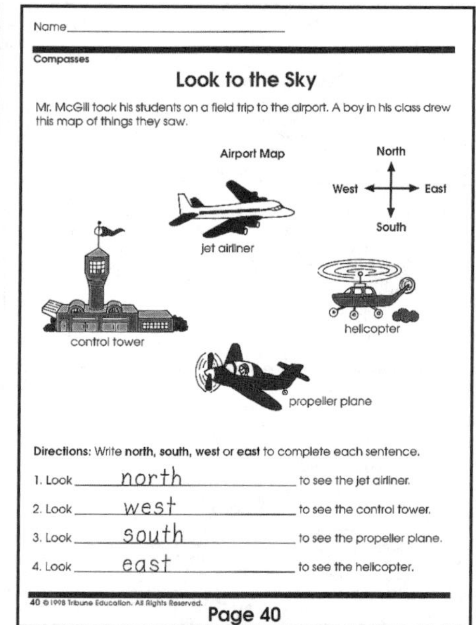
Name____________________

Compasses

Look to the Sky

Mr. McGill took his students on a field trip to the airport. A boy in his class drew this map of things they saw.

Airport Map

Directions: Write **north, south, west** or **east** to complete each sentence.

1. Look north to see the jet airliner.
2. Look west to see the control tower.
3. Look south to see the propeller plane.
4. Look east to see the helicopter.

Page 40

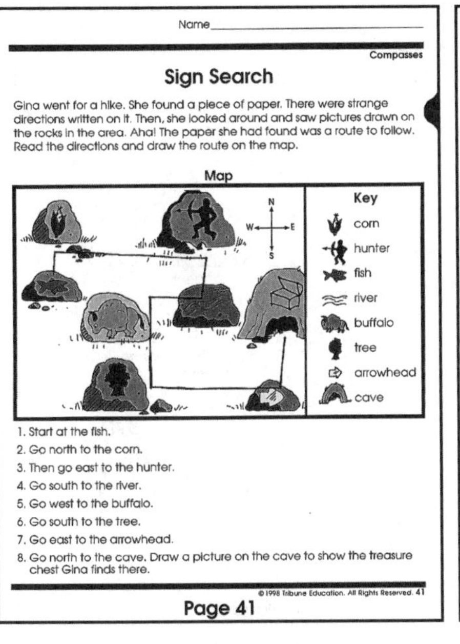

Name________________________

Compasses

Sign Search

Gina went for a hike. She found a piece of paper. There were strange directions written on it. Then, she looked around and saw pictures drawn on the rocks in the area. Aha! The paper she had found was a route to follow. Read the directions and draw the route on the map.

Map

1. Start at the fish.
2. Go north to the corn.
3. Then go east to the hunter.
4. Go south to the river.
5. Go west to the buffalo.
6. Go south to the tree.
7. Go east to the arrowhead.
8. Go north to the cave. Draw a picture on the cave to show the treasure chest Gina finds there.

Page 41

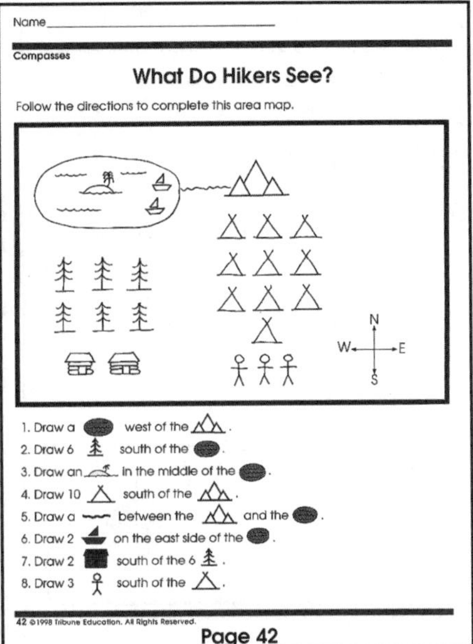

Name________________________

Compasses

What Do Hikers See?

Follow the directions to complete this area map.

1. Draw a [lake] west of the [mountains].
2. Draw 6 [trees] south of the [lake].
3. Draw an [island] in the middle of the [lake].
4. Draw 10 [tents] south of the [mountains].
5. Draw a [river] between the [mountains] and the [lake].
6. Draw 2 [boats] on the east side of the [lake].
7. Draw 2 [cabins] south of the 6 [trees].
8. Draw 3 [people] south of the [tents].

Page 42

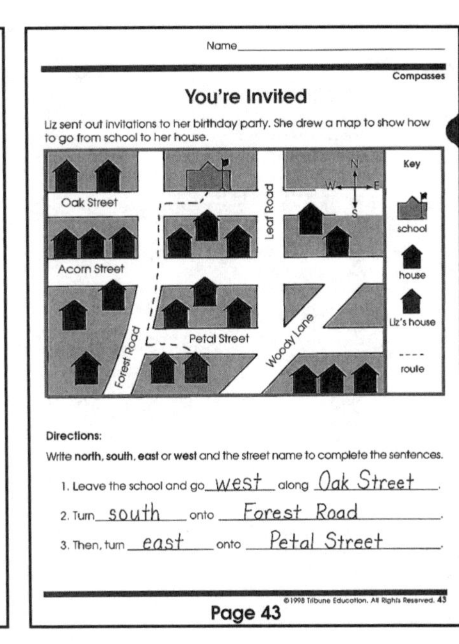

Name________________________

Compasses

You're Invited

Liz sent out invitations to her birthday party. She drew a map to show how to go from school to her house.

Directions:

Write **north, south, east** or **west** and the street name to complete the sentences.

1. Leave the school and go west along Oak Street.
2. Turn south onto Forest Road.
3. Then, turn east onto Petal Street.

Page 43

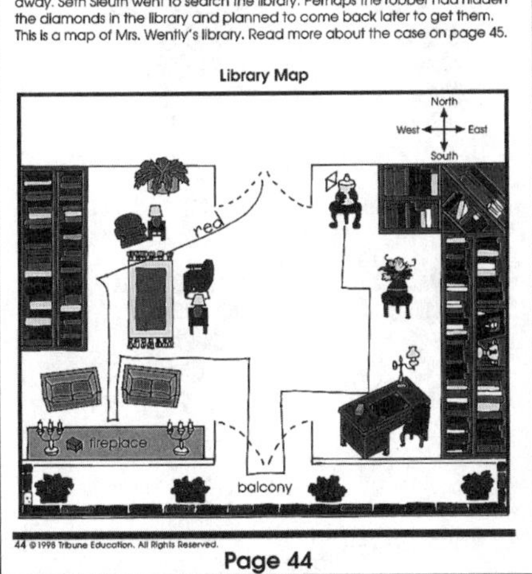

Name________________________

Compasses

Missing Diamonds

Mrs. Wently's diamonds are missing. Seth Sleuth has been hired to find them. He listens to Mrs. Wently's story. She had seen the robber run through the library and out onto the balcony. Then, he jumped to the ground and ran away. Seth Sleuth went to search the library. Perhaps the robber had hidden the diamonds in the library and planned to come back later to get them. This is a map of Mrs. Wently's library. Read more about the case on page 45.

Library Map

Page 44

Name________________________

Compasses

Ice Cream!

Ding. Ding. Ding-a-ling! Here comes the ice-cream truck. On hot summer days, Stan drives his ice-cream truck around the neighborhood. He takes the same route every day. This map shows the neighborhood where Stan drives. Follow the directions on page 47.

Ice-Cream Truck Route Map

Page 46

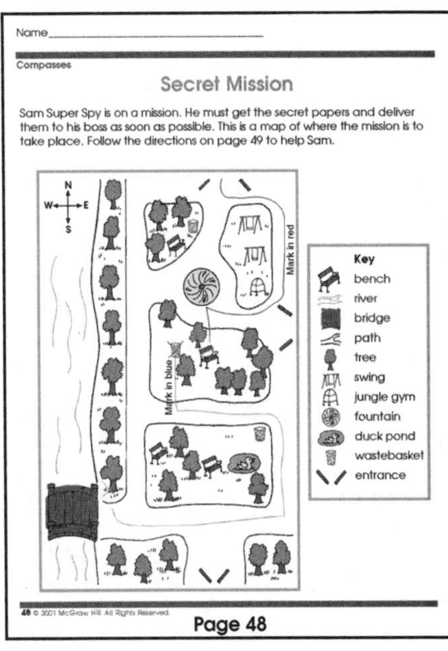

Name________________________

Compasses

Secret Mission

Sam Super Spy is on a mission. He must get the secret papers and deliver them to his boss as soon as possible. This is a map of where the mission is to take place. Follow the directions on page 49 to help Sam.

Page 48

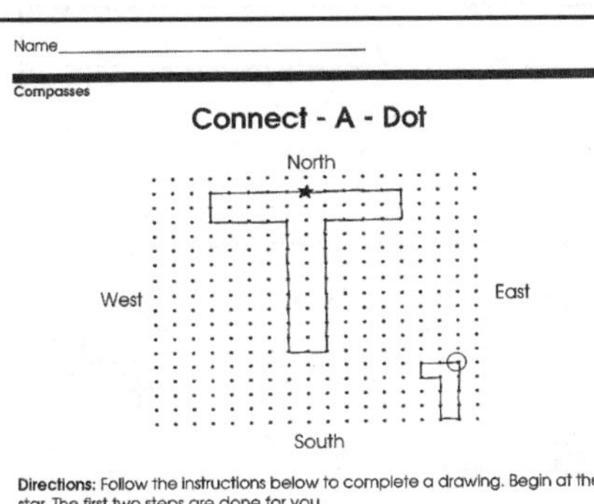

Name________________________

Compasses

Connect - A - Dot

Directions: Follow the instructions below to complete a drawing. Begin at the star. The first two steps are done for you.

Draw a straight line . . .

1. Five spaces west.
2. Two spaces south.
3. Four spaces east.
4. Nine spaces south.
5. Two spaces east.
6. Nine spaces north.
7. Four spaces east.
8. Two spaces north.
9. Five spaces west.

What letter did you draw? T

Begin at the circle to complete another drawing.

Draw a straight line . .

1. Four spaces south.
2. One space west.
3. Three spaces north.
4. One space west.
5. One space north.
6. Two spaces east.

What number did you draw? 7

Page 50

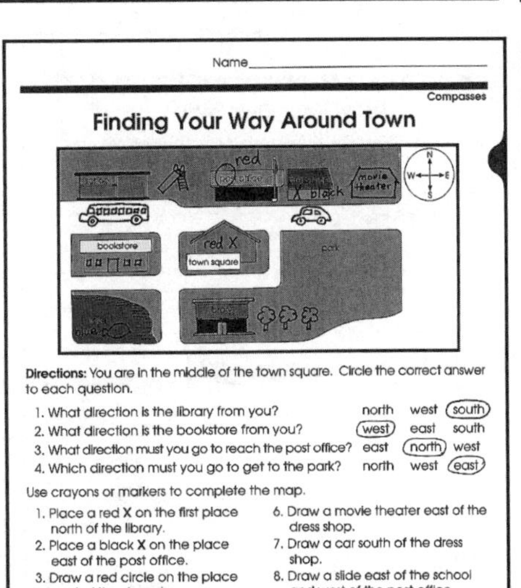

Name________________________

Compasses

Finding Your Way Around Town

Directions: You are in the middle of the town square. Circle the correct answer to each question.

1. What direction is the library from you?	north	west	(south)
2. What direction is the bookstore from you?	(west)	east	south
3. What direction must you go to reach the post office?	east	(north)	west
4. Which direction must you go to get to the park?	north	west	(east)

Use crayons or markers to complete the map.

1. Place a red X on the first place north of the library.
2. Place a black X on the place east of the post office.
3. Draw a red circle on the place west of the dress shop.
4. Draw a blue fish on the place south of the bookstore.
5. Draw three trees east of the library.
6. Draw a movie theater east of the dress shop.
7. Draw a car south of the dress shop.
8. Draw a slide east of the school and west of the post office.
9. Draw doors and windows on the first building north of the lake.
10. Draw a yellow bus south of the place which is west of the post office.

Page 51

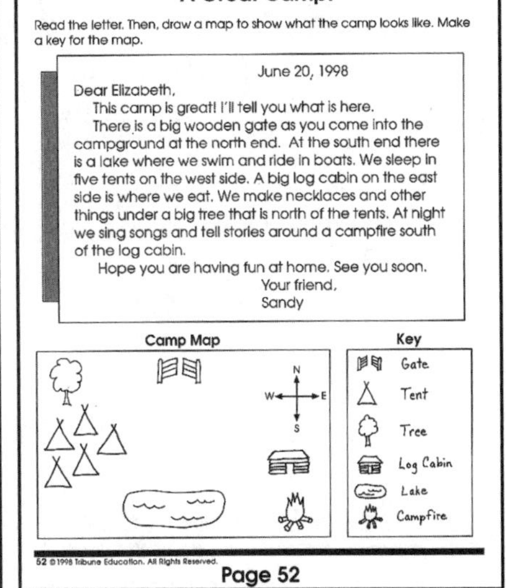

Name________________________

Compasses

A Great Camp!

Read the letter. Then, draw a map to show what the camp looks like. Make a key for the map.

June 20, 1998

Dear Elizabeth,

This camp is great! I'll tell you what is here.

There is a big wooden gate as you come into the campground at the north end. At the south end there is a lake where we swim and ride in boats. We sleep in five tents on the west side. A big log cabin on the east side is where we eat. We make necklaces and other things under a big tree that is north of the tents. At night we sing songs and tell stories around a campfire south of the log cabin.

Hope you are having fun at home. See you soon.

Your friend,

Sandy

Camp Map

Page 52

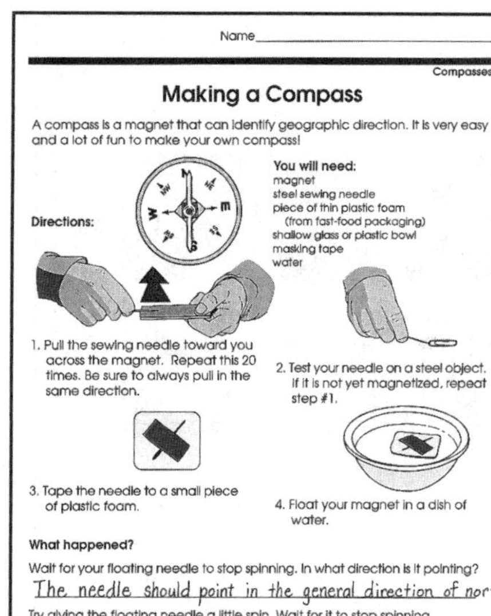

Name____________________

Compasses

Making a Compass

A compass is a magnet that can identify geographic direction. It is very easy and a lot of fun to make your own compass!

You will need:
magnet
steel sewing needle
piece of thin plastic foam (from fast-food packaging)
shallow glass or plastic bowl
masking tape
water

Directions:

1. Pull the sewing needle toward you across the magnet. Repeat this 20 times. Be sure to always pull in the same direction.
2. Test your needle on a steel object. If it is not yet magnetized, repeat step #1.
3. Tape the needle to a small piece of plastic foam.
4. Float your magnet in a dish of water.

What happened?

Wait for your floating needle to stop spinning. In what direction is it pointing? The needle should point in the general direction of north

Try giving the floating needle a little spin. Wait for it to stop spinning.

Now what direction is it pointing? It should point to the north.

©1998 Tribune Education. All Rights Reserved. 53

Page 53

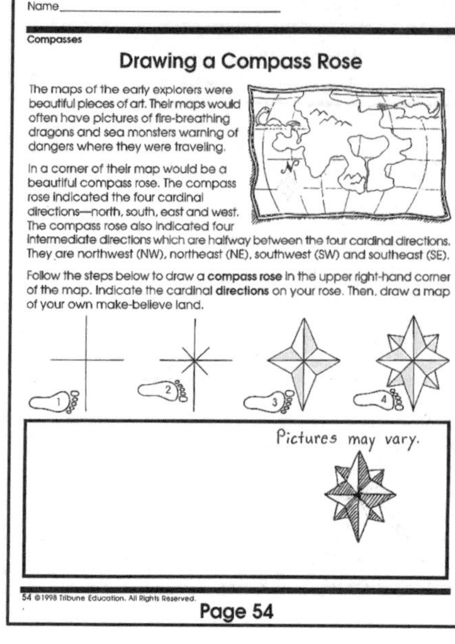

Name____________________

Compasses

Drawing a Compass Rose

The maps of the early explorers were beautiful pieces of art. Their maps would often have pictures of fire-breathing dragons and sea monsters warning of dangers where they were traveling.

In a corner of their map would be a beautiful compass rose. The compass rose indicated the four cardinal directions—north, south, east and west. The compass rose also indicated four intermediate directions which are halfway between the four cardinal directions. They are northwest (NW), northeast (NE), southwest (SW) and southeast (SE).

Follow the steps below to draw a **compass rose** in the upper right-hand corner of the map. Indicate the cardinal **directions** on your rose. Then, draw a map of your own make-believe land.

1 2 3 4

Pictures may vary.

54 ©1998 Tribune Education. All Rights Reserved.

Page 54

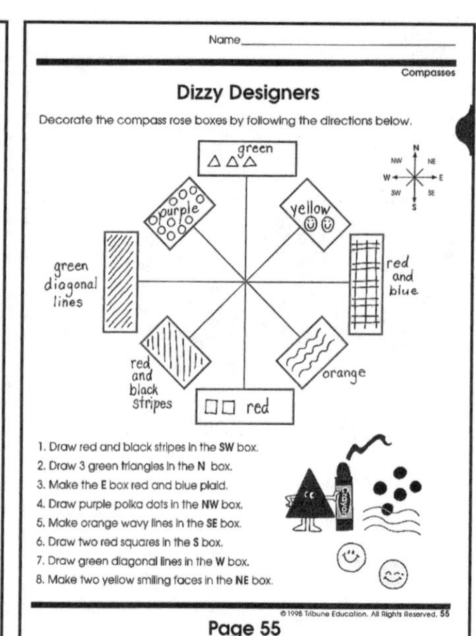

Name____________________

Compasses

Dizzy Designers

Decorate the compass rose boxes by following the directions below.

1. Draw red and black stripes in the **SW** box.
2. Draw 3 green triangles in the **N** box.
3. Make the **E** box red and blue plaid.
4. Draw purple polka dots in the **NW** box.
5. Draw orange wavy lines in the **SE** box.
6. Draw two red squares in the **S** box.
7. Draw green diagonal lines in the **W** box.
8. Make two yellow smiling faces in the **NE** box.

©1998 Tribune Education. All Rights Reserved. 55

Page 55

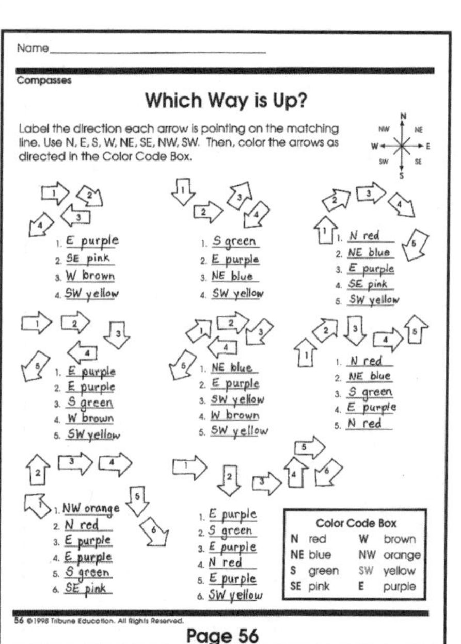

Name____________________

Compasses

Which Way is Up?

Label the direction each arrow is pointing on the matching line. Use N, E, S, W, NE, SE, NW, SW. Then, color the arrows as directed in the Color Code Box.

1. E purple
2. SE pink
3. W brown
4. SW yellow

1. S green
2. E purple
3. NE blue
4. SW yellow

1. N red
2. NE blue
3. E purple
4. SE pink
5. SW yellow

1. E purple
2. E purple
3. S green
4. W brown
5. SW yellow

1. NE blue
2. E purple
3. SW yellow
4. W brown
5. SW yellow

1. N red
2. NE blue
3. S green
4. E purple
5. N red

1. NW orange
2. N red
3. E purple
4. E purple
5. S green
6. SE pink

1. E purple
2. S green
3. E purple
4. N red
5. E purple
6. SW yellow

Color Code Box

N	red	W	brown
NE	blue	NW	orange
S	green	SW	yellow
SE	pink	E	purple

56 ©1998 Tribune Education. All Rights Reserved.

Page 56

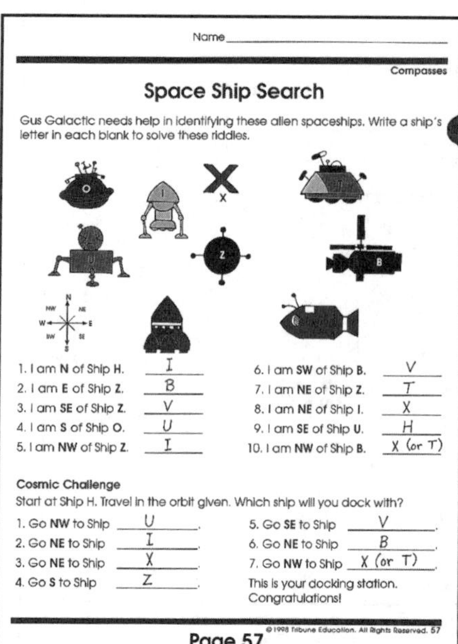

Name____________________

Compasses

Space Ship Search

Gus Galactic needs help in identifying these alien spaceships. Write a ship's letter in each blank to solve these riddles.

1. I am **N** of Ship **H**. I
2. I am **E** of Ship **Z**. B
3. I am **SE** of Ship **Z**. V
4. I am **S** of Ship **O**. U
5. I am **NW** of Ship **Z**. I
6. I am **SW** of Ship **B**. V
7. I am **NE** of Ship **Z**. T
8. I am **NE** of Ship **I**. X
9. I am **SE** of Ship **U**. H
10. I am **NW** of Ship **B**. X (or T)

Cosmic Challenge

Start at Ship H. Travel in the orbit given. Which ship will you dock with?

1. Go **NW** to Ship U.
2. Go **NE** to Ship I.
3. Go **NE** to Ship X.
4. Go **S** to Ship Z.
5. Go **SE** to Ship V.
6. Go **NE** to Ship B.
7. Go **NW** to Ship X (or T).

This is your docking station. Congratulations!

©1998 Tribune Education. All Rights Reserved. 57

Page 57

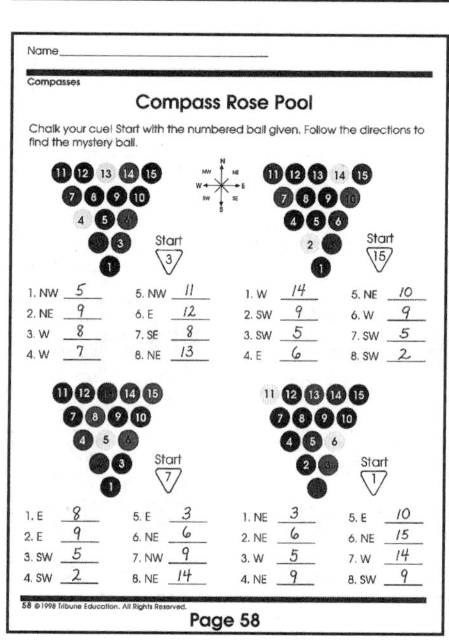

Name____________________

Compasses

Compass Rose Pool

Chalk your cue! Start with the numbered ball given. Follow the directions to find the mystery ball.

Start 3

1. NW 5
2. NE 9
3. W 8
4. W 7
5. NW 11
6. E 12
7. SE 8
8. NE 13

Start 15

1. W 14
2. SW 9
3. SW 5
4. E 6
5. NE 10
6. W 9
7. SW 5
8. SW 2

Start 7

1. E 8
2. E 9
3. SW 5
4. SW 2
5. E 3
6. NE 6
7. NW 9
8. NE 14

Start 1

1. NE 3
2. NE 6
3. W 5
4. NE 9
5. E 10
6. NE 15
7. W 14
8. SW 9

58 ©1998 Tribune Education. All Rights Reserved.

Page 58

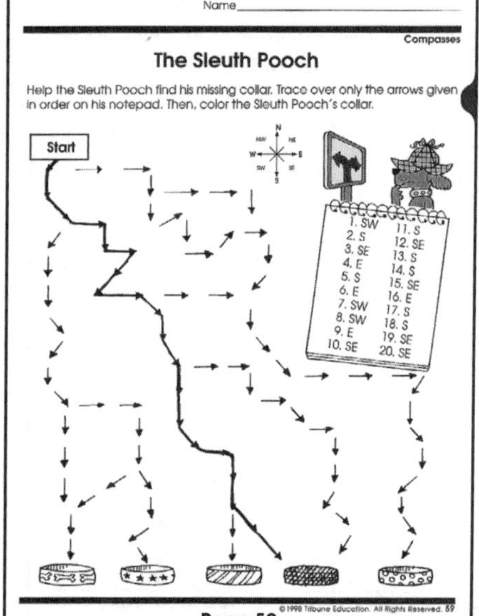

Name____________________

Compasses

The Sleuth Pooch

Help the Sleuth Pooch find his missing collar. Trace over only the arrows given in order on his notepad. Then, color the Sleuth Pooch's collar.

Start

1. SW
2. S
3. SE
4. E
5. S
6. E
7. SW
8. SW
9. E
10. SE
11. S
12. SE
13. S
14. S
15. SE
16. E
17. S
18. SE
19. SE
20. SE

©1998 Tribune Education. All Rights Reserved. 59

Page 59

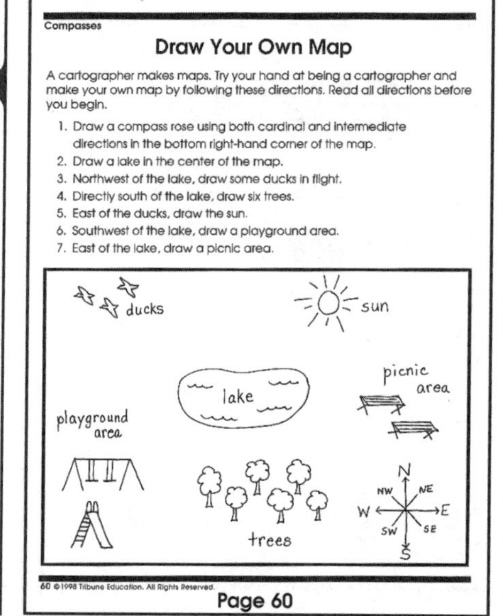

Name____________________

Compasses

Draw Your Own Map

A cartographer makes maps. Try your hand at being a cartographer and make your own map by following these directions. Read all directions before you begin.

1. Draw a compass rose using both cardinal and intermediate directions in the bottom right-hand corner of the map.
2. Draw a lake in the center of the map.
3. Northwest of the lake, draw some ducks in flight.
4. Directly south of the lake, draw six trees.
5. East of the ducks, draw the sun.
6. Southwest of the lake, draw a playground area.
7. East of the lake, draw a picnic area.

60 ©1998 Tribune Education. All Rights Reserved.

Page 60

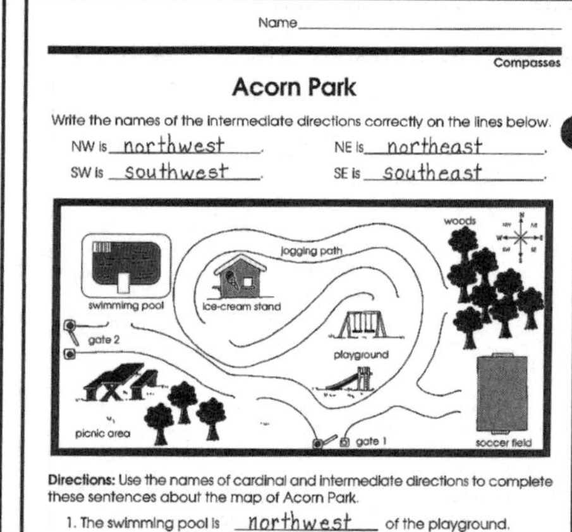

Name____________________

Compasses

Acorn Park

Write the names of the intermediate directions correctly on the lines below.

NW is northwest. NE is northeast.
SW is southwest. SE is southeast.

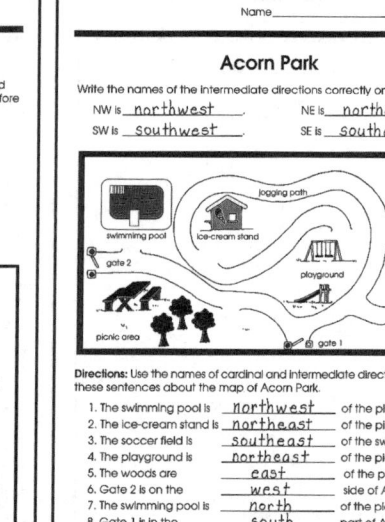

Directions: Use the names of cardinal and intermediate directions to complete these sentences about the map of Acorn Park.

1. The swimming pool is northwest of the playground.
2. The ice-cream stand is northeast of the picnic area.
3. The soccer field is southeast of the swimming pool.
4. The playground is northeast of the picnic area.
5. The woods are east of the playground.
6. Gate 2 is on the west side of Acorn Park.
7. The swimming pool is north of the picnic area.
8. Gate 1 is in the south part of Acorn Park.
9. The woods are northeast of gate 1.

©1998 Tribune Education. All Rights Reserved. 61

Page 61

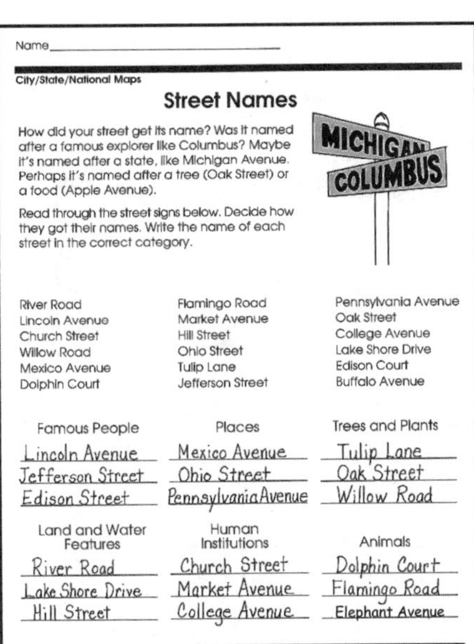

Name________________

City/State/National Maps

Street Names

How did your street get its name? Was it named after a famous explorer like Columbus? Maybe it's named after a state, like Michigan Avenue. Perhaps it's named after a tree (Oak Street) or a food (Apple Avenue).

Read through the street signs below. Decide how they got their names. Write the name of each street in the correct category.

River Road
Lincoln Avenue
Church Street
Willow Road
Mexico Avenue
Dolphin Court
Flamingo Road
Market Avenue
Hill Street
Ohio Street
Tulip Lane
Jefferson Street
Pennsylvania Avenue
Oak Street
College Avenue
Lake Shore Drive
Edison Court
Buffalo Avenue

Famous People	Places	Trees and Plants
Lincoln Avenue	Mexico Avenue	Tulip Lane
Jefferson Street	Ohio Street	Oak Street
Edison Street	Pennsylvania Avenue	Willow Road

Land and Water Features	Human Institutions	Animals
River Road	Church Street	Dolphin Court
Lake Shore Drive	Market Avenue	Flamingo Road
Hill Street	College Avenue	Elephant Avenue

Page 62

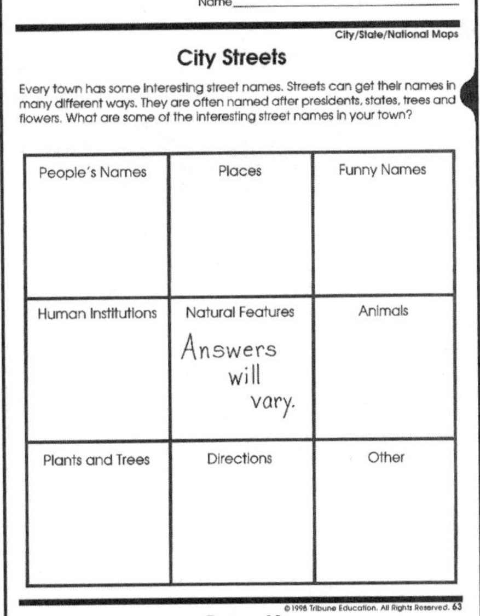

Name________________

City/State/National Maps

City Streets

Every town has some interesting street names. Streets can get their names in many different ways. They are often named after presidents, states, trees and flowers. What are some of the interesting street names in your town?

People's Names	Places	Funny Names
Human Institutions	**Natural Features**	**Animals**
	Answers will vary.	
Plants and Trees	**Directions**	**Other**

Page 63

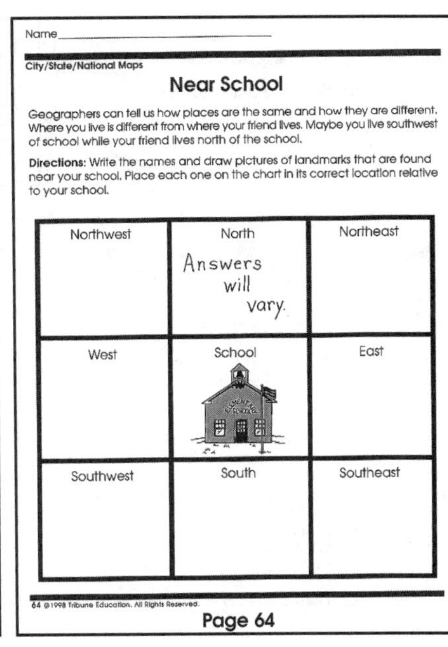

Name________________

City/State/National Maps

Near School

Geographers can tell us how places are the same and how they are different. Where you live is different from where your friend lives. Maybe you live southwest of school while your friend lives north of the school.

Directions: Write the names and draw pictures of landmarks that are found near your school. Place each one on the chart in its correct location relative to your school.

Northwest	North	Northeast
	Answers will vary.	
West	**School**	**East**
Southwest	**South**	**Southeast**

Page 64

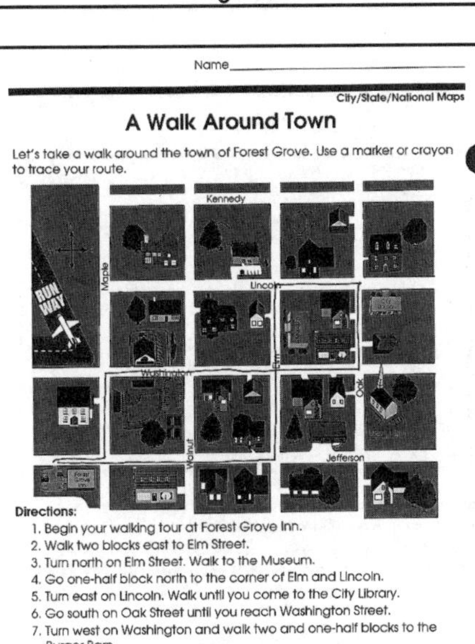

Name________________

City/State/National Maps

A Walk Around Town

Let's take a walk around the town of Forest Grove. Use a marker or crayon to trace your route.

Directions:

1. Begin your walking tour at Forest Grove Inn.
2. Walk two blocks east to Elm Street.
3. Turn north on Elm Street. Walk to the Museum.
4. Go one-half block north to the corner of Elm and Lincoln.
5. Turn east on Lincoln. Walk until you come to the City Library.
6. Go south on Oak Street until you reach Washington Street.
7. Turn west on Washington and walk two and one-half blocks to the Burger Barn.
8. Lunch is over. Take the shortest way back to Forest Grove Inn.

Page 65

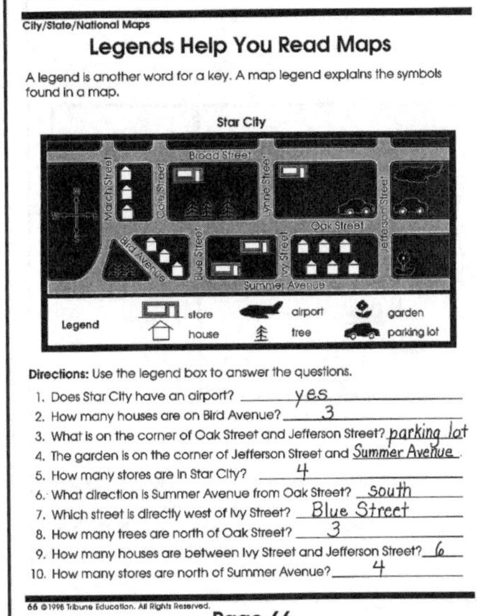

Name________________

City/State/National Maps

Legends Help You Read Maps

A legend is another word for a key. A map legend explains the symbols found in a map.

Directions: Use the legend box to answer the questions.

1. Does Star City have an airport? yes
2. How many houses are on Bird Avenue? 3
3. What is on the corner of Oak Street and Jefferson Street? parking lot
4. The garden is on the corner of Jefferson Street and Summer Avenue.
5. How many stores are in Star City? 4
6. What direction is Summer Avenue from Oak Street? South
7. Which street is directly west of Ivy Street? Blue Street
8. How many trees are north of Oak Street? 3
9. How many houses are between Ivy Street and Jefferson Street? 6
10. How many stores are north of Summer Avenue? 4

Page 66

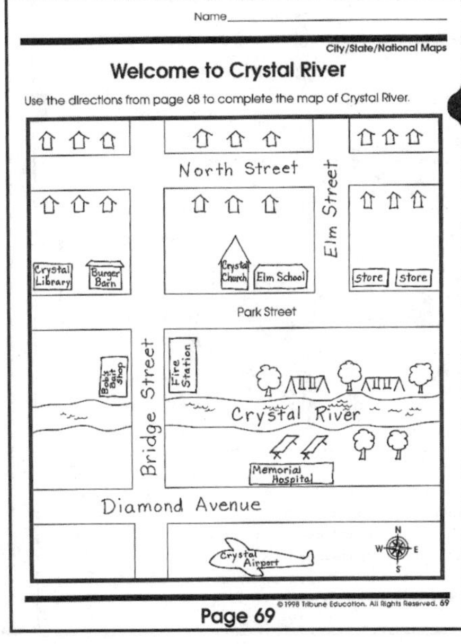

Name________________

City/State/National Maps

Welcome to Crystal River

Use the directions from page 68 to complete the map of Crystal River.

Page 69

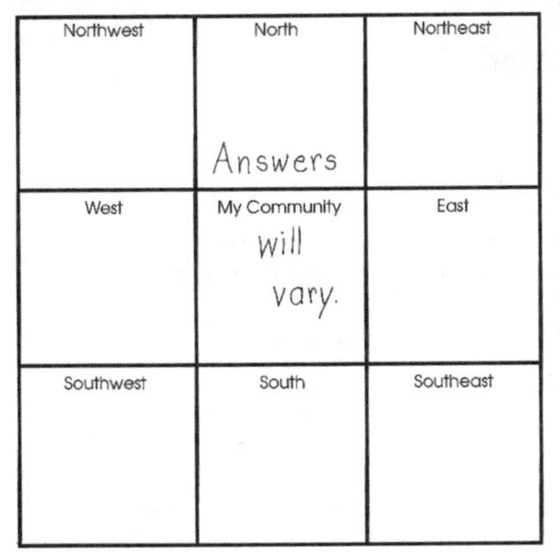

Name________________

City/State/National Maps

Near My Community

Use a state map to locate your community. Then, write the names of other communities, cities, towns, lakes, places to visit and other well-known landmarks on the chart below. Write each one in its correct location relative to your community.

Northwest	North	Northeast
	Answers	
West	**My Community**	**East**
	will vary.	
Southwest	**South**	**Southeast**

Page 70

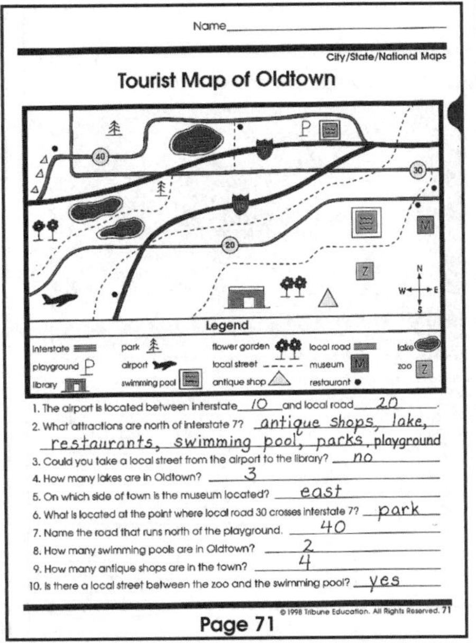

Name________________

City/State/National Maps

Tourist Map of Oldtown

1. The airport is located between interstate 10 and local road 20.
2. What attractions are north of interstate 7? antique shops, lake, restaurants, swimming pool, parks, playground
3. Could you take a local street from the airport to the library? no
4. How many lakes are in Oldtown? 3
5. On which side of town is the museum located? east
6. What is located at the point where local road 30 crosses interstate 7? park
7. Name the road that runs north of the playground. 40
8. How many swimming pools are in Oldtown? 2
9. How many antique shops are in the town? 4
10. Is there a local street between the zoo and the swimming pool? yes

Page 71

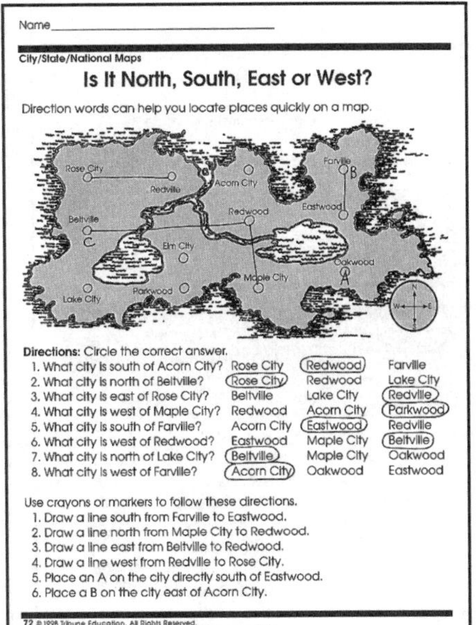

Name________________

City/State/National Maps

Is It North, South, East or West?

Direction words can help you locate places quickly on a map.

Directions: Circle the correct answer.

1. What city is south of Acorn City? Rose City (Redwood) Farville
2. What city is north of Beltville? (Rose City) Redwood Lake City
3. What city is east of Rose City? Beltville Lake City (Redville)
4. What city is west of Maple City? Redwood Acorn City (Parkwood)
5. What city is south of Farville? Acorn City (Eastwood) Redville
6. What city is west of Redwood? Eastwood Maple City (Beltville)
7. What city is north of Lake City? (Beltville) Maple City Oakwood
8. What city is west of Farville? (Acorn City) Oakwood Eastwood

Use crayons or markers to follow these directions.

1. Draw a line south from Farville to Eastwood.
2. Draw a line north from Maple City to Redwood.
3. Draw a line east from Beltville to Redwood.
4. Draw a line west from Redville to Rose City.
5. Place an A on the city directly south of Eastwood.
6. Place a B on the city east of Acorn City.

Page 72

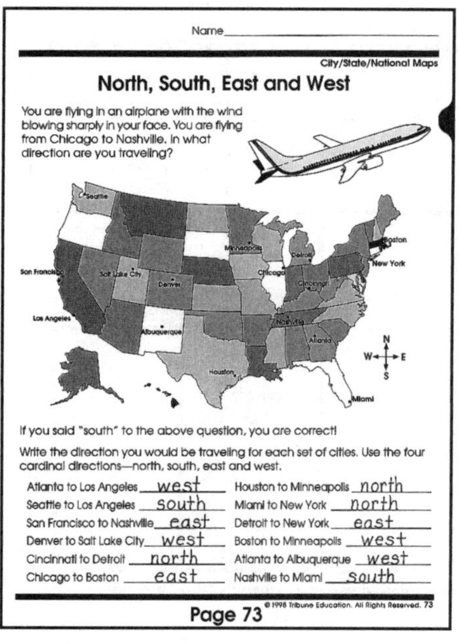

Name________________

City/State/National Maps

North, South, East and West

You are flying in an airplane with the wind blowing sharply in your face. You are flying from Chicago to Nashville. In what direction are you traveling?

If you said "south" to the above question, you are correct!

Write the direction you would be traveling for each set of cities. Use the four cardinal directions—north, south, east and west.

Atlanta to Los Angeles	west	Houston to Minneapolis	north
Seattle to Los Angeles	south	Miami to New York	north
San Francisco to Nashville	east	Detroit to New York	east
Denver to Salt Lake City	west	Boston to Minneapolis	west
Cincinnati to Detroit	north	Atlanta to Albuquerque	west
Chicago to Boston	east	Nashville to Miami	south

©1998 Tribune Education. All Rights Reserved. 73

Page 73

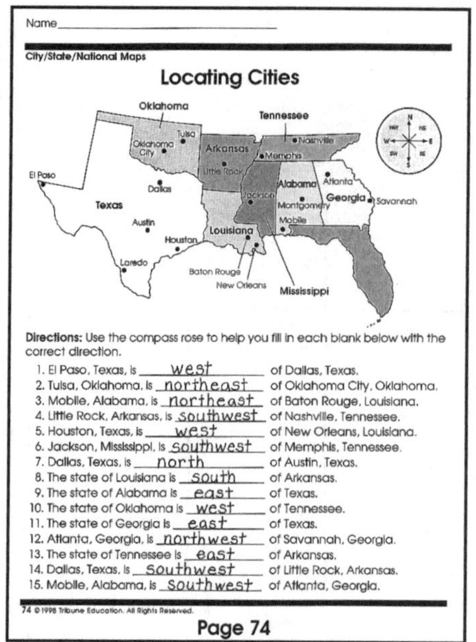

Name________________

City/State/National Maps

Locating Cities

Directions: Use the compass rose to help you fill in each blank below with the correct direction.

1. El Paso, Texas, is west of Dallas, Texas.
2. Tulsa, Oklahoma, is northeast of Oklahoma City, Oklahoma.
3. Mobile, Alabama, is northeast of Baton Rouge, Louisiana.
4. Little Rock, Arkansas, is southwest of Nashville, Tennessee.
5. Houston, Texas, is west of New Orleans, Louisiana.
6. Jackson, Mississippi, is southwest of Memphis, Tennessee.
7. Dallas, Texas, is north of Austin, Texas.
8. The state of Louisiana is south of Arkansas.
9. The state of Alabama is east of Texas.
10. The state of Oklahoma is west of Tennessee.
11. The state of Georgia is east of Texas.
12. Atlanta, Georgia, is northwest of Savannah, Georgia.
13. The state of Tennessee is east of Arkansas.
14. Dallas, Texas, is southwest of Little Rock, Arkansas.
15. Mobile, Alabama, is southwest of Atlanta, Georgia.

74 ©1998 Tribune Education. All Rights Reserved.

Page 74

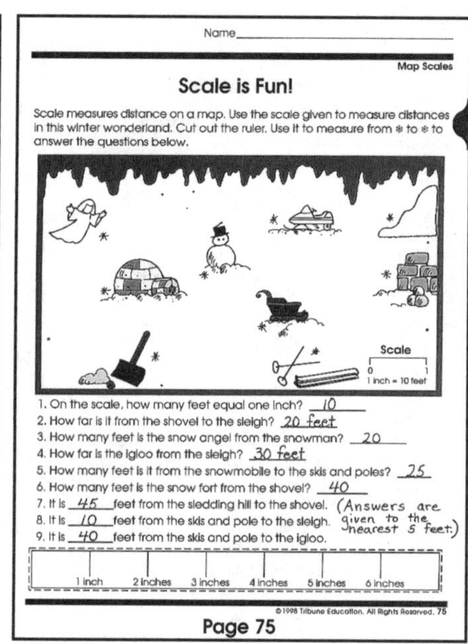

Name________________

Map Scales

Scale is Fun!

Scale measures distance on a map. Use the scale given to measure distances in this winter wonderland. Cut out the ruler. Use it to measure from ✻ to ✻ to answer the questions below.

Scale 1 inch = 10 feet

1. On the scale, how many feet equal one inch? 10
2. How far is it from the shovel to the sleigh? 20 feet
3. How many feet is the snow angel from the snowman? 20
4. How far is the igloo from the sleigh? 30 feet
5. How many feet is it from the snowmobile to the skis and poles? 25
6. How many feet is the snow fort from the shovel? 40
7. It is 45 feet from the sledding hill to the shovel.
8. It is 10 feet from the skis and pole to the sleigh.
9. It is 40 feet from the skis and pole to the igloo.

(Answers are given to the nearest 5 feet.)

1 inch 2 inches 3 inches 4 inches 5 inches 6 inches

©1998 Tribune Education. All Rights Reserved. 75

Page 75

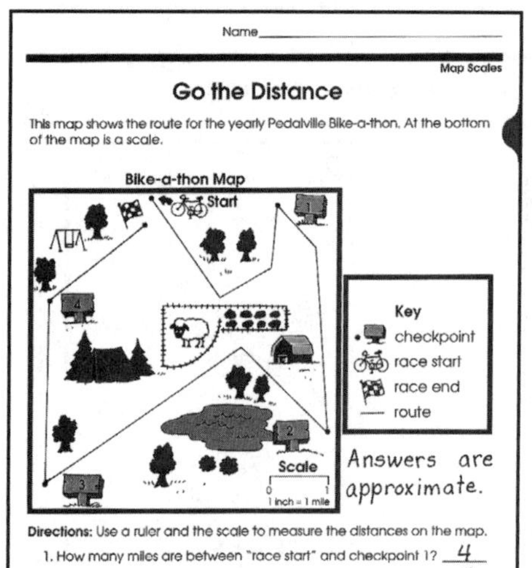

Name________________

Map Scales

Go the Distance

This map shows the route for the yearly Pedalville Bike-a-thon. At the bottom of the map is a scale.

Bike-a-thon Map

Key: checkpoint, race start, race end, route

Scale 1 inch = 1 mile

Answers are approximate.

Directions: Use a ruler and the scale to measure the distances on the map.

1. How many miles are between "race start" and checkpoint 1? 4
2. How many miles are between checkpoint 1 and checkpoint 2? 4
3. How many miles are between checkpoint 2 and checkpoint 3? 6
4. How many miles are between checkpoint 3 and checkpoint 4? 3
5. How many miles are between checkpoint 4 and "race end"? 2

©1998 Tribune Education. All Rights Reserved. 77

Page 77

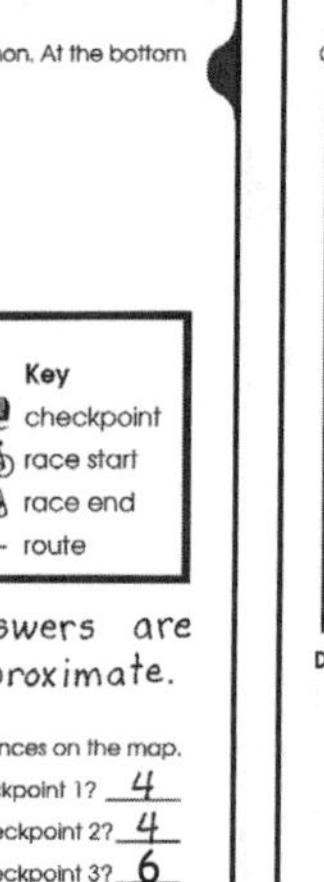

Name________________

Map Scales

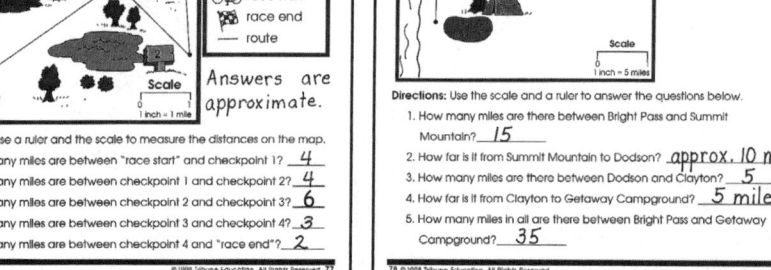

Are We There Yet?

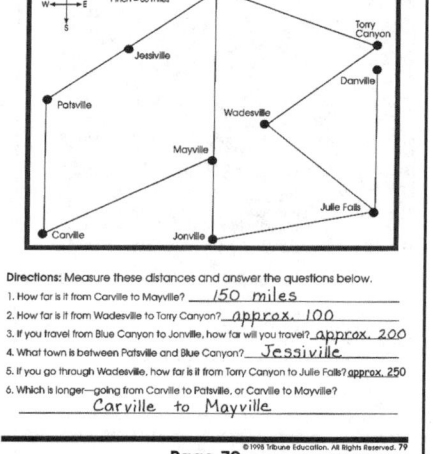

Calvin is going on a vacation to Getaway Campground.

Key: town, route, Getaway Campground

Scale 1 inch = 5 miles

Directions: Use the scale and a ruler to answer the questions below.

1. How many miles are there between Bright Pass and Summit Mountain? 15
2. How far is it from Summit Mountain to Dodson? approx. 10 miles
3. How many miles are there between Dodson and Clayton? 5
4. How far is it from Clayton to Getaway Campground? 5 miles
5. How many miles in all are there between Bright Pass and Getaway Campground? 35

78 ©1998 Tribune Education. All Rights Reserved.

Page 78

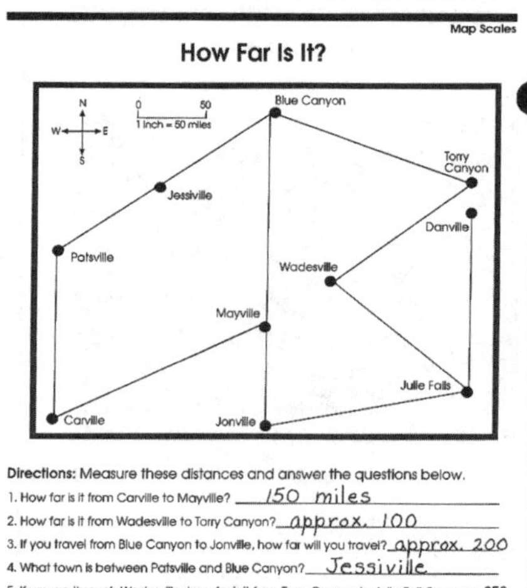

Name________________

Map Scales

How Far Is It?

1 inch = 50 miles

Directions: Measure these distances and answer the questions below.

1. How far is it from Carville to Mayville? 150 miles
2. How far is it from Wadesville to Torry Canyon? approx. 100
3. If you travel from Blue Canyon to Jonville, how far will you travel? approx. 200
4. What town is between Patsville and Blue Canyon? Jessiville
5. If you go through Wadesville, how far is it from Torry Canyon to Julie Falls? approx. 250
6. Which is longer—going from Carville to Patsville, or Carville to Mayville? Carville to Mayville

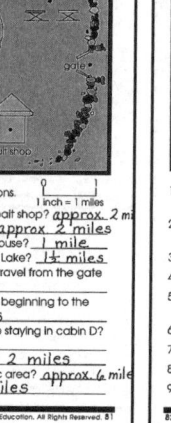

©1998 Tribune Education. All Rights Reserved. 79

Page 79

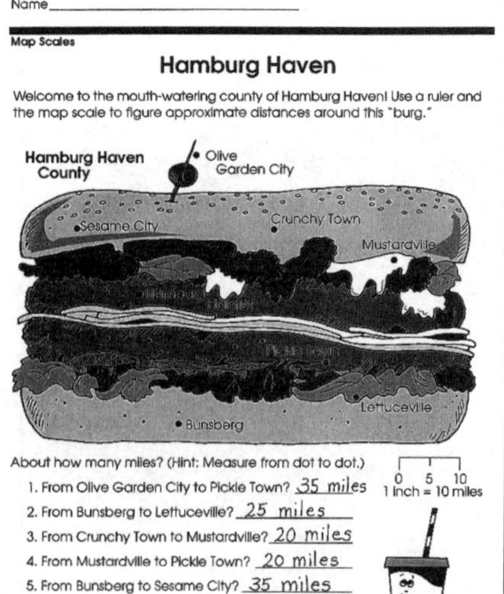

Name________________

Map Scales

Hamburg Haven

Welcome to the mouth-watering county of Hamburg Haven! Use a ruler and the map scale to figure approximate distances around this "burg."

Hamburg Haven County

1 inch = 10 miles

About how many miles? (Hint: Measure from dot to dot.)

1. From Olive Garden City to Pickle Town? 35 miles
2. From Bunsberg to Lettuceville? 25 miles
3. From Crunchy Town to Mustardville? 20 miles
4. From Mustardville to Pickle Town? 20 miles
5. From Bunsberg to Sesame City? 35 miles
6. From Hamburg Hamlet to Lettuceville? 40 miles
7. From Crunchy Town to Bunsberg? 30 miles

80 ©1998 Tribune Education. All Rights Reserved.

Page 80

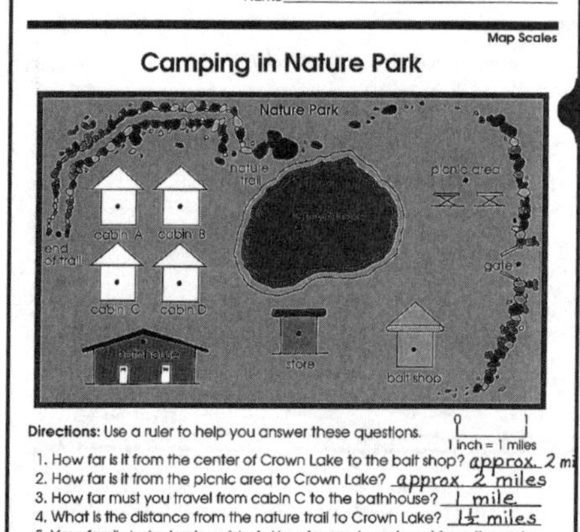

Name________________

Map Scales

Camping in Nature Park

1 inch = 1 miles

Directions: Use a ruler to help you answer these questions.

1. How far is it from the center of Crown Lake to the bait shop? approx. 2 mi
2. How far is it from the picnic area to Crown Lake? approx. 2 miles
3. How far must you travel from cabin C to the bathhouse? 1 mile
4. What is the distance from the nature trail to Crown Lake? 1½ miles
5. Your family is staying in cabin A. How far must you travel from the gate to the cabin? approx. 5½ miles
6. What is the approximate distance in miles from the beginning to the end of the nature trail? approx. 4 miles
7. How far must your family travel to the store if you are staying in cabin D? 2 miles
8. How far is it from the store to cabin B? approx. 2 miles
9. The end of the nature trail is how far from the picnic area? approx. 6 miles
10. How far is the bathhouse from cabin A? 2 miles

©1998 Tribune Education. All Rights Reserved. 81

Page 81

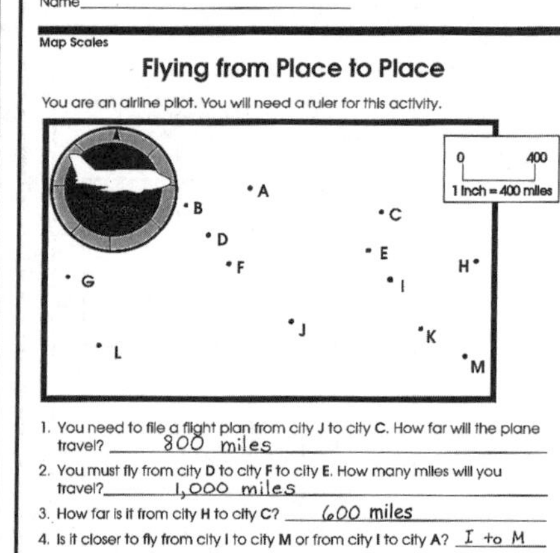

Name________________

Map Scales

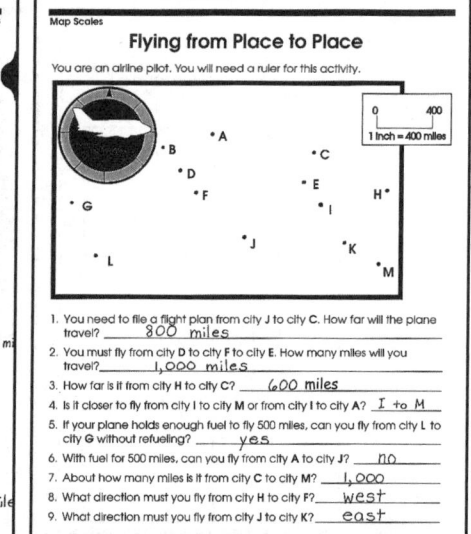

Flying from Place to Place

You are an airline pilot. You will need a ruler for this activity.

1 inch = 400 miles

1. You need to file a flight plan from city J to city C. How far will the plane travel? 800 miles
2. You must fly from city D to city F to city E. How many miles will you travel? 1,000 miles
3. How far is it from city H to city C? 600 miles
4. Is it closer to fly from city I to city M or from city I to city A? I to M
5. If your plane holds enough fuel to fly 500 miles, can you fly from city L to city G without refueling? yes
6. With fuel for 500 miles, can you fly from city A to city J? no
7. About how many miles is it from city C to city M? 1,000
8. What direction must you fly from city H to city F? west
9. What direction must you fly from city J to city K? east

82 ©1998 Tribune Education. All Rights Reserved.

Page 82

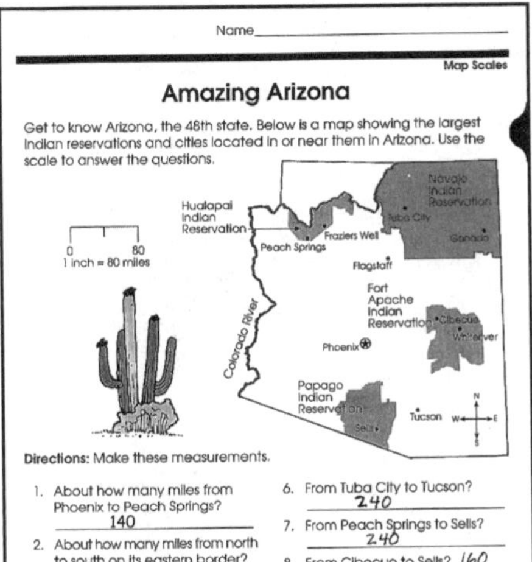

Name____________

Map Scales

Amazing Arizona

Get to know Arizona, the 48th state. Below is a map showing the largest Indian reservations and cities located in or near them in Arizona. Use the scale to answer the questions.

Directions: Make these measurements.

1. About how many miles from Phoenix to Peach Springs? 140
2. About how many miles from north to south on its eastern border? 320
3. About how many miles from Flagstaff to Ganado? 120
4. From Tucson to Flagstaff? 160
5. From Whiteriver to Ganado? 120
6. From Tuba City to Tucson? 240
7. From Peach Springs to Sells? 240
8. From Cibecue to Sells? 160
9. The Fort Apache Indian Reservation from north to south at its greatest distance. 80 miles
10. The Navajo Indian Reservation from east to west at its greatest distance. 140 miles

Page 83

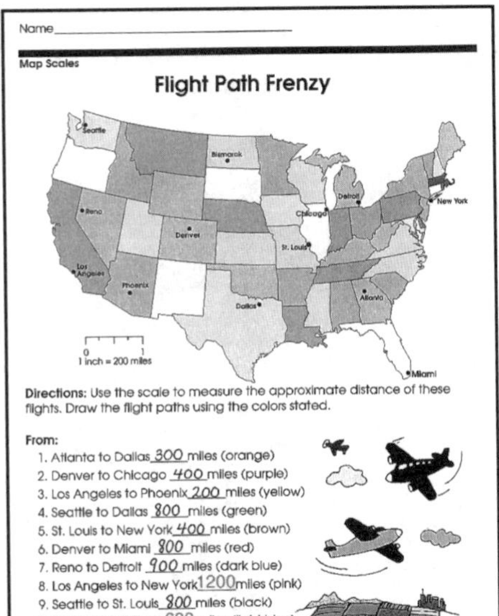

Name____________

Map Scales

Flight Path Frenzy

Directions: Use the scale to measure the approximate distance of these flights. Draw the flight paths using the colors stated.

From:

1. Atlanta to Dallas 300 miles (orange)
2. Denver to Chicago 400 miles (purple)
3. Los Angeles to Phoenix 200 miles (yellow)
4. Seattle to Dallas 800 miles (green)
5. St. Louis to New York 400 miles (brown)
6. Denver to Miami 800 miles (red)
7. Reno to Detroit 900 miles (dark blue)
8. Los Angeles to New York 1200 miles (pink)
9. Seattle to St. Louis 800 miles (black)
10. Chicago to Miami 600 miles (light blue)

Page 84

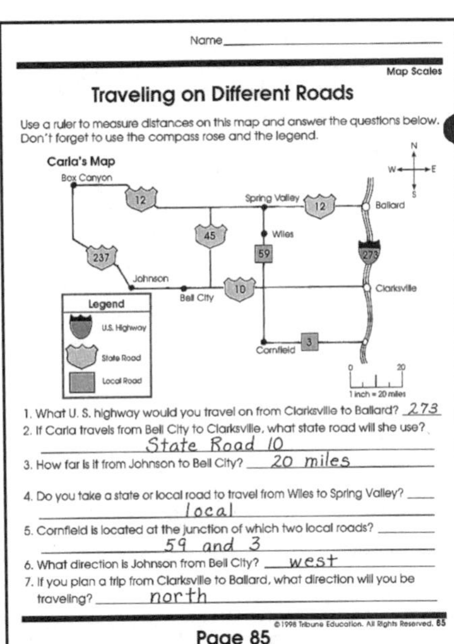

Name____________

Map Scales

Traveling on Different Roads

Use a ruler to measure distances on this map and answer the questions below. Don't forget to use the compass rose and the legend.

1. What U. S. highway would you travel on from Clarksville to Ballard? 273
2. If Carla travels from Bell City to Clarksville, what state road will she use? State Road 10
3. How far is it from Johnson to Bell City? 20 miles
4. Do you take a state or local road to travel from Wiles to Spring Valley? local
5. Cornfield is located at the junction of which two local roads? 59 and 3
6. What direction is Johnson from Bell City? west
7. If you plan a trip from Clarksville to Ballard, what direction will you be traveling? north

Page 85

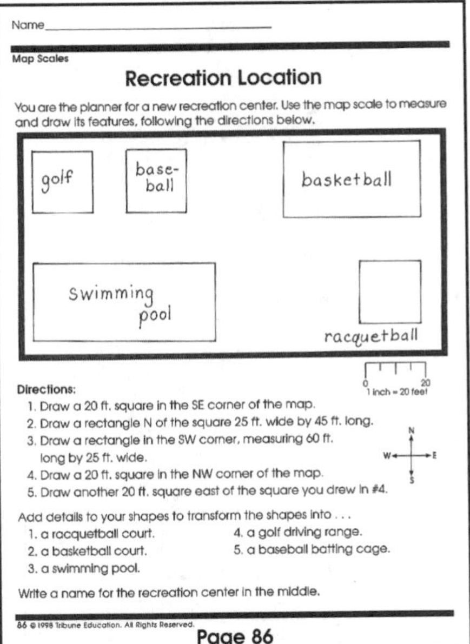

Name____________

Map Scales

Recreation Location

You are the planner for a new recreation center. Use the map scale to measure and draw its features, following the directions below.

Directions:

1. Draw a 20 ft. square in the SE corner of the map.
2. Draw a rectangle N of the square 25 ft. wide by 45 ft. long.
3. Draw a rectangle in the SW corner, measuring 60 ft. long by 25 ft. wide.
4. Draw a 20 ft. square in the NW corner of the map.
5. Draw another 20 ft. square east of the square you drew in #4.

Add details to your shapes to transform the shapes into . . .

1. a racquetball court.
2. a basketball court.
3. a swimming pool.
4. a golf driving range.
5. a baseball batting cage.

Write a name for the recreation center in the middle.

Page 86

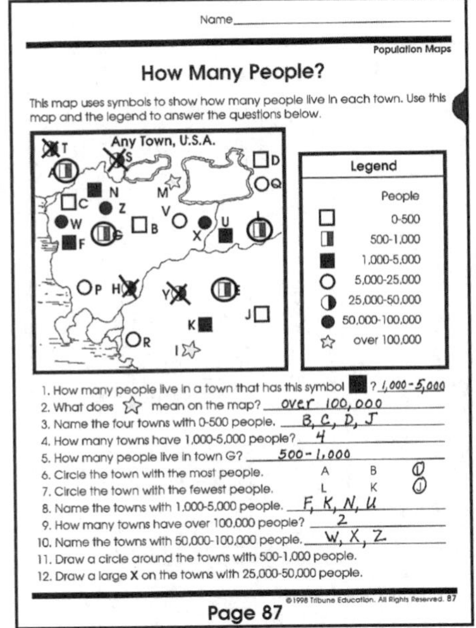

Name____________

Population Maps

How Many People?

This map uses symbols to show how many people live in each town. Use this map and the legend to answer the questions below.

1. How many people live in a town that has this symbol ■? 1,000-5,000
2. What does ☆ mean on the map? over 100,000
3. Name the four towns with 0-500 people. B, C, D, J
4. How many towns have 1,000-5,000 people? 4
5. How many people live in town G? 500-1,000
6. Circle the town with the most people. A B I (circled)
7. Circle the town with the fewest people. L K J (circled)
8. Name the towns with 1,000-5,000 people. F, K, N, U
9. How many towns have over 100,000 people? 2
10. Name the towns with 50,000-100,000 people. W, X, Z
11. Draw a circle around the towns with 500-1,000 people.
12. Draw a large **X** on the towns with 25,000-50,000 people.

Page 87

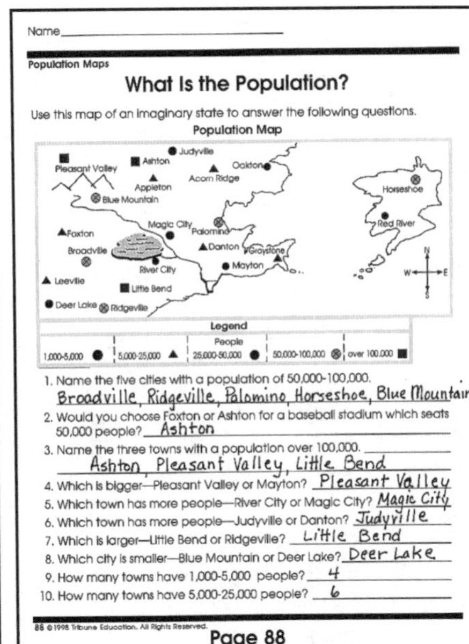

Name____________

Population Maps

What Is the Population?

Use this map of an imaginary state to answer the following questions.

1. Name the five cities with a population of 50,000-100,000. Broadville, Ridgeville, Palomino, Horseshoe, Blue Mountain
2. Would you choose Foxton or Ashton for a baseball stadium which seats 50,000 people? Ashton
3. Name the three towns with a population over 100,000. Ashton, Pleasant Valley, Little Bend
4. Which is bigger—Pleasant Valley or Mayton? Pleasant Valley
5. Which town has more people—River City or Magic City? Magic City
6. Which town has more people—Judyville or Danton? Judyville
7. Which is larger—Little Bend or Ridgeville? Little Bend
8. Which city is smaller—Blue Mountain or Deer Lake? Deer Lake
9. How many towns have 1,000-5,000 people? 4
10. How many towns have 5,000-25,000 people? 6

Page 88

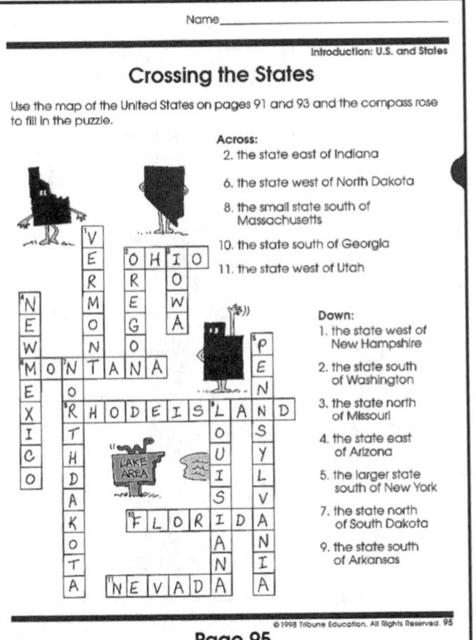

Name____________

Introduction: U.S. and States

Crossing the States

Use the map of the United States on pages 91 and 93 and the compass rose to fill in the puzzle.

Across:

2. the state east of Indiana
6. the state west of North Dakota
8. the small state south of Massachusetts
10. the state south of Georgia
11. the state west of Utah

Down:

1. the state west of New Hampshire
2. the state south of Washington
3. the state north of Missouri
4. the state east of Arizona
5. the larger state south of New York
7. the state north of South Dakota
9. the state south of Arkansas

Page 95

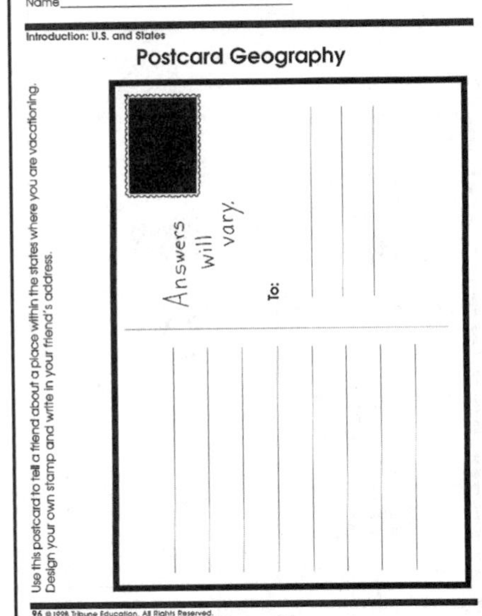

Name____________

Introduction: U.S. and States

Postcard Geography

Use this postcard to tell a friend about a place within the states where you are vacationing. Design your own stamp and write in your friend's address.

Answers will vary.

To:

Page 96

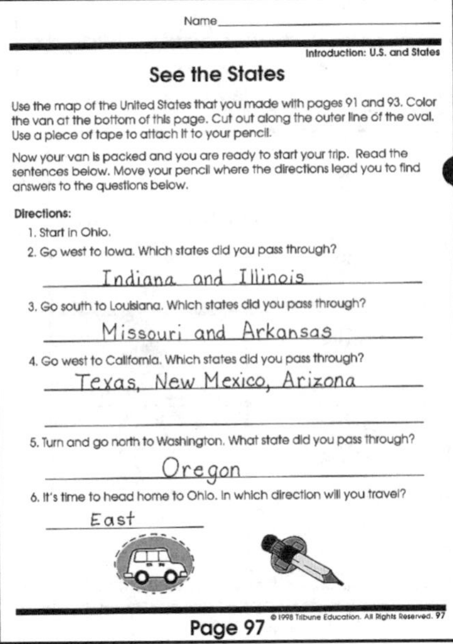

Name____________

Introduction: U.S. and States

See the States

Use the map of the United States that you made with pages 91 and 93. Color the van at the bottom of this page. Cut out along the outer line of the oval. Use a piece of tape to attach it to your pencil.

Now your van is packed and you are ready to start your trip. Read the sentences below. Move your pencil where the directions lead you to find answers to the questions below.

Directions:

1. Start in Ohio.
2. Go west to Iowa. Which states did you pass through? Indiana and Illinois
3. Go south to Louisiana. Which states did you pass through? Missouri and Arkansas
4. Go west to California. Which states did you pass through? Texas, New Mexico, Arizona
5. Turn and go north to Washington. What state did you pass through? Oregon
6. It's time to head home to Ohio. In which direction will you travel? East

Page 97

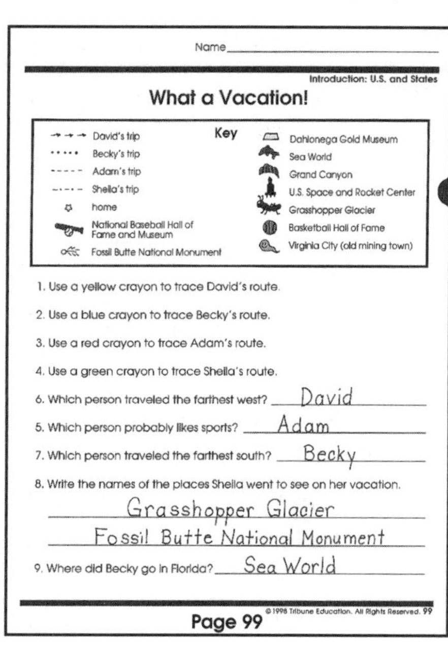

Name

Introduction: U.S. and States

What a Vacation!

1. Use a yellow crayon to trace David's route.
2. Use a blue crayon to trace Becky's route.
3. Use a red crayon to trace Adam's route.
4. Use a green crayon to trace Sheila's route.
6. Which person traveled the farthest west? David
5. Which person probably likes sports? Adam
7. Which person traveled the farthest south? Becky
8. Write the names of the places Sheila went to see on her vacation. Grasshopper Glacier; Fossil Butte National Monument
9. Where did Becky go in Florida? Sea World

Page 99

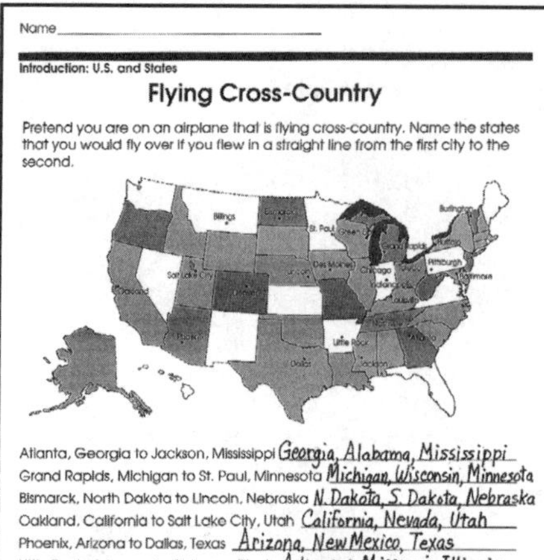

Name

Introduction: U.S. and States

Flying Cross-Country

Pretend you are on an airplane that is flying cross-country. Name the states that you would fly over if you flew in a straight line from the first city to the second.

Atlanta, Georgia to Jackson, Mississippi: Georgia, Alabama, Mississippi
Grand Rapids, Michigan to St. Paul, Minnesota: Michigan, Wisconsin, Minnesota
Bismarck, North Dakota to Lincoln, Nebraska: N. Dakota, S. Dakota, Nebraska
Oakland, California to Salt Lake City, Utah: California, Nevada, Utah
Phoenix, Arizona to Dallas, Texas: Arizona, New Mexico, Texas
Little Rock, Arkansas to Chicago, Illinois: Arkansas, Missouri, Illinois
Toledo, Ohio to Green Bay, Wisconsin: Ohio, Michigan, Wisconsin
Pittsburgh, Pennsylvania to Burlington, Vermont: Pennsylvania, New York, Vermont
Denver, Colorado to Billings, Montana: Colorado, Wyoming, Montana
Nashville, Tennessee to Indianapolis, Indiana: Tennessee, Kentucky, Indiana
Des Moines, Iowa to Louisville, Kentucky: Iowa, Illinois, Indiana, Kentucky
Baltimore, Maryland to Buffalo, New York: Maryland, Pennsylvania, New York

Page 100

Name

Introduction: U.S. and States

State Snatcher

The State Snatcher has stolen some of the abbreviations of the states. Write in the missing abbreviations. Use another U.S. map to help you.

Postal Abbreviations Chart

State	Abbr.	State	Abbr.	State	Abbr.	State	Abbr.
Alabama	AL	Indiana	IN	Nebraska	NE	South Carolina	SC
Alaska	AK	Iowa	IA	Nevada	NV	South Dakota	SD
Arizona	AZ	Kansas	KS	New Hampshire	NH	Tennessee	TN
Arkansas	AR	Kentucky	KY	New Jersey	NJ	Texas	TX
California	CA	Louisiana	LA	New Mexico	NM	Utah	UT
Colorado	CO	Maine	ME	New York	NY	Vermont	VT
Connecticut	CT	Maryland	MD	North Carolina	NC	Virginia	VA
Delaware	DE	Massachusetts	MA	North Dakota	ND	Washington	WA
Florida	FL	Michigan	MI	Ohio	OH	West Virginia	WV
Georgia	GA	Minnesota	MN	Oklahoma	OK	Wisconsin	WI
Hawaii	HI	Mississippi	MS	Oregon	OR	Wyoming	WY
Idaho	ID	Missouri	MO	Pennsylvania	PA		
Illinois	IL	Montana	MT	Rhode Island	RI		

Page 101

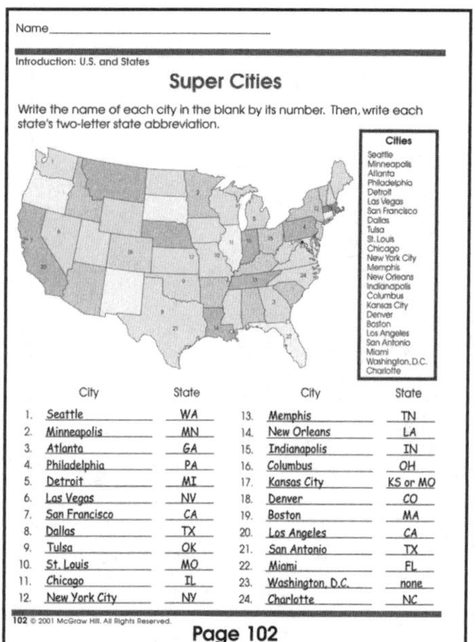

Name

Introduction: U.S. and States

Super Cities

Write the name of each city in the blank by its number. Then, write each state's two-letter state abbreviation.

	City	State		City	State
1.	Seattle	WA	13.	Memphis	TN
2.	Minneapolis	MN	14.	New Orleans	LA
3.	Atlanta	GA	15.	Indianapolis	IN
4.	Philadelphia	PA	16.	Columbus	OH
5.	Detroit	MI	17.	Kansas City	KS or MO
6.	Las Vegas	NV	18.	Denver	CO
7.	San Francisco	CA	19.	Boston	MA
8.	Dallas	TX	20.	Los Angeles	CA
9.	Tulsa	OK	21.	San Antonio	TX
10.	St. Louis	MO	22.	Miami	FL
11.	Chicago	IL	23.	Washington, D.C.	none
12.	New York City	NY	24.	Charlotte	NC

Page 102

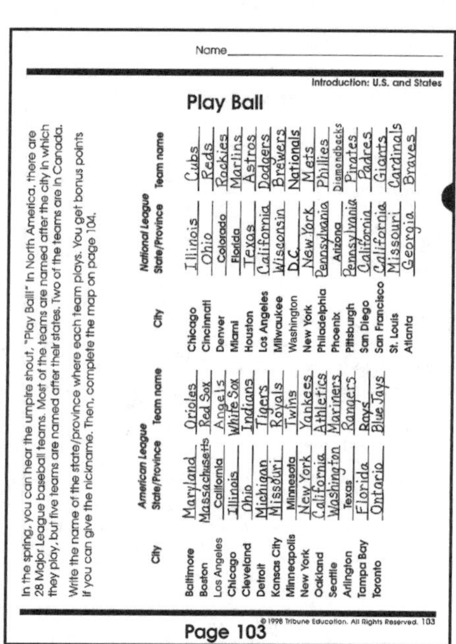

Name

Introduction: U.S. and States

Play Ball

In the spring, you can hear the umpire shout, "Play Ball!" in North America. There are 28 Major League baseball teams. Most of the teams are named after the city in which they play, but five teams are named after their states. Two of the teams are in Canada. Write the name of the state/province where each team plays. You get bonus points if you can give the nickname. Then, complete the map on page 104.

American League

City	State/Province	Team name
Baltimore	Maryland	Orioles
Boston	Massachusetts	Red Sox
Los Angeles	California	Angels
Chicago	Illinois	White Sox
Cleveland	Ohio	Indians
Detroit	Michigan	Tigers
Kansas City	Missouri	Royals
Minneapolis	Minnesota	Twins
New York	New York	Yankees
Oakland	California	Athletics
Seattle	Washington	Mariners
Arlington	Texas	Rangers
Tampa Bay	Florida	Rays
Toronto	Ontario	Blue Jays

National League

City	State/Province	Team name
Chicago	Illinois	Cubs
Cincinnati	Ohio	Reds
Denver	Colorado	Rockies
Miami	Florida	Marlins
Houston	Texas	Astros
Los Angeles	California	Dodgers
Milwaukee	Wisconsin	Brewers
Washington	D.C.	Nationals
New York	New York	Mets
Philadelphia	Pennsylvania	Phillies
Phoenix	Arizona	Diamondbacks
Pittsburgh	Pennsylvania	Pirates
San Diego	California	Padres
San Francisco	California	Giants
St. Louis	Missouri	Cardinals
Atlanta	Georgia	Braves

Page 103

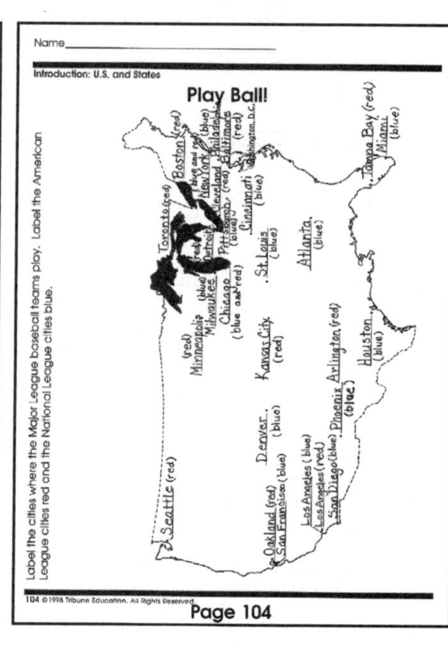

Name

Introduction: U.S. and States

Play Ball!

Label the cities where the Major League baseball teams play. Label the American League cities red and the National League cities blue.

Page 104

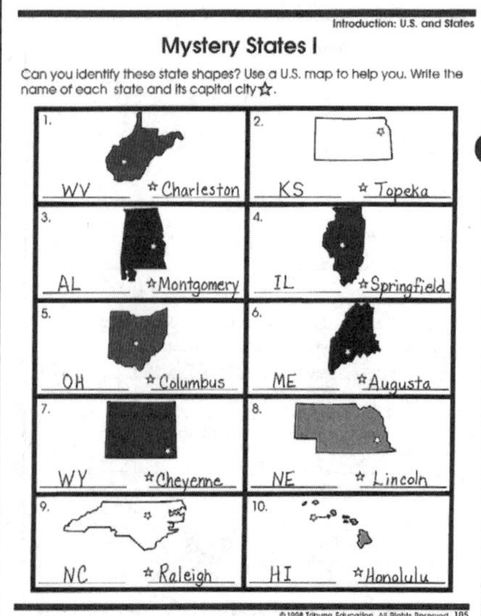

Name

Introduction: U.S. and States

Mystery States I

Can you identify these state shapes? Use a U.S. map to help you. Write the name of each state and its capital city ☆.

1. WV ☆ Charleston
2. KS ☆ Topeka
3. AL ☆ Montgomery
4. IL ☆ Springfield
5. OH ☆ Columbus
6. ME ☆ Augusta
7. WY ☆ Cheyenne
8. NE ☆ Lincoln
9. NC ☆ Raleigh
10. HI ☆ Honolulu

Page 105

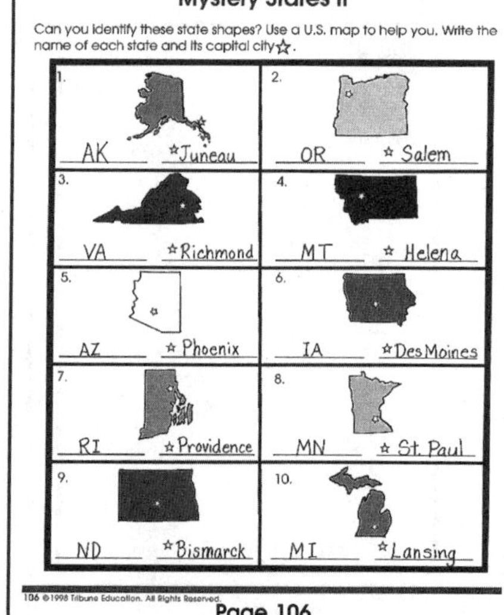

Name

Introduction: U.S. and States

Mystery States II

Can you identify these state shapes? Use a U.S. map to help you. Write the name of each state and its capital city ☆.

1. AK ☆ Juneau
2. OR ☆ Salem
3. VA ☆ Richmond
4. MT ☆ Helena
5. AZ ☆ Phoenix
6. IA ☆ Des Moines
7. RI ☆ Providence
8. MN ☆ St. Paul
9. ND ☆ Bismarck
10. MI ☆ Lansing

Page 106

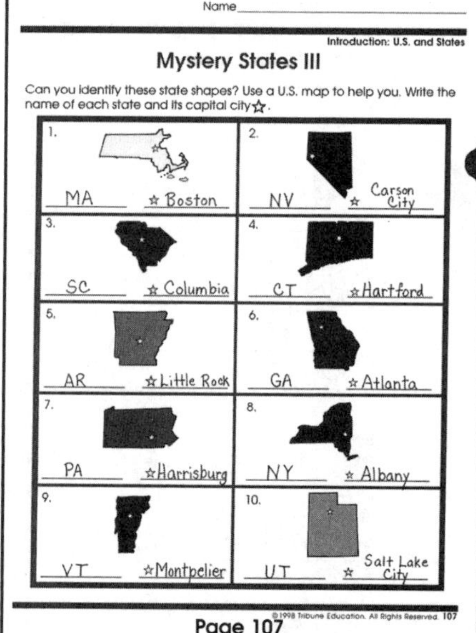

Name

Introduction: U.S. and States

Mystery States III

Can you identify these state shapes? Use a U.S. map to help you. Write the name of each state and its capital city ☆.

1. MA ☆ Boston
2. NV ☆ Carson City
3. SC ☆ Columbia
4. CT ☆ Hartford
5. AR ☆ Little Rock
6. GA ☆ Atlanta
7. PA ☆ Harrisburg
8. NY ☆ Albany
9. VT ☆ Montpelier
10. UT ☆ Salt Lake City

Page 107

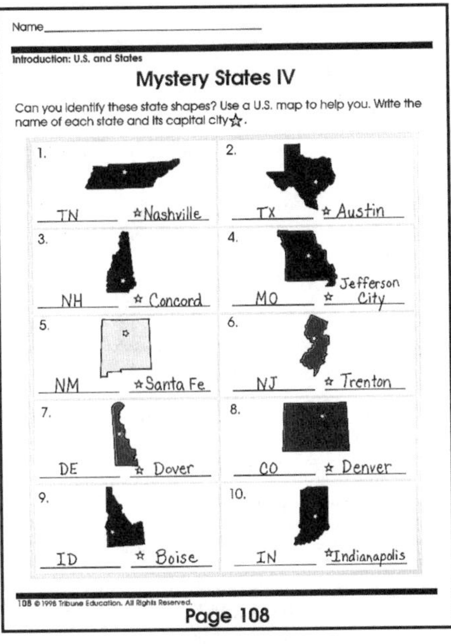
Name____________________

Introduction: U.S. and States

Mystery States IV

Can you identify these state shapes? Use a U.S. map to help you. Write the name of each state and its capital city☆.

1. TN ☆Nashville
2. TX ☆Austin
3. NH ☆Concord
4. MO ☆Jefferson City
5. NM ☆Santa Fe
6. NJ ☆Trenton
7. DE ☆Dover
8. CO ☆Denver
9. ID ☆Boise
10. IN ☆Indianapolis

Page 108

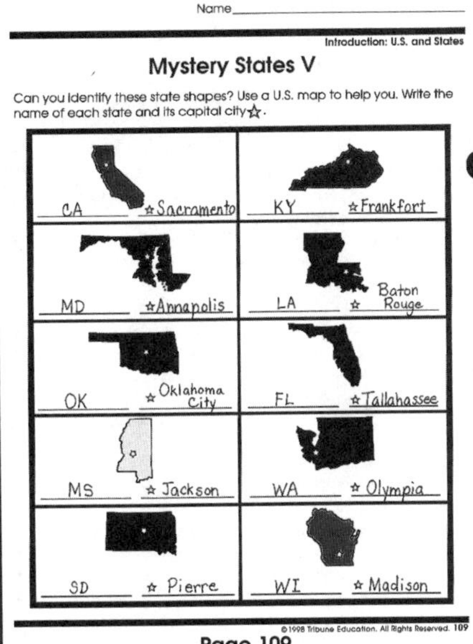
Name____________________

Introduction: U.S. and States

Mystery States V

Can you identify these state shapes? Use a U.S. map to help you. Write the name of each state and its capital city☆.

CA ☆Sacramento	KY ☆Frankfort
MD ☆Annapolis	LA ☆Baton Rouge
OK ☆Oklahoma City	FL ☆Tallahassee
MS ☆Jackson	WA ☆Olympia
SD ☆Pierre	WI ☆Madison

Page 109

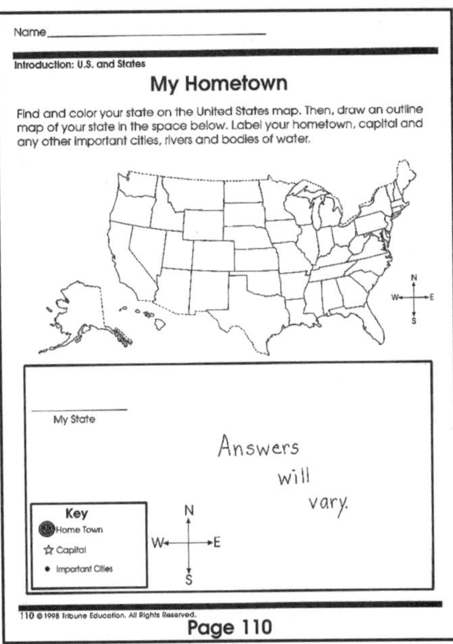
Name____________________

Introduction: U.S. and States

My Hometown

Find and color your state on the United States map. Then, draw an outline map of your state in the space below. Label your hometown, capital and any other important cities, rivers and bodies of water.

Page 110

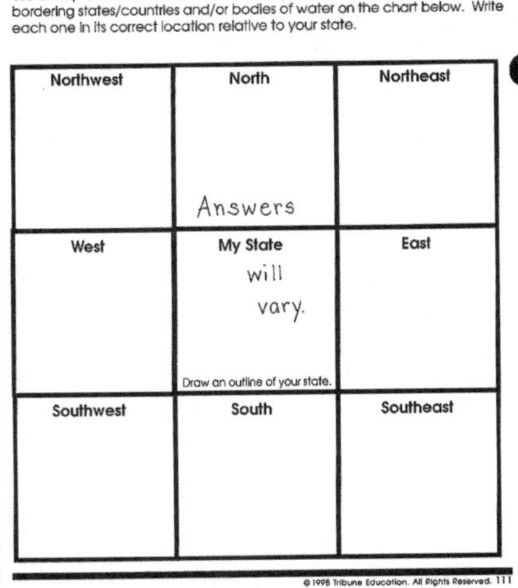
Name____________________

Introduction: U.S. and States

Near My State

Use a map of the United States to locate your state. Write the names of the bordering states/countries and/or bodies of water on the chart below. Write each one in its correct location relative to your state.

Northwest	North	Northeast
	Answers	
West	My State will vary. Draw an outline of your state.	East
Southwest	South	Southeast

Page 111

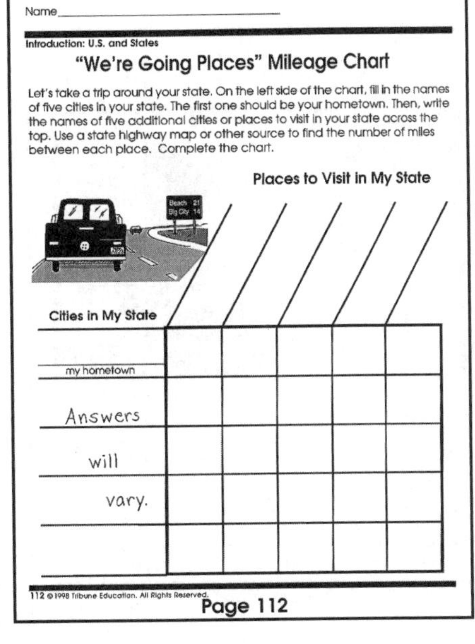
Name____________________

Introduction: U.S. and States

"We're Going Places" Mileage Chart

Let's take a trip around your state. On the left side of the chart, fill in the names of five cities in your state. The first one should be your hometown. Then, write the names of five additional cities or places to visit in your state across the top. Use a state highway map or other source to find the number of miles between each place. Complete the chart.

Places to Visit in My State

Cities in My State

my hometown

Answers will vary.

Page 112

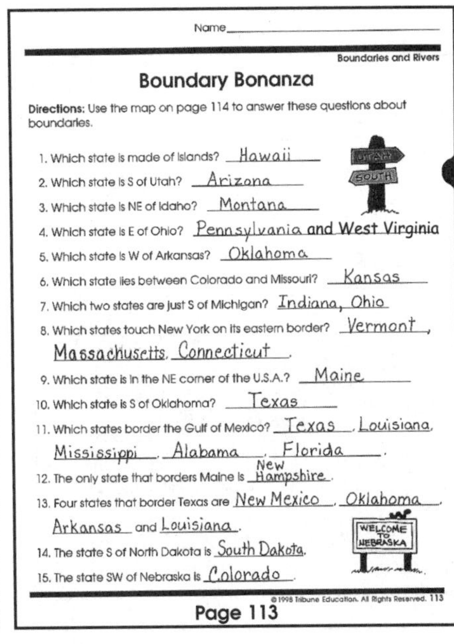
Name____________________

Boundaries and Rivers

Boundary Bonanza

Directions: Use the map on page 114 to answer these questions about boundaries.

1. Which state is made of islands? Hawaii
2. Which state is S of Utah? Arizona
3. Which state is NE of Idaho? Montana
4. Which state is E of Ohio? Pennsylvania and West Virginia
5. Which state is W of Arkansas? Oklahoma
6. Which state lies between Colorado and Missouri? Kansas
7. Which two states are just S of Michigan? Indiana, Ohio
8. Which states touch New York on its eastern border? Vermont, Massachusetts, Connecticut.
9. Which state is in the NE corner of the U.S.A.? Maine
10. Which state is S of Oklahoma? Texas
11. Which states border the Gulf of Mexico? Texas, Louisiana, Mississippi, Alabama, Florida.
12. The only state that borders Maine is New Hampshire.
13. Four states that border Texas are New Mexico, Oklahoma, Arkansas and Louisiana.
14. The state S of North Dakota is South Dakota.
15. The state SW of Nebraska is Colorado.

Page 113

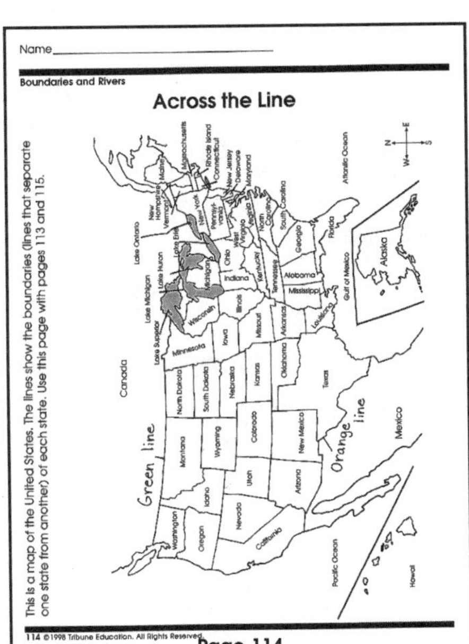
Name____________________

Boundaries and Rivers

Across the Line

This is a map of the United States. The lines show the boundaries (lines that separate one state from another) of each state. Use this page with pages 113 and 115.

Page 114

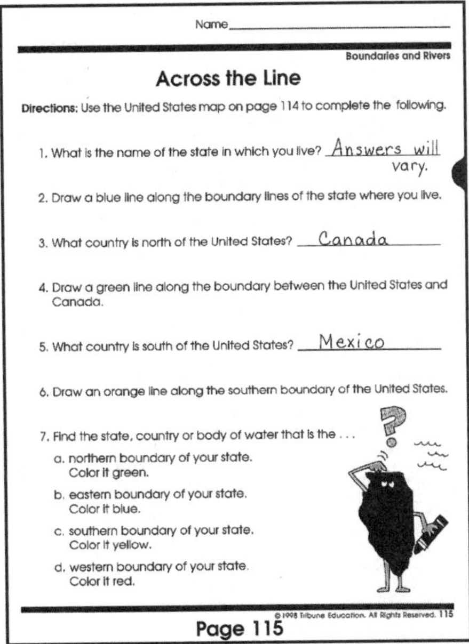
Name____________________

Boundaries and Rivers

Across the Line

Directions: Use the United States map on page 114 to complete the following.

1. What is the name of the state in which you live? Answers will vary.
2. Draw a blue line along the boundary lines of the state where you live.
3. What country is north of the United States? Canada
4. Draw a green line along the boundary between the United States and Canada.
5. What country is south of the United States? Mexico
6. Draw an orange line along the southern boundary of the United States.
7. Find the state, country or body of water that is the . . .
   a. northern boundary of your state. Color it green.
   b. eastern boundary of your state. Color it blue.
   c. southern boundary of your state. Color it yellow.
   d. western boundary of your state. Color it red.

Page 115

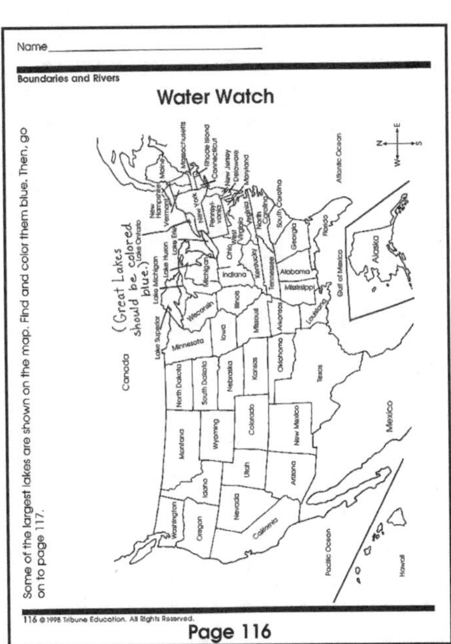
Name____________________

Boundaries and Rivers

Water Watch

Some of the largest lakes are shown on the map. Find and color them blue. Then, go on to page 117.

Page 116

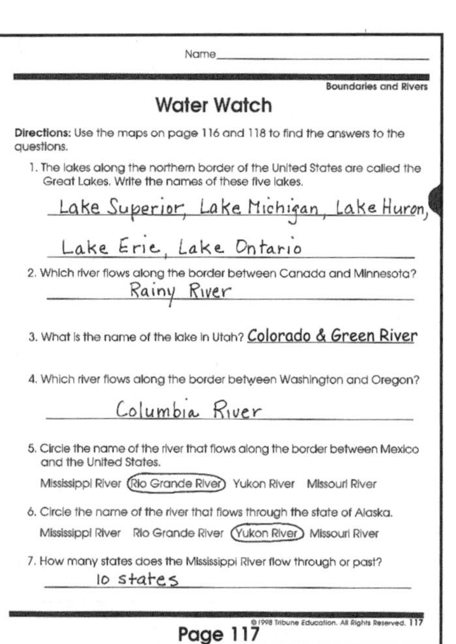

Name

Boundaries and Rivers

Water Watch

Directions: Use the maps on page 116 and 118 to find the answers to the questions.

1. The lakes along the northern border of the United States are called the Great Lakes. Write the names of these five lakes.
   Lake Superior, Lake Michigan, Lake Huron, Lake Erie, Lake Ontario
2. Which river flows along the border between Canada and Minnesota? Rainy River
3. What is the name of the lake in Utah? **Colorado & Green River**
4. Which river flows along the border between Washington and Oregon? Columbia River
5. Circle the name of the river that flows along the border between Mexico and the United States.
   Mississippi River (Rio Grande River) Yukon River Missouri River
6. Circle the name of the river that flows through the state of Alaska.
   Mississippi River Rio Grande River (Yukon River) Missouri River
7. How many states does the Mississippi River flow through or past? 10 states

©1998 Tribune Education. All Rights Reserved. 117

Page 117

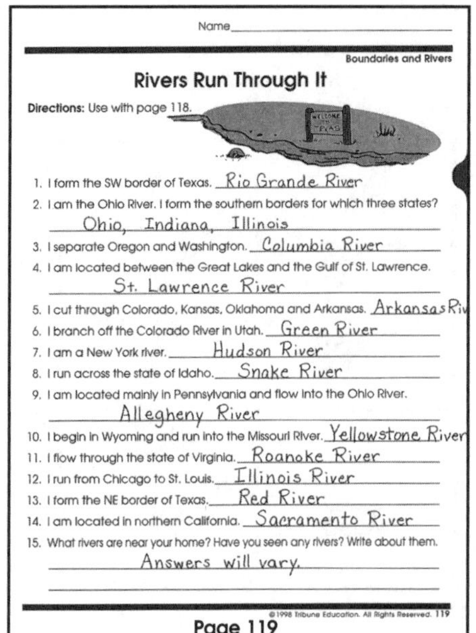

Name

Boundaries and Rivers

Rivers Run Through It

Directions: Use with page 118.

1. I form the SW border of Texas. Rio Grande River
2. I am the Ohio River. I form the southern borders for which three states? Ohio, Indiana, Illinois
3. I separate Oregon and Washington. Columbia River
4. I am located between the Great Lakes and the Gulf of St. Lawrence. St. Lawrence River
5. I cut through Colorado, Kansas, Oklahoma and Arkansas. Arkansas River
6. I branch off the Colorado River in Utah. Green River
7. I am a New York river. Hudson River
8. I run across the state of Idaho. Snake River
9. I am located mainly in Pennsylvania and flow into the Ohio River. Allegheny River
10. I begin in Wyoming and run into the Missouri River. Yellowstone River
11. I flow through the state of Virginia. Roanoke River
12. I run from Chicago to St. Louis. Illinois River
13. I form the NE border of Texas. Red River
14. I am located in northern California. Sacramento River
15. What rivers are near your home? Have you seen any rivers? Write about them. Answers will vary.

©1998 Tribune Education. All Rights Reserved. 119

Page 119

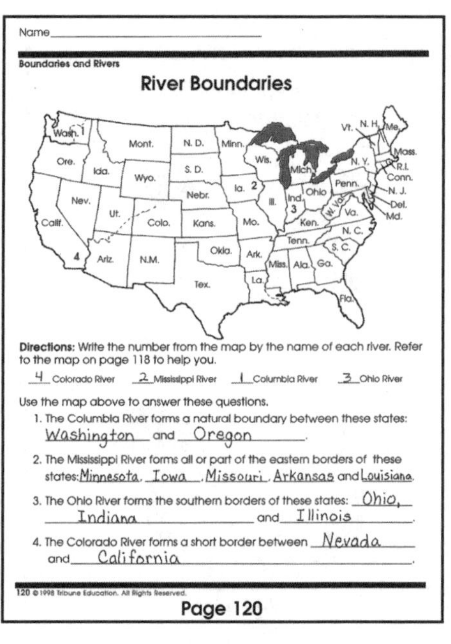

Name

Boundaries and Rivers

River Boundaries

Directions: Write the number from the map by the name of each river. Refer to the map on page 118 to help you.

4 Colorado River 2 Mississippi River 1 Columbia River 3 Ohio River

Use the map above to answer these questions.

1. The Columbia River forms a natural boundary between these states: Washington and Oregon.
2. The Mississippi River forms all or part of the eastern borders of these states: Minnesota, Iowa, Missouri, Arkansas and Louisiana.
3. The Ohio River forms the southern borders of these states: Ohio, Indiana and Illinois.
4. The Colorado River forms a short border between Nevada and California.

120 ©1998 Tribune Education. All Rights Reserved.

Page 120

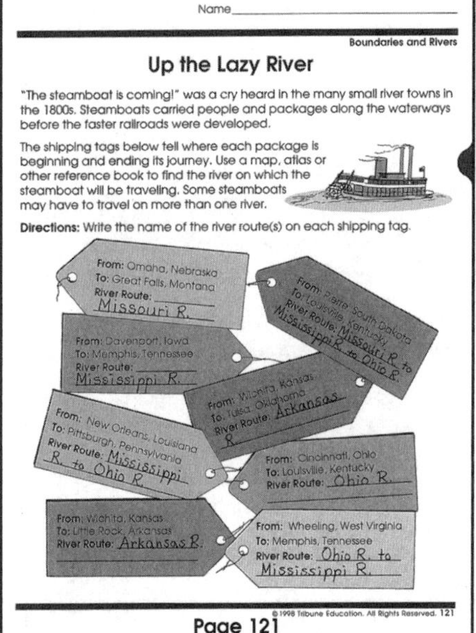

Name

Boundaries and Rivers

Up the Lazy River

"The steamboat is coming!" was a cry heard in the many small river towns in the 1800s. Steamboats carried people and packages along the waterways before the faster railroads were developed.

The shipping tags below tell where each package is beginning and ending its journey. Use a map, atlas or other reference book to find the river on which the steamboat will be traveling. Some steamboats may have to travel on more than one river.

Directions: Write the name of the river route(s) on each shipping tag.

From: Omaha, Nebraska
To: Great Falls, Montana
River Route: Missouri R.

From: Pierre, South Dakota
To: Louisville, Kentucky
River Route: Missouri R. to Mississippi R. to Ohio R.

From: Davenport, Iowa
To: Memphis, Tennessee
River Route: Mississippi R.

From: Wichita, Kansas
To: Tulsa, Oklahoma
River Route: Arkansas

From: New Orleans, Louisiana
To: Pittsburgh, Pennsylvania
River Route: Mississippi R. to Ohio R.

From: Cincinnati, Ohio
To: Louisville, Kentucky
River Route: Ohio R.

From: Wichita, Kansas
To: Little Rock, Arkansas
River Route: Arkansas R.

From: Wheeling, West Virginia
To: Memphis, Tennessee
River Route: Ohio R. to Mississippi R.

©1998 Tribune Education. All Rights Reserved. 121

Page 121

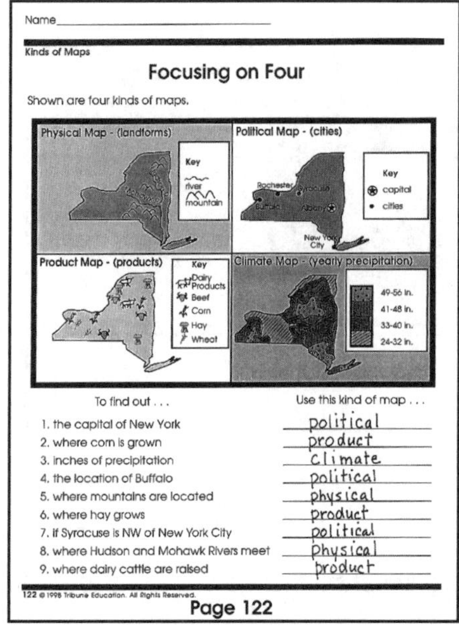

Name

Kinds of Maps

Focusing on Four

Shown are four kinds of maps.

To find out . . .	Use this kind of map . . .
1. the capital of New York	political
2. where corn is grown	product
3. inches of precipitation	climate
4. the location of Buffalo	political
5. where mountains are located	physical
6. where hay grows	product
7. If Syracuse is NW of New York City	political
8. where Hudson and Mohawk Rivers meet	physical
9. where dairy cattle are raised	product

122 ©1998 Tribune Education. All Rights Reserved.

Page 122

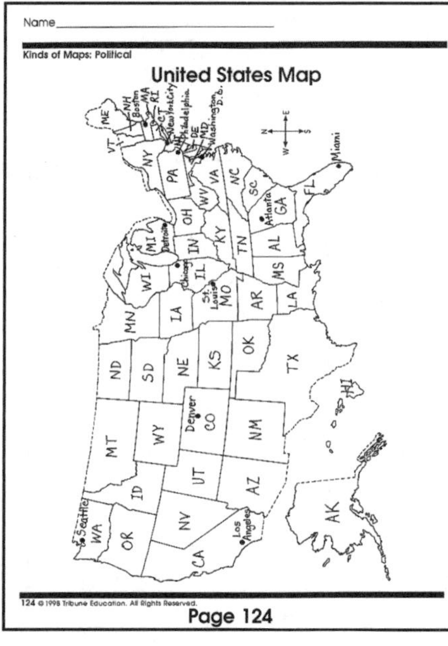

Name

Kinds of Maps: Political

United States Map

124 ©1998 Tribune Education. All Rights Reserved.

Page 124

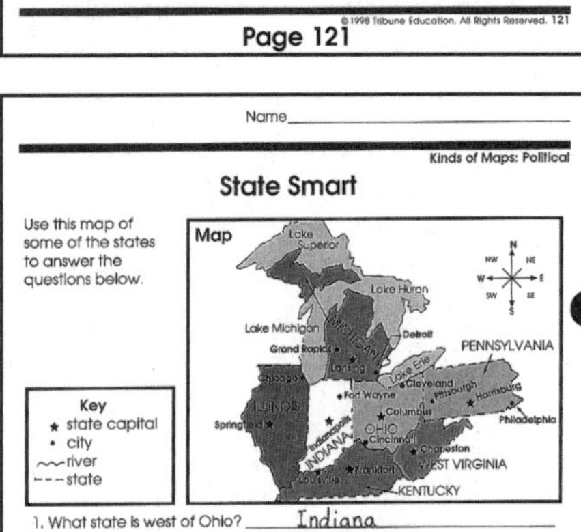

Name

Kinds of Maps: Political

State Smart

Use this map of some of the states to answer the questions below.

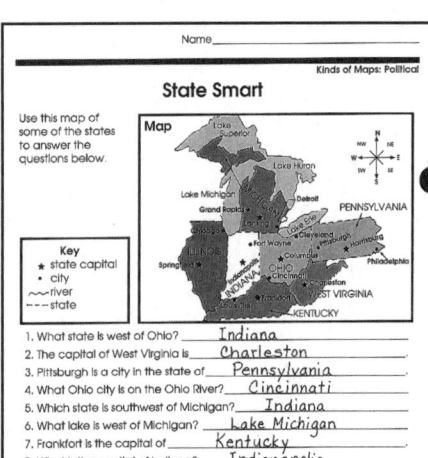

1. What state is west of Ohio? Indiana
2. The capital of West Virginia is Charleston
3. Pittsburgh is a city in the state of Pennsylvania
4. What Ohio city is on the Ohio River? Cincinnati
5. Which state is southwest of Michigan? Indiana
6. What lake is west of Michigan? Lake Michigan
7. Frankfort is the capital of Kentucky
8. What is the capital of Indiana? Indianapolis
9. Springfield is the capital of Illinois
10. Chicago is northeast of Springfield, Illinois.
11. What Ohio city is northeast of Columbus? Cleveland
12. Grand Rapids is northwest of Lansing, Michigan.
13. What state is east of Illinois? Indiana
14. What lake forms the northern border of Ohio? Lake Erie

©1998 Tribune Education. All Rights Reserved. 125

Page 125

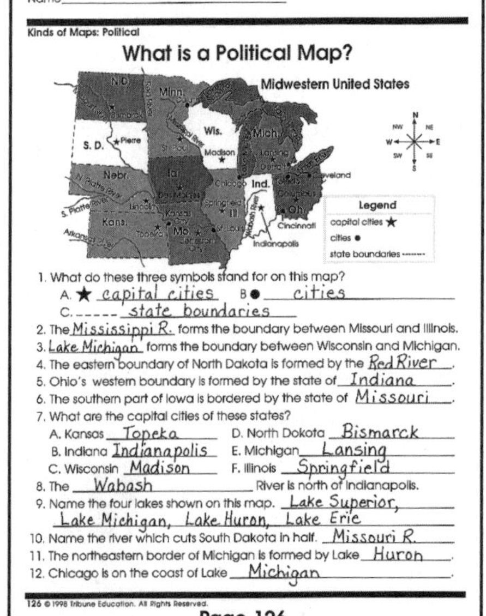

Name

Kinds of Maps: Political

What is a Political Map?

1. What do these three symbols stand for on this map?
   A. ★ capital cities B. ● cities
   C. ------ state boundaries
2. The Mississippi R. forms the boundary between Missouri and Illinois.
3. Lake Michigan forms the boundary between Wisconsin and Michigan.
4. The eastern boundary of North Dakota is formed by the Red River.
5. Ohio's western boundary is formed by the state of Indiana.
6. The southern part of Iowa is bordered by the state of Missouri.
7. What are the capital cities of these states?
   A. Kansas Topeka D. North Dakota Bismarck
   B. Indiana Indianapolis E. Michigan Lansing
   C. Wisconsin Madison F. Illinois Springfield
8. The Wabash River is north of Indianapolis.
9. Name the four lakes shown on this map. Lake Superior, Lake Michigan, Lake Huron, Lake Erie
10. Name the river which cuts South Dakota in half. Missouri R.
11. The northeastern border of Michigan is formed by Lake Huron.
12. Chicago is on the coast of Lake Michigan.

126 ©1998 Tribune Education. All Rights Reserved.

Page 126

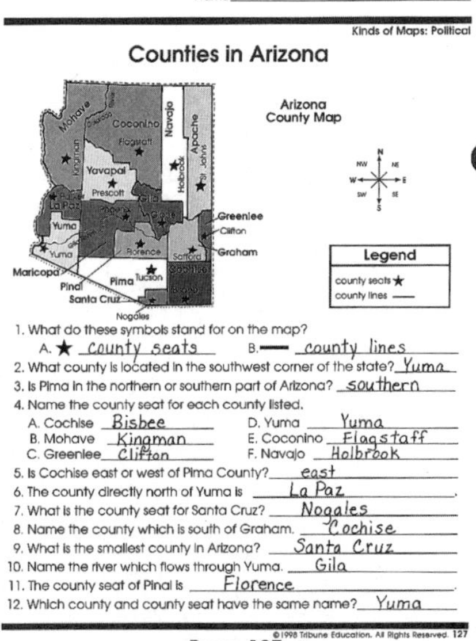

Name

Kinds of Maps: Political

Counties in Arizona

1. What do these symbols stand for on the map?
   A. ★ county seats B. ▬ county lines
2. What county is located in the southwest corner of the state? Yuma
3. Is Pima in the northern or southern part of Arizona? southern
4. Name the county seat for each county listed.
   A. Cochise Bisbee D. Yuma Yuma
   B. Mohave Kingman E. Coconino Flagstaff
   C. Greenlee Clifton F. Navajo Holbrook
5. Is Cochise east or west of Pima County? east
6. The county directly north of Yuma is La Paz.
7. What is the county seat for Santa Cruz? Nogales
8. Name the county which is south of Graham. Cochise
9. What is the smallest county in Arizona? Santa Cruz
10. Name the river which flows through Yuma. Gila
11. The county seat of Pinal is Florence.
12. Which county and county seat have the same name? Yuma

©1998 Tribune Education. All Rights Reserved. 127

Page 127

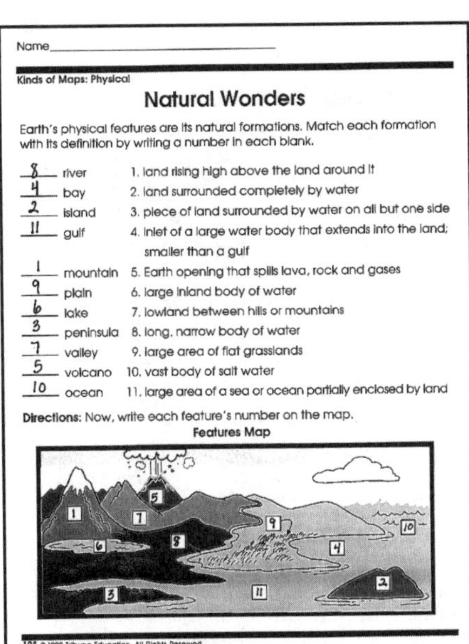

Name______________________

Kinds of Maps: Physical

Natural Wonders

Earth's physical features are its natural formations. Match each formation with its definition by writing a number in each blank.

8	river	1. land rising high above the land around it
4	bay	2. land surrounded completely by water
2	island	3. piece of land surrounded by water on all but one side
11	gulf	4. inlet of a large water body that extends into the land; smaller than a gulf
1	mountain	5. Earth opening that spills lava, rock and gases
9	plain	6. large inland body of water
6	lake	7. lowland between hills or mountains
3	peninsula	8. long, narrow body of water
7	valley	9. large area of flat grasslands
5	volcano	10. vast body of salt water
10	ocean	11. large area of a sea or ocean partially enclosed by land

Directions: Now, write each feature's number on the map.

Features Map

Page 128

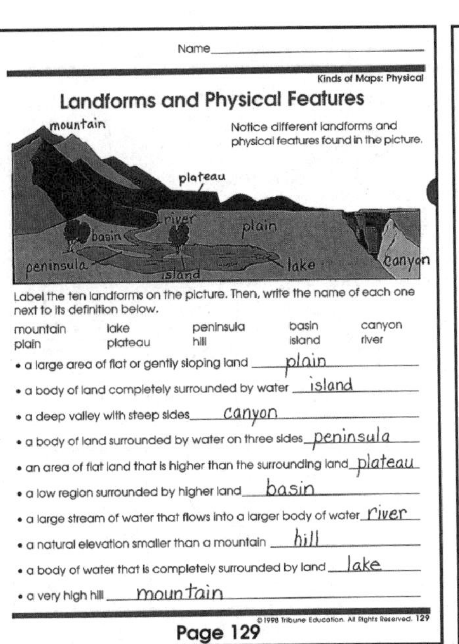

Name______________________

Kinds of Maps: Physical

Landforms and Physical Features

Notice different landforms and physical features found in the picture.

Label the ten landforms on the picture. Then, write the name of each one next to its definition below.

mountain lake peninsula basin canyon
plain plateau hill island river

- a large area of flat or gently sloping land plain
- a body of land completely surrounded by water island
- a deep valley with steep sides canyon
- a body of land surrounded by water on three sides peninsula
- an area of flat land that is higher than the surrounding land plateau
- a low region surrounded by higher land basin
- a large stream of water that flows into a larger body of water river
- a natural elevation smaller than a mountain hill
- a body of water that is completely surrounded by land lake
- a very high hill mountain

Page 129

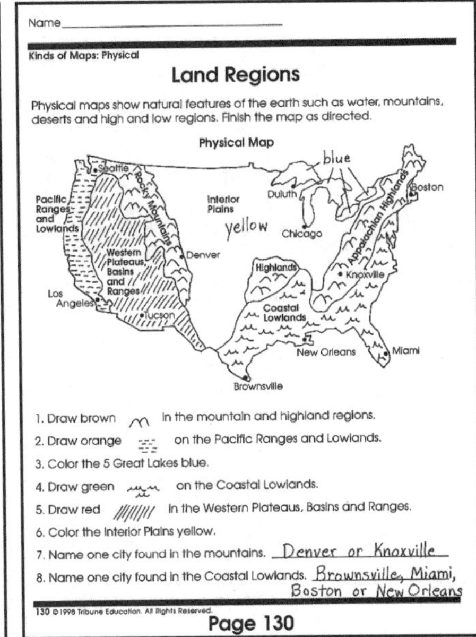

Name______________________

Kinds of Maps: Physical

Land Regions

Physical maps show natural features of the earth such as water, mountains, deserts and high and low regions. Finish the map as directed.

Physical Map

1. Draw brown in the mountain and highland regions.
2. Draw orange on the Pacific Ranges and Lowlands.
3. Color the 5 Great Lakes blue.
4. Draw green on the Coastal Lowlands.
5. Draw red ////// in the Western Plateaus, Basins and Ranges.
6. Color the Interior Plains yellow.
7. Name one city found in the mountains. Denver or Knoxville
8. Name one city found in the Coastal Lowlands. Brownsville, Miami, Boston or New Orleans

Page 130

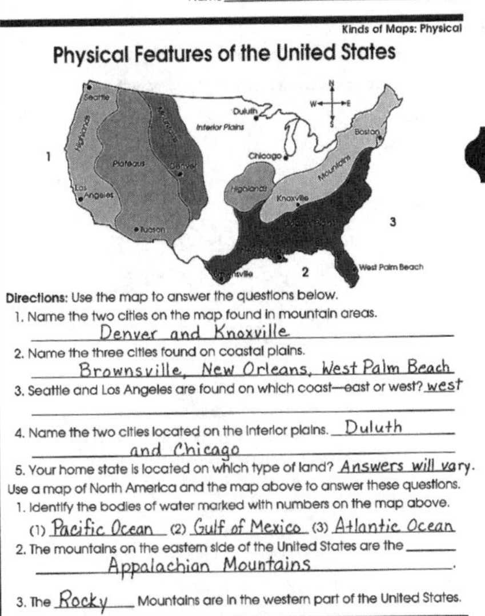

Name______________________

Kinds of Maps: Physical

Physical Features of the United States

Directions: Use the map to answer the questions below.

1. Name the two cities on the map found in mountain areas. Denver and Knoxville
2. Name the three cities found on coastal plains. Brownsville, New Orleans, West Palm Beach
3. Seattle and Los Angeles are found on which coast—east or west? west
4. Name the two cities located on the interior plains. Duluth and Chicago
5. Your home state is located on which type of land? Answers will vary.

Use a map of North America and the map above to answer these questions.

1. Identify the bodies of water marked with numbers on the map above. (1) Pacific Ocean (2) Gulf of Mexico (3) Atlantic Ocean
2. The mountains on the eastern side of the United States are the Appalachian Mountains.
3. The Rocky Mountains are in the western part of the United States.

Page 131

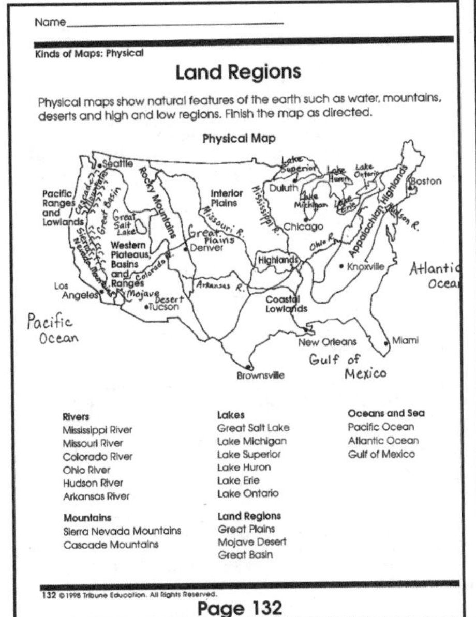

Name______________________

Kinds of Maps: Physical

Land Regions

Physical maps show natural features of the earth such as water, mountains, deserts and high and low regions. Finish the map as directed.

Physical Map

Rivers	Lakes	Oceans and Sea
Mississippi River	Great Salt Lake	Pacific Ocean
Missouri River	Lake Michigan	Atlantic Ocean
Colorado River	Lake Superior	Gulf of Mexico
Ohio River	Lake Huron	
Hudson River	Lake Erie	
Arkansas River	Lake Ontario	

Mountains	Land Regions
Sierra Nevada Mountains	Great Plains
Cascade Mountains	Mojave Desert
	Great Basin

Page 132

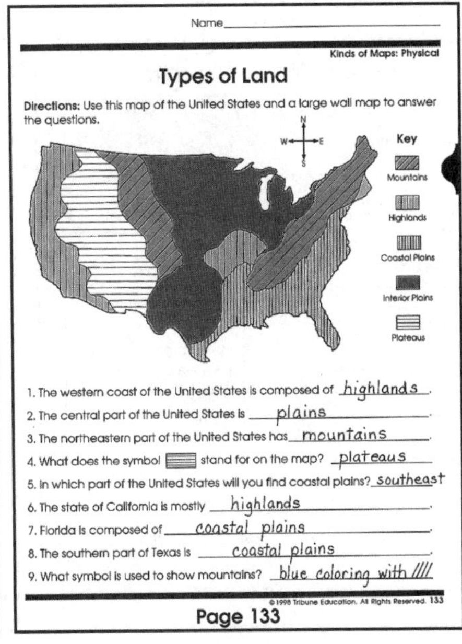

Name______________________

Kinds of Maps: Physical

Types of Land

Directions: Use this map of the United States and a large wall map to answer the questions.

1. The western coast of the United States is composed of highlands.
2. The central part of the United States is plains.
3. The northeastern part of the United States has mountains.
4. What does the symbol stand for on the map? plateaus
5. In which part of the United States will you find coastal plains? southeast
6. The state of California is mostly highlands.
7. Florida is composed of coastal plains.
8. The southern part of Texas is coastal plains.
9. What symbol is used to show mountains? blue coloring with ////

Page 133

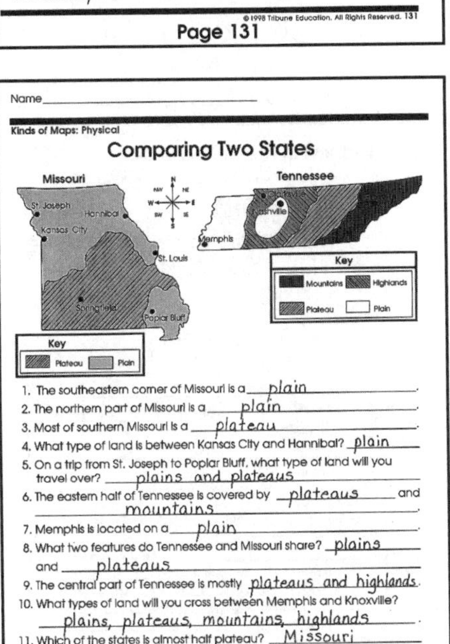

Name______________________

Kinds of Maps: Physical

Comparing Two States

1. The southeastern corner of Missouri is a plain.
2. The northern part of Missouri is a plain.
3. Most of southern Missouri is a plateau.
4. What type of land is between Kansas City and Hannibal? plain
5. On a trip from St. Joseph to Poplar Bluff, what type of land will you travel over? plains and plateaus
6. The eastern half of Tennessee is covered by plateaus and mountains.
7. Memphis is located on a plain.
8. What two features do Tennessee and Missouri share? plains and plateaus
9. The central part of Tennessee is mostly plateaus and highlands.
10. What types of land will you cross between Memphis and Knoxville? plains, plateaus, mountains, highlands
11. Which of the states is almost half plateau? Missouri

Page 134

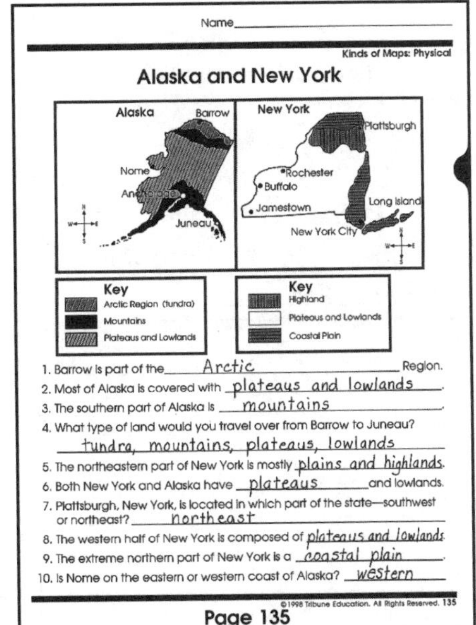

Name______________________

Kinds of Maps: Physical

Alaska and New York

1. Barrow is part of the Arctic Region.
2. Most of Alaska is covered with plateaus and lowlands.
3. The southern part of Alaska is mountains.
4. What type of land would you travel over from Barrow to Juneau? tundra, mountains, plateaus, lowlands
5. The northeastern part of New York is mostly plains and highlands.
6. Both New York and Alaska have plateaus and lowlands.
7. Plattsburgh, New York, is located in which part of the state—southwest or northeast? northeast
8. The western half of New York is composed of plateaus and lowlands.
9. The extreme northern part of New York is a coastal plain.
10. Is Nome on the eastern or western coast of Alaska? western

Page 135

Name______________________

Kinds of Maps: Physical

Poetic Forms

Just as there are many kinds of landforms and physical features, there are also many forms of poetry. Let's use what you know about landforms and physical features to write a diamanté poem. Look at the sample below.

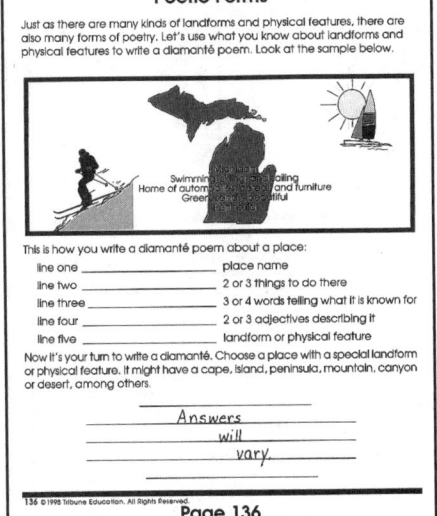

Michigan
Swimming, skiing, sailing
Home of automobiles and furniture
Green, wet, beautiful
Peninsulas

This is how you write a diamanté poem about a place:

line one	______________	place name
line two	______________	2 or 3 things to do there
line three	______________	3 or 4 words telling what it is known for
line four	______________	2 or 3 adjectives describing it
line five	______________	landform or physical feature

Now it's your turn to write a diamanté. Choose a place with a special landform or physical feature. It might have a cape, island, peninsula, mountain, canyon or desert, among others.

Answers
will
vary.

Page 136

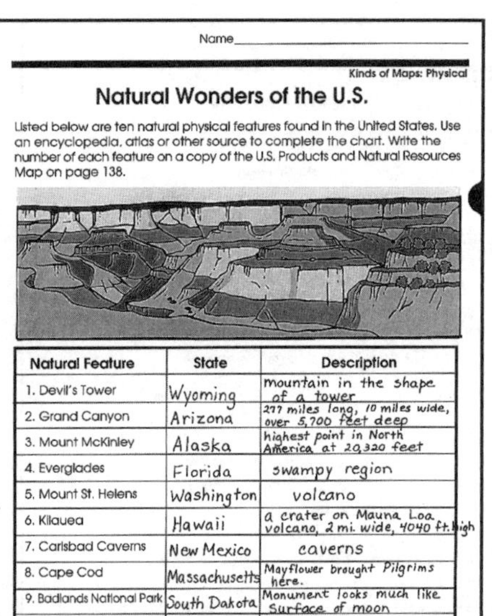

Name____________________

Kinds of Maps: Physical

Natural Wonders of the U.S.

Listed below are ten natural physical features found in the United States. Use an encyclopedia, atlas or other source to complete the chart. Write the number of each feature on a copy of the U.S. Products and Natural Resources Map on page 138.

Natural Feature	State	Description
1. Devil's Tower	Wyoming	mountain in the shape of a tower
2. Grand Canyon	Arizona	277 miles long, 10 miles wide, over 5,700 feet deep
3. Mount McKinley	Alaska	highest point in North America at 20,320 feet
4. Everglades	Florida	swampy region
5. Mount St. Helens	Washington	volcano
6. Kilauea	Hawaii	a crater on Mauna Loa volcano, 2 mi. wide, 4040 ft. high
7. Carlsbad Caverns	New Mexico	caverns
8. Cape Cod	Massachusetts	Mayflower brought Pilgrims here.
9. Badlands National Park	South Dakota	Monument looks much like surface of moon
10. Mojave Desert	California	15,000 square miles

Page 137

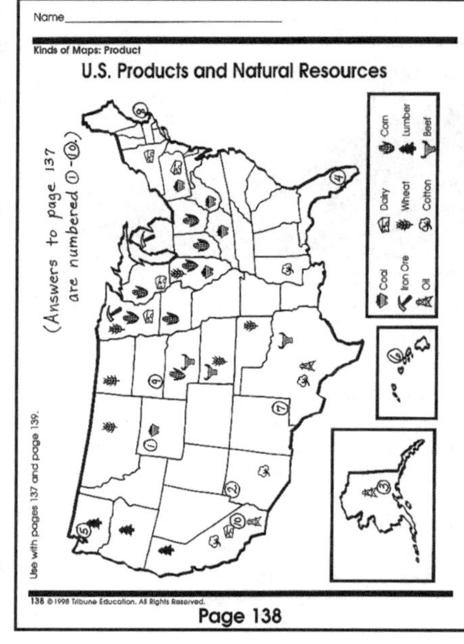

Name____________________

Kinds of Maps: Product

U.S. Products and Natural Resources

Page 138

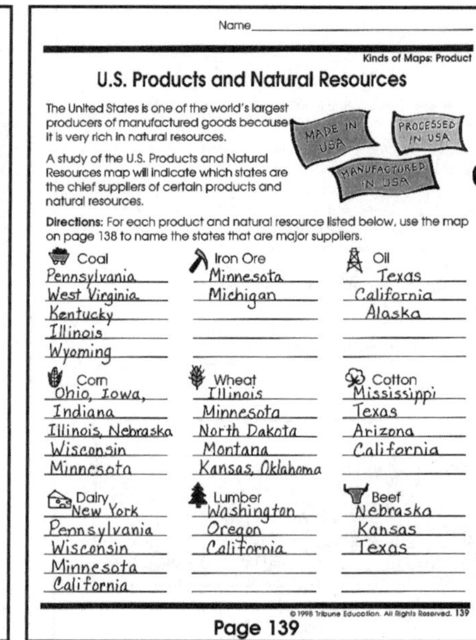

Name____________________

Kinds of Maps: Product

U.S. Products and Natural Resources

The United States is one of the world's largest producers of manufactured goods because it is very rich in natural resources.

A study of the U.S. Products and Natural Resources map will indicate which states are the chief suppliers of certain products and natural resources.

Directions: For each product and natural resource listed below, use the map on page 138 to name the states that are major suppliers.

Coal: Pennsylvania, West Virginia, Kentucky, Illinois, Wyoming

Iron Ore: Minnesota, Michigan

Oil: Texas, California, Alaska

Corn: Ohio, Iowa, Indiana, Illinois, Nebraska, Wisconsin, Minnesota

Wheat: Illinois, Minnesota, North Dakota, Montana, Kansas, Oklahoma

Cotton: Mississippi, Texas, Arizona, California

Dairy: New York, Pennsylvania, Wisconsin, Minnesota, California

Lumber: Washington, Oregon, California

Beef: Nebraska, Kansas, Texas

Page 139

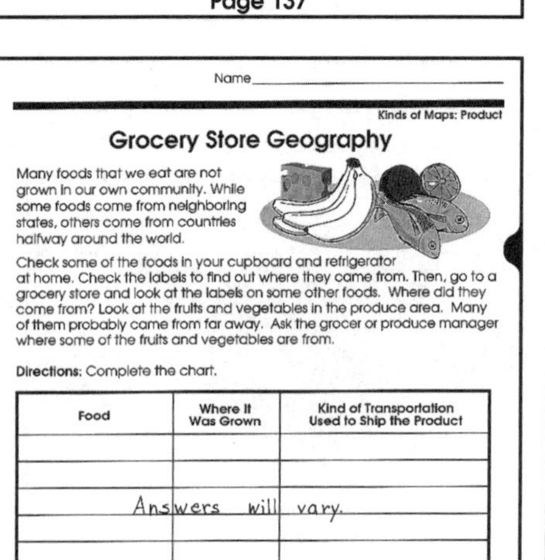

Name____________________

Kinds of Maps: Product

Grocery Store Geography

Many foods that we eat are not grown in our own community. While some foods come from neighboring states, others come from countries halfway around the world.

Check some of the foods in your cupboard and refrigerator at home. Check the labels to find out where they come from. Then, go to a grocery store and look at the labels on some other foods. Where did they come from? Look at the fruits and vegetables in the produce area. Many of them probably came from far away. Ask the grocer or produce manager where some of the fruits and vegetables are from.

Directions: Complete the chart.

Food	Where It Was Grown	Kind of Transportation Used to Ship the Product
Answers	will	vary.

On a map, locate where these foods were grown.

Which was shipped the greatest distance? Answers

How far did it have to travel to reach your grocery store? will vary.

Page 141

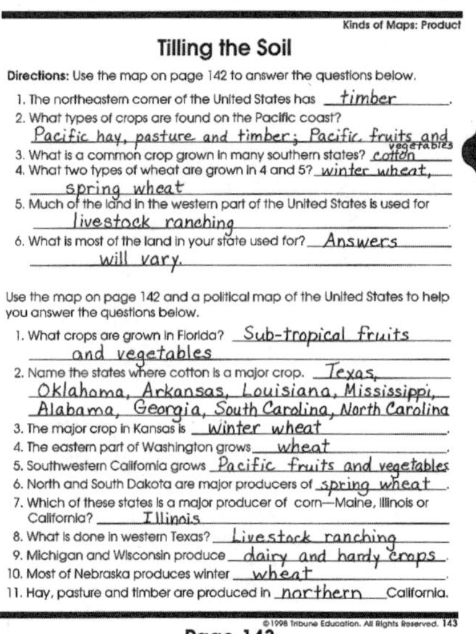

Name____________________

Kinds of Maps: Product

Tilling the Soil

Directions: Use the map on page 142 to answer the questions below.

1. The northeastern corner of the United States has timber.
2. What types of crops are found on the Pacific coast? Pacific hay, pasture and timber; Pacific fruits and vegetables
3. What is a common crop grown in many southern states? cotton
4. What two types of wheat are grown in 4 and 5? winter wheat, spring wheat
5. Much of the land in the western part of the United States is used for livestock ranching.
6. What is most of the land in your state used for? Answers will vary.

Use the map on page 142 and a political map of the United States to help you answer the questions below.

1. What crops are grown in Florida? Sub-tropical fruits and vegetables
2. Name the states where cotton is a major crop. Texas, Oklahoma, Arkansas, Louisiana, Mississippi, Alabama, Georgia, South Carolina, North Carolina
3. The major crop in Kansas is winter wheat.
4. The eastern part of Washington grows wheat.
5. Southwestern California grows Pacific fruits and vegetables.
6. North and South Dakota are major producers of spring wheat.
7. Which of these states is a major producer of corn—Maine, Illinois or California? Illinois
8. What is done in western Texas? Livestock ranching
9. Michigan and Wisconsin produce dairy and hardy crops.
10. Most of Nebraska produces winter wheat.
11. Hay, pasture and timber are produced in northern California.

Page 143

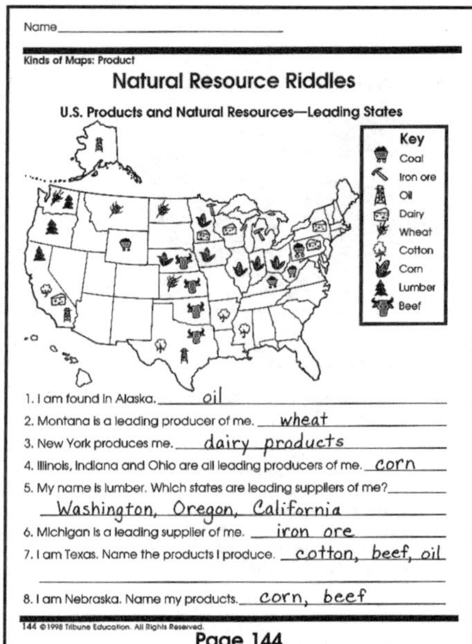

Name____________________

Kinds of Maps: Product

Natural Resource Riddles

U.S. Products and Natural Resources—Leading States

1. I am found in Alaska. oil
2. Montana is a leading producer of me. wheat
3. New York produces me. dairy products
4. Illinois, Indiana and Ohio are all leading producers of me. corn
5. My name is lumber. Which states are leading suppliers of me? Washington, Oregon, California
6. Michigan is a leading supplier of me. iron ore
7. I am Texas. Name the products I produce. cotton, beef, oil
8. I am Nebraska. Name my products. corn, beef

Page 144

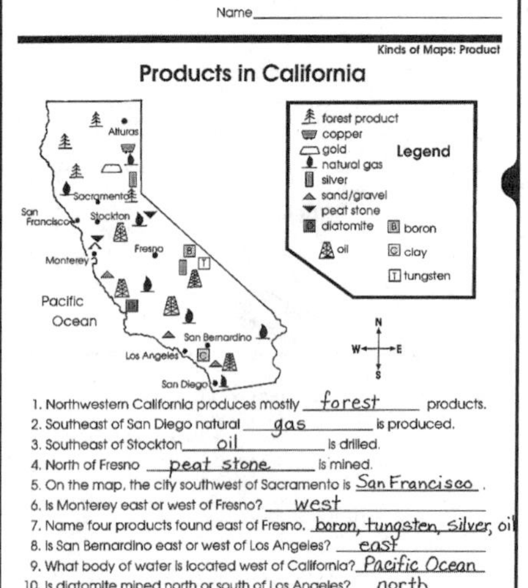

Name____________________

Kinds of Maps: Product

Products in California

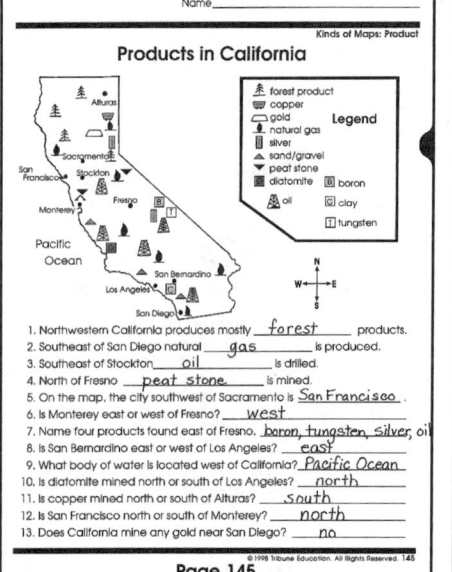

1. Northwestern California produces mostly forest products.
2. Southeast of San Diego natural gas is produced.
3. Southeast of Stockton oil is drilled.
4. North of Fresno peat stone is mined.
5. On the map, the city southwest of Sacramento is San Francisco.
6. Is Monterey east or west of Fresno? west
7. Name four products found east of Fresno. boron, tungsten, silver, oil
8. Is San Bernardino east or west of Los Angeles? east
9. What body of water is located west of California? Pacific Ocean
10. Is diatomite mined north or south of Los Angeles? north
11. Is copper mined north or south of Alturas? south
12. Is San Francisco north or south of Monterey? north
13. Does California mine any gold near San Diego? no

Page 145

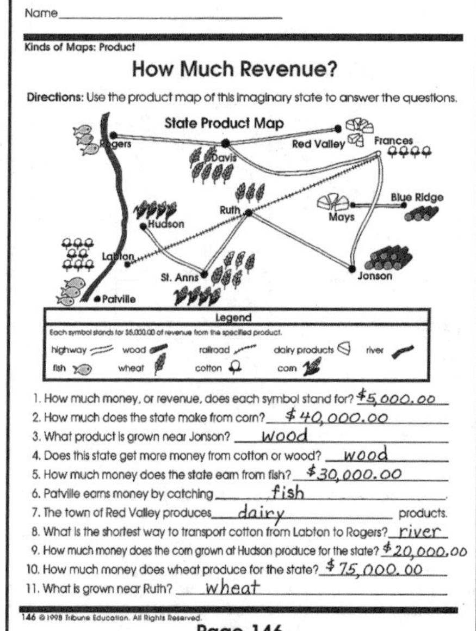

Name____________________

Kinds of Maps: Product

How Much Revenue?

Directions: Use the product map of this imaginary state to answer the questions.

1. How much money, or revenue, does each symbol stand for? $5,000.00
2. How much does the state make from corn? $40,000.00
3. What product is grown near Jonson? wood
4. Does this state get more money from cotton or wood? wood
5. How much money does the state earn from fish? $30,000.00
6. Patville earns money by catching fish
7. The town of Red Valley produces dairy products.
8. What is the shortest way to transport cotton from Labton to Rogers? river
9. How much money does the corn grown at Hudson produce for the state? $20,000.00
10. How much money does wheat produce for the state? $75,000.00
11. What is grown near Ruth? wheat

Page 146

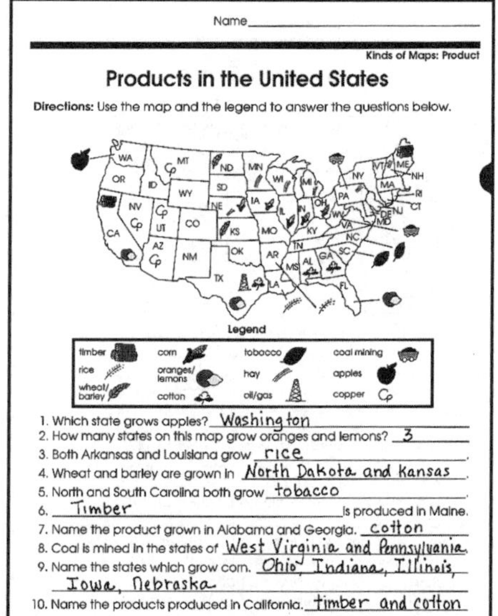

Name____________________

Kinds of Maps: Product

Products in the United States

Directions: Use the map and the legend to answer the questions below.

1. Which state grows apples? Washington
2. How many states on this map grow oranges and lemons? 3
3. Both Arkansas and Louisiana grow rice.
4. Wheat and barley are grown in North Dakota and Kansas.
5. North and South Carolina both grow tobacco.
6. Timber is produced in Maine.
7. Name the product grown in Alabama and Georgia. cotton
8. Coal is mined in the states of West Virginia and Pennsylvania.
9. Name the states which grow corn. Ohio, Indiana, Illinois, Iowa, Nebraska
10. Name the products produced in California. timber and cotton

Page 147

Name________________________

Kinds of Maps: Climate

How Much Did It Rain?

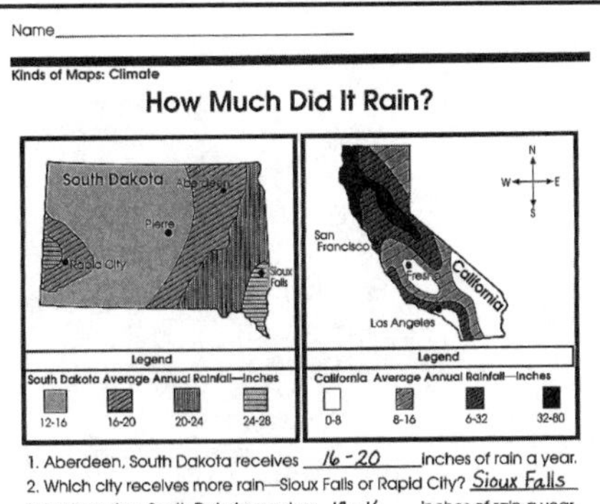

1. Aberdeen, South Dakota receives 16-20 inches of rain a year.
2. Which city receives more rain—Sioux Falls or Rapid City? Sioux Falls
3. Northwestern South Dakota receives 12-16 inches of rain a year.
4. How much rain does Pierre, South Dakota usually receive? 12-16 inches
5. The southeastern corner of South Dakota receives 24-28 inches of rain.
6. What does the symbol ☐ mean on the map of California? 0-8 inches of annual rainfall
7. Southeastern California receives 0-8 inches of rain a year.
8. Los Angeles, California, receives an average of 8-16 inches of rain a year.
9. The northeastern part of California receives 8-16 inches of rain.
10. What does this symbol ■ mean on the map of California? 32-80 inches of annual rainfall
11. Fresno, California, receives an average of 0-8 inches of rain.
12. Which city receives more rain—Sioux Falls, South Dakota or Fresno, California? Sioux Falls, South Dakota
13. The extreme northwestern corner of California receives 32-80 inches of rain a year.

Page 148

Name________________________

Kinds of Maps: Climate

Temperature Ranges

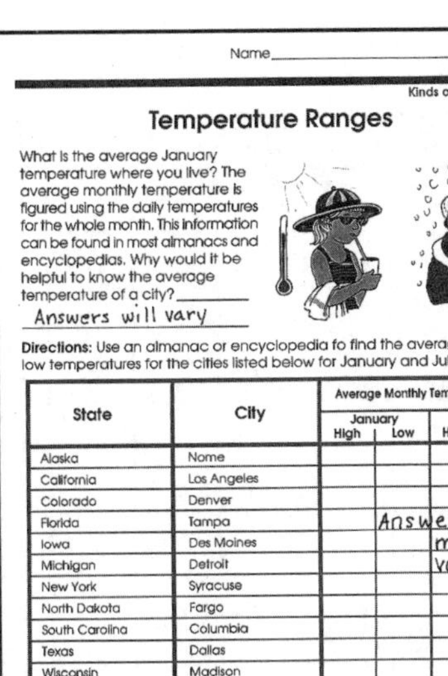

What is the average January temperature where you live? The average monthly temperature is figured using the daily temperatures for the whole month. This information can be found in most almanacs and encyclopedias. Why would it be helpful to know the average temperature of a city? Answers will vary

Directions: Use an almanac or encyclopedia to find the average high and low temperatures for the cities listed below for January and July.

State	City	Average Monthly Temperatures (F°) January High	January Low	July High	July Low
Alaska	Nome				
California	Los Angeles				
Colorado	Denver				
Florida	Tampa		Answers		
Iowa	Des Moines		may		
Michigan	Detroit		vary.		
New York	Syracuse				
North Dakota	Fargo				
South Carolina	Columbia				
Texas	Dallas				
Wisconsin	Madison				
State of your choice:					

Circle the highest temperature in each "high" column and the lowest temperature in each "low" column.

Page 149

Name________________________

Kinds of Maps: Climate

U.S. Climate Zones

The word climate is used to describe the weather in a particular place over a long period of time. Because the United States covers such a large area, it has a number of different climate zones. Some areas have long, cold winters and short, cool summers, while other areas are always warm in both the summer and the winter.

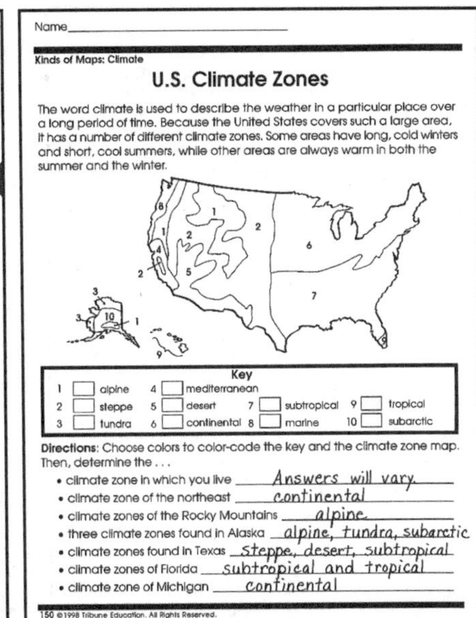

Key

1 ☐ alpine 4 ☐ mediterranean
2 ☐ steppe 5 ☐ desert 7 ☐ subtropical 9 ☐ tropical
3 ☐ tundra 6 ☐ continental 8 ☐ marine 10 ☐ subarctic

Directions: Choose colors to color-code the key and the climate zone map. Then, determine the . . .

- climate zone in which you live Answers will vary.
- climate zone of the northeast continental
- climate zones of the Rocky Mountains alpine
- three climate zones found in Alaska alpine, tundra, subarctic
- climate zones found in Texas steppe, desert, subtropical
- climate zones of Florida subtropical and tropical
- climate zone of Michigan continental

Page 150

Name________________________

Pacific States

Fill in the "Five Fundamental Themes of Geography" for each state. After "discovering" a state, fill in all the columns of the chart except **Regions**. When you have finished with all of the states in a section, fill in **Regions**.

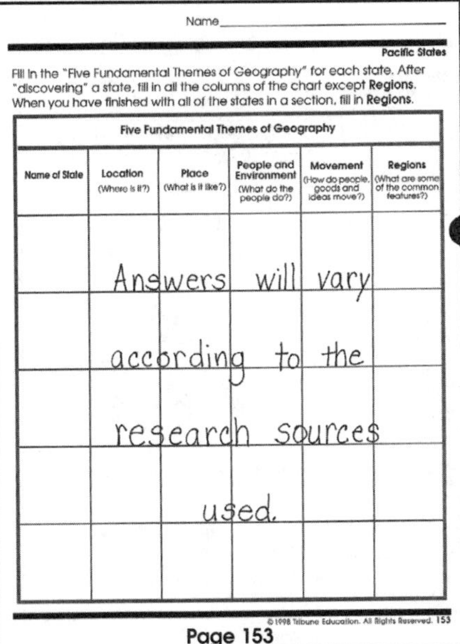

Five Fundamental Themes of Geography					
Name of State	Location (Where is it?)	Place (What is it like?)	People and Environment (What do the people do?)	Movement (How do people, goods and ideas move?)	Regions (What are some of the common features?)
	Answers will vary				
	according to the				
	research sources				
	used.				

Page 153

Name________________________

Pacific States

Washington

The Evergreen State

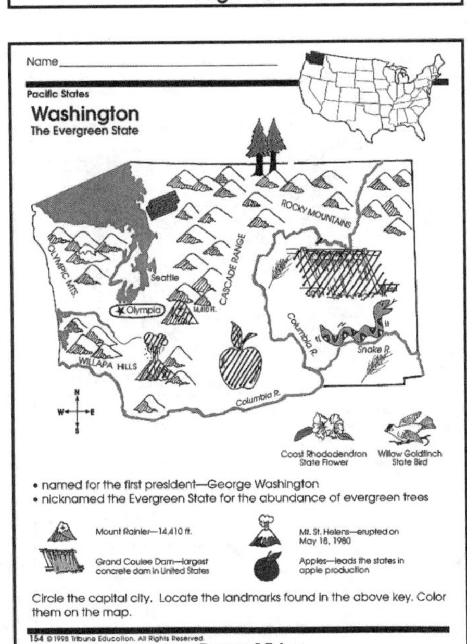

- named for the first president—George Washington
- nicknamed the Evergreen State for the abundance of evergreen trees

Mount Rainier—14,410 ft.

Mt. St. Helens—erupted on May 18, 1980

Grand Coulee Dam—largest concrete dam in United States

Apples—leads the states in apple production

Circle the capital city. Locate the landmarks found in the above key. Color them on the map.

Page 154

Name________________________

Pacific States

Oregon

The Beaver State

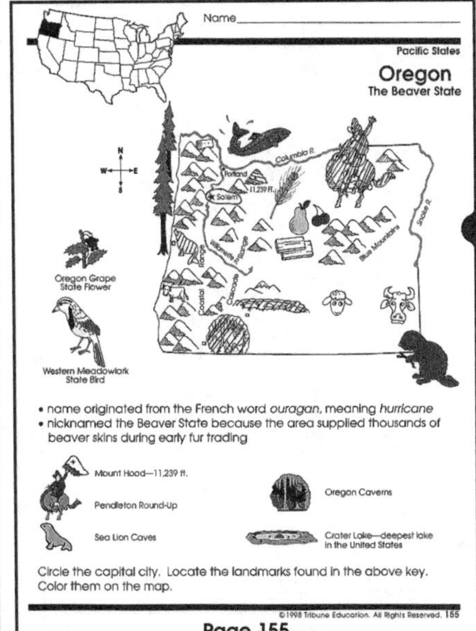

- name originated from the French word *ouragan*, meaning *hurricane*
- nicknamed the Beaver State because the area supplied thousands of beaver skins during early fur trading

Mount Hood—11,239 ft.

Oregon Caverns

Pendleton Round-Up

Sea Lion Caves

Crater Lake—deepest lake in the United States

Circle the capital city. Locate the landmarks found in the above key. Color them on the map.

Page 155

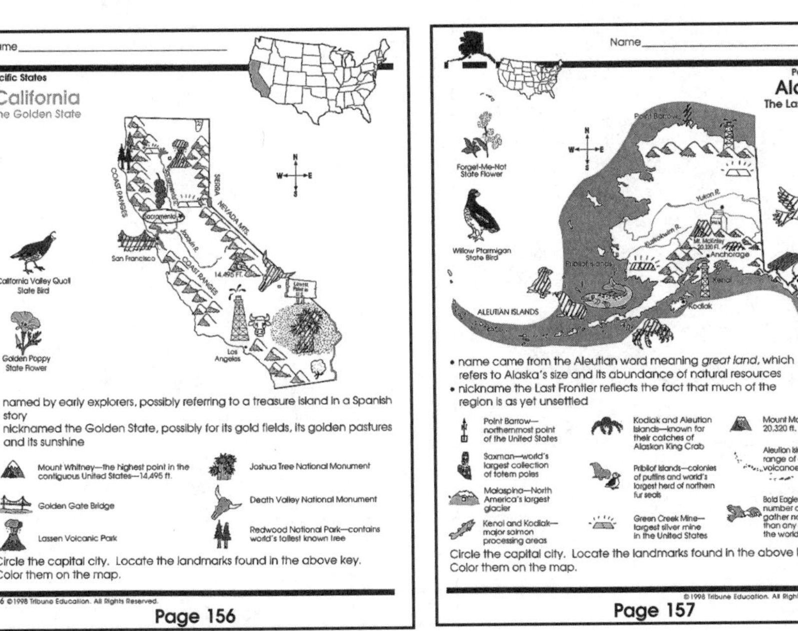

Name________________________

Pacific States

California

The Golden State

- named by early explorers, possibly referring to a treasure island in a Spanish story
- nicknamed the Golden State, possibly for its gold fields, its golden pastures and its sunshine

Mount Whitney—the highest point in the contiguous United States—14,495 ft.

Joshua Tree National Monument

Golden Gate Bridge

Death Valley National Monument

Lassen Volcanic Park

Redwood National Park—contains world's tallest known tree

Circle the capital city. Locate the landmarks found in the above key. Color them on the map.

Page 156

Name________________________

Pacific States

Alaska

The Last Frontier

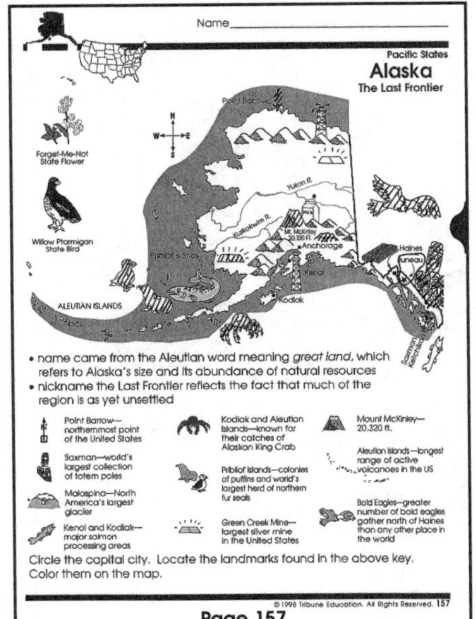

- name came from the Aleutian word meaning *great land*, which refers to Alaska's size and its abundance of natural resources
- nickname the Last Frontier reflects the fact that much of the region is as yet unsettled

Point Barrow—northernmost point of the United States

Kodiak and Aleutian Islands—known for their catches of Alaskan King Crab

Mount McKinley—20,320 ft.

Saxman—world's largest collection of totem poles

Pribilof Islands—colonies of puffins and world's largest herd of northern fur seals

Aleutian Islands—longest range of active volcanoes in the US

Malaspina—North America's largest glacier

Green Creek Mine—largest silver mine in the United States

Bald Eagles—greater number of bald eagles gather north of Haines than any other place in the world

Kenai and Kodiak—major salmon processing areas

Circle the capital city. Locate the landmarks found in the above key. Color them on the map.

Page 157

Name________________________

Pacific States

Hawaii

The Aloha State

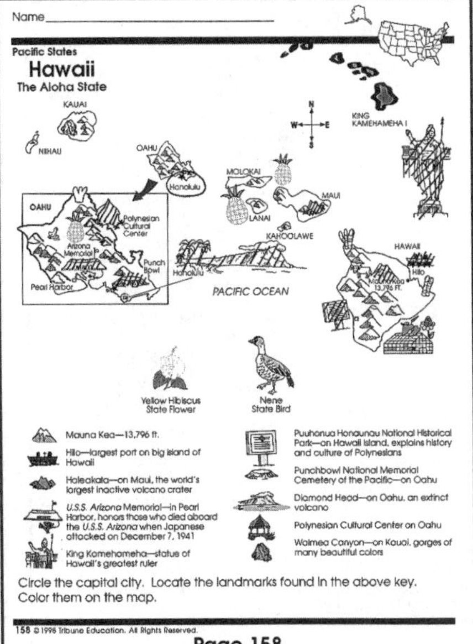

Mauna Kea—13,796 ft.

Hilo—largest port on big island of Hawaii

Haleakala—on Maui, the world's largest inactive volcano crater

U.S.S. Arizona Memorial—in Pearl Harbor, honors those who died aboard the *U.S.S. Arizona* when Japanese attacked on December 7, 1941

King Kamehameha—statue of Hawaii's greatest ruler

Puuhonua Honaunau National Historical Park—on Hawaii island, explains history and culture of Polynesians

Punchbowl National Memorial Cemetery of the Pacific—on Oahu

Diamond Head—on Oahu, an extinct volcano

Polynesian Cultural Center on Oahu

Waimea Canyon—on Kauai, gorges of many beautiful colors

Circle the capital city. Locate the landmarks found in the above key. Color them on the map.

Page 158

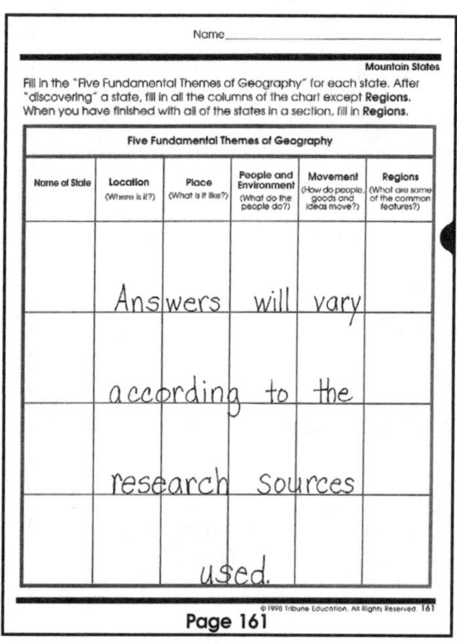

Name____________________________

Mountain States

Fill in the "Five Fundamental Themes of Geography" for each state. After "discovering" a state, fill in all the columns of the chart except **Regions**. When you have finished with all of the states in a section, fill in **Regions**.

Five Fundamental Themes of Geography					
Name of State	Location (Where is it?)	Place (What is it like?)	People and Environment (What do the people do?)	Movement (How do people, goods and ideas move?)	Regions (What are some of the common features?)
	Answers will vary according to the research sources used.				

Page 161

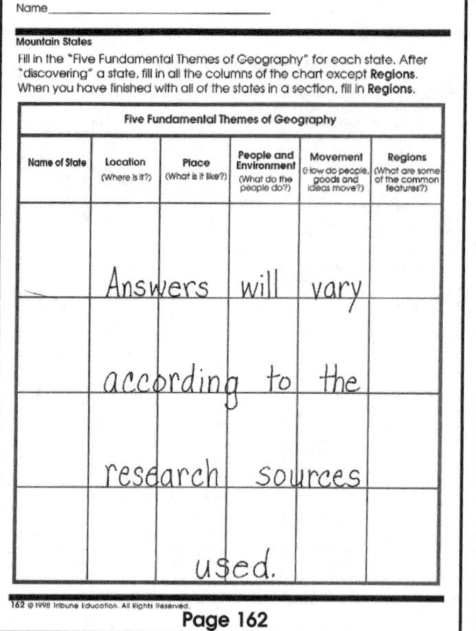

Name____________________________

Mountain States

Fill in the "Five Fundamental Themes of Geography" for each state. After "discovering" a state, fill in all the columns of the chart except **Regions**. When you have finished with all of the states in a section, fill in **Regions**.

Five Fundamental Themes of Geography					
Name of State	Location (Where is it?)	Place (What is it like?)	People and Environment (What do the people do?)	Movement (How do people, goods and ideas move?)	Regions (What are some of the common features?)
	Answers will vary according to the research sources used.				

Page 162

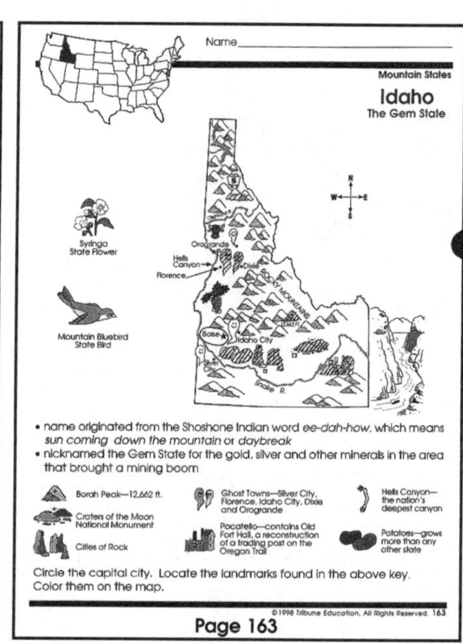

Name____________________________

Mountain States

Idaho

The Gem State

- name originated from the Shoshone Indian word *ee-dah-how*, which means *sun coming down the mountain* or *daybreak*
- nicknamed the Gem State for the gold, silver and other minerals in the area that brought a mining boom

Borah Peak—12,662 ft. · Craters of the Moon National Monument · Cities of Rock · Ghost Towns—Silver City, Florence, Idaho City, Dixie and Orogrande · Pocatello—contains Old Fort Hall, a reconstruction of a trading post on the Oregon Trail · Hells Canyon—the nation's deepest canyon · Potatoes—grows more than any other state

Circle the capital city. Locate the landmarks found in the above key. Color them on the map.

Page 163

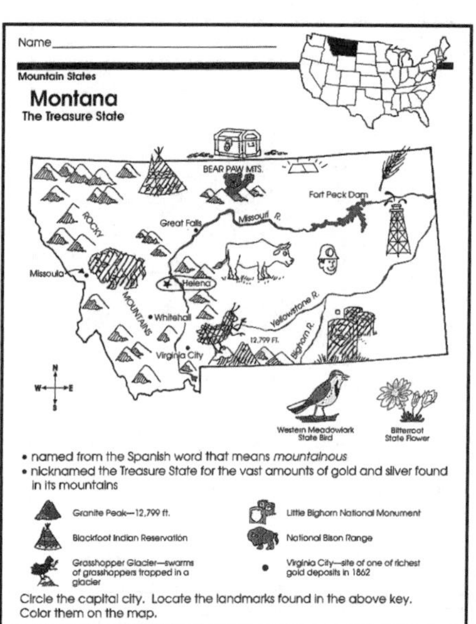

Name____________________________

Mountain States

Montana

The Treasure State

- named from the Spanish word that means *mountainous*
- nicknamed the Treasure State for the vast amounts of gold and silver found in its mountains

Granite Peak—12,799 ft. · Blackfoot Indian Reservation · Grasshopper Glacier—swarms of grasshoppers trapped in a glacier · Little Bighorn National Monument · National Bison Range · Virginia City—site of one of richest gold deposits in 1862

Circle the capital city. Locate the landmarks found in the above key. Color them on the map.

Page 164

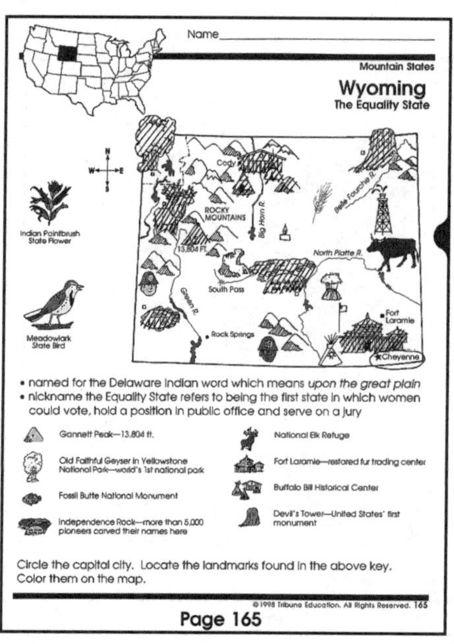

Name____________________________

Mountain States

Wyoming

The Equality State

- named for the Delaware Indian word which means *upon the great plain*
- nickname the Equality State refers to being the first state in which women could vote, hold a position in public office and serve on a jury

Gannett Peak—13,804 ft. · Old Faithful Geyser in Yellowstone National Park—world's 1st national park · Fossil Butte National Monument · Independence Rock—more than 5,000 pioneers carved their names here · National Elk Refuge · Fort Laramie—restored fur trading center · Buffalo Bill Historical Center · Devil's Tower—United States' first monument

Circle the capital city. Locate the landmarks found in the above key. Color them on the map.

Page 165

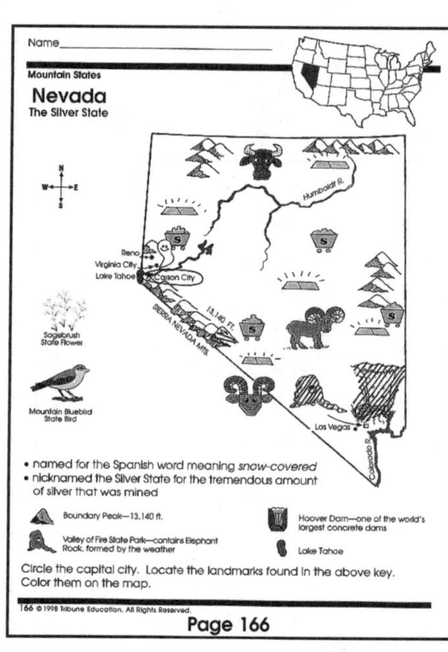

Name____________________________

Mountain States

Nevada

The Silver State

- named for the Spanish word meaning *snow-covered*
- nicknamed the Silver State for the tremendous amount of silver that was mined

Boundary Peak—13,140 ft. · Valley of Fire State Park—contains Elephant Rock, formed by the weather · Hoover Dam—one of the world's largest concrete dams · Lake Tahoe

Circle the capital city. Locate the landmarks found in the above key. Color them on the map.

Page 166

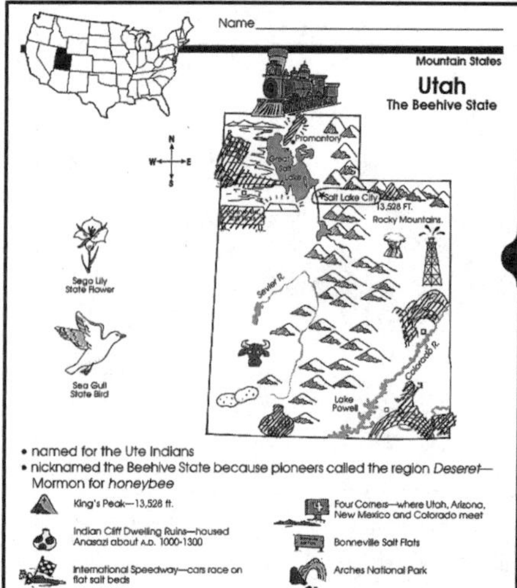

Name____________________________

Mountain States

Utah

The Beehive State

- named for the Ute Indians
- nicknamed the Beehive State because pioneers called the region *Deseret*—Mormon for *honeybee*

King's Peak—13,528 ft. · Indian Cliff Dwelling Ruins—housed Anasazi about A.D. 1000–1300 · International Speedway—cars race on flat salt beds · Promontory—first transcontinental railroad completed in 1869 · Four Corners—where Utah, Arizona, New Mexico and Colorado meet · Bonneville Salt Flats · Arches National Park · Rainbow Bridge National Monument—world's largest natural stone bridge

Circle the capital city. Locate the landmarks found in the above key. Color them on the map.

Page 167

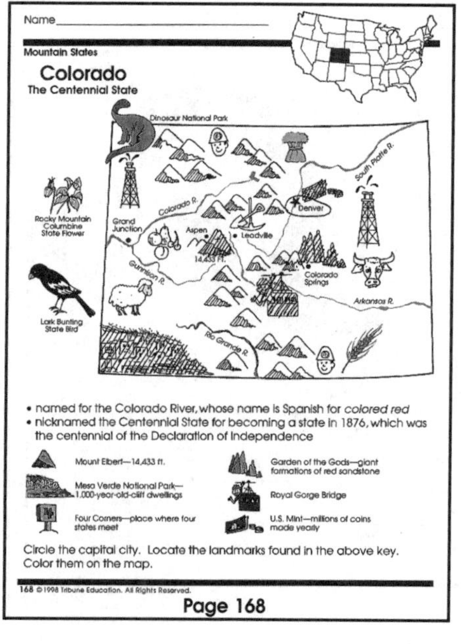

Name____________________________

Mountain States

Colorado

The Centennial State

- named for the Colorado River, whose name is Spanish for *colored red*
- nicknamed the Centennial State for becoming a state in 1876, which was the centennial of the Declaration of Independence

Mount Elbert—14,433 ft. · Mesa Verde National Park—1,000-year-old-cliff dwellings · Four Corners—place where four states meet · Garden of the Gods—giant formations of red sandstone · Royal Gorge Bridge · U.S. Mint—millions of coins made yearly

Circle the capital city. Locate the landmarks found in the above key. Color them on the map.

Page 168

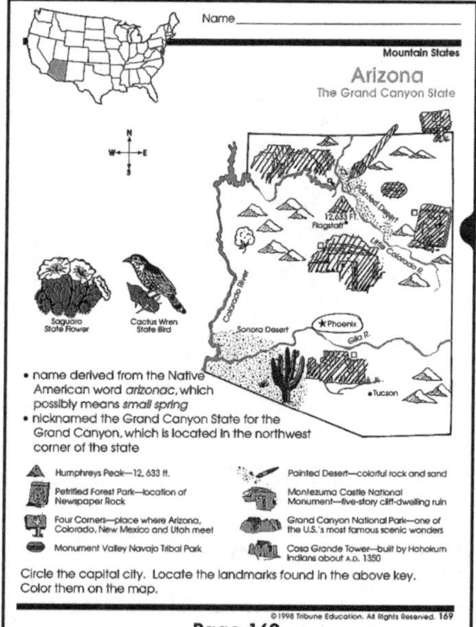

Name____________________________

Mountain States

Arizona

The Grand Canyon State

- name derived from the Native American word *arizonac*, which possibly means *small spring*
- nicknamed the Grand Canyon State for the Grand Canyon, which is located in the northwest corner of the state

Humphreys Peak—12,633 ft. · Petrified Forest Park—location of Newspaper Rock · Four Corners—place where Arizona, Colorado, New Mexico and Utah meet · Monument Valley Navajo Tribal Park · Painted Desert—colorful rock and sand · Montezuma Castle National Monument—five-story cliff-dwelling ruin · Grand Canyon National Park—one of the U.S.'s most famous scenic wonders · Casa Grande Tower—built by Hohokum Indians about A.D. 1350

Circle the capital city. Locate the landmarks found in the above key. Color them on the map.

Page 169

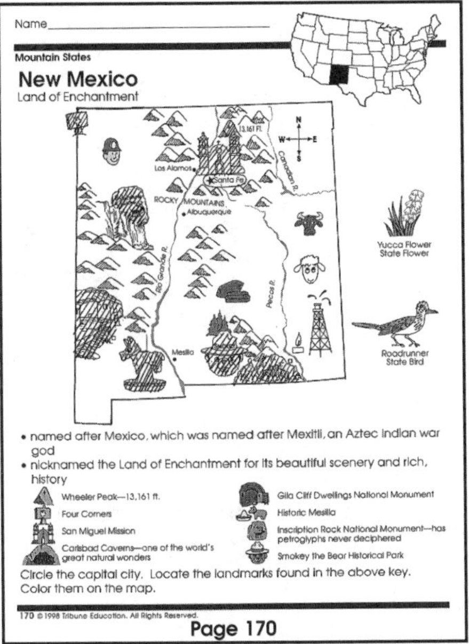
Name________________________

Mountain States

New Mexico
Land of Enchantment

- named after Mexico, which was named after Mexitli, an Aztec Indian war god
- nicknamed the Land of Enchantment for its beautiful scenery and rich, history

Wheeler Peak—13,161 ft. · Four Corners · San Miguel Mission · Carlsbad Caverns—one of the world's great natural wonders · Gila Cliff Dwellings National Monument · Historic Mesilla · Inscription Rock National Monument—has petroglyphs never deciphered · Smokey the Bear Historical Park

Circle the capital city. Locate the landmarks found in the above key. Color them on the map.

Page 170

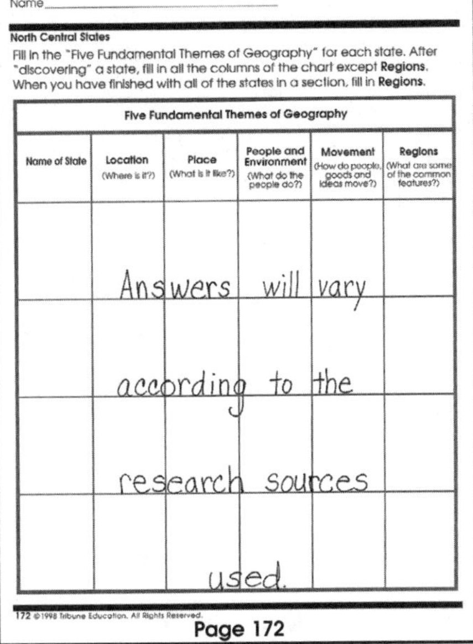
Name________________________

North Central States

Fill in the "Five Fundamental Themes of Geography" for each state. After "discovering" a state, fill in all the columns of the chart except **Regions**. When you have finished with all of the states in a section, fill in **Regions**.

Five Fundamental Themes of Geography

Name of State	Location (Where is it?)	Place (What is it like?)	People and Environment (What do the people do?)	Movement (How do people, goods and ideas move?)	Regions (What are some of the common features?)
Answers will vary according to the research sources used.					

Page 172

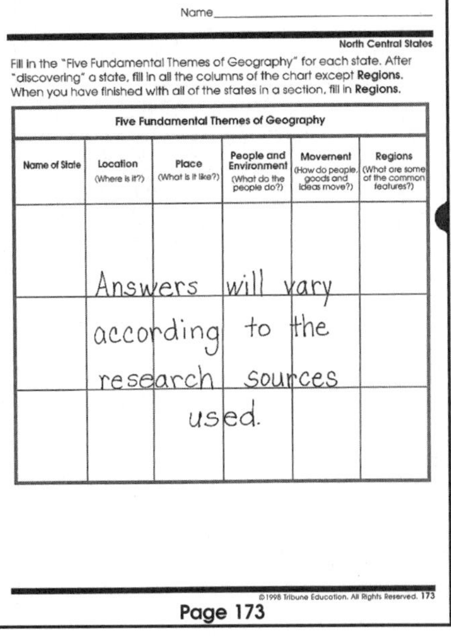
Name________________________

North Central States

Fill in the "Five Fundamental Themes of Geography" for each state. After "discovering" a state, fill in all the columns of the chart except **Regions**. When you have finished with all of the states in a section, fill in **Regions**.

Five Fundamental Themes of Geography

Name of State	Location (Where is it?)	Place (What is it like?)	People and Environment (What do the people do?)	Movement (How do people, goods and ideas move?)	Regions (What are some of the common features?)
Answers will vary according to the research sources used.					

Page 173

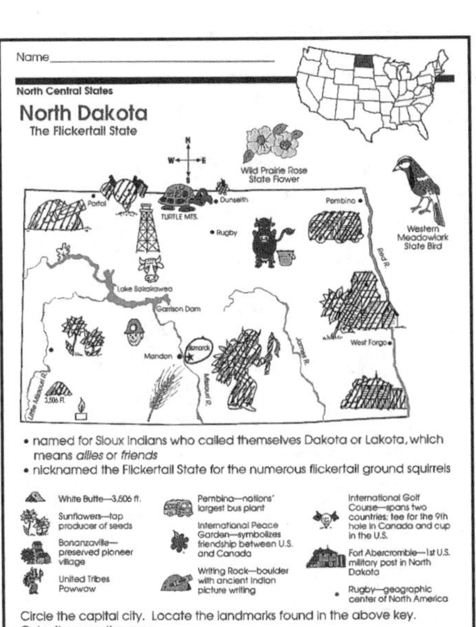
Name________________________

North Central States

North Dakota
The Flickertail State

- named for Sioux Indians who called themselves Dakota or Lakota, which means *allies* or *friends*
- nicknamed the Flickertail State for the numerous flickertail ground squirrels

White Butte—3,506 ft. · Sunflowers—top producer of seeds · Bonanzaville—preserved pioneer village · United Tribes Powwow · Pembina—nations' largest bus plant · International Peace Garden—symbolizes friendship between U.S. and Canada · Writing Rock—boulder with ancient Indian picture writing · International Golf Course—spans two countries; tee for the 9th hole in Canada and cup in the U.S. · Fort Abercrombie—1st U.S. military post in North Dakota · Rugby—geographic center of North America

Circle the capital city. Locate the landmarks found in the above key. Color them on the map.

Page 174

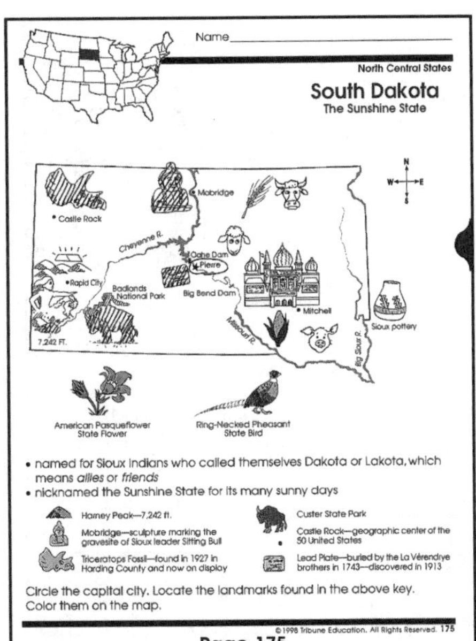
Name________________________

North Central States

South Dakota
The Sunshine State

- named for Sioux Indians who called themselves Dakota or Lakota, which means *allies* or *friends*
- nicknamed the Sunshine State for its many sunny days

Harney Peak—7,242 ft. · Mobridge—sculpture marking the gravesite of Sioux leader Sitting Bull · Triceratops Fossil—found in 1927 in Harding County and now on display · Custer State Park · Castle Rock—geographic center of the 50 United States · Lead Plate—buried by the La Vérendrye brothers in 1743—discovered in 1913

Circle the capital city. Locate the landmarks found in the above key. Color them on the map.

Page 175

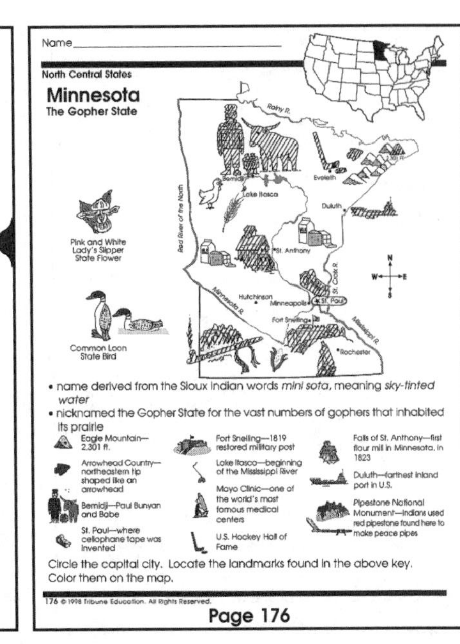
Name________________________

North Central States

Minnesota
The Gopher State

- name derived from the Sioux Indian words *mini sota*, meaning *sky-tinted water*
- nicknamed the Gopher State for the vast numbers of gophers that inhabited its prairie

Eagle Mountain—2,301 ft. · Arrowhead Country—northeastern tip shaped like an arrowhead · Bemidji—Paul Bunyan and Babe · St. Paul—where cellophane tape was invented · Fort Snelling—1819 restored military post · Lake Itasca—beginning of the Mississippi River · Mayo Clinic—one of the world's most famous medical centers · U.S. Hockey Hall of Fame · Falls of St. Anthony—first flour mill in Minnesota, in 1823 · Duluth—farthest inland port in U.S. · Pipestone National Monument—Indians used red pipestone found here to make peace pipes

Circle the capital city. Locate the landmarks found in the above key. Color them on the map.

Page 176

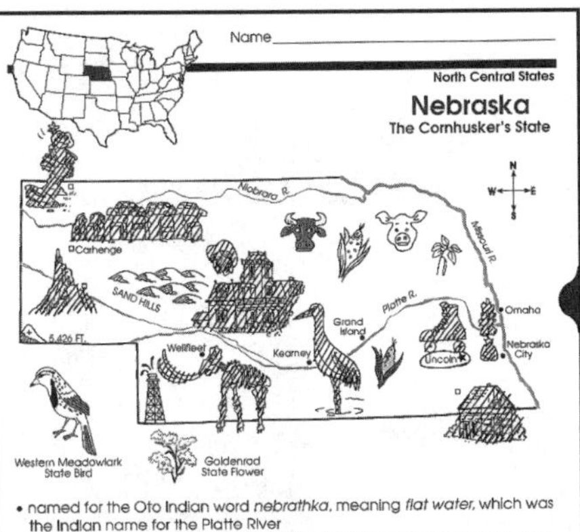
Name________________________

North Central States

Nebraska
The Cornhusker's State

- named for the Oto Indian word *nebrathka*, meaning *flat water*, which was the Indian name for the Platte River
- nicknamed the Cornhusker State for the state's leading crop of corn and for the cornhusking contests that used to be held in the fall

Toadstool Park—in the Badlands, has rock formations resembling toadstools · Wellfleet—largest mammoth fossil ever found · National Museum of Roller Skating · Arbor Lodge—home of Julius Sterling Morton, founder of Arbor Day · Chimney Rock National Historic Site · Carhenge—replica of Stonehenge made of cars · Cranes—about 500,000 stop along the Platte River every spring as they migrate north · Buffalo Bill's home · Homestead National Monument of America—site of the first piece of land claimed under the Homestead Act

Circle the capital city. Locate the landmarks found in the above key. Color them on the map.

Page 177

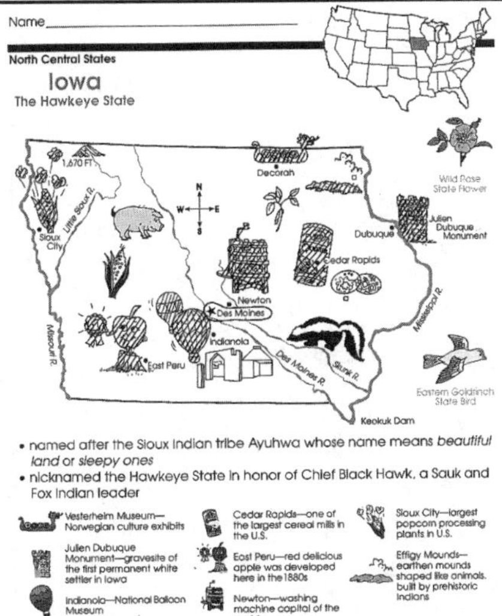
Name________________________

North Central States

Iowa
The Hawkeye State

- named after the Sioux Indian tribe Ayuhwa whose name means *beautiful land* or *sleepy ones*
- nicknamed the Hawkeye State in honor of Chief Black Hawk, a Sauk and Fox Indian leader

Vesterheim Museum—Norwegian culture exhibits · Julien Dubuque Monument—gravesite of the first permanent white settler in Iowa · Indianola—National Balloon Museum · Cedar Rapids—one of the largest cereal mills in the U.S. · East Peru—red delicious apple was developed here in the 1880s · Newton—washing machine capital of the world · Sioux City—largest popcorn processing plants in U.S. · Effigy Mounds—earthen mounds shaped like animals, built by prehistoric Indians

Circle the capital city. Locate the landmarks found in the above key. Color them on the map.

Page 178

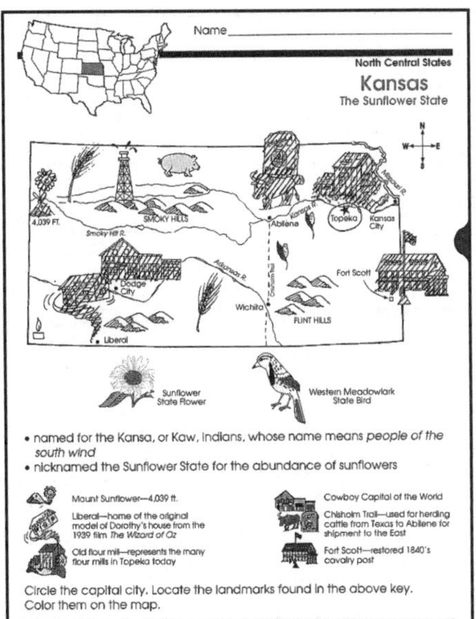
Name________________________

North Central States

Kansas
The Sunflower State

- named for the Kansa, or Kaw, Indians, whose name means *people of the south wind*
- nicknamed the Sunflower State for the abundance of sunflowers

Mount Sunflower—4,039 ft. · Liberal—home of the original model of Dorothy's house from the 1939 film *The Wizard of Oz* · Old flour mill—represents the many flour mills in Topeka today · Cowboy Capital of the World · Chisholm Trail—used for herding cattle from Texas to Abilene for shipment to the East · Fort Scott—restored 1840's cavalry post

Circle the capital city. Locate the landmarks found in the above key. Color them on the map.

Page 179

Name

North Central States

Missouri

The Show Me State

- named for an Indian word meaning *town of the long canoes*
- nickname the Show Me State related to an 1899 speech by Congressman Vandiver in which he indicated he was unimpressed with speeches and wanted to be shown results

Taum Sauk Mountain—1,772 ft.
Pony Express—carried mail from St. Joseph, Missouri to Sacramento, California from 1860 to 1861
Hannibal—contains the home and museum of Mark Twain, who wrote *Tom Sawyer*
Fulton—has a 1990 sculpture using eight Berlin Wall sections
Gateway Arch—tallest monument in U.S.
Boot Heel Country—named because the shape resembles a boot heel
Silver Dollar City—reconstructed 1880s mining town
First ice-cream cone—at Louisiana Purchase Centennial Expo in St. Louis in 1904

Circle the capital city. Locate the landmarks found in the above key. Color them on the map.

Page 180

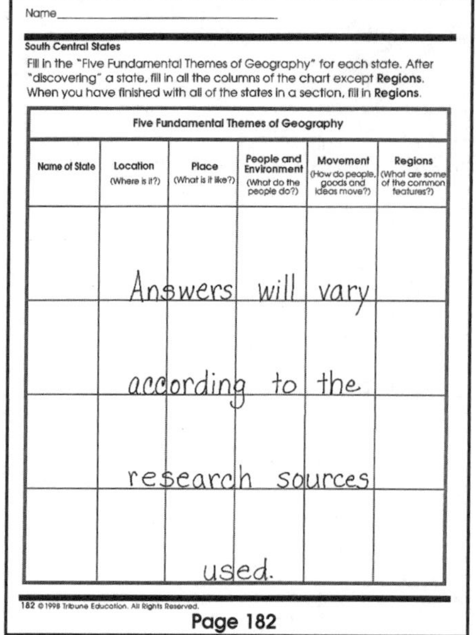

Name

South Central States

Fill in the "Five Fundamental Themes of Geography" for each state. After "discovering" a state, fill in all the columns of the chart except **Regions**. When you have finished with all of the states in a section, fill in **Regions**.

Five Fundamental Themes of Geography

Name of State	Location (Where is it?)	Place (What is it like?)	People and Environment (What do the people do?)	Movement (How do people, goods and ideas move?)	Regions (What are some of the common features?)

Answers will vary according to the research sources used.

Page 182

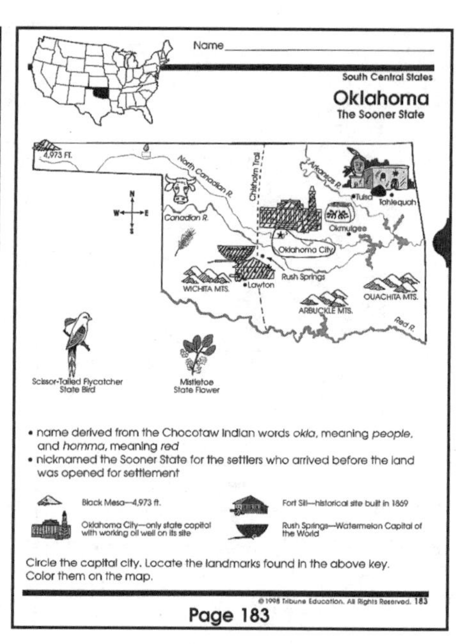

Name

South Central States

Oklahoma

The Sooner State

- name derived from the Chocotaw Indian words *okla*, meaning *people*, and *homma*, meaning *red*
- nicknamed the Sooner State for the settlers who arrived before the land was opened for settlement

Black Mesa—4,973 ft.
Oklahoma City—only state capitol with working oil well on its site
Fort Sill—historical site built in 1869
Rush Springs—Watermelon Capital of the World

Circle the capital city. Locate the landmarks found in the above key. Color them on the map.

Page 183

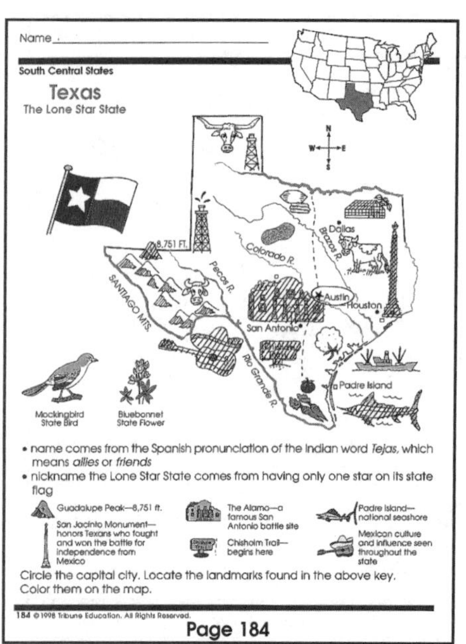

Name

South Central States

Texas

The Lone Star State

- name comes from the Spanish pronunciation of the Indian word *Tejas*, which means *allies* or *friends*
- nickname the Lone Star State comes from having only one star on its state flag

Guadalupe Peak—8,751 ft.
San Jacinto Monument—honors Texans who fought and won the battle for independence from Mexico
The Alamo—a famous San Antonio battle site
Chisholm Trail—begins here
Padre Island—national seashore
Mexican culture and influence seen throughout the state

Circle the capital city. Locate the landmarks found in the above key. Color them on the map.

Page 184

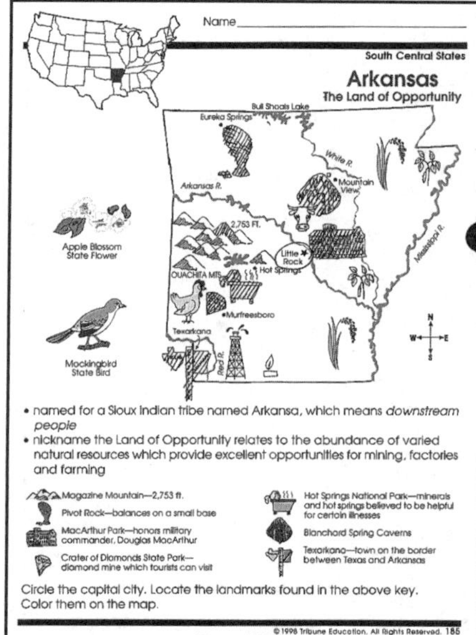

Name

South Central States

Arkansas

The Land of Opportunity

- named for a Sioux Indian tribe named Arkansa, which means *downstream people*
- nickname the Land of Opportunity relates to the abundance of varied natural resources which provide excellent opportunities for mining, factories and farming

Magazine Mountain—2,753 ft.
Pivot Rock—balances on a small base
MacArthur Park—honors military commander, Douglas MacArthur
Crater of Diamonds State Park—diamond mine which tourists can visit
Hot Springs National Park—minerals and hot springs believed to be helpful for certain illnesses
Blanchard Spring Caverns
Texarkana—town on the border between Texas and Arkansas

Circle the capital city. Locate the landmarks found in the above key. Color them on the map.

Page 185

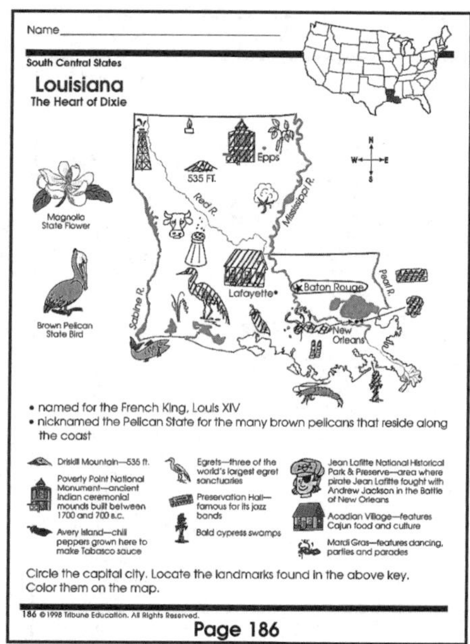

Name

South Central States

Louisiana

The Heart of Dixie

- named for the French King, Louis XIV
- nicknamed the Pelican State for the many brown pelicans that reside along the coast

Driskill Mountain—535 ft.
Poverty Point National Monument—ancient Indian ceremonial mounds built between 1700 and 700 B.C.
Avery Island—chili peppers grown here to make Tabasco sauce
Egrets—three of the world's largest egret sanctuaries
Preservation Hall—famous for its jazz bands
Bald cypress swamps
Jean Lafitte National Historical Park & Preserve—area where pirate Jean Lafitte fought with Andrew Jackson in the Battle of New Orleans
Acadian Village—features Cajun food and culture
Mardi Gras—features dancing, parties and parades

Circle the capital city. Locate the landmarks found in the above key. Color them on the map.

Page 186

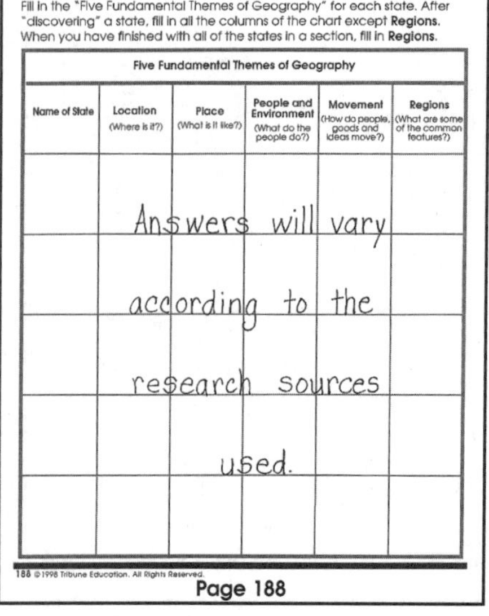

Name

Midwest States

Fill in the "Five Fundamental Themes of Geography" for each state. After "discovering" a state, fill in all the columns of the chart except **Regions**. When you have finished with all of the states in a section, fill in **Regions**.

Five Fundamental Themes of Geography

Name of State	Location (Where is it?)	Place (What is it like?)	People and Environment (What do the people do?)	Movement (How do people, goods and ideas move?)	Regions (What are some of the common features?)

Answers will vary according to the research sources used.

Page 188

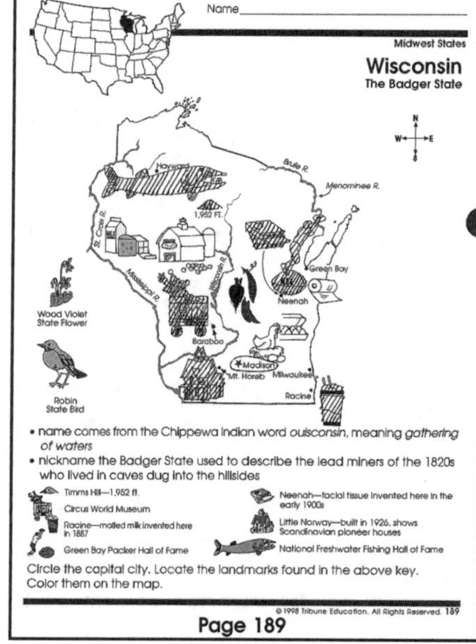

Name

Midwest States

Wisconsin

The Badger State

- name comes from the Chippewa Indian word *ouisconsin*, meaning *gathering of waters*
- nickname the Badger State used to describe the lead miners of the 1820s who lived in caves dug into the hillsides

Timms Hill—1,952 ft.
Circus World Museum
Racine—malted milk invented here in 1887
Green Bay Packer Hall of Fame
Neenah—facial tissue invented here in the early 1900s
Little Norway—built in 1926, shows Scandinavian pioneer houses
National Freshwater Fishing Hall of Fame

Circle the capital city. Locate the landmarks found in the above key. Color them on the map.

Page 189

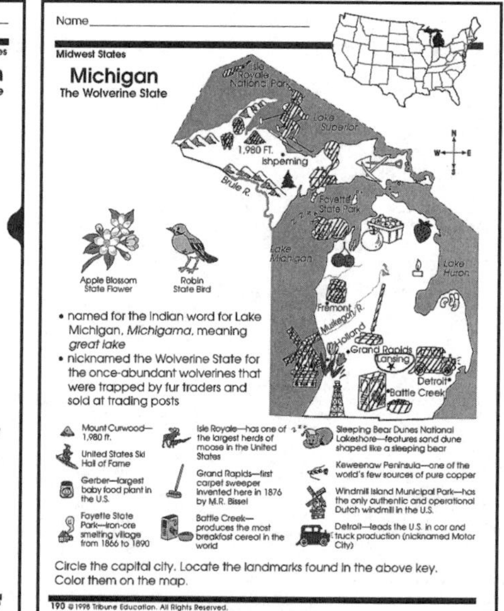

Name

Midwest States

Michigan

The Wolverine State

- named for the Indian word for Lake Michigan, *Michigama*, meaning *great lake*
- nicknamed the Wolverine State for the once-abundant wolverines that were trapped by fur traders and sold at trading posts

Mount Curwood—1,980 ft.
United States Ski Hall of Fame
Gerber—largest baby food plant in the U.S.
Fayette State Park—iron-ore smelting village from 1866 to 1890
Isle Royale—has one of the largest herds of moose in the United States
Grand Rapids—first carpet sweeper invented here in 1876 by M.R. Bissel
Battle Creek—produces the most breakfast cereal in the world
Sleeping Bear Dunes National Lakeshore—features sand dune shaped like a sleeping bear
Keweenaw Peninsula—one of the world's few sources of pure copper
Windmill Island Municipal Park—has the only authentic and operational Dutch windmill in the U.S.
Detroit—leads the U.S. in car and truck production (nicknamed Motor City)

Circle the capital city. Locate the landmarks found in the above key. Color them on the map.

Page 190

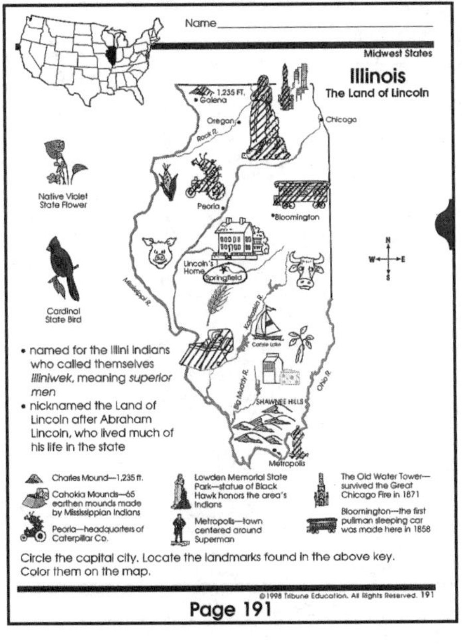
Name____________________________

Midwest States

Illinois

The Land of Lincoln

- named for the Illini Indians who called themselves *Illiniwek*, meaning *superior men*
- nicknamed the Land of Lincoln after Abraham Lincoln, who lived much of his life in the state

Charles Mound—1,235 ft.

Cahokia Mounds—65 earthen mounds made by Mississippian Indians

Peoria—headquarters of Caterpillar Co.

Lowden Memorial State Park—statue of Black Hawk honors the area's Indians

Metropolis—town centered around Superman

The Old Water Tower—survived the Great Chicago Fire in 1871

Bloomington—the first pullman sleeping car was made here in 1858

Circle the capital city. Locate the landmarks found in the above key. Color them on the map.

©1998 Tribune Education. All Rights Reserved. 191

Page 191

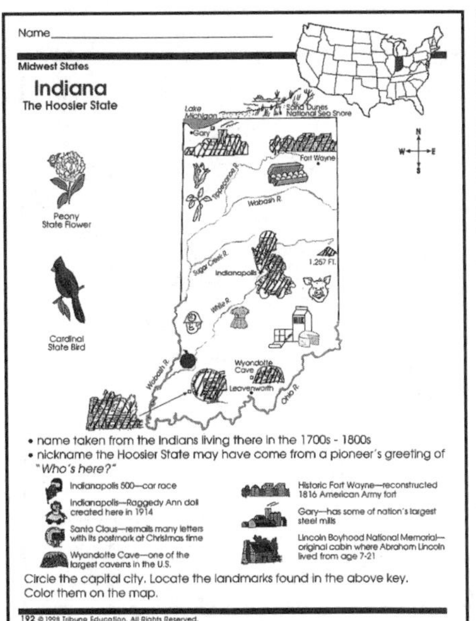
Name____________________________

Midwest States

Indiana

The Hoosier State

- name taken from the Indians living there in the 1700s - 1800s
- nickname the Hoosier State may have come from a pioneer's greeting of "*Who's here?*"

Indianapolis 500—car race

Indianapolis—Raggedy Ann doll created here in 1914

Santa Claus—remails many letters with its postmark at Christmas time

Wyandotte Cave—one of the largest caverns in the U.S.

Historic Fort Wayne—reconstructed 1816 American Army fort

Gary—has some of nation's largest steel mills

Lincoln Boyhood National Memorial—original cabin where Abraham Lincoln lived from age 7-21

Circle the capital city. Locate the landmarks found in the above key. Color them on the map.

192 ©1998 Tribune Education. All Rights Reserved.

Page 192

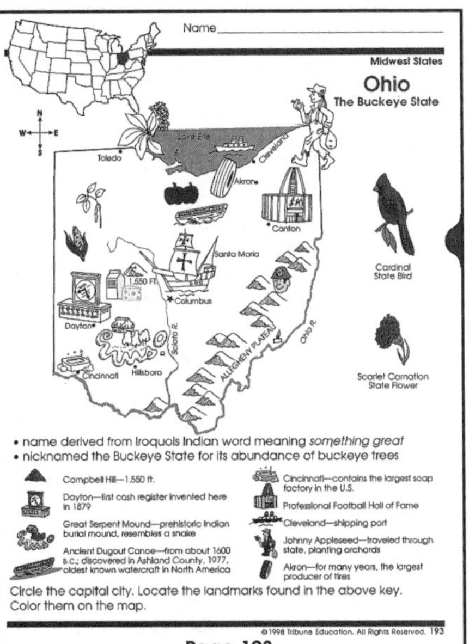
Name____________________________

Midwest States

Ohio

The Buckeye State

- name derived from Iroquois Indian word meaning *something great*
- nicknamed the Buckeye State for its abundance of buckeye trees

Campbell Hill—1,550 ft.

Dayton—first cash register invented here in 1879

Great Serpent Mound—prehistoric Indian burial mound, resembles a snake

Ancient Dugout Canoe—from about 1600 B.C.; discovered in Ashland County, 1977, oldest known watercraft in North America

Cincinnati—contains the largest soap factory in the U.S.

Professional Football Hall of Fame

Cleveland—shipping port

Johnny Appleseed—traveled through state, planting orchards

Akron—for many years, the largest producer of tires

Circle the capital city. Locate the landmarks found in the above key. Color them on the map.

©1998 Tribune Education. All Rights Reserved. 193

Page 193

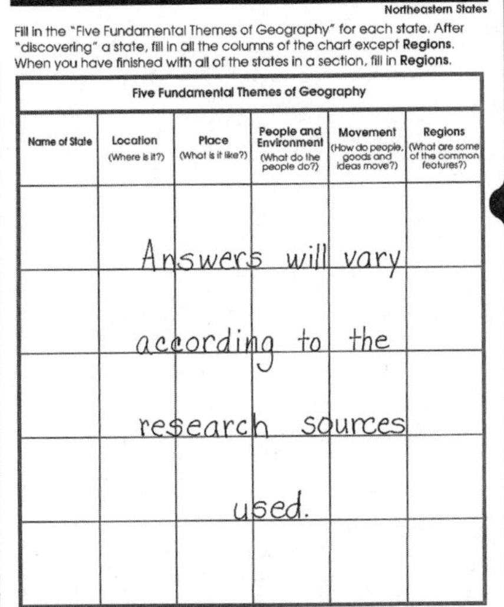
Name____________________________

Northeastern States

Fill in the "Five Fundamental Themes of Geography" for each state. After "discovering" a state, fill in all the columns of the chart except **Regions**. When you have finished with all of the states in a section, fill in **Regions**.

Five Fundamental Themes of Geography					
Name of State	Location (Where is it?)	Place (What is it like?)	People and Environment (What do the people do?)	Movement (How do people, goods and ideas move?)	Regions (What are some of the common features?)
	Answers will vary according to the research sources used.				

©1998 Tribune Education. All Rights Reserved. 195

Page 195

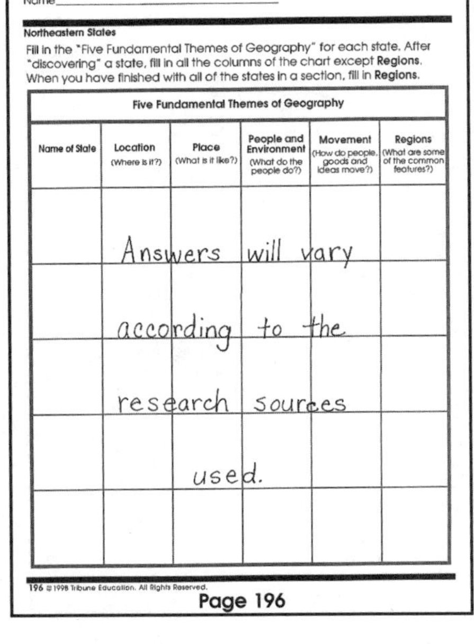
Name____________________________

Northeastern States

Fill in the "Five Fundamental Themes of Geography" for each state. After "discovering" a state, fill in all the columns of the chart except **Regions**. When you have finished with all of the states in a section, fill in **Regions**.

Five Fundamental Themes of Geography					
Name of State	Location (Where is it?)	Place (What is it like?)	People and Environment (What do the people do?)	Movement (How do people, goods and ideas move?)	Regions (What are some of the common features?)
	Answers will vary according to the research sources used.				

196 ©1998 Tribune Education. All Rights Reserved.

Page 196

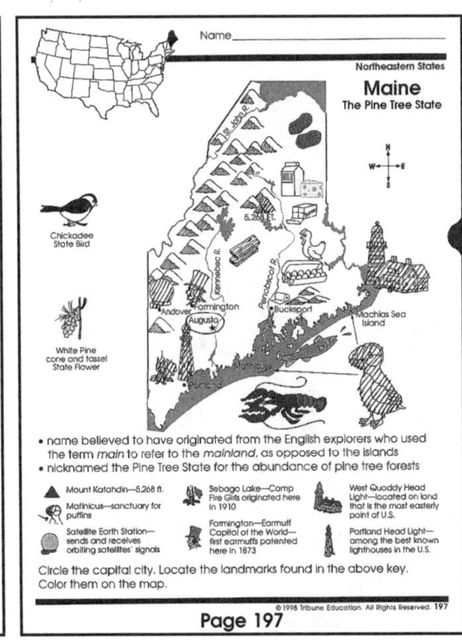
Name____________________________

Northeastern States

Maine

The Pine Tree State

- name believed to have originated from the English explorers who used the term *main* to refer to the *mainland*, as opposed to the islands
- nicknamed the Pine Tree State for the abundance of pine tree forests

Mount Katahdin—5,268 ft.

Matinicus—sanctuary for puffins

Satellite Earth Station—sends and receives orbiting satellites' signals

Sebago Lake—Camp Fire Girls originated here in 1910

Farmington—Earmuff Capital of the World—first earmuffs patented here in 1873

West Quoddy Head Light—located on land that is the most easterly point of U.S.

Portland Head Light—among the best known lighthouses in the U.S.

Circle the capital city. Locate the landmarks found in the above key. Color them on the map.

©1998 Tribune Education. All Rights Reserved. 197

Page 197

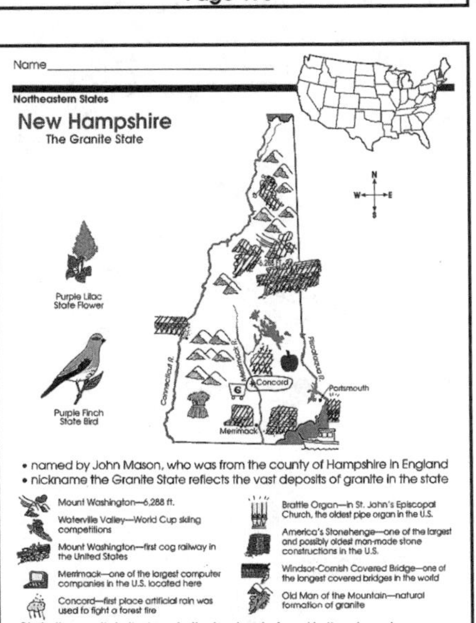
Name____________________________

Northeastern States

New Hampshire

The Granite State

- named by John Mason, who was from the county of Hampshire in England
- nickname the Granite State reflects the vast deposits of granite in the state

Mount Washington—6,288 ft.

Waterville Valley—World Cup skiing competitions

Mount Washington—first cog railway in the United States

Merrimack—one of the largest computer companies in the U.S. located here

Concord—first place artificial rain was used to fight a forest fire

Brattle Organ—in St. John's Episcopal Church, the oldest pipe organ in the U.S.

America's Stonehenge—one of the largest and possibly oldest man-made stone constructions in the U.S.

Windsor-Cornish Covered Bridge—one of the longest covered bridges in the world

Old Man of the Mountain—natural formation of granite

Circle the capital city. Locate the landmarks found in the above key. Color them on the map.

198 ©1998 Tribune Education. All Rights Reserved.

Page 198

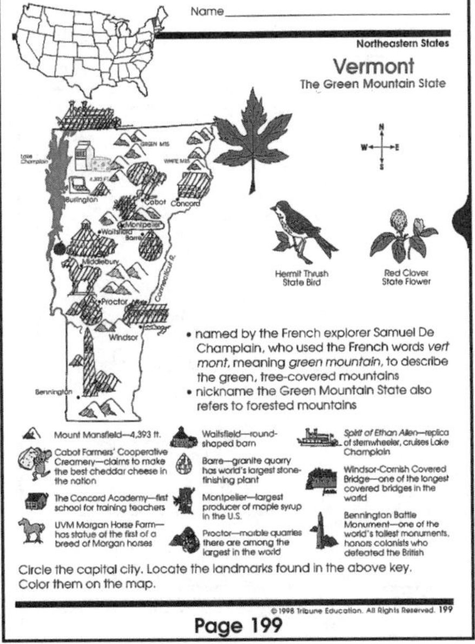
Name____________________________

Northeastern States

Vermont

The Green Mountain State

- named by the French explorer Samuel De Champlain, who used the French words *vert mont*, meaning *green mountain*, to describe the green, tree-covered mountains
- nickname the Green Mountain State also refers to forested mountains

Mount Mansfield—4,393 ft.

Cabot Farmers' Cooperative Creamery—claims to make the best cheddar cheese in the nation

The Concord Academy—first school for training teachers

UVM Morgan Horse Farm—has statue of the first of a breed of Morgan horses

Waitsfield—round-shaped barn

Barre—granite quarry has world's largest stone-finishing plant

Montpelier—largest producer of maple syrup in the U.S.

Proctor—marble quarries there are among the largest in the world

Spirit of Ethan Allen—replica of sternwheeler, cruises Lake Champlain

Windsor-Cornish Covered Bridge—one of the longest covered bridges in the world

Bennington Battle Monument—one of the world's tallest monuments, honors colonists who defeated the British

Circle the capital city. Locate the landmarks found in the above key. Color them on the map.

©1998 Tribune Education. All Rights Reserved. 199

Page 199

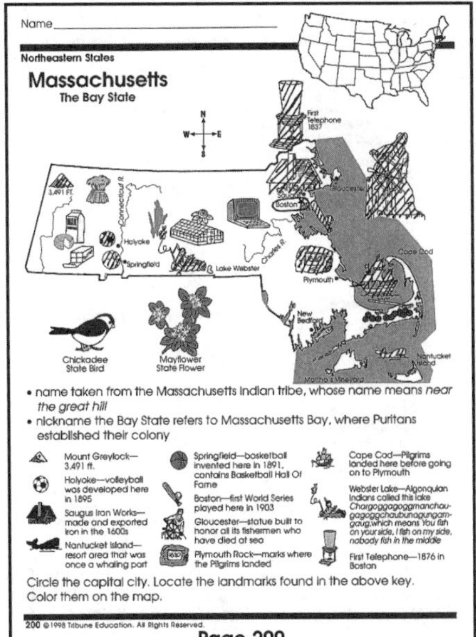
Name____________________________

Northeastern States

Massachusetts

The Bay State

- name taken from the Massachusetts Indian tribe, whose name means *near the great hill*
- nickname the Bay State refers to Massachusetts Bay, where Puritans established their colony

Mount Greylock—3,491 ft.

Holyoke—volleyball was developed here in 1895

Saugus Iron Works—made and exported iron in the 1600s

Nantucket Island—resort area that was once a whaling port

Springfield—basketball invented here in 1891, contains Basketball Hall Of Fame

Boston—first World Series played here in 1903

Gloucester—statue built to honor all its fishermen who have died at sea

Plymouth Rock—marks where the Pilgrims landed

Cape Cod—Pilgrims landed here before going on to Plymouth

Webster Lake—Algonquian Indians called this lake *Chargoggagoggmanchaugagoggchaubunagungamaugg*, which means *You fish on your side, I fish on my side, nobody fish in the middle*

First Telephone—1876 in Boston

Circle the capital city. Locate the landmarks found in the above key. Color them on the map.

200 ©1998 Tribune Education. All Rights Reserved.

Page 200

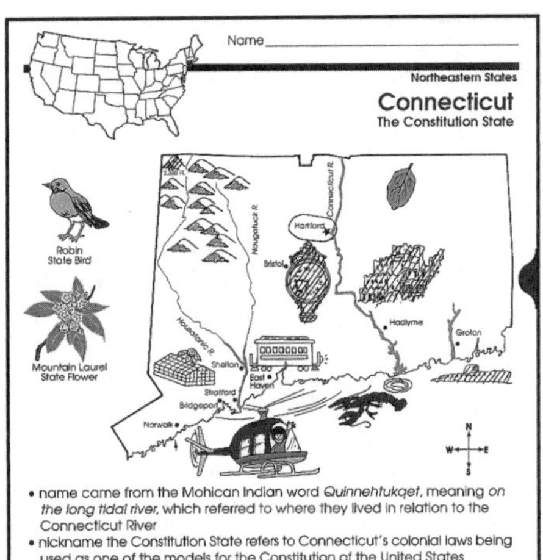

Name ______________________

Northeastern States

Connecticut
The Constitution State

Robin
State Bird

Mountain Laurel
State Flower

- name came from the Mohican Indian word *Quinnehtukqet*, meaning *on the long tidal river*, which referred to where they lived in relation to the Connecticut River
- nickname the Constitution State refers to Connecticut's colonial laws being used as one of the models for the Constitution of the United States

Mount Frissel—2,380 ft.
Great American Clock and Watch Museum
Gillette Castle
Groton—United States Naval Submarine Base

Circle the capital city. Locate the landmarks found in the above key. Color them on the map.

Page 201

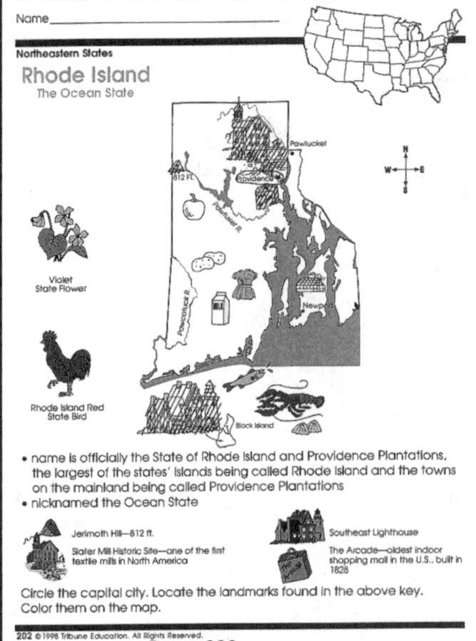

Name ______________________

Northeastern States

Rhode Island
The Ocean State

Violet
State Flower

Rhode Island Red
State Bird

- name is officially the State of Rhode Island and Providence Plantations, the largest of the states' islands being called Rhode Island and the towns on the mainland being called Providence Plantations
- nicknamed the Ocean State

Jerimoth Hill—812 ft.
Slater Mill Historic Site—one of the first textile mills in North America
Southeast Lighthouse
The Arcade—oldest indoor shopping mall in the U.S., built in 1828

Circle the capital city. Locate the landmarks found in the above key. Color them on the map.

Page 202

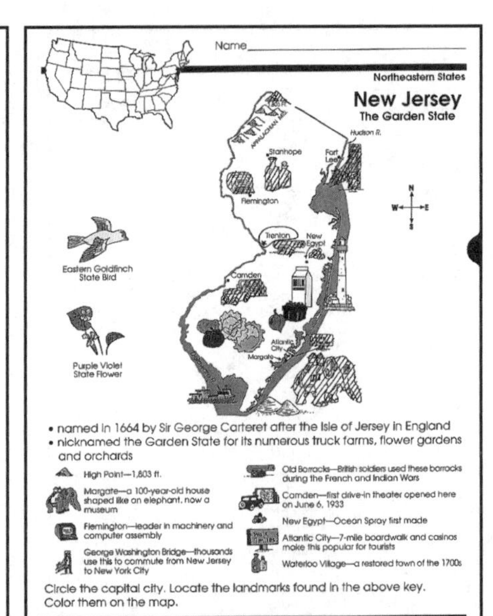

Name ______________________

Northeastern States

New Jersey
The Garden State

Eastern Goldfinch
State Bird

Purple Violet
State Flower

- named in 1664 by Sir George Carteret after the Isle of Jersey in England
- nicknamed the Garden State for its numerous truck farms, flower gardens and orchards

High Point—1,803 ft.
Margate—a 100-year-old house shaped like an elephant, now a museum
Flemington—leader in machinery and computer assembly
George Washington Bridge—thousands use this to commute from New Jersey to New York City
Old Barracks—British soldiers used these barracks during the French and Indian Wars
Camden—first drive-in theater opened here on June 6, 1933
New Egypt—Ocean Spray first made
Atlantic City—7-mile boardwalk and casinos make this popular for tourists
Waterloo Village—a restored town of the 1700s

Circle the capital city. Locate the landmarks found in the above key. Color them on the map.

Page 203

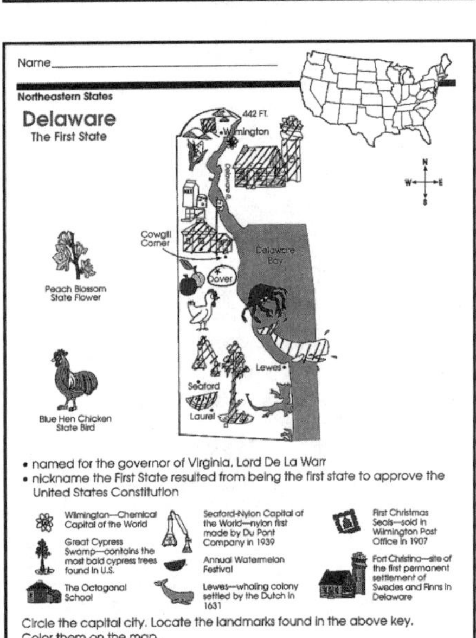

Name ______________________

Northeastern States

Delaware
The First State

Peach Blossom
State Flower

Blue Hen Chicken
State Bird

- named for the governor of Virginia, Lord De La Warr
- nickname the First State resulted from being the first state to approve the United States Constitution

Wilmington—Chemical Capital of the World
Great Cypress Swamp—contains the most bald cypress trees found in U.S.
The Octagonal School
Seaford-Nylon Capital of the World—nylon first made by Du Pont Company in 1939
Annual Watermelon Festival
Lewes—whaling colony settled by the Dutch in 1631
First Christmas Seals—sold in Wilmington Post Office in 1907
Fort Christina—site of the first permanent settlement of Swedes and Finns in Delaware

Circle the capital city. Locate the landmarks found in the above key. Color them on the map.

Page 204

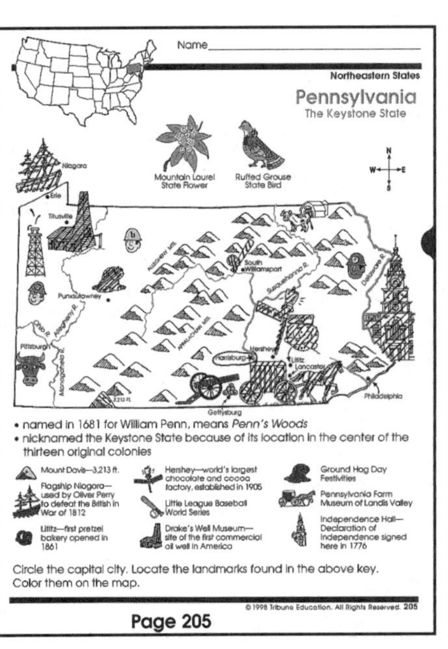

Name ______________________

Northeastern States

Pennsylvania
The Keystone State

Mountain Laurel
State Flower

Ruffed Grouse
State Bird

- named in 1681 for William Penn, means *Penn's Woods*
- nicknamed the Keystone State because of its location in the center of the thirteen original colonies

Mount Davis—3,213 ft.
Flagship Niagara—used by Oliver Perry to defeat the British in War of 1812
Lititz—first pretzel bakery opened in 1861
Hershey—world's largest chocolate and cocoa factory, established in 1905
Little League Baseball World Series
Drake's Well Museum—site of the first commercial oil well in America
Ground Hog Day Festivities
Pennsylvania Farm Museum of Landis Valley
Independence Hall—Declaration of Independence signed here in 1776

Circle the capital city. Locate the landmarks found in the above key. Color them on the map.

Page 205

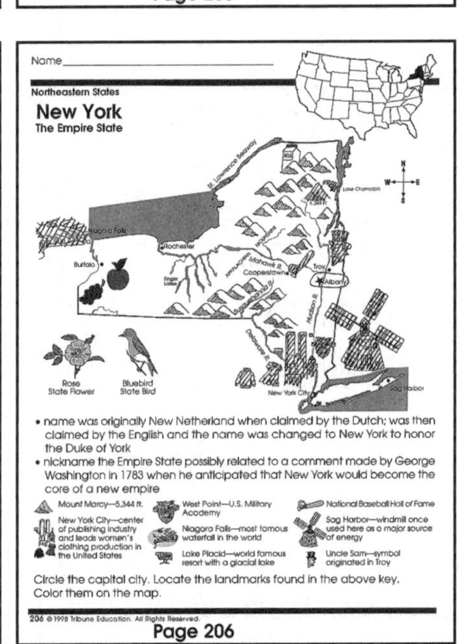

Name ______________________

Northeastern States

New York
The Empire State

Rose
State Flower

Bluebird
State Bird

- name was originally New Netherland when claimed by the Dutch; was then claimed by the English and the name was changed to New York to honor the Duke of York
- nickname the Empire State possibly related to a comment made by George Washington in 1783 when he anticipated that New York would become the core of a new empire

Mount Marcy—5,344 ft.
New York City—center of publishing industry and leads women's clothing production in the United States
West Point—U.S. Military Academy
Niagara Falls—most famous waterfall in the world
Lake Placid—world famous resort with a glacial lake
National Baseball Hall of Fame
Sag Harbor—windmill once used here as a major source of energy
Uncle Sam—symbol originated in Troy

Circle the capital city. Locate the landmarks found in the above key. Color them on the map.

Page 206

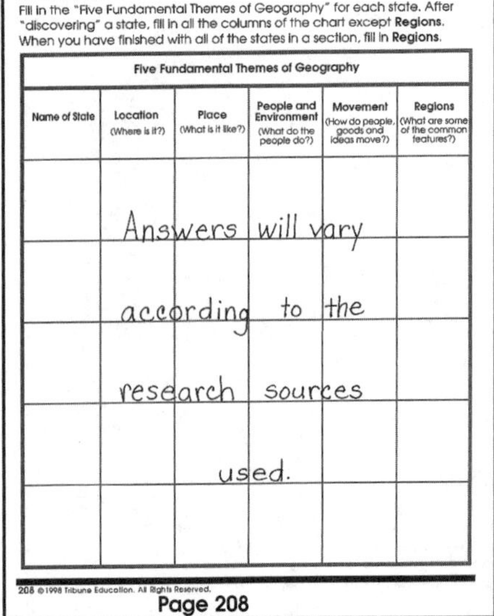

Name ______________________

Southeastern States

Fill in the "Five Fundamental Themes of Geography" for each state. After "discovering" a state, fill in all the columns of the chart except **Regions**. When you have finished with all of the states in a section, fill in **Regions**.

Five Fundamental Themes of Geography

Name of State	Location (Where is it?)	Place (What is it like?)	People and Environment (What do the people do?)	Movement (How do people, goods and ideas move?)	Regions (What are some of the common features?)

Answers will vary according to the research sources used.

Page 208

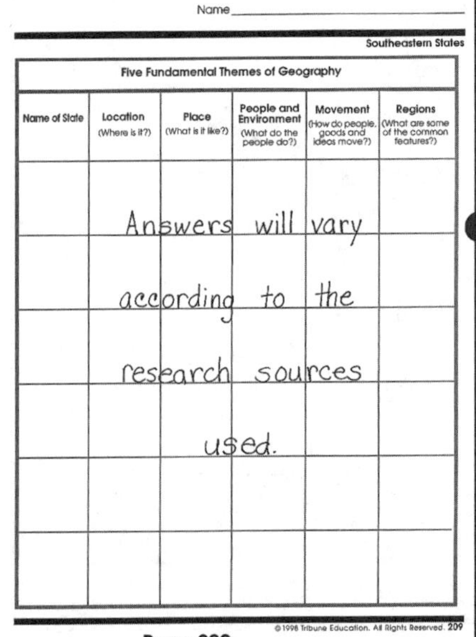

Name ______________________

Southeastern States

Five Fundamental Themes of Geography

Name of State	Location (Where is it?)	Place (What is it like?)	People and Environment (What do the people do?)	Movement (How do people, goods and ideas move?)	Regions (What are some of the common features?)

Answers will vary according to the research sources used.

Page 209

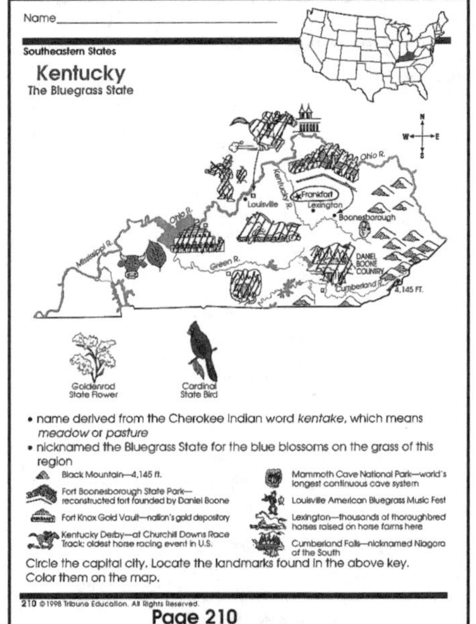

Name ______________________

Southeastern States

Kentucky
The Bluegrass State

Goldenrod
State Flower

Cardinal
State Bird

- name derived from the Cherokee Indian word *kentake*, which means *meadow* or *pasture*
- nicknamed the Bluegrass State for the blue blossoms on the grass of this region

Black Mountain—4,145 ft.
Fort Boonesborough State Park—reconstructed fort founded by Daniel Boone
Fort Knox Gold Vault—nation's gold depository
Kentucky Derby—at Churchill Downs Race Track; oldest horse racing event in U.S.
Mammoth Cave National Park—world's longest continuous cave system
Louisville American Bluegrass Music Fest
Lexington—thousands of thoroughbred horses raised on horse farms here
Cumberland Falls—nicknamed Niagara of the South

Circle the capital city. Locate the landmarks found in the above key. Color them on the map.

Page 210

Name____________________

Southeastern States

West Virginia
The Mountain State

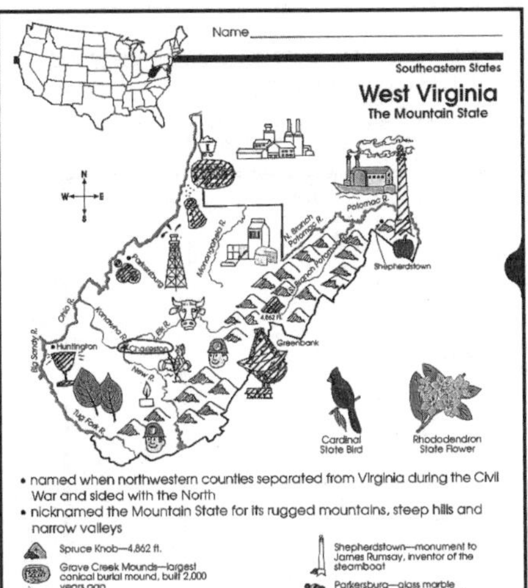

- named when northwestern counties separated from Virginia during the Civil War and sided with the North
- nicknamed the Mountain State for its rugged mountains, steep hills and narrow valleys

- Spruce Knob—4,862 ft.
- Grave Creek Mounds—largest conical burial mound, built 2,000 years ago
- Marshall County—underground salt mines
- Huntington—famous for its glassware and pottery
- Shepherdstown—monument to James Rumsay, inventor of the steamboat
- Parkersburg—glass marble manufacturing center of U.S.
- National Radio Astronomy Observatory

Circle the capital city. Locate the landmarks found in the above key. Color them on the map.

Page 211

Name____________________

Southeastern States

Maryland
The Old Line State

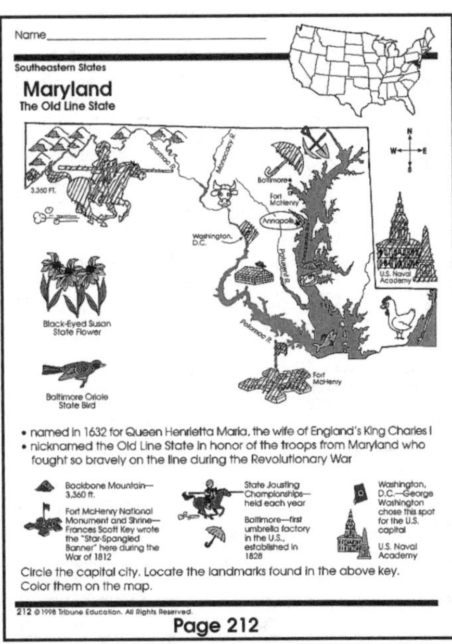

- named in 1632 for Queen Henrietta Maria, the wife of England's King Charles I
- nicknamed the Old Line State in honor of the troops from Maryland who fought so bravely on the line during the Revolutionary War

- Backbone Mountain—3,360 ft.
- Fort McHenry National Monument and Shrine—Frances Scott Key wrote the "Star-Spangled Banner" here during the War of 1812
- State Jousting Championships—held each year
- Baltimore—first umbrella factory in the U.S., established in 1828
- Washington, D.C.—George Washington chose this spot for the U.S. capital
- U.S. Naval Academy

Circle the capital city. Locate the landmarks found in the above key. Color them on the map.

Page 212

Name____________________

Southeastern States

Virginia
Old Dominion

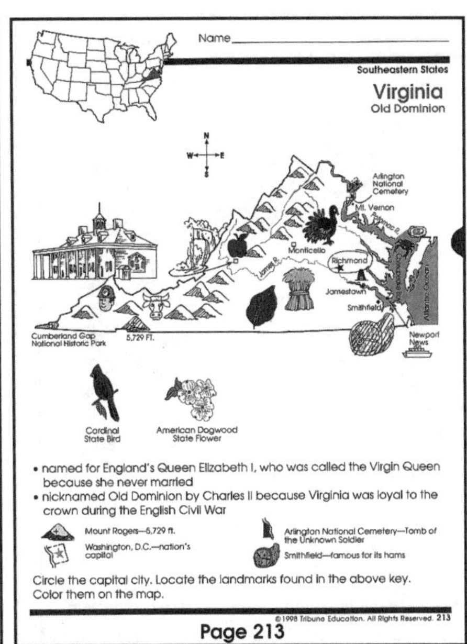

- named for England's Queen Elizabeth I, who was called the Virgin Queen because she never married
- nicknamed Old Dominion by Charles II because Virginia was loyal to the crown during the English Civil War

- Mount Rogers—5,729 ft.
- Washington, D.C.—nation's capital
- Arlington National Cemetery—Tomb of the Unknown Soldier
- Smithfield—famous for its hams

Circle the capital city. Locate the landmarks found in the above key. Color them on the map.

Page 213

Name____________________

Southeastern States

Tennessee
The Volunteer State

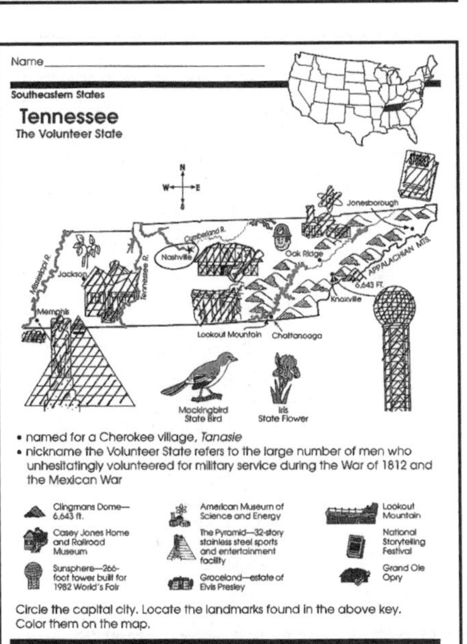

- named for a Cherokee village, *Tanasie*
- nickname the Volunteer State refers to the large number of men who unhesitatingly volunteered for military service during the War of 1812 and the Mexican War

- Clingmans Dome—6,643 ft.
- Casey Jones Home and Railroad Museum
- Sunsphere—266-foot tower built for 1982 World's Fair
- American Museum of Science and Energy
- The Pyramid—32-story stainless steel sports and entertainment facility
- Graceland—estate of Elvis Presley
- Lookout Mountain
- National Storytelling Festival
- Grand Ole Opry

Circle the capital city. Locate the landmarks found in the above key. Color them on the map.

Page 214

Name____________________

Southeastern States

North Carolina
The Tarheel State

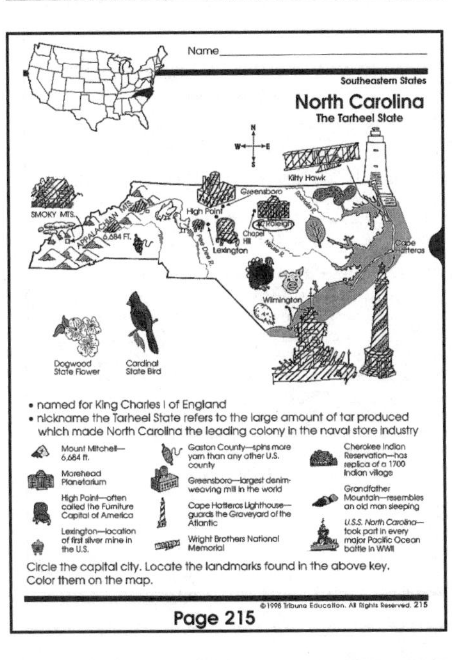

- named for King Charles I of England
- nickname the Tarheel State refers to the large amount of tar produced which made North Carolina the leading colony in the naval store industry

- Mount Mitchell—6,684 ft.
- Morehead Planetarium
- High Point—often called the Furniture Capital of America
- Lexington—location of first silver mine in the U.S.
- Gaston County—spins more yarn than any other U.S. county
- Greensboro—largest denim-weaving mill in the world
- Cape Hatteras Lighthouse—guards the Graveyard of the Atlantic
- Wright Brothers National Memorial
- Cherokee Indian Reservation—has replica of a 1700 Indian village
- Grandfather Mountain—resembles an old man sleeping
- *U.S.S. North Carolina*—took part in every major Pacific Ocean battle in WWII

Circle the capital city. Locate the landmarks found in the above key. Color them on the map.

Page 215

Name____________________

Southeastern States

South Carolina
The Palmetto State

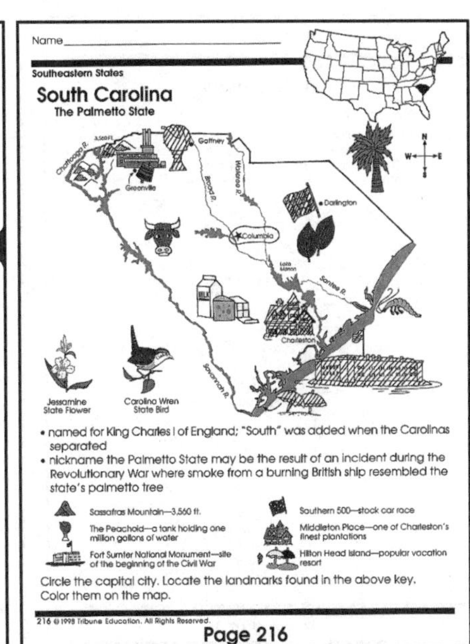

- named for King Charles I of England; "South" was added when the Carolinas separated
- nickname the Palmetto State may be the result of an incident during the Revolutionary War where smoke from a burning British ship resembled the state's palmetto tree

- Sassafras Mountain—3,560 ft.
- The Peachoid—a tank holding one million gallons of water
- Fort Sumter National Monument—site of the beginning of the Civil War
- Southern 500—stock car race
- Middleton Place—one of Charleston's finest plantations
- Hilton Head Island—popular vacation resort

Circle the capital city. Locate the landmarks found in the above key. Color them on the map.

Page 216

Name____________________

Southeastern States

Mississippi
The Magnolia State

- name taken from two Indian words, *misi* and *sipi* meaning *big river* or *great water*
- nickname the Magnolia State refers to the many magnolia trees that grow in the state

- Woodall Mountain—806 ft.
- Delta Blues Museum—dedicated to blues musicians and music
- Shrimp Festival—chief shrimp-packing port
- Elvis Presley Park—site of famous rock 'n' roll singer's birthplace
- Vicksburg—site where Coca-Cola was first bottled in 1894
- *Delta Queen*—built in 1926, tours the Mississippi River
- Natchez—oldest town on the Mississippi River

Circle the capital city. Locate the landmarks found in the above key. Color them on the map.

Page 217

Name____________________

Southeastern States

Alabama
The Heart of Dixie

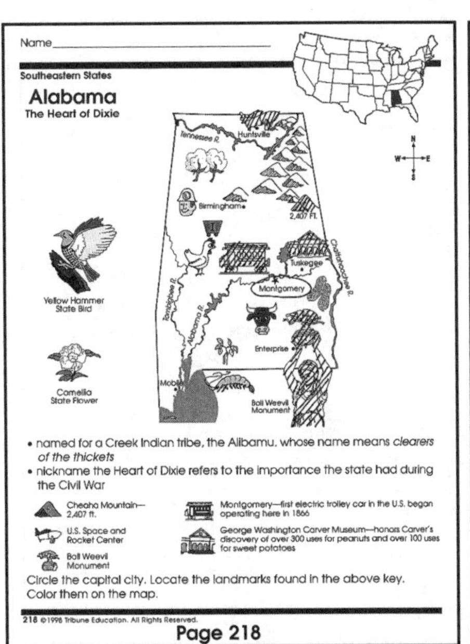

- named for a Creek Indian tribe, the Alibamu, whose name means *clearers of the thickets*
- nickname the Heart of Dixie refers to the importance the state had during the Civil War

- Cheaha Mountain—2,407 ft.
- U.S. Space and Rocket Center
- Boll Weevil Monument
- Montgomery—first electric trolley car in the U.S. began operating here in 1866
- George Washington Carver Museum—honors Carver's discovery of over 300 uses for peanuts and over 100 uses for sweet potatoes

Circle the capital city. Locate the landmarks found in the above key. Color them on the map.

Page 218

Name____________________

Southeastern States

Georgia
The Empire State of the South

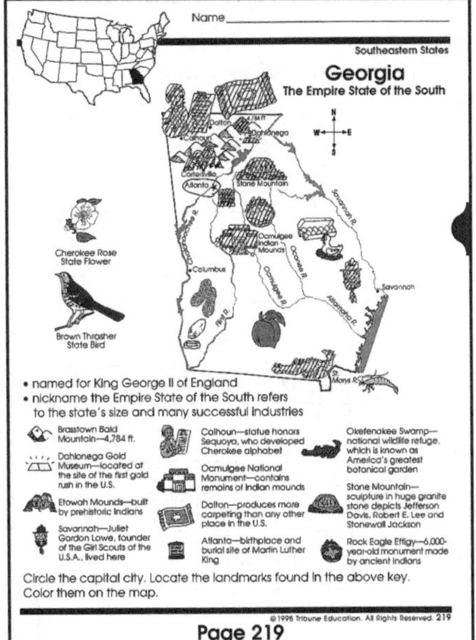

- named for King George II of England
- nickname the Empire State of the South refers to the state's size and many successful industries

- Brasstown Bald Mountain—4,784 ft.
- Dahlonega Gold Museum—located at the site of the first gold rush in the U.S.
- Etowah Mounds—built by prehistoric Indians
- Savannah—Juliet Gordon Lowe, founder of the Girl Scouts of the U.S.A., lived here
- Calhoun—statue honors Sequoya, who developed Cherokee alphabet
- Ocmulgee National Monument—contains remains of Indian mounds
- Dalton—produces more carpeting than any other place in the U.S.
- Atlanta—birthplace and burial site of Martin Luther King
- Okefenokee Swamp—national wildlife refuge, which is known as America's greatest botanical garden
- Stone Mountain—sculpture in huge granite stone depicts Jefferson Davis, Robert E. Lee and Stonewall Jackson
- Rock Eagle Effigy—6,000-year-old monument made by ancient Indians

Circle the capital city. Locate the landmarks found in the above key. Color them on the map.

Page 219

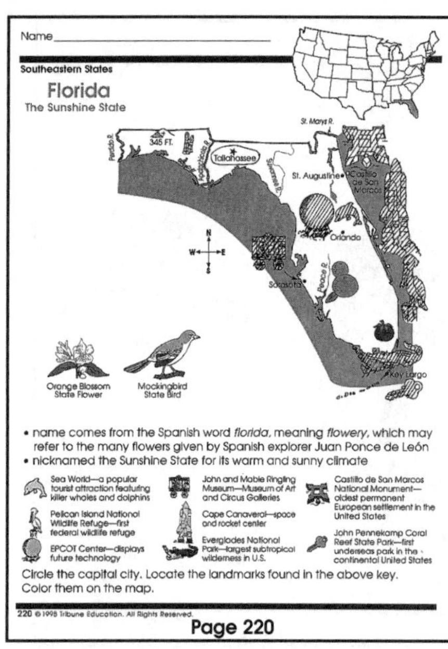
Name________________________

Southeastern States

Florida

The Sunshine State

- name comes from the Spanish word *florida*, meaning *flowery*, which may refer to the many flowers given by Spanish explorer Juan Ponce de León
- nicknamed the Sunshine State for its warm and sunny climate

Sea World—a popular tourist attraction featuring killer whales and dolphins

Pelican Island National Wildlife Refuge—first federal wildlife refuge

EPCOT Center—displays future technology

John and Mable Ringling Museum—Museum of Art and Circus Galleries

Cape Canaveral—space and rocket center

Everglades National Park—largest subtropical wilderness in U.S.

Castillo de San Marcos National Monument—oldest permanent European settlement in the United States

John Pennekamp Coral Reef State Park—first undersea park in the continental United States

Circle the capital city. Locate the landmarks found in the above key. Color them on the map.

Page 220

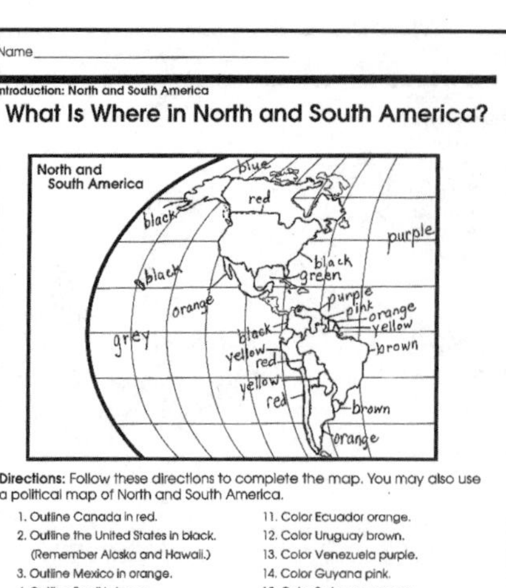
Name________________________

Introduction: North and South America

What Is Where in North and South America?

Directions: Follow these directions to complete the map. You may also use a political map of North and South America.

1. Outline Canada in red.
2. Outline the United States in black. (Remember Alaska and Hawaii.)
3. Outline Mexico in orange.
4. Outline Brazil in brown.
5. Outline Chile in red.
6. Outline Argentina in orange.
7. Outline Paraguay in yellow.
8. Outline Colombia in black.
9. Outline Bolivia in red.
10. Color Peru yellow.
11. Color Ecuador orange.
12. Color Uruguay brown.
13. Color Venezuela purple.
14. Color Guyana pink.
15. Color Suriname orange.
16. Color French Guiana yellow.
17. Color the Gulf of Mexico green.
18. Color the Arctic Ocean blue.
19. Color the Pacific Ocean grey.
20. Color the Atlantic Ocean purple.

Page 222

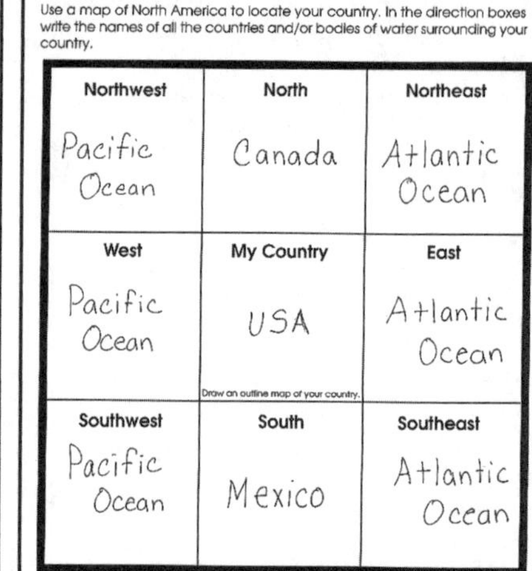
Name________________________

Introduction: North and South America

Neighboring Countries

Use a map of North America to locate your country. In the direction boxes write the names of all the countries and/or bodies of water surrounding your country.

Northwest	North	Northeast
Pacific Ocean	Canada	Atlantic Ocean
West	**My Country**	**East**
Pacific Ocean	USA Draw an outline map of your country.	Atlantic Ocean
Southwest	**South**	**Southeast**
Pacific Ocean	Mexico	Atlantic Ocean

Page 223

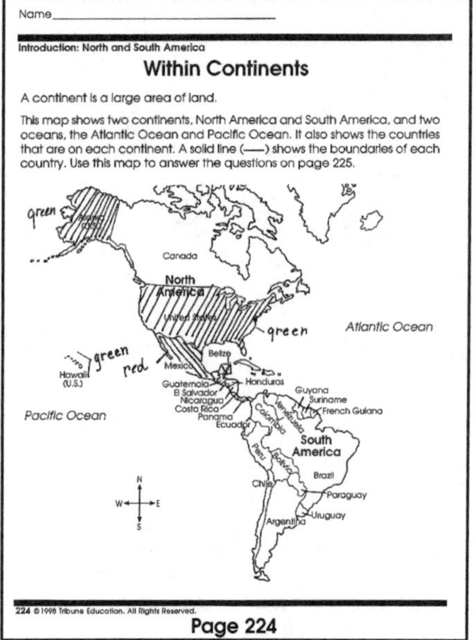
Name________________________

Introduction: North and South America

Within Continents

A continent is a large area of land.

This map shows two continents, North America and South America, and two oceans, the Atlantic Ocean and Pacific Ocean. It also shows the countries that are on each continent. A solid line (——) shows the boundaries of each country. Use this map to answer the questions on page 225.

Page 224

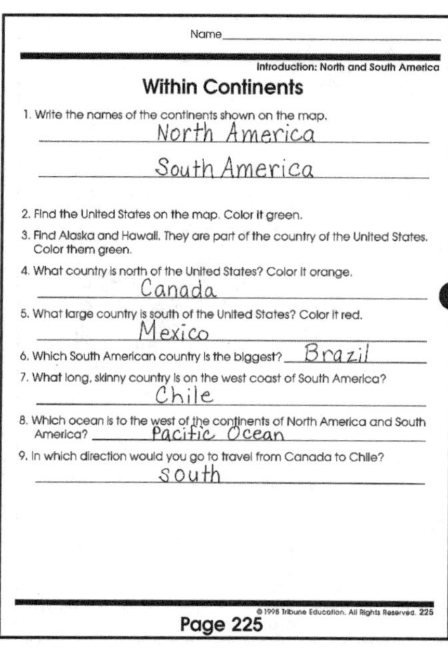
Name________________________

Introduction: North and South America

Within Continents

1. Write the names of the continents shown on the map. North America / South America
2. Find the United States on the map. Color it green.
3. Find Alaska and Hawaii. They are part of the country of the United States. Color them green.
4. What country is north of the United States? Color it orange. Canada
5. What large country is south of the United States? Color it red. Mexico
6. Which South American country is the biggest? Brazil
7. What long, skinny country is on the west coast of South America? Chile
8. Which ocean is to the west of the continents of North America and South America? Pacific Ocean
9. In which direction would you go to travel from Canada to Chile? south

Page 225

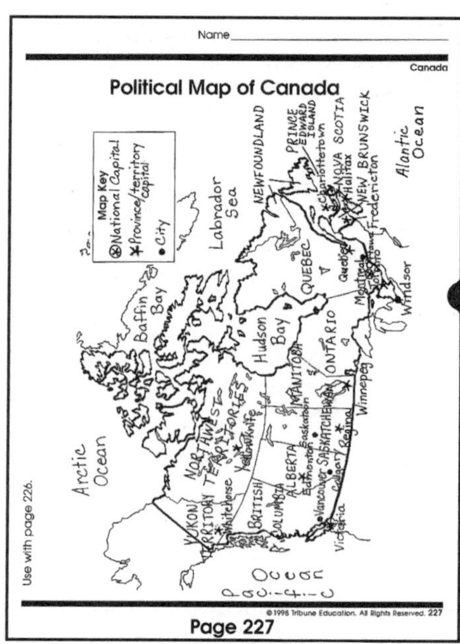
Name________________________

Canada

Political Map of Canada

Page 227

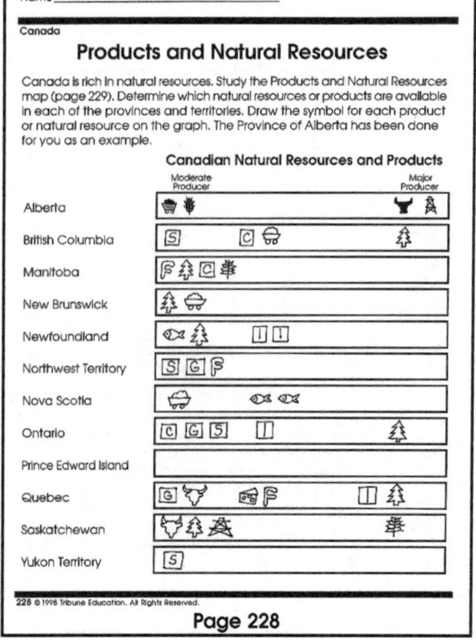
Name________________________

Canada

Products and Natural Resources

Canada is rich in natural resources. Study the Products and Natural Resources map (page 229). Determine which natural resources or products are available in each of the provinces and territories. Draw the symbol for each product or natural resource on the graph. The Province of Alberta has been done for you as an example.

Canadian Natural Resources and Products

Moderate Producer — Major Producer

Alberta

British Columbia

Manitoba

New Brunswick

Newfoundland

Northwest Territory

Nova Scotia

Ontario

Prince Edward Island

Quebec

Saskatchewan

Yukon Territory

Page 228

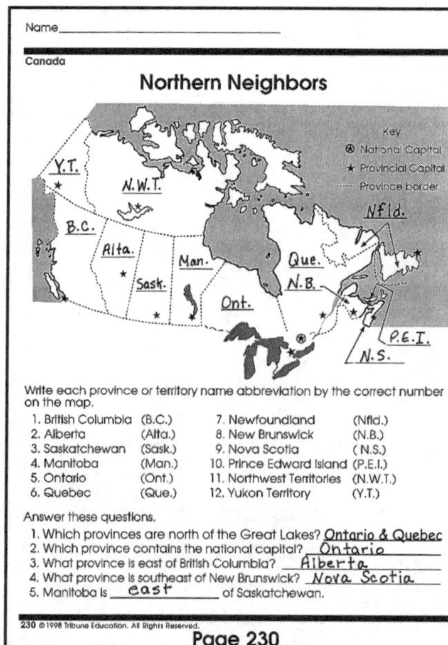
Name________________________

Canada

Northern Neighbors

Write each province or territory name abbreviation by the correct number on the map.

1. British Columbia (B.C.)
2. Alberta (Alta.)
3. Saskatchewan (Sask.)
4. Manitoba (Man.)
5. Ontario (Ont.)
6. Quebec (Que.)
7. Newfoundland (Nfld.)
8. New Brunswick (N.B.)
9. Nova Scotia (N.S.)
10. Prince Edward Island (P.E.I.)
11. Northwest Territories (N.W.T.)
12. Yukon Territory (Y.T.)

Answer these questions.

1. Which provinces are north of the Great Lakes? Ontario & Quebec
2. Which province contains the national capital? Ontario
3. What province is east of British Columbia? Alberta
4. What province is southeast of New Brunswick? Nova Scotia
5. Manitoba is east of Saskatchewan.

Page 230

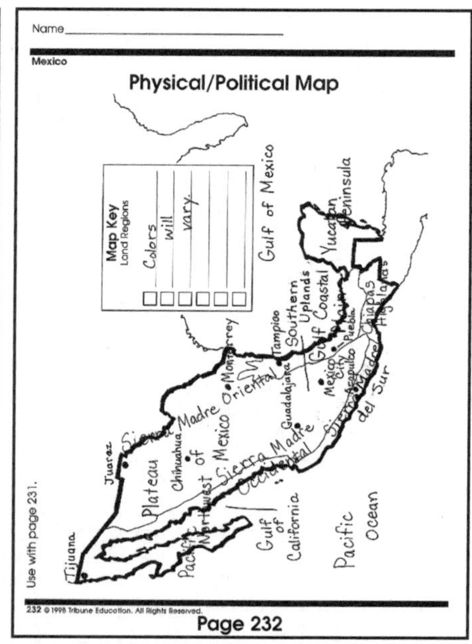
Name________________________

Mexico

Physical/Political Map

Page 232

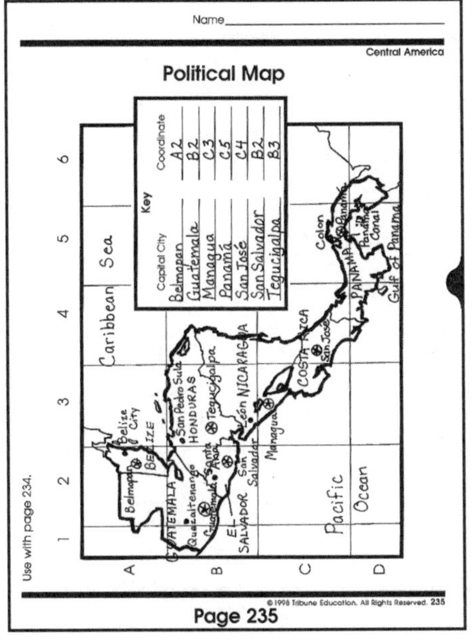
Name______________

Central America

Political Map

Capital City	Coordinate
Belmopan	A2
Guatemala	B2
Managua	C3
Panamá	C5
San José	C4
San Salvador	B2
Tegucigalpa	B3

Use with page 234.

Page 235

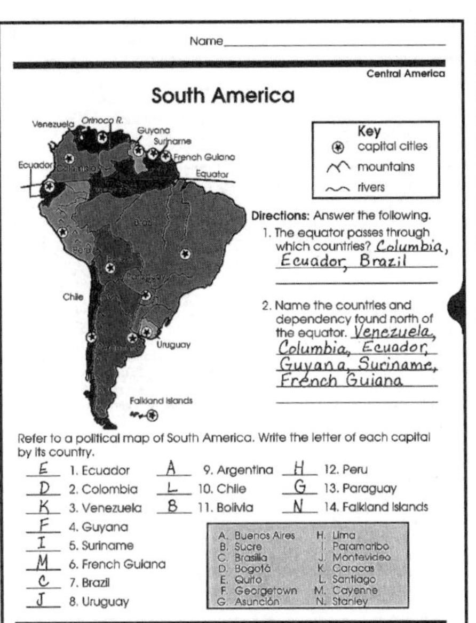
Name______________

Central America

South America

Key
- capital cities
- mountains
- rivers

Directions: Answer the following.

1. The equator passes through which countries? *Columbia, Ecuador, Brazil*
2. Name the countries and dependency found north of the equator. *Venezuela, Columbia, Ecuador, Guyana, Suriname, French Guiana*

Refer to a political map of South America. Write the letter of each capital by its country.

E	1. Ecuador	*A*	9. Argentina	*H*	12. Peru
D	2. Colombia	*L*	10. Chile	*G*	13. Paraguay
K	3. Venezuela	*B*	11. Bolivia	*N*	14. Falkland Islands
F	4. Guyana				
I	5. Suriname				
M	6. French Guiana				
C	7. Brazil				
J	8. Uruguay				

A. Buenos Aires	H. Lima
B. Sucre	I. Paramaribo
C. Brasília	J. Montevideo
D. Bogotá	K. Caracas
E. Quito	L. Santiago
F. Georgetown	M. Cayenne
G. Asunción	N. Stanley

Page 237

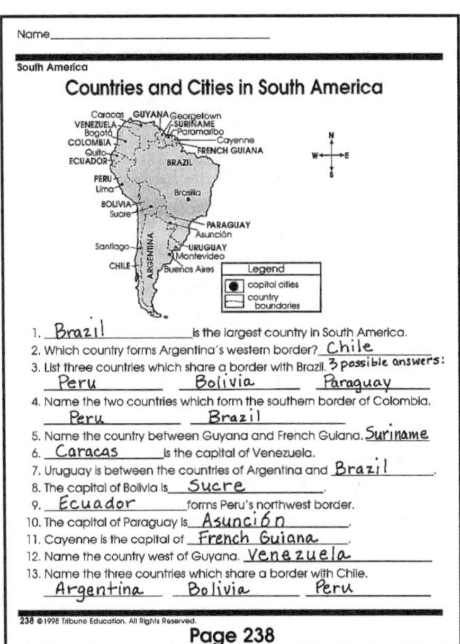
Name______________

South America

Countries and Cities in South America

1. *Brazil* is the largest country in South America.
2. Which country forms Argentina's western border? *Chile*
3. List three countries which share a border with Brazil. *3 possible answers: Peru, Bolivia, Paraguay*
4. Name the two countries which form the southern border of Colombia. *Peru, Brazil*
5. Name the country between Guyana and French Guiana. *Suriname*
6. *Caracas* is the capital of Venezuela.
7. Uruguay is between the countries of Argentina and *Brazil*.
8. The capital of Bolivia is *Sucre*.
9. *Ecuador* forms Peru's northwest border.
10. The capital of Paraguay is *Asunción*.
11. Cayenne is the capital of *French Guiana*.
12. Name the country west of Guyana. *Venezuela*
13. Name the three countries which share a border with Chile. *Argentina, Bolivia, Peru*

Page 238

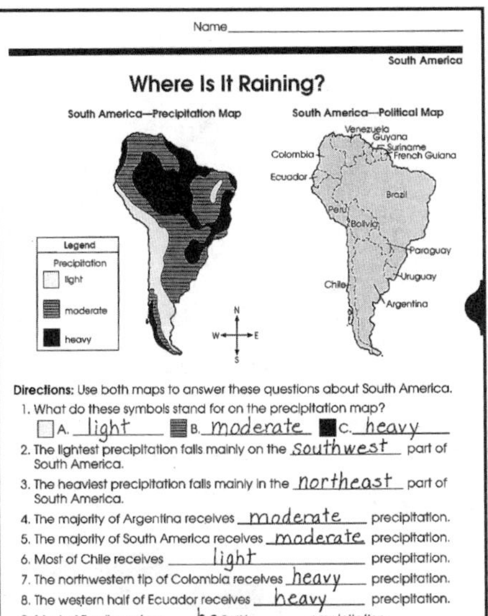
Name______________

South America

Where Is It Raining?

South America—Precipitation Map / South America—Political Map

Directions: Use both maps to answer these questions about South America.

1. What do these symbols stand for on the precipitation map? A. *light* B. *moderate* C. *heavy*
2. The lightest precipitation falls mainly on the *southwest* part of South America.
3. The heaviest precipitation falls mainly in the *northeast* part of South America.
4. The majority of Argentina receives *moderate* precipitation.
5. The majority of South America receives *moderate* precipitation.
6. Most of Chile receives *light* precipitation.
7. The northwestern tip of Colombia receives *heavy* precipitation.
8. The western half of Ecuador receives *heavy* precipitation.
9. Most of Brazil receives *heavy* precipitation.

Page 239

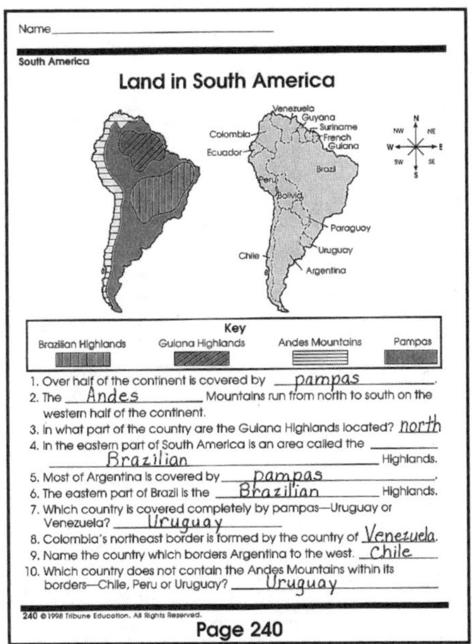
Name______________

South America

Land in South America

1. Over half of the continent is covered by *pampas*.
2. The *Andes* Mountains run from north to south on the western half of the continent.
3. In what part of the country are the Guiana Highlands located? *north*
4. In the eastern part of South America is an area called the *Brazilian* Highlands.
5. Most of Argentina is covered by *pampas*.
6. The eastern part of Brazil is the *Brazilian* Highlands.
7. Which country is covered completely by pampas—Uruguay or Venezuela? *Uruguay*
8. Colombia's northeast border is formed by the country of *Venezuela*.
9. Name the country which borders Argentina to the west. *Chile*
10. Which country does not contain the Andes Mountains within its borders—Chile, Peru or Uruguay? *Uruguay*

Page 240

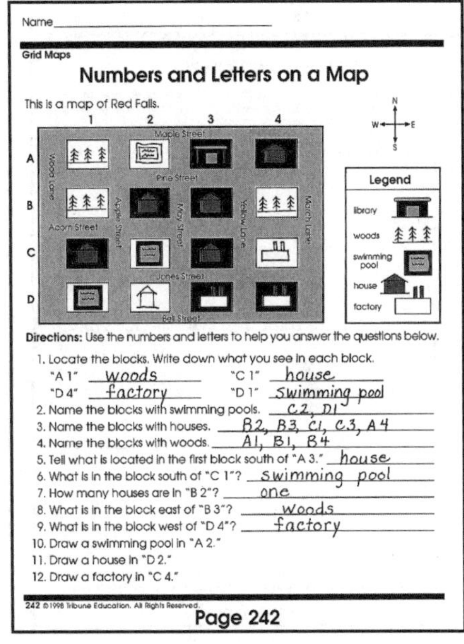
Name______________

Grid Maps

Numbers and Letters on a Map

This is a map of Red Falls.

Directions: Use the numbers and letters to help you answer the questions below.

1. Locate the blocks. Write down what you see in each block. "A 1" *woods* "C 1" *house* "D 4" *factory* "D 1" *swimming pool*
2. Name the blocks with swimming pools. *C2, D1*
3. Name the blocks with houses. *B2, B3, C1, C3, A4*
4. Name the blocks with woods. *A1, B1, B4*
5. Tell what is located in the first block south of "A 3." *house*
6. What is in the block south of "C 1"? *swimming pool*
7. How many houses are in "B 2"? *one*
8. What is in the block east of "B 3"? *woods*
9. What is in the block west of "D 4"? *factory*
10. Draw a swimming pool in "A 2."
11. Draw a house in "D 2."
12. Draw a factory in "C 4."

Page 242

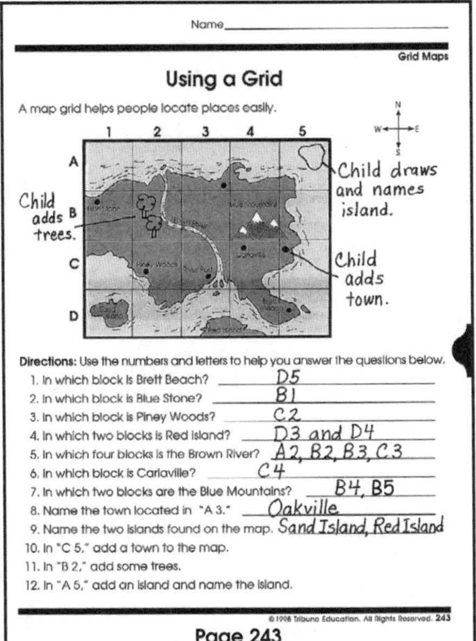
Name______________

Grid Maps

Using a Grid

A map grid helps people locate places easily.

Directions: Use the numbers and letters to help you answer the questions below.

1. In which block is Brett Beach? *D5*
2. In which block is Blue Stone? *B1*
3. In which block is Piney Woods? *C2*
4. In which two blocks is Red Island? *D3 and D4*
5. In which four blocks is the Brown River? *A2, B2, B3, C3*
6. In which block is Carlaville? *C4*
7. In which two blocks are the Blue Mountains? *B4, B5*
8. Name the town located in "A 3." *Oakville*
9. Name the two islands found on the map. *Sand Island, Red Island*
10. In "C 5," add a town to the map.
11. In "B 2," add some trees.
12. In "A 5," add an island and name the island.

Page 243

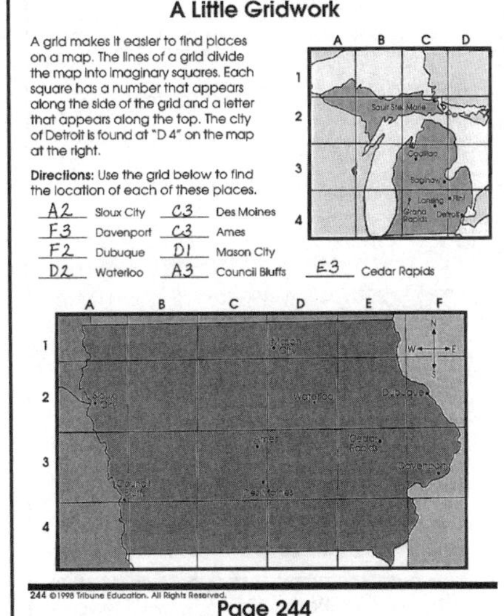
Name______________

Grid Maps

A Little Gridwork

A grid makes it easier to find places on a map. The lines of a grid divide the map into imaginary squares. Each square has a number that appears along the side of the grid and a letter that appears along the top. The city of Detroit is found at "D 4" on the map at the right.

Directions: Use the grid below to find the location of each of these places.

A2	Sioux City	*C3*	Des Moines
F3	Davenport	*C3*	Ames
F2	Dubuque	*D1*	Mason City
D2	Waterloo	*A3*	Council Bluffs
E3	Cedar Rapids		

Page 244

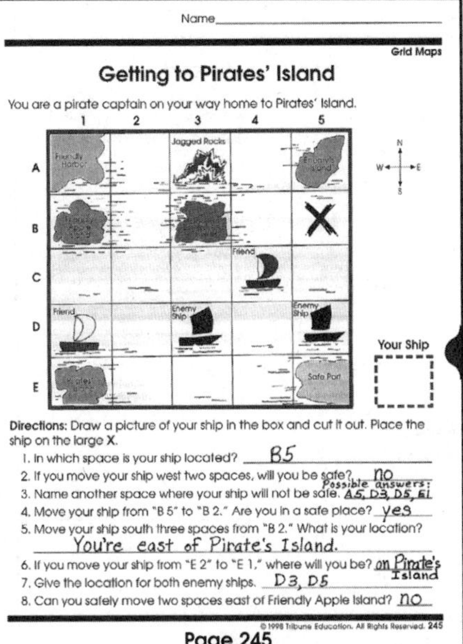
Name______________

Grid Maps

Getting to Pirates' Island

You are a pirate captain on your way home to Pirates' Island.

Directions: Draw a picture of your ship in the box and cut it out. Place the ship on the large X.

1. In which space is your ship located? *B5*
2. If you move your ship west two spaces, will you be safe? *no*
3. Name another space where your ship will not be safe. *Possible answers: A5, D3, D5, E1*
4. Move your ship from "B 5" to "B 2." Are you in a safe place? *yes*
5. Move your ship south three spaces from "B 2." What is your location? *You're east of Pirate's Island.*
6. If you move your ship from "E 2" to "E 1," where will you be? *on Pirate's Island*
7. Give the location for both enemy ships. *D3, D5*
8. Can you safely move two spaces east of Friendly Apple Island? *no*

Page 245

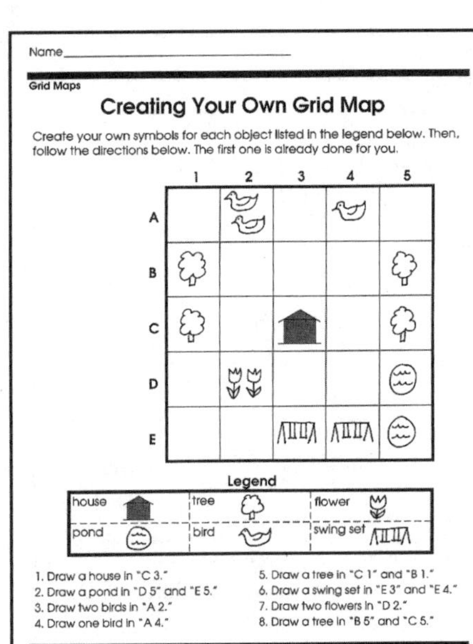

Name______________________

Grid Maps

Creating Your Own Grid Map

Create your own symbols for each object listed in the legend below. Then, follow the directions below. The first one is already done for you.

Legend: house, tree, flower, pond, bird, swing set

1. Draw a house in "C 3."
2. Draw a pond in "D 5" and "E 5."
3. Draw two birds in "A 2."
4. Draw one bird in "A 4."
5. Draw a tree in "C 1" and "B 1."
6. Draw a swing set in "E 3" and "E 4."
7. Draw two flowers in "D 2."
8. Draw a tree in "B 5" and "C 5."

246 ©1998 Tribune Education. All Rights Reserved.

Page 246

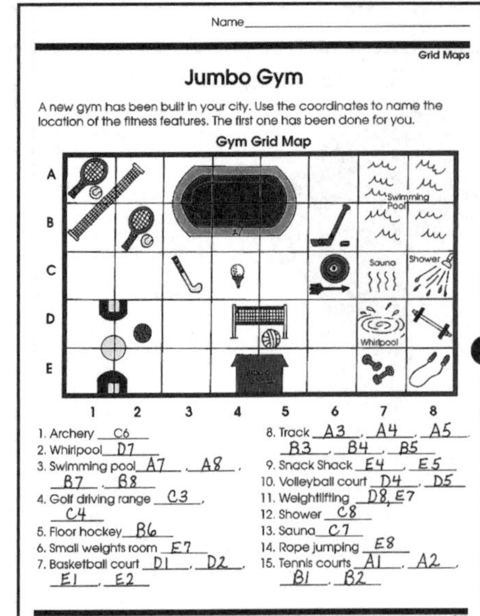

Name______________________

Grid Maps

Jumbo Gym

A new gym has been built in your city. Use the coordinates to name the location of the fitness features. The first one has been done for you.

Gym Grid Map

1. Archery C6
2. Whirlpool D7
3. Swimming pool A7, A8, B7, B8
4. Golf driving range C3, C4
5. Floor hockey B6
6. Small weights room E7
7. Basketball court D1, D2, E1, E2
8. Track A3, A4, A5, B3, B4, B5
9. Snack Shack E4, E5
10. Volleyball court D4, D5
11. Weightlifting D8, E7
12. Shower C8
13. Sauna C7
14. Rope jumping E8
15. Tennis courts A1, A2, B1, B2

©1998 Tribune Education. All Rights Reserved. 247

Page 247

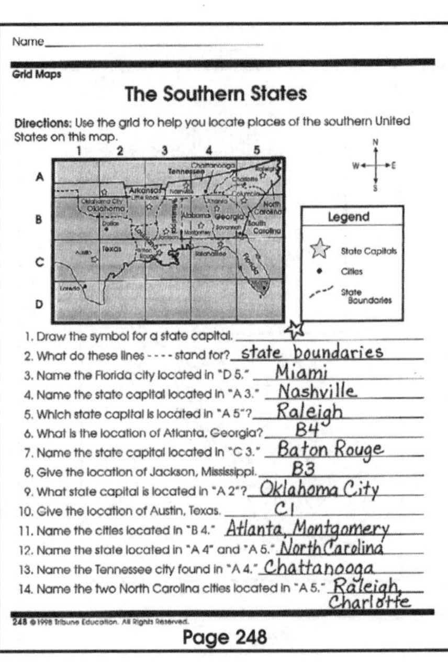

Name______________________

Grid Maps

The Southern States

Directions: Use the grid to help you locate places of the southern United States on this map.

1. Draw the symbol for a state capital. ☆
2. What do these lines - - - - stand for? state boundaries
3. Name the Florida city located in "D 5." Miami
4. Name the state capital located in "A 3." Nashville
5. Which state capital is located in "A 5"? Raleigh
6. What is the location of Atlanta, Georgia? B4
7. Name the state capital located in "C 3." Baton Rouge
8. Give the location of Jackson, Mississippi. B3
9. What state capital is located in "A 2"? Oklahoma City
10. Give the location of Austin, Texas. C1
11. Name the cities located in "B 4." Atlanta, Montgomery
12. Name the state located in "A 4" and "A 5." North Carolina
13. Name the Tennessee city found in "A 4." Chattanooga
14. Name the two North Carolina cities located in "A 5." Raleigh, Charlotte

248 ©1998 Tribune Education. All Rights Reserved.

Page 248

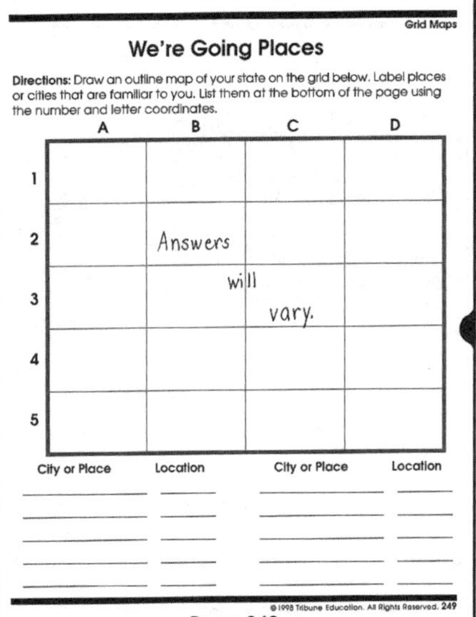

Name______________________

Grid Maps

We're Going Places

Directions: Draw an outline map of your state on the grid below. Label places or cities that are familiar to you. List them at the bottom of the page using the number and letter coordinates.

Answers will vary.

City or Place	Location	City or Place	Location

©1998 Tribune Education. All Rights Reserved. 249

Page 249

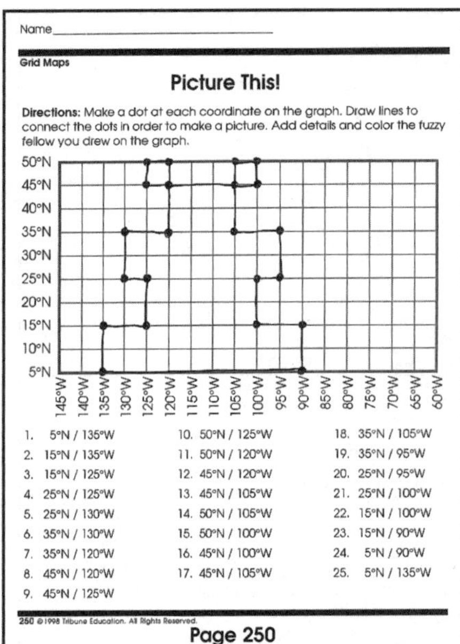

Name______________________

Grid Maps

Picture This!

Directions: Make a dot at each coordinate on the graph. Draw lines to connect the dots in order to make a picture. Add details and color the fuzzy fellow you drew on the graph.

1. 5°N / 135°W
2. 15°N / 135°W
3. 15°N / 125°W
4. 25°N / 125°W
5. 25°N / 130°W
6. 35°N / 130°W
7. 35°N / 120°W
8. 45°N / 120°W
9. 45°N / 125°W
10. 50°N / 125°W
11. 50°N / 120°W
12. 45°N / 120°W
13. 45°N / 105°W
14. 50°N / 105°W
15. 50°N / 100°W
16. 45°N / 100°W
17. 45°N / 105°W
18. 35°N / 105°W
19. 35°N / 95°W
20. 25°N / 95°W
21. 25°N / 100°W
22. 15°N / 100°W
23. 15°N / 90°W
24. 5°N / 90°W
25. 5°N / 135°W

250 ©1998 Tribune Education. All Rights Reserved.

Page 250

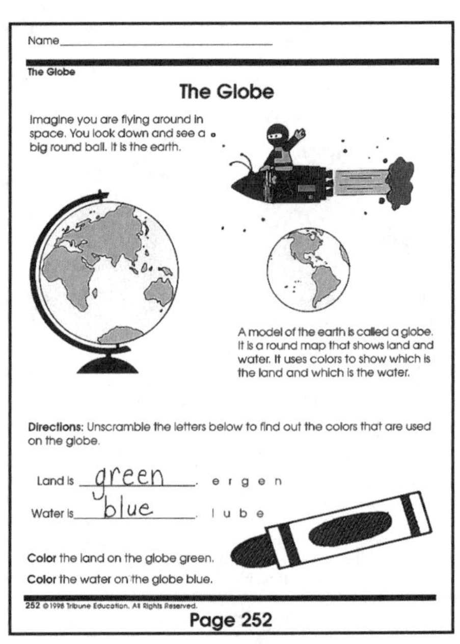

Name______________________

The Globe

The Globe

Imagine you are flying around in space. You look down and see a big round ball. It is the earth.

A model of the earth is called a globe. It is a round map that shows land and water. It uses colors to show which is the land and which is the water.

Directions: Unscramble the letters below to find out the colors that are used on the globe.

Land is green. e r g e n

Water is blue. l u b e

Color the land on the globe green.

Color the water on the globe blue.

252 ©1998 Tribune Education. All Rights Reserved.

Page 252

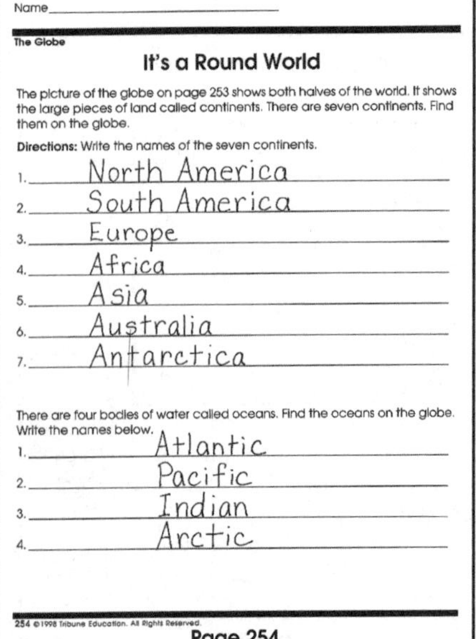

Name______________________

The Globe

It's a Round World

The picture of the globe on page 253 shows both halves of the world. It shows the large pieces of land called continents. There are seven continents. Find them on the globe.

Directions: Write the names of the seven continents.

1. North America
2. South America
3. Europe
4. Africa
5. Asia
6. Australia
7. Antarctica

There are four bodies of water called oceans. Find the oceans on the globe. Write the names below.

1. Atlantic
2. Pacific
3. Indian
4. Arctic

254 ©1998 Tribune Education. All Rights Reserved.

Page 254

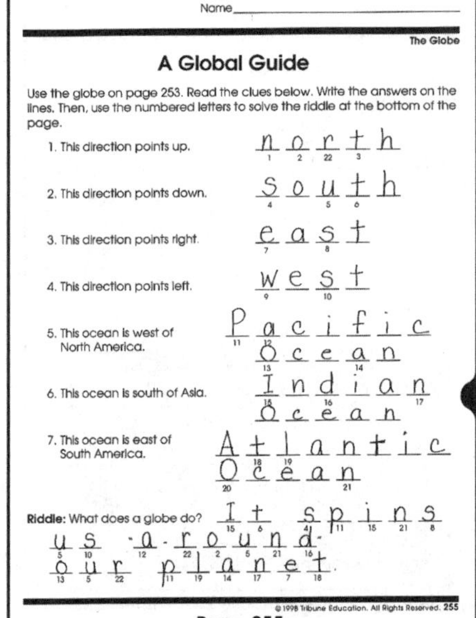

Name______________________

The Globe

A Global Guide

Use the globe on page 253. Read the clues below. Write the answers on the lines. Then, use the numbered letters to solve the riddle at the bottom of the page.

1. This direction points up. north
2. This direction points down. south
3. This direction points right. east
4. This direction points left. west
5. This ocean is west of North America. Pacific Ocean
6. This ocean is south of Asia. Indian Ocean
7. This ocean is east of South America. Atlantic Ocean

Riddle: What does a globe do? It spins us around our planet.

©1998 Tribune Education. All Rights Reserved. 255

Page 255

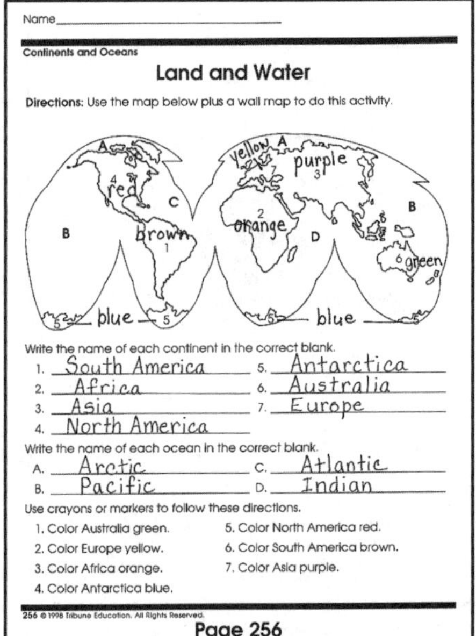

Name______________________

Continents and Oceans

Land and Water

Directions: Use the map below plus a wall map to do this activity.

Write the name of each continent in the correct blank.

1. South America
2. Africa
3. Asia
4. North America
5. Antarctica
6. Australia
7. Europe

Write the name of each ocean in the correct blank.

A. Arctic
B. Pacific
C. Atlantic
D. Indian

Use crayons or markers to follow these directions.

1. Color Australia green.
2. Color Europe yellow.
3. Color Africa orange.
4. Color Antarctica blue.
5. Color North America red.
6. Color South America brown.
7. Color Asia purple.

256 ©1998 Tribune Education. All Rights Reserved.

Page 256

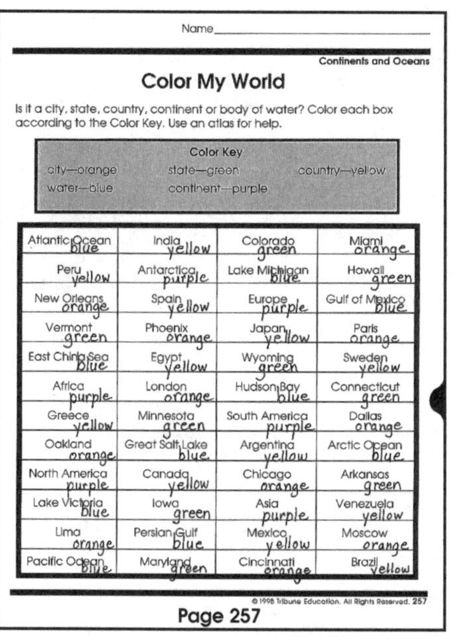

Name
Continents and Oceans
Color My World
Is it a city, state, country, continent or body of water? Color each box according to the Color Key. Use an atlas for help.
Color Key
city—orange state—green country—yellow
water—blue continent—purple
Atlantic Ocean blue
India yellow
Colorado green
Miami orange
Peru yellow
Antarctica purple
Lake Michigan blue
Hawaii green
New Orleans orange
Spain yellow
Europe purple
Gulf of Mexico blue
Vermont green
Phoenix orange
Japan yellow
Paris orange
East China Sea blue
Egypt yellow
Wyoming green
Sweden yellow
Africa purple
London orange
Hudson Bay blue
Connecticut green
Greece yellow
Minnesota green
South America purple
Dallas orange
Oakland orange
Great Salt Lake blue
Argentina yellow
Arctic Ocean blue
North America purple
Canada yellow
Chicago orange
Arkansas green
Lake Victoria blue
Iowa green
Asia purple
Venezuela yellow
Lima orange
Persian Gulf blue
Mexico yellow
Moscow orange
Pacific Ocean blue
Maryland green
Cincinnati orange
Brazil yellow
©1998 Tribune Education. All Rights Reserved. 257

Page 257

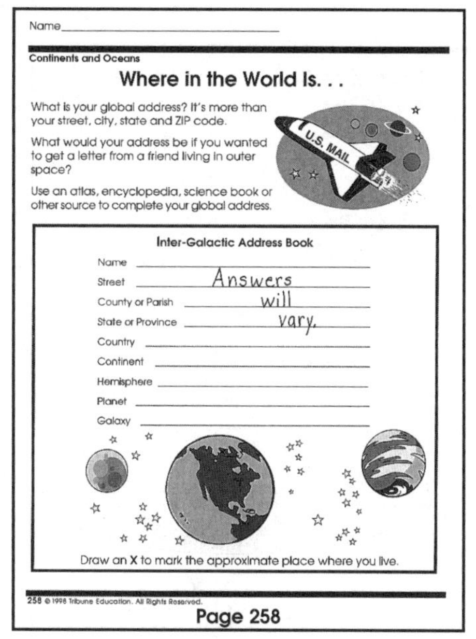

Page 258

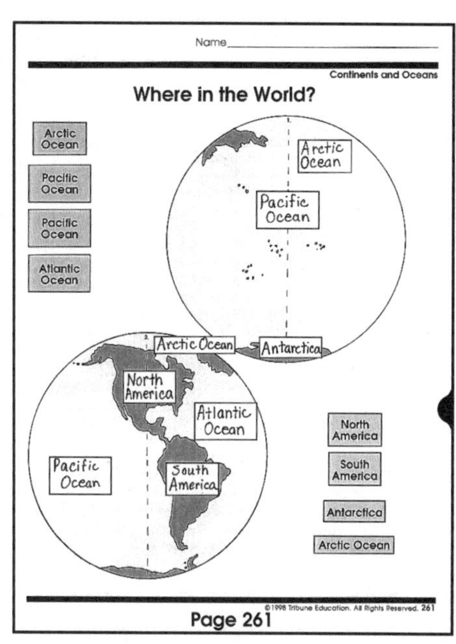

Page 261

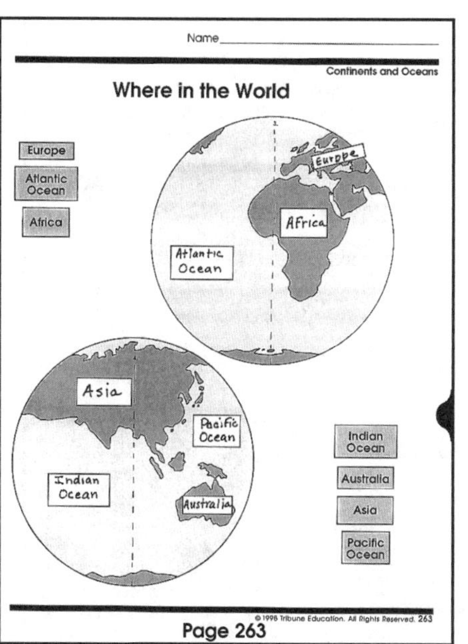

Page 263

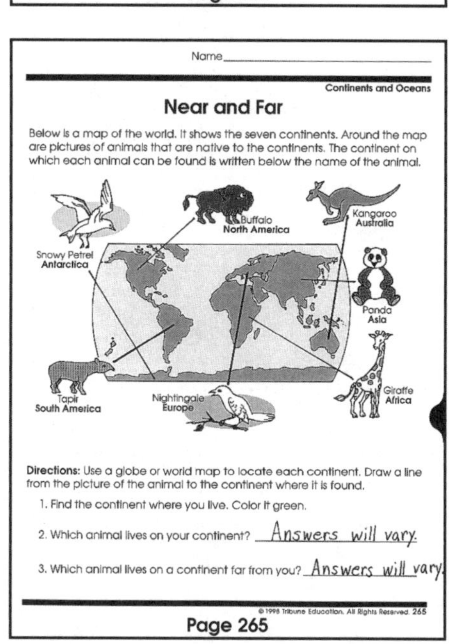

Name
Continents and Oceans
Near and Far
Below is a map of the world. It shows the seven continents. Around the map are pictures of animals that are native to the continents. The continent on which each animal can be found is written below the name of the animal.
Buffalo North America
Kangaroo Australia
Snowy Petrel Antarctica
Panda Asia
Giraffe Africa
Tapir South America
Nightingale Europe
Directions: Use a globe or world map to locate each continent. Draw a line from the picture of the animal to the continent where it is found.
1. Find the continent where you live. Color it green.
2. Which animal lives on your continent? Answers will vary.
3. Which animal lives on a continent far from you? Answers will vary.
©1998 Tribune Education. All Rights Reserved. 265

Page 265

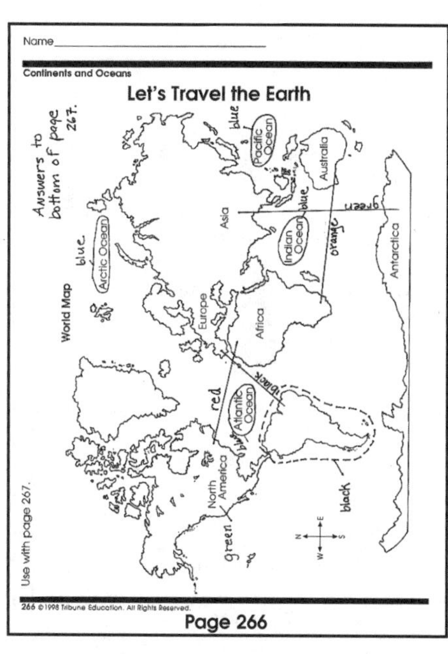

Page 266

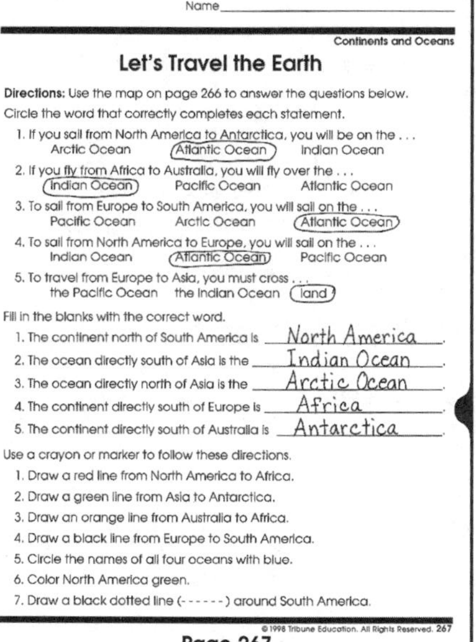

Page 267

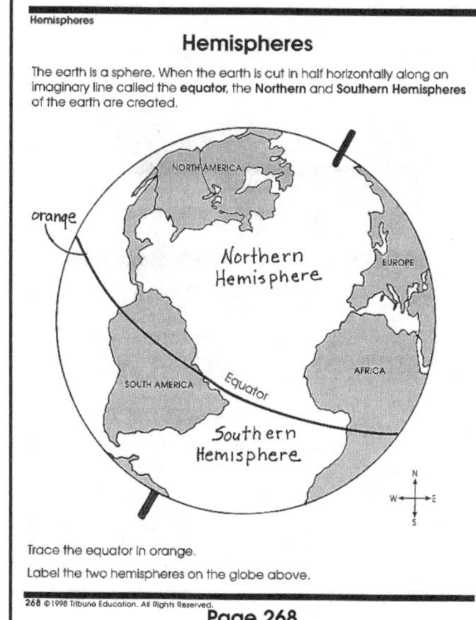

Name
Hemispheres
Hemispheres
The earth is a sphere. When the earth is cut in half horizontally along an imaginary line called the equator, the Northern and Southern Hemispheres of the earth are created.
NORTH AMERICA
orange
Northern Hemisphere
EUROPE
SOUTH AMERICA
Equator
AFRICA
Southern Hemisphere
Trace the equator in orange.
Label the two hemispheres on the globe above.
268 ©1998 Tribune Education. All Rights Reserved.

Page 268

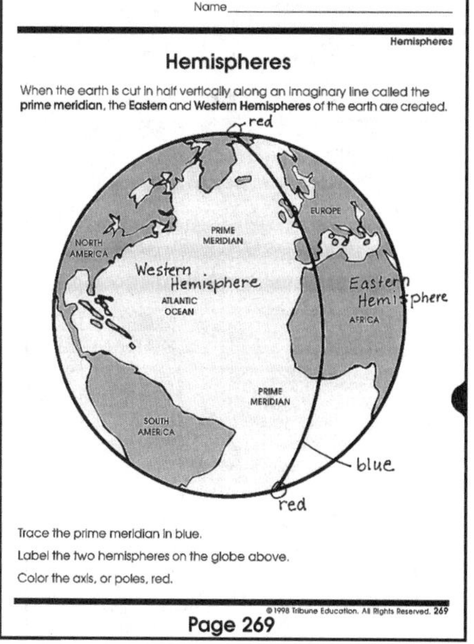

Page 269

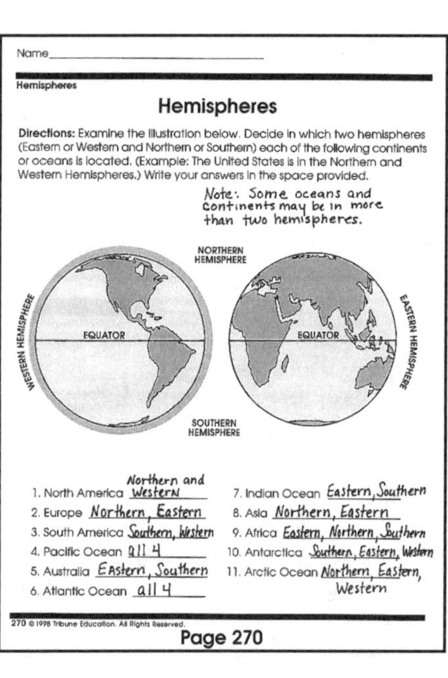

Name

Hemispheres

Hemispheres

Directions: Examine the illustration below. Decide in which two hemispheres (Eastern or Western and Northern or Southern) each of the following continents or oceans is located. (Example: The United States is in the Northern and Western Hemispheres.) Write your answers in the space provided.

Note: Some oceans and continents may be in more than two hemispheres.

1. North America Northern and Western
2. Europe Northern, Eastern
3. South America Southern, Western
4. Pacific Ocean all 4
5. Australia Eastern, Southern
6. Atlantic Ocean all 4
7. Indian Ocean Eastern, Southern
8. Asia Northern, Eastern
9. Africa Eastern, Northern, Southern
10. Antarctica Southern, Eastern, Western
11. Arctic Ocean Northern, Eastern, Western

270 ©1998 Tribune Education. All Rights Reserved.

Page 270

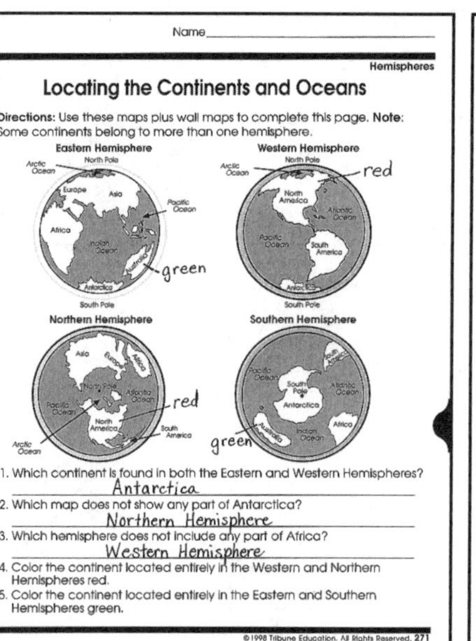

Name

Hemispheres

Locating the Continents and Oceans

Directions: Use these maps plus wall maps to complete this page. **Note:** Some continents belong to more than one hemisphere.

1. Which continent is found in both the Eastern and Western Hemispheres? Antarctica
2. Which map does not show any part of Antarctica? Northern Hemisphere
3. Which hemisphere does not include any part of Africa? Western Hemisphere
4. Color the continent located entirely in the Western and Northern Hemispheres red.
5. Color the continent located entirely in the Eastern and Southern Hemispheres green.

©1998 Tribune Education. All Rights Reserved. 271

Page 271

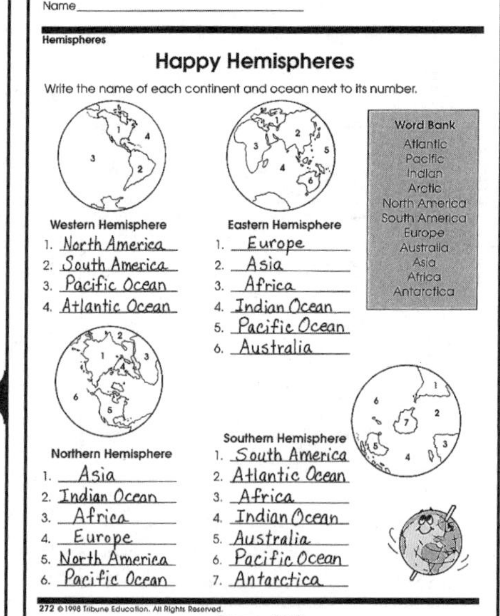

Name

Hemispheres

Happy Hemispheres

Write the name of each continent and ocean next to its number.

Word Bank: Atlantic, Pacific, Indian, Arctic, North America, South America, Europe, Australia, Asia, Africa, Antarctica

Western Hemisphere
1. North America
2. South America
3. Pacific Ocean
4. Atlantic Ocean

Eastern Hemisphere
1. Europe
2. Asia
3. Africa
4. Indian Ocean
5. Pacific Ocean
6. Australia

Northern Hemisphere
1. Asia
2. Indian Ocean
3. Africa
4. Europe
5. North America
6. Pacific Ocean

Southern Hemisphere
1. South America
2. Atlantic Ocean
3. Africa
4. Indian Ocean
5. Australia
6. Pacific Ocean
7. Antarctica

272 ©1998 Tribune Education. All Rights Reserved.

Page 272

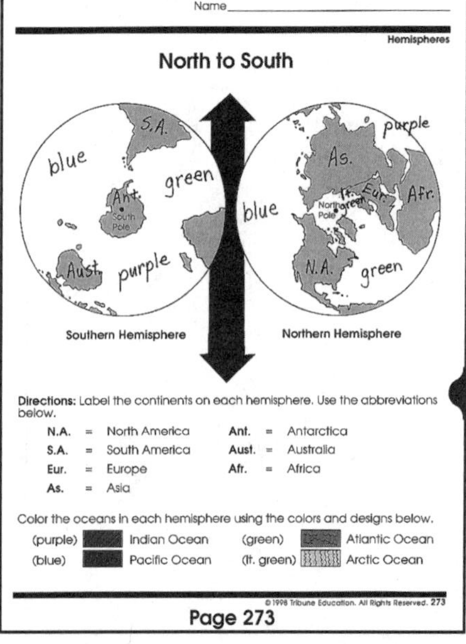

Name

Hemispheres

North to South

Directions: Label the continents on each hemisphere. Use the abbreviations below.

N.A.	=	North America	Ant.	=	Antarctica
S.A.	=	South America	Aust.	=	Australia
Eur.	=	Europe	Afr.	=	Africa
As.	=	Asia			

Color the oceans in each hemisphere using the colors and designs below.

(purple) Indian Ocean (green) Atlantic Ocean
(blue) Pacific Ocean (lt. green) Arctic Ocean

©1998 Tribune Education. All Rights Reserved. 273

Page 273

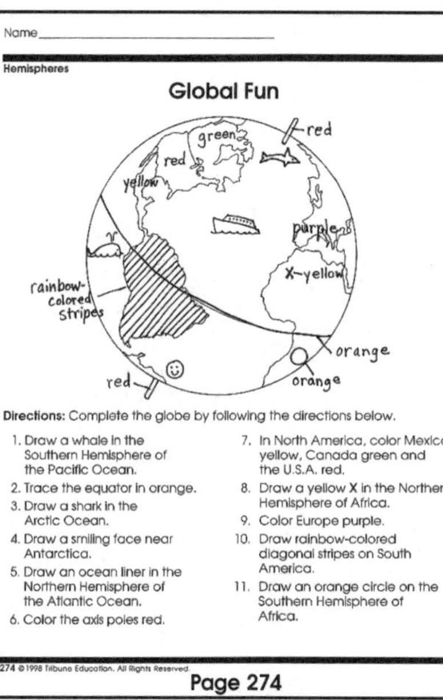

Name

Hemispheres

Global Fun

Directions: Complete the globe by following the directions below.

1. Draw a whale in the Southern Hemisphere of the Pacific Ocean.
2. Trace the equator in orange.
3. Draw a shark in the Arctic Ocean.
4. Draw a smiling face near Antarctica.
5. Draw an ocean liner in the Northern Hemisphere of the Atlantic Ocean.
6. Color the axis poles red.
7. In North America, color Mexico yellow, Canada green and the U.S.A. red.
8. Draw a yellow X in the Northern Hemisphere of Africa.
9. Color Europe purple.
10. Draw rainbow-colored diagonal stripes on South America.
11. Draw an orange circle on the Southern Hemisphere of Africa.

274 ©1998 Tribune Education. All Rights Reserved.

Page 274

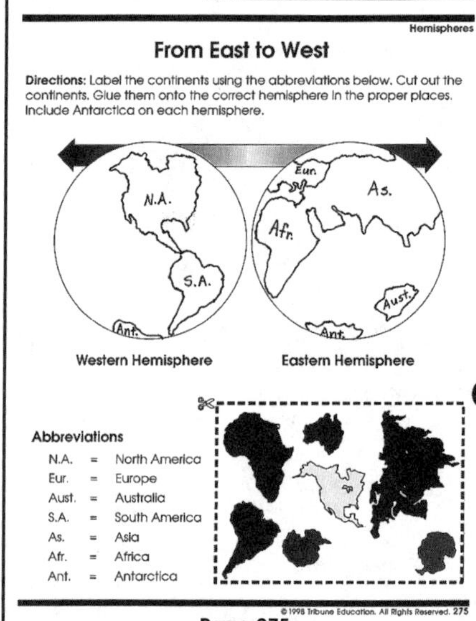

Name

Hemispheres

From East to West

Directions: Label the continents using the abbreviations below. Cut out the continents. Glue them onto the correct hemisphere in the proper places. Include Antarctica on each hemisphere.

Abbreviations

N.A.	=	North America
Eur.	=	Europe
Aust.	=	Australia
S.A.	=	South America
As.	=	Asia
Afr.	=	Africa
Ant.	=	Antarctica

©1998 Tribune Education. All Rights Reserved. 275

Page 275

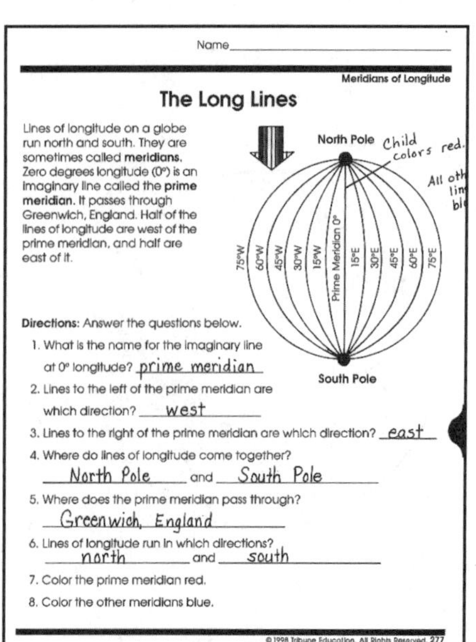

Name

Meridians of Longitude

The Long Lines

Lines of longitude on a globe run north and south. They are sometimes called **meridians**. Zero degrees longitude (0°) is an imaginary line called the **prime meridian**. It passes through Greenwich, England. Half of the lines of longitude are west of the prime meridian, and half are east of it.

Directions: Answer the questions below.

1. What is the name for the imaginary line at 0° longitude? prime meridian
2. Lines to the left of the prime meridian are which direction? west
3. Lines to the right of the prime meridian are which direction? east
4. Where do lines of longitude come together? North Pole and South Pole
5. Where does the prime meridian pass through? Greenwich, England
6. Lines of longitude run in which directions? north and south
7. Color the prime meridian red.
8. Color the other meridians blue.

©1998 Tribune Education. All Rights Reserved. 277

Page 277

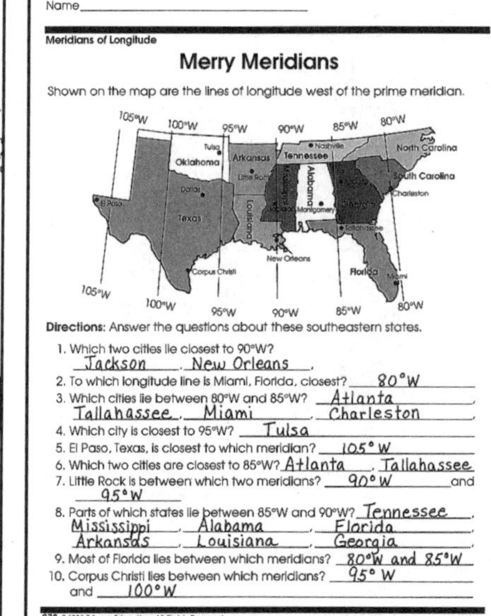

Name

Meridians of Longitude

Merry Meridians

Shown on the map are the lines of longitude west of the prime meridian.

Directions: Answer the questions about these southeastern states.

1. Which two cities lie closest to 90°W? Jackson, New Orleans
2. To which longitude line is Miami, Florida, closest? 80°W
3. Which cities lie between 80°W and 85°W? Atlanta, Tallahassee, Miami, Charleston
4. Which city is closest to 95°W? Tulsa
5. El Paso, Texas, is closest to which meridian? 105°W
6. Which two cities are closest to 85°W? Atlanta, Tallahassee
7. Little Rock is between which two meridians? 90°W and 95°W
8. Parts of which states lie between 85°W and 90°W? Tennessee, Mississippi, Alabama, Florida, Arkansas, Louisiana, Georgia
9. Most of Florida lies between which meridians? 80°W and 85°W
10. Corpus Christi lies between which meridians? 95°W and 100°W

278 ©1998 Tribune Education. All Rights Reserved.

Page 278

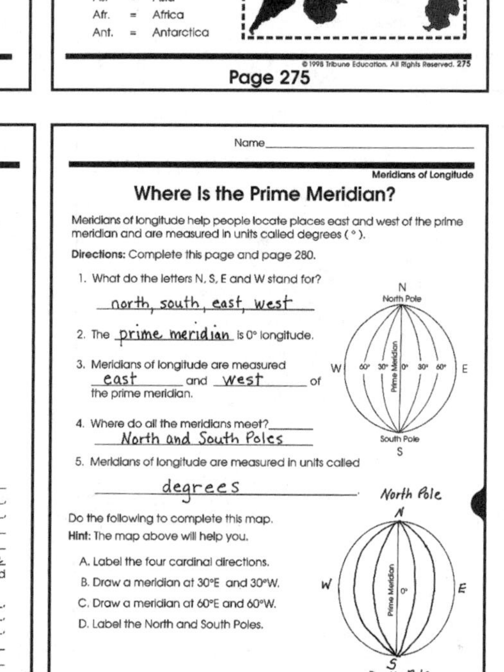

Name

Meridians of Longitude

Where Is the Prime Meridian?

Meridians of longitude help people locate places east and west of the prime meridian and are measured in units called degrees (°).

Directions: Complete this page and page 280.

1. What do the letters N, S, E and W stand for? north, south, east, west
2. The prime meridian is 0° longitude.
3. Meridians of longitude are measured east and west of the prime meridian.
4. Where do all the meridians meet? North and South Poles
5. Meridians of longitude are measured in units called degrees.

Do the following to complete this map.
Hint: The map above will help you.

A. Label the four cardinal directions.
B. Draw a meridian at 30°E and 30°W.
C. Draw a meridian at 60°E and 60°W.
D. Label the North and South Poles.

©1998 Tribune Education. All Rights Reserved. 279

Page 279

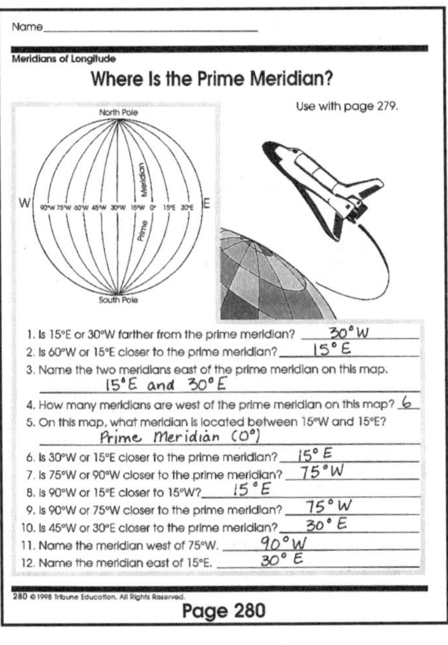
Name________________________

Meridians of Longitude

Where Is the Prime Meridian?

Use with page 279.

1. Is 15°E or 30°W farther from the prime meridian? 30° W
2. Is 60°W or 15°E closer to the prime meridian? 15° E
3. Name the two meridians east of the prime meridian on this map. 15°E and 30°E
4. How many meridians are west of the prime meridian on this map? 6
5. On this map, what meridian is located between 15°W and 15°E? Prime Meridian (0°)
6. Is 30°W or 15°E closer to the prime meridian? 15° E
7. Is 75°W or 90°W closer to the prime meridian? 75° W
8. Is 90°W or 15°E closer to 15°W? 15° E
9. Is 90°W or 75°W closer to the prime meridian? 75° W
10. Is 45°W or 30°E closer to the prime meridian? 30° E
11. Name the meridian west of 75°W. 90° W
12. Name the meridian east of 15°E. 30° E

280 ©1998 Tribune Education. All Rights Reserved.

Page 280

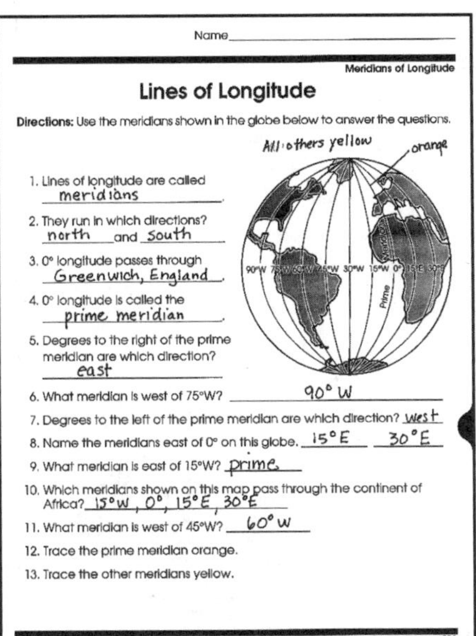
Name________________________

Meridians of Longitude

Lines of Longitude

Directions: Use the meridians shown in the globe below to answer the questions.

All others yellow / orange

1. Lines of longitude are called meridians
2. They run in which directions? north and south
3. 0° longitude passes through Greenwich, England
4. 0° longitude is called the prime meridian
5. Degrees to the right of the prime meridian are which direction? east
6. What meridian is west of 75°W? 90° W
7. Degrees to the left of the prime meridian are which direction? west
8. Name the meridians east of 0° on this globe. 15° E 30° E
9. What meridian is east of 15°W? prime
10. Which meridians shown on this map pass through the continent of Africa? 15° W, 0°, 15° E, 30° E
11. What meridian is west of 45°W? 60° W
12. Trace the prime meridian orange.
13. Trace the other meridians yellow.

©1998 Tribune Education. All Rights Reserved. 281

Page 281

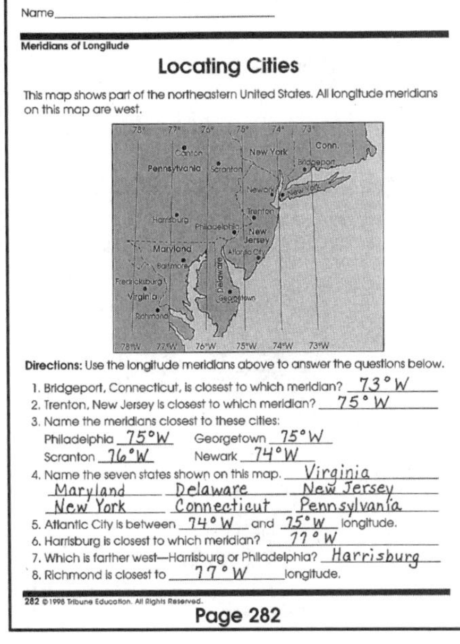
Name________________________

Meridians of Longitude

Locating Cities

This map shows part of the northeastern United States. All longitude meridians on this map are west.

Directions: Use the longitude meridians above to answer the questions below.

1. Bridgeport, Connecticut, is closest to which meridian? 73° W
2. Trenton, New Jersey is closest to which meridian? 75° W
3. Name the meridians closest to these cities:
   Philadelphia 75° W Georgetown 75° W
   Scranton 76° W Newark 74° W
4. Name the seven states shown on this map. Virginia, Maryland, Delaware, New Jersey, New York, Connecticut, Pennsylvania
5. Atlantic City is between 74° W and 75° W longitude.
6. Harrisburg is closest to which meridian? 77° W
7. Which is farther west—Harrisburg or Philadelphia? Harrisburg
8. Richmond is closest to 77° W longitude.

282 ©1998 Tribune Education. All Rights Reserved.

Page 282

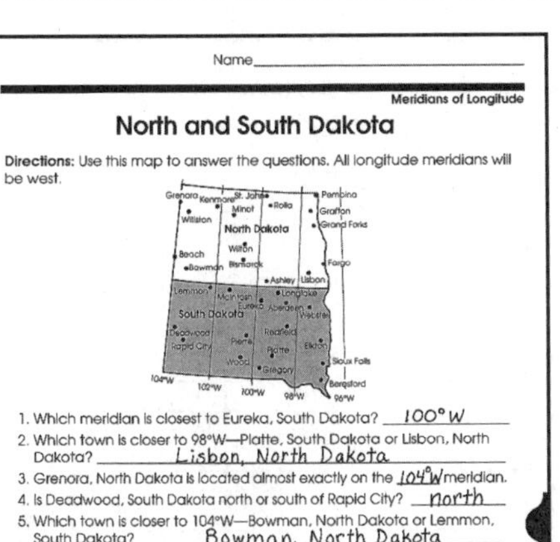
Name________________________

Meridians of Longitude

North and South Dakota

Directions: Use this map to answer the questions. All longitude meridians will be west.

1. Which meridian is closest to Eureka, South Dakota? 100° W
2. Which town is closer to 98°W—Platte, South Dakota or Lisbon, North Dakota? Lisbon, North Dakota
3. Grenora, North Dakota is located almost exactly on the 104°W meridian.
4. Is Deadwood, South Dakota north or south of Rapid City? north
5. Which town is closer to 104°W—Bowman, North Dakota or Lemmon, South Dakota? Bowman, North Dakota
6. If you were traveling east from Rapid City, which meridian would you arrive at first? 102° W
7. Which meridian would you reach first when traveling east from Sioux Falls, South Dakota? 96° W
8. Bismarck is in the state of North Dakota.
9. Lemmon, South Dakota is closest to the 102° W meridian.
10. Name the North Dakota cities located east of 98°W longitude. Pembina, Grafton, Grand Forks, Fargo, Lisbon, Webster, Elkton, Sioux Falls, Beresford

©1998 Tribune Education. All Rights Reserved. 283

Page 283

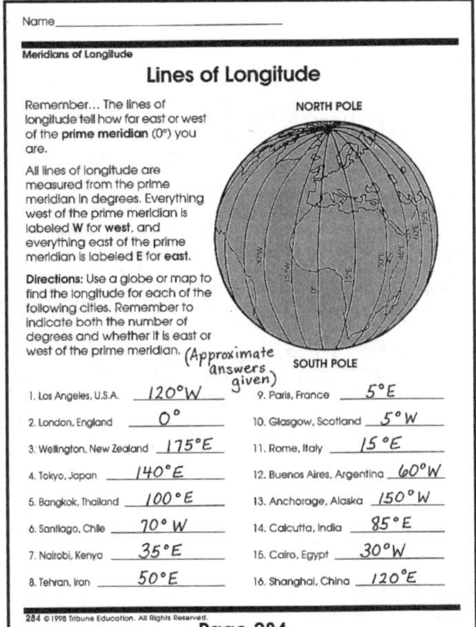
Name________________________

Meridians of Longitude

Lines of Longitude

Remember... The lines of longitude tell how far east or west of the **prime meridian** (0°) you are.

All lines of longitude are measured from the prime meridian in degrees. Everything west of the prime meridian is labeled **W** for **west**, and everything east of the prime meridian is labeled **E** for **east**.

Directions: Use a globe or map to find the longitude for each of the following cities. Remember to indicate both the number of degrees and whether it is east or west of the prime meridian. (Approximate answers given)

NORTH POLE / SOUTH POLE

1. Los Angeles, U.S.A.	120° W	9. Paris, France	5° E
2. London, England	0°	10. Glasgow, Scotland	5° W
3. Wellington, New Zealand	175° E	11. Rome, Italy	15° E
4. Tokyo, Japan	140° E	12. Buenos Aires, Argentina	60° W
5. Bangkok, Thailand	100° E	13. Anchorage, Alaska	150° W
6. Santiago, Chile	70° W	14. Calcutta, India	85° E
7. Nairobi, Kenya	35° E	15. Cairo, Egypt	30° W
8. Tehran, Iran	50° E	16. Shanghai, China	120° E

284 ©1998 Tribune Education. All Rights Reserved.

Page 284

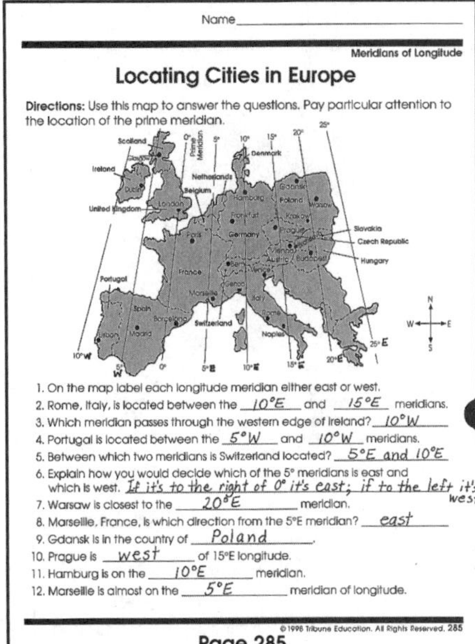
Name________________________

Meridians of Longitude

Locating Cities in Europe

Directions: Use this map to answer the questions. Pay particular attention to the location of the prime meridian.

1. On the map label each longitude meridian either east or west.
2. Rome, Italy, is located between the 10° E and 15° E meridians.
3. Which meridian passes through the western edge of Ireland? 10° W
4. Portugal is located between the 5° W and 10° W meridians.
5. Between which two meridians is Switzerland located? 5° E and 10° E
6. Explain how you would decide which of the 5° meridians is east and which is west. If it's to the right of 0° it's east; if to the left it's west
7. Warsaw is closest to the 20° E meridian.
8. Marseille, France, is which direction from the 5°E meridian? east
9. Gdansk is in the country of Poland.
10. Prague is west of 15°E longitude.
11. Hamburg is on the 10° E meridian.
12. Marseille is almost on the 5° E meridian of longitude.

©1998 Tribune Education. All Rights Reserved. 285

Page 285

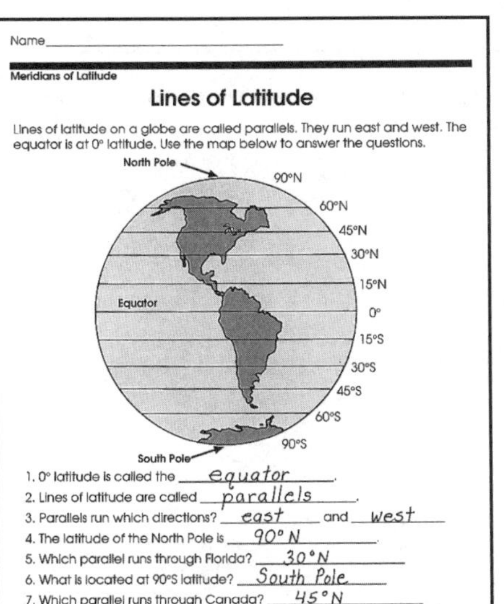
Name________________________

Meridians of Latitude

Lines of Latitude

Lines of latitude on a globe are called parallels. They run east and west. The equator is at 0° latitude. Use the map below to answer the questions.

1. 0° latitude is called the equator.
2. Lines of latitude are called parallels.
3. Parallels run which directions? east and west
4. The latitude of the North Pole is 90° N.
5. Which parallel runs through Florida? 30° N
6. What is located at 90°S latitude? South Pole
7. Which parallel runs through Canada? 45° N
8. Lines of latitude above the equator are which direction? north
9. Below the equator, the parallels are which direction? south

286 ©1998 Tribune Education. All Rights Reserved.

Page 286

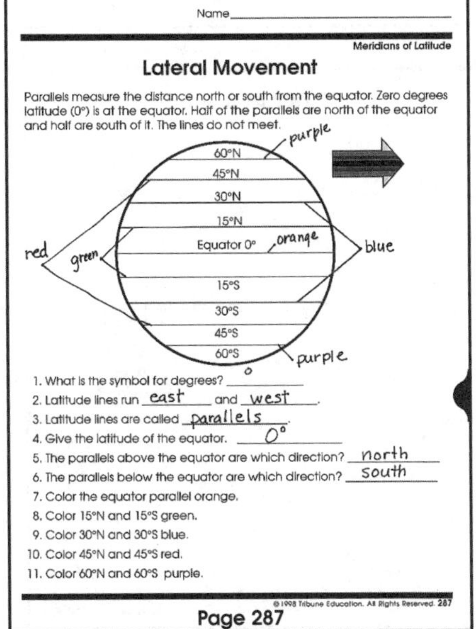
Name________________________

Meridians of Latitude

Lateral Movement

Parallels measure the distance north or south from the equator. Zero degrees latitude (0°) is at the equator. Half of the parallels are north of the equator and half are south of it. The lines do not meet.

1. What is the symbol for degrees? °
2. Latitude lines run east and west.
3. Latitude lines are called parallels.
4. Give the latitude of the equator. 0°
5. The parallels above the equator are which direction? north
6. The parallels below the equator are which direction? south
7. Color the equator parallel orange.
8. Color 15°N and 15°S green.
9. Color 30°N and 30°S blue.
10. Color 45°N and 45°S red.
11. Color 60°N and 60°S purple.

©1998 Tribune Education. All Rights Reserved. 287

Page 287

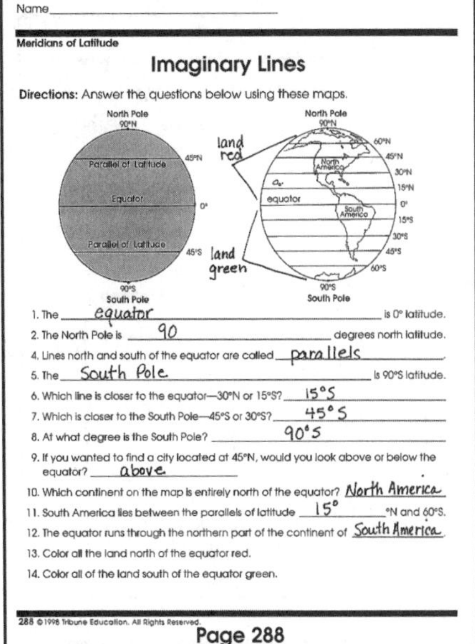
Name________________________

Meridians of Latitude

Imaginary Lines

Directions: Answer the questions below using these maps.

1. The equator is 0° latitude.
2. The North Pole is 90 degrees north latitude.
4. Lines north and south of the equator are called parallels.
5. The South Pole is 90°S latitude.
6. Which line is closer to the equator—30°N or 15°S? 15° S
7. Which is closer to the South Pole—45°S or 30°S? 45° S
8. At what degree is the South Pole? 90° S
9. If you wanted to find a city located at 45°N, would you look above or below the equator? above
10. Which continent on the map is entirely north of the equator? North America
11. South America lies between the parallels of latitude 15° °N and 60°S.
12. The equator runs through the northern part of the continent of South America.
13. Color all the land north of the equator red.
14. Color all of the land south of the equator green.

288 ©1998 Tribune Education. All Rights Reserved.

Page 288

Name

Lines of Latitude

What's My Line?

There are several important lines of latitude on the globe which have special names.

Directions: Use a map, globe or other resource to identify the special lines on the illustration of the globe below.

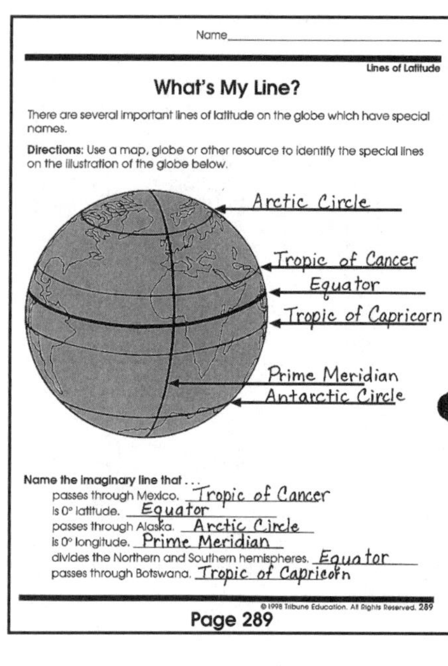

Name the imaginary line that . . .

passes through Mexico. Tropic of Cancer
is 0° latitude. Equator
passes through Alaska. Arctic Circle
is 0° longitude. Prime Meridian
divides the Northern and Southern hemispheres. Equator
passes through Botswana. Tropic of Capricorn

Page 289

Name

Lines of Latitude

Across the U.S.A.

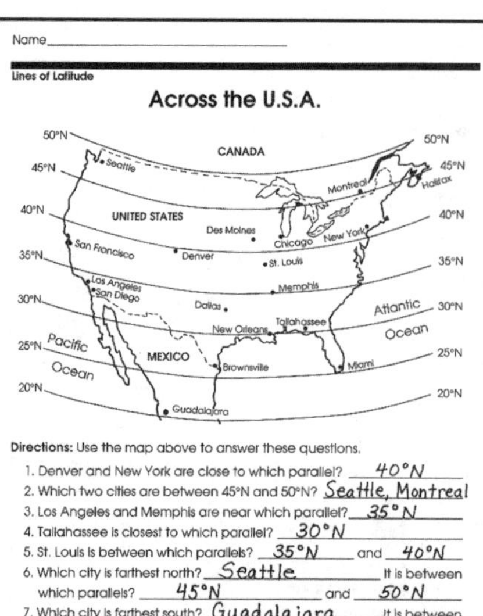

Directions: Use the map above to answer these questions.

1. Denver and New York are close to which parallel? 40°N
2. Which two cities are between 45°N and 50°N? Seattle, Montreal
3. Los Angeles and Memphis are near which parallel? 35°N
4. Tallahassee is closest to which parallel? 30°N
5. St. Louis is between which parallels? 35°N and 40°N
6. Which city is farthest north? Seattle It is between which parallels? 45°N and 50°N
7. Which city is farthest south? Guadalajara It is between which parallels? 20°N and 25°N
8. San Francisco is halfway between 35°N and 40°N.

Page 290

Name

Lines of Latitude

Latitude in North America

Directions: Use the map on page 291 to answer the questions below.

1. The Arctic Circle is located between 60°N and 70 °N.
2. Is Chicago closer to 40°N or 50°N? 40°N
3. Name the three United States cities located between 20°N and 30°N. Brownsville New Orleans Miami
4. New York is closest to the 40°N parallel of latitude.
5. Name the eight United States cities located between 30° N and 40°N. San Francisco San Diego St. Louis Dallas Los Angeles Denver Memphis Tallahassee
6. The Atlantic Ocean is on the eastern side of the United States.
7. Mexico is the country south of the United States.
8. Canada is the country north of the United States.
9. On the west, the United States is bordered by the Pacific Ocean.
10. Montreal is in the country of Canada
11. Seattle is located closest to the 50°N parallel of latitude.
12. What part of the United States does the Arctic Circle cross? Alaska
13. Memphis is located between the 30°N parallel and the 40°N parallel.
14. Is Dallas north or south of the 30°N parallel of latitude? north
15. Name the four United States cities located between 40°N and 50°N. Seattle Des Moines Chicago New York
16. Denver is closest to the 40°N parallel of latitude.
17. San Francisco is located near 40 °N.
18. Does the Arctic Circle pass through Greenland? yes
19. Which parallel of latitude on the map goes through Florida? 30°N
20. Guadalajara is located in what country? Mexico

Page 292

Name

Lines of Latitude

Parallels Help With Location

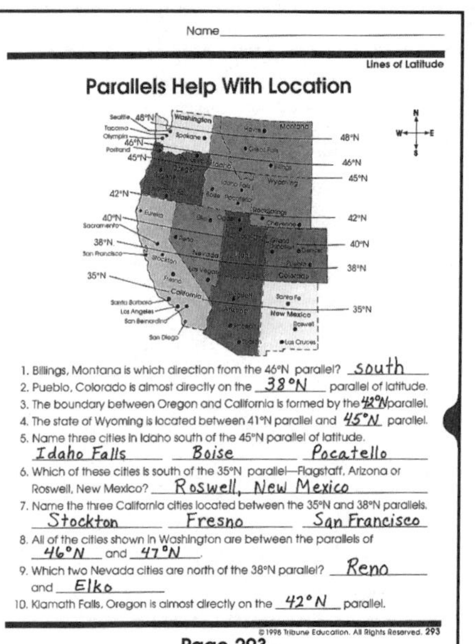

1. Billings, Montana is which direction from the 46°N parallel? south
2. Pueblo, Colorado is almost directly on the 38°N parallel of latitude.
3. The boundary between Oregon and California is formed by the 42°N parallel.
4. The state of Wyoming is located between 41°N parallel and 45°N parallel.
5. Name three cities in Idaho south of the 45°N parallel of latitude. Idaho Falls Boise Pocatello
6. Which of these cities is south of the 35°N parallel—Flagstaff, Arizona or Roswell, New Mexico? Roswell, New Mexico
7. Name the three California cities located between the 35°N and 38°N parallels. Stockton Fresno San Francisco
8. All of the cities shown in Washington are between the parallels of 46°N and 47°N.
9. Which two Nevada cities are north of the 38°N parallel? Reno and Elko
10. Klamath Falls, Oregon is almost directly on the 42°N parallel.

Page 293

Name

Latitude and Longitude

Picture It!

Directions: Coordinates are sets of numbers that show where lines of latitude and longitude meet. Place a dot at each latitude / longitude coordinate on the graph. Draw lines to connect the dots in order.

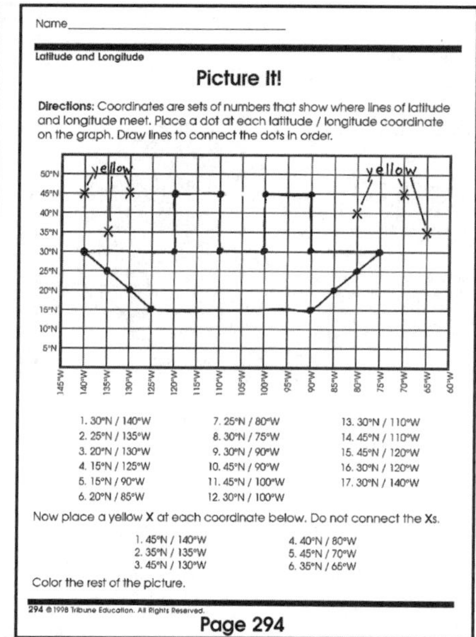

1. 30°N / 140°W
2. 25°N / 135°W
3. 20°N / 130°W
4. 15°N / 125°W
5. 15°N / 90°W
6. 20°N / 85°W
7. 25°N / 80°W
8. 30°N / 75°W
9. 30°N / 90°W
10. 45°N / 90°W
11. 45°N / 100°W
12. 30°N / 100°W
13. 30°N / 110°W
14. 45°N / 110°W
15. 45°N / 120°W
16. 30°N / 120°W
17. 30°N / 140°W

Now place a yellow **X** at each coordinate below. Do not connect the Xs.

1. 45°N / 140°W
2. 35°N / 135°W
3. 45°N / 130°W
4. 40°N / 80°W
5. 45°N / 70°W
6. 35°N / 65°W

Color the rest of the picture.

Page 294

Name

Latitude and Longitude

What Will They Be?

Directions: Place a dot at each of these latitude and longitude points on the graph.

1. 45°N / 105°W
2. 40°N / 110°W
3. 35°N / 115°W
4. 30°N / 120°W
5. 25°N / 125°W
6. 20°N / 120°N
7. 15°N / 115°W
8. 10°N / 110°W
9. 5°N / 105°W
10. 10°N / 100°W
11. 15°N / 95°W
12. 20°N / 90°W
13. 25°N / 85°W
14. 30°N / 90°W
15. 35°N / 95°W
16. 40°N / 100°W

Draw a line to connect the dots in order. What have you drawn? diamond

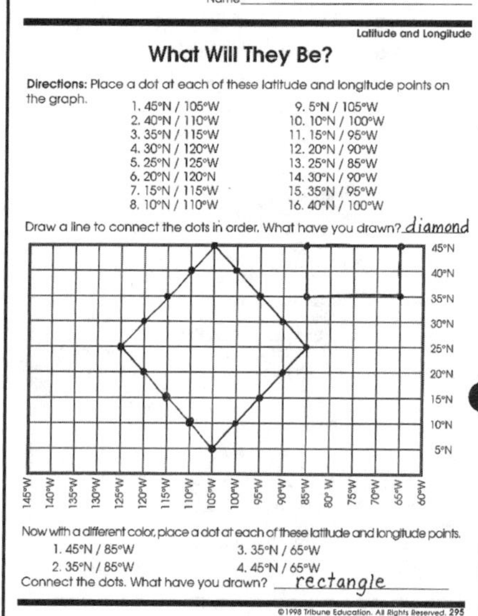

Now with a different color, place a dot at each of these latitude and longitude points.

1. 45°N / 85°W
2. 35°N / 85°W
3. 35°N / 65°W
4. 45°N / 65°W

Connect the dots. What have you drawn? rectangle

Page 295

Name

Latitude and Longitude

Using Lines to Draw a State

Directions: Place a dot on the grid for each point given. The first two have been done for you.

1. 38°N / 99°W
2. 38° N / 102°W
3. 36°N / 102°W
4. 34°N / 102°W
5. 34°N / 104°W
6. 34°N / 106°W
7. 33°N / 105 1/2°W
8. 32 1/2°N / 105°W
9. 32°N / 104 1/2°W
10. 31°N / 104°W
11. 30°N / 104°W
12. 29 1/2°N / 103°W
13. 30°N / 102°W
14. 30°N / 101°W
15. 29°N / 101°W
16. 28°N / 100°W
17. 27 1/2°N / 99°W
18. 26 1/2°N / 97 1/2°W
19. 28°N / 97 1/2°W
20. 29°N / 96 1/2°W
21. 30°N / 95°W
22. 31°N / 94°W
23. 33°N / 94°W
24. 35°N / 94°W
25. 35°N / 96°W
26. 35°N / 99°W
27. 37°N / 99°W

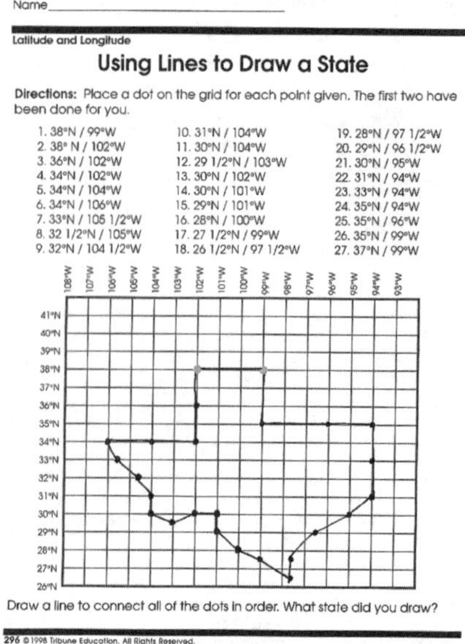

Draw a line to connect all of the dots in order. What state did you draw?

Page 296

Name

Latitude and Longitude

Casey's Island

Directions: Use the map above to answer the questions below.

1. The whales are between which two latitude lines? 20°N and 30°N
2. The coast guard station is located between which longitude lines? 130°E and 150°E
3. If the whales go north to 55°N latitude, what will they hit? rocks
4. The boats must cross what longitude lines to get to the sunken ship? 140°E, 130°E, 120°E
5. If you draw a latitude line at 35°N, what will you cross? Casey's Island
6. If the whales cross 90°E longitude, what will they reach? dock
7. Name the items crossed by the 55°N latitude line. coast guard station sharks, airplanes, seagulls, rocks
8. Which longitude lines cross Casey's Island? 100°E, 110°E, 120°E, 130°E

Page 297

Name

Latitude and Longitude

State Search

Which state is roughly between the coordinates given? After locating the state, color it on the map as directed.

	Latitude	Longitude	State	Color
1.	45°N / 50°N	105°W / 115°W	Montana	orange
2.	40°N / 45°N	75°W / 80°W	Pennsylvania	tan
3.	44°N / 50°N	67°W / 70°W	Maine	red
4.	25°N / 30°N	80°W / 85°W	Florida	yellow
5.	40°N / 45°N	90°W / 95°W	Iowa	gray
6.	30°N / 35°N	85°W / 90°W	Alabama	green
7.	43°N / 47°N	87°W / 93°W	Wisconsin	blue
8.	31°N / 36°N	104°W / 109°W	New Mexico	pink
9.	36°N / 38°N	82°W / 89°W	Kentucky	lt. green
10.	36°N / 39°N	76°W / 84°W	Virginia	gold
11.	26°N / 34°N	94°W / 107°W	Texas	purple
12.	41°N / 45°N	104°W / 111°W	Wyoming	lt. blue
13.	36°N / 41°N	90°W / 95°W	Missouri	brown

Page 298

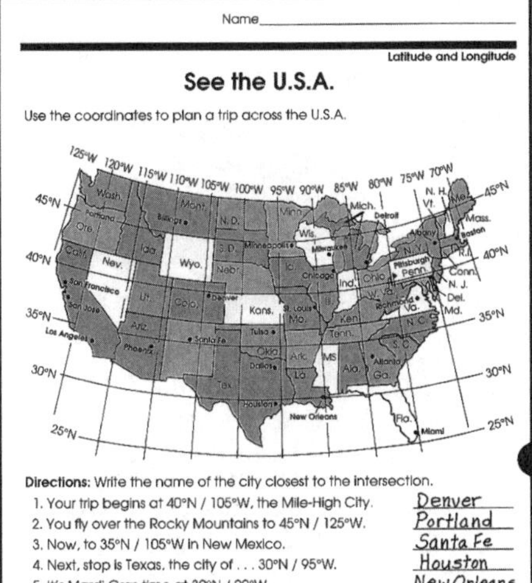
Name________________

Latitude and Longitude

See the U.S.A.

Use the coordinates to plan a trip across the U.S.A.

Directions: Write the name of the city closest to the intersection.

1. Your trip begins at 40°N / 105°W, the Mile-High City. Denver
2. You fly over the Rocky Mountains to 45°N / 125°W. Portland
3. Now, to 35°N / 105°W in New Mexico. Santa Fe
4. Next, stop is Texas, the city of . . . 30°N / 95°W. Houston
5. It's Mardi Gras time at 30°N / 90°W. New Orleans
6. Then, fun in the sun and the Atlantic Ocean 25°N / 80°W. Miami
7. To the Gateway Arch in the city of . . 40°N / 90°W. St. Louis
8. The Steelers play football here—40°N / 80°W. Pittsburgh
9. Next, to the capital of New York—40°N / 75°W. Albany

 299

Page 299

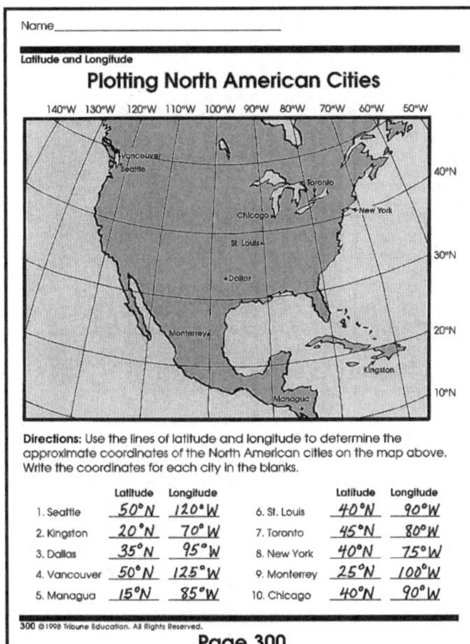
Name________________

Latitude and Longitude

Plotting North American Cities

Directions: Use the lines of latitude and longitude to determine the approximate coordinates of the North American cities on the map above. Write the coordinates for each city in the blanks.

	Latitude	Longitude		Latitude	Longitude
1. Seattle	50°N	120°W	6. St. Louis	40°N	90°W
2. Kingston	20°N	70°W	7. Toronto	45°N	80°W
3. Dallas	35°N	95°W	8. New York	40°N	75°W
4. Vancouver	50°N	125°W	9. Monterrey	25°N	100°W
5. Managua	15°N	85°W	10. Chicago	40°N	90°W

300

Page 300

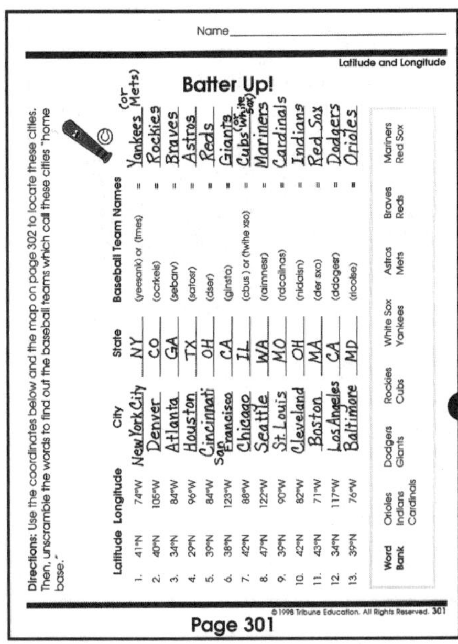
Name________________

Latitude and Longitude

Batter Up!

Directions: Use the coordinates below and the map on page 302 to locate these cities. Then, unscramble the words to find out the baseball teams which call these cities "home base."

	Latitude	Longitude	City	State	Baseball Team Names	
1.	41°N	74°W	New York City	NY	(yeesankr) or (tmes)	Yankees (or Mets)
2.	40°N	105°W	Denver	CO	(ockeisr)	Rockies
3.	34°N	84°W	Atlanta	GA	(sebarv)	Braves
4.	29°N	96°W	Houston	TX	(sotsar)	Astros
5.	39°N	84°W	Cincinnati	OH	(dser)	Reds
6.	38°N	123°W	San Francisco	CA	(ginsta)	Giants
7.	42°N	88°W	Chicago	IL	(cbus) or (twihe xso)	Cubs (or White Sox)
8.	47°N	122°W	Seattle	WA	(rainmes)	Mariners
9.	39°N	90°W	St. Louis	MO	(rdcalnas)	Cardinals
10.	42°N	82°W	Cleveland	OH	(nidaisn)	Indians
11.	43°N	71°W	Boston	MA	(der sxo)	Red Sox
12.	34°N	117°W	Los Angeles	CA	(ddogesr)	Dodgers
13.	39°N	76°W	Baltimore	MD	(riolose)	Orioles

Word Bank: Orioles, Indians, Cardinals, Dodgers, Giants, Rockies, Cubs, White Sox, Yankees, Astros, Mets, Braves, Reds, Mariners, Red Sox

 301

Page 301

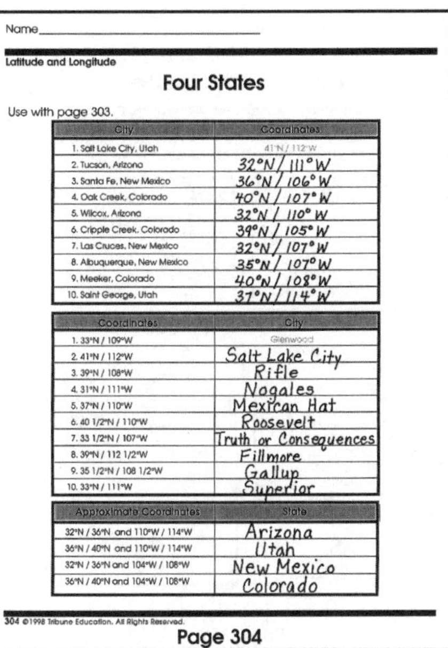
Name________________

Latitude and Longitude

Four States

Use with page 303.

City	Coordinates
1. Salt Lake City, Utah	41°N / 112°W
2. Tucson, Arizona	32°N / 111°W
3. Santa Fe, New Mexico	36°N / 106°W
4. Oak Creek, Colorado	40°N / 107°W
5. Wilcox, Arizona	32°N / 110°W
6. Cripple Creek, Colorado	39°N / 105°W
7. Las Cruces, New Mexico	32°N / 107°W
8. Albuquerque, New Mexico	35°N / 107°W
9. Meeker, Colorado	40°N / 108°W
10. Saint George, Utah	37°N / 114°W

Coordinates	City
1. 33°N / 109°W	Glenwood
2. 41°N / 112°W	Salt Lake City
3. 39°N / 108°W	Rifle
4. 31°N / 111°W	Nogales
5. 37°N / 110°W	Mexican Hat
6. 40 1/2°N / 110°W	Roosevelt
7. 33 1/2°N / 107°W	Truth or Consequences
8. 39°N / 112 1/2°W	Fillmore
9. 35 1/2°N / 108 1/2°W	Gallup
10. 33°N / 111°W	Superior

Approximate Coordinates	State
32°N / 36°N and 110°W / 114°W	Arizona
36°N / 40°N and 110°W / 114°W	Utah
32°N / 36°N and 104°W / 108°W	New Mexico
36°N / 40°N and 104°W / 108°W	Colorado

304

Page 304

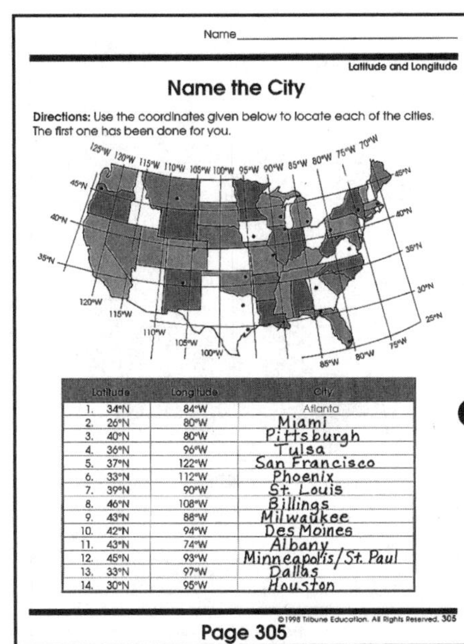
Name________________

Latitude and Longitude

Name the City

Directions: Use the coordinates given below to locate each of the cities. The first one has been done for you.

	Latitude	Longitude	City
1.	34°N	84°W	Atlanta
2.	26°N	80°W	Miami
3.	40°N	80°W	Pittsburgh
4.	36°N	96°W	Tulsa
5.	37°N	122°W	San Francisco
6.	33°N	112°W	Phoenix
7.	39°N	90°W	St. Louis
8.	46°N	108°W	Billings
9.	43°N	88°W	Milwaukee
10.	42°N	94°W	Des Moines
11.	43°N	74°W	Albany
12.	45°N	93°W	Minneapolis/St. Paul
13.	33°N	97°W	Dallas
14.	30°N	95°W	Houston

 305

Page 305

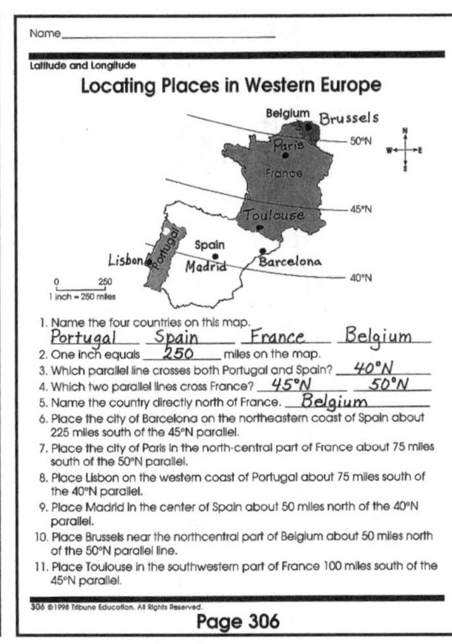
Name________________

Latitude and Longitude

Locating Places in Western Europe

1. Name the four countries on this map. Portugal Spain France Belgium
2. One inch equals 250 miles on the map.
3. Which parallel line crosses both Portugal and Spain? 40°N
4. Which two parallel lines cross France? 45°N 50°N
5. Name the country directly north of France. Belgium
6. Place the city of Barcelona on the northeastern coast of Spain about 225 miles south of the 45°N parallel.
7. Place the city of Paris in the north-central part of France about 75 miles south of the 50°N parallel.
8. Place Lisbon on the western coast of Portugal about 75 miles south of the 40°N parallel.
9. Place Madrid in the center of Spain about 50 miles north of the 40°N parallel.
10. Place Brussels near the northcentral part of Belgium about 50 miles north of the 50°N parallel line.
11. Place Toulouse in the southwestern part of France 100 miles south of the 45°N parallel.

306

Page 306

Name________________

Latitude and Longitude

Where in Europe?

Directions: Estimate and write the coordinates and countries for these European cities using the map on page 307. The first one has been done for you.

City	Latitude	Longitude	Country
1. London	52°N	0°	United Kingdom
2. Belgrade	45°N	20°E	Serbia
3. Warsaw	57°N	21°E	Poland
4. Stockholm	59°N	18°E	Sweden
5. Athens	38°N	23°E	Greece
6. Helsinki	61°N	25°E	Finland
7. Paris	48°N	3°E	France
8. Munich	47°N	12°E	Germany
9. Copenhagen	56°N	13°E	Denmark
10. Oslo	60°N	11°E	Norway
11. Glasgow	56°N	6°E	United Kingdom
12. Prague	50°N	14°E	Czech Republic
13. Bern	47°N	8°E	Switzerland
14. Hamburg	53°N	10°E	Germany
15. Dresden	52°N	13°E	Germany
16. Dublin	53°N	6°W	Ireland
17. Rome	42°N	13°E	Italy
18. Budapest	43°N	18°E	Hungary
19. Vienna	48°N	16°E	Austria
20. Amsterdam	53°N	5°E	Netherlands

308

Page 308

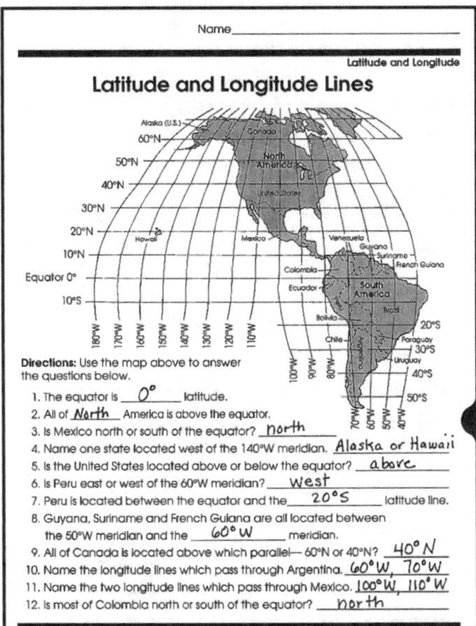
Name________________

Latitude and Longitude

Latitude and Longitude Lines

Directions: Use the map above to answer the questions below.

1. The equator is 0° latitude.
2. All of North America is above the equator.
3. Is Mexico north or south of the equator? north
4. Name one state located west of the 140°W meridian. Alaska or Hawaii
5. Is the United States located above or below the equator? above
6. Is Peru east or west of the 60°W meridian? west
7. Peru is located between the equator and the 20°S latitude line.
8. Guyana, Suriname and French Guiana are all located between the 50°W meridian and the 60°W meridian.
9. All of Canada is located above which parallel— 60°N or 40°N? 40°N
10. Name the longitude lines which pass through Argentina. 60°W, 70°W
11. Name the two longitude lines which pass through Mexico. 100°W, 110°W
12. Is most of Colombia north or south of the equator? north

 309

Page 309

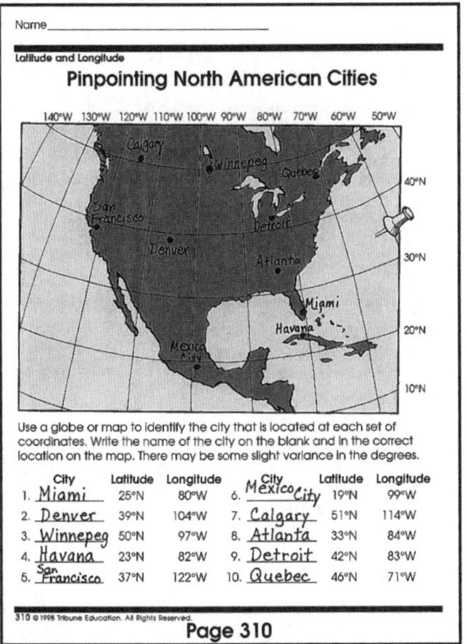
Name________________

Latitude and Longitude

Pinpointing North American Cities

Use a globe or map to identify the city that is located at each set of coordinates. Write the name of the city on the blank and in the correct location on the map. There may be some slight variance in the degrees.

City	Latitude	Longitude	City	Latitude	Longitude
1. Miami	25°N	80°W	6. Mexico City	19°N	99°W
2. Denver	39°N	104°W	7. Calgary	51°N	114°W
3. Winnepeg	50°N	97°W	8. Atlanta	33°N	84°W
4. Havana	23°N	82°W	9. Detroit	42°N	83°W
5. San Francisco	37°N	122°W	10. Quebec	46°N	71°W

310

Page 310

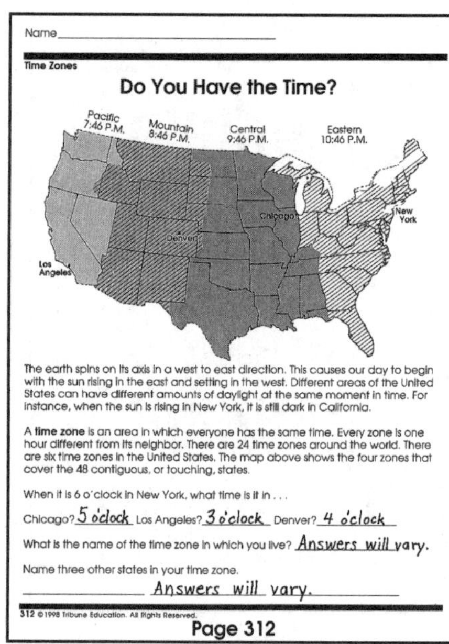

Name______________________

Time Zones

Do You Have the Time?

The earth spins on its axis in a west to east direction. This causes our day to begin with the sun rising in the east and setting in the west. Different areas of the United States can have different amounts of daylight at the same moment in time. For instance, when the sun is rising in New York, it is still dark in California.

A **time zone** is an area in which everyone has the same time. Every zone is one hour different from its neighbor. There are 24 time zones around the world. There are six time zones in the United States. The map above shows the four zones that cover the 48 contiguous, or touching, states.

When it is 6 o'clock in New York, what time is it in . . .

Chicago? 5 o'clock Los Angeles? 3 o'clock Denver? 4 o'clock

What is the name of the time zone in which you live? Answers will vary.

Name three other states in your time zone.

Answers will vary.

Page 312

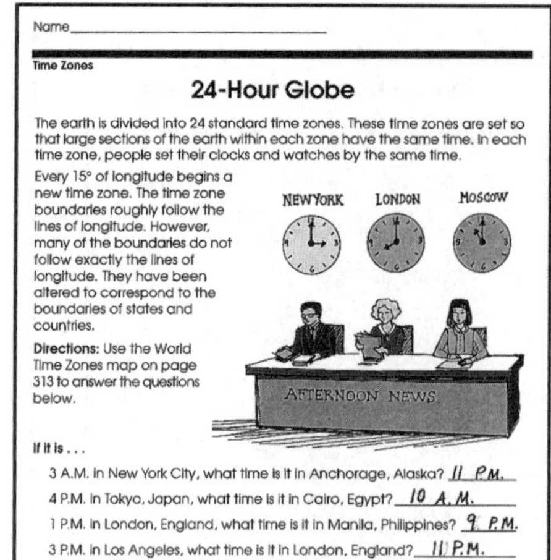

Name______________________

Time Zones

24-Hour Globe

The earth is divided into 24 standard time zones. These time zones are set so that large sections of the earth within each zone have the same time. In each time zone, people set their clocks and watches by the same time.

Every 15° of longitude begins a new time zone. The time zone boundaries roughly follow the lines of longitude. However, many of the boundaries do not follow exactly the lines of longitude. They have been altered to correspond to the boundaries of states and countries.

Directions: Use the World Time Zones map on page 313 to answer the questions below.

If it is . . .

3 A.M. in New York City, what time is it in Anchorage, Alaska? 11 P.M.
4 P.M. in Tokyo, Japan, what time is it in Cairo, Egypt? 10 A.M.
1 P.M. in London, England, what time is it in Manila, Philippines? 9 P.M.
3 P.M. in Los Angeles, what time is it in London, England? 11 P.M.
10 A.M. in Denver, what time is it in Paris, France? 5 P.M.
9 P.M. in Chicago, what time is it in Mexico City, Mexico? 9 P.M.
4 A.M. in Anchorage, what time is it in Rome, Italy? 2 P.M.
1 P.M. in Paris, France, what time is it in Chicago? 8 A.M.
11 P.M. in New York City, what time is it in Paris, France? 4 A.M.

Page 314

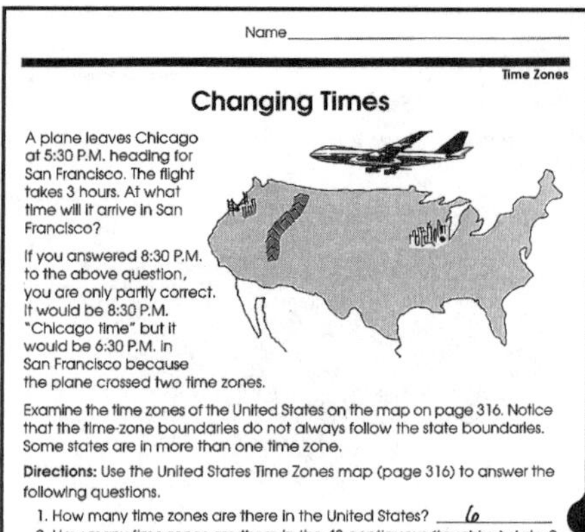

Name______________________

Time Zones

Changing Times

A plane leaves Chicago at 5:30 P.M. heading for San Francisco. The flight takes 3 hours. At what time will it arrive in San Francisco?

If you answered 8:30 P.M. to the above question, you are only partly correct. It would be 8:30 P.M. "Chicago time" but it would be 6:30 P.M. in San Francisco because the plane crossed two time zones.

Examine the time zones of the United States on the map on page 316. Notice that the time-zone boundaries do not always follow the state boundaries. Some states are in more than one time zone.

Directions: Use the United States Time Zones map (page 316) to answer the following questions.

1. How many time zones are there in the United States? 6
2. How many time zones are there in the 48 contiguous (touching) states? 4
3. Name the time zones in all 50 states. Eastern, Central, Mountain, Pacific, Alaska, Hawaii
4. If it is 3:30 P.M. in your state, what time is it in . . . Answers will vary.
   California? ______ Iowa? ______
   New York? ______ Colorado? ______
5. What time is it right now in . . . Answers will vary.
   Miami, Florida? ______ Portland, Oregon? ______
   Grand Rapids, Michigan? ______ Dallas, Texas? ______
   Cody, Wyoming? ______ Richmond, Virginia? ______

Page 315

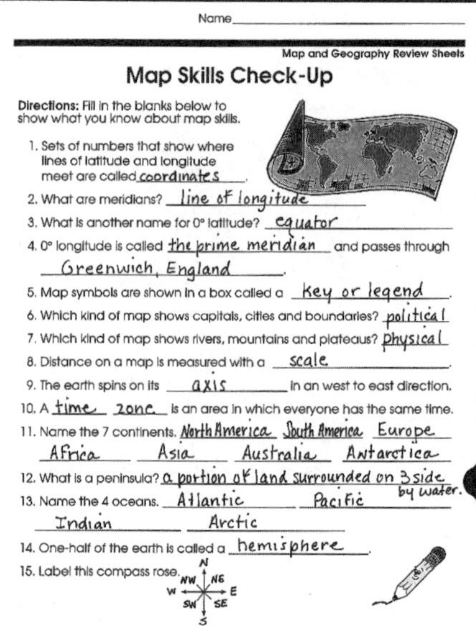

Name______________________

Map and Geography Review Sheets

Map Skills Check-Up

Directions: Fill in the blanks below to show what you know about map skills.

1. Sets of numbers that show where lines of latitude and longitude meet are called coordinates.
2. What are meridians? line of longitude
3. What is another name for 0° latitude? equator
4. 0° longitude is called the prime meridian and passes through Greenwich, England
5. Map symbols are shown in a box called a key or legend.
6. Which kind of map shows capitals, cities and boundaries? political
7. Which kind of map shows rivers, mountains and plateaus? physical
8. Distance on a map is measured with a scale.
9. The earth spins on its axis in an west to east direction.
10. A time zone is an area in which everyone has the same time.
11. Name the 7 continents. North America South America Europe Africa Asia Australia Antarctica
12. What is a peninsula? a portion of land surrounded on 3 side by water.
13. Name the 4 oceans. Atlantic Pacific Indian Arctic
14. One-half of the earth is called a hemisphere.
15. Label this compass rose. N NE E SE S SW W NW

Page 317

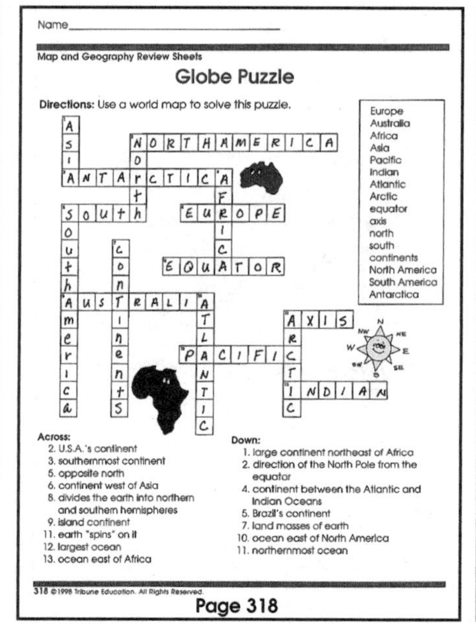

Name______________________

Map and Geography Review Sheets

Globe Puzzle

Directions: Use a world map to solve this puzzle.

Europe, Australia, Africa, Asia, Pacific, Indian, Atlantic, Arctic, equator, axis, north, south, continents, North America, South America, Antarctica

Across:
2. U.S.A.'s continent
3. southernmost continent
5. opposite north
6. continent west of Asia
8. divides the earth into northern and southern hemispheres
9. island continent
11. earth "spins" on it
12. largest ocean
13. ocean east of Africa

Down:
1. large continent northeast of Africa
2. direction of the North Pole from the equator
4. continent between the Atlantic and Indian Oceans
5. Brazil's continent
7. land masses of earth
10. ocean east of North America
11. northernmost ocean

Page 318

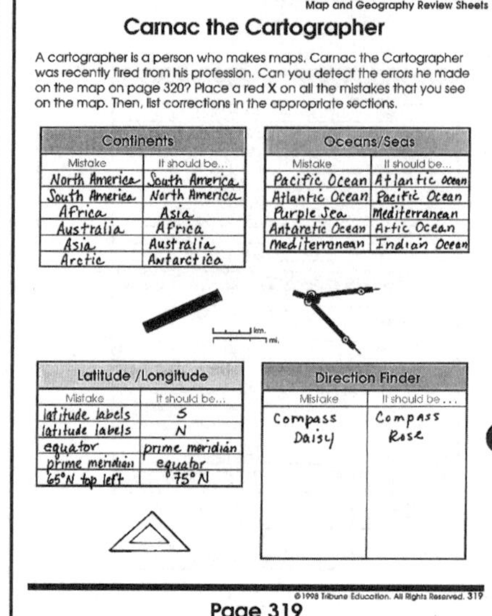

Name______________________

Map and Geography Review Sheets

Carnac the Cartographer

A cartographer is a person who makes maps. Carnac the Cartographer was recently fired from his profession. Can you detect the errors he made on the map on page 320? Place a red X on all the mistakes that you see on the map. Then, list corrections in the appropriate sections.

Continents	
Mistake	It should be...
North America	South America
South America	North America
Africa	Asia
Australia	Africa
Asia	Australia
Arctic	Antarctica

Oceans/Seas	
Mistake	It should be...
Pacific Ocean	Atlantic Ocean
Atlantic Ocean	Pacific Ocean
Purple Sea	Mediterranean
Antarctic Ocean	Artic Ocean
Mediterranean	Indian Ocean

Latitude/Longitude	
Mistake	It should be...
latitude labels	S
latitude labels	N
equator	prime meridian
prime meridian	equator
65°N top left	75°N

Direction Finder	
Mistake	It should be...
Compass Daisy	Compass Rose

Page 319

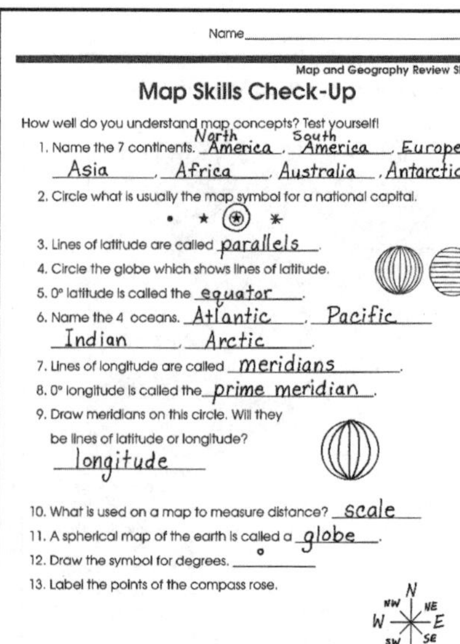

Name______________________

Map and Geography Review Sheets

Map Skills Check-Up

How well do you understand map concepts? Test yourself!

1. Name the 7 continents. North America, South America, Europe, Asia, Africa, Australia, Antarctica
2. Circle what is usually the map symbol for a national capital.
3. Lines of latitude are called parallels.
4. Circle the globe which shows lines of latitude.
5. 0° latitude is called the equator.
6. Name the 4 oceans. Atlantic, Pacific, Indian, Arctic.
7. Lines of longitude are called meridians.
8. 0° longitude is called the prime meridian.
9. Draw meridians on this circle. Will they be lines of latitude or longitude? longitude
10. What is used on a map to measure distance? scale
11. A spherical map of the earth is called a globe.
12. Draw the symbol for degrees. °
13. Label the points of the compass rose. N NE E SE S SW W NW

Page 321

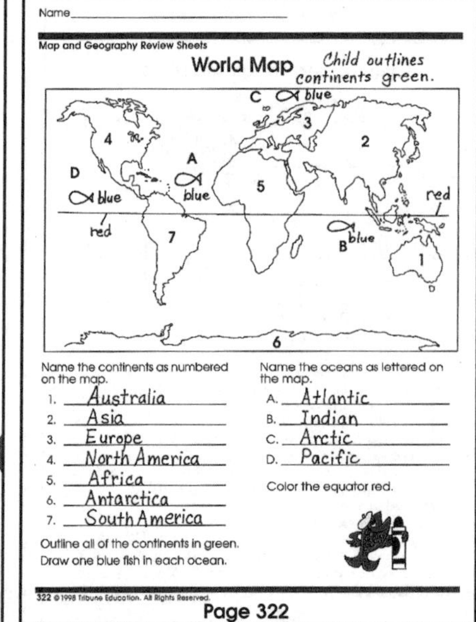

Name______________________

Map and Geography Review Sheets

World Map

Child outlines continents green.

Name the continents as numbered on the map.

1. Australia
2. Asia
3. Europe
4. North America
5. Africa
6. Antarctica
7. South America

Name the oceans as lettered on the map.

A. Atlantic
B. Indian
C. Arctic
D. Pacific

Color the equator red.

Outline all of the continents in green.
Draw one blue fish in each ocean.

Page 322

Reading a Map

A **map** is a drawing of all or part of the earth's surface. Because this map shows the round earth as a flat rectangle, the areas near the North and South Poles are stretched out of size.

Lines of **latitude** (←→) and lines of **longitude** (↕) help you find places on a map. Can you find the city of Cairo? It is located near 30°N latitude and 30°E longitude.

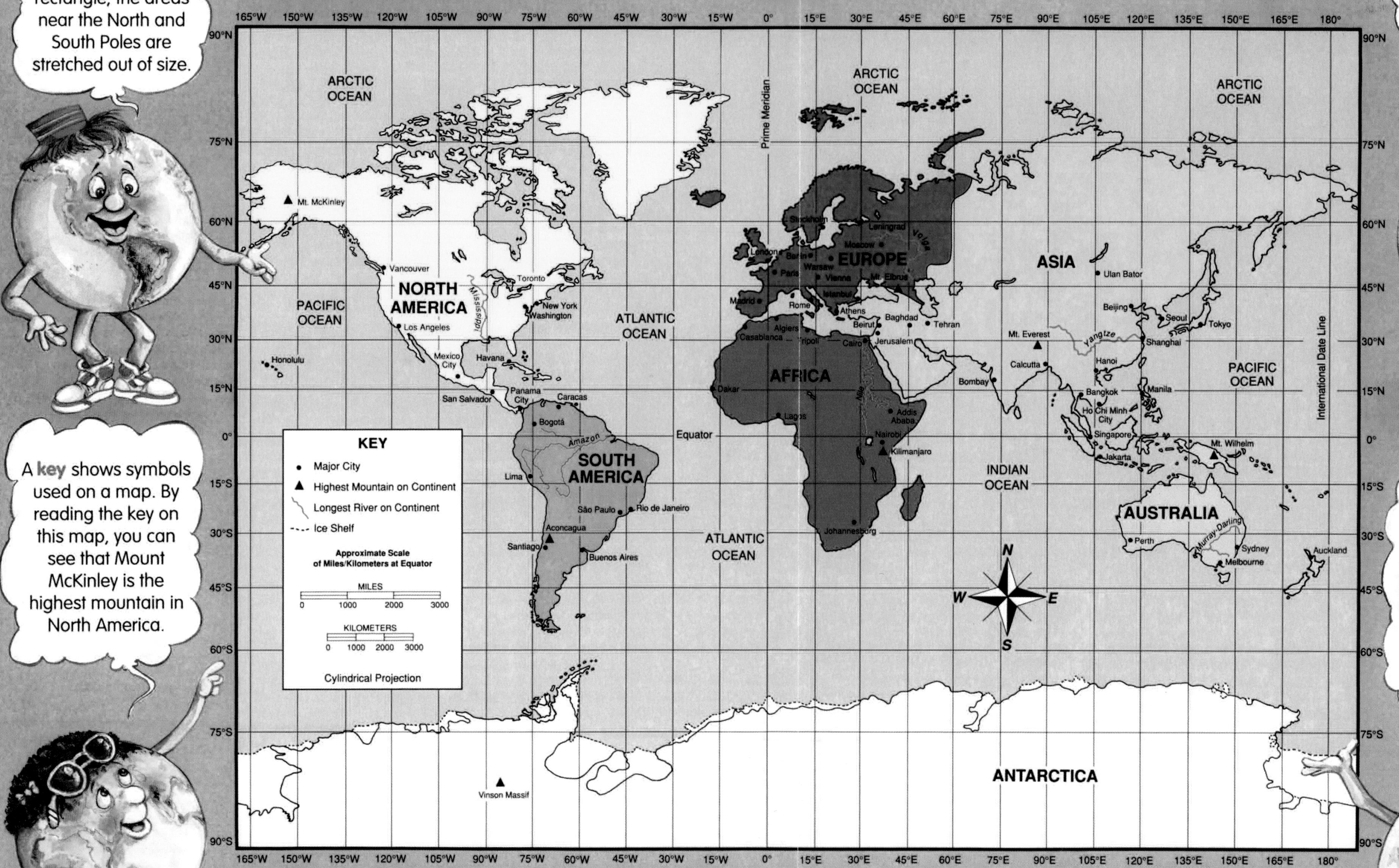

A **key** shows symbols used on a map. By reading the key on this map, you can see that Mount McKinley is the highest mountain in North America.

A **compass rose** shows directions on a map. By checking the compass rose on this map, you can see that Australia is southeast of Europe.